STRAVINSKY
Chronicle of a Friendship

Stravinsky

Chronicle of a Friendship

Revised and Expanded Edition

❧ Robert Craft

VANDERBILT UNIVERSITY PRESS

Nashville and London • *1994*

Original edition published by Knopf, 1972

Revised and expanded edition published by Vanderbilt University Press, 1994
94 95 96 97 98 99   5 4 3 2 1

This publication is made from recycled paper and meets the minimum requirements of American
National Standard for Information Sciences—Permanence of Paper for Printed Library Materials ∞

Library of Congress Cataloging-in-Publication Data
Craft, Robert
Stravinsky: chronicle of a friendship / Robert Craft. —Rev. and expanded ed.
p.   cm.
Includes indexes.
ISBN 0-8265-1258-5
1. Stravinsky, Igor, 1882–1971—Friends and associates. 2. Composers—Biog-
raphy. 3. Craft, Robert—Diaries. I. Title.
ML410.S932C8 1994
780' .92—dc20
[B]
                                                            94-12666
                                                              CIP
                                                              MN

Manufactured in the United States of America

They went quietly down into the roaring streets, inseparable
and blessed; and as they passed along in sunshine and shade,
the noisy and the eager, and the froward and the vain, fretted
and chafed, and made their usual uproar.

Little Dorrit

Ce n'est pas tout à la fois, mais grain par grain qu'on goute le passé.

Proust

Look, what thy memory cannot contain

Sonnet LXXVII

Contents

Illustrations

Acknowledgments

I wish to thank Mark Wait, one of America's front-rank pianists and dean of Vanderbilt University's Blair School of Music, for bringing this new edition of my *Chronicle* to the attention of Charles Backus, director of Vanderbilt University Press. I take pleasure in thanking the staff of the Press, especially Bard Young, my meticulous editor, and Gary Gore, whose design has added appeal to this book's new life. Thanks also go to Professor David Lowe of the Vanderbilt Slavic Languages faculty for regularizing the transliterations of Russian words and phrases, and to Christopher Frommer for patiently typing my untidy manuscript. I am grateful to my wife, Alva, to my sister, Phyllis Crawford, and to Stanley Baron for suggesting improvements.

Preface

TO THE REVISED AND EXPANDED EDITION

travinsky: Chronicle of a Friendship 1948-1971, a selection from my diaries, first appeared in 1972 and was soon out of print. Dissatisfied with my choice of the contents—the book had been hastily put together to meet a publication schedule that coincided with The New York City Ballet's Stravinsky Festival in June 1972—I did not want it reissued. I had included nothing at all for 1954, only a single occurrence on a single day for 1948, 1950, 1957, and no more than a few paragraphs for 1953 and 1955. Furthermore, the entries for 1951 and 1956 did not substantiate my thesis that these were crucial in Stravinsky's later years, 1951 because it brought his California isolation to an end and changed his musical horizons, 1956 because of the effects of a near fatal illness.

The period from early October 1956, in Munich, when Stravinsky's life was measured in anxious hours, to his seventy-fifth birthday the following June is the annus mirabilis of his American years. In eight months he rose from his hospital bed to compose most of *Agon*, that masterpiece of the reborn young man. From then on, his health was his most immediate and constant concern. During the final decade and a half, living under the threat of a paralyzing or mortal stroke, he visited doctors, or they him, almost daily. In addition, he was subjected to at least one hematological analysis a week and obliged to interrupt his work in order to adhere to a complex schedule of medications. Stravinsky's own record of his changing platelet count and prothrombin (coagulation) time would be another person's full-time job. So far as can be determined, none of this diminished his creativity, nor did it substantially curtail his extremely active life.

After the Munich crisis, Stravinsky was invited to appear in most of the musical capitals of the globe, the distances increasing, it seemed, in proportion to the decline of his own bodily mobility. That a man so constantly in orbit could compose so much new-thought music, conduct so much, read and write so much, and accomplish so much else continues to amaze me. I was a third his age when I first knew him, half his age at the time of his last creations, yet I could scarcely keep pace with him even physically. I should mention that I wrote down no descriptions of concerts, except in the USSR, where they revealed so much of Stravinsky in his background, simply because I was too busy conducting to write: rehearsing not only my own portions of his programs, but his as well, in the later years trying to prepare the music so that no more, and often even less, than a run-through would be required of him.

Another shortcoming of the original *Chronicle* was that essential, if snippety, contexts were missing for the 1960s, meaning that Stravinsky was therefore represented by his ancillary activities—touring, recording, compiling books of "conversations"—rather than by his creative work. These contexts naturally include his associations with friends, and though I attempted to describe his close relationship with Aldous Huxley, I felt incapable of doing the same for those with Gerald Heard and Christopher Isherwood, both of whom saw him more frequently and over a longer period. To repair the omission in Heard's case, I have included a letter of his that is strikingly similar to his talk. ("Letters written by eyewitnesses," Horace Walpole wrote, "are genuine history; and as far as they go, more satisfactory than formal premeditated narratives.") At each entry beginning "Gerald for dinner," the reader should try to imagine two or three hours of verbal wit and personal grace of the kind displayed in his communication of August 1956. (How I miss those evenings with the California Free English!)

* * *

I began my Stravinsky diary as an aide-mémoire, a simple record of matters of fact, not a storehouse of observations and impressions, still less a confidant, or mirror for self-contemplation. At the time, the diaries that were in vogue were those of the existentialist self-analysts, Kierkegaard, Amiel, Kafka, Pavese; the writers' notebooks, of which Henry James's is the most highly evolved example; and the philosophical journal—Canetti's comes to mind—in which the world is interpreted as well as recorded. None of them, of course, was a suitable model for my purpose. (My favorite diary, then and now, is the uncategorizable one by Jules Renard.) Unlike these "professional" writers, I tried to present a simple accumulation of isolated moments of reality, "writing up" the most memorable of them, leaving most in the form of bald facts to which to return later for leisurely elaboration—as I mistakenly thought, forgetting how quickly emotions and even significances evaporate, and that after a few years all memories are bound to be revisionist.

Near the beginning (the summer of 1949), I tried to describe close-up, eyepeeling behavior, but the novelty of Stravinsky's soon wore off. Coleridge observed that "an inquisitiveness into the minutest circumstance or casual sayings of eminent contemporaries is . . . quite natural," and Cyril Connolly, encouraging me to keep this record (and referring to Hazlitt's "My First Acquaintance With Poets"), convinced me that the small talk of the great is rarer than their empyrean big talk and will last longer. However that may be, I did take down some of the talk that amused me, as Auden's always did. But I wrote because I wanted to put a fence around my experience. In doing so I discovered an alter ego of which I am not especially fond but which, being opposed to capital punishment, I could not put to death.

In an attempt to provide a connecting thread and overall, perspectival view of the main events and changing moods, I have added a brief post-script to each of the twenty-three complete years of the Chronicle. A Postlude concludes the whole, ending with Vera Stravinsky's death in 1982.

R.C.

STRAVINSKY
Chronicle of a Friendship

❧ 1948

March 31. Washington, D.C. Arriving at the Raleigh Hotel for my appointment with Stravinsky this morning, I find Auden pacing the lobby—in the same suit he wore in a photograph taken a decade ago in China. "The night train from Pittsburgh was late," he says, "and the Stravs aren't receiving yet." In that case, I ask, would he join me in a second breakfast? But no, he wouldn't, because "there are no hard rolls in America." He drinks two glasses of beer instead, and lay-analyses "the old boy, in whose case, obviously, the mother figure is money." Suddenly remembering *The Rake's Progress*, he delves into a battered briefcase and brings forth a copy of the libretto wrapped in the *New York Times*. Evidently counting on only a short wait, he opens the typescript to the final scene and hands it to me saying, "This might interest you." While I read, he turns to the *Times* obits, at which he registers disappointment, then to the book page, which provokes a groan. Thereafter he watches me at a tangent, no doubt trying to place me. I tell him that we met after one of his Barnard College lectures in the spring of 1946.

When I say that I think the Bedlam scene contains some of the most beautiful lines ever intended for an opera, he grants me ten additional minutes for the rest of the text, or approximately the time it would take *him* to read it. I have hardly finished Scene One when he jumps up exclaiming, "Surely the old boy must be ready by now," and fire-chases back to ring the apartment.

"The Lily Pons Suite, 704–705" the brass nameplate says, but we are admitted by the tall, queenly beautiful Mrs. S., wearing a blue turban and white piqué housecoat. Mr. S., in a burgundy bathrobe, waits behind her; and he continues to hide behind and to depend on her throughout the meeting, like a small pet mouse with a large friendly cat. They greet me warmly and smother Auden with Russian-style kisses. They have not seen him since the scenario-planning in Hollywood more than four months ago, but lovable, even kissable though he may be, Auden is a Public School Englishman, plainly horrified by such open demonstrations of affection.

1

1948 He winces and quickly poses a number of deflecting questions about the S.s' health, household, lovebirds, parrots. Then yes, too, dear me, we are forgetting the opera. The manuscript is again delved for and handed in, like a schoolboy's exam. Mr. S. receives it solemnly, even superstitiously, asking Mrs. S. ("Verusha" this time, at other times "Vierotchka") to bring whiskey—not Auden's preferred drink, but he takes it. Toasting the opera, we rapidly sink four toothglass tumblers-full, after which I feel less nervous, if also a little too well oiled. Why have I not been more nervous in the first place? Is it because Mr. S., from his music and from the New York rehearsals and concerts in which I have watched him, seems like someone I already know very well?

He talks about his new Concerto for Strings, the "Basiliensis," and his performance of it in Mexico City last month. Whereas all his exchanges with Mrs. S. are in Russian (a long one in which they are probably deciding what to do about me with regard to seating strategy at luncheon), the language of this narrative is an assortment of handy French, German, and English phrases. His pursuit of verbal exactitude and his self-interruptions searching for English equivalents of foreign expressions could become exasperating. At one point he wants edification on the difference between a cad and a bounder, words encountered in a detective story read on the train last night; but apart from Auden's distinction that one of the terms applies chiefly to moral, the other chiefly to social, behavior, I do not catch his would-have-been-immortal answer, being obliged in that instant to open the door for the waiter.

According to popular concepts of the changing evolutionary design of human physique, Mr. S. is something of a throwback. He is physically so extraordinary, in any case, that nothing less than a life-size statue (not merely a head or bust), or scaled-to-life-size drawing (Picasso's seated portrait is especially misleading), could convey his uniqueness: the pygmy height, bandy legs, fleshlessness, football player's shoulders, large hands and wide knuckles, tiny head with recessive frontal lobes, sandy hair (black in photographs), smooth red neck and high, Woody Woodpecker back hairline. He is so absorbing to watch that to attend to what he says requires an effort. And when that predicament is overcome, a greater one arises in knowing how to respond. Some of his remarks are so sweeping, absolute, exclusive, as well as so exaggerated and *parti-pris*, that I am uncertain whether or not my leg is being pulled. Add to this the difficulties that agreement is obviously expected for no matter what he says, and that the composer in person, insofar as colleagues are concerned, frequently seems to be saying the opposite of his autobiography. Thus, the mention of his *Symphonies of Wind Instruments*—of which his forthcoming New York performance is the subject of today's meeting—provokes a tirade against Ansermet and his recent NBC Symphony broadcast of the piece.

Still, respond one must. I do so easily to a joke about "Hollywood composers who farm out their orchestrations and whose scores should be marked 'Coloring Added,' like the labels on food cans." But I have no idea how to react to a verbal thumbs down on the Beethoven Violin Concerto because "That D sharp in the first movement is such an ugly note"; or to a Nietzschean argument denying the Germanness of German music, "Because Bach was Saxon, Beethoven Flemish, Haydn Croatian, Mozart Bavarian." I do not quarrel with these attributions or propose other candidates, but then neither does Auden, and he cannot think them less preposterous than I do.

We pair off for a moment, Mr. S. and Auden to discuss the libretto, Mrs. S. and myself to talk about books. Her English is as charming as everything else about her. "I tried to but could not read *The Nak'd and the Dead*," she says (whereas at table she defends American food to the extent of saying that our "ba-ked potatoes are good"). She says "here it's"—the logical reversal of "it's here"—and "fas-ten" for "fasten." But her accent is more French than Russian. "Tell me, please, what means 'doctrine'?" and the word comes out so French-sounding—"doctreene"—that I answer "a female doctor." Do I agree, she asks, long cilia fluttering slowly over large blue eyes, that women appreciate flowers more than men, and that intellectual men hardly notice and are rarely able to identify any flowers except carnations and roses? "Auden not only failed to sniff our bouquets, but he deposited his coat on a cluster of gardenias still lying in their box. Eager loves flowers," she goes on, leaving me no time to consider the relationship between male intellect and floral indifference. "He always has fresh flowers in his room while he works, and he cuts and waters them himself. He gardens every day, too, if he has time." But Eager's delectation of blossoms is less apparent to me than his compulsive folding up and tidy tucking away of wrapping paper and ribbons.

My business with him, in connection with our forthcoming Town Hall concert, amounts to two questions: how much rehearsal time will he have, and how many strings will I have for the Symphony in C? Knowing that both totals are insufficient, I am tempted to fudge the answers, but, hearing the truth, he merely tells me to add more. He demands definite answers and does not accept provisional ones. During this conversation he asks me for the best way to render *"se rendre compte"* in English. I fail to satisfy, of course, and he turns to Auden who is equally nonplussed. Impatient at this, Mr. S. grunts and slaps his knee, exposing some of his animal energy. Otherwise he is graciousness itself, the Roi Soleil of Saint-Simon's *"Jamais homme si naturellement poli."*

Lunch is welcome more for the relief it brings from the tonnage of Mr. S.'s tête-à-tête concentration than gustatorily. But we get smashed. I do, anyway, and my head turns like a pinwheel halfway through the third bottle of Bordeaux, at which time Auden, intellect unbowed, begins to chat about linguistic science as a key to thought structure (it is no such thing,

1948 he thinks) versus the "British nanny as the true source of all philosophy in the Empiric Isles." He deprecates philosophy still further with the statement that "it can be no more than a game anyway, for St. Paul's reason that 'We are part of what we know.'" Besides this, I recall only Mr. S.'s fuss about a wobble in the table, his annoyance with a butter-fingered waiter, his obsession with scraping up crumbs, and his exculpatory rubbing out of two spots on the tablecloth. (What is he apologizing for? Surely the "clean-slate" theory doesn't apply to him.) He remarks, marvelously, "Music is the best means we have of digesting time," and talks at some length about words. This involves a great deal of slow-fishing translation of which, probably because of its nonlogicality, I retain only the information that the Russian for "ladybug" means, literally, "God's little cow." After several demi-cups of espresso, he retires for a "catnap," which, Mrs. S. predicts, will last until dinner.

After a walk along the Potomac, elated but apprehensive about the fate of my concert, I return to the Lily Pons at 7. Here it seems that whatever has been concluded about me, and they have surely noticed that whereas I am tongue-tied with them, I talk freely with Auden, their curiosity has been aroused and perhaps some sympathy, for they are very gentle and outgoing.

Dinner in the Raleigh restaurant offers a study in contrasts of culture, temperament, and mind. On another level, the shabby, dandruff-speckled, and slightly peculiar-smelling poet (attributes easily offset by his purity of spirit and intellectual punctiliousness) and the neat, sartorially perfect, and liberally eau-de-cologned composer could not be more unlike each other. Auden devours—bolts—his lamb chops, potatoes, and sprouts as if eating were a chore to be accomplished as quickly as possible and gulps the carefully chosen Margaux oblivious to its qualities. Mr. S., in contrast, fusses over his food, and sniffs, sips, and savors the wine. In Auden's case, the senses seem to be of negligible importance, while in Mr. S.'s the affective faculties appear to be kin to instruments of thought. Powerful observer though he is, Auden shows little interest in the visual world and is evidently purblind to painting and even to "poetic" nature, being more concerned with the virtues of gardening than with the beauty of flowers. And whatever the acuteness of his aural sense, the idea of music appeals to him more than music itself, music with words—opera and Anglican hymns—more than Haydn quartets. That the music of Auden's poetry is not its strongest feature should not be surprising. He is a conceptualizer in quest of intellectual order, a social, moral, and spiritual diagnostician above all.

Auden refers to a forthcoming performance of Mr. S.'s *Oedipus Rex* at Juilliard and says that, according to the announcement, the entire text, not just the Narrator's part, is to be sung in a new translation by e.e. cummings. Seeing that this alarms Mr. S., Auden vouches for cummings's awareness of the composer's intentions and is certain that only the speeches will be in

4

English—which indicates that he is at least acquainted with the work. Thereafter the talk about music turns to the Wagner and Strauss operas that he most admires but that are far from Mr. S.'s present interest. Auden does not subscribe to Strauss's view of himself as an epigone of Wagner, for the reason that "Wagner is a giant without issue."

Begging indulgence for her English, Mrs. S. asks the poet how to improve it. "Take a new word and use it in ten different sentences," he says. She chooses "fastidious" and with no implicit criticism of her new mentor goes on: "My *husband* is very fastidious!" Auden is aware that his articulation and accent are obstacles for the S.s, but the supplementary words that he offers in German only add to the confusion, since his pronunciation of the language, and more so of French, constitute a further impediment. He writes *"au fond"* on the tablecloth before the S.s understand what he is saying. His vocabulary is odd, too, not in rare or classical-root words but in such British expressions as "fribbled" and "grouting."

Answering a question about his travel plans, Auden says, "I like to fly and am not afraid of crashing. It is simply a matter of whether one's time is up. My time will be up when I am eighty-eight." Mr. S. suddenly switches from "Ow-den" to "Wystan" and is enthusiastically met on the same basis with "EE-gawr," a cultural *faux pas*, the use of the given name without the patronymic being inadmissible to these old-fashioned Russians. After the dinner, Auden tries to depart but is detained by the S.s' Russian-style hugs and kisses, to which he responds with pumping handshakes and a charge toward the door.

April 1. I accompany Mr. S. to his morning rehearsal with the National Symphony Orchestra in Constitution Hall. At intermission, in his dressing room, he tells me that the bass clarinet at the end of the first movement of the Symphony in Three is "a kind of laughing or nose-thumbing."

April 2. Again with Mr. S. to his rehearsal. In the evening we go together to a Mozart concert at Dumbarton Oaks, myself on an admission card with Auden's name: he has returned to New York. Jennie Tourel sings arias and songs, Mitch Miller stars in the oboe quartet, and Ralph Kirkpatrick in the C minor Fantasy and Trio K. 502. The S.s are inordinately amused when I say that the name of our host, John Thatcher, reminds me of Mr. S.'s song *Yicher-Yacher (Jackdaw)*.

April 3. Fly to New York to make final arrangements for the concert.

April 4. Sunday. Back to Washington, with Vera Kassman (my roommate at 313 W. 91st Street). In the green room following the matinee concert, Mrs. S. helps her husband remove a sopping shirt and undershirt, and douses him with Kölnisches Wasser. When friends and autograph seekers are admitted, he slips around them in order to close the last half-inch of a window. In the Lily Pons afterward, with Nicolas Nabokov and his new wife Patricia, Mrs. S. invites us to join them at dinner but then realizes that Miss Kassman understands Russian and withdraws the invitation, with the excuse that they are tired and will be going to bed early. But all of us meet on the same night train to New York. The S.s now call me "Bobb"—long, very deep "o," close to "u."

April 7. Lunch with the S.s and Alexei Haieff at the Ambassador Hotel. Mr. S. orders smoked salmon for me and obliges me to swallow a glass of straight Bols gin with it. Afterward we go with Haieff to my rehearsal at Nola Studios. I know the Symphony in C better than Mr. S. does. Haieff encourages me and tries to cover up for my gaucheness and inadequacies.

April 11. Town Hall. During our dress rehearsal, Mrs. S. approaches a man listening from the side, tells him the rehearsal is "closed," and identifies herself as the wife of the conductor. "And I'm the father of the conductor," my father answers. The Stravinsky-conducted first half of the concert goes smoothly, though the immediate repeat of the Symphonies is a mistake: the second performance should have come at the end of the evening. An awful moment occurs in my half, in the finale of the Capriccio, when the pianist, Elly Kassman, jumps the famous "general pause" measure and I try to follow, instead of sticking to the strict count of measures and leaving the reunion problem to her. Cacophony ensues, but we end together. Mr. S. tells me afterward that conductors cannot make orchestras understand such things, and must go with the beat and the large ensemble no matter what. But I once saw Stokowski, in a concert in the 55th Street Mosque Theater, sort out a mess of the same kind in Schoenberg's *Pelleas.* The Symphony in C is ragged in places but effective nevertheless.

April 14. I.S. shows me a letter from Stark Young about the Town Hall concert: ". . . wondering—as happens to me very rarely in art—how these incredible patterns of form and tone appear to any soul, how can the wonder and beauty of what you say come to us like that . . . all the miracle of the ancient, barbaric, passionate world are there, and all the human heart is there. . . ."

April 15–19. I am with the S.s every day and most of the day and night. Balanchine and Maria Tallchief come daily, too, and since the Russians speak Russian together, Maria and I become friends. I.S. sees my underarm *Introductory Lectures on Psychoanalysis* and makes some criticisms that show he understands nothing about Freud.

April 18. Sunday. I am the subject of Virgil Thomson's column in today's *Herald Tribune,* "Gift For Conducting." Without telling me, I.S. wrote to him, pointing out that his review of the concert "failed to notice the talents of this accomplished musician." Thomson refers to "the excellence of this young conductor," and calls me "musically most impressive." He says that although I come from "the Berkshire Music School at Tanglewood, as so many of the better young do nowadays," I "show no influence of the Tanglewood-Koussevitzky platform elegance," which is a nice way of understating my clumsiness on the podium, but he continues speaking of the thoroughness of my musical preparation and performance.

6

April 20. With the S.s to the Juilliard School's dress rehearsal of *Oedipus Rex*, sets by Frederick Kiesler, conducted by my old teacher Edgar Shenkman. Having been a student here only two years ago, this visit with Stravinsky is awkward, and the faculty people obviously regard me as an impostor.

April 21. I invite the S.s and their friend Lisa Sokolov to lunch at the Town and Country on Park Avenue, forgetting that the restaurant has no wine list and specializes in popovers. On discovering this, Mr. S. says he wants to leave, but Lisa and Mrs. S. restrain him. My three Russians annoy the stiff and prim waiters and the animosity is mutual. I resolve never again to expose the S.s to American food—how did they escape it in ten years in this country?—and promise myself to remember Paul's advice to Timothy: "Drink no longer water, but use a little wine for thy stomach's sake." A fiasco.

April 23. Nabokov takes the S.s and me to see Mary McCarthy in a debate at the New School for Social Research, where I used to attend Bertrand Russell's lectures on Plato, Leibniz, J. S. Mill, and D. H. Lawrence. (Russell pretended that Frieda L. really wrote the books). Mary is quite contrary, but I am distracted by memories of Russell, always late, dropping his coat on the floor by the rostrum, and beginning to talk before reaching it. Afterward, choosing from the raised hands, he would say either nothing at all or "Very silly question."

April 26. With Mr. S. to his Ballet Theater *Apollo* rehearsal at the Metropolitan Opera. In the evening, I share a box there with Mrs. S. and Haieff.

April 28. I.S. conducts the first performance of *Orpheus* with the New York City Ballet, Mosque Theater, West 55th Street, on a program with Mozart's Sinfonia Concertante. I meet their California physician, Maximilian Edel, and we all go to a party at Harold Clurman's.

May 4. After our lunch at "Maria's," where the S.s see Prince Troubetzkoy, I help them pack and go with them to the train for Los Angeles. They are very affectionate now, with kisses and hugs and invitations to come to Denver in July and to Hollywood after that.

June 17. I drive to the airport to fetch Soulima Stravinsky, his wife Françoise, and their three-year-old son, John. Suffering from a migraine after the long flight from Paris, she goes to bed as soon as we reach the Ambassador Hotel. Soulima's manners resemble his father's, but so do his mannerisms. He speaks sketchy English, less resourceful than his father's but less thickly accented. Dinner with Soulima and his friend Luc Bouchage.

July 20. Denver. A message at the Brown Palace Hotel asks me to come to the house of Charles Bayly, where the male S.s are running through the Capriccio, and the females are being photographed. Saul Caston, conductor of the Denver Symphony, is there, but fortunately he

1948 does not recognize in me the fifteen-year-old student he once auditioned at the Curtis Institute in Philadelphia.

July 22. Rehearsal in Red Rocks. In the evening to *Così fan tutte* in . Central City, conducted by Emile Cooper, with whom, afterward, I.S. speaks Russian. While driving us to Central City, Caston tries to pry from I.S. an answer to how he composed *The Rite of Spring*: "My ear was very experienced." (Thanks.) When Caston exclaims on the beauty of the Rockies, I.S. says that he is "indifferent to mountains" and especially dislikes this "Wagnerian view." Mrs. S. tells me later that what attracts him in a landscape is composition, frame, dimension perspectivized by architecture—the castle on the Italian hilltop, the arch of the ruined aqueduct in the pasture. The unique landscape on the walls of his studio, she says, is a Zen-like drawing by Rembrandt of a black fence bisecting a snow field.

July 24. I go with the S.s to a performance of Virgil Thomson's *The Mother of Us All* at the University of Denver. After a few minutes, I.S. wants to depart, but Mrs. S. tells him that he is being watched by Thomson and everyone else. Françoise does flee, unable to overcome a fit of *fou rire*.

The S.s convince me to visit Mexico en route to California.

July 25. I leave for El Paso on a Greyhound, whose driver tells me that he has witnessed countless tender farewells, "but an hour later even the most broken-hearted end up on the back seat with a stranger."

July 26. El Paso. I wait in the railroad station from dawn to midday for the train to Mexico City, change $100 to pesos (5 to $1) in Juarez, obtain a tourist visa, and buy a ticket—Pullman: second-class passengers sit on the floor and first class on hard benches. At dinner time, the Indians cook tortillas in their compartments. Stop at Chihuahua in the night.

July 27. The landscape is wild and empty. I go out at each station to watch the bargaining between the passengers and the Indians but do not stray far from the steps of the train, since it leaves without warning and does not follow a schedule; we are already half a day late. At most stations, crippled children point to their maimed limbs and cry: "*no trabajo.*" Children and women are barefoot. At some stations Indians sell shawls, woven garments, sombreros, cooked-in-oil food, and pulque. But I continue with my diet of bananas, Coca-Cola, and the small edible part of the immense T-bone steaks that are brought to my compartment an hour after I order them. Thirst is a torture, but I hold out against the water.

July 28. Today the towns and the people look slightly more prosperous, the population is denser than in the northern desert, and much of the land is farmed. Weary from the jerking and bumping of the train, I would like to count the hours but cannot find out how many are *thought* to remain. We reach Mexico City in the afternoon. My room at the Hotel Reforma costs $7 a day.

July 29. Eat in Sanborn's, then go to the Cathedral and Chapultepec. I buy an alligator-skin briefcase. The newspapers say that the polio epidemic is greater here than in the United States where the Mexican children in Los Angeles do not contract it, but only the gringos. Telegraph the S.s to expect me tomorrow.

July 30. Fly to Monterrey and Nogales, where we leave the plane, undergo a medical inspection, and pass Immigration. Los Angeles from the air: even the smallest bungalow seems to have a swimming pool. Taxi to 1260 North Wetherly Drive, where the S.s are waiting dinner for me. I sleep on the couch in the den adjoining I.S.'s studio. The heights of predecessors here, including Auden, are notched and penciled inside the door of the closet; before I am allowed to go to bed, my measurement is added— below the elevation of the tallest guests, Aldous Huxley and Charles Olson, but far above that of the shortest, Beata Bolm.

July 31. I.S. exercises for nearly an hour before breakfast, including 15 minutes of hatha yogi head-stands. His breakfast consists of espresso and two raw eggs, swallowed in single gulps. After it, he takes me to his *sanctum sanctorum* and plays his Mass and as much as he has composed of the first scene of the *Rake*. His piano is a tacky-sounding and out-of-tune upright dampened with felt. A plywood board is attached to its music rack, and quarto-size strips of thick manila paper are clipped to it. All the staves are drawn with his styluses. To the side of the piano is a kind of surgeon's operating table on which the cutlery consists of an electric pencil-sharpener, an electric metronome, four different sizes of styluses, colored pencils, gums, a stopwatch. "Singing" all the time, facial muscles swelling, mouth quivering, veins bulging, he skips from part to part, searching for notes on the piano and groaning until he finds them, or, when the reach is too wide, asking me to play them. All of this is animal-like, or at least very physical, especially the grunts of satisfaction when the right chord is sounded exactly together. At the end, covered with perspiration, he mops his face with a towel from the table by the piano. The surprising part of the audition is the discovery that he wants reassurance. Mrs. S. had advised me: "If you like it, tell him"; but I cannot think of anything to say.

August 2. Nicolas Nabokov's description of the S. house leaves out a great deal. Much smaller than expected, this one-bedroom cottage is an overstocked museum, albeit a tidy one, and bright and cozy, with white walls and light-colored upholstery, pillows, rugs. Flowers are everywhere, and floppy rubber plants fill the dining room. The furniture does not include any antiques, and both pianos in I.S.'s studio are in poor condition. The library is largely Russian and French (a second edition—98 volumes— of Voltaire, surprisingly), with shelves of *romans policiers* and a complete set of German-language Baedekers. There are large collections of glass *presse-papiers* (marble weights, *piédouche* weights, torsades, swirls); coral; lapis lazuli; Russian cups, samovars, pyrogravure boxes; I.S.'s family silverware (huge tureens and ladles bearing the crown-shaped Kholodovsky coat-of-arms); pre-Columbian statuettes; and glass cases of tropical entomological

1948 specimens stuffed and mounted.

The house is a gallery of icons, paintings and drawings, among them ten Picassos (including the full-face line portrait of I.S.), several Tanguys, Tchelichevs, a Léger. I.S.'s bathroom is cluttered with blue-and-white porcelain apothecary jars; a tray of syringes; hot-water bottles, pill boxes with aperients, carminatives, and charcoal tablets, vials of medicines all neatly labeled in Russian by I.S. himself. Powders, unguents and ointments, drops, herbs (aconite, belladonna, henbane, calomel, valerian, veronal) and other *materia medica* crowd his night-table.

August 3. With the S.s to the Farmers Market, then to Forest Lawn: I.S. is very keen on *The Loved One*. He pronounces Whispering Glades, "glads," as in gladiolas. Dinner (*lapin*) *chez* Françoise, a marvelous cook. I.S. is the least indolent man I have ever observed: if he is not composing or orchestrating, writing or typing letters, he sets to work "making order" in his files.

August 4. Lunch and dinner with the S.s and to the Pickwick Book Store where I choose a small library for them.

August 6. Ingolf Dahl and Sol Babitz for dinner, but Popka, I.S.'s psittacine pet, is the center of attention, not I.S. The parrot waddles the length and breadth of the table scattering food and soiling the cloth. I.S. tickles the bird's underside, strokes its head feathers, and feeds it from his mouth, extending pieces of bread on his tongue. Fortunately, Popka, no linguist or verbal mimic, does not talk or even squawk.

August 8. Eugene Berman for lunch. In the afternoon we see *Birth of a Nation* in a cinema on Sunset Boulevard, then dine with him at the "Naples" restaurant (good zabaglione).

September 17. New York. I meet Soulima's flight and drive him to Baldwin Piano, where he practices for his Sunday concert.

September 18. With Soulima and Claudio Spies to the former's rehearsal of Mozart's Concerto K. 503 with the Columbia Broadcasting Symphony.

November 18. Card from Auden: ". . . would love to hear the *Mavra* records if you would say when and where. Just off to Washington. Back on Sunday night."

November 29. I conduct *Mavra* in a concert at the YMHA.

December 23. Letter from Auden agreeing to read three new poems in my February 26 concert.

🐚 **Postscript 1994.** On December 26–27, 1947, New York was buried under the heaviest snowfall since the blizzard of 1888. I was among the passengers incarcerated for more than twenty-four hours in one of hundreds of buses stalled on the approaches to the paralyzed city. But for me the worst part of the experience was that this intrusion of force majeure kept me from the only rehearsal of Stravinsky's Piano Concerto, which I was to conduct in Town Hall two days later. My failure to appear was particularly embarrassing in that all the orchestra players, residents of Brooklyn or Manhattan, were present and that I had been responsible in the first place for convincing the pianist, Elly Kassman, to include the piece in her recital program and her husband to pay for it.

Following a hastily-organized last-minute rehearsal, the concert took place and the performance went smoothly. But the ordeal had exhausted me. My father, about to leave for Florida, invited me to go with him for a rest. On January 1 we drove to Richmond and the next night to St. Augustine, going from grey to blue skies, barren trees and frozen rivers to lush green land and the aquamarine coast. During the following weeks we lived in a rented house near Palm Beach, and spent much of our time in automobile excursions to Orlando, the Lake Okeechobee sugar mills, Sarasota, the Everglades, and the Keys. At the end of January and the longest visit I had had with my father since my prep-school years, I returned to New York and prepared for my April concert.

By this time I had changed the repertory of my part of the program. Originally, Miss Kassman was to have repeated her performance of the Concerto. I now asked her to play the Capriccio instead, since I had decided to perform the Symphony in C, which included the necessary strings, and which was neglected at the time in favor of the Symphony in Three Movements. This made for a difficult program, and we were able to budget only three rehearsals. None of the music was familiar, and by the standards of the time all of it was rhythmically tricky. An additional problem for me was that the Symphony score was a very faint photocopy of Stravinsky's manuscript. Anxiously aware of my limited conducting experience, I set about to learn the music so thoroughly that somehow, perhaps by rote, singing each part for each player, I would manage to communicate it. My only guide was a radio air-check acetate recording, fuzzy and full of fade-outs, of Stravinsky's 1944 broadcast with the Boston Symphony.

Immediately after my return from California in August (via San Francisco, Yosemite, Chicago), I began to make plans for a second Town Hall concert, in which Stravinsky had already agreed to conduct the American premiere of his Mass, and had promised to prepare Latin versions of his Russian Sacred Choruses as companion pieces.

Two years after Stravinsky's death, B. H. Haggin's *Decade of Music* (Horizon Press) included an account of the first Town Hall concert and of my relationship with Stravinsky at that time. It provides a perspective from the outside. Neither of us ever met Haggin:

> Part of the Stravinsky story of recent years was the love seen in the relationship of Stravinsky and Robert Craft that began in 1948. As it happened, I heard Craft's first concerts at that time, and reported the remarkable performances of difficult works of Stravinsky that

11

1948 he produced with only two or three rehearsals of his small pick-up orchestra, chorus and soloists—performances in which he demonstrated his impressive gifts as a musician and conductor in his knowledge of every detail of the works that was evident in what he asked of performers and was able to get them to achieve. And I heard the concert in which Stravinsky participated, conducting his *Symphonies of Wind Instruments* and *Danses concertantes*. It became known that Craft had written to Stravinsky about the *Symphonies* in connection with the performance he was planning, and that the letter had so impressed Stravinsky that he offered to conduct the piece himself, and had done so without fee when Craft had told him he had no money. The understanding and feeling about Stravinsky's music that Craft had revealed in the letter, the gifts he revealed at the rehearsals and the concert, made understandable the continuing and close professional relation of Stravinsky and Craft in the years that followed.

🐝 *1949*

January 3. Telegram from I.S.: "Happy your *Mavra* success. Congratulations. Delighted Auden participation and your program suggestion. Just yesterday wired Richard Mohr my acceptance to record Mass on five sides with Russian Choruses on the sixth one. Now if these choruses eliminated wonder how to cut Mass without harm otherwise than if five sides."

January 9. From Auden: "Congratulations on the *Mavra* performance which seemed to me *excellent*. . . . Hope to see you soon."

January 23. Letter from Evelyn Waugh, Piers Court: "I shall be back in New York (Plaza Hotel) for a week from Jan. 28th. . . . Please let us meet and let us not miss the great honor of meeting Mr. Stravinsky."

January 26. Letter from Soulima: "Father will play *Rake*'s score to you and Auden, *nobody* else. So keep it an absolute secret, don't tell anybody (even Rieti or Nabokov). Will you arrange this meeting of, strictly, Auden, Father and Vera, at the Baldwin House, to make it absolutely incognito, sometime in the afternoon on February 3?"

February 3. 6:55 A.M., Pennsylvania Station. With Auden to meet the S.s' train, he from his Seventh Avenue apartment, presumably; me from my 415 West 53rd Street coldwater walk-up. Explaining that he has jury duty today, Auden asks I.S. to postpone the audition of Act One until evening. At dinner in the S.s' suite at the Ambassador, Auden is elated at "having hung the jury and obstructed injustice in the trial of a taxi driver who would have been a victim of the prejudice of automobile owners." When the S.s confess that they have never voted, he lectures them sternly on their civic responsibilities. We go to Sasha Schneider's for the *Rake*. Nabokov and Patricia are already there, and Balanchine who, with Auden, follows the score over I.S.'s shoulder at the piano. I turn pages, a tricky business, often either too soon or too late, and involving guess-work as to whether I.S. has remembered the last chord at the end of the page. Auden seems unaware that his violations of the strict rule of silence have irritated I.S. to an explosive degree. At the conclusion of the Act, Auden asks him

13

1949 to change the soprano's final note to a high "C." The word is wrong, I.S. says, whereupon Auden, after much "uh-uh-uh"-ing and "now-let's-see"-ing, comes up with a new last line ending in "heart." In the future, Auden advises I.S., take fewer pains to make every word audible (I.S., in the interests of verbal distinctness, having alternated, more often than blended, the voices in duets and trios).

February 4. The Waughs arrive at the S.s' suite in the Ambassador Hotel in evening dress—"for a late party at the Astors'," they say—the glittering perfection of which seems to exaggerate the crumples in our own everyday togs. Mrs. W. is fair and lovely, Mr. W. is pudgy, ruddy, smooth-skinned, and too short. He offers favorable comments on the temperature of the S.s' hotel rooms, complaining that he must keep the windows of his own rooms at the Plaza open or suffocate, a confession that may help to account for both his icy exterior and his inner heat. I.S. replies in French, attempting to excuse the switch in language with a compliment on the French dialogue in Mr. W.'s *Scott-King's Modern Europe*. Mr. W. cuts in, however, disclaiming any conversational command of the tongue, whereupon Mrs. W. contradicts him—"That's silly, darling, your French is very good"—and is sharply reprimanded.

I mention Mr. W.'s lecture in Town Hall last week on Graham Greene's *The Heart of the Matter*, the coolest performance of the sort I have ever seen, but he disparages it. Unencumbered by notes, he faced the audience like a ramrod and was able to study it, even to turn the tables on it, to judge by the ruthlessly observed details in his descriptions of three people who walked out.

Mr. W. prefers to talk about the undertaking industry and the ban it has imposed against burying him should he, as the industry must fervently hope, expire in the United States. "I have arranged to be buried at sea," he says. Keenly interested in our own burial plans, he is eager to know whether my *beaux restes* are destined for a family vault. But this down-to-earth talk makes I.S. uneasy.

A crisis occurs when Waugh refuses the S.s' whiskey, and their vodka and caviar, not so much because of his rudeness—"I never drink whiskey before wine"—but because the S.s exchange a few words in Russian, a pardonable recourse for them in many instances, but not now; and V.'s pretense, as she talks, of referring to the cigarettes she rummages for in her handbag does not take in Waugh who, naturally and correctly, deduces that the subject of the exchange is himself. A new impasse looms when Mr. W. asks I.S. about his American citizenship, says he deplores the American Revolution, and hears I.S. praise the Constitution. Thereupon I.S. proposes that we go to dinner, thus bringing the abstemious and uncomfortable half-hour to a close.

Mr. W.'s spirits take an upward turn during the freezing and, in his case, coatless, block-and-a-half walk to "Maria's." The sight of the Funeral

Home at the corner of Lexington Avenue and Fifty-Second Street so restores his *joie de vivre* that for a moment we fear he may actually take leave of us and explore the service entrance. "Maria's," small, dark, crowded, is the wrong restaurant: the W.'s are too swanky here. But the starchiness and defensive sparring that the S.s think of as the normal English method of making acquaintance vanish with the Valpolicella, which the temperature-sensitive Mr. W. mulls. It seems to me, too, that the novelist, like everyone who meets V., is succumbing to her charm. He begins to behave gallantly to her, in any case, and even the suspicion in the glowering glances he directs to I.S. diminishes.

With the fettucine the conversation turns—no apparent connection—to the Church. Here I.S. shines, showing himself to be at least as ultramontanist as Mr. W., as well read in Chesterton and Péguy, and as prone to believe in the miraculous emulsification of St. Januarius's blood. From some of the novelist's remarks, I would guess that he supposes the composer to be one of Maritain's Jewish converts, which is a common and, so far as the Maritain influence is concerned, partly accurate supposition.

Another crisis confronts us when V. mentions the forthcoming New York premiere of I.S.'s Mass and invites the W.s to attend. Explaining that the piece is liturgical, I.S. says, marvelously: "One composes a march to help men march; and it is the same way with my Credo: I hope to provide some help with the text. The Credo is long. There is a great deal to believe."

Mrs. W. handles this, sincerely regretting that they have already "booked passage home." Lest the conversation continue in this dangerous direction, her husband adds, with a bluntness that seems to show that he has been inwardly lacerating all evening by the threat of I.S.'s cacophonous art: "All music is painful to me." The statement can only be ignored, and V. does so, elegantly, with a compliment to Mr. W. on *his* art, and a comparison between his *Decline and Fall* and Sade's *Justine*. When at length Mr. W. realizes that the S.s have read everything he has published, a new character emerges in him, as magnanimous and amusing as the old one was unbending and priggishly precise.

If the novelist does not brook the literary talk of literary types, he certainly seems to enjoy it from outsiders like (though no one is like) the S.s and even from semi-insiders like (there are many like) me, for I admire Mr. W.'s fictions and no longer complain that chance and arbitrariness play too important a part in them. We seek to draw him out on other writers but are rewarded with only one acidulated reference to his fellow lecture-touring compatriots, the Sitwells, and the commendation, in which the last two adjectives are wickedly emphasized, of Christopher Isherwood as "a good young American novelist."

The meal concluded, Mr. W. asks permission to smoke a cigar. Choosing one from a case in his breast pocket, he holds it under his nose,

15

1949 where it looks like a grenadier's mustache, circumcises the sucking end with a small blade, passes a match under the other end as if he were candling a pony of precious cognac, avidly stokes and consumes it. Holy Smoke!

February 6. Afternoon train with I.S. to Boston, the Sheraton Hotel.

February 8. Morning rehearsal of *Orpheus* with the Boston Symphony, and evening concert in Sanders Theatre, Cambridge. Lunch at Edward Forbes's with Dr. Max Reinkel.

February 21. New York. A birthday lunch for Auden, after which we record the Piano Concerto for RCA in Manhattan Center. I.S. conducts, Soulima plays the solo, and I play the fourth trumpet part.

February 23. A visit from Koussevitzky. In the evening I rehearse the Mass for I.S. at 30 Rockefeller Plaza, Studio B.

February 26. 5:30 P.M. Town Hall. I begin the concert with the Octet, which the New York Philharmonic musicians play much less well than the Juilliard students three years ago. Soulima plays I.S.'s Sonata and, with Beveridge Webster, the Concerto for Two Solo Pianos. I.S. conducts the Mass twice. In the first part of the concert, Auden reads his poems, "In Praise of Limestone," "The Duet," and "Music is International." In contrast to his normally untidy, unwashed, uncombed, and unpressed appearance, he looks uncomfortably well-groomed. Stagefright intensifies his restlessness and impatience and, since the event takes place before martini hour, he shortens the distance between the links in his chain-smoking. He leads with his chin, moves awkwardly, and twice wipes his nose on his sleeve. The voice splutters and barks, thus adding to the impression he sometimes gives of a a very gentle hound. Yet by sheer force of intellect he is always in total command of the audience. He acknowledges the warm applause with a surprised grin, spastic bow, and the rapid exit that he makes at dinner parties on discovering that the hour is past his bedtime.

February 27. The three of us to lunch at "Maria's" with Coco Chanel. Dinner with Balanchine, Nabokov, and Dushkin.

February 28. The S.s leave for Chicago on the Twentieth Century Limited.

March 5. A letter from Aaron Copland answering my invitation to play one of the pianos in *Noces*:

> Through an unfortunate series of circumstances the final concert of the League of Composers had to be postponed until April 10. You can imagine how disappointed I am, both from the standpoint of not being able to appear as pianist, and from the standpoint of our running rival events. As for Marc Blitzstein's participating as pianist I think it would be more effective if you invited him yourself. He knows who you are, of course, and can certainly appreciate the sentimental value of the occasion. His address is: 4 East 12th Street. Good luck on the concert. Yours cordially.

April 19. I conduct *Noces* (pianos: Charles Rosen, Elly Kassman,
Leonid Hambro, Robert Cornman), *Histoire du Soldat* (Isadore Cohen, David
Oppenheim, Bernard Garfield, *et al.*), and *Pastorale* (Ralph Gomberg, *et al.*),
on a program with Bartok's Sonata for Two Pianos and Percussion.

May 1. Princeton University Chapel. I assist Carl Weinrich in a program of Gabrieli, Schütz, Ruggles (*Angels*, in which I play trumpet), I.S.'s
Mass.

May 7. From I.S.: "I had already read your brilliant article in *Musical
America*. Has it been printed in full there? . . . I doubt it. Remember June
1st—Love, ISTR."

May 14. McMillan Theater, Columbia University. In a concert sponsored by the American Academy and the National Institute of Arts and
Letters, I conduct the Princeton and Bryn Mawr choirs in I.S.'s Mass and
conduct a piece for strings by Louis Mennini. The program includes four
sonatas for prepared piano by Cage, and six songs by Stefan Wolpe.

May 25. Telegram from I.S.: "Happy to see you dearest Bob. Please
come directly Wetherly Drive for early breakfast with us."

May 31. Leave Newark Airport on a non-scheduled flight for Los
Angeles via Philadelphia, Washington, Pittsburgh, Nashville, Oklahoma
City, Albuquerque, Phoenix.

June 1. Taxi to the S. house at 5 P.M.!

June 3. David Diamond for lunch says that he visited Schoenberg, who
glared at his summer print shirt "and wanted it then and there. The
Juilliards were there to play his four quartets to him."

June 14. At tonight's *Soldat* rehearsal, Royce Hall, UCLA, I.S. intro-
duces me to Bronislava Nijinsky, who is deaf and fat. The staging is by
Henry Schnitzler, the son of the playwright. Antonia Cobos dances the
Princess.

June 18. I.S.'s birthday. Drive in silence to and from the Russian
Church. Home, after Confession, he prays before the icon in his studio.
The meaning of the *Symphony of Psalms* dedication, he says, is St. Thomas's
"art is a way to God." He remains in a foul mood until late afternoon when
Balanchine and about 20 others come for a party. Balanchine says that he,
Maria Tallchief, and Nicky Magallanes drove out from New York via
Oklahoma in only five days.

June 20. I.S. says that he feels closer to some animals than to some humans, and he tells me that he kept a clutch of chickens when he first lived
in California, and would have added cows, goats, and a whole *Renard* barn-
yard as well but for zoning laws and neighbors who "want every lawn to
look as neatly manicured as a cemetery or golf course." The house even
now is a rookery, a bird cage, and from time to time a wildlife refuge.
Canaries have the run of the living room, munching the leather book bindings, target-practicing on the lampshades, and as many as forty lovebirds—
some making love, some just necking—can be counted in the kitchen. At

1949 table, the same parakeets as last summer, gifts of Emil Ludwig, take turns pecking food directly from I.S.'s mouth, and depositing nibs, feathers and unmentionable other matter uncomfortably near the *déjeuner*. An extraordinarily un-shy hummingbird, frequenting the back patio, alights in I.S.'s hand.

June 21. At lunch time, today and every day, V. comes to the door of the living room and claps her hands, her way of calling I.S. If his studio door is open, and he hears her, he applauds back. If in a good mood, he comes quickly and gives her a resounding osculation.

June 22. I.S.'s equivalent gesture for head-scratching, which, with his unwigged dome, he cannot do, is to clamp his left hand over his mouth.

July 1. I.S. does not have perfect pitch; he cannot, out of the clear, distinguish G from F-sharp, and if his record player happened to transmit the *Jupiter* Symphony in B instead of C, he would complain about the slow tempo but probably not about the key.

I.S. does not know how to whistle—he tells me that St. Petersburg droshky drivers whistled to provoke their horses to urinate—and, except while composing, he rarely sings. When he does, it is a "ta-ta-ta" solfeggio, far from the actual pitches. Apart from his work in progress on the *Rake*, the only tune I have heard him "carry" is from the *Dreigroschenoper*, which he "sang" not for the music but for the words.

When composing, I.S. must be alone, and on composing days he is incommunicado. He holes up in his studio, shutting the outer doors of the foyer and the double doors of his soundproof room, quite literally sealing himself in. On emerging, he is silent or grumpy, and his temper tantrums are more frequent and longer than normally. No information is forthcoming about work-in-progress, the crisis in the soul in his case being reflected by moody silences. Another reliable sign that creative problems are under attack is a return to the Eighteenth Amendment, which is repealed the moment they have been solved.

While orchestrating, he likes companionship, and asks me to read to him, interrupting from time to time to say "just a moment" (*i.e.*, "be quiet"), then, a moment later, "And?" When V. did not feel well and remained in bed one afternoon last week, he brought a table from his studio to her bedside and orchestrated there, ostensibly to keep her company, but *he* was the one who did not want to be alone.

He talks constantly about rules in art and the necessity of obeying them. When he says that musical composition has its rules, he means the textbook kind, those that have been deduced and formulated from the works of the masters. Yet his own supreme rule is that of thumb (*i.e.*, ear).

I.S. likes to copy music. He has duplicated entire scores of his own as well as, when he wishes to learn a piece thoroughly, of other composers. This is a hobby and a relaxation, but it is also the exercise of his talents as calligrapher.

I.S. seems to enjoy total recall of his intensely active, creative, and often technicolor dreams, and these form one of the two main subjects of his breakfast conversation. (The other is the revoltingly vivid description of the morning's bowel movement, which includes form and texture—"minestrone" or "consommé," and even perfume, whether sulfurous or acrid.) The origins of many of his compositions, as well as the solutions of musical problems, have come in dreams. As Sir Thomas Browne wrote, "the slumber of the body seems to be but the working of the soul."

Beneath the intellectual lurks the athlete, all muscle and bone. Very vain of his physique, I.S. likes to show off his stomach muscles, lying flat on the floor and, like the strong man in the circus side-show, inviting people of twice his weight to stand on him between rib cage and abdomen. Ordinarily my first view of him each morning, on the awninged concrete porch adjoining the living room, is upside down. He will hold this inverted position, head on a straw mat, legs skyward, for as long as ten minutes, then execute a whole manual of toe-touching, torso-twisting, knee-bending exercises, concluding with a dozen "chins" on the metal crossbar in his bedroom closet. Only when he wraps himself in his white terrycloth robe and sets off for the shower am I reminded of how completely this particular athlete is lacking in brawn.

I.S., the musical miniaturist, needs to surround himself with tiny objects, including thumbnail photos in minuscule polyptic fold-out frames.

No one is allowed to disturb the sacred rite of afternoon tea. This is served not in a cup but in a glass with a metal holder (*podstakannik*) under the glass. The tea must be very hot and very weak ("In St. Petersburg, we could see Kronstadt through the tea") and served with pumpernickel or black bread, jams, cakes. He eats some of the bread immediately but does not drink the tea until just before rising to leave, by which time, as he says, it is "lukey-warm." Tea-time is for mental digestion, a period of thought, a half-hour "break," but without conversation. During it he always plays a game of solitaire—two, if he loses the first.

A half hour before dinner, I.S. drinks Scotch, or a tumbler of straight Bols gin from a terracotta bottle, and eats a piece of Gruyère or prosciutto. Depending on the quality of the day's work, he will drink to the point of inebriation. As Drummond of Hawthornden observed of Ben Jonson, drink is "one of the elements in which he liveth." Dinner is washed down with a bottle of white Burgundy, a bottle of claret—I.S. is a carnivore— and, at the end, a bottle of champagne.

July 4. Though professing to loathe parties, when attending one I.S. quickly becomes its voluble epicenter. (V. recalls that in their first years in Hollywood they would return from movie stars' parties and read Dostoevsky together, "to remind ourselves about human beings.") We go to a poolside reception for him at Harold English's, but the guest of honor keeps well away from water, internally and externally.

1949 I.S. retains the Russian gender pronouns in English. After swatting a fly, for example, he refers to the corpse as "she." But the idiosyncrasies of his English are not always traceable to Russian constructions. "I finded it," he will say, "later one" (for later "on"), "close the towel" (for "fold"), "rape" ("*rapez*") the cheese. Conductors and critics are *un*competent—music critics are hemorrhoids—and, though very rarely in relation to him, a review is "eulogious." "It doesn't arrange me" means "suit me."

In Russian, I.S. is by no means shy of the earthy and indelicate. His customary response to ribald gossip, a result, perhaps, of his early training in law school, is "*Kto derzhal ikh za nogi?*" ("Who was holding their legs?"), and among his workaday critical expressions are "*u menia ne stoit*" ("It doesn't give me an erection"), "*khuy golandsky*" ("Dutch penis," this in reference to someone of exceptional *mental* density), and "*mandit*," which is not found in his Russian dictionaries. He also uses the portmanteau word "*podmyvatsya*," meaning to wash one's private parts; a few days ago he told a wine steward who had served a corky Chablis to "pour it into a bidet and *podmyvatsya*." Among the words classified by his Russian friends as Stravinskyisms is "*krivossachka*," which he uses to refer to a woman who cannot urinate straight, but only in a curve. Always graphic, he illustrates the difficulty with pencil and paper, drawing a "*priyamaya linia*" (————) and a "*krivaya linia*" (～～). "*Mentalité*" is a much used word, but always deprecatingly: "What a *mentalité!*" "*Emmerder*" is one of the handiest expressions in his vocabulary; a driver moving at first-gear speed in the road in front of us is an "*emmerdeur*."

I.S. is especially devoted to the word "drag," which he first learned as a musical direction in a score by Henry Purcell and now employs while rehearsing orchestras, as well as in his business correspondence: "Don't drag, please." According to V., he has a substantial Ukrainian vocabulary, though all that I have learned of it (apart from words like "*hospodar*," which are in the English dictionary) is "*ne vihiliates*," the laconic direction in railway cars that I.S. likes to contrast to the German version: "*Das Hinauslehnen des Oberkorpers aus dem Fenster ist gegen der damit verbundenen Lebensgefahr strengstens verboten*." German usages are frequent targets of his ridicule, though many of his favorite words and sayings are in that language: "*plopper*" (for someone who talks too much and to no purpose); "*fificus*"—though the French "*tapette*" occurs at least as often; "*feine Gesellschaft*"; "*mit langen Zähnen*"; and Wilhelm Busch's "*Erstens ist es anders, Zweitens als man denkt*." Not surprisingly, I.S.'s English is as polyglot as *Finnegans Wake*, from the morning's first "so-so la-la" (a standard response to "How do you feel?") to the last comment of the evening on the performance of a piece of music: "*grosso modo*."

I.S. is addicted to inter-language puns, especially those involving words that are proper in one tongue but improper ("*unanständig*," he prefers to say) in another; yet V. says that he is an inveterate punster in Russian as well. (The tendency to play with words as things in themselves, and thus diminish their primary value as sign functions, is supposed to be a withdrawal-from-reality symptom, but in I.S.'s case no other behavior corroborates the diagnosis.) At the moment he is interested in paronyms, such as differ and defer, and in homophones, such as "puny" and "puisne," and especially those with diametrically opposite meanings, like "raise" and "raze," "seize" and "cease." A part of his daily conversation is concerned with word investigations and lexical comparisons. He will not allow an uncertain term to pass until satisfied with a full etymological, as well as current-usage, understanding of it, and his pursuit of English equivalents for Russian, German, and French idioms can interrupt a meal or conversation for a quarter of an hour while he disappears among his dictionaries and obliges us to await his findings. He is fond of declensions and can be launched on them by such accidents as my use at dinner yesterday of "enthusiasm," which is the same word in Russian: "Enthusiasmum is the accusative, enthusiasma the dative, enthusiasmu the. . . ."

July 8. A hospital bed is installed in I.S.'s room to help relieve the pain from the pinched nerve in the shoulder of his writing arm.

July 9. This morning's household routine is shattered by the discovery that Popka is female. Yvgenia Petrovna has found an egg in the parakeet's nest, a wine-bottle basket in the kitchen closet. Popka is the most pampered of I.S.'s feathered pets. Though occasionally caged or held in jesses, the bird more often has the run of the house, including the dinner table, where it tramples the food, eats and excretes, tracks butter on the linen—until I.S. extends a forefinger, orders it to perch there, then, like Long John Silver, lifts it to his shoulder.

I.S. abhors clumsiness in any form, and goes into conniptions when people drop, spill, stumble. He is prejudiced against anyone with a loud voice, including his friend the Reverend James McLane; V. attributes some of the perfect harmony of their marriage to her very quiet one. *All* noise is painful to I.S. He will jump out of his chair if Yvgenia Petrovna smashes a cup, and even the most distant bombination of a hammer or drill drives him "mad." He notices noises heard by no one else, having an especially keen ear for discrepancies, from one block to the next, in the engine of his wife's automobile.

I.S. has a rich lore of Russian folk stories, of which I like best the one about the peasant who, asked what he would do if he were made Tsar, says: "I would steal everything I could carry and run as fast as possible."

July 11. Efrem Kurtz, conductor of the Houston Symphony, for lunch. The S.s clearly like him, as they like and feel at home with all Russians. Dr. Engelman comes in the evening for I.S.'s shoulder pains.

July 12. The S.s often play *Patience royale* together, V. steering, I.S. ruddering. The game occupies only a small and automatic part of his mind, leaving his musical digestion—a favorite I.S. expression—uncompetitively to its own processes; it is the perfect pastime for him between spells of

1949 composing. When playing by himself, he grunts and curses; an eavesdropper collecting late-Tsarist-period Russian *gros mots* would surely be able to increase his or her vocabulary.

July 21. To Hollywood Bowl to see Vera Zorina in *Jeanne d'Arc au bûcher*.

July 24. Lobster lunch with the S.s at Malibu. They now call me Bobe exclusively; the word as they pronounce it means bean in Russian. An afternoon visit from Ralph Hawkes, en route to London from Australia. He wants the *Rake* premiere for the Edinburgh Festival.

July 27. Aldous and Maria Huxley for dinner, she petite and eager, with large, believing eyes in a small, pinched face, he even taller than anyone had warned. But I look first at his silver-point features, especially the slightly hooked, slightly haughty nose. I had expected his blind eye to be buffed, but a milky film, like clouded glass, covers the right cornea and he turns the unflawed, rapidly nictitating left eye to us. His skin is desiccated—from the desert sun during his anchorite period, one would suppose, except that he is also chlorotic. Apart from the big weedy brows, everything about him suggests not the out-of-doors, but the tightly sealed edifices of learning. What strikes me next is that he seems so out of scale in the diminutive, I.S.-size house, crouching under the low ceilings, ducking through the doorways, flinching from a chandelier, reaching out for the table. One feels that it may really be unsafe for him here, that he could actually trap himself in I.S.'s tiny WC and never get out.

We are still more aware of his visual limitations at dinner, when he feels for his knife, fork, and plate with the palpations of a blind man. His wife helps him to find the food, and she continues to direct him throughout the meal in quiet asides. *"Un tout petit peu à gauche, chéri,"* she whispers when his knife fails to find a purchase on the chicken (which his brand of vegetarianism allows), and in the same voice she advises him how long to uptilt the salt shaker; but he would not welcome, indeed would resent, any solicitude from another source. Conversation is in French, partly because it is the H.s' domestic language, partly because I.S. is not attuned to Huxleyan English, having been confined to my backwoods American. The word "issue," for example, a clean, sibilant "iss-u" in Mr. H.'s mouth, is a gooey "ish-shoe" in mine. I do not know what the S.s make of "my-thology" and "skies-ophrenia."

I.S. seems to think of Mr. H. as an English-born Frenchman, quintessentially English in manners (good in I.S.'s book), but in other respects more civilized (French). Language apart, the two men inhibit each other. If Mr. H. is the wrong size, he is also the wrong culture. That sovereignty of scientific rationalism, the blueprint of his intellectual heredity, is a planet away from I.S.'s mystagogic view of human existence. I.S. has not followed any science or philosophy since his University of St. Petersburg years, at which time he was immersed in Kant, and he is in terror all evening lest

22

Mr. H. dwells on scientific theories and deeds. Yet Mr. H. is as self-conscious of his own limitations in being unable to stem the flow of his thoughts long enough to approach the world of the other from the other's bias. The two men watch each other like champions of two mutually incomprehensible games, but for basic toeholds rather than gambits.

Mr. H.'s voice, a lambent, culture-saturated purr, is as memorable as his head. His stories ripple musically through pursed lips, the longer anecdotes beginning in dove-tones and rising toward what promise to be explosive finishes, but knotting instead, or fizzling out at the climactic high note. And what a storyteller he is! As family history alone, his autobiography would contain the richest material of any writer alive, while to judge from tonight's tales of Joyce, Pound, Eliot, and Yeats, such a book could also be one of the most entertaining for the 1920s. Best of all, he betrays no mark of the repertory company. Good as these performances are, the most astonishing occurs when he examines I.S.'s collection of sea shells. Holding each specimen under a magnifying glass two inches from his left eye, Mr. H. casually provides a breathtaking conchological commentary, apologizing the while for his knowledge and begging our pardon each time he drops another Latin name.

The hunching and cringing from the confines of Lilliput begin all over again on the way back to the living room, though having charted the reefs in his memory he now moves with a gliding, if slightly rubbery walk. We ensconce him in the largest chair, from which he seems to squirm away— parts of him anyway—like a cornered cephalopod, now stretching its peripatetic tentacles to alarming length, now cupping them in. As he listens to us, his fingers plait and unplait, or tickle the fenders of his chair, but when he talks, his arms move continuously and rapidly in large illustrative gestures so that, like Vishnu, he seems to have several pairs of them.

And what does he talk about? The finding of bacteria at ocean depths; the heightening of erotic sensibilities through breathing exercises; the sexual customs of the American utopias, especially the Oneida experiment in training adolescent boys on women past the menopause; the greater sexual appeal of the larger and lower-voiced male Tingara frog (the *Physalaemus pustulossus*); Baudelaire's Latin poems, which "demonstrate wide reading in the type of poem but complete ignorance of stress, merely duplicating the number of syllables"; problems of multiple meanings in Pali, "which is not a subtle language, but has thirty different words for 'knowledge' "; Augustus Hare (whose taste for oddity seems to me rather like Mr. H.'s own); the possibility of flights to the moon within a decade if enough money were to be diverted to the project, although Mr. H. says that his only interest in visiting another planet would be to establish contact with an older civilization. This river of learning is continually nourished by tributaries of quotations—a clerihew, the whole of *Le vierge, le vivace et le bel aujourd'hui*, which he recites as though he were reading from an oculist's

1949 chart, except for one small stumble of memory, from which he picks himself up with an air of surprise that none of us had caught him as he tripped. No doubt Mr. H. can provide as much Bartlett on any topic, and no doubt the anthology automatically flicks open to the right page.

July 29. Dinner at Jean Renoir's. The French is too fast for me and I remain silent.

August 4. Balanchine for dinner.

August 7. The Balanchines for lunch.

August 8. I.S. is obsessed with mirrors, not out of a desire to multiply himself or any metaphysical wish to go through the looking glass (unlike Alice, he *is* "quite sure what I'm going to be, from one minute to another"), but simply to reassure himself, constantly and from all angles, that everything is in place. (Curiously, he does not recognize his voice on a record, as he mentioned in a recent interview: "Why is this? I have asked many engineers. No one can explain it.") Still another of his obsessions is with scissors, apparently because, like many nearly bald men, he is forever trimming remnants of "haars," a form of the plural that he insists should be admitted in cases such as his. But many utensils fascinate him, including dentists' tools. Hardware stores are magnetic lures whose spell can be broken only by the purchase of a bag of nails, a shiny new monkey wrench, or an implement for his gardening or carpentering. One of his hobbies is making picture frames, for which he has had a diamond glass-cutter built to his specifications.

I.S. collects small ivory, metal, leather, wood, papier-maché boxes; he has no fewer than forty, of which he alone remembers the contents. Inordinately, even fetishistically, fond of the smell of leather, he will hold a wallet or pouch to his nose as others would sniff a carnation. Otherwise, his favorite odors are of coffee—especially the aroma when a tin of it has been newly opened ("Coffee never tastes as good as it smells")—and tobacco. He rolls his own cigarettes, partly for the olfactory gratification, but also because the handwork appeals to him. He is the most tactile man I have ever known. He likes to touch wood, to wrap packages, to feel: one of his favorite expressions is: "I have to touch the music" (*i.e.,* through the piano).

I.S. perfectly fits Freud's description of the anal personality: the cataloguing; the thrift; the accumulating, retaining, hoarding (he saves every rubber band and string); the exactness and exactingness; the tidiness and neatness: he cannot resist wiping the ring left on a table by the glass of a guest or dinner companion; the possessiveness, which extends to people (he demands fealty from friends, subservience from servants); the superstitious fears—of funerals, of illnesses (he will leave a room in which someone has coughed or sneezed), of being without money, of intestinal irregularities (especially oppilations). For this last, the sheer volume of his talk about *govno* is impressive, but what compels him to publish his cloacal news of the day ("soft," "hard") on each morning's "bulletin board"? The Russian word, which also means "black," is more literally pertinent than the French, German, and English words because of the charcoal that he munches before drinking, and against the acidity of, champagne. He uses the word *perdit*—crepitation—with great frequency and even in his music (*Renard*). On "hard" days no breakfast passes without reference to his *"poire"* (syringe), and three times this summer he has described a childhood auto-coprophagous experiment (*"sans gout"*). Anyone who happened to see I.S.'s surprisingly large collection of photographs of himself in the nude might conclude that he is exhibitionistic. Whatever the truth of this, he is proud of his muscles, and he likes to sunbathe stark naked—though perhaps he does not wear a bathing suit simply because, being unable to swim, he does not have one.

I.S.'s sexual utopia is mammary, his sexual type the opulent Rubens goddess (the uberous bosoms, that is; the mesial features of the back do not excite him to the same extent). The psychogenesis of the attraction might well have been an insufficiency on the part of his wetnurse, but it is not an undifferentiated desire (any port in a storm), perhaps not even a desire at all, but a fixation. Inspired by a ro-busty woman at a neighboring table in a restaurant, he will wean himself from the view just long enough to sketch the "heaving embonpoint" on the tablecloth. And whereas his drawings of Picasso, Catherine (the first Mrs. Stravinsky), Ramuz, Diaghilev, Tansman, and myself, are characterized by radical abbreviation, *these* forms are fully filled (*formosa*) and complete with areolas.

I.S. is vain to the extent that he will not go out to dinner because of a pimple on his nose. And he is a dandy, a collector of silk scarves, handkerchiefs, pajamas, cravats, gloves. He will spend as much as ten minutes in selecting the proper neckwear, and V. recalls that after the premiere of Falla's *Retablo* at the Princesse de Polignac's, its composer and I.S. were observed conversing animatedly in a corner, not about the new opus, as V. learned, but about Falla's necktie. (Schoenberg said that he would like to have watched Mahler tying his necktie.) Before going out to dinner tonight, I.S. says, "I'll wear a sincere tie."

August 10. Lunch at the Farmers Market with the S.s., Huxleys—cooing at each other today like newlyweds, or oldlyweds making up after a spat—and Christopher Isherwood. Because of the extensive variety of its salads, seeds (Aldous eats quantities of sunflower seeds, for his eyes), nuts, health foods, fruit (Milton: "The savoury pulp they chew, and in the rind"), the restaurant is a Huxleyan haunt. Most of the other tables are held down by drugstore cowboys, movie stars, Central European refugees, and—to judge by the awed glances in our direction—Aldine and Igorian admirers. All are vegetarians, for the nonce, and all nibble at their greens like pasturing cows.

One immediately sees what Virginia Woolf meant by likening

1949 Isherwood to a jockey. Nothing in his clothes, of course, suggests the furlong post, the track and turf, or the pari-mutuel window, but they are less conspicuously suited to Hollywood than those of Aldous or I.S. (both of them sporting much too resonant neckwear, as if they had lost their sense of the dapper at this remove from more discriminating and conservative centers of haberdashery). It is a question of the slight stature, bantam weight, somewhat too short legs, and disproportionately, even simianly, long arms, a comparison forced on the attention because of their frequent employment for metrical purposes. It is in the build of the man that one understands Mrs. Woolf.

Isherwood's manner is casual, vagabondish, lovelorn. One does not imagine him in a fit of anger, or behaving precipitately, or enduring extended states of great commotion. At moments he might be thinking of things beyond and above, from which the conversation brusquely summons him back to earth. He is a listener and an observer, with the observer's habit of staring, rather than an initiator, a propounder and expatiator, of new subjects; his trancelike eyes will see more deeply through us and record more essential matter about us than this verbosity of mine is doing about him. At the same time, his sense of humor is very ready, and he maintains a chronic or semi-permanent smile (a network of small creases about the mouth), supplementing it with chuckles and an occasional fullthrottle laugh, during which the tongue lolls. But he is not at ease in spite of the drollery. Underneath—for he is as multi-layered as a *mille* (in practice rarely more than a *six* or a *huit*) *feuille*—are fears, the uppermost of which might well be of a musical conversation or high general conversation about The Arts. But I could be miles off. Perhaps he is merely suffering from the prohibition rule of the Farmers Market, and in this case the contents of I.S.'s thermos bottles will come as an agreeable surprise.

Issyvoo conveys greetings to "All-deuce," as he pronounces it, from a swami. The voice, both in pitch and volume, is too high, and the words are too deliberated. Aldous, replying, digresses to make room for a ribald story, which Isherwood follows like an eager schoolboy, exclaiming "Oh, boy!" and rubbing his knees in anticipation of the outcome. He also says "heck!," "swell!," "by golly!," "gosh!," "gee whiz!," and "gee whillikers."

Apart from their very evident mutual affection, how do the two men regard each other? Isherwood cannot match the softly orating Huxleyan delivery or the Huxleyan intellectual ammunition (a stunning aside on the "haeccities of the later Persian mystics," an apt quote from the *Biathanatos*, and the most recent information about amino acids and cellular differentiation). But then, the younger man has made his name partly on his wariness of fluency at supernal intellectual altitudes. Is he gently baiting the sage, tweaking his proboscis a bit by that credulous way of asking those further questions about the marvelous, the horrendous, and the barely believable that are so much a part of All-deuce's talk? Or does he regard him as ever so slightly unbalanced from too much book learning? Not really deranged, like Don Quixote, but a bit "off" nevertheless?

And am I wrong in sensing the faintest tinge of doubt on the Huxley side as to the hundred-percent impregnability of his younger colleague's spiritual dedication and final severance from The World?, in detecting just the hint of a suspicion that one last unburned boat may still be hidden somewhere in the reeds? We suppose, in any case—it is the S.s' impression as well as my own—that the younger man is obliged to apply himself to those spiritual exercises that the older one masters merely by turning his mind to them. The Huxley universe is the larger of the two, but the author of the Isherwood books sits no less securely in the center of *his*, and partly for this reason—the critical acuteness in the books—to meet Isherwood is more of an encounter than to meet Aldous. Another reason is simply that most of us are little more than enchanted audiences for Aldous, not because he wills it that way, but because we have no choice. Whatever the truth of these speculations, how improbable a team to represent Vedanta in the Wild West!

I.S., as I know him, is even less comfortable than Isherwood. He dislikes being outnumbered by Englishmen speaking their language, and these particular Englishmen probably seem to him too freely, richly verbal; in I.S.'s world, the important things cannot be said. But I.S. presents an almost exaggerated contrast in other ways as well: in his deep diapason, versus their duet of flute-stops; in his love of concreteness: the Englishmen's talk about religion is too abstract for him; he believes in the physical existence of the Devil and his Infernal Regions, as at one time people believed in mermaids; and in the autocracy and absoluteness of his views, though these can seem more extreme than they are simply because of his imperfect command of the flutey language's syntactic qualifying paraphernalia.

I would exchange some, if less than half, of my kingdom for a peek at the picture these two observers draw of I.S. Will they discover that the epigrams, paradoxes, *bons mots*, conceal nothing at all in their line? Or will they conclude that the treasures are being kept to the deeps out of reticence, to be surfaced again on other, more favored days? Whatever the answer, and both conclusions would be wrong, the polite side of I.S., that Bellona's armor of will in the man and of style in the music ("Music may symbolize, but it cannot express"), is the only side anyone except V. ever sees.

Why, then, have people mistaken I.S. for an "intellectual"? Primarily, I think, because it is his own preferred image of himself. Vain of his "factual knowledge," he would actually like to be regarded as a *summa* of erudition, the wielder of the ultimate gavel of sophisticated judgment. Nor will he tolerate such terms as "instinct" and "genius" in relation to himself, pretending instead that "brains" and "technique," meaning the perfection of the ear

1949 and the mastery of means, constitute the composer's full equipment. "Emotions," it follows, are scarcely admitted to be an ingredient. Moreover, he seems to think of the affective functions as physiologically zoned, like the separation of emotion and intelligence in Comte's *tableau cérébral*.

Little as it matters, I.S.'s intellectual world apart from music has been formed to a great extent by his intimates. He is radically susceptible to personal influence, which I say because I can see effects that I myself have had on him. (V. says that I am the only friend in his adult life who has disagreed with him and survived, a dubious distinction both as conduct and consequence.) For my own part, and though it hardly requires saying, I entertain few if any fixed views capable of withstanding "rigorous intellectual investigation" (I.S. has made me more aware than I was before that I am a "feeler" rather than a "thinker"), and I certainly want no responsibility for any of them, musical or otherwise, settling on such a man. But I.S.'s susceptibility is in question, not *whose* view.

The chief influence was Diaghilev. V. cites certain aesthetic attitudes as virtually parroted from him, and she insists that "Before age and America changed Stravinsky's character, he opened his heart only to Diaghilev; furthermore, Diaghilev's criticisms were the only ones Stravinsky ever heeded." Since Diaghilev's death, and throughout the subsequent years of concert nomadism, Stravinsky has carried a locket containing a miniature icon that Diaghilev admired. Ramuz and Cingria were later influences—the *homo faber* philosophy and the ideal of the village virtues, meaning the moral superiority of simple things—*les vins honnetes*, for instance, meaning Grade B. Arthur Lourié, proselytizing for Maritain, was still another, as were Nabokov and Suvchinsky: a philosophy compiled of Herzen and Berdyaev in the case of the former, of Rozanov and Shestov in the case of the latter.

Certainly these and the very few others who knew I.S. intimately must have realized that, while his artistic intelligence is uncanny and the palettes of his sense perceptions are acute and varied, his critical range is peculiarly limited. What he offers are judgments without trials in a no-man's-land of likes and dislikes. At a time when no-man's-lands quickly become so much real estate crossed by so many beaten paths, the hazard to himself hardly requires spelling out. "Taste," as we grow older, is a narrowing tyranny. I would like to have put many questions to these illustrious predecessors but must put some prior ones to myself. What, for a beginning, of Chamfort's warning that "A philosopher attached to the train of a great man finds it necessary to conceal his true feelings?"

August 19. To the Huxleys for tea—parsley tea with crystal sugar, and a tray of molasses cookies, wheat germ, raw carrots, small wedges of non-fattening fruit cake. Architecturally, the house—on King's Road, where large homes hide behind woods and hedges—would satisfy the taste in mansions of a retired Kenya colonial. The furnishings are so spare, the large rooms so unadorned, that one is tempted to inquire when the occupants expect to move in to stay. The place is in contrast in most other ways as well to the S. house, which, like the composer himself, is small, snug, brightly lighted, not forbiddingly private, and as packed as a provincial art gallery. The lights are off as we enter, drawn curtains notwithstanding, and the sole evidence of Edison is a lamp in Mr. H.'s study, which could be a consulting office, except for the overflow of books, or a secret room for third-degree interrogations. The walls are bare, apart from a few of Mr. H.'s own watercolors, Cézanne-inspired landscapes with trees and rocks. The chairs are Mies-like and severe.

I.S. does not scintillate in such surroundings. And when Mrs. H. withdraws, taking V. with her so that the boys may have a smoking-room chat, he is not only uncomfortable but positively frightened of having to face Mr. H. without V.'s support. As I know I.S., he is whetting for a whiskey, but the display of health foods and Mrs. H.'s gingerly proffered carafe of sherry (after a slightly snickering reference to booze) intimidate him, and he does not ask for it. The sepulchral lighting and raftered baronial hall dampen the conversation, too. Mr. H. is serious here, and we are reverent and hushed, though for my part I could not have contributed more than a twig or two to the blaze of Mr. H.'s talk, and these I hold back, not because of the bleakness of the decor but because of self-consciousness in delivering my verbal congestions.

But no matter, Mr. H. alone and uninterrupted could hardly be bettered, and I am soon regretting that no tape machine has preserved him today on the culinary mortifications of St. Philip Neri. Mr. H. is far more engaging to listen to than to read, the conversation outclassing the writing in at least two ways: the talk is comparatively free of the late-Tolstoy sermonizing that has become such a heavy part of the books; and the talker embroiders his main thematic paths with a luxury of odd links, an anastomosis of curious connections (the style is beginning to affect me!) that the writer could not—no writer could—afford to pursue.

What is Mr. H. to I.S.? First of all, a kind of handy, neighborhood university. I.S., like a quiz-contest master of ceremonies, is forever wanting immediate answers to random matters of fact. He will leave the dinner table to trace some scrap of information and return thirty minutes and two cold courses later—empty-handed, as often as not, for lack of a methodology. But if Mr. H. is in town, I.S. need only pick-up the telephone, as he did yesterday when he wanted a rundown on the history of scissors. I.S. is convinced that Mr. H. suffers from, and is a prisoner of, his encyclopedic erudition, though the Tao of his seemingly unquenchable quest could also be freedom through possession.

And I.S. to Mr. H? A "creative genius"—or, as scientists prefer, "hopeful monster"—is the simple, but I think complete, answer: one of the few in-

1949 vested with the power to create. Mr. H. prostrates himself before the mystery of this power and even regards it as justification for the existence of the human species. In the early years, D. H. Lawrence was Mr. H.'s creative genius, and whatever qualities, Lawrentian or otherwise, the words represent for Mr. H. now, he still thirsts for them as others do for religious inspiration. He would disclaim the possession of even a pinch of creative genius in himself, allowing the classification "creative writer" to be used with reference to himself only if he were attempting to explain his low income to a tax collector. He writhes at the hint of a reference to his work, and a direct question about a book-in-progress would, I think, dissolve him altogether. Contrast this with I.S., who beams with satisfaction at the mention of *his* tiniest opus. But I.S. *is* a creator.

Mr. H. also mistakenly looks to I.S. as a source of knowledge *about* music, and not only for the secrets of art, but for the plainest musicological facts as well. His appetite for this knowledge appears to be insatiable, moreover, though he already commands a large store of music history and a tune-humming acquaintance with the repertory which, on that level, may be as wide as I.S.'s. That such knowledge has no interest for, or bearing on, the mind of the composer, or that the composer's stock of prejudices might be narrow and cranky *because* of creative preoccupations, Mr. H. does not seem to have considered. How long, I wonder, will it take Mr. H. to discover that I.S.'s genius is wrapped—for *protection* from musical data—in a vacuum?

August 28. Listening to the CBS broadcast of I.S.'s *Orpheus* this afternoon, the composer conducts along with the actual conductor throughout, beating meter patterns and giving cues, as he does even while listening to a piano sonata, in which case he cues themes. Balanchine delivers a short speech.

August 30. Koussevitzky comes at 5.

August 31. To Alma Mahler's birthday party.

September 1. I.S. would be happy going to the cinema every day, and the worse the film, bad Westerns preferred, the more he seems to enjoy it. "Good" cinema, on the other hand—socially significant drama, Method acting—annoys him. In these three months I have seen more films than in the previous three years.

V. tells a story that reveals an aspect of I.S.'s character. It seems that Cocteau's *Les Enfants terribles* provoked a wave of shoplifting in Paris. She tried it herself, in fact, pocketing a magnet while accompanying I.S. to a hardware store. When she told him, he stalked out in anger without making his own purchase, and when she discovered that the stolen article was not magnetized, he claimed that this retributive justice was divinely inspired.

September 2. Before we drive to San Diego this evening, I.S. obliges us to sit for a minute in silence, as Arabs do before traveling, then to stand while he makes the sign of the cross. This *"priesest"* is to ensure our safe return, a Russian superstition, like throwing spilt salt over one's left shoulder, or dabbing one's fingers in spilt wine (or mopping it with bread, like intinction) and touching behind the ears with them, which the Stravs never fail to do.

We eat with Isherwood at Ted's in Santa Monica, then drive to San Diego, the Grant Hotel.

September 4. I fetch Eugene Berman and Ona Munson in La Jolla and we go with them to Tijuana for the *corrida*. Arriving there two hours ahead of time, we continue to Ensenada, where, to my surprise, I.S., always super-squeamish about the cleanliness of cutlery, plates, drinking glasses, does not scruple to eat a tortilla that has been bare-handled by the vendor. Our seats are on the sunny side of the arena, which inspires I.S. to make a sombrero from a newspaper, a work of art no matter how unfashionable as a hat.

I.S. regards himself as an aficionado, but what he likes about bullfighting is the pageantry, the parade of the matadors and their *cuadrillas*, as well as, for a wonder, the noise, the shouts, boos, catcalls, fanfares, blaring brass band. He watches transfixed as the bull charges into the ring, and shouts "bravo" when the animal vaults a barrera and scatters the hecklers in the front row, but during a crisis, when the crowd leaps to its feet, he cringes and cannot bring himself to look. He is plainly horrified, too, when a picador's nag is gored, spilling steaming entrails; when a muleta misses its mark and blood expulses from the bull's wound like water from a hand pump; and when a team of mangy plough horses drags each carcass away, while workers in overalls sprinkle sand over the glutinous ground as matter-of-factly as if the ring were a stockyard and the sacred taurobolai a purely commercial transaction. Then, for a moment anyway, he would make over his estate to the SPCA.

On our return to the United States, an immigration officer asks I.S. where he was born. "St. Petersburg," he says, hoping to pass as a Floridian, but his accent leads to further questions and eventually to "Russia." Ordered to "pull over," he is subjected to a barrage of inane questions ("the color of your grandmother's hair," as he retells it), and this infuriates *me*, because he suffers from the refugee's abiding fear of border police and customs inspectors. During World War II he felt humiliated by being required to carry an Alien Registration Card. Back in Hollywood, he complains bitterly of being a "second-class citizen."

September 10. New York. Note from I.S.: "Dearest Bob, happy to have your wire—1000 thanks. Provided you keep your word and we see you here in Dec. Enclosed an incredible letter from an unknown idiot after the *Orpheus* broadcast. Send it back for my collection, please. Expecting now your letter. Much love, ISTR."

September 13. Soulima arrives in New York for the premiere of his and Antonia Cobos's Scarlatti ballet, *The Mute Wife*. A note from I.S. regarding

1949 the receipt of Act II, Scene I, of the *Rake* score: "Dearest Bob, please see to it that they [Boosey & Hawkes] send me a *decent acknowledgment....*"

September 14. Letter from V. "To tell you how we miss the month of August with you staying here . . . I read now F. Scott Fitzgerald and enjoy it. Scott on the rocks."

September 19. Card from Isherwood: "I'm telling Random House to mail you [a copy of *The Condor and the Cow*] as a gift . . . when I come East, I hope to see you. We hardly had time to get to know each other as well as, I, at any rate, should have liked."

September 24. Write to I.S. saying Peter Bartok told me that his parents had recorded I.S.'s Concerto for Two Solo Pianos in Europe before the war.

October 7. I.S. writes: "Dearest Bobsky, today just this . . . the *Pribaoutki* material I sent you one week ago via B[oosey] & H[awkes]. Please, acknowledge! Paul Sacher (of Basel) was here the other day—on his way (from Mexico) to New York. He will be there on October 10th at the Ambassador Hotel. I promised him to write you—he wanted so much to get in touch with you and to come to your concert. He leaves New York on October 26th. Let us hear from you very soon."

October 14. Telegram from I.S.: "Dearest Bob what a joy for us your coming here in December. Hope for a long time. Soulimas definitely leaving Hollywood for New York mid-December. Affectionately, Stravinsky."

October 16. Letter from Isherwood:

> Dear Robert, I really do appreciate your sweet letter. I would dearly like to believe the things you write about the book—especially coming from you, who can be, as I know, a merciless critic; but what matters to me much more is the personal feeling you imply. This is mutual, believe me. I wish I could come to your concert. I wish I could see you under any circumstances. But, right now, I can't get away. Money has to be earned. And I want to drag my novel over the first hump, at any rate. However, things have a way of opening up unexpectedly. When they do, I shall probably leave for New York at very short notice. I'll let you know at once. I bought Wystan's Greek Portable and am enjoying it. But haven't read his *Horizon* article yet. Some friends here have it. Bill asks to be remembered. And don't forget me, either. Christopher.

October 21. Telegram from I.S.: "Happy Birthday to you dearest Bob. Wishing you heartily a very successful concert. . . . Love, Kisses, Stravinsky."

October 22. Town Hall. 5:30. I conduct a program of I.S.'s Suite No. 1 for Small Orchestra, and *Renard*; Mozart's Clarinet Concerto (with Reginald Kell); Falla's Concerto for Harpsichord (with Sylvia Marlowe); Berg's Chamber Concerto (with Isadore Cohen and Robert Cornman).

Also on the program is Arthur Berger's Duo (played by Joseph Fuchs and **1949** Leo Smit). Dinner afterward with Auden and his cellist friend, then fly to Los Angeles.

October 31. Los Angeles. With the S.s to the San Francisco Opera's *Don Giovanni*, at the Shrine Auditorium.

November 3. I.S. plays the Terzetto for me.

November 12. New York. Letter from Aaron Copland: "I had a good time at your last concert, but, like everybody else, thought you gave us rather too much to swallow all at one time."

November 20. My Carnegie Hall dress rehearsal is cut short when Toscanini suddenly calls an NBC Symphony rehearsal there. Concert at 8:30: the complete *Pulcinella*, Four Etudes, *Zvezdoliki*, *Perséphone*. Auden reads "Prime," "Memorial for the City," "Atlantis."

December 10. New York. Town Hall. 5:30. I conduct Monteverdi's *Orfeo*, playing the recitatives at the keyboard, on a double bill with *Mavra*.

🌒 **Postscript 1994.** I spent the beginning of the year organizing the February Town Hall concert, inviting Robert Shaw to prepare and conduct the Sacred Choruses, and Soulima Stravinsky and Beveridge Webster to play the Concerto for Two Pianos. The instrumentalists this time, on the insistence of RCA, which recorded the Mass, were members of the New York Philharmonic. I also had to find a boys' choir for the Mass. Lincoln Kirstein helped me with this, but Stravinsky was not satisfied with the one we found, which was less well trained and coarser in sound than the English all-male choirs of his experience; he did not mention this to me at the time, but confided it in a letter to Nadia Boulanger. The concert, nevertheless, with Auden reading three of his new poems, was a memorable occasion.

At some point during rehearsals, Stravinsky invited me to spend the summer in his home in California, sorting out and cataloguing his manuscripts recently received from Paris. I promised to come, of course, though I would not be paid—then or ever, until the mid-1960s when a lawyer remarked that the advantage to him in tax-deductions would be considerable. I spent the months of April and May preparing myself by reading Russian literature.

During June I lived in the Stravinsky home, sleeping on the couch in the small, book-filled anteroom to his studio. In July I moved a few blocks away to a house that Stravinsky had rented for his son and family; they were temporarily at the Music Academy of the West at Carpenteria (Santa Barbara), where Soulima taught piano. The vacated house, belonging to the actor Vladimir Sokolov and standing behind his own larger one at 8624 Holloway Drive, had three bedrooms and bathrooms, a fireplace, a kitchen, as well as one of Stravinsky's pianos and part of his music library. On one side was a Catholic school and on the other the home of the conductor Fritz Zweig. The composer Eric Zeisl, whose daughter was to marry

1949 Ronald Schoenberg, the composer's elder son, lived around the corner.

I walked from 8624 Holloway Drive to 1260 North Wetherly every morning, uphill all the way, and breakfasted with Stravinsky. His mail delivery was very early, and before starting to compose he wanted me to help with the problems it never failed to contain. Immediately after breakfast we would consider the various strategies to be used in his replies, after which we drafted and corrected the letters. I dreaded these sessions; Stravinsky could be stubborn and unreasonable, and in his impatience to go to his piano, he often became petulant.

Mrs. Stravinsky breakfasted still earlier and, in order to avoid the discussions about correspondence, quickly disappeared in her automobile. In the course of these escape outings—she loved to drive—she bought household implements and ornaments, flowers and plants, seeds for the Stravinsky aviary, as well as all comestibles for Wetherly Drive and, during June, Holloway Drive.

She liked to browse in second-hand bookstores, which partly accounted for the somewhat tattered appearance of the Stravinsky library. I wondered why they had acquired the 98-volume Voltaire, but I knew that their Bronte collection dated from Stravinsky's wish to compose music for Orson Welles's film *Jane Eyre*, and I was aware that the books by Martin du Gard, Marc Chadourne, and Stark Young (the only American on their shelves at that time) were there because the authors were the composer's personal friends. Julian Green, Henri de Montherlant, Saint-Exupéry, and Raymond Roussel were well represented. The Russian, French, and German classics were, of course, in the original languages.

When I arrived at the Stravinsky home the music manuscripts from Paris were still crated. I piled them on the wooden table in the living room, where Stravinsky passed them several times a day en route to and from his studio without looking at or betraying any curiosity about them.

An hour or so before dinner he would go to his wine cellar, in the patio just outside the kitchen behind the house, and choose a white Burgundy and a red Bordeaux; he enjoyed viticultural talk, and would explain to me why Burgundies are not usually decanted and exactly how short a time a really old Bordeaux should be allowed to "breathe." In addition to straight Bols gin and whiskey (Scotch only; he disliked Bourbon, which he thought "sweet"), he sometimes drank rum because of its thermostatic properties, warming and cooling according to the season.

Almost no day passed without visitors. Guests came for lunch, for dinner, and for pre-dinner drinks and *zakousky*. Sokolov was a regular, as were the Sol Babitzes and the Ingolf Dahls. The Soulimas and Marions came frequently, and Adolph and Beata Bolm once or twice a week. The Bolms were eager to tell me their stories about the early Diaghilev years, passionately interesting the first time around but not for Stravinsky who would retire to his studio after dinner and resume work on the *Rake*.

❧ *1950*

January 22. (Sunday). Baron Osten-Sacken for lunch. I go to the Schoenberg matinee concert (Trio, *Ode to Napoleon*) in the Los Angeles County Museum. An interview with Schoenberg about his paintings is broadcast during intermission: a soft, pained voice.

January 24. To the Huxleys'. Most of Aldous's friends are specialists: Hubble the astronomer, Stravinsky the musician, Dr. Kiskadden the surgeon, Moller the geneticist, a cetologist from Monterey, an eminent hypnotist, an automatic-writing instructor from La Jolla, a master *vitrailleur*, a parapsychologist from Duke, a monk who has a secret formula for manuscript preservation. Aldous says that barnacles were introduced into the Salton Sea by a seaplane and that every boat there is encrusted with them now. Someone asks if they are edible, and since Aldous does not answer, I am tempted to say "yes," on the gamble that if he doesn't know, nobody does.

January 27. An hour before her wedding ceremony in the Stravinsky livingroom, Ona [Munson] goes to V.s bedroom, weeps on her shoulder, says she does not love [Eugene] Berman. But since this was always perfectly evident, today does not seem to be quite the right time to say so. Berman, too, has been late in deciding that he is not a believer and therefore a judge should perform the ceremony instead of a rabbi. At 4 o'clock I.S.'s lawyer, Aaron Sapiro, comes with a gentleman from the bench and, in front of the Stravinsky fireplace, and with me as best man, Berman and Ona, a necrophiliac homosexual and a lesbian, are briskly pronounced man and wife.

February 1. Breakfast with Varvara Karinska, Balanchine's costume designer. Afterward I drive Yvgenia Petrovna to San Pedro. This is the end of the Western world: in Southern California ocean and land meet back to back with no estuarial commingling. From here we look eastward to New York and Europe, not westward to China.

February 5. The Huxleys and Isherwood for dinner, Aldous talking about dianetics.

1950   **February 6.** We leave for New York by automobile, staying at the Barbara Worth Hotel in El Centro.

February 21. New York, the Lombardy Hotel, East 56th Street. I.S. conducts *Firebird* at the City Center Ballet, on a program with Blitzstein's *The Guests* and Bizet's Symphony in C.

February 27. To Eliot's *Cocktail Party*. A postcard for me from Evelyn Waugh, forwarded from Wetherly Drive: " 'Anthony who sought things that were lost' appeared in an undergraduate magazine, has not been reprinted and will not be in my life time. . . . My instinct is to suppress or destroy more and more juvenilia. . . . *Work Suspended* has too few short stories I wish to preserve."

March 1. Auden for lunch and to work with I.S., who is now visualizing every detail of the action. Wondering how long it will take to wheel the bread machine on stage, I.S. holds his stopwatch like a starter at a track meet, while Auden, responding as if he might have had a great deal of experience with baby carriages, jumps to his feet and crosses the room pushing an imaginary perambulator—all of which is to no useful purpose, since the dimensions of the stage on which the opera will be performed are unknown.

March 7. I.S. poses for Marino Marini. Dinner with Stark Young.

March 17. I.S. works with Auden.

March 25. Dinner with Poulenc.

March 27. Lunch with Carlos Chavez, then to *Death of a Salesman*.

March 28. A cocktail party at Clare Booth Luce's, after which we go with Poulenc to the Philadelphia Orchestra concert in Carnegie Hall: Sibelius's Seventh, Virgil Thomson's Cello Concerto.

March 29. Huntington Hartford comes at 5. I.S. still wants an American premiere of the *Rake*, preferably in a small New York theater where he thinks the opera could have a short run, a notion that has possessed him since he saw Menotti's *The Consul*. Kirstein thinks Hartford might be the "angel" for this, but I.S. refuses to play the score for any non-musician.

April 8. Death of Nijinsky. I.S. does not comment and appears to be unaffected, but who knows?

April 13. I.S. goes with me to Mitropoulos's concert at Carnegie Hall: *A Survivor From Warsaw.*

April 20. I.S. and Marcelle de Manziarly play the *Rake* four-hands at her apartment for a group of musician friends. Unknown to I.S., Billy Rose, whose opinion about a possible Broadway run is sought, if not his money, is smuggled in among the S.s' friends, like Odysseus and Polyphemus's sheep. Watching Rose's expression from the side of the room, I quickly realize that a performance in a commercial theater is out of the question.

April 29. (Saturday). Town Hall. 5:30. I conduct my Chamber Art

Society ensemble in a concert of the Divertimento K. 251, *Pribaoutki* and *Berceuses du Chat*, Webern's Concerto, Schoenberg's Serenade. The players—Izzy Cohen, Seymour Barab, Ralph Gomberg, Samuel Baron, Robert Nagel—are super, and the songs are beautifully sung by Arline Carmin.

May 8. We leave for Los Angeles by car, staying in Bedford, Pennsylvania.

June 21. Los Angeles. With Ingolf Dahl to Peter Viertel's, where we work with him, his uncle Eduard Steuermann, and Isherwood on the English translation of *Pierrot Lunaire.*

June 23. Letter from Dahl about the translation:

> No. 1: shuddering instead of shivering??
> Measure 25: the moon pours down in waves at nightfall
> No. 3: sable instead of ebon??
> Measure 24: What shall I put on today
> > or
> > What make-up to wear today
> > or
> > What sort of make-up to wear
>
> ———
>
> He's tired of the rouge
> No. 5: As a pallid drop of blood stains the white lips
>
> ———
>
> > Wild and joyful
>
> ———
>
> > Haunting my imagination
> No. 6: So feverish, grown so great
> No. 8: Giant mothwings, dark and baleful (black enshadowed) killed the splendid blaze of sun. Out of fume of lower darkness comes a breath
> No. 10: Pierrot descends
>
> That's all I have. Seems a rather meager harvest for so many hours of impassioned argument. The Christopher Fry is disarmingly delightful . . . but it is *no* opera libretto! Good luck, see you soon (in the meantime, I expect to read about your *Pierrot* performance in *Variety*).
> P.S. Isherwood used the expression "Gothic washstand" in *Berlin Stories.* What was all the fuss about?

June 24. With I.S. to Isherwood's East Rustic Road house, under sycamores, beside a creek, and near the beach. Salka Viertel, widow of the movie director-hero in *Prater Violet* and Steuermann's sister, joins us for lunch. Isherwood's language is more British with her ("I like him most

1950 awfully"), and he is more inhibited alone with I.S. (without V.).

June 29. With the S.s to *Kind Hearts and Coronets*. Letter from Schoenberg, dated June 26:

> Your plans interest me very much, among them especially your intention to translate and perform the choral pieces of Opus 27 and 28. If the translation becomes so good as that of *Pierrot Lunaire*, I would be very pleased.
>
> Who will play the piano part in the Suite Op. 29? You know that this is one of my most difficult piano writings, but perhaps for the young people of today it might already be easier.
>
> The records of *Pierrot Lunaire* which I possess have been played, in German, under my direction and are issued by Columbia Records. Whether it is not sold out at present, I don't know. But I am ready to let you have my set, as you said, for a few hours to make a copy. I have no record of the English version which Mr. Dahl conducted. Evidently, as Mr. Dahl does not have a record, it has not been recorded. The best time to call for the album would be 11 a.m. But in any case I recommend you to telephone in the morning. Sincerely yours,
>
> Arnold Schoenberg

July 5. Not only angels fear to tread! Not until after my visit to Schoenberg today am I aware of having walked from the street to his house on the grass, instead of on the noisy gravel driveway, of tiptoeing to the door, and of waiting there in the hope of being seen and not having to ring the bell. His pretty daughter sees me, however, and leads me to the living room, abandoning me there, except for occasional peeps at me from the kitchen. The only picture in the room is a photograph of Kokoschka's portrait of Schoenberg. The only furnishings are a light gravy-colored leather armchair, a sofa, and a piano covered with the tennis trophies of the composer's elder son.

Schoenberg enters, walking slowly and with the help of his wife. Stooped and wizened, but as suntanned as an athlete, he seems thinner than in even the most recent photograph—that pained, sensitive face, difficult to look into and impossible not to—and the bulging veins in his right temple are even more prominent. His ears also appear to have grown larger; they *are* larger than I.S.'s (the concha and outward antitragus), which I remark because the oversized hearing apparatus of both composers is their outstanding sculptural feature. He sits in the gravy-colored *fauteuil*, on the edge of the cushion and without repose; seated, he seems even smaller, as well as older than his years. Beginning to talk, he adjusts caster-thick eyeglasses heretofore dangled from his neck by a part-ribbon and part-rubber-band tether. His voice is soft, but as pained and sensitive as his face, and almost unbearably intense.

He seeks to convince me to use an English translation for my forthcoming New York performance of *Pierrot,* and he recommends Dahl's version. In answer to my question about performing his a cappella male choruses, he suggests that I double each line with an instrument offstage and transmit the instrumental performances to the singers through individual earphones. Since I also plan to present his Septet-Suite, he proposes that we listen to the private recording of it made at the Paris premiere which he conducted. He criticizes the performance during nearly every page-turn in the score, and at length during each pause to change the record side. "This is the most difficult of all my piano writings," he remarks at one point, but I am thinking that the clarinet parts are as much of a problem. He listens to the music—what can be heard of it beneath the crackling surface noise—as though he had forgotten having written it, and the rediscovery leaves him radiant. At the end, he entrusts the records to me, which is very like I.S., who will also play acetates of his radio broadcasts and lend them out to prospective performers.

A question of mine concerning his *Lieder,* Opus 22, seems to surprise him—agreeably, I think. He wants to know how I know the work, and with total ingenuousness confesses his guilt "in using too many instruments, though orchestras of that size were not impracticable at the time the music was composed." He remarks, not complainingly, that "the songs had to wait twenty years for a performance," which makes me want to tell him that I think they are the most beautiful orchestral songs ever written, but I refrain partly because of the text of his canon for G.B. Shaw and partly because one does not gush to Schoenberg—though later I regret that I did not say it. He is still more surprised to discover that I know the score of *Von Heute auf Morgen,* and even less able to conceal his pleasure in recalling this long-buried opera. The fact of these reactions is shocking evidence of the neglect of his music. How, in the age of. . . ? But that's it, exactly.

He knows of my association with I.S., but does not allude to it, nor do I, not having come on I.S.'s account. I think he is curious, though, and would at least like to inquire after I.S.'s health, even though his own is so frail and though age has so suddenly crushed him. When his younger son tears through the room yelping like a bloodhound, and Schoenberg calls after him, making a show of shrinking from the noise and begging him not to play in the house, any observer not aware of the relationship would assume that the composer was the grandfather instead of the parent. As I prepare to go, he autographs my score of *Pierrot Lunaire,* and he invites me to visit him again next week.

Outdoors, my feeling of lightness is a measure of the intensity of the man, as well as of the strain created by the danger of crossing the circle of his pride; his fathomless humility is plated all the way down with a hubris

1950 of stainless steel.

July 8. With the S.s and Isherwood to Sequoia National Park, five hours across a desert furnace. The small trees are at the beginning of the ascent, the giants, scarred from lightning-kindled forest fires, are at the top, above the seven-thousand-foot level. Here are ferns, woods, snow-capped peaks, clear and exhilarating air. A bibulous picnic. On the return, dinner in Bakersfield. Isherwood thinks that Lawrence's *St. Mawr* is "the greatest book to have been inspired by the American West."

August 2. Aspen, the Four Seasons Hotel. I.S. conducts a matinee concert—Divertimento, *Firebird*, Tchaikovsky's Second—in a tent and in blue jeans, the railroad strike having stopped the shipping of his baggage from Los Angeles.

August 3. With Victor Babin and Vitya Vronsky, in two cars, over the Independence Pass—snow on the roadsides—to Taos, the Sagebrush Inn.

August 4. Visits to Frieda Lawrence—loud voice, ear-splitting laugh—and Mabel Dodge, then drive to Santa Fe and Santo Domingo Pueblo to see several hundred totally inebriated Indians in a corn dance. After dinner, en route in the dark to Bishop's Lodge, I make a wrong turn on a dirt road, discover that I am driving in a dried creek bed with piñon and sage on the banks, but thanks to a bright moon am able to retrace my path.

September 1. With I.S. to the Koussevitzky-Vladimir Horowitz rehearsal in Hollywood Bowl, then to Koussevitzky's hotel. Saul Steinberg for dinner at the S.s'.

October 21. New York. My concert in Town Hall: *Pierrot* and the Septet.

Between October 24 and 28. Otto Klemperer comes for lunch. Seeing a score of Gerald Strang's Concerto Grosso under my arm, he grabs it, points to the notes of the first measure, counts loudly from "one" to "twelve," says, "Nowadays no one is doing anything else." Klemperer is too tall for the small S. dining room and too big for the small glass-topped table. Most of the conversation is in German. I.S. shows him the orchestra score of *Rake* Act I. I drive Klemperer home.

October 29. I.S. completes the sketch score of Act II, and I take him to Klemperer's concert at U.S.C.: Brandenburg No. 1, with Adolph Koldofsky playing the violino piccolo, and No. 5, with Alice Ehlers playing the keyboard part. O.K. does not acknowledge the applause at the beginning, except to glare angrily at the audience. At the end, he refuses to bow with Ehlers, and takes only a curt one himself, from the side of the stage. His tempi are very fast, but at least the music, new in its own time, does not sound artificially archaic.

November 2. Drive Yvgenia Petrovna to Balboa in the afternoon, through an unvaried scenery of used car lots, billboards, hideous buildings. Ferruccio Busoni on Los Angeles in 1911: "How such a town, so tasteless and bare could be built in such a country. Why must this marvelous gift of

Nature be besmeared in such a way?"

November 10. To the San Francisco Opera's *Magic Flute*, briskly conducted by Paul Breisach. I.S. never glances at the stage, or even once looks up from the orchestra score, which he follows with a pocket torch. His talk after the performance indicates that he believes Mozart was poisoned by Masons for having revealed their secrets, while at the same time he contends that Mozart was not really interested in Freemasonry, but had embraced it for political reasons.

November 13. Letter from Schoenberg:

> Dear Mr. Craft: Thank you very much for the good news of the successful performances of the Septet-Suite and *Pierrot Lunaire*. I am very interested in your intention to perform my opus 27 and 28, and it is very flattering to me that through your comparison with the *Musikalisches Opfer*, though overestimating me, you put me in the neighborhood of Bach. Where did you get the canon for the Concertgebouw? Was it published? Of course you can perform it in the manner mentioned. I am sure you did not overlook that A means A major, S [Es] means E flat major, C means C major and G (not E) means G major. In other words there are four different tonalities and the task of the cello part is to make them understandable. But it must be checked, whether the cello part is not only to be used when all the four voices are together. Probably I have examined it at the time, but I don't recall it. In case the sound is disturbing with the fifth voice, the cello so near to the bass voice, I recommend to double the cello in the lower octave by the double-bass. Could you make me a record of these performances? The chorus *Dreimal Tausend Jahre* is only one of three choruses, the third of which is not yet finished. It would be better to wait until this opus is complete. I have no transcription of the piano concerto for 12 instruments. Such a transcription would ask for at least 20 to 24 instruments, doubling some of the strings, using enough brass. Ask Schirmer whether he would order such an arrangement. I know people who would be ready to make it. I hope to hear from you. Most cordially yours,
>
> Arnold Schoenberg.

December 1. We spend the afternoon with Walter Arensberg, who shows us his collections of pre-Columbians, Brancusi, Duchamp, Picasso, Klee, Kandinsky, Cézanne. Sherry and cake at the end of the three-hour tour.

December 31. At work on the *Rake*, I.S. composes the end of the scene "Methinks it is no shame," has an ozalid copy made, and wraps it for mailing to London. How, sending the score to the printer piecemeal, can he be certain that the as-yet-unwritten music will not require adjustments in

1950 the already completed parts? But there have been no changes in the earlier part of the opera in all the two-and-a-half years of work on it. Now, more than ever during that time, I.S. is fearful of dying and leaving the opera unfinished.

Ingolf Dahl and I concoct a skit, a satire on a German composer's "inspiration," a photograph of a voluptuous nude, and act it out at the S.s' New Year's party for the Marions, Edel, Louriés. Afterward, we drive on Mulholland. The sparkle of lights in the clear night reaches all the way to Long Beach.

ঌ **Postscript 1994.** At the beginning of January 1950, my breathing was constricted by sharp pains in both sides of my chest. The cold that I had caught on the bus from New York was diagnosed as double pleurisy. I was confined to bed and saturated with penicillin. In the interim, the Soulima Stravinskys had moved to New York—conveniently, since the Igor Stravinsky house had only one small bedroom and the couch could not be used as a sick-bed in the daytime. After a year and a half in Los Angeles, Soulima's wife had realized that the smaller tree would not grow in the shadow of the larger one; she wanted her husband to make a new beginning in New York. Moreover, she had been disturbed to see her husband revert to his childhood role, described by Nijinsky after a visit to the composer in 1916: "Stravinsky treats his children like soldiers."

My diary for January gives a brief description of Eugene Berman's wedding, but neglects to say that he had been courting the actress Ona Munson since he had first seen her in *Gone with the Wind*. The diary for February mentions only the first road-stop on the way to New York, and a few of the concerts, spectacles, and social functions attended on arrival there. I should have noted that the hotel in El Centro did not accept Stravinsky's personal check, and that this led to a vexatious scene with the manager and a serious reduction in our supply of cash. In 1950 automobiles were inspected at the Arizona border and citrus fruit found in vehicles traveling from one state to the other was confiscated; at Yuma we were obliged to join a queue of automobiles with open-trunks. The drive to Del Rio, Texas, the day after, was the longest and loneliest, and the landscape the most deserted and melancholy that any of us had ever been through. We found no restaurant of any kind on the way, and the ration of Russian cutlets in Yvgenia Petrovna's hamper had been reduced to one for each of us. Stravinsky gobbled his but slowly savored the contents of his thermos (Chateau Margaux) and flask (Armagnac).

In San Antonio we found the Sunday edition of the *New York Herald Tribune*, in which Virgil Thomson's column comparing Webern's music to "spun steel" and publicizing René Leibowitz as his disciple irked Stravinsky. My Town Hall concert in late April included a piece by Webern, but Stravinsky was ill and did not attend.

I should have expanded the entries that record the stages of our return to California in May, a happier, more romantic trip than the one to New York. In the little town of Gillette, Wyoming, we stayed in an ancient and miserable hotel but enjoyed ourselves nevertheless. After consuming the filet portions of huge T-bone steaks in the hotel dining room, we sat through a terrible western in a small, tatterdemalion movie house across the street. The lights remained on until the seats had filled, nearly all of them with cowboys wearing boots with spurs, wide leather chaps with fringes, and ten-gallon hats. The Stravinskys began to comment on this scene in Russian, surely not identified as such by the other members of the audience who nevertheless grew quiet and, I thought, began to regard the elderly foreign-looking pair with suspicion, thereby making me slightly nervous. The next day's drive through Montana, part of it along the Little Big Horn River, fascinated my beloved Russians as it did me. We stopped for yet another T-bone at a diner inevitably called "Custer's Last Stand." That night we were the only guests in a motel at the northern entrance to Yellowstone Park.

Back in the Rocky Mountains in late July, Stravinsky began a rehearsal in Aspen one morning by raising his arms, and signaling the downbeat for Tchaikovsky's Second Symphony. "Happy Birthday" sounded instead, the wife of one of the players having given birth during the night, but Stravinsky had not been informed of this and was not amused. Incredibly, he did not know the tune, which at that time was not crooned in his kind of restaurant, but he remembered it and five years later used it in the *Greeting Prelude*, thereby repeating the expensive error of 1911 when he incorporated a snippet of hurdy-gurdy street music in *Petrushka*: the still-living composers of both melodies were awarded sizable percentages of his royalties.

❧ *1951*

January 1. Read Saltykov-Schedrin's *A Family of Noblemen* to I.S. while he orchestrates. So many characters are killed off in the first part that new ones are introduced (without preparation) and old ones brought back in flashbacks. Yudushka is a great bore, and why Arina Petrovna gives in to him is far from clear. Since almost everything in the novel is overstated and too obvious, one wonders how Aldous and Isherwood can consider working on a movie script of it, or even mention it in the same breath with *Oblomov*.

January 2. Schoenberg writes to Mr. and Mrs. Fritz Stiedry, "My young friend Mr. Craft is slowly working himself into my music by performing my music a lot and finally he will succeed. I would like to see all of my friends encourage such people as Craft."

January 31. Lunch with Baron d'Osten at the Brown Derby. Huxleys for dinner. Aldous eats two helpings of chicken and drinks three glasses of Margaux, a remarkable improvement over his usual diet of salad, goat cheese, and water. He performs a demonstration, asking me to dangle a ring on a 30-inch string and to hold it rigidly. "Make a positive wish," he says, and when I do the ring vibrates outward from my body. "Make a negative wish," he says, and when I comply the ring makes circular and left-and-right pendulum movements, the result, supposedly, of subconscious muscular flexes.

February 15. Working on my new verse:

> *Spiders' Sakes*
> (Concerning Blake's "The Fly")
>
> Why should I
> Free the fly
> Death-wound
> In spiders' down?
> Why god become

To flies undone?
Why insert man
In god's fly plan?
The Greater Phase
We cannot know:
Heed then the ways
That god does show.
Thus poets' lives
Envy their lot
Watching flies
All else forgot.

February 16. Dinner with Jean Renoir, Rumer Godden, and the Indian girl, star of his film *The River*. At one point, when the S.s say that they like rodeos, the visitor from the land of sacred cows remarks: "I am always embarrassed to see people make fools of themselves with animals."

February 17. I.S. completes the recitative, "Where have you hidden her?" After dinner we go with the Huxleys to *The Blue Angel*. Aldous, in the front row, raises his magnifying glass at each close-up of Dietrich's charms.

February 19. Letter from Auden, who seems to know about I.S.'s contract with the Biennale: "Dear Bob, It's wonderful news about Venice. But there are one or two matters which—strictly *entre nous*—Chester and I would like to know about. It seems to us that, if there is, as I understand, a *large* sum of money being paid for the premiere rights, we are entitled to ten percent thereof. What do you think? As the contract is not being negotiated through Boosey Bean, we are completely in the dark as to the facts. Could you use your discretion and, if circumstances are propitious, mention the matter to *Il Maestro*? Hope Cuba is fun. Love, Wystan."

February 20. Leave for Miami by automobile. Picnic near Indio. Blythe to Wickenburg, the Crest Villa Hotel. Finish Burkhardt's *Renaissance*.

February 21. A plaque on a tree near a gas station: "Outlaws were chained to this tree before a jail was built in these parts." Drive to Phoenix, Deming, and El Paso. I.S. is fascinated by the alligators in a pool in the El Paso plaza.

February 23. Lunch in Dallas, sleep in Shreveport. To my surprise, the news of Gide's death disturbs I.S.; I have never heard a good word from him about the *Perséphone* libretto or its librettist. At sunset, hundreds of blackbirds in a tree in the town square begin to sing.

Louisiana: mud swamps, wood fires, unpainted cabins, brick towns, old railroad stations, Baptist churches, creeks, pine woods, pigs on the roadside, black men riding horses bareback, red dirt, river air (the Red River), fragrances of spring. In Shreveport, a buxom black lady with red bandanna shows us to our rooms, chuckling all the way.

1951 February 28. Miami. Leaving the car in a garage for repairs, we taxi to the airport and fly to Havana in a Cuban airplane. From the air, lower Florida, beyond a rim of sheened, indigo sea is a brocade of swampy islands. The sand and coral floors slope away in trellises from the Keys, and the colors of the Caribbean shimmer like shot silk. Near Key West, which looks like a fortress on an old map, the contour of the islands is like the skeleton tail of an ice-age mammoth. At the Havana airport, our stewardess, a soubrette with a retroussé nose, says: "This is Cuba." I.S.: "It better be."

The Customs officers bring us frozen daiquiris, which is nice but no compensation for the loss of our luggage. Havana is an aromatic city, preponderantly of cooking oil and coffee, the latter thick enough, it seems, to filter out of the air. Going directly to a press conference in the bar of the El Presidente, we are greeted with more daiquiris and *entusiasmo*. Lunch follows, at La Zaragosana (two lisps), in an atmosphere of Habana Habana smoke. Afterward to Wilfredo Lam, who puts on a private exhibition of his paintings, accompanying it with a great deal of talk about his gods, Stravinsky and Picasso.

Dinner at the hacienda of Fifi Tarafa: a carafe of daiquiris this time. She displays photographs of, and many recordings by, *her god*, Toscanini. Partly for this reason, I.S. elects to sit in the patio, which is paved with eighteenth-century terra cotta beer bottles, bottoms up, and which looks toward a garden with a statue of Benjamin Franklin. I.S. is impatient to go home and finish the *Rake*.

March 1. A late afternoon breeze relieves the oppressive heat. In the cobblestone streets of the old city: open-air cafés in which café-au-lait people sip rum drinks. Near the harbor the alleys are narrow, single-file. The Hotel El Presidente features tile floors and men smoking Romeo y Juliet No. 4 cigars, from which they burn off the ends with wood torches, then nibble the air holes.

March 10. During lunch at Fort Smith, a woman approaches I.S., says she is a reporter for the local newspaper, asks his name, does not recognize it, asks him to write it down, still doesn't, asks V. if she is a movie actress.

March 21. Hollywood. Nabokov arrives from India at 4 A.M. and sleeps on I.S.'s couch.

March 22. Isherwood and Nabokov for dinner.

March 23. Aldous for dinner. Nabokov is droll about Auden's difficulties in India finding drink and in suffering through female dance entertainments. Says that when the applause had stopped after one hip-grinding number, Auden was heard saying, loudly and crankily, "Not my cup of tea."

April 7. Play the *Rake* Epilogue with I.S. four-hands. It is too long, and the chord at the climax would be less out of place in a Coca-Cola jingle.

April 12. Letter from Darius Milhaud about *Socrate*: "I always heard it with only one singer when Satie played it."

April 16. Adolph Bolm is dead. I.S. has known him since the 1910 **1951**
Firebird and, since 1940, as a close friend and Hollywood neighbor; both
I.S. and V. are shocked and saddened. They knew that he had been in a La
Jolla hospital recently but not that he was seriously ill. His death, from
myocardial infarction, occurred shortly before 8 A.M. The milkman, looking through the open window of Bolm's room, noticed that he was not
breathing, rang the doorbell, and told Mrs. Bolm to "say a prayer before
you go to wake your husband."

During an afternoon drive with us, the widow tearfully recalls the first
time that V. met her "Adya," in Paris, on V.'s name day, September 30,
1920. My own memories of Adya are of a kind and considerate man, the
most helpful to me of I.S.'s friends when I came to live in California. True,
his account of the first, Washington, D.C., *Apollon Musagètes*, in which he
wore a Louis Quatorze costume ("exactly what Igorfyodorovitch wanted"),
had become familiar, and his fund of anecdotes about Nijinsky's and the
Uruguayan marriage was by no means inexhaustible. Clearly, too, Bolm's
culture-enthusiasm barked at I.S.'s shins, though *he* played Patience during
it, drumming his fingers on the table and nodding noncommittally. But
when I.S. had the floor, Adya would prostrate himself at the composer's
feet: "*Da, da, Igorfyodorovitch,*" he would say, making a synaloepha of the
first syllables of the patronomic, and reducing the rest of it to "itch."

Expressions of condolence seek to convince the bereaved that the
deceased is "better off where he is now," wherever that may be, on grounds
that if he or she had lived, then she or he would only have had to endure
more suffering. In this way the object of grief is switched from the dead to
the living, and the mourner, released from the obligation to mourn, can
continue with plans for his own deathless future.

April 17. An afternoon with Universal Knowledge. Aldous calls, asking me to read to him; he has overtaxed his "good" eye. I nevertheless find
him typing the *Devils of Loudun*, in the den at the end of the darkened corridor, and on a table stacked ominously with publications in Braille. He
does this wearing his "Chinese glasses," black cellulose goggles with,
instead of lenses, perforations that prevent staring by forcing the pupils to
move nystagmically, or stroboscopically. He has taped a bandage over the
pinholes on the right side, which means that he has no sight at all in his
opaline right eye.

He seems pleased to be interrupted but is clearly less hungry for a dose
of reading than for a discussion of his work—except that he refuses to talk
about it as *his*: he will give himself no credit, even for the discoveries of his
research. Without any stepping-stone small talk he dives into the depths
of the *Malleus Maleficarum* and the "appalling materialism of the Church to
which it testifies." In developing this thesis he shirks no opportunity for
scatological descriptions, and, of course, the torturing of witches provides
an abundance of such occasions. Is there any Swiftian compulsiveness in

1951 this, or is it merely the yeast in his ongoing argument as to the pervasiveness of human cruelty and vileness? At one point, telling me how bellows and tongs were used to exorcise the Devil from a child's stomach, he is put in mind of a cartoon by Wilhelm Busch, and the thought of this fellow misanthrope seems to leave him gay and exhilarated. "Has anyone ever detested humanity more?," he asks in a mordantly bright voice.

The thought strikes me today, not for the first time, that Aldous's most pronounced characteristics are his search for clarity and, at the same time, his credulity. They make a very odd team. On the one side is an apparently unshakable *credo ut intelligam* (which includes logic and the analytic disciplines), and on the other, a radical susceptibility to the nostrums of quacksalvers and spiritual confidence men. The clarity side is descended by school and family from nineteenth-century philosophers for whom there could be no unruly ideas, which is not quite the right inheritance for the verbally elusive "perennial philosophy." But what of the team mate? What school is he from, Paracelsus High?

And where was this other half at the time of *Antic Hay*, one would like to know, and what has befallen the author of the early novels that he can now look for salvation in a pill? The man who was always hurrying to expose the *paradis artificiels* of yesterday has become the readiest exponent, even the guinea pig, for those of today. Why, as it appears, is he grasping at straws? As a so-called uncommitted liberal, does he feel committed to try everything, to give every idea its due? An explanation would surely have to explore backwards, to Victorian roots. It seems to me that Aldous is a shocked Victorian, capable of being shocked by what to most people are common happenings. His hardest-worked word is "extraordinary," and the runner-up word, "absolutely," functions as its geminate. Only the extraordinary and the exaggerated seem to interest him, so that at times one thinks he has ceased to believe in ordinary human beings. Whereas he allows that some of the shocks, the creations of Mozart, are ennobling, most of them are the contrary. And it is the larger statistic that offers so much satisfaction for the anti-meliorist in him. Irony is the surfacing trick of the shocked Victorian, but irony grows stale with the speed of yesterday's events, and how much of Aldous's will outlive him?

The point about ordinary and "whole" people is the crux of Aldous's failure as a novelist—though "failure" is unfair because in the accepted sense he never set out to succeed; and why should he not write about extraordinary people? A readable journal is rarer than a readable novel, and its characters and records of events, being "true," are at least as likely to endure, at any rate the characters and events in a journal by Aldous Huxley. Such a journal, containing the unfictionalized raw material, the ideas and speculations, the thumbnail portraits, the highlights of conversations, the commentaries about books—the cross-references in his annotations of Evans-Wentz's *Tibetan Book of the Dead* draw on a whole unknown-to-

me library—would be a treasure indeed. As far back as *Point Counter Point,* **1951**
Philip Quarles's musings indicated that a journal was Aldous's form par
excellence; except that in-person Aldous is far superior to Aldous under
any guise.

April 22. We listen to Mitropoulos's broadcast of *Wozzeck.*

April 24. With the Huxleys to Escondido, the Felicitas Motel. Late
walk in the clear night, Aldous identifying the stars.

April 25. At the San Diego Zoo Aldous reassures us on the subject of
how much healthier and longer-lived the animals are in captivity. But
Aldous himself is the most interesting creature here. He tells us the Latin
name of each animal, the facts of habitats, and of longevity. *Viz:* "This
bird has a remarkable mutant discovered by the Sumatra expedition last
year." He compares the condor cage to a house by Neutra, and when a
lion roars says that the qualities of the sound indicate acute constipation.
The eagles, he says, look like General MacArthur. On the Korean War:
"My friend at the UN tells me that China never wanted to arrange a peace
and is having the time of its life killing American imperialists."

At the San Diego Museum of Art, Alfred Frankfurter, who escorts us,
removes paintings from walls for close-up viewing. When he says that
"Our best Guardi has gone to Venice," Aldous mentions a "similar one with
a marvelous shadow, now in Budapest." Aldous looks at pictures through
an enormous magnifying glass, the Bausch and Lomb Ortho-Fusor No. 2.
On a picture of the Infant Jesus and another baby, "The one is a Mongolian
idiot and the other suffers from a pituitary deficiency." Frankfurter gives
I.S. a photo of Zurburan's Paschal Lamb.

April 26. Drive via the Palomar and San Bernardino mountains to
Llano, Aldous's Mojave Desert home during his *Perennial Philosophy* period.
Rain falls, mercifully, most of the way. The desert is in bloom and the
Joshua trees are flaming torches. But the Llano lunch is not I.S.'s meat; the
Huxleys eat nothing but vegetables. The husband of Maria's sister, who
lives here, is apparently unpresentable. Home in late afternoon, inspired
to educate myself.

April 28. Tonight's Russian Easter Midnight Mass is presided over by a
Bishop, for which reason, probably, the crowd is greater than last year.
The little white church with the blue onion dome, hopelessly lost in con-
crete-and-steel downtown Hollywood, is filled to capacity. We join two or
three hundred other latecomers who pack the grounds and spill into the
street, where the service is relayed through a sputtery public-address system. "Displaced Persons," with close-shaven *en brosse* heads, ill-fitting,
donated clothes, and faraway eyes, comprise the majority of this outdoor
congregation. The others are the White Russian regulars, a loud clan, locally, with whom the S.s have little traffic and by whom, in consequence, they
are snubbed. Both factions appear to be deeply homesick tonight, flamboyant professional exiles no less than the timid and indigent D.P.s; or so I

1951 judge from the soulful singing of a hymn—not only soulful but also drastically out of tune, like an atonal version of the beginning of Tchaikovsky's "*1812*." Even the mire, after a week of heavy rain, seems to contribute to the nostalgia by responding to footsteps with Russian-size squelches.

Shortly before midnight all of us in the open-air congregation light tapers. Then at exactly 12 o'clock the church doors open and the clergy and congregation pour forth into our dense and now literally inflammable human chandelier. A deacon in a newly starched alb heads the procession, swinging the censer and spreading incense over us with a vengeance. Behind him, the Bishop, in a scarlet, white, and gold samite, pauses on the top steps and sings *"Khristos voskrese"* ("Christ is Risen"), to which the whole crowd cries, *"Voistinu voskrese"* ("He is Risen Indeed"), though it does not come out that way but tumbles around the church letter by letter, like noodles in alphabet soup. Next in the procession is a priest carrying a tall cross, and after him a train of acolytes displaying icons, *baroogve* (holy banners or icons made of cloth), and the globe and scepter of Christ the King; these clerics have long, soft, Spanish-moss beards. Three times around the church they parade, and thrice, in tow, the D.P.s follow, though their attention is directed more and more to their wilting and dripping candles. *"Khristos voskrese,"* sings the Bishop as he launches each successive trip, and each time the *"Voistinu voskrese"* wobbles around the church in response. The service concludes with an orgy of congregational kissing, in the sequence left cheek, right cheek, and again left, and with everyone you know or cannot escape, Easter kisses being unrefusable.

At the S.s' afterward, the Lenten fast is symbolically broken—not having been physically observed—by eating *kulich*, the Easter bread with a paper rose; and *paskha*, the million-calorie (sugar, milk, cheese, eggs, raisins, tutti-frutti) Easter cake. After draining in its obelisk mold for almost a week, the *paskha* was taxied to church today by Yvgenia Petrovna to be blessed. The mold and a cheesecloth wrapper are now removed, revealing the "X.B." imprint—"Christ is Risen"—on the front of the decanted cake, as well as Easter flower designs on the sides.

May 6. To Conrad Lester's Bedford Drive home to see his collection of paintings—Toulouse-Lautrec's *Oscar Wilde*—and to discuss the program of I.S.'s January concert with the Los Angeles Chamber Orchestra.

May 22. With the Huxleys to the Huntington Library in Pasadena. We are allowed to handle a Shakespeare folio, an illuminated Chaucer from 1400, and music manuscripts including Wagner's beautiful copy of Haydn's Symphony 104. The walls are covered with portraits of eighteenth-century British capitalists. Tea afterwards at the home of the astronomer Edwin Hubble. Aldous says that Hubble had been a Rhodes Scholar but settled down as a small-town Kansas lawyer before he began to study astronomy. Hubble worships Bertrand Russell and lets me borrow two of Russell's books. Augustus John's portrait of Eddington is on the wall. Hubble's cat is called Nicolas Copernicus.

May 23. A letter from Andrés Segovia at 248 Central Park West saying that Egon Wellesz showed him the guitar part of Schoenberg's Serenade in Vienna in, he thinks, 1925 and that he, Segovia, said that certain things would have to be modified. He adds that he "will be glad to work on it and to play the part in my performance" if Schoenberg will accept "suggestions." He won't.

June 4. Koussevitzky's death upsets I.S., but only as an untimely surprise: he expresses not a single word of regret, and when a reporter calls and asks for a statement, gives one so grudging, so ungenerous and condescending that it cannot be used. Sometimes he shows too clearly that he tends to regard people as useful or not useful—no longer useful in Koussevitzky's case—rather than as people for themselves.

June 18. Work on my Webern poem: numbers and notes, imprisoned music awaiting the sanction of feeling, in circles singing round.

I.S.'s birthday begins, as it does each year, in a black mood. This seems to be owing to nothing more grave than the postponement of breakfast until after Confession; he will complain of cramps at the first crinkle of hunger, and demand food immediately, no matter where he is or in what company. On the way to church this morning he growls like a hungry tiger, and since this is the year's second most sacred anniversary (just below Christmas), the growl is the only sound permitted. The Confession and the Mass following it last two hours, most of which is knelt through on an uncushioned and rugless floor. When we enter the church, I.S. goes directly to the altar rail and prostrates himself, spread-eagled, flat on the floor. A minute or so later an acolyte appears, rattling a thurible and smothering us with incense. A priest enters next, half-concealing himself behind a rood screen, like an *intrigant* in a Restoration comedy. He signals I.S. to approach the screen, where—furtively, as if he were demanding the password in a speakeasy—he asks the name of his patron saint. From this point I.S. is "Igor" (correctly pronounced "Eager" only by V., who, at the same time, is the only person he will allow to pronounce it). "What, Igor, do you have on your conscience?" the confessor inquires (in Russian), and, whatever it is, I.S. tells him standing. For the Absolution, the priest holds a partlet over the suppliant's head, recites a prayer, and extends the pectoral cross to his lips. The church doors are then opened, and stray people enter to join in the Mass and form a chorus, of sorts, in the "*Gospodi pomiluy.*" A second acolyte carries the monstrance for the priest and follows the Communion cup with a red cloth with which to wipe away pendant drops. After taking the sacraments, I.S. prays with his head to the floor, like a Muslim.

The ride from the church, like the ride going, is silent, but at least the odor of sanctimony is dispelled by the odor of whiskey and Russian cutlets. At home, I.S. goes directly to his studio and prays, crossing himself again

1951 and again before the icon that watches over him as he composes, the mediator in the renewal of his divine gift. From noon on, friends call, bringing gifts and offerings, and dozens of telegrams from the faithful but far away pile up on the hall table. But I.S. is removed and untalkative to the end of the day.

June 22. With Aldous to a private screening of Renoir's *The River*, which no one likes. Afterward to Aldous's, to listen to the *Musical Offering* and to a fascinating talk by him on Malebranche. Maria says that Aldous recognized Catherwood's engraving of New York harbor from Governor's Island, now on their wall, at an auction and at a distance of ten feet, even though he can scarcely see that far and though the picture was similar to several others.

June 27. To Schoenberg's, while the S.s are at the Castelnuovo-Tedescos'. I borrow the tape of Tibor Varga's performance of the Violin Concerto.

July 6. Call on Schoenberg to return the tape. Two sculptured heads of him are in the living room, one from *ca.* 1936, the other, of recent date, shrunken, it seems, to two-thirds of the former size. He is unwell today and unable to come downstairs, but his voice is audible from the bedroom, and from there he inscribes my scores of *Erwartung* and *Die glückliche Hand*, besides sending me a gift of the facsimile of *Dreimal Tausend Jahre*. He also sends a message inviting me to stay and listen to the Concerto. (I have been doing little else all week.) "He likes to hear it," Mrs. Schoenberg explains, "whatever he can hear of it upstairs; it is his favorite among his orchestral works, as the String Trio is of his chamber music." After I listen twice through, she shows me Schoenberg's studio, which is as small and crowded as I.S.'s, but without I.S.'s finicky aesthetic arrangement of working paraphernalia, and without the tinsel and decor. The desk is tinted with red, yellow, and blue light from a stained-glass window. This is spooky, but less so than Schoenberg's self-portraits, obsessive about eyes. Manuscripts and papers cover a desk, a table, and an old harmonium, and every inch of shelf space is stuffed with music (including miniature orchestra scores of *Otello* and *Falstaff*) and bound sets of books (Strindberg, Ibsen, Byron). A mandolin, wistful reminder of the Serenade and *Pierrot*, hangs from a peg on the wall.

July 11. The Huxleys for dinner, with Signor Ungaro, the Italian Consul, Passinetti, the novelist, and the Baroness d'Erlanger. Aldous talks about Sir Aurel Stein, and about second-century Bodhisattvas. He mentions 20 books that I want to read immediately.

July 14. While we are at breakfast, Mary Jeanette Brown, secretary of Evenings on the Roof, telephones me with the news of Schoenberg's death during the night. I inform V. first, and she waits until I.S. is in his studio to tell him. Returning, she says that he was deeply moved. Half an hour later, he emerges to show me the telegram he has composed to Mrs. Schoenberg: "Deeply shocked by saddening news of terrible blow inflicted

to all musical world by loss of Arnold Schoenberg. Please accept my *1951*
heartfelt sympathy. Igor Stravinsky."

V. telephones it to Western Union. During lunch, I.S. does not talk or
mention the death. Ingolf Dahl calls in the afternoon to say that the message was greatly appreciated. A little later, Dick Hoffmann calls with
information about the funeral service, which I.S. wants to attend but
decides not to, believing his presence could only be seen as ironic. I.S. is
far more upset by this death than he was a few weeks ago by
Koussevitzky's, a man he knew well. Schoenberg's death ends a uniquely
tangential relationship, a *concidentia oppositorum*, a bond formed by a 40-year
antinomical coupling of the composers' names (rather than their music).
Apart from this they knew practically nothing about, yet were deeply
interested in, each other. "*Soirée* at the Werfels' with Stravinsky," Thomas
Mann wrote in 1943 in the *Entstehung des Doktor Faustus*: "Talked about
Schoenberg."

July 15. Berman, for dinner, brings us a "*court et inepte Baedeker pour l'Italie*,"
actually 18 pages of descriptions of cities, galleries, restaurants, museums,
and people, with their addresses, telephone numbers, and even classifica-
tions of psychological types—"neurasthenic," "cold," etc.

July 16. Dinner at the Huxleys', in the open lean-to behind their house.
Julian Huxley is there, and Gerald Heard, Isherwood, Haddow (the British
Consul), the Hubbles, the Kiskaddens, and Aldous's brother-in-law Joep
Nicolas. In different clothes, Sir C. A. Haddow, son of the music critic,
could be mistaken for a Viking.

Conversation is highly competitive in the display of up-to-date scientific information, but Aldous and Gerald are so quick at the game, battledores
and shuttlecocks, that no one else has a chance to play. In gatherings such
as this one, Aldous speaks trippingly (as always), Gerald with a just noticeable strut. At one point, when Aldous advances a somewhat shaky hypoth-
esis, his brother gently teases him about his credulity. But compared to
Gerald's rasher speculations, Aldous is skepticism itself. Still, the essential
difference between the two Angeleno sages is one of temperament. Aldous
would shine most appealingly in a girls' college, Gerald in a lamasery—if
such inextinguishable and entertaining verbosity is imaginable in a holy
place. What bravura performers both!

July 19. At 4, I bring Aldous to a cocktail party at the Baroness's, then
go with the S.s to dinner at Alma Mahler-Werfel's. She has the bosom of a
pouter pigeon and the voice of a barracks bugle in one of her first husband's symphonies. Some of the conversation is difficult to follow, partly
because it is in German, partly because this survivor of distinguished husbands and consorts is deaf. Moreover, her wines, champagne, and cordials
are befuddling but unrefusable, being required for toast-making. To I.S.,
she quotes Mahler's "Only those who can create can interpret," letting us
know that the remark is aimed at her next-door neighbor, Bruno Walter.

1951 When the subject turns to Schoenberg, she tells the story of the composer's objection to the illogical American system of addressing mail with the number before the street. To demonstrate the illogicality, Schoenberg instructed a taxi driver: "Take me to number forty-five. I will give you the name of the street when we get there." Recalling the night of Schoenberg's death, she says that because the downstairs clock was several minutes fast, Mrs. Schoenberg thought midnight had passed and, with it, her husband's triskadekaphobic crisis. She then went to his bedroom, found him lifeless, and noticed that the clock in his room had stopped before twelve.

After dinner, Anna Mahler, Frau Alma's sculptress daughter, stops by and offers to show I.S. Schoenberg's death mask. As she unwraps it, I.S. is visibly moved, the more so after she tells him that he, of all people, is the first to see it. Here, a foot away, is the face of the man who has haunted him since 1912, but whom he scarcely saw and since 1912 never at close range, the face, in death, of the one composer whose supremacy in twentieth-century music challenges I.S.'s. *Absit omen!*

July 20. A note from Aldous about his role in suggesting Auden to do the libretto of the *Rake*: *"Je ne suis au plus que l'intermédiaire qui a combiné heureusement le rencontre de ces deux éminentes lesbiennes Musique et Poésie dont le collage, depuis trente siècles est si notoire."*

July 28. I am gripped by high fever and piercing abdominal pain. Dr. Edel comes in the afternoon, then, late at night, Dr. Bower, who, hinting at polio, drives me to Cedars of Lebanon Hospital.

August 3. Released from the hospital with no explanation for the fever and pains, and groggy from antibiotic saturation bombing, I spend the night at the McLanes'.

August 4. Fly to New York, feeling very weak.

August 7. We sail for Naples on the SS *Constitution*.

August 11. I.S. has pneumonia, a result, he believes, of the powerful and unadjustable air-cooling system in his stateroom (No. 118). At 1:30 P.M. we sight the Azores and the west-bound SS *Independence*.

August 13. Anchored at Gibraltar for three hours, our ship is surrounded by a bobbing bazaar of small boats. The partners of the oarsmen hold up bottles of wine, dresses, jackets, berets, scarves, rope sandals, jewelry, souvenirs of the Rock, matadors' hats, muletas, and spangled pants. Ropes are thrown up, fastened to the deck rails, then used as pulleys to hoist baskets containing the merchandise. Buyer and seller negotiate with fingers representing dollars, the former always showing at least one digit less than the asking price. The deal made, the money is dropped in the baskets. Prices are lower on the lower decks, and, as the *Constitution* raises anchors to depart, on the upper ones as well.

August 15. On the dock at Naples: Auden and Kallman in soiled white suits, and Theodore, Denise, and Kitty Stravinsky. Auden's first question to me: "How did the old boy react to Schoenberg's death? Did he dance and drink champagne?"

With Auden to Papagallo's, a small, four-table restaurant on a hillside, with a caged parrot. Last seen sprawled on the floor of his New York apartment, surrounded by open volumes of Saintsbury's prosody and the OED, Auden looks outstandingly non-aboriginal in these surroundings, especially with his hennaed hair, skin raw with sunburn, once-white Panama suit. A gang of gamins singles out and pursues him as we walk, and when he shouts *"Basta"* at them, the foreign ring of the word in his mouth increases his plight.

His right hand flaps circularly as he talks. When the subject is serious, the movement becomes more forceful and the static between words increases. His arguments are always categorical: "Actually, there are just two points: (a) . . . (b). . . ." Another of his characteristics is a contempt for ill-health. "Bad weather does not exist if it is ignored," he says, and on the strength of this philosophy he will eschew a coat and catch cold. Puzzle games, quizzes, quests, hypotheses delight him. Tonight he contends that "Italian and English are the languages of Heaven, 'Frog' the language of Hell." I am supposed to follow this by inventing celestial and infernal usages, but can think of none, and, anyway, he is already developing the idea that "The 'Frogs' were expelled from Heaven in the first place because they annoyed God by calling him *cher maitre"*—this in reaction to Dr. Musella who is attending I.S. and uses the form of address in every sentence. Auden has a prodigious repertory of unintentionally funny C. of E. hymns and of opera prima donna anecdotes. He is very proper, even a Puritan, except about sexual matters—indecorous stories amuse him, but not gastrointestinal ones (mine about my German friend who when ill in Paris swallowed a suppository thinking it a strange kind of French pill). His brilliant all-seeing brown eyes are set in a rumpled face (I.S.: "Soon we will have to smooth him out to see who it is"), but his actual eyesight is poor, and without spectacles he may fail to apprehend furniture; he once waded through the glass front door of his own apartment building. We drink grappas in the Galleria, but he is able to stay awake only long enough to swallow his sleeping pills. He tips the table over as we leave, having forgotten it was there.

August 16. A charabanc to San Martino, partly to see the portrait gallery of musicians: the Scarlattis, Farinelli, Zingarelli, Bellini, and Cimarosa, a fat man seated at a clavicembalo.

August 17. At the National Gallery, the Pompeii mosaics—cubes of blue glass and polished marble as fine as the smallest point in a pointillist picture—are a natural history of birds, animals, fish. We go to the *pinacoteca* for Titian's portrait of Pope Paul III with his nephews Alessandro—the patron of Lasso and Filippo di Monte—and Ottavio Farnese, the latter bowing like a ballet dancer. One feels that the old Pope has not been taken in by his obsequious *nipoti.*

1951 A drive on the tree-lined Royal Way to Caserta where the English gardens imitate Pompeii, which was excavated while Caserta was being built. The grotto and its ruins—weeds and roots growing out of the walls, fragments of ancient frescoes, holes in the ceiling—are all artificial.

From the balcony of the S.s' rooms at the Excelsior: soft blues of bay and sky, Sorrento and Castellemare, Vesuvio and the islands. In spite of these views, our eyes are fixed on the waterfront below, an arena of strolling Americans and the touts who prey on them with Swiss watches, fountain pens, black market rates of exchange, offers to the favors of their sisters. These salesmen lean against the seawall, pretending to be absorbed in the view, then pounce around and harrow the victim at close quarters until he or she buys something "to get rid of the nuisance."

The shores are crowded with bathers, and the bay is white with sails. Beneath the balcony to the left are the docks of the Capri excursion boats where, every half-hour or so, a small steamer leaves or lands low in the water with tourists. To the right of the hotel are a restaurant, the Transatlantico, and the Castle of Lucullus, now a jail. Another restaurant, the Zi'Teresa, faces these incongruous buildings across a small inlet, and at night the rival names are spelled out in brightest Neapolitan neon. Chinese lanterns festoon the façades of each establishment, and from each we hear the same music: guitars and soulful tenors. In the morning, table laundry flutters from both their porches, and this morning, too, we hope to recover from an intestinal instability, the result of yesterday's lunch at one of them.

August 18. My fellow passengers on an excursion bus to Pompeii and the peninsula are a group of Italian shoe manufacturers from Boston and a young woman school teacher from Oklahoma, who comes aboard loudly condemning Neapolitan cabmen and the Italian character in general, thereby offending the cobblers. Our guide is elderly, extremely laconic, and prone to fall asleep, in spite of the driver's habit of creeping up behind ant-paced tomato carts and murderously blasting his horn. The guide's first words announce a rest stop, but because no one could be tired, except from the claxoning, we are curious to see what waylay has been devised. This proves to be a cameo factory, whose contract with the bus company must have specified that we are to stay there until a dozen brooches are sold. In the back rooms, pale boys, magnifying glasses strapped to their heads like optometrists, sit carving at poorly lighted tables.

In the Pompeii museum, Miss Oklahoma wishes to know whether the lava cast in the shape of a man contains a man's skeleton, but the guide will say no more than "obviously" (not "obviously yes" or "no"). The streets are broader than many Naples alleys today, but the curbs are high and the stepping stones that divide the road at crossings are too tall for automobiles to pass over, though they would be well below chariot axles. The ruins are hot, efts and lizards always underfoot. Though Auden contends that Pompeii was only a kind of Atlantic City, the view of Vesuvius is worth the trip.

At the Villa dei Misteri, the women are asked to remain outside while the men line up for a look at two faded frescoes of love-making, and a not very authentic-looking representation of the Scales of Justice on which a heap of gold is easily overbalanced by a grossly exaggerated lingam. The inscription *SALVE LUCRUM* at the house of Vedius Siricus would amuse I.S. We trek to an oil shop, a wine shop, a granary, to sites of excavation-in-progress, to the amphitheater, to the Villa of the Dioscuri.

After Amalfi, I lean from the sea side of the bus to the mountain side, but we round each hairpin turn at high speed and on the wrong side of the road. The afternoon is spent in Sorrento and Castellamare in bus-franchised shopping areas.

August 20. The boat to Ischia, an absurdly class-segregated pocket steamer, is crowded and smelly; I am obliged to stand all the way to Casamicciola, where I finally find a seat next to a man who is reading Goldoni and trying to memorize a passage he evidently thinks extremely funny. Transferring at Forio to a trawler, and rowed ashore, I find Auden, barefoot and with "the bottoms of his trousers rolled," waiting on the tiny dock. He carries my bag through the toy-like town to the Via Santa Lucia and his house, the street level of which is an empty stable and carriage room. The upstairs rooms are ample, bright, and surprisingly tidy, except for burnt offerings—stubbed cigarettes—in unemptied ashtrays, a protest presumably, against the sterility of American cleanliness. Americans are not responsible, in any case, but a handsome Neapolitan Ganymede with a manner like his not quite believable name, Giocondo. While Giocondo spreads the lunch, we move to a patio, the domain of a cat and a dog, Moisè, for whom Wystan throws a ball, or pretends to, taking in the eager retriever again and again with the same feint, and once cuffing the poor cur for barking, which alters the quality of noise to something resembling a screech owl.

Giocondo does not understand Wystan's Italian, and it must be a relief to him, as it certainly is to me, when the poet resumes the language of his muse. What, he asks, will become of I.S.'s promised Ischian visit? It can take place, I tell him, only if the doctors allow it, and when I.S. is prepared to brave the gauntlet of journalists standing round-the-clock guard in the hotel lobby. "Oh," Wystan says, "in Italy one gets rid of journalists simply by saying you believe in the Church. Then they will scatter as if you had the plague." In this instant a courier arrives with an express letter which Wystan passes to me without so much as a glance at the envelope, asking for a précis. It is an invitation from the Intendente of La Scala to "assist" at the *Rake* at La Scala's expense. Wystan tries but is unable to conceal his pleasure.

We walk to a beach in the afternoon, Wystan at high speed, wearing

1951 plimsolls, in spite of the heat and, himself excepted, the universal indolence; the water is bathtub warm, and only Moisè, still starting at every false throw, is aquatically inclined. On the return we meet Chester Kallman, just back from a visit to another part of the island. Wystan is always happier in tandem with Chester, and the best of his former good spirits are doldrums in comparison. He dotes on the younger man, in fact, listening admiringly to his talk, calling attention to jeweled bits of it, and supplying helpful interruptions for rougher gems though, as a rule, if Chester appears to be even on the verge of speaking, Wystan remains silent. When the younger man goes to the kitchen for a moment, Wystan tells me: "He is a good poet and a far cleverer person than I am." Whatever the truth of these judgments, Chester *is* a good cook. By some oversight, however, the spinach has not been washed, and after what sounds like a painfully gritty bite, Wystan reports a large presence of sand; then, lest we think him persnickety, he quickly adds that he doesn't in the least mind, and even manages to suggest that he has become quite fond of it. When conversation turns to the opera, Wystan repeats his story about Benjamin Britten liking the *Rake* very much, "Everything but the music" (a story I.S. did not find at all funny).

His talk flows with generalizations, not all of them, at first flush, a hundred percent self-evident. "Jews are more complicated than Gentiles," he says, which, coming from him, seems a vulnerable thesis. But while his Manichean mind is almost continually engaged with polarizing moral distinctions, he goes about sorting the Good and the Evil as if it were a game and without the assumption of any rectitude of his own. The language of this is oddly diocesan and Sunday-school-like, as when, with vigorous rotary movements of his right hand and his always uptilted head held still farther back, he declares himself "very cross with Stalin" because the tyrant has been "naughty." (Stalin's icons compete on Forio's walls with those of the Virgin and the Madonna.)

At *passeggiata* time, we go to a trattoria in the piazza with Harold Acton, a tall gentleman, very kind to Wystan, and so much better dressed than anyone in the vicinity as to be conspicuous. There the librettists repeatedly raise their glasses to the *Rake* premiere—"Prosit!" from Wystan, whose natural foreign language even in Ischia is German. On the return to the Via Santa Lucia, he sings parts of Fricka's waffling scene in *Die Walküre*, which sounds odd in this deserted—the whole town has gone to bed by 10 o'clock—Mascagni scenery.

August 21. At 6 A.M., Wystan, barefoot in spite of cold flagstones, escorts me to a bus that meets the Naples boat at Laccoameno; and only just meets it, for we stop at every turn to collect still more passengers and to tie still more bundles and cardboard suitcases to the roof. The boat being overcrowded as well, I debark at Pozzuoli and return to Naples by taxi. The driver is a testy type, very free with oaths. His favorites are, at

high speed, "*Cretino!*," and, at low speed, "*Mezzo-culiliello!*" (half-assed). The **1951**
latter is directed largely to inattentive pedestrians and animals. Once we
nearly collide with a vegetable cart hauled by a poor Rosinante: "*Mezzo-culiliello!*"

I reach the hotel just as Dottore Musella, on his rounds, is ordering
I.S.—thin and aquiline, knees hunched to chin, a pack of hot compresses
on his crown—to remain in bed for the balance of the week. The Dottore,
like most of I.S.'s physicians around the world, is eager to chat with his
patient about the arts. But when the name of Eleanora Duse is mentioned,
V. provides the talk, describing a performance of *A Doll's House*, seen in
Moscow as a child, with Duse playing Nora in Italian supported by a
Russian-speaking cast. When Musella departs, V. attempts to dissuade I.S.
from conducting *The Rake* even if he *has* fully recovered, attributing some of
his desire to conduct to vanity. I.S. answers that he *is* a performer, hence
an actor, but not a vain one. "Acting," he continues, "is an element in my
make-up. My father was as renowned for his dramatic talent as for his
voice. Besides, I *like* to perform."

After this burst of off-telling, I accompany V. to a *farmacia* to fetch I.S.'s
new medicines. We join a queue of American tourists, all purchasing paregoric and all looking intensely uncomfortable as V., in turn, asks for milk of
magnesia.

August 22. The Naples aquarium is dim, dirty, and reeking of urine,
and many of the tanks are as slimy outside as within. Behind one murky
window an eel quivers against a rock like a paper ribbon in a breeze.
Behind another a cuttlefish discharges an inky obnubilation. An attendant
is feeding sardines to the scorpion fish, but smaller fish dart around these
monsters and snatch the food themselves. The scorpion fish move to the
surface slowly and along the sides of the tank, using their long red feelers,
lobster claws, and trolley-car-antennae legs. One of them makes a reflection on the under-surface but shatters it like a mirror when he invades it.
Are they blind? One old *joli-laide* crustacean reminds me of the line, "liquid
prisoner pent in walls of glass."

We explore the hillside streets behind the hotel, climbing stone staircases and wandering through dark alleys wall-papered with oleograph
Madonna images. In one open place, an old woman is sewing on an
ancient Singer in the better light of the middle of a street. Suddenly a
small boy throws a tomato against a wall with the intention of spattering
us, which ought to but does not relieve our guilt feelings for having come
in our richer state to look at the poor.

August 25. On the morning boat to Capri, loudspeakers blare Caruso
recordings. At the dock, I transfer to a smaller boat for the Blue Grotto
and am rowed along the cliffs to join a queue waiting for two-minute turns
in the cave. The seasickness rate in the choppy water outside the bottle-
neck entrance is high, and the complexion of most passengers is verdigris.

1951 Going inside, we switch to tiny skiffs and lie flat on the floor while the oarsman grips a chain attached to the cave and, between waves, pulls us through. The water inside is indeed azure and transparent, but this hardly justifies the singing of "Santa Lucia" by the extended-open-palms oarsmen. "No one has ever visited the Blue Grotto twice," Norman Douglas wrote. I spend the afternoon in upper Capri and return to Naples on the 6 o'clock steamer.

August 26. To Milan. The train, a *rapido*, is wobbly, sooty, and two hours late. I.S.: "Italians do not believe without exaggeration. The expression '*una cosa tremenda*' is applied to something of no great moment, and '*brutissimo*' and '*repellente*' are used with reference to quite minor inconveniences. As you see, too, the slowest and least punctual trains are called *rapido*,' '*accelerato*,' '*direttismo*.'" Harold Acton, a fellow passenger, stops to greet I.S. A film star's reception for I.S. at the Duomo Hotel in Milan: the entire street is blocked off and the entranceway cordoned by ropes.

August 27. Auden arrives during the evening rehearsal. Having neglected to make hotel reservations, he and Kallman have had to take rooms, rented by the hour, in a *bordello*. "The girls are very understanding," Auden says, "but it is too expensive." The front of Auden's white linen suit is now polka-dotted with Chianti stains.

The first full orchestra rehearsal: the excitement of hearing the music learned at the piano during three years is like seeing a color film after viewing frames of black-and-white negatives. I.S. repeats some passages more than need be simply out of his "composer's curiosity." Afterward, Signor Ratto shows us his *maquettes*. The colors are Italian rather than English, and the Bedlam is a Piranesi prison. Auden objects to the Neapolitan-ice-cream-colored "London," as well as to Trulove's country home: "With a house as grand as that, the Rake would be better off marrying the daughter right away and foregoing his progress."

August 28. At the Sforzesco, V. buys one of the gas-filled balloons for sale by the front entrance and releases it, to watch it float away over the moat and castle, but the balloon vendor is offended.

Auden has been assigned to coach the chorus's English, not a word of which can be understood, and to advise the *maestro della scena*. But he disapproves of everything in the staging: "It could hardly be worse if the director were Erwin Piscator and the singers were climbing and descending ladders."

September 2. Bellagio. We lunch by the lake across from Tremezzo (where Pliny lived and Mussolini was hanged by the heels). When I.S. casts some breadcrumbs on the water, fish rise toward the surface in the hope of being fed. Return to Milan via Bergamo, dine with W.H.A. and C.K., and go with them to Giordano's unintentionally funny *Fedora*. This disappoints us, after Kallman's lively preview of it during dinner, at which time Auden relinquishes the stage, except for contributions of background information or to alert the S.s to imminent high points in Chester's narrative. He looks on beaming as Chester talks.

September 4. To Certosa di Pavia, a warm, drowsy afternoon sweet with the smell of new mown grass.

September 5. To Venice, the cast, chorus, and orchestra in three reserved railroad cars. The S.s, Auden and I are in the restaurant car when the train stops at Verona and an American tourist, across the aisle, says to his companion: "Hey, didn't Shakespeare live here?" Auden, interjecting: "Surely it was Bacon." Then Vicenza, Padua, Mestre, the land's end, the long trestle, and the bell towers, churches, and chimneys of the Serenissima.

Venice. Finding that his Scala-sponsored accommodations at the Bauer are bathless and viewless, Auden retreats to the S.s' large, over-upholstered and luxuriously uncomfortable Royal Suite and bursts into tears. V. calls the "Direzione," explaining that Maestro Auden is the co-author of "*La Carriera d'un Libertino*" and a poet "who has been received at Buckingham Palace by the King." A better room is promptly found, but Wystan's tears, exposing so much frustration and wounded pride, have watered us all a bit, partly because he is beyond the most appropriate age for them, and partly because his mind is so superior to such behavior.

The Piazza. The great quadriga of bronze horses on the façade of St. Mark's. The bell tower is disproportionately big. Pigeon love: the male treads and turns, blinks, treads again, chases. The bands playing on each side of the Piazza sound like the two Milhaud string quartets played together. Auden talks about Venice in *The Wings of the Dove*.

September 6. Rehearsal of Act II in the afternoon, Act III in the evening. Still no syllable of the Scala chorus sounds English. Afterwards to Harry's Bar, but Auden, seeing the girl who has been following him from New York, bolts. A midnight gondola ride with him, drunk now and full of song (*Die Walküre*), to the Zanipolo. I.S. says that Colette once sang Wagner to him when they were drunk together in a Paris-Nice train. A large rat runs along the molding of a wall two feet from our boat. "The D.T.s," Auden says.

September 7. During I.S.'s rehearsal in the Fenice, Jennie Tourel misses a cue, but he conducts to the end of her piece before realizing that she isn't singing.

September 8. To the exhibition *I Fiamminghi in Italia* at the Ducal Palace. Philippe Heugel at noon, Nadia Boulanger for lunch, then Louis MacNeice and Auden at Florian's, and at night Verdi's Requiem at the Fenice, rousingly conducted by de Sabata, and wonderfully sung by Schwarzkopf and Stignani.

September 9. Afternoon at the Lido, where we swim in seaweed and garbage. Nabokov arrives. I.S.'s dress rehearsal at 9 P.M.

September 10. Spender arrives and Ferdinand Leitner conducts *his*

1951 dress rehearsal. With Lukas Foss, Claudio Spies, and Leo Smit at the Monaco.

September 11. I meet Leopold Survage, Maria Freund, Markevitch, Boris Kochno, Domenico De' Paoli, Herbert Fleischer, Michel Georges-Michel. Telegrams from Lifar, Jean Renoir, Marguerite Caetani, Poulenc, Sauguet, Stark Young, Aldous, Balanchine.

"La Prima Assoluta." An afternoon and evening of stifling heat, the sirocco blowing like a bellows. The alleys near the theater have been roped off to keep the lower orders at bay, and hours before curtain time the Fourth Estate begins to line up along the wider streets. They have actually come to applaud the parade of the rich, most of whom, however, arrive in gondolas and motor launches and are deposited at the canal-side entrance; in Venice, 1789 is a long way in the future. Our own pedestrian party includes Nadia Boulanger, who carries I.S.'s valises, Auden and Kallman, both nervous in spite of liquid fortifications (a moat of martinis), and Louis MacNeice (handsome, silent, but perhaps pickled).

The vaguely familiar face of Zinovy Peshkov, Maxim Gorky's adopted son, last seen by V. in the Caucasus during the Revolution, veers toward her as we enter the foyer, but she is quickly besieged by old friends from Paris. Soldiers wearing tricornes and cross-webbing are positioned at the side entrances, and at the front they hold candelabras.

La Fenice glitters and bouquets of roses, like debutantes' corsages, are pinned to each loge. The beauty of these hideouts is even less than skin deep, however, the red plush having suffered moth-pox and being badly in need of deodorants. Another discomfort is that the seats are like European railroad compartments: the occupants on the side nearer the stage face in the wrong direction, as if, like grasshoppers, their ears were encased in their legs and abdomens. The audience is in formal dress, everyone except the *New York Times*'s Howard Taubman.

During the delay before the curtain, thoughts drift back through the three weeks of preparation, the conferences with stage directors and music coaches, the discovery of echoes in the opera of I.S.'s so-called private life, such as the card game, which stems from his fondness for Patience, the harpsichord arpeggios being an imitation of his way of shuffling cards, and the instrument's staccato chords recalling the way he snaps playing cards on a table. Auden may well have observed I.S. playing solitaire. V. says, too, that in the Epilogue, the idea of pointing to the audience—"you and you"—was inspired by Walter Huston in *The Devil and Daniel Webster*, a film I.S. liked.

At 21:35, a prompt thirty-five minutes late, I.S. enters the pit and acknowledges the warm welcoming applause of both the ultra *mondaine* and the boisterous bravos in the top galleries. Expectancy is high: the last great master is presenting his largest-scale work. He turns quickly to the orchestra, so that we can see only his occipital bumps and small, vital beat.

As the opera unfolds, the audience seems to become aware that Stravinsky has achieved a new and greater breadth, that the short, tight movements that were his trademark have given way to lyrically free arias and scenas, and that in spite of lapidary orchestration, the *Rake* is a singers' opera, with long melodic lines. The Rake, Robert Rounseville, though not fully emerged from his film career and manner, is aptly cast; Elisabeth Schwarzkopf is a cool and perfect Anne, musically superior to all the other singers; Hugues Cuénod is a subtle and mysterious Sellem; and Tourel as Baba could swagger through her grand exit on an elephant without risking a snigger from the audience. During the first-act intermission we drink *espresso* in the Campo San Fantin, mercifully rescued from impertinent judgments on the music occasioned by the stunning effect on everyone of Fräulein Schwarzkopf's "C." During the second act intermissions, people who would not have understood Pound's remark, "beauty is a brief gasp between one cliché and another," questioned Stravinsky's use of operatic conventions and formulas, but the majority are conceding him anything and following him raptly.

The performance is tentative and shows more "might" as the preterite of "may" than in the sense of power. At most changes of tempo, the ensemble falls apart and there are a dozen near-disastrous entrances. Some crucial lines are lost, or misunderstood; e.g., the Rake's "My wife? I've buried her," is taken as a pointedly redundant "I've married her." But the opera survives, and we and most of the audience are deeply moved. When the performance ends, at 1 A.M., Stravinsky receives an ovation.

The post mortem party at the Taverna does not expire until the bleary dawn. During it we play a tune-detection game; V. thinks the Mourning Chorus begins like the *Volga Boat Song*; the beginning of Act III, and especially the woodwind trill with the *fermata*, reminds Auden of the dance of the apprentices in *Meistersinger*; I say that the Terzetto is Tchaikovskyan, and the Epilogue a vaudeville or pasquinade, à la *Seraglio* or *L'Heure espagnole*. But what beautiful inventions the score contains: the modulation to "O willful powers," the transformations of the Ballad-Tune in the final two scenes, and the double appoggiaturas in the graveyard scene, those style-embalmed representations of Tom's fear that return during his mad scene. But the finest moments of all are in the final pages, the music of "Venus, mount thy throne," of "In a foolish dream," and—perhaps the most personal music I.S. ever wrote—"Where art thou, Venus?"

To bed at 6 A.M., under stifling mosquito netting.

September 12. Lunch with Igor Markevitch. To San Michele with V. to place flowers on Diaghilev's grave.

September 13. The S.s, Claudio Spies, and I go to tea at the Palazzo Curtis (Palazzo Barbarigo), where Henry James lived. To the second *Rake* in the evening.

September 14. The S.s, Michelangelo Spagno, Claudio, and I go to

1951 Chioggia, a two-hour ride even in our fast motorboat. South of the "island of the insane," San Servolo (*sans cervelles?*), when the propeller strangles in seaweed, we call for help from a passing coal barge—in return for which I.S. shakes hands with the boatmen. North of Chioggia, near the passageway to the open sea, sails swarm over the lagoon, some of them decorated with portraits of saints and Madonnas—a Madonna of the Kettledrums among them —who grow fat or lean according to the Adriatic wind.

Parking in the canal of San Domenico, mooring to the outermost fishing boat, we scramble to a cobblestone street, where the Chioggetti applaud I.S. and follow him over canal bridges and past rundown Venetian-style palazzi with flowerpot chimneys to the center of the city. Women in clogs and barefoot men and children are unable to turn their eyes from V.'s golden sandals.

The whole city stinks overpoweringly of fish, for which reason we stop at a café on the main street and swallow Fernet Brancas. A moment later an old and dilapidated automobile bleats its way through the crowd and to our table—Chioggia's unique taxi, so its driver claims, though just then two other ancient jalopies come rattling and racing each other in our direction. Not knowing which to choose—the early bird might not be the hungriest, and the chirping and flapping of the others can hardly be ignored—we hire all three and set out on a tour, each of us in his own chariot. Mine has a wooden bench for a seat and a hole in the floor as large as the windows. Hands reach in offering lottery tickets, toy gondolas, religious medals.

At the *pescheria*, fishermen are putting their boats to bed under tarpaulins. We leave our taxis here, exchange innumerable *addios*, and motorboat to San Domenico, a bare church except for Carpaccio's *St. Paul*, invisibly high on the south wall, and a large wooden crucifix, "miraculously" discovered in the canal, like a piece of driftwood. The sacristan, a small boy, unlocks two tall doors, draws a velvet curtain, and swings the statue out where we can see it from all angles. The gaunt, larger-than-human Christ, with bulging rope-like veins, is strangely alive. To judge by the rococo curls in the beard and hair, the stylized halo and crown of thorns, the carving dates from the late eighteenth century and could be the work of a Tyrolean peasant. Half of it remains a tree trunk, and whereas the slumped-to-the-side head is fully formed, the torso and legs are disproportionately elongated, the arms, still the limbs of a tree, unnaturally thin. Coming upon the raw material in the woods, the carver, like the men who fished the sculpture from the water, must have experienced an apparition, and it survives in this sunny church, the ghost in the closet, the "*Ecce Homo*" behind the altar's too sweet Christ and Mary dolls.

The lagoon, in the gloaming hour, is rich in mirages. From time to time birds rest on our prow. Venice is dark, and the gondolas gliding by might be bearing coffins to the islands for secret burial.

September 15. With Marion Sachs to Torcello, where we climb the bell tower—a stone ramp with two steps at each corner's turn—and, on top, surprise a man and woman in an advanced stage of courtship. In the low-tide lagoon, birds in ankle-deep water appear to be walking on the surface, while emerging part-time islands return ducks and other amphibians to their gressorial ways.

September 17. With Baron Raffaello de Banfield Tripcovich, in his Lancia, to Padua (the Scrovegni Chapel), Vicenza (the Teatro Olimpico), and, on the Brenta, the Baroness d'Erlanger's Villa Malcontenta. Here we sip tea with the Grand Duchess Maria Pavlova, the Grand Duke Vladimir's widow, with whom, surprisingly, the S.s actually seem shy. I am more impressed by the Baron and his faultless English and German. His mother's tutors in these tongues were Joyce and Rilke—in his Duino period—Trieste being the family seat.

September 18. With the Baron again, to Ferrara and Ravenna—San Vitale, Galla Placidia, Dante's tomb, S. Apollinare in Nuovo, S. Apollinare in Classe: dark eyes in beautiful mosaics.

September 20. Letter from Auden in Forio d'Ischia:

> Dear Bob, I was so sorry to miss you all after the performance on Thursday to say au revoir, but you seemed to have disappeared. I hope Friday went even better. Am just beginning to recover from the stress of the last three weeks. I hope (though I doubt it) that you are getting a little rest now. Two requests: 1) As Ballo never answers letters, could you see that someone in the office sends us ten (10) copies of the programme book. This address will do. 2) Could you find out what is being done about copies of the tape recording of the performance. We were promised one.
>
> Overleaf are some possible suggestions for more lyrics for that mezzo-soprano cycle, all from the *P[oets of the] E[nglish] L[anguage]*. Much love to Igor, Vera and yourself from us both, Wystan. Rumors reach us that La Scala are thinking of having Ebert again for their production. It seems incredible. You must sink it, if true. P.S. Give Ballo and the Hotel this address in case of mail to be forwarded.
>
> Vol. I
> P. 497. Sidney. My true love hath my heart, as I have his.
> Vol. II
> 63. Anon. Weep O mine eyes and cease not.
> 65. George Peele. Hot sunne, coole fire, tempered with sweet aire.
> 95. Campion. Harke, all you ladies that do sleep.
> 100. Campion. So quicke, so hot, so mad is thy fond sute.

1951

325. Ben Jonson. Slow, slow, fresh fount, keepe time with my salt teares.

458. George Herbert. I gave to Hope a watch of mine.

501. Vaughan. Unfold, unfold! take in his light.

Vol. III

183. Herrick. A Gygis Ring they beare about them still.

426. Pope. When other ladies to the shades go down.

Vol. IV

1. Blake. The wild winds weep;

Burns. O whistle and I'll come to you, my lad.

Vol. V

Christina Rossetti. Never on his side of the grave again.

Not in anthology: the song of the Veronic in *Comus*: "Sweet tale, sweetest nymph that livst unseen."

September 29. Milan. I.S.'s La Scala concert: Symphony in Three, *Petrushka* Suite, *Scherzo à la Russe, Norwegian Moods, Circus Polka, Divertimento*. An embarrassing scene in the dressing room afterward, as a young man falls to his knees in front of I.S.

October 3. Basel, the Three Kings Hotel. After the morning in the museum, we take the train via Freiburg, Heidelberg, and Mainz to Cologne, where Eric Winkler meets us. Many one-armed and one-legged ex-soldiers in shabby uniforms and no coats are begging in the freezing railroad station.

October 4–8. Rehearsals. Cologne is more ruined than Pompeii: façades without houses and vice versa, steps without porches, gaping holes in the earth, grass growing from third-floor rooms, duck-board sidewalks, and people living in makeshift shelters in the rubble. Next to the Cathedral, still closed because of falling bits of stone, is a bomb shelter with a floor of Roman mosaics discovered in 1942. A twisted bridge still lies in the Rhine. The radio station is not yet completely built, but the orchestra is good and the *Oedipus* chorus excellent.

October 6. At the Rundfunk, I.S. and I listen to a tape of Scherchen's Darmstadt performance of Schoenberg's *The Golden Calf*.

At 3 A.M. I mistakenly press the button for the *Gepäckträger* who promptly appears with his hand cart and is properly but illogically annoyed with me for waking him: where would I or anyone be going at this hour?

October 8. I.S.'s concert: *Apollo, Symphonies of Winds, Oedipus Rex*. A rigidly attentive and appreciative audience, straight backs, thick necks.

October 9. The 11:41 A.M. Rheingold Express to Baden-Oos. Heinrich Strobel meets our train and we go in two cars to the Brenners Park Hotel, Baden-Baden. The city supports a large garrison of French soldiers. Walk by the brook. Autumn woods. Hans Rosbaud for dinner.

October 14. Nabokov arrives. I.S. conducts a broadcast concert of

Symphony in C, *Ode, Scènes de Ballet, Petrushka*. At a party in the hotel afterwards, a German musician of my age tells me that he first heard *Pierrot
Lunaire* in Schoenberg's recording while a prisoner of war in Tennessee.

October 15. Lunch at a mountain tavern in the Schwarzwald with
Count Salm, the Mathias Grünewald expert. At the Rundfunk, we listen to
tapes of Webern's Variations, which I.S. asks to hear *three times*! also a tape
of Rosbaud's Donaueschingen performance of Boulez's *Polyphonie X*.

October 20. Munich. To a Max Ernst show and to the Franke Gallery,
which is offering 12 good Klees for modest prices. At the Museum of
Science a uniformed guard recognizes I.S. and plays the antique keyboard
instruments for us—amazingly well.

October 22. Train to St. Gall. In our compartment, two German ladies
who do not recognize I.S. talk about his concert: *"Ist die Musik von
Strawinsky atonal?"* Then at Lindau, when the Customs official collects his
autograph, they flee in embarrassment. We stay in a hotel in St. Gall
where Wagner once lived.

October 23. To the monastery and rococo library where we skate over
the polished oak floor in felt slippers. Illuminated sixth- to tenth-century
Celtic manuscripts. To the cathedral and Museum of Natural History.
Train to Berne, the Schweizerhof. A letter from I.S.'s cousin, Docteur V.
Nossenko, Villa Casias, Leysin, Avenue Evian, requesting a social visit, puts
him in a fractious mood.

October 24. To the Klee Museum, then the lakeside train, trying to
imagine Byron and Shelley in a wherry in the summer of 1816. Geneva,
the Hotel des Bergues.

October 26. We collide with Ernest Ansermet in a tram, the first face-to-
face encounter between him and I.S. since the 1937 quarrel about *Jeu de cartes*.

October 30. Drive to Gruyère via Clarens, where I.S. shows me "Les
Tilleuls," in which most of *Sacre* was composed. Stop at the church of St.
Pierre to see Gino Severini's mosaics, and at Notre-Dame du Valentin to
see his fresco based on the Theotokos at Torcello. I.S. says that he was on
good terms with Severini in Paris.

November 4. Geneva, Victoria Hall. I.S. conducts the Orchestre de la
Suisse Romande in *Orpheus, Norwegian Moods, Circus Polka*, Divertimento.
Party at Dr. Maurice Gilbert's, with Denis de Rougemont.

November 9. Rome. Meet Fernandel in the Hassler hotel, and, in the
Piazza St. Ignazio, Osbert Sitwell. On the Via dei Cappellari, the bordello
alley leading from the end of Piazza Navona, a plaque identifies No. 29 as
the birthplace of Metastasio.

November 10. To the catacombs of Sant'Agnese, then the Vatican
Museum. In Gentile da Fabriano's *Nicolas of Bari*, the Saint, levitating outside the upper window of a brothel, tosses gold coins through it to a bed
to stop the women inside from prostituting themselves, but the fallen
females do not seem to have understood his motive. They are shapely in a

1951 twentieth-century way, with comely backs: modern notions of the voluptuous are older than art criticism allows.

November 12. Naples, the Excelsior Hotel. A Mozarteum Concert at San Carlo, Paumgartner conducting, Clara Haskill playing K. 459.

November 18. Rome. We spend the afternoon at Hadrian's Villa, then visit Jean Renoir—Ingrid Bergman is there—and go to a concert in the Argentina to hear a piece by Petrassi. Meet Roman Vlad there.

November 19. Animals, sculptured and in mosaics, in the Vatican Museum: a scorpion stinging a bull's testicles; a crane biting the head of a serpent; monkeys, lions, peacocks, eagles. In the *pinacoteca*, a Nativity in which the Tuscan hills seethe with miracles. To Corrado Cagli's studio. I.S.'s concert for flood victims.

November 22. New York. Auden and Isherwood meet us at the airport and stay for Thanksgiving dinner at the Lombardy Hotel.

November 25. I.S. conducts *Le Baiser de la fée* at the City Ballet.

November 29. I.S. sees Robbins's *The Cage*, and is nonplussed but pleased with the success.

December 29. Train for Los Angeles.

&❧ **Postscript 1994.** I cannot excuse the impudence of my critique of Aldous Huxley, whom I loved very deeply. But I might try to improve my appearance by emphasizing that the real target is not him but my own growing pains. He had had a considerable influence on me long before I knew him, and in my prep school and early college years the appearance of each new book by him was an exciting event bringing new notions and new bearings for old ones. I should add that in the year of my discovery of him his reputation had begun to suffer because of his pacifism, more that than his espousal of a religious philosophy which was on the way to a wartime vogue. He had recently published the *Encyclopedia of Pacifism* and a shorter tract urging pacifism as a practical policy. The argument of the latter broke ground with the claim that "feeling, willing, thinking are the three modes of ordinary human activity." Not action? Kierkegaard says somewhere, "In Greece, philosophizing was a mode of action," and it was certainly that with Aldous himself. But the oversight was unfortunate, polemically speaking, and so was the title of his pamphlet, *What Are You Going To Do About It?* which fairly begged for C. Day Lewis's rejoinder, *We're Not Going to Do Nothing*.

My role in Stravinsky's life greatly expanded in 1951. I read to him while he orchestrated, as the entry for January 1 indicates, but also during free evenings when Mrs. Stravinsky would sit next to him doing needle work. He now entrusted me with vetting his manuscripts and correcting his proofs. He was not pleased with my laundry lists of errors both trivial (misspellings, missing rests, the wrong number of beams on and between notes) and important (wrong notes, faults in transposition), nor were my suggestions for adding dynamics always well received: loud(er) or soft(er) was sufficient, he thought, since the gradations, always relative, require adjustment in rehearsals and performances. *"Pianissimo"* was a much more common marking in his music of the time than *"fortissimo."*

I had also begun to do some of the driving, especially in the evenings, when Mrs. Stravinsky's eyesight was unreliable; but Stravinsky was happier when she drove and he could sit next to her and direct.

My diary entries for the three months in Europe fail to include any observations concerning the renewed effects of the Old World on Stravinsky's personality and behavior, though from the moment of our arrival in Italy I could see that he felt more at home there than in California. For one change, he now spoke only French and German (his Italian was sketchy and, apart from *"andiamo,"* used everywhere, unsuitably operatic). Never having heard him speak German before, to any extent, I was surprised by his fluency in the language. I did not feel left out, however, as I did a decade later in Russia, and I even began to try out my own rudimentary, school-taught French and German. Stravinsky quickly re-adapted to Italian, German, and Swiss manners and class distinctions, and because he was familiar with the cities and other places that we visited, he showed them to me in a proprietary way that resembled mine in our travels in America.

Stravinsky had conducted opera only once before, a quarter of a century earlier, and during his *Rake* rehearsals and premiere he was capable of cue-ing singers too soon as well as too late. At La Scala, rather than conduct himself he preferred to audit the rehearsals of Ferdinand Leitner, his assistant conductor, and he did not undertake a run-through until the last day in Venice.

When we left Rome for New York, November 21, I was homesick for the States. European hotel rooms were barely heated, the lighting was usually too weak to read by, the skies had become leaden, and the cities, after dark, were dreary. Our airplane put down in Paris, where Arthur Sachs invited us to dinner in a private lounge. We stopped at Shannon, then, airborne again, climbed step-ladders to train-like bunks above the seats, claustrophobic but comfortable. The transatlantic flight took more than 30 hours, and we refueled at Gander and Boston. What I saw of the U.S.A. between the New York airport and Manhattan, the brick bunga-lows, the factories of Queens, and the grossness of American automobiles, reversed my homesickness: I wanted to return to Italy.

The next day(!) Stravinsky rehearsed the City Ballet orchestra and two days later conducted a performance. After that, and until we left for California a month later, we spent most evenings at the opera, the ballet, the theater, party-going.

On one of my trips to Kingston, my mother confided that our beloved old Victorian home had been sold.

৯ 1952

January 4. Walk in the hills at the summit of Doheny. Red-hot pokers in bloom everywhere. In a euphoric mood, I work on a poem but fumble it and the mood drains away, leaving me with a handful of empty sophistries. Dinner at the Huxleys'. Aldous's workroom, with its several different kinds of lamps, over-stuffed bookshelves, relaxing chair—he is always first with the latest gadgets—resembles a physician's consulting office. He insists that the only prose he can read is of the point-by-point Voltaire kind, as distinguished from the molten-mass Kierkegaard kind, but most of his books, treatises by mystics, belong to the latter category.

January 7. Orchids for V.'s Russian-calendar birthday. She begins work on a commission from the Baroness d'Erlanger to copy an 18th-century Venetian picture of acrobats forming a standing-on-shoulders pyramid, a human lattice. Aldous says that in Vendrell, in Catalonia, these human towers are erected with children on top.

January 8. After an afternoon of playing English virginal music, I.S. says he prefers Gibbon. We listen to recordings of Joyce and Gertrude Stein, the two extremes of thin and thick. I read Freud's *New Introductory Lectures* to the S.s. Three years ago the thought of the book horrified him.

January 9. The clarity of the sky and the ocean today is unreal, and both remain separate, as in the pictures made with butterfly wings that my father brought back from Bermuda when I was a small child: bright, glossy surfaces on different levels of superposition.

January 10. I.S. receives Simon Harcourt-Smith's script for the proposed *Odyssey* film and asks me to read it and advise him. Verdict: Wagner, not Stravinsky: storms, wars, gods.

January 12. Aldous, for lunch, says that Maria is in the hospital after a mastectomy. The absence of any hint of this when we saw them eight days ago seems odd—"very British behavior," the S.s explain. And even now, Aldous's tone forbids further inquiry. When I drive him to the hospital afterward, he gives me the typescript of *The Devils of Loudun* and an interesting article from the *American Journal of Science* on antibiotics. I.S.

rehearses 7–9 P.M.

January 13. Aldous, for lunch again, says that the current rains, "A sea storm, of course, since nothing comes our way landwards," are the first of such duration and force since 1934. I show him the *Odyssey* script and he digresses on the superiority of the scenes in Ithaca, then gives me his copy of Victor Bérard's *Homer*.

January 15. Royce Hall is full, but the concert begins an hour late because the trombonist has been caught on the wrong side of a flood-formed nullah. I.S. is very nervous during *Histoire, Dumbarton*, and the Octet but calm in the second-half, *Danses concertantes.* Reception afterward at Alma Mahler-Werfel's, the S.s and Aldous in a private room (where Werfel died). Aldous is amusing on Max Reinhardt's *Faust* and on a set of *transition* on a bookshelf here, observing that "Backwards it spells 'no it isn[t] art.'" Frau Alma shows us some Klees, some Kafka relics, and, removing them from glass display boxes, her Kokoschka fans. I drive Aldous home at 1 A.M., and return for the S.s at 2, water now up to the wheel hubs.

January 16. Sunset Boulevard at La Rue's (Sunset Plaza) is blocked with windshieldhigh mud slides and abandoned cars. Two people have drowned in cars in Culver City. We listen to a recording of *Idomeneo*.

January 21. V. finishes her 22-figure human-pyramid painting. A Mendelssohn evening: the complete *Midsummer Night's Dream* music, the Opus 49 Trio, and Tchaikovsky's Third Symphony (the Scherzo is Mendelssohnian).

January 22. Aldous suggests that I apply myself to writing an "early American sex history, a Kinsey report on Shakers, Mormons, Mennonites, and pioneer wife-exchanging." Philistinism from Aldous: "Why should we trust Mondrian as an abstract painter when we know that before becoming abstract he was a very mediocre academic painter?" But Cézanne, by his own admission, could not draw in an academically correct manner, and shouldn't we judge an artist on what he has done, not on what he once could not do?

January 27. To the Huxleys' at 6:30, Maria very pale, and Frieda Lawrence with spouse, Angelo Ravagli (Lady Chatterley's lover), and from there to Brian Aherne's beach house in Santa Monica (formerly the Barbara Hutton-Cary Grant home) with Ludovic Kennedy, Moira Shearer (white skin, flaming hair), and Frederick Ashton. Monet, Picasso, Monticelli, Rowlandson on the walls. Dinner in the Miramar with Frieda, who remembers the place from 1922 with D.H.L.

January 31. I.S. writes to Boosey & Hawkes about the ballet project: "I have not heard a thing from Dali. I guess the matter must have been dropped. . . . Auden must have given you the last correction of the word 'initiated.'" I help I.S. answer Kallman's arguments against the grouping of four scenes into the second act of the *Rake* and two in the third: "I do not quite agree with your estimate of advantages compared to disadvantages in

1952 either solution." We play Isaac's *Constantinus Choralis* four-hands.

February 2. I.S. composes "Westron Wind." Later we go to the beach, which is patrolled by vigilant sandpipers in squadron formation. Evening at the Huxleys' listening to Safford Cape's Dufay recording; Aldous, in a chipper mood, dances a hoe-down.

February 11. To the Huxleys'. Aldous plays a recording of Haydn's Trumpet Concerto for I.S., and we borrow a recording of Bach's *St. John*.

February 12. I.S. comes to my rehearsal of Schoenberg's Septet, questioning me afterward about the construction of the music. He has many prejudices.

February 13. Read Gilbert White's *Natural History of Selborne* to the S.s: "Worms, though in appearance a despicable link in the chain of nature, yet, if lost, would make a lamentable chasm." Tired, after "composing strict canons all day," I.S. wants to go to a movie, and we end up at a dull one about Africa, *Latuka*.

February 14. A touching valentine from my never-forgetting mother. With the S.s to Pacific Palisades and Thomas Mann's house. The mimosas are in almond blossom, and the pepper trees are blood red. During dinner I.S. says, "Tradition carries the good artist on its shoulder as St. Christopher carried the Lord."

February 20. I.S. is now completely absorbed in the Schoenberg, which we talk about for two hours after tonight's rehearsal.

February 23. Before leaving for Pasadena with the S.s and Huxleys, Aldous asks me to witness his will. Exhibition at the Huntington Library of Turner watercolors, most of them brown-yellow, pale-red, and sepia. Most, too, focus on a dark spot, or a clean white one, that composes the page. A remarkable self-portrait as a high-cheek-boned young man. Marvelous pictures of misty Swiss and Scottish lakes, as well as Venetian and Roman scenes. Stop at the Hubbles' for tea. Aldous chats with him about Flammarion galaxies and about the duration of the Big Bang—if there was any duration, which is to say any *time*. Augustus John's portrait of Sir Arthur Eddington is on the wall.

February 25. I.S. plays me "Tomorrow shall be my dancing day." As casually as possible, I draw his attention to the unrelieved length of the flute parts.

February 29. Listen to Josquin with I.S., who telegraphs Carlos Chavez to postpone the Mexican concerts until late March.

March 4. "Tomorrow shall be my dancing day" is now rescored with oboes. A beautiful piece, but tonally static.

March 8. We drive to Palmdale for lunch, spareribs in a cowboy-style restaurant, Bordeaux from I.S.'s thermos. A powdering of snow is in the air, and, at higher altitudes, on the ground: Angelenos stop their cars and go out to touch it. During the return, I.S. startles us, saying he fears he can no longer compose; for a moment he actually seems ready to weep. V. gently, expertly, assures him that whatever the difficulties, they will soon pass. He refers obliquely to the Schoenberg Septet and the powerful impression it has made on him. After 40 years of dismissing Schoenberg as "experimental," "theoretical," "*démodé*," he is suffering the shock of recognition that Schoenberg's music is richer in substance than his own. I suggest that he divert himself by orchestrating one of his earlier pieces and propose the Concertino, which would be useful for his concerts.

March 13. I.S. shows me his 12-instrument version of Concertino, a marvel of translation that also sheds light on accentuation and phrasing, and that improves on the original in the 4th measure of [5] and the 2nd measure of [7], which sounds congested in the quartet, and, in the interest of compactness, in the 5-beat cut at [7]. But the most curious difference from the original quartet piece is in the reduction of dissonance in the opening scale. In general, the changes of color in the mixed-timbre version will bring the musical ideas into greater relief and provide transparency in the dense low-register textures that are a feature of the piece. The new score also forms motives out of what were simple changes of harmony in the quartet (*cf.* 2 measures before [21]). Finally, the jazz spirit in the second Allegro, especially "cool" in the music for clarinet, bassoon, and cello at [27], promises to be more pronounced in the 12-instrument version. The choice of flute, clarinet, oboe, English horn, and of bassoons, trumpets, and trombones in pairs, was dictated by the instrumentation of the companion pieces, the Octet and the Cantata, that he has already chosen for the concert at which the Concertino will be performed.

March 18. At lunch, I.S. says he believes in a physically present but invisible devil: "The Devil wants us to believe he is only an idea, since that would make it easier for him."

March 19. Michael Powell comes with plans for the *Odyssey* film, promising that the script will be by Dylan Thomas.

March 20. With the S.s to a slow-moving movie, *Rashomon*. Good angles, but tundras of waiting and silence.

March 24. Aldous has just returned from a trip in the desert, and, as always after a spell in depopulated regions, is refreshed and in high spirits. He has brought back a garland of rare-blossoming, once-in-a-decade lilies. But Aldous himself is a far more rare and spectacular burgeoning. "Cacti," he says, "grow no more than an inch in five years, hence the large ones are among the world's most venerable plants." He is excited by his discovery that "desert whippoorwills hibernate. They are genetically related to hummingbirds, you remember, and humming birds were the only species heretofore known to hibernate. The early Hindu philosophers called them 'sleeping birds.'" With this he digresses for a fascinating quarter of an hour on the "Trochilidea family, what the onomatopoeic Mayans called the Dzunum. . . ." He gives me his copy of Apollinaire's *Le Joujou des Demoiselles*, saying that the risqué verse will improve my French and that it was given

1952 to him in his youth for the same purpose.

I drive him to the summit of Doheny Hill, the start of one of his favorite rambles, even though it has a reputation for rattlesnakes. We follow rutted tracks into a wilderness area, the daddy-long-legs easily ahead. His intellectual pace is even faster, of course, and here he stays a sprint in front, making me, in pursuit, feel mentally pigeon-toed. He digresses on Catharism, and drops dendrological information as if we were on an arboricultural tutorial; I learn and forget all sorts of things about flora to the right and left of the path, from the tallest pedunculates to the tiniest sessile organisms, though one wonders how, purblind, he can tell.

Not until the return trek does he switch to a subject I am able to follow, "the lit-t'ry cult of dirt, Auden's 'Nor make love to those who wash too much.' Ford Madox Ford may have been the least frequently washed of modern novelists." My unique contribution is to quote the dirt-specialist historian Lecky, but no sooner is this out than I realize I have mistakenly attributed the remark to J. B. Bury, whose name I mispronounce, as though it had to do with graveyards. Aldous is momentarily taken aback by his ignorance of this author, and then dawn breaks: "Oh, you mean Professor Bewry." His most interesting remarks of the afternoon are about "Tom Eliot," whose criticism he compares to "A great operation that is never performed: powerful lights are brought into focus, scalpels are laid out, anesthetists and assistants are posted, instruments are prepared. Finally the surgeon arrives, opens his bag, then closes it again and goes off." He says that "the marriage in *The Cocktail Party* was inspired, if that is the word, by Tom's own marriage. His wife, Vivienne, was an ether addict. Her face was mottled, as if with ecchymotic spots, and the house smelled like a hospital. All that dust and despair in Eliot's poetry can be traced back to the wedding. *The Family Reunion* is a play about murdering one's wife."

On the way home we drive to an ice-cream parlor in Beverly Hills and eat banana splits. "Cerebretonics should eat bananas every day," Aldous says.

April 8. I rent the small house behind the Baroness d'Erlanger's large one and move my things there.

April 9. The typescript of Auden's *Delia, a Masque of Night* arrives, and I read it aloud to I.S. Six characters—Sacrapant (Sarastro, Klingsor), Delia (a tame Kundry), Orlando (Tamino, Parsifal), Bungay (Papageno), Xantippe (Baba the Turk), Old Crone (the goddess in disguise)—are in search of I do not know what. The libretto is too involved for a fairy tale, too prolix for musical setting, and dramatically static; it contains a sizable quintet, perhaps to atone for the absence of ensembles in the *Rake*, a diverting round (the owl and the mouse), and, in the pageant of Time (Death and Mutability), beautiful poetry.

April 11. The S.s go to St. Matthias. In the evening, I rehearse the Serenade in Schoenberg's house in the presence of the composer's widow and daughter, Nuria, and Richard Hoffmann, Leonard Stein, Paco

Lagerstrom, and, on the wall, Schoenberg's death mask.

April 13. I.S. gives me the Cantata's original manuscript page for the passage, "And through the glass window shines the sun," inscribing it "To Bob whom I love."

April 19. The S.s buy a new Buick, to be picked up June 16 in Flint, Michigan. At 11 P.M., we go to the Russian Easter service. An enormous crowd of "Displaced Persons": close-shaven bullet heads, Tolstoy noses, deep eyes, deep male voices. *"Khristos voskrese,"* the Bishop cries from the open door of the church, and the D.P.s respond with *"Voistinu,"* then march three times around the church behind the censer, crosses, banners, icons, lighted candles. Embracing and cheek-kissing follow. On the way home to eat paskha, I.S. says that the last Russian church he attended in Paris was located over a nightclub, which had to be bribed to keep quiet for a few minutes before midnight. Then when the band and the customers heard *"Khristos voskrese,"* the jazz would recommence with a vengeance.

April 27. New York. With I.S. to a theater on West 65th Street, to hear Alexei Haieff's Piano Concerto, played by Leo Smit, conducted by Stokowski. Party afterward at Sylvia Marlowe's with Berman, Eleanor Clark, Arthur Gold and Robert Fizdale. I.S. goes with Kallman and Protetch to *Four Saints in Three Acts,* in order not to hear it under more conspicuous circumstances in Paris next month.

April 28. Fly to Geneva via Gander and Paris. A clear, low-altitude view of Mont-St.-Michel. During the stopover in Paris, Nabokov comes with photographers and reporters. Discussion of programs, rehearsals, last-minute changes. I.S. drinks too much Scotch and eats too much *jambon cru.* Telegram from Cocteau: "I am busy working for you which is the reason I am not with you." At the Geneva airport, Theodore, Denise, and Kitty (celebrating her adoption by the Theodores), and A.M. Held, supervisor of stage spectacles for Switzerland. I.S. gives an interview in which he compares the red sunrise, from the plane, to the decors in the *Prince Igor* ballet. Taxi to the Hotel des Bergues. In the evening, without having had time to unpack, we attend a *Rake* rehearsal: the decors are by Theodore, and Samuel Baud-Bovy conducts. Hugues Cuénod's Sellem is the highlight of this very provincial, underprepared presentation, in which the main interest is in the comical sound of the French. Below my window, the honking of the swans in the cove by Rousseau Island keeps me awake.

May 2. After lunch with Cuénod, I join I.S. at 40 rue du Marche, where he is being filmed, then with V. to buy a Klee ink drawing ($350) in the Moos Gallery. At intermission in the *Rake* performance, a collection is taken up, like passing the plate in a church, to help pay the orchestra.

May 3. We leave the land of Protestant theology (Calvin, Zwingli) and child psychology (Rousseau, Pestalozzi, Piaget) and fly to Paris (Plaza-Athénée). Dinner with Nicolas and Patricia Nabokov in the Café Relais, then to the Vienna Opera's *Wozzeck* at the Théâtre des Champs-Elysées, in

1952 a loge with Albert Camus and Mme André Malraux. At intermission the S.s introduce me to Arthur Honegger, Auric, Roland-Manuel, and Helene Berg. Dinner afterward at the Relais with Camus and Josette Day, "Beauty" in Cocteau's *Beauty and the Beast*. Camus is unsociable-to-surly, at first, opening with the pronouncement: *"Pylon* is Faulkner's greatest work." He plans to devote an essay to Melville, he tells us, "the greatest American writer, an infinitely more important one than the pederast-voyeur Henry James."

When the talk switches to Büchner and Berg, it is apparent that the music made little impression on Camus—in comparison with the permanent dent in me—but he is attentive to whatever is said about the play. I.S. suggests that the only contemporary of Büchner's with whom he might be compared is Gogol. Büchner lacks Gogol's sense of humor, but Büchner's social vision was infinitely more radical (Gogol was a reactionary), and he threw off the social blinkers of his time with a greater power of poetry. Consider Wozzeck's: "People like us, if we ever did get into Heaven, they'd put us to work on the thunder." I.S. thinks that the last orchestral interlude is a mistake: "Until this point the artist stays behind his constructions, but here he comes up front to tell us exactly how he feels about it all and how we should feel." As if there had ever been any doubt about how anyone felt. Yet it is difficult to see how Berg could have avoided this apotheosis and ended with the Doktor's *"Jetzt ganz still"* or the Hauptmann's *"Kommen Sie schnell."*

Camus says that, like Caliban, Wozzeck sees and hears with an animal being, a radar that reaches into Nature itself. That he is under the spell of an enchanted nature is already established in the foraging scene, where he sees a strange fire while his companion sees only a man experiencing visions. And again in the scene with the Doctor, the Nature that Wozzeck seeks to understand is hardly ever absent. "If only one could read the lines and figures in the toadstools," he says—a reminder of De Quincey's "great alphabet of Nature"*—but the medical materialist kills the thought, telling Wozzeck that *his* Nature is the merest superstition. At times Wozzeck might be describing the effects of a hallucinatory drug: "The world gets dark, and you have to feel around with your hands and everything keeps slipping, like a spider's web." The Fool is also subject to visions, and though he is something of a stock character, his visions place him on the the same wavelength as Wozzeck.

At this point, I.S. says that the great feat of the Fool's scene is in the music: Berg really does succeed in creating the impression that the concertina, the band, the soldiers' chorus are being improvised then and there for a one and only performance. But this is also the greatest achievement of the opera as a whole: the audience's sense of a totally spontaneous cre-

---

* And today of Michel Foucault's "The madman sees nothing but resemblances everywhere; for him all signs resemble one another, and all resemblances have the value of signs."

ation from a score compounded of strict formal devices.

Camus says that Wozzeck's alienation is defined a minute after the curtain goes up, as he talks to the Captain and, without communicating, the Captain to him. In the next three scenes it is the same between Wozzeck and his comrade, Wozzeck and his wife, Wozzeck and the man of science, that proto-Nazi doctor who is the most prescient creation of all, though Büchner's doctor is less evil—he has to tell himself "not to let a mere man upset you"—than the Nazi scientists who treated people purely as laboratory specimens. The catechism in the doctor scene contains an amazing anticipation in the way Marie's name comes to Wozzeck's lips, and in the failure of the scientific-materialist doctor to perceive this "Freudian slip." The meaning of this scene, and of the opera, is that when the man of true human nature—"the dumb soul of humanity," as Rilke described Wozzeck—is delivered to his tormentor, the tormentor is destroyed, disintegrating as a human being as his indifference to suffering progresses. So, too, with the Captain at the end of the play, when he hears Wozzeck drowning and says, "Come away, it is not good to listen," a statement that stands as the antithesis to all those questions in which Wozzeck seeks the meaning of Nature.

May 4. Lunch at Arthur Sachs's rue de l'Université home, the one-time residence of Frederick the Great. High fence, paved court, porte cochère, six stables, and, on the dining room walls, Lorenzo Lotto, Boudin, Bonington, Manet, Goya, Vuillard, Monet. Sachs's car and chauffeur take me to Orly to meet my sister's flight from New York. Dinner at Marie Blanche de Polignac's with Poulenc and Sauguet.

May 5. In the Louvre for three hours with the S.s. while the contents of their room at the Plaza-Athénée are moved to apt. 740 on the 7th floor. Cocteau comes to fetch I.S. for dinner at Le Grand Véfour. He is very simple at first, then goes off like a Catherine's wheel. I eat with V. and my sister at La Coupole, then join I.S. and Cocteau, who draws his *Oedipus* set and costume designs for the edification and approval of I.S., who then passes them to me for safekeeping. Back to the hotel with Cocteau, in his car and with his chauffeur.

May 7. With I.S. to a 5 o'clock concert at the Comédie des Champs-Elysées to hear Boulez's *Structures*, which he plays with Messiaen on two pianos. When a young woman bursts into mock applause, a young man bounds across three vacant rows and resoundingly slaps her, whereupon the gendarme by the exit leads him away. All of this takes place without interrupting the performance.

May 8. With I.S. to Monteux's Boston Symphony *Sacre*, which ends with an ovation for I.S. His comments are becoming increasingly Parisian: "I remember Diaghilev saying: '*Monteux est un petit monsieur de l'orchestre qui fait l'amour probablement très bien parce que les dames l'aiment beaucoup. Mais comment avec ce ventre?*' " The greater part of the conversation of those with whom we dine at noon is malicious gossip about the people with whom we dine in the evening; and vice versa. As I.S. says: "People who talk this way *to* you obviously talk the same way *about* you. 'The Judgment of Paris' is not a pretty picture."

May 10. After a dinner in a bistro near the Invalides, we go with Balthus to the Deux Magots. Slim, pale, handsome, bittersweet, dandyish, he is femininely conscious of his clothes, which are evidently meant to identify him as a Hebridean laird, or, at any rate, to conceal that his work could have anything to do with paint. He will say nothing about art, except to vent scorn on "the latest daubs of Chagall," but to steer him away from music, Schubert's above all, is difficult. The conversation centers on the Reverend James McLane, pioneer Balthus collector but known to Balthus only as a friend of the S.s, and I.S. is soon performing missionary and ambassadorial roles for both artist and buyer, Balthus being as curious about his clergyman admirer as the reverse. But Balthus adroitly skirts the first question that is surely in his mind as well as in the Los Angeles Reverend's: the possibly inverted erotic inclinations of the other.

What about Balthus's portrait of Eros? Do his open-legged, mirror-fixated, pubescent girls represent joyful innocence, as Camus and Artaud have claimed? Or do they, as I think, project a lesbian fantasy, for it seems to me that the girl in *The Guitar Lesson* openly dreams of being fingered by an older woman. And all of Balthus's girls are either flushed with desire or pale with satisfaction (or is it the other way around?). They are definitely not little girls to gratify boys of any age, but then, those barely budding bosoms and itchily selfconscious pudenda, girl-bodies with acromegalic boys' heads, stubby legs, edematous calves, puppy-fat ankles, teeny feet are a long way from *my* vision of *volupté*.

I also fail to glean any insight from the man concerning the other oddities of his artistic *eidos*. Why, master of technique that he is, does he seem at times hardly to know how to draw? And why, apart from juvenile would-be-delinquents, is his work in no way concerned with the contemporary? A list of influences would read like a catalog of loans from the Louvre: Piero; Carpaccio; Caravaggio; Velázquez (the dwarfs, duennas, cats, mirrors, goldfish bowls); the French 17th century; Corot; Courbet; Ingres; Seurat; Cézanne. Whatever the answers, Balthus is peerless among living portraitists—his "Miró" and, above all (because more wicked), his "Derain"—and the same could be said, in their genre, of his landscapes, especially those with trees reminiscent of early Mondrian. He stands no less alone in another dimension, the representation of Evil. I am thinking of *La Chambre*, in which, surely, the sexually ambivalent Satanic dwarf cannot be ignored, the picture meaning far more than, as I.S. would have it, spatial architecture and chiaroscuro.

May 14. Leaving the rue Chambiges with my sister at sunrise, we luckily find a taxi to the Gare d'Austerlitz in time for the train to Souillac. In our compartment, the man opposite withdraws behind his newspaper as if he felt personally guilty for the "Go Home Americans" graffiti on almost every suburban wall. We enter the dining car at Chateauroux, and leave it, six courses and one bottle later, at Limoges.

At Souillac I hire a 1932 Studebaker, the only available car, and we go to wild, holy Rocamadour to ascend the famous 143 helical steps, grooved by the knees of expiators including those of Thomas-à-Becket's murderer, Henry II. The shrine of the Black Virgin, a worm-perforated doll with crown and streaming tulle, is venerated in a chapel clinging to the crag like a clematis. She is a hypnotizing totem, her eyes abjuring the world and fixing to a point beyond, her smile radiating a higher wisdom. Pilgrims prostrate themselves before it and piously tell their beads.

The precipice from here to the top is a Stations-of-the-Cross, with a stone bench at each Station, in which we discover wavy trilobite imprints, which leaves us wondering what the medieval masons supposed these fossil patterns to be—remembering that Xenophanes predicated his cyclical theory of geological history on the fossil imprints of fish in the marble quarries at Syracuse.

From the summit we walk back to Rocamadour village on an automobile road leading to the twelfth-century gate. Now, in late afternoon, some of the chimneys of the windowless, tomblike stone dwellings are emitting smoke, a macabre effect in the absence of other signs of life. The *Guide Bleu's* claim that these houses have never been restored is obviously true; what is more difficult to believe is that people still inhabit them.

The Notre Dame de Rocamadour hotel has not been disturbed by post-medieval developments in plumbing, but the restaurant is reasonably recent and is recommended for truffles. We dine on a terrace overlooking the Alzou River. Women are spreading laundry on its banks and long after dark the smack of wet clothes on stone flip-flaps through the valley.

May 15. Wholly or partly boarded-up cave entrances line the road during the 40-mile ride to Lascaux, and some of the names on the route signs, Les Eyzies, Les Combarelles, Font-de-Gaume, are renowned in archeology, the last of them for its wall paintings of mastodons. As if to compete in kind with these attractions of the region, the road plunges the 20-year-old Studebaker to its fenders in craters. The name Lascaux does not appear until Montignac-sur-Vézère, the town nearest that most celebrated of Magdalenian painted caves. A mile or so up a hill beyond Montignac, a footpath leads through pine woods to the cave entrance. There, posted to a tree, is a notice of visiting days and hours that leaves me wondering why this possibly ruinous information was not available in Paris, and marveling at my uncharacteristic luck in having coincided with one of the rare times of admission.

Our guide is one of the discoverers of the cave, one of the former schoolboys who stumbled on it 12 years ago while searching for a ball that

1952   had disappeared in a golf-sized hole. Probing with sticks, and eventually digging their way in, these youths were the first to behold the buried Sistine Chapel of Stone Age art. The actual entrance has never been found, probably having been closed by geological faulting, and the one we use, an airlock with double sets of iron doors, was only recently installed.

The ground just beyond as well as just before the door is flooded with seepage from overhead rocks. But, on choice, I prefer the clamminess and the thought of the creepy-crawlies to the twinges of claustrophobia and fear of entombment that afflict me when we pass from the airlock propylaea to the cave proper. These anxieties are dispelled as soon as our eyes are accustomed to the dim glow of a dozen feeble footlights, supplemented by the guide's electric torch, and begin to distinguish glistening black lines, and brilliant patches of red and yellow, on the walls and ceilings ahead and overhead; the footlights themselves are eery because they suggest the grease lamps, or resin torches, of the ancient troglodyte artists. When a system of these lines and colors forms a bull, we suspect an ocular trick, until the beauty and power of the animal, and the rhythm of it on the rough surface, inspire an awe such as I have never felt in any terranean temple, the stronger, no doubt, because Stone Age man, when I try to imagine him, provokes a vague loathing. But who could not be humbled before the spectacle of so much bursting life, after that instant of incredulity attributable to the incomprehensible gulf of 20,000 years?

The cave is toothlike, in that the two principal chambers branch from the main rotunda like dental roots, and because the right root contains a cavity that bores into the earthen gums to a depth of about eight feet. The unique representation of the human animal is found in this cavity, and the visit there is the turning point of the tour. Before seeing it, our experience is primarily aesthetic, and after it, largely concerned with meaning. The human figure is schematically scratched, a stick man with a bird head. Its other most conspicuous feature is its horim-extended, whether or not tumescent, sex. Whether the picture represents a shaman or a hunter, the contrast between its crudeness and the naturalistically perfect depictions of animals implies a complex mental relationship between human being and beast, which, in turn, involves a system of natural gods and divine attributes (zoomorphism), and a system of sympathetic magic: a matching bird-headed wand is etched near the birdman, along with a club and an arrow. In short, this stick-man confronts us with the symbol-making power, with evidence for the existence some two to three hundred centuries ago of a dualistic belief system.

Even so, this discovery of a metaphysical caveman is not more astonishing than the discovery of his refinement of artistic technique and delicacy of artistic feeling. After all, he must have lived very like the beasts he killed, yet his art, even by academic standards, is the least primitive imaginable. The purity of the artists' emotion—the animals are real and breathingly alive—is matched by a mastery of proportion, a power of line, an *1952* intelligence in abbreviation as canny as in the greatest pictorial creations of any historical period.

At the outset, to acquaint us with the profusion of the paintings, the guide plays his torch panoramically over all the decorated surfaces of the ovalshaped main room. At first, the superimposition of animal on animal by successive generations of artists is bewildering; yet the form of whichever individual outline the eye seeks to trace stands out clearly. This, I think—as if I could "think" anything about the state of consciousness of supposedly prelogical minds so many millennia ago—is because each artist must have had his own view of a painted area, and composed his own picture according to his own new and different scale. In every case the contours and surface qualities of the calcite walls are determining factors in the composition. The line of a vertebra will run congruently with a crack in the rock, an eyesocket prove to be a hole or indentation from which locus the entire animal has been designed. No animal is placed in a rectangular field, and none seems to have been composed to a sight-line or beholder's eye other than the artist's, which reminds us that in spite of all the framed squares of paint in rectangular rooms throughout the world, neither Nature nor the human eye is box-shaped.

By similar tokens, photographs and drawings are no preparation for the 3-D effects of the convexities and concavities of the surfaces, while all photographs mislead as to color and scale, the sizes of the animals being so various, the colors so vivid. We expected to see faint, partly flaked lines, scarcely visible in the dark, and forms as faded as Uccello's Noah frescoes, instead of reds, yellows, and blacks that glisten as if they had been newly varnished and not yet had time to dry: the *Last Supper* is in immeasurably worse condition. This extraordinary state of preservation, the reason for that initial moment of disbelief, is explained as good geological luck. The cave must have been sealed like a jar for thousands of years.

The right wall of the right root, from the main room to the crypt of the bird-headed man, is traced with engravings. Beyond that, the bulging and hollowing, and never artificially smoothed or flattened, surface is covered with horses and bison, deer and aurochs, until it coils navel-like into the earth. The left root is even more richly embellished, and it funnels away even more suddenly and deeply. Arrows are depicted in greater numbers here than anywhere else in the cave, implanted in their ungulate targets as well as on the ground.

Reminding us that visits to the cave are limited to one hour, owing to the small ration of air, and that a longer stay would corrupt the paintings, the guide terminates our tour. But a longer one would provoke visual indigestion—in me, at any rate, for I attribute my momentary feeling of suffocation and intoxication outside, in the morning sun, not so much to the cave's anemic air as to its teeming chthonian life. The silence of the cave

1952 continues to reverberate outside, where I suffer a kind of aerial, or rather, lacking a time decompressor or Wellsian time machine to throw me back into the present, temporal embolism. The cave is still and must always have been a sacred place, a great temple. Climbing the hill above it and emerging from the woods into a field of blue cornflowers and wild poppies, I feel haunted by the experience and know that in some degree I will be haunted by it all my life.

We are back in Paris in time for a late dinner in the Tremouille with Roland-Manuel and I.S., who gives me a book and a note from Nadia Boulanger: *"Je voulais offrir ce livre à Bob Craft. . . . Donc,* I will leave it with you this evening to give it to Bob for me."

May 16. Tea with Louis MacNiece in the Hotel des Deux Mondes, and a rehearsal of *Façade* with his wife, Hedli Anderson. In the evening, the S.s and I go to the Salle Gaveau for a session of the writers' jamboree on the subject "The Country as Good, the City as Evil," but only Stephen Spender sticks to it—on Baudelaire, Blake, Kafka, Lorca (New York). The rest is oratory from such culture hams as Salvador de Madariaga.

May 17. To the exhibition of Italian medieval art in the Petit Palais: Byzantine ivories, stone pieces from Ravenna, manuscripts, jeweled crosses. Then to a film documentary, narrated by Cocteau, of Carpaccio's *Mystery of St. Ursula.*

May 18. To Chartres in Arthur Sachs's car, and, back in Paris, with Nadia Boulanger, Rosbaud, Ansermet, Cocteau to I.S.'s evening rehearsal.

May 19. With I.S. to Rosbaud's *Erwartung* rehearsal. I.S. does not like the music. Lunch with Nabokov and Edgar Wind, then with Auden and Boris Kochno to the *Oedipus* rehearsal. At the evening performance, I.S. conducts erratically. Cocteau's *tableaux vivants* are not devoid of ideas—the parricide's mask at the end, eyes popped out like *truite au bleu*—but the presentation is campy, and when Cocteau announces that *"le tableau vivant représente le complex d'Œdipe"* the audience titters. A party at Hervé Dugardin's.

May 20. A letter for I.S. from a copyist, Gilbert Goeme, about the first performance of *Sacre.*

I.S. and Cocteau record the Narrator's speeches in *Oedipus* for the Columbia Records tape made in Cologne last year. Lunch with Cocteau at the Tremouille.

At the theater tonight, I.S. introduces me to Charles-Albert Cingria. After *Erwartung,* the younger audience retreats. During Cocteau's last *Oedipus* speech, the upper balcony explodes with boos, whistles, hissing, shouts of *"Assez avec Cocteau."* When the protest subsides, Cocteau shrewdly asks the public to show respect for *Stravinsky's* work, at which point I.S., in the seat next to me, heads for the hotel. The request provokes applause, followed by more boos and counter-applause, and the war between the claques resumes at the end of the performance.

May 21. With V. to her rue de l'Assomption apartment, and to several dealers in search of pictures by Nicolas de Stael. Go with I.S. to hear *1952* Milhaud conduct, and Suzanne Danco sing, *Socrate*. Michael Ayrton and Peter Watson afterward. Dinner in the Relais with Nadia B.

May 22. Lunch at Lucien's, *rive gauche*. At MacNeice's in the afternoon, with Auden. I.S.'s concert: the *Capriccio*, well-played by Monique Haas, and his 1940 and 1945 symphonies.

May 23. With I.S. to Fricsay's Berlin Philharmonic Bartok concert, Geza Anda soloist, a study in contrasts between German and French orchestras: the former are dead serious, the men—many pink, bald heads—sit stiffly and with shoulders back, and play loudly and with military precision; the latter slump in their seats, talk and smoke throughout rehearsals—which never begin on time—and in the concerts are bored, inattentive, slack. During intermission I chat with Herbert Read about Lascaux. To the Café Relais, where we meet Sir Charles Mendl and Yvonne, his new, very young wife.

May 24. I conduct *Façade* in the Comédie des Champs-Elysées. The S.s and Edith Sitwell are in the audience.

May 25. With the S.s to the exhibition of Mexican art at the Musée d'Art Moderne. The many photographs of the Dresden Codex show Mayan computations of time. Lunch at the Tremouille with Virgil Thomson and Nabokov, who says that Faulkner, drunk and grousing, is holing up in his room because the all-black cast of *Four Saints* is billeted in his hotel: "Why did you bring all those negroes here?" is the question of the man whom Malraux, Camus, and Sartre venerate to the extent that they will appear only if he does.

With I.S. and Nadia to a soirée of Musique Concrète from which we soon flee. Dinner in Nadia's apartment, which is like a funeral parlor—the organ, the creaky floors, the flowers, the photos of the dead (Paul Valéry).

May 26. Lunch with Auden. He tells us that Edith Sitwell broke wind while she was recording *Façade* and did not notice it during playbacks though everyone else heard it distinctly. In the afternoon, Sachs's car takes us to the Gare du Nord, where Cingria sees us off. In Brussels at 10:30, Paul Collaer meets our train and escorts us to the Palace Hotel.

May 27. Brussels. After lunch at Collaer's, the Musée Ancien (Brueghel's *Icarus* and Bosch's *Temptation of St. Anthony*) and the Museum of Modern Art (Ensor). Collaer promises to send I.S. his tapes of the Webern cantatas.

May 28. Lunch with Marguerite Long, whom I.S. last saw with Ravel, and Collaer, who describes Alban Berg in Brussels for a performance of his *Kammerkonzert*. To the Musée Cinquantenaire: beautiful twelfth-century Brabançon crosses.

May 29. Pierre Janlet, director of the Beaux Arts, shows us his collection of Klee, Picasso, Schwitters. Drink Schiedam with him. Lunch at Collaer's with Peter Pears. I.S.'s concert in the evening—how can he drink

1952 so much and still conduct?—begins with the national anthem, during which everyone stands and faces the Queen's loge. After the concert, we go with Artur Rubinstein to the Taverne Royale and drink Beychevelle.

May 30. I.S. goes to lunch with Queen Elisabeth and her daughter, Marie-José, the ex-Queen of Italy. V. declines the invitation, telling the equerry who calls that she wants to look at pictures in Malines and Antwerp (Memling's angels, Antonella's *Crucifixion*, the Rembrandts and the Van Eycks), thereby creating a minor scandal: *"On ne refuse pas à une Reine, Madame,"* Mme Collaer says indignantly. *"Je suis Américaine,"* V. answers, and I have never admired her more.

May 31. To Ghent, to see the Van Eycks in St. Bavon, also the Philippe de Champagne exhibition, which is very dull, despite I.S.'s defense, which seems to be based on the eminence of his sitters: Pascal, Richelieu, Colbert, Mazarin, Mansard. To Bruges for the Memlings, and to Vlissingen for the ferry. The Frisian Islands: windmills, dikes, new-mown hay, poppies and purple rhododendrons, tile roofs, dog carts, long, straight rows of trees, German concrete "pill boxes" and tank traps from 1944. Bergen-op-zoom, Breda, Dordrecht, Rotterdam. The Hotel des Indes in the Hague provides only one bathroom for the three of us.

June 2. To the Boymans Museum in Rotterdam. In Jeorg Ratgeb's *Last Supper*, the disciples, drunk, or asleep (heads on the table), are blowing their noses on the floor and pay not the slightest attention to the Lord. To Delft, to see the Prinsenhof Rembrandt etchings. Canals, tow-headed children, cows, cobbled streets, bicycles. The countrywomen wear *sabots* and huge white sailboat hats.

June 3. Rehearsal of *The Nightingale* and *Oedipus* in Amsterdam. In the former, the Debussyist-prelude is long enough to launch a four-hour opera, but nothing in the following 40 minutes relates to it. To the Frans Hals Museum at Haarlem; Utrecht, where, as we enter the Cathedral, the organist is playing Bach's St. Anne Fugue; and to Mies van der Rohe's Kröller-Müller Museum, to see Van Gogh's potato-diggers and the early Mondrians. Return via s'Hertogenbosch. Back in the Hague, I finish Francis Parkman's *The Conspiracy of Pontiac*.

June 4. A concert in the Ridderzaal in I.S.'s honor, opening the Holland Festival. Queen Juliana and her ministers, ambassadors, generals: I have never seen so much pomp and gold galloon, so many epaulettes, medals, and swords. I.S. and I are the only males not in uniform or white tie. Green plush chairs sustain the overfed, half-drunk, half-asleep audience. At intermission, following a drastically cut performance of Mozart's Serenade, K. 361, the Queen sends for I.S., bids him sit next to her, declares her admiration for his "works," and is not only taken aback but also struck dumb by his response: "And which of my works do you admire, Your Majesty?" The program ends with his String Concerto, in which nearly everything, including the tempo relationships in the first movement, is wrong. When the conductor, Van Otterloo, presented to I.S. afterward, asks how he liked the performance, I.S. snaps: "Do you want a conventional answer or the truth?" Van O. manfully opts for the latter, which is "Horrible!"

June 5. A drive across the Zuider Zee dike, which is guarded by soldiers and grazed by sheep. Red-roofed barns in the polders. After *The Nightingale* and *Oedipus* in the evening, a surprise 70th birthday party for I.S., at U.S. Ambassador Chapin's, 13 days too soon, as it happens, June 5 being the Old Style Russian date.

June 15. (Sunday). Detroit. A birthday article on I.S. in the *N.Y. Times* by Olin Downes contains a paragraph about me. To escape the heat wave we go to an airconditioned theater and a film, *Outcast of the Islands*. Taxi to Flint, the Durant Hotel.

June 18. Duluth. We attempt to celebrate I.S.'s birthday in a restaurant called The Flame, but the proper liquid ingredients are lacking, and the only available wine, a Beaujolais *rouge*, comes in an ice-filled bucket. Never having adjusted to the improbability of finding well-stocked wine cellars in hinterland America, I.S. is furious, and Alexei Haieff's giggling fit only partly defuses him. Reverting to his restaurant routine, I.S. blows his nose in the linen napkin; orders the waiter to remove the ice-water and bring an empty glass, which becomes an *étui* for his spectacles; tests the legs of the table for unevenness (discovering a wobble, he inserts wedges under all four legs); demands *"un couteau qui coupe,"* even before trying the one that he has; insists that empty dishes be cleared away immediately, and, when this does not happen, loads them on a vacant table himself.

V. drives in the afternoon, while I.S., next to her, gives unneeded directions from a road map spread on his knees. Not having been sufficiently slaked by the ice-cold Beaujolais, he uncorks a thermos, thereby flooding the car with a redolence of whiskey and a phosphorescence of discourse. Birch woods, lakes, the green of Spring. At night, in a motel in Bemidji, Minnesota, V. comes to tell Alexei that I.S. is offended because we neglected to include him in our backseat chat about Bach, which we had thought too trivial to interest him.

June 19. Grand Forks and Minot, North Dakota (Clarence Parker Hotel). Tall grain elevators, prairies, black birds with orange wing spots, ducks. Share a room with Alexei, a stentorian snorer.

June 20. In the Williston oil basin: trailers with Texas license plates. The Missouri River valley. Stop to watch a cattle auction in a corral. Horses in silhouette on a hilltop, deer in a game refuge, cows, Scotch thistles, gray sage, black-eyed Susans, stiles, fences, soft blue skies. Sleep in Havre (Havre Hotel).

June 21. The Hungry Horse Dam. Sleep in a log-cabin motel in Kalispell with bearskins on the walls.

June 22. The Going-to-the Sun Highway in Glacier National Park is a

1952 frighteningly narrow, steep, curving road, with no guide rails. From time to time, bears and deer appear at the side of the road. Mist. We cross the Continental Divide in a howling wind. Glaciers and flowers (bluebells), cascades, numerous tunnels. I.S. dislikes this Wagnerian scenery: "I despise mountains; they tell me nothing." Lunch in Babb, on a Blackfeet Indian Reservation. The roads on both sides of the Canadian border are unpaved and very rough. We spend the night in Calgary, in the old and comfortable Canadian Pacific Hotel Palliser.

June 23. Lake Louise. Very grumpy because alcohol is forbidden, I.S. insists that we continue to Radium Hot Springs, where people are bathing in a 115° pool.

July 2. Hollywood. I.S.'s gardeners, Varzhinsky and Dmitri Stepanitch, neither of whom speaks any English, carry a sofa, desk, and three chairs down the hill from the S. house at 1260 North Wetherly Drive to mine at 1218, behind the Baroness d'Erlanger's.

July 21. Violent shaking from an earthquake at 4:52 A.M. In I.S.'s studio, objects are hurled from shelves and glass frames are broken. "Ravel knocked down Debussy," he says. He completes the full score of Cantata.

July 24. Edward James for dinner. According to the Baroness, his mother was the daughter of Lady Forbes, Edward the VII's mistress. He brings expensive vanity press editions of his books and a repertory of amusing stories about assorted English and French eccentrics, and his appanage at West Dene. The mysterious B. Traven apparently lives on Edward's coffee finca near Tampico.

July 25. Dinner at the Huxleys' with the Edwin Hubbles and Mary Louise Kent, whose arm is as weighted with bracelets as an African king's, and who, in her 90s, smokes marijuana. Aldous remarks that the most popular words rhyming with his name are tremendous, stupendous, horrendous, and hazardous.

August 7. Huxleys in the evening. He says that breathing exercises heighten erotic sensibilities. Also talks about water shortage and irrigation in Southern California, 1800-1850.

August 12. With Aldous and the Baroness to I.S.'s concert in Hollywood Bowl, which, Aldous observes, looks like "a cross-section of the womb." Delectable performances by I.S. of the *Fingal's Cave* Overture and Tchaikovsky's Second Symphony, less good ones of his own Capriccio and *Firebird*.

August 17. With the S.s and James—he and his ex-wife Tilly (Ottilie) Losch, the Austrian ballet dancer, unexpectedly encounter and then ostentatiously avoid each other—to Gerald Heard's lecture in the Ivar Street Temple. It is a terrific show, beginning with an intense silence, an inspirational heavenward look, a grasping of the top of the pulpit by his long thin fingers—he doesn't "shoot" until we can see the whites of his knuckles—and, finally, the high, nasal voice. He does not glance at notes, never gropes for a word, forms perfect sentences, and manages to tie up even the most disparate digressions. Lunch with him and James at the Bel Air. Isherwood for dinner.

August 31. With Janet Gaynor and Adrian to Gerald's lecture, "Play," in the Ivar Street Temple. His vocabulary today— *anaphoric, ankylosis, dermopteral*—is as far-flung as his subjects are far-fetched: Thales of Miletus, the salt content in the hypothalamus, Fénelon as psychologist, Velikovsky, Rudolf Carnap. At lunch with him afterward, I scribble a squib under the table: "A marmoreal mask / His intellect deserves / To disguise the task / Of being Gerald Heard."

Groddeck (*The World of Man*) says that the German lullaby, *Eia Popeia, eia popei* (*Wozzeck*) is a Greek verse with the accents shifted, e.g., *eude my paidion eude mu pai* (sleep then my baby, sleep then my child).

September 13. Scorching desert wind. Two rehearsals. Dinner at Huxleys' with Robert Hutchins. Aldous's talk about sterpiculture is intended to titillate.

September 14. To Gerald's Vedanta Society lecture. Afterward, he and Aldous chat about molecular structure, the endocrine correlates of schizophrenia, and viscosity as a function of pressure.

September 29. Alma Mahler and Bruno Walter come to my rehearsal of *Petrushka* and Haydn's *La Reine* and Symphony No. 31 in John Burroughs High School.

September 30. V.'s name day. James gives her an Indian brooch: a maharajah and spouse formed of emeralds, rubies, diamonds.

October 9. Luigi Dallapiccola for lunch at the S.s'. He describes his wartime (1942) meeting with Webern in Vienna. His public (UCLA) lecture today is mistranslated for him, paragraph by paragraph.

October 18. Dinner at the Huxleys' with Gregor Piatigorsky, who is amusing about Sam Goldwyn. I remind him of a symposium at Tanglewood, in July 1946, in which he defended Heifetz for refusing to learn I.S.'s Violin Concerto because of the "unviolinistic" first chords, and of Harold Shapero's defense of the piece as perfectly playable. I drive him to his Bundy Avenue home later, and as we approach the porte cochère, the Piatigorsky-Rothschild private police follow us.

October 20. Birthday present from I.S.: a black cashmere sweater. V. goes to Dr. Mauer for X-rays of her thyroid. The esophagus is being pressed out of shape and an operation is necessary, the sooner the better, he says.

October 22. Wanda, the Baroness's new helper, is a very pretty French-Polish girl with a charming lisp and sultry manner. The Baroness herself has the soul of a panderer; the heart, too, and she is trying to deliver this attractive but married woman into my clutches.

October 31. Halloween. Fearful of curious neighborhood children, I.S. turns out all the lights and hides under his bed.

1952   November 10. Finish Focillon's *Life of Forms in Art*. I.S. is interviewed by a Miss Kennedy of *Time*. To Dr. Edel's office to see Howard Warshaw's new mural: a pitcher, a book, a candlestick (good title for John Van Druten) in black, white, and *merde*.

November 11. Royce Hall. I.S. conducts his Concertino and Cantata, after which we go to a reception at Conrad Lester's with Aldous and Piatigorsky.

November 13. I drive I.S. to the hospital at 9:30 in the morning, 14 miles of dense traffic. At 11:30 Mauer announces that the operation is a success. An hour later, V., ashen, eyes half-open and full of castor oil against the anesthetic, arms, neck, and hands with a rash as though from a vesicant, is wheeled down the hall on a gurney. We return to the hospital at 5, after which I rehearse the *Ode to Napoleon*.

December 17. Depart for New York on the *Chief*, which climbs slowly over the San Bernardino mountains to Barstow. The desert: Joshua trees, knurled and gnomic. At Needles we go out for a 10-minute walk in warm light rain.

December 18. Draft a poem as we cross Arizona and New Mexico:

In the Desert near Las Vegas

No green hope braves the brown eternity
And among the sun-worshippers no saint
(I think of the Thebaid in the fourth century)
Hears or heeds the body's deluxe complaint

   O where do lions go
   to have their thorns removed?

Receding seas ebbed this startled ground
Where Pleistocene shapes, still struggling as they drowned,
Pillory the eye on their weird halt
And impillar fleeing gamblers turned to salt.

   O where is the old man's cave
   The old man whom lions trust?

By noon snowflakes begin to fall on the tumbleweed and piñon, and I long to be outside with the cool sting in my face. At Lamy a youngish man wearing a Stetson, spiv suit, string tie, and brown suede shoes boards the train, proceeds to the bar, and leaves the change from $20 minus the price of a Scotch and soda. He responds to the first call for lunch. Following a little later, we find him seated at a separated corner table with a portable charcoal broiler on which he is broiling a steak. Smoke and commotion fill the dining car. A man entering from the other end, no doubt thinking the train ablaze, turns and flees. Four others, coming from the bar and showing effects thereof, stop and gawk, like the "Celebrated Persian Physicians Examining the Stools of King Darius" in Ensor's mock-Rembrandt drawing. Soon the audacious cook pokes a thermometer into the meat, appears satisfied with the result, extinguishes the flame, seasons and eats it. A waiter tells us that we have been in the presence of The World's Champion Steak Eater, a familiar figure on the train, and a popular one—the size of the perquisite in the bar. He keeps his own steaks aboard in a special refrigerator.

December 20. New York, the Gladstone Hotel. With Arthur Berger and Milton Babbitt to I.S.'s dress rehearsal at Town Hall. Auden and Kallman afterward.

December 21. Town Hall. The New Friends of Music concert, I.S. conducting the Cantata, Concertino, *Soldat*. Leonard Bernstein comes to the dressing room. Dinner at Maria's with Auden. To Balanchine's *Metamorphoses*, which makes Hindemith's music palatable and is memorable for the dancing, with attached wings, of three "angels." Auden claims that "if two rectangles can be described on a face with certain common points, the face is that of an angel."

December 22. I.S. records the Cantata, and I go with him afterward to the Met's *Don Giovanni*, intelligently conducted (Max Rudolf) and sung (Erich Kunz's Leporello). With I.S. and Vittorio Rieti to Toffenetti's restaurant.

December 23. Party for I.S. at Jennie Tourel's with Auden, Copland, Virgil Thomson, Kirstein. Auden, the worse for gin, is overheard by nearly everyone including the subject saying that "Virgil looks like Coleridge's death mask" and is "not top drawer."

December 26. Dinner at Auden's 23rd and Seventh Avenue walk-up. He kisses us as we enter, the prerogative being a sprig of mistletoe dangling over the barricade of book-filled crates by the door, which does not shut tightly enough to be locked and exposes the place to footpads. Shuffling about in *pantoufles* (bunion-accommodating babouches), he distributes fetchingly wrapped and ribboned Christmas presents: for me a copy of his new poem, "The Woods," his essay on Sidney Smith, and a volume of Paul Tillich's theology. He tells I.S. that the Cantata impressed him deeply and explains that " 'lyke-wake' means the watch kept at night over the corpse—lyke means lych which means corpse—and that the corpse is placed at the lych gate before burial. The 'whinny-muir' is the gorse moor on which souls are ceaselessly nettled, and the 'brig o'dred' is the narrow bridge to Purgatory from which wicked souls topple into Hell. The Baily, of course, is the Mayor," and 'Tomorrow Shall Be My Dancing Day,' is a popular "ballad carol."

The apartment is filled with stale, boozy air, and strewn with empty bot-

1952 tles, unwashed martini glasses, papers, books, phonograph records, assorted junk. We compete for the most recently occupied, and therefore most likely to be dusted, chairs, all of them looking as if they had been purchased with Green Stamps, then choose drinks, tipping out cigarette butts and ashes, dregs of earlier drinks and other detritus from the glasses in which the new concoctions are likely to be served.

Shortly before dinner, the fine line between decor and reality momentarily confuses V. Going to the lavatory and finding shaving utensils and other matter sloshing in the sink, a glass containing a set of Auden's "snappers" (store teeth), a mirror in which it would be impossible even to *recognize* oneself, a towel that would require the user to wash again, and on the floor a basin of dirty fluid, she unthinkingly empties the basin and fills it with fresh water. Not until dessert time do we discover, with mixed emotions, that she has flushed Chester's chocolate pudding down the drain.

At dinner, Wystan diverts us with stories about the "miching mouse" (Herrick) that shares the apartment with him, apparently born and brewed there. "I leave scraps enough lying about for the poor dear to eat," he says (and we fully believe, silently speculating about other livestock boarding there). And not just "lying about," either: the plates and silverware are greasy, and, such is the dishwasher's myopia, by no means free of hardened remnants of previous meals. The dinner—smoked clams, steak, potatoes with dill—is edible, nevertheless, and Wystan tucks in like Oliver Twist, which helps to account for his new, marsupial-sized paunch: his plate soon looks as if it had been attacked by locusts. Five bottles of Pommard, from a case deposited on the floor at the end of the table, are emptied as well; but whereas I am heavylidded in consequence, Wystan remains a beacon of intelligence. Moreover, he does not wear his mortarboard tonight. Christmas merriment is intruded upon only once, by a telephone call from his female admirer, the same who followed him to Venice for the *Rake*, and from whom, like Casanova but for a very different reason, he was forever escaping, once jumping into a passing gondola and almost taking a header into a canal.

After dinner he plays bits of *Dido*, *Nabucco*, and *Die Walküre*. Though well aware of being courted with the Wagner, I.S. is not in a compliant mood, and after 20 restless minutes he puts it down as "improvisation." Which visibly disappoints Wystan.

December 27. At 5, Edith and Osbert Sitwell come for cocktails, in the S.s' Gladstone Hotel suite, escorted by Auden. "Now remember," he had said, briefing us on the telephone, "Edith drinks like a fish." Acting on this tip, V. places standing orders for double martinis and double scotches to be sent up at regular intervals. But the poetess merely sips from her glass, and her brother, shaking from Parkinson's Disease and unable to hold his, sits on his hands during the entire meeting. The toping is carried out entirely by Wystan himself and by I.S., who, between them, siphon off the contents of a full tray.

Dr. Edith's accoutrements include the famous gold Urim and Thummim, tubular gold bracelets, huge rings, a rosewood walking stick, a strong dose of scent. She does not actually wear a coign, but a flat something of the sort swathed in black silk, thereby denying verification of Wystan's assurance that she is "as bald as a coot," which, in conjunction with her most estimable Roman nose, evokes a likeness, in profile, to a pileated woodpecker. The triangular, spectral blanc-de-chine face might have come from a tapestry, or beneath the swirling *lettrine* of an illuminated manuscript. But her eyes are more remarkable still. Heavily underpenciled with blue, like the woad dye of an early Briton warrior, they squint as narrowly as the slits in a medieval helmet.

Dr. Edith enters the room peeling long black gloves and claiming that a gorilla in the Ringling Brothers Circus at Sarasota, watching her do this, tried to do the same with his hands. Failing, he reached from his cage and kissed hers, a homage that appears neither to have surprised nor to have frightened her, whereas the animal's trainer, she reports, is still in hospital recuperating from the shock. And who, having met this Eleanor of Aquitaine, would presume to doubt the story?

Directing the talk to Hollywood and her forthcoming visit there, she asks I.S. about "the extent to which Aldous *really* believes in Tantra." Whatever he thinks of Aldous's beliefs, I.S.'s mind turns like a compass needle to the center of his own: "Sacrifice is the basis of religion," he says, "and sleeping on beds of nails and living on diets of grass are not sacrifices but experiments." Notwithstanding, he resolves, later in the evening, to bone up on the Upanishads.

Shortly after the departure of the Plantagenets, Sonia Orwell, our upstairs neighbor, tells us that she had been giving a party in her rooms at the same time as ours, and that the bar service was very slow: "When I complained to the waiter, he advised me to 'Do like those Russians on the seventh floor, lady, order doubles.'"

December 28. To the ISCM Webern concert at the 92nd Street "Y": the string-quartet pieces, the Canons, and the Trakl songs. The abolition of harmony and of the consonance-dissonance relationship strikes me tonight as too great a loss. And why was Webern so obsessed with limitations? In the Quartet, Opus 28, the series is identical in its retrograde and inverted forms, meaning that only three intervals are possible, minor seconds and major and minor thirds. This is architecture with no furniture.

December 31. Dinner at Lucia Davidova's. At 11:30 Lincoln Kirstein escorts us to Balanchine's New Year's party, a subdued celebration of his marriage today to Tanaquil LeClerq. Even Karinska and Kopeikin are quiet. Lincoln drives us to the Gladstone at 1 A.M.

&❧ **Postscript 1994.** The 1952 chronicle touches on all of the main events

1952 of the year. But if Stravinsky's return to Paris after 13 years and a world war had any profound emotional effect on him, it was never evident. He did not visit the sites of his former homes and did not seek out old friends.

From our first evening in Paris, I found the French Stravinsky as different from the Italian and German versions of the year before as *they* had been from the American. Suffice to say that he dominated every gathering, and that I had no trouble imagining him doing the same during the *entre deux guerres*. For myself, I felt less awkward sitting in silence at a dinner table with Jean Cocteau, or Albert Camus, than I did in the company of the rich and titled who, unlike the writers, expected their guests, or fellow guests, to participate in conversations and to possess at least a modicum of drawing-room punctillio. By this time Stravinsky was speaking French with me more frequently than English.

The Paris festival, underwritten, as we subsequently learned, by the CIA and Julius Fleischmann, favored products made in the U.S.A. Stravinsky himself was presented as an American, partly by having some of his music introduced by the New York City Ballet and by having *The Rite of Spring* played by the Boston Symphony. He had scarcely been aware of the assault on his American-period music in Paris at the end of the war, nor did he suspect that the hisses and boos that greeted Cocteau and his staging of *Oedipus Rex* animadverted on the music as well. *The Cage* was the one American period opus that interested the Parisian audience, but this was entirely owing to Jerome Robbins's choreography, in which the females, with their simulated orgasms (bee-stings), win the battle of the sexes.

Vera Stravinsky, who had lived in Paris during the first four months of the *drole de guerre*, would have been happy to have stayed there and never return to Los Angeles, unlike her husband, who defended his adopted country at every opportunity. Unlike the year before, he did not respond to any new music in Paris, but, then, he attended only one avant-garde concert and only a few minutes of a demonstration of *"Musique Concrète."*

1952 was a watershed year for me, partly because I conducted in Europe for the first time, but mainly because I began to conduct regularly for the Evenings on the Roof, later the Monday Evening Concerts, in Los Angeles. Some of the music performed in our Schoenberg memorial series in the autumn had not been heard before in the United States, and though its effect on the status quo was insignificant, the effects on Stravinsky were powerful and permanent. He had completed his Cantata in July and the first two movements of his Septet by November 6 (the third in January 1953), which is to say that this first late-period venture into atonality began during, and to some extent as a result of, those four Schoenberg concerts in our homely little West Hollywood Auditorium.

❧ *1953*

January 1. A marvelous New Year's present from I.S., the manuscript score of the second movement of the Symphony in C, which Hindemith has just returned to him, having been entrusted with it by Willy Strecker in 1939. To the ballet: *Metamorphoses* and *Scotch* Symphony. I.S. likes the Mendelssohn "except for the Protestant ending."

January 7. Auden comes to the hotel to celebrate V.'s and Kallman's birthdays. He complains about a difficult morning with "My mad woman," the same who followed him to Venice a year and a half ago. We go to *Bohème* at the Met, to hear the tenor who will sing Tom Rakewell next month. I.S., hardly remembering the opera, is struck by "the perfect lengths of the scenes and acts and the finesse of the orchestration."

January 9. A piano rehearsal of the *Rake* conducted by a truculent, dictatorial Fritz Reiner, who insults all of us and practically tells I.S. to shut up. Auden stays but I leave before the end.

January 10. Meet Adolph Gottlieb and Archibald MacLeish at the exhibition of the former, then go to the Stamos show. With his handlebar mustaches and black eyes, Stamos himself is more memorable than his pictures.

January 13. David Protech takes us to a concert performance of *Euryanthe* in Carnegie Hall. I.S., making a case for Weber, will not admit the pervading dullness of the opera, the heavy Liederkranz-style choruses and protracted *Tannhäuser*-like, off-stage horn music.

January 19. To the revival of Lillian Hellman's *Children's Hour*, which the S.s hate, and in truth the real plot is delayed too long and the last scene is unnecessary and unmercifully protracted. But I.S.'s dislike is rooted in his disagreement with the author at the time of her film *North Star*, for which he composed the never-used *Scherzo à la russe*.

January 20. With the S.s to an exhibition of Spanish painting that includes attractive drawings and watercolors by García Lorca. Dushkin, for lunch, says that I.S. was stopped at Immigration in 1939 and asked if he wanted to change his name. When Dushkin proposed a second U.S. tour

1953 with I.S. to the concert manager Marks Levine, the answer was "Stravinsky again? He's been here."

January 21. Dinner at Maria's with Auden, his friend Wayne, Kallman, and Protetch. W.H.A. is whey-faced, shaken by the latest trials with his female admirer, who finally "had to be taken to the coop. She was ringing up every few minutes, hammering at the door in the middle of the night, even bribing the manager of the building to let her into my apartment, where she took measurements of my old suit in order to buy me a new one. She had begun to shout in public that we had had intercourse together, though both God and she know that I met her only once, at the request of her psychiatrist. Still, it is unpleasant to commit someone: the ambulance, the white coats, the straitjacket, that sort of thing."

He talks about the Yale Younger Poets series, and his job of introducing a sheaf of poems by the winnowed finalist: "Everyone is writing fragments now, but I continue to look for good whole lines. . . . 'Originality' and 'striking images' are the very last qualities I care about." He discourses on whiskey cultures versus wine cultures, dividing Europe by this measure, as Feuerbach divided it into bean and potato cultures. After dinner, we pile into a taxi to go to *Pal Joey*, but, with not enough room for all, Wystan elects to take the subway. He is shocked by the bawdiness of the musical, and when the chorus girls bump their "bare" bottoms audiencewards, revealing bouquets of violets fixed like tail feathers in the clefts, he dashes from the theater and does not reappear.

January 25. I.S. is in bed with 'flu. I go to Jennie Tourel's Town Hall concert: two dull Scarlatti arias; two Mozart lieder; Monteverdi's *Lamento*, for which her voice is too dry; Purcell's Mad Bess; and Hindemith's *Die junge Magd*, conducted by the composer, whose hands are oddly small, extending from such a stocky, no-neck body. His cues are as business-like as his dark blue suit, but the music is charmless and the slow tempo, repetition, lack of variety are soporifics. Afterward the Hindemiths pay a "short visit" to I.S. at the hotel, but stay more than an hour, which must arouse a suspicion that his illness is not unrelated to the concert.

January 26. To Thomas Scherman's concert: Isaac Stern in Prokofiev's First Concerto, Hindemith's lumpy Horn Concerto, Purcell's Fantasy on One Note (*over* one note).

January 27. To a cocktail party at Auden's and a bad play set in Venice, *Time of the Cuckoo*.

January 28. After their lecture at the Met Opera, Auden and Kallman come to the hotel for two hours of steep drinking. When Kallman remarks that a certain woman has a complexion like a peach, Auden says, "Yes, yellow and hairy," and he goes on about pubic wigs (merkins), the pubic symphysis, the oriental practice of "depilating the female copse."

Dinner at Lucia Davidova's, then to Town Hall to hear Ralph Kirkpatrick play Rameau, a group of Scarlatti sonatas in manic-depressive sequence, and, on a reconstructed 18th-century Challis piano, Haydn's Forty-Sixth Sonata.

January 30. With David Protetch at midnight to P.J. Clarke's Third Avenue sawdust bar, a crowded version of the Black Hole of Calcutta. After elbowing our way to the bar rail, we remain pinioned there, while the girl next to me picks lint from my coat—not a fixation but an expedient: she does not have room at her sides to lower her arms. Crew-cuts bristle everywhere, even under bowlers, tipped back to expose them. Bright green, red, and orange vests are also in fashion, and "boiled" collars, pin-striped shirts, and gray topcoats with black felt lapels. The queasy expression of a man propped up half by the bar and half by me is worrying in that if he becomes sick, we are too tightly trussed together to move. A voice somewhere behind: "Eddy got a phone call from a ladypsychiatrist who said she had a female patient suffering from a case on him, and would he mind having an affair with the patient."

January 31. Finish *The Year With Mother* and *In My Solitary Life*, the abridgement of Augustus Hare's Victorian autobiography. Augustus was brought up in Hurstmonceaux, the ancestral castle in Sussex, where the language at family repasts was Greek—if brought-up is the term for being obliged to sleep with only one blanket in mid-winter, for being forbidden to speak or to make any kind of noise, and for being locked up on Sundays in a burial vault for enforced meditation. On Sundays, his grandmother was accompanied to church by a beautiful white doe that stood at her pew door during the service. When Augustus's Aunt Esther saw how Augustus loved his cat Selma, she demanded that he give the cat to her. "Soon there came a day when Selma was missing: Aunt Esther had ordered her to be hanged." In one of his examinations at Southgate School, Augustus was required to "give the size, population, and government of Nineveh; the route of Jonah to Nineveh from Joppa; where you suppose Tarshish to be, and the reason for your supposition." At Oxford, he was required to name "all the prophecies in the Old Testament in their order relating to the coming of Christ; and all the relationships of Abraham and all the places he lived in." Somehow Augustus's story-telling gift survived this brutal and useless education: "Just as [Cardinal] Newman was coming forward within the altar-rail, and was in the act of reading the Communion Service, a black cat sprang from one of the rafters of the roof and came crashing down upon him, falling upon the hem of his surplice. Newman's face never changed a muscle, and quietly, reverently, and slowly, he went on reading the service without moving: but it must have seemed like a demon."

February 9. To Peter Bartok's and then to the Periscope Bookshop, where Edmund Wilson walks in and asks for "anything by Denton Welch. My wife likes him very much; I don't like him at all." Roaming about, he mislays a bundle of papers, which I find and restore to him, noticing a Russian newspaper among them: "Thank you, thank you very much."

1953 Brayton Lewis: "There are some good new English novels." E.W.: "I have given up reading English novels." B.L.: "Are American novels much better?" E.W.: "No, it is because there are so many good English novels. Evelyn Waugh's last one was good. He's off to a fine start on this trilogy. An excellent novel, really. Have you got Cyril Connolly's little book about the disappearing diplomats? He promised but has forgotten to send it." B.L.: "Have you read Augustus Hare?" E.W.: "No, I suppose I should read it. I have so much systematic reading to do, you know. I'm at Princeton now." Short, stocky, pot-bellied, slightly shabby, he belongs to the upstate cracker-barrel American tradition.

February 12. Dress rehearsal of the *Rake*. I.S. conducts along with Reiner, which is embarrassing because the balconies are full and every eye in them is trained on I.S. Auden complains about the Americanized diction. "The 'don' in *Adonis* should be pronounced like the 'don' in *don't*." We go with Balanchine afterward to Radio City Music Hall to scoff at a movie about Hurok, *Tonight We Sing*, in which Ezio Pinza is Chaliapin, Toumanova is Pavlova, and Stern is Ysaÿe.

February 14. Premiere of the *Rake* at 2 P.M., the S.s in Rudolph Bing's box, myself between Alma Mahler-Werfel and Paco Lagerstrom, close to the orchestra pit. An hour and a half before curtain time Edward James arrives, preceded by numerous telegrams from several addresses in Mexico, and telephone calls from towns on the U.S. side of the Rio Grande. It seems that Plutarco, Edward's major domo, was to have delivered Edward's clothes, toiletries, and one of his cars to him at Juarez but misunderstood his instructions; or, more likely, Edward had forgotten or misunderstood them himself. In the event, Edward hired a taxi to drive him along the U.S. side of the river while Plutarco was driving in the opposite direction on the Mexican side. Edward then flew from El Paso to New York clad only in gray silk trousers, a silk shirt and shoes—without socks, tie, jacket, overcoat—and this on the coldest day of the New York winter. Turning up at the Gladstone as the S.s are preparing to leave, he does not try to stop V. from rushing to Saks to buy hosiery for him or stop I.S. from lending him an ill-fitting jacket, Edward being nearer I.S.'s size than mine. Naturally Edward has no ticket, and this too is left to the opera's composer to provide.

Party afterward at Lucia's with Auden, Kallman, Balanchine, Kirstein, James. Kallman, revolted by Blanche Thebom's voluptuously female performance, says that "Baba is, and must be played by, a dyke."

February 19. To the second performance of the *Rake* with I.S., back with James from the Baltimore concert. The libretto now strikes me as overendowed with conceits and too pedagogic; Auden is forever telling the audience: "Well, you can see that we know about the 18th century." And too literary, though he is proud of his learned derivations: "Restore [the] age of gold," from Dryden's version of the *Aeneid*, Book VI, and "I am exceeding weary" from *Henry IV Part 2*. It is nonsense to pretend, as Virgil Thomson does, that there is method in I.S.'s stresses on prepositions and conjunctions, the truth being that his settings of them are hit and miss.

February 21. To Shaw's *Misalliance* at City Center, a poorly organized play, bellowingly underlined by the actors. Afterward James invites us to the 21 Club.

February 25. Afternoon visit from Nicolas de Stael—tall, good looking, likable—who speaks Russian with the S.s. Afterward to Inge's *Picnic*: "Mother, what can we do with the love we have?" Then to the Barbery Room where we meet Copland, Bernstein, Blitzstein.

February 26. At I.S.'s Philharmonic concert, I stay backstage chatting with Dmitri Mitropoulos about Schoenberg.

February 28. With Louis MacNeice and Ruthven Todd at Tim's Bar on Third Avenue. Todd is unkempt, tight, and repetitious. MacNeice says he can't understand what Americans see in Wallace Stevens.

March 1. Between 6:30 and midnight, I.S. records one hour of the *Rake* at Columbia's East 30th Street studio. I stay in the control room. Bernstein and Oscar Levant come for part of the session.

March 4. To *The Merchant of Venice*, then the Oak Room. William Faulkner, Ruth Ford, and Bill Inge are at the next table.

March 5. With the S.s and Edward James to the Baroque Room in the St. Regis Hotel for lunch with Salvador and Gala Dali. Her eyes are small, close together, and furtive, and she does not bother to hide her irritation with us. She is the male, and seeing them together makes one believe that his soft watches symbolize impotence. The effort not to stare at his waxed mustache is a constant preoccupation, but his stiff shirt and collar and conspicuous tie-pin are also hard to ignore. He is shrewd, heartless, intolerably narcissistic, but also lively and amusing. He says that he could not resist telling Philip Johnson that "in my view the houses of the future will be soft and hairy." "Freud's brain was like an *escargot de Bourgogne*," he remarks, but when did he see it? Conversation is in French, but at one point he turns to me saying: "I speak English very well for profound things, have big vocabulary, but very badly for other things." He has short-fingered, pudgy, feminine hands. When the "*addition*" arrives, he peeks at it, then quickly passes it to James. Avida dollars, indeed.

March 6. To Bernstein's brassy musical *Wonderful Town* (Winter Garden), performed in a don't-give-it-a-chance-to-fall-apart manner. At least one laugh: Soda jerk: "Do you want to eat indoors or outdoors?" Tough guy: "Which is this?"

March 8. The news of Prokofiev's death seems to have had no effect on I.S., but V. is very upset. The second recording session of *Rake*, 11:30–6:00.

March 9. With I.S. to Arthur Berger's for a private concert by the New Music Quartet: Haydn, Opus 74, No. 3, Webern's *Bagatelles* and Opus 28 Quartet, I.S.'s Three Pieces and Concertino. I.S. finds numerous faults with the performances of his own pieces and spends an hour coaching the players. James comes with Templeton Strong, whom I.S. knew in Geneva in 1915, and who copied the parts and score of the Three Pieces at that time.

March 18. Hollywood. To the Schoenbergs' to help Gertrud S. serve her Viennese-style *Kaffee* and *Küchen*. She gives me the facsimile score of *Das goldene Kalb*, and takes me through Schoenberg's rooms, in which some 40 of his paintings are on the wall or lying about. Some of them are on cardboard, some are on canvas, and some of the canvases are painted on both sides, Schoenberg having been too poor to afford separate ones. The self-portrait from the back, walking in a street, is the most astonishing picture, together with the all-eyes *Vision of Christ*, but the portraits of critics are nightmares. The middle pane of yellow glass in one of the front windows is eerie, and one wonders how Schoenberg could have liked it, if he did. The cluttered library contains Christian prayer books and is said to contain a score of *Histoire du Soldat* critically annotated by Schoenberg.

March 23. Reading Winthrop Sargent's article on him in the latest issue of *Life*, I.S. wastes a quarter hour underscoring the errors. Next to the sentence, "Stravinsky loves to read theologians like St. Thomas Aquinas and Kierkegaard and is fairly regular in his attendance at the Russian Orthodox Church," he red-pencils the phrase about his church attendance, and writes in the margin: "Sorry, it is not true." In another margin, following the statement, "In his relations with people, Stravinsky can be warm or frosty, depending on his mood," he writes: "No, depending on the people I meet."

April 1. Augustus Hare: "A peasant would not take off his hat before a new wooden cross because he knew it when it was a pear tree."

April 4. At the Russian Church, 11:30 P.M., a large crowd of poor refugees indoors and out, broad faces, big-boned types with large, believing eyes, the men wearing ill-fitting suits, the women black shawls. At midnight the archimandrite—crown, red and gold robe, metal-rimmed spectacles—emerges from the church, proclaims *"Khristos voskrese,"* hears the response of the congregation, begins a mournful, or at any rate far from jubilant, chant and circles the church three times, followed by clerics bearing a sentimental Christ icon, a banner of a saint, and a Greek cross: the Trinity is less solidly hypostatic in Russia than in the West. Easter well-wishers exchange kisses, candles droop and drip, and colored eggs are sold in the street.

April 5. Kulich and paskha for breakfast. Lunch with the Milhauds at Florence Heifetz's (ex-Mrs. Jascha and, after him, Mrs. King Vidor). Eggs *à la Turque*. Darius's face, without frown or wrinkle, is like a mask. Though hobbled by arthritis, he does not complain. "Come to my concert," he says, "I'm playing a lovely thing by Rameau" (not "I'm playing *my*. . ."). He describes Leon Kirchner's music as "convulsive."

April 12. Mrs. Schoenberg and Nuria come at 6:45. "This should have happened 20 years ago," she says to V., adding: "The fault was not Schoenberg's and not Stravinsky's, but that of intermediaries." Both women are nervous, but caviar and vodka help. Nuria is tanned, quiet, beautiful. Her mother asks to see I.S.'s workroom, and V. obliges. Dinner at the Knickerbocker Hotel, where James joins us. Mrs. Schoenberg says she "admired the man Alban Berg" and "disliked the school teacher Webern, who tried to surpass Schoenberg in small ways." Afterward to Hancock Auditorium for a concert by the New Music Quartet, but the performances of Berg's Quartet, Schoenberg's Trio, and Webern's Opus 28 are ragged, an off-night.

April 13. To the Huxleys'. Aldous describes his visit to the new steel mill at Fontana, in such a way that he seems to be testing his memory in order to be certain that he had understood everything.

April 18. With V. to Royce Hall for the *Symphony of Psalms* and *Survivor From Warsaw*, then to the Schoenbergs'. At night, the house has a Charles Addams feeling not dispelled by champagne and Viennese *Küchen*. The Leonard Steins are there, Dick Hoffmann, Sharpless Hickman, Nuria and her escort. Mrs. Schoenberg plays a recording of Schoenberg lecturing on his Orchestra Variations in Frankfurt in 1930. A warm, soft Viennese voice: *"Das ist meine Situation.* A Lindberg flies the Atlantic and everyone hails the new achievement. But a new achievement in the arts is reviled." The Frankfurt Radio Orchestra plays the theme of the Variations as written, then in Schoenberg's curious tonal harmonization.

April 20. Fetch Aldous before my concert. He is in an exalted mood, chuckling over a book by an 18th-century art critic who gave grades in composition, color, and line: "Giovanni Bellini received a zero in expression." We arrive in time to hear the witless last movement of Roy Harris's piece for 18 horns. I conduct Bach's cantatas 60 and 187, then go with Aldous to eat a banana split.

April 28. New York. I.S. tells us about his Venezuelan concerts, about seeing an ape (pronounced "ap") in the jungle outside Caracas and a wildcat crossing the road in front of his car. He says that the nighttime noise of the jungle focuses around F sharp. I drive to Boston (the Sheraton Hotel) to begin *Rake* rehearsals.

May 10. Boston. A scandal at today's rehearsal: I.S. screams at Ralph Kirkpatrick and orders him to leave. R.K. tells me his eyes are bad and he could not see I.S.'s beat.

May 21. From *Conversations with Kafka* by Gustav Janouch, for my commonplace book:

> I lent Kafka a German translation of the *Bhaghavad Gita*. Kafka said . . . "All the yogis and sorcerers rule over the life of nature not because of their burning love of freedom but because of a concealed and icy hatred of life. The source of Indian religious devo-

tions is bottomless pessimism."

The path from the head to the pen is much longer and harder than from the head to the tongue. Much is lost on the way.

Alfred Doblin makes on me the impression that he looks on the external world as something quite incomplete, to which he must give the final creative touches by his writing.

May 22. Dylan Thomas comes at 11 A.M., red- and pimple-faced, bulbous-nosed, glazed-over eyes. He is in a bad way and nervous, to boot, about meeting I.S. In bed himself, I.S. cannot relieve Thomas's tension by drinking with him, although the whiskey he pours for the tubby poet calms *him* so effectively that an attack of the D.T.s seems slightly less imminent.

Propping himself up, I.S. explains what he requires in an opera libretto. Thomas says he has a science-fiction idea, "at least to be going on with. It is about the rediscovery of the planet after an atomic misadventure; and about the re-creation of language: a person, an object, a word." He worries aloud about his wife, who "is losing her mind," but seeing that this isn't sufficient explanation for his chain-smoking and trembling hands, adds that the gout is torturing him. "Still, the cure is worse. They shove bayonets into you." Talking about the *Rake*, which he heard "on the wireless from Venice," he says, making sure that we understand, "Auden is the most skillful of us all, but I am not like him in any way, you know." Then switching to Yeats, "the greatest lyric poet since Shakespeare," he declaims "daybreak and a candle's end."

June 5. Los Angeles. Postcard from the Huxleys in Jackson Hole, Wyoming: "We think you should start a restaurant. Vera will paint, Igor will play the piano, Maria will cook (God help the customers), and I will write the advertisements. Love, Aldous. And will Bob entertain the Signore?? Love Maria."

June 19. To the Schoenbergs' after lunch. The interiors have been painted white and, in other regards as well, the house is less gloomy. All three children are there, and Mrs. Schoenberg shows me the manuscripts of *Moses und Aron*; of Webern's *opera* 1,6,9,10,11; of the *Kammersymphonie* interlude in *Wozzeck*—which Berg sent to Schoenberg; the *tutti* orchestra is in red ink, the *Kammersymphonie* in black—and of the *Lulu* Prologue, which Berg copied out in score and sent with a letter saying he could not afford any other birthday present (for September 13, 1935). Of all of these, the *Moses* score is the most beautifully written. Mrs. Schoenberg says that "Mr. Schoenberg"—she never refers to him any other way—started work on *Lulu*, but when he discovered that the marginal performance direction "to be sung in the manner of a Polish Jew" was not in Wedekind's original text, gave it up. She rants about the anti-Semitism of the Weberns. And she says that Schoenberg had applied to the Guggenheim family for financial help as long ago as 1931, when he lived in Barcelona, but was refused on grounds that he was an "established artist." "All the more reason to help me," he answered, with perfect logic, adding, "My students can receive money but not I."

June 25. The Huxleys for dinner and to the film *A Queen Is Crowned*. Aldous is no monarchist: "The Duke of Edinburgh might have stepped from an Arrow Collar ad," he says, and "The Dean of Westminster—we were in school together at St. Christopher's—is the stupidest person I've ever known." He comes away remarking on how "the coronation is an affair of the Church, which otherwise has no power at all."

June 28. Lunch with the Huxleys and Gerald at the Beverly Wilshire, after Gerald's sermon in the Ivar Street Temple, an hour of eloquence and élan marred only by a reference, quite regular when I.S. is in the congregation, to "atonal music," which Gerald seems to think is something I.S. invented. At table, Gerald, still high, displays what Maugham claimed for him, that "affluence of conversation which Dr. Johnson loved in Burke." He goes on and on, fascinatingly, about the engram complex, the Adamites and chiliasm, and hyperthyroids through the ages: "Ambrose of Milan, Teresa of Avila, Joseph of Copertino—all had pop-eyes, gaping mouths and swollen throats." As we leave, I.S. mentions the necessity of disposing of his favorite canary because "it is old and Yvgenia Petrovna devotes too much time to it." Aldous says, "But old canaries can be taught new tunes; surely you remember the serinette, the organ, mentioned by Diderot, used for teaching it."

In the afternoon, I.S. plays his Septet with me, four hands. At night, anxious about his forthcoming prostatectomy and unable to sleep, he asks me to fetch Aldous, who massages and then hypnotizes him.

June 29. Tea at Gerald's. "I doubt," he says as we stroll in his garden, "that Bernard Shaw ever had an aesthetic experience. When I used to go through the National Gallery with him, he managed to find something clever to say about every picture, but that was as far as it went." Gerald describes the endemic diseases of the over-forties as "senile optimism" and "the triumph of hope over experience." When he refers to his ancestors he does not mean grandpa and grandma but the creatures who lived in the treetops.

To the Huxleys' in the evening. Aldous talks about the Mormons baptizing their ancestors: "Since no one before Joseph Smith could go to Heaven, everyone with an earlier birth date had to be provided with a genealogy going back to Abraham." Aldous is excited by his latest experiences with mescalin. The drug peyotl induces a state of hyper-perception and at the same time of indifference to the world that is similar to schizophrenia—which, it follows, might be curable or controlled chemically. Mescalin is non-toxic, he says, and the autonomic nervous system and mental activity remain normal under it, at which time the works of men do

1953 not attract, whereas the beauty of Nature—flowers, grass, the blue of the sky—is overwhelming. It seems that the drug places in abeyance one or more of the hormone systems that feed the brain with glucose, and that the brain, which is to say the focusing instrument that enables us to work but keeps the mind in tow, opens up the mind—which, roughly, was Bergson's distinction. Aldous says that under mescaline "one sees what Traherne and Blake meant by 'things in themselves.' The only music that holds up under it is Bach's."

July 1. To the Huxleys' to meet Christopher Wood, who is polite, gentle, and rather loose-jointed. Maria talks about Aldous's first meeting with Gerald in 1929, about their lecture tours together, about Peggy Kiskadden's infatuation with Gerald—to the extent that he had to leave her house.

July 8. To the Huxleys'. They have a new relaxing gadget that consists of copper wire nets that are put over the head like a veil; if right-handed, you must cover your eyes with your left hand. Aldous also has a new palming technique according to which one hand is placed on the solar plexus, for warmth. Maria is touching: "We do these things because two years ago both of us thought we were going blind and now Aldous's eyes are much better and I no longer have my cataracts. But, if we *had* been blind, we would still have had each other." Aldous plays a record of Yves Tremayne singing Nicolas Gombert. He gives me Dryden's *Absalom* and a book by Logan Smith's mother, *Religious Fanaticism*.

July 22. With the Huxleys to the Wilshire Ebell Theater to see Tara Bey, their Lebanese fakir protegé. He "kills" himself before our eyes—two "doctors" testify that his pulse, heart, breathing have stopped—then comes back to life by "the power of his will." At one point his robes are shifted to expose his jowlish genitalia. Difficult to face the Huxleys after this embarrassing farce.

July 27. Reading Caesar's *Commentaries*: how sly and talented he is at inventing pretexts; Ford Maddox Ford's *Provence*, which is fussy, fastidious chat that could go on indefinitely; and Baron Corvo's *The Desire and Pursuit of the Whole*, for which Auden's preface is much less good than D. H. Lawrence's Corvo essay (Auden's "paranoia" is Lawrence's "imagining enemies"). With Gerald and the Hubbles to Aldous's birthday party.

July 29. To the Schoenbergs' for dinner with Balanchine, his wife and her mother, Mrs. Schoenberg and her mother (Kolisch), and Dick Hoffmann. When I arrive, Balanchine is already cooking skewered slabs of shish kebab over a charcoal fire in the yard. During dinner, indoors, various Schoenberg pieces are discussed as potential vehicles for a ballet. Because Balanchine does not know any of them and, in truth, is here only because he thinks it is time to do a piece by Schoenberg, I cover for him and suggest the *Begleitmusik*. Hoffmann doubts that a ballet orchestra can do justice to the score, but I argue that the City Ballet Orchestra plays much more difficult modern pieces than the New York Philharmonic and plays them all the time. A tense moment follows, during which I wait to see if Stravinsky's name is mentioned, which could be a cue for Hoffmann to say that the *Begleitmusik* is more difficult than any Stravinsky. After a suitable silence, I propose the Second Chamber Symphony, especially for its second movement, but Balanchine wants a twelve-tone piece, without understanding exactly what the term means. Finally, after agreeing that I will work with him on the *Begleitmusik*, he leaves early, not at all happy with the tone of the discussion. I drive Mrs. Kolisch home with Nuria joining for the ride.

July 30. I play the *Begleitmusik* for Balanchine three times through; he grasps the form of the piece but not the note construction.

August 9. Going to the S.s for breakfast I find a baby hummingbird on the stones outside my door, its left wing broken. Quiet and unprotesting in my hands, it is so small that, except for its bill, it would fit into a tea bag. I.S. places it in an old parrot cage and we lower honeysuckle blossoms to within its reach, supplementing this diet with honeyed water squeezed on the flowers from an eyedropper. Soon the bird goes directly to the dropper, which we fill and suspend just above. The mother hovers outside the window, its bright eye-beads full of "understanding." At night we wrap the cage in cloth, but the wing will probably not mend, and the bird is already tame and therefore destroyed.

August 11. Isherwood for lunch. He will be 50 in two weeks but looks as boyish as ever. Almost everything I say seems to surprise him, and his studying blue eyes strike me, now as always, as seeing and knowing at a deeper level than his conversation indicates. Still, he is more relaxed and easy than he used to be, perhaps because he has just finished his novel, though he claims to have no idea why he wrote it, and says that he might rewrite it in another way. He talks about his trip to Canyon de Chelly, where he asked the Indians living under a huge, menacing boulder if they were afraid it might fall. The answer is " 'It hasn't ever fallen yet.' "

August 14. Fetch Aldous at 3 for our visit from the William Waltons. Aldous, in the car: "I am always amazed at the resources of malice in French people of a certain class and at the total selfishness and lack of public spirit on the part of the French of all classes." The Waltons arrive in a sleek Jaguar convertible, driven by Sir William's brother from Vancouver. Sir William is easy but awkwardly quiet, and I.S. does not understand his accent, hence the encounter, except for the dalliance-inviting exposure of Lady W.'s bosom, is dull.

August 15. A disaster on our return from the ocean: Edward James, no socks, hair overgrown, beard unkempt, is sitting at the dining room table correcting his poems. He infuriates the S.s, never appearing anywhere on time, always without pocket money, giving no advance notice but walking in during dinner, never sensing when the time has come to leave, abandoning cars with flat tires and buying new cars, forgetting appointments, repeating ad infinitum the same anecdotes about his Aunt Fenicia. Yet we spend most of our time with him sharing his laughter. I remember the evening when, having had enough, V. lectured him on his shortcomings, only to be told: "My, how your English has improved!" But James is intimidated by I.S. and always on his best mettle with him. The mystery is that I.S. has been seriously considering a commission to set one of James's poems to music (leaving the choice of text to me, alas) and that James can actually accept this after I.S. had made it clear that *his* interest is strictly in the size of the commission.

August 23. To Gerald's morning lecture on the difference between "abandon" in de Coussade's *L'Abandonnement* and a real victory over what we "abandon." James and Tilly Losch are there, avoiding each other, but perhaps he does have feelings for her; his one memorable couplet, from "My Love dies hard," is: "knowing you will yet wound and try to kill,/it [my heart] is ashamed to find it loves you still." Gerald, at lunch, holds forth on termites and white ants. More at ease with I.S. than before, he invites us to tea with the philosopher C. D. Broad.

August 24. Finish Pope-Hennessy's *Giovanni di Paolo*. To the Schoenbergs' in the evening. I talk about Rilke and Kafka to Nuria, boring and also irritating her when I say that she does not know enough about her great father's world. She says that the Mad Scene from *Lucia*, sung by Tetrazzini, is her favorite record. Later she shows me her father's library: three volumes of Gautama Buddha (in German); Shestov's *All Things Are Possible*; Tieck, Wieland, and Count Platen, all in good bindings; an unopened volume of the German edition of *Doktor Faustus*; Byron in German with the composer's marginalia around the *Ode to Napoleon*. Scraps of manuscripts are lying on tables. The music library includes the complete Bach with markings in Schoenberg's hand, and bound Eulenberg scores.

September 6. An overflowing crowd for Gerald's Sunday morning, his subject being a defense of the Kinsey Report: "We can explain nature only by the accumulation of facts." At lunch he says that St. Thomas had 20 definitions of "nature" but contradicted them all when trying to prove why a woman couldn't become Pope.

To Aldous's for dinner, with Gerald, Hubble, Robert Hutchins, and Julian Huxley. Gerald, in his element, talks down even these professional talkers. Hutchins does an imitation of Alfred North Whitehead speaking so softly that his lectures were understood only when he raised his head to say, in a slightly louder voice, "for example," after which he returned to the mumble. Also an imitation of Niels Bohr's English. Julian is more critical than Aldous—no truck with J. B. Rhine—but much less kind.

September 20. With the Huxleys for Tara Bey's second performance. The trappings this time include a velvet curtain, spotlight, an elderly white-haired doctor who does not understand a word of Tara Bey's French but will not relinquish his place to any bilingual colleague who offers to take it. Telepathic tricks are played with members of the audience; a rabbit and a chicken are hypnotized; the magician himself is buried for ten minutes in a coffin filled with sand, revived from a cataleptic seizure, pierced with knives and knitting-size needles that members of the audience are invited to extricate. He reclines on a bed of spikes while a heavy-set man stands on him, and reclines on two swords with, on his stomach, a 100-pound stone that an assistant sledge-hammers into small pieces. At one point, his testicles are again accidentally unswaddled. Can Aldous really believe that this exhibitionistic Houdini possesses supernatural and occult powers?

October 4. My deepest problem: I have changed families and at a terrible cost substituted my ideal for my real one. Where I am now is exactly where I thought I wanted to be ten years ago, the old story of getting what you think you want. If only analyses were solutions instead of beginnings!

October 11. After conducting Schoenberg's Quintet in the Los Angeles County Museum, I dine at the Schoenbergs'. Frau S. gives me a paper on which Schoenberg wrote "Encourage Craft." Later, Nuria and I go to Lukas Foss, who has rented Anna Mahler's house, and then to the ocean at Malibu.

October 19. I.S. comes to my dress rehearsal and the concert of his "jazz," which attracts the largest audience we have ever had. The premieres of *Preludium* and *Tango*. With Aldous to a party at the Louriés'.

October 20. I.S. gives me Picasso's one-line drawing—sketch for a cover for *Ragtime*—of an ithyphallus, inscribing it in relation to last night's concert.

November 9. I.S. is informed of Dylan Thomas's death in the cruelest way, a cable from a London newspaper asking for comment.

December 31. With V., the Baroness d'Erlanger, and Countess Claude de Biéville to a New Year's party at Hormel's (Hormel ham) in Bel Air. The house is attractively festooned, but the action takes place outside, in a tent warmed by braziers. The food, caviar and breasts of partridge, and the champagne are from Romanoff's, the starlets are courtesy of MGM. At midnight, the Baroness makes "whoopee" in a paper hat, blowing a horn, and at midnight Countess Claude says, "Don't be shy" and sticks her tongue down my throat. Home at 2.

≈ **Postscript 1994.** The first two-and-a-half months of 1953, the only year between 1950 and 1967 in which the Stravinskys did not go to Europe, were spent in New York at the Gladstone, a small hotel on the south side of 52nd street between Park and Lexington Avenues. They resided there on their return from Europe in November 1951, and they stayed there during each subsequent visit to New York until December

1953 1960, when they moved to the St. Regis. The Gladstone treated Stravinsky royally, or whiggishly, reducing its rates for him and catering to his every wish. Before each of his arrivals a small upright Baldwin was installed in his bedroom, and he would work there uninterrupted for three or four hours every day; the Septet was completed there. The food was not to American tastes, but this may have been hotel policy, most of its guests being German and British.

In January 1953, as in December 1951 and 1952, we attended performances at the Metropolitan Opera at least twice weekly, usually in Rudolph Bing's loge, sometimes joined there by Risë Stevens or another Met diva. Stravinsky was acclimatizing himself for the February premiere of the *Rake*. My diary gives none of my impressions about the opera's New York premiere. Stravinsky had a music stand and light installed for the dress rehearsal only a few rows behind Fritz Reiner, in the pit, and conducted along with the conductor, interrupting him every few minutes as well, and, to his ill-concealed annoyance, advising him on matters of tempi, articulation, and balance. The singers were disturbed by this, but neither they nor anyone else was prepared to ask the composer to keep quiet. I was sitting next to Stravinsky and could feel the awful focus of 2,000 pairs of eyes, but I was unable to restrain him. Most insulting of all, to the bourgeoisie (Flaubert: *"Tout le monde est bourgeois"*), were his exchanges in Russian with Balanchine across the pit and the footlights. As I remember, Mrs. Stravinsky hid somewhere in the last row, while Auden and Kallman held court for their own admirers in another part of the house. In Stravinsky's defense, I must say that he always conducted along with any performance of any music, even cueing a pianist playing a solo, or a singer in a piano-accompanied song. In the case of the Met's *Rake*, he was studying the score for his forthcoming recording sessions.

After a brief interlude in California in March, Stravinsky and his son-in-law journeyed to Cuba and Venezuela for concerts. Seeing the composer in New York on his return, I thought he looked peaked, and in Boston two weeks later, at the time of his meeting with Dylan Thomas,* he was confined to bed for more than a week.

In July, back in Hollywood, Stravinsky underwent a prostatectomy. He was never the same afterward. Perhaps the spinal anesthetic had injured his sciatic nerve. Whatever the reason, his walk was much slower after the surgery—before it he had been the fastest-moving septuagenarian I had ever seen, out-distancing even his youngest companions—and he suffered dizzy spells for many months; this was a preview of his old age. His daily exercises came to an end, and though he continued to venture alone down Wetherly Drive to his Sunset Boulevard barber and branch of the Bank of America, then back up the hill, his pace was much less sprightly.

* See Robert Craft, *Stravinsky: Glimpses of a Life* (New York: St. Martin's, 1993).

๙ 1954

January 2. I write to I.S. in New York urging him to set "Do Not Go Gentle" for voice and string quartet. Aldous and Maria come with New Year's wishes.

January 5. Evening with Aldous, who plays a recording of Andrea Gabrieli's *Pater Peccavi* Mass and quotes Edward Lear ("a major poet") extensively. Verlaine's *Hombres* is "dedicated to buggery," he says, adding that "he preferred starving boys, one of whom smelled like Stilton cheese. You remember Rimbaud's 'his feet fermented in his shoes'?"

February 3. Meet I.S.'s flight from New York and stay up with him until 2 A.M. He says that Ansermet came to see him and talked exclusively about phenomenology.

February 22. Aldous and Gerald Heard for dinner, witty and unstoppable.

March 9. My character: indecisiveness wedded to impulsiveness.

March 12. With Aldous to a cocktail party at Isherwood's in honor of Auden, who gives me a nicely inscribed copy of *Delia* ("the driven snow" from *A Winter's Tale*). Talk with him about Robert Graves's "Gospels" and David Jones's *Anathemata*. Iris Tree is there, and, for her benefit, Aldous tells the story of her father, Sir Herbert Beerbohm Tree, in a bad play whose cast included a live horse. At one point the animal answered the call of nature on stage, thereby inspiring Sir H. to address the audience: " 'This horse is a better critic than an actor.' "

March 16. I.S. plays and sings "Do Not Go Gentle . . ." for me. Auden, Isherwood, and Don Bachardy for dinner, Auden looking as if he had just returned from Shangri-La, which is to say that his face now has the craquelure of an Old Master—which, of course, he is, but not *that* old. Becoming more moral by the hour ("It is profoundly wicked not to pay one's bills by return mail"), he will soon be sounding like Moses. More dangerous still, he seems to be growing fonder of ugly words, especially those associated with mining (tump, adit, buddle, gangue). He says that I was wrong to change "The Jews on me" passage in the Cantata. "By any definition *The*

1954 Merchant of Venice is anti-Semitic," he goes on, "but we can't change it." And, "anti-Semitism has nothing to do with Biblical texts." But surely it has everything to do with them, and he must be forgetting his own argument that the Immaculate Conception is anti-Semitic, being the ultimate denial of the Jewishness of the Christian God. Borrowing I.S.'s copy of Von Hügel's *St. Catherine of Genoa*, the lecture-circuit bard departs, listing heavily from the effects of five martinis and two decanters of wine. "Only the man who has secrets refuses to drink," he says, quoting Baudelaire. God rest his liver. I.S. says that when Auden was living with him while working on the *Rake* scenario, Yvgenia Petrovna reported that the soap, towels, and wash-cloths put out each day were never used, and that she never found a trace of moisture in the shower or sink. During the same visit, when Lisa Sokolov sat next to Auden at dinner and observed aloud to him that his fingernails were remarkably dirty, he did not reply but asked I.S. afterward: "Who was that extraordinary woman?"

April 7. Rome. With I.S. to Henze's *Boulevard Solitude* (Magda Laszlo as Manon Lescaut) at the Opera, but not being in evening dress we are not admitted. A fist-fight breaks out between Nicolas Nabokov and a guard, after which an exception is to be made for I.S., but not for me, whereupon he returns with me to the hotel.

April 8. Last night's encounter at the Opera has made the front page of the *New York Times*. We spend the afternoon in Tivoli, then chat with Roland-Manuel in the Hassler. With I.S. to a dreadful concert of Poulenc, Britten, Prokofiev in the Foro Italico.

April 17. Lunch with the Caetanis in their Botteghe Oscure palace: ancient concierges, shaky lifts, and a circular staircase leading out of an enormous empty room to their book-filled, Balthus-filled apartments. The lunch is frugal and the conversation does not scintillate. Princess Margherita's venerable husband, Roffredo, Duke of Sermoneta, resembles Liszt so closely that he could be a stand-in, and I.S. says later that according to Diaghilev, Liszt *was* the father. To I.S.'s *Oedipus* concert in the Foro.

April 21. Rain, cold, fog. To Siena, stopping in Orvieto; the cathedral, alternating black and white Pisan-style horizontal stripes, is near freezing. The only light, in the San Brizio chapel, is directed to Signorelli's images of the end of the world. After checking in at the primitive Hotel Siena, we go to the Duccio room in the Cathedral Museum.

April 22. To Arezzo, and the cracked and corroded tatters of Piero's *Legend of the True Cross*. Large spaces are empty and others are totally color-less. Seepage at the point of convergence between the church and the bell tower, erected a century after Piero, is the principal and obvious cause of damage, since the adjacent "Death of Adam" is in the poorest condition of any of the frescoes. In the absence of lighting we are scarcely able to make out many of the figures in this drab decay of what must have been one of the most resplendently chromatic rooms in the world, and apart from

Piero's plan—open air scenes forming the top layer, ceremonial scenes the middle, battles the bottom—the effect of the whole is one of utmost confusion. The Emperor Constantine's tent is intact, but this could have been executed by someone else. The most memorable image is the Zoroastrian rooster.

April 23. San Gemignano, Poggibonsi, and Pisa.

April 24. Lucca, Pistoia, and Florence, in rooms overlooking the Arno.

April 25. From the Uffizzi to the Palazzo Strozzi exhibition of Piero, Uccello, Andrea del Castagno, Domenico Veneziano. Uccello's windows and some of his most faded frescoes are on view for the first time ever at eye level. But Domenico Veneziano is the discovery of a lifetime.

April 26. To the Duomo and Baptistry, the Pitti Palace, and the Medici Chapel.

April 27. Santa Croce, Santa Maria in Novella, the Bargello, and the Brancacci Chapel.

April 28. Train to Milan, and from there in an old Packard to Lugano. I.S. will brook no criticism of anything Swiss, and he does not see the point when I complain of (symbolic) bats in the stuffy old hotel.

April 29. Afternoon at the Thyssen Collection. A reception after I.S.'s concert with the Lugano Radio Orchestra. I keep trying and keep failing to read the *Tractatus;* the famous definition, "superstition is the belief in the causal nexus," is too cutely roundabout, and the same could be said of countless other beliefs.

April 30. A ferry across Lago Maggiore: Byronic mists and distant storms. Train from Stresa to Geneva, Hotel des Bergues, followed all the way by photographers from *Paris-Match.*

May 1. Dinner at Theodore's with Ansermet, who says that when he conducted *Daphnis et Chloé* in Vienna in 1940, Webern told him he had never heard it before.

May 2. Train to Baden-Oos, changing in Lausanne and Basel.

May 3. I conduct three rehearsals with the sluggish Rundfunk orchestra.

May 4. Three more rehearsals. Dinner with the Strobels in their apartment.

May 5. Record Schoenberg's Second Chamber Symphony, the Bach-Webern Ricercar, I.S.'s *Moods* and Septet.

May 6. Train to Frankfurt, where an elderly porter with Bismarck mustaches helps us transfer from the Bahnhof to an airport bus. Fly to Dusseldorf and, through thunderstorms and hail, to London, where V. receives a telegram from I.S. in Geneva: he has canceled his Cologne concert because of a sore throat; he has gargled with the wrong medication. A long delay in Shannon.

May 7. New York. Leaving the plane, I receive a telegram asking me to call home: my mother's mother has died in her sleep and the funeral was

1954 yesterday. Unfortunately I have an unpostponable rehearsal in Hollywood tomorrow and cannot go home. Alexei Haieff waits with us for the noon flight and the Baroness meets us at the Los Angeles airport.

May 9. Los Angeles. A letter from I.S. in Geneva explains that his sore throat was the result of a mistake in bottle labeling: he has gargled with formaldehyde, but what was he doing with that?

June 7. Postcard from I.S. in Lisbon: "Love from I Str and from an extremely charming, clean, light pink, light green, light gray, silver-white city. The red color of the roofs [on the card] is completely wrong. People inside and outside very calm. So much thanks for your after-Ojai letter. Reading with delight *Under Milk Wood.*"

June 11. Fetch I.S. at the airport at 7 P.M. So far from being tired after his Lisbon-New York-Los Angeles flights, he wants a musical evening. After we play the *Vom Himmel hoch* variations, four-hands, I suggest that he transcribe it for instruments. I show him passages in *Paideia* that I have marked for him, one of which, a commentary on Prometheus, "I am bound here in this rhythm," he copies, as he often does in the case of words and music that he wishes to remember: "Rhythm is that which imposes bonds of movement and confines the flux of things. . . . The original conception which lies beneath the Greek discovery of rhythm in music and dancing is not flow but pause, the steady limitation of movement. . . ."

July 9. Dinner with Balanchine and Nicolas Kopeikin, washed down with Dutch gin and three bottles of white wine. Lesson from I.S. in *sommelier*-manship: a wine bottle must be held in pronation position, never in supination.

July 24. With the S.s and the Baroness to Jules Stein's fake-Norman home on Angelo Drive where we meet Luis Domínguín. Jean Stein is nice, very pretty, too young and too well-bred for the likes of me. The Stein library consists entirely of bound sets, but the house has some good furniture and an interesting collection of metal fish from India. Jean and sister Susan have their own outdoor ice-cream bar, playhouse, and pool. Jean's French fiancé is a titled coxcomb. Her father does not like losing to me at ping-pong, and it is virtually impossible not to win against him.

July 28. The rhetoric in Gerald's UCLA lecture this afternoon is more sweeping than he allows himself in his Sunday morning sermons, but he amuses, nevertheless, especially when the order of his slides gets muddled and they come out upside down. A large audience in spite of wilting heat.

August 1. Visit from Isherwood and Nicolas Magallanes. At the Baroness's, Jean Stein and her Duc. She is attractive, chic, pale, bosomy, and I am shy, stiff, pedantic.

August 12. I.S. names his new ballet *Agon.* At the rehearsal of the Ives ballet, Greek Theater, Balanchine describes one section as a "juvenile delinquents' dance in Central Park." In "In the Night," the whole company crosses the stage on knees, like Lourdes. To Hitchcock's *Rear Window.*

September 20. Opening of the Monday Evening Concerts season: flowers from Jean and a telegram from I.S.: "Wishing you as much personal enjoyment as you will be giving us. Tonight should prove to be your finest reward for job so remarkably done. Affectionate thoughts Igor Stravinsky." *In Memoriam Dylan Thomas* is played before and after intermission. The first half of the concert, apart from the premiere, consists of Andrea Gabrieli's *Ricercar del 12 tono,* Purcell's *Funeral Music for Queen Mary,* a Willaert ricercar, Schütz's *Absalom,* five Gesualdo madrigals, a speech by Aldous, and a recording of Thomas reading. The second half concludes with Bach's *Gottes Zeit.* Marilyn Horne is great. Party with Aldous.

October 15. With Gerald and Isherwood to a dinner at Huxleys' for brother Julian, who is academic, arrogant, jokey and in every way unlike Aldous. Gerald does not expound his harebrained science in this company.

October 25. My Monday Evening Concert: Bach's Cantata 160; Monteverdi's *Zefiro torna,* and two marvelous Schütz sacred symphonies, *Anima mea* and *Adjuro vos.* Also on the program, Andre Previn and Dorothy Wade in the Bartok Second Rhapsody. Aldous, afterward, talks about St. Catherine of Siena's letter to Sir John Hawkwood asking him to fight pagans instead of Christians.

ᕉ **Postscript 1994.** The 1954 diary records the significant events of the year, but elaborates on none of them. The principal development in my life was the resolve to record the complete works of Carlo Gesualdo and Anton Webern; I succeeded in taping all of Webern's songs with instruments, as well as some of the chamber music, and in finishing two records of Gesualdo madrigals—collectors' items today because the twenty-year-old Marilyn Horne was one of the five singers. Stravinsky was in the control room during all of these sessions, learning the music and occasionally offering suggestions about performance. He was also with me in the editing cubicle and by the end of the summer had become deeply immersed in the music of both composers.

In 1954 the Evenings on the Roof became the Monday Evening Concerts, but we continued to present the same kind of program, Bach cantatas and early music alongside nineteenth- and twentieth-century pieces. The concerts of the Ojai Festival—1954 was the first of my six years as Musical Director there—differed from those offered on Monday evenings in West Hollywood only in that the resources were greater.

The turning point of the year came with our participation in Nicolas Nabokov's April festival in Rome and our travels elsewhere in Italy before and after it. Depending on rehearsal schedules, we took almost daily excursions to the Etruscan towns, to the Castelli Romani, and to the great villas and gardens both north (Bagnaia) and south (Ninfa). We already knew that we wanted to live in Italy and did not do so only because Stravinsky's American doctors told us that he required constant and sophis-

1954 ticated (*i.e.*, American) medical attention.

We heard more new music in Rome than in Paris the year before and attended many more operas and concerts, some of them conducted by Hermann Scherchen, one of a very few in the profession I respected. Our social life in Rome was much less formal than it had been in Paris, and we dined more frequently in trattorias in Trastevere than we did in the great transpontine palaces. Mrs. Stravinsky's return-to-Europe campaign became outspoken to the extent that during a reception at the American Academy she was heard to denounce California as unliveable for the reason that "there is no one to talk to," a sure-fire story as repeated by Virgil Thomson and others, but wrongly taken to be an indication of Stravinsky's attitude as well as his wife's. Yet Stravinsky was aware that his music *was* more regularly and widely performed in Europe than in America and that European musical life stimulated him far more.

1954 was a year of new-found creative energies for Stravinsky. His *In Memoriam Dylan Thomas*, composed in the early days of the year, is one of his most moving pieces, and the burst of invention that marked the beginning of *Agon*, completed through the Sarabande by November, was matched in later years only by *The Flood* (1962).

❧ 1955

January 8. Lunch at Gerald's: hand-holding around the table before settling down to a feast of yogurt, wheat germ, salad: "to perish of starvation and green fruit," as Byron wrote of Shelley's vegetarianism. Gerald's homosexuality is more noticeable, and he is more imperious with his disciples, when the S.s are absent.

January 25. New York. Auden at 6, directly from grand jury duty, recommends books for I.S.'s St. Mark's Passion. His face falls when I tell him that I.S. had been tantalized by the thought of using Picander's libretto, but rises again when I repeat I.S.'s remark that he could only write a Passion in English. To Menotti's *Saint of Bleecker Street.*

February 5. Hollywood. Peggy Kiskadden comes to tell us that Maria Huxley is dying—"a matter of hours." It seems that when the cancer spread to her liver two weeks ago, she was hospitalized with "jaundice." Peggy is no more able to explain than we are why Aldous refused to acknowledge that the disease *was* cancer, as we all knew two years ago. Now, according to Peggy, the shock has blinded him.

February 6. While we are at Gerald's for tea, Aldous phones. A few minutes later, Gerald comes back in a state of euphoria: "At last, the mask will soon be off; how much happier she will be out of the body." I.S. is horrified.

February 12. Maria dies at 6 A.M.

February 14. To the funeral, at St. Matthias, an agony for pale, red-eyed Aldous. Isherwood is also red-eyed, and only Maria's mother, whose arm Aldous holds at the head of the recessional, betrays no sign of great grieving. The grave is next to the cemetery wall. I take the S.s for a drive on the ocean highway. A gray, foggy day.

February 16. Aldous for dinner, thin, deathly pale. Maria's name is not mentioned, and we talk too fast trying to cover the expanding silences. Matthew fetches his father.

February 28. Finish reading Amiel's journals to the Baroness. This self-centered prig is nevertheless a considerable psychologist and aphorist:

1955

Practical life is sullied by a crude contradiction; it pursues the good and cannot tell what the good is.

Psychology has replaced morality. Do not prefer clarity to truth.

The religion of the French: words. Their loves are variations of egoism, their promises variations of duplicity.

Carnal pleasure is only a storm of the soul, and sex merely a limitation of the spirit.

Mary Magdalene could have become a Saint in Heaven, but she could not have been presented in any salon in Rome.

The frightful thing about this existence is that, since we are deprived of acquired experience and former practice by each new case, we do not know what to do.

March 5. In the Dome car of the train for Chicago, we sit with a man who tells us he is from Omaha, "which we call the Middle West but which you would call the East; yes sir-ee, all things are relative." He has been employed by the Union Pacific Railroad for 33 years: "You know, from San Barneydoo into Los Angeles"—the "Los" is pronounced emphatically, the "Angeles" in diminuendo—"we rent the Santa Fe tracks. Haven't got our own." When we leave he tells us how much he has "enjoyed the visit," and that he hopes he hasn't bored us.

March 14–15. New York. At 2 P.M. we fly to the Azores and Lisbon, the S.s in berths. In Santa Maria in the Azores, while we drink tea in a musty waiting room in the middle of the night, the painter William Congdon, a fellow passenger, introduces himself, and the S.s invite him for dinner in Lisbon. Portugal comes into view shortly after sunrise, a layer of deep green between cliffs and clouds. Minutes later we are over the coast but see nothing until a long orchard and, at the end of it, almost too late, the airport runway. I.S.'s friend Constantine Varela Cid meets us with a car and takes us through the pink and pistachio city to the Aviz Hotel.

This stable for millionaires—twenty of them, each with five hotel servants—is also a temple of gastronomy. In the restaurant after dinner, a blackamoor boy in red and gold *Rosenkavalier* uniform goes from table to table lighting cigars. We drive to the Church of Belem to see its Manueline cloister; to Mafra; and to blue and white Atlantic-blown Ericeira, its coves studded with seines and lobster cages. Return across a moor with white windmills, via Sintra and Queluz.

I.S. has just begun to nap when a reporter calls requesting an interview about the Sibelius Prize, a sum of $18,000 which, he says, I.S. has won. "What will you do with the money?" the reporter asks. "I will try to sell it to Calouste Gulbenkian," I.S. answers, referring to the oil billionaire whose rooms are next to ours and whose low, dry cough coming through the wall makes me think of the goat in *Gerontion*. To avoid the interview, I.S. pretends he has a cold, then superstitiously fears he is catching one.

March 16. To Evora, a Roman city south of Lisbon, via the Rossio ferry, Setubal, and, on a high road overlooking the sea, Arrabida. Here, far below, are sand bars, a slow rolling surf, gulls, and, on the slope every ten yards or so from cliff top to sea, the small circular towers of Franciscan hermits, each structure facing a slightly different direction to help reduce neighborly encounters.

The proprietor of the Evora restaurant is absorbed in a newspaper, on the back page of which is a photograph of I.S. illustrating a story about the Sibelius Prize. Soon the paper will be turned around, glances will be directed toward us, and I.S. will be caught, one consequence of which could be the gift of a new *spécialité de la maison*—the one now facing us is a soup of rancid olive oil—which we would somehow have to eat. In the event, the proprietor sends for a certain professor, the most learned of the guides, the only one worthy of us. By the time he arrives, the local wine, a drop of which would have cured the insomnia of the Thane of Cawdor, has made us feel like narcoleptics. To make matters worse, the pertinacious professor indicates that our tour will not be a *Reader's Digest* version. We follow him to a charnelhouse in which we are meant to shudder (and do); to São Brás, a cathedral whose wide buttresses and knobbed finials suggest the legs of a colossal grasshopper; to the Roman temple of Diana; and to a convent school, whose classroom walls tell the story of Portugal's heroic age in bright blue *azulejos*.

Back in Lisbon we stop to see the Golden Coaches of Belem, a museum of horse-drawn carriages, all heavily gilt and with rococo furbelows. Lifting a seat cushion and discovering a privy-shaped aperture, I.S. is delighted to find that the passenger could relieve nature in transit, like the horses.

At the Aviz, a batch of congratulatory telegrams for the Sibelius Prize await I.S., some of them also soliciting contributions, and one asking for a loan.

Congdon for dinner. We talk about the exhibition of fake art, Van Meegerens and such, in Amsterdam three years ago, and how we thought the fake late Mondrians, which one would suppose comparatively easy to do, the least convincing pictures in the show. "It is a question of tensions," Congdon says. "We cannot be certain about the tension of a work of art in a different period than our own, but we instantly feel the lack or falsity of it in a contemporary work."

March 18. To Seville, via Badajoz, where the Spanish Customs contains too many photographs of El Caudillo Franco and too large a contingent— is an invasion expected?—of his soldiers. The chief clerk ignores us until he has finished flipping through a magazine, but after stamping our declarations and allowing us to return to our car, he suddenly detains I.S. with a request for an autograph—not in connection with the Sibelius Prize, or

1955 even because of a suspicion that I.S. might be a film producer (that fatal "Hollywood" in his passport), but for the reason, as we see after he signs and the clerk shows the name to a guard: *"Es un famoso violinista."* (*"No me gusta,"* the guard says.)

The narrow Guadiana bridge is choked with purple pigs coming from the other side. At the approach of our car, they turn and flee in the opposite direction, curdling the air with their squeals. In contrast to the clean, pink and blue Portuguese cities, Badajoz is dirty white; and in contrast to the colorful Portuguese folk dress, clothes are black. The small Lusitanian valleys give way to great vistas of plowed red earth in which the black vine shoots look like cloves in ham. Olive trees cover the hills, and herds of merinos and their shepherds, red-faced men in leather clothes with wine skins slung over their shoulders like the bags of a bagpipe. Automobiles are much rarer than on the Portuguese side, and donkey carts are almost the only traffic all the way to Roman Italica.

Entering Seville in late afternoon on the Triana Bridge, we go directly to the Cathedral. After groping in the total dark, afraid of losing each other behind the giant pillars, we are startled by cries of *"Estravinsky, Estravinsky!"* *"Qu'y a-t-il, mon père?"* I.S. says, when he sees that they are coming from a padre. *"Vous êtes riche maintenant, n'est-ce pas?"* the cleric inquires. *"Comment?"* *"Le prix d'Esibelius."* I.S. quickly dampens this enthusiasm with *"Peut-être je suis riche, mon père, mais je suis très avare."* With this, our new companion identifies himself as the organist, which could account for his having descried I.S. in the *noche oscura* of the cathedral but does not explain why he is on the lookout for him in Seville in the first place, since we have not yet registered in the hotel. He says that he had as quickly recognized Richard Strauss and Ravel on their visits here (no doubt surprising them as much as he did us). Enveloped in his auréole of garlic, we follow this priestly picaro on a tour of the paintings, the reliquaries, and the treasuries; he has the authority to unlock doors and light lights.

After dinner in our hotel, the Alfonso XIII, where I.S. stayed with Diaghilev during Holy Week 1921, we buy mohair scarves and walk by the Guadalquivir and through balconied streets.

March 19. A portion of the road near Córdoba is occupied by a young people's bicycle race—in its last lap, evidently, to judge by the tottering of the vehicles and the slow-motion pumping of the exhausted boys. In Córdoba, the elaborate Moorishness of the *Mezquita* overwhelms the Christian altar, and the building is most unconvincing as a church. Carmone and Ecija are white towns in yellowgreen fields of flax.

After Jaen, the red hills erupt and aspens relieve the olive-tree landscape. The approach to Granada is decorated by a sudden spate of roadside advertising in which the signs all end in *"mejores no hay."* North of Granada, a crowd of bereted farmers and workers gaze wonderstruck at an in-construction dam, like a scene in an early Soviet film. We climb from the white city, set in blue, snowpeaked mountains, to the Alhambra and, shivering in cold winds, follow gravel paths to gardens, shrubbery, stagnant pools. Our rooms in the Hotel Alhambra overlook the tiled roofs of the town below. Thornton Wilder is seated at a neighboring table in the hotel restaurant, but we do not disturb him. We drink Fundador to keep warm, and I read Washington Irving's *Tales of the Alhambra* to the S.s.

March 20. To Madrid. Lunch in a Parador near Bailen. Pink and white almond trees, then barren land which, nearer Madrid, explodes into butte-like escarpments. We stop in a cave city, where each cave-front is a wall of whitewashed stone. In one glaring white La Mancha town, traffic is halted for a funeral procession led by a baroque black and silver hearse. We stop again at Aranjuez, then, with virtually no transition from country to city, go directly from the blasted heath to the Ritz.

March 21. The Prado. One of the Primitives rooms contains a picture of a drowned St. Vincent—a stone tied around his neck—being fished out by a rope attached to his nimbus. Next to this is a predella of the ascent into Heaven: feet sticking out below a dark cloud in the first panel are pulled out of sight in the second, leaving a wake of fiery light, a "before and after" advertisement. The Lady of Elche makes us wish for more ancient Iberian art, and I would like to spend a year looking at Velasquez, the reticent, the silent, the supreme.

During a taxi tour, the driver flicks his radio dial in search of a program he thinks might suit us, but when *Symphony of Psalms* comes on he switches off in disgust.

I.S. is deeply shocked by the news of the death—the suicide?—of the 41-year-old Nicolas de Stael.

March 22. Walk from the Puerta del Sol through the fish markets behind the Plaza Major: tubs of turtle claws, mouse-mustachioed langoustines, and fish, barreled heads toward the hubs like rose windows.

Ataulfo Argenta—lean, tall, Greco-ish—tells us that when he conducted Schoenberg's Variations in Milan, the audience hissed all the way through.

The S.s dine with Alvide Lees-Milne, I with I.S.'s concert agent, Felicitas Keller. From midnight until 2 we and the S.s watch flamenco dancing in the Zamora Club, a tiny room full of Americans and smoke. The dancers and singers sit semi-circle on a small stage flanking two guitarists, an old man and a boy. One of the male singers encourages his songs with his left hand, tracing patterns with it as elaborate as the melismas and ornaments of the music. The limbering-up period is livened with clapping, stomping, and "Olé"-ing, but a worst-first protocol rules the order of the solo performances. The male dancers affect not to notice the audience, but every gesture of the females (tight torsos and pleated skirts), especially of one Rosa, the beauty of the troupe in spite of badly blemished skin, is *ad captandem vulgis*.

March 23. To Illescas and Toledo in the car of Señor de las Eras, the

1955 Minister of Education. A nun in white habit shows us the Grecos in the Church of Santa Maria of Illescas. Toledo is a gauntlet of vendors and rapacious would-be guides, persistent as flypaper and uninsultable. In San Juan de los Reyes, the clumps of chains hanging from the walls, supposedly worn by Christians freed by the Crusaders, look heavy enough to weigh the anchors of a modern battleship. More impressive than El Greco's house is Samuel Levi's Synagogue del Transito, where Hebrew script survives just under the terebinth ceiling. At 11 P.M.(!) I go to a special concert by the Banda Municipal de Madrid in the Teatro Español, to hear Julian Menendez's transcription of *Sacre* for winds, cellos, and basses. The players are good and the conductor, Arambarri, is good enough, but the performance has been put on for I.S., who is comfortably in bed, not for a proxy, and his non-attendance is difficult to explain.

March 24. A ceremony for the installation of the new American Ambassador. Moors in shiny blue helmets and buff uniforms, mounted on horses with gilded hooves, patrol the walks of the Royal Palace. The guards outside the main gate are apparelled in pink uniforms and white capes, the horse troops inside in orange and white ones. Close up, scars are visible on many of the horses. From the bull ring?

To another concert, again deputizing for I.S., with the odd combination of the Mass and *Histoire du Soldat*.

March 25. After the morning rehearsal we go to San Antonio de la Florida to see the Goyas. I.S.'s concert is at 7, which in Madrid is practically a matinee.

March 26. To the Escorial with Prince Eugenio Bourbon, who so resembles his uncle, Alfonso XIII, especially in the Habsburg mandibles, that I.S. is reminded of meeting the King at a Ballets Russes performance in 1916, and of an excursion to the Escorial with Diaghilev the next day. Leaving the city we see sheep on our left, a sign of (!) good luck at the beginning of a journey, according to the Prince. In spite of our winter coats we shiver on the cold pavements and in the draughty corridors of the Escorial, but the Prince, wearing only a light suit, does not complain. Cellini's life-size marble Crucifix in the Monastery of San Lorenzo el Real is deeply affecting. Prince Eugenio describes the arrival of the statue from Madrid, carried by fifty human porters (Philip would not trust such a treasure to a mule train), and the King's shock on seeing that the Christ was naked—he covered the private parts with a handkerchief, thereafter venerated as a relic—the sculpture lacking in all *gravidad y decoro;* the figure is Cellini's least serpentine and seductive, however, and at an opposite extreme from his Narcissus or Ganymede. When we descend to the marble vaults, Prince Eugenio recounts how Philip ordered the exhumation of eight royal corpses and their re-entombment in the Escorial, also how funeral processions led by bishops converged from all over Spain—Yuste, Granada, Valladolid, Talavera de la Reina, Tordesillas—and deposited their catafalques here. Charles V's tomb is uppermost. Below and next to his are the tombs of his insane mother, his wife the Empress Isabella, his sister the queen of France, his other sister Mary of Hungary, his second son, his third son (the Infante Don Juan), and Philip's wife, Maria of Portugal.

Back in Madrid, we spend the evening with Ortega y Gasset and the young, very pretty Marquesa de Slauzol, who warns us in advance that the philosopher is deaf and who helps him with bits of conversation that he fails to catch. Except for a hearing aid and piercingly intelligent brown eyes, his head might be that of one of the Roman senators in the Vatican Museum. Short—only two inches taller than I.S.—he speaks r-rolling French in a husky voice: "Russell has written nothing since the *Principia*, which was mainly the work of Whitehead. . . . Heidegger produced nothing of value during his last twenty-five years." He talks about the troglodyte history in Spain, explaining the cave life we saw en route as a continuation of tradition rather than the result of poverty. When we talk about our tours to the cathedrals north of Lisbon, he pokes fun at the Portuguese: "They are far older than the Spanish, and their art probably reflects their confused memory of China and of pagodas." Telling us that he saw I.S. conduct *Orpheus* and *Oedipus* in Munich four years ago, he mentions the appearance of his own new book in German, and in Germany, without underlining the anomaly of his prophet-without-honor status in Franco's Spain. Recalling his visit to Aspen in 1949, he says that Thornton Wilder had translated for him, but that the audience "had already understood because of my extravagant gestures." Taking out his wallet, he proudly shows us a photograph of himself in Aspen with Gary Cooper.

Everything about the man is vivid, his clothes—natty blue jacket, bow tie, pearl cuff-links, and cigarette holder—no less than his mind. He is resonant, too, and so, heeding the Marquesa, are we. The chorus of deaf men's voices grows louder, moreover, as we ply each other with whiskey, a "fifth" of which is emptied before Ortega departs, leaving us wonderfully elated, not to say high.

March 27. Fly at noon, over red plains and gullies, and thereafter thick clouds, to Rome.

March 28. I.S. is in bed with flu. To the Obelisco Gallery to see the arrangement of V.'s paintings; then to a film on Lurçat's tapestries.

March 29. V.'s vernissage attracts a large crowd that includes Mimi Pecci-Blunt, Iris Tree, Aldous's niece Claire, the Roberts from the American Academy, and the American, Russian, and French colonies. Substituting for I.S. at dinner chez Orso (spigola, *poire belle Hélène*), I sit next to Irene Brin (Signora del Corso), a glamorous lady with whom I have been secretly, lustfully, in love for the last year and a half.

March 31. To *La Cenerentola* at the Rome Opera, with a recovered I.S. The audience of uncorseted females in furs, silks and jewels has B.O.

April 1. We spend most of the day in the excavations at Palestrina, then

1955 go to Segovia's concert in the Teatro Argentina. His unamplified guitar is scarcely audible at first, but when the sellout audience grows quiet we hear very clearly, or, rather, overhear, for the music of this most personal of instruments, the consolation of loneliness, is meant for the player alone.

April 7. Nabokov for lunch, very funny on India in a take-off on Stephen Spender and a Sanskrit poet reciting their verses to each other. Yvan Nabokov comes, and we compare notes on *The Man Without Qualities*. After talking with Alessandro Piovesan about the *"passione secondo San Marco,"* I.S. decides to go to Venice and test the acoustics in the Salute and the Frari in the event that San Marco is not available.

April 10. (Easter). With the S.s to St. Peter's. I.S. protests when the Pope appears on the balcony, and the crowd applauds and holds up its *bambini*: "These people are an audience at a spectacle, not communicants in a ceremony. Furthermore, I want to say, 'My Father who art in heaven,' not '*our* Father.' " We place flowers on the graves of Keats and Shelley, by the pyramid of Cestius Caesar, then go to the Villa Aurelia (American Academy) to meet the young Prince of Hesse.

April 12. In an interview with Mario Rinaldi, just-published, I.S. says that he is actually working on a *"passione secondo San Marco."* He also speaks of his trips around Rome to Tarquinia and Avezzano (though he was not with me on the visit to the latter). He mentions the Sibelius medal but says that he will not go to Finland because it is very far away as well as "too near a certain city that I have no desire to see again." He says that he was asked to attend a concert in the Vatican conducted by Mario Rossi but refused because he did not have the proper clothes. Rinaldi writes: "To be near Stravinsky, one immediately has the impression that this man is *al corrento* concerning the whole literary and artistic activity of the world. Of his Roman friends he spoke especially about the books of Carlo Levi, the paintings of Guttuso. His knowledge of old music is profound. . . . He says that 'Webern has opened many doors.' " Rinaldi describes I.S. as "climbing the Spanish Steps which are full of azaleas before Easter."

April 17. A walk with Laszlo in the Gianicolo, just before the train. In Venice, Piovesan and Count Alessi meet us at the station with a *motoscaffo*. Overcoats in the Piazza, where I sit, beneath the horses of Lycippus, thinking of *bella Roma*, the Rome of the senses, the sounds of fountains at night (the Tritone, the four rivers in the Navona, the Quattro Fontane, the Campidoglio); the colors of Rome (apricot, and the ochre of the Villa Medici); the flowers of Rome (the floral displays in the Campo Fiori; and on the Spanish Steps, not to mention the displays there of all-sex whores); and the gardens (the Pincio); the aqueducts, the gates (Porto San Sebastiano); the arches and columns; the city of smart clothing shops and of catacombs (Sant'Agnese, where we held flickering candles in a dark, damp and draughty passage lined with skulls and bones and crosses); the city of ancient walls and sidewalk cafes; the city of churches with dark-eyed shepherds in mosaics; the city of dancing angels—Bernini's, on the bridge—of bells, of obelisks (the Trinità dei Monte).

April 18. (Venice.) A motorboat takes us to the Salute where a chorus and musicians from the Fenice sing and play a motet by Croce. The reverberation is too long, and we continue to the Frari, in which the same music, with rapid 16th-note passages, is more distinct. Lunch at Harry's Bar with Count Alessi.

April 25. From Innsbruck to Mittersill with a garrulous driver. Alpine country with fir trees, castles, wooden villages, wooden people. The road narrows after Kitzbühl, near the castle where French Premier Daladier was interned during the war, and Schloss Mittersill, where Nijinsky was interned. Webern's grave, in Mittersill churchyard, is marked only by an Iron Cross and name tag. We cover the plot with wild flowers and return to Innsbruck feeling oppressed by this melancholy place and the events that took place there in 1945.

May 6. Copenhagen to Greenland, Winnipeg, Los Angeles. Clear views of Greenland at midnight in a bright, rosy-tinged sky. After passing over an eery wilderness of ice and snow with black mountain sides, we land on a narrow lip beneath a costal cliff, a former U.S. air base, and enter a rudimentary terminal through a heavily insulated bridge-tunnel. Even the ocean is frozen—frazil ice and vuggy ice. In Los Angeles, I.S. is greeted by TV, reporters, photographers.

June 2. I.S., immersed in Edmund Wilson's *Dead Sea Scrolls*, is devastated by the idea of an Essene prototype.

June 28. I.S. shows me the libretto of his *Cantata Sacrae Sanctissimi Marcus*, also the orchestra score of the Dedicatio, for tenor, baritone and trombones, and the first chorus, which specifies boy sopranos (never higher than E).

June 30. Letter from Aldous in Guilford, Connecticut:

> . . . I expect to return to LA in September, but shall (I hope) have to come back here in November for rehearsals [of *The Genius and the Goddess*] (if there is a production in December or January, which I hope, but don't yet know). . . . There is a wonderful loan exhibition at the M. of Modern Art, pictures in private collections, from Cézanne to Picasso. Such marvels: and on the floor above is a show called "The New Decade"—five or six acres of non-representational ennui, produced since the end of the war. How very cruel to juxtapose the two shows! And why on earth should these last years have been so fearfully barren? Unanswerable question. My love to you all. Yours, Aldous H.

July 23. At Ernst Krenek's, listening to his *Medea* and the Symphony from *Pallas Athene Weint*. He provides I.S. with the title *Canticum Sacrum Ad*

1955 *Honorem Sancti Marci Nominis.*

August 14. I.S. is in a tizzy because Heinrich Strobel's book about him says that he was introduced to Debussy's music by Diaghilev: "I played *l'Après-midi* to Rimsky years before I had ever heard of Diaghilev."

September 24. Dinner on the pier, at "Jack's at the Sea," then to the amusement park, where I.S. and V. drive electric bumper cars, I.S. very slowly and cautiously. Also the spook house and fun house with distorting mirrors. Throwing darts at a straw target, V. wins a rubber statue of a hula dancer.

October 17. My Monday Evening Concert: Monteverdi, Gesualdo, and a group of pieces for brass, fanfare by Josquin, Canzona by Luzzaschi, Ricercar by Andrea Gabrieli, and Purcell's Funeral Music for Queen Mary. During Aldous's lecture on Gesualdo, Mrs. Nys, his mother-in-law, in the third row, fidgets and changes position when the subject of sex seems imminent. Marilyn Horne again triumphant.

October 20. My birthday. Edward James suddenly appears from Mexico with a female(!) secretary. He knows one of the actresses in the Ivar Street theater production of *The Plough and the Stars*, and obliges us to go with him to the gabby play.

December 23. New York. Auden and Chester, too early for dinner, take up the slack with too many martinis, supplementing them with a bottle of Pouilly, in I.S.'s room, and two bottles of Piesporter during the meal. Chester, as always, talks about opera and his gods, Wagner and Strauss. Also, "My book of poems will be the best since the discovery of Robert Lowell, which isn't much, of course, but I'm barnstorming now, what with NBC's *Magic Flute* and my records and books." He looks a fright—boiled eyes, receding hairline, piggish neck. Auden, bright as ever but didactic, says that as an undergraduate, Tolkien fell in love with the Phoenician language. He describes the masque by Campion that "King James commissioned for one of his *eromenoi*, and which has music by Ferrabosco."

&⬩ **Postscript 1994.** The Stravinskys knew how highly Maria valued their friendship with Aldous, who was so much more remote and abstract than she was, and knew that she reaffirmed it much more frequently than he might have done by himself. Maria, moreover, Belgian-born and French-speaking was capable of intimacy and affection. Stravinsky, who was in the habit of locking arms with his male friends, and hugging and kissing them in the Russian manner, left, right, left, felt that Aldous's English reticence, rather than his height, forbade such behavior. Maria's death, and Aldous's pain, cast a pall over February and March.

More deaths with special meaning for the Stravinskys were in store for them in 1955: Ortega y Gasset, Thomas Mann, Oscar Moss (sponsor of the Monday Evening Concerts), and the suicides of Eugene Berman's wife, Ona, and Nicolas de Stael.

The main event of the year in Vera Stravinsky's life was her exhibition, the first anywhere, at the Galleria Obelisco in Rome at the end of March. This was a happy occasion, except that Stravinsky was in the hospital, and a second vernissage had to be arranged for him a few days later.

Creatively, with the composition of the *Canticum Sacrum*, Stravinsky turned in a new direction. Soon after accepting the commission, in Venice, in April, he began to talk about his musico-theological-architectual concepts. By the time he began to compose, at the end of May, he had planned a structure of five-movements, like the domes of St. Mark's, with a middle movement in three parts representing the virtues in the order *Caritas, Spes, Fides*. Thus "hope" would stand at the center of the entire work. The symbolic number five appears in the first and last choruses as well, in the organ responses, which consist of five parallel lines, each confined to its own modal group of, from top to bottom, five pitches, four pitches, three pitches, two pitches, and six pitches. But the *Canticum* is new in every way. Starting with *Surge aquilo*, the second movement, Stravinsky began to explore the world of twelve-pitch serial music. *Surge aquilo* was completed on July 20, "Charity" on August 7, "Hope" and "Faith" by September 30, Mrs. Stravinsky's name day, the day of the three virtues in the Orthodox Church. *Brevis motus* is dated November 2, *Illi autem* November 21. Stravinsky also wrote the first of his Bach variations in 1955, in New York in December, where we had decided to spend the holidays after six uninterrupted months in Los Angeles.

❧ 1956

January 1. New York. Always the same resolves, but no matter, since none is likely to survive the week. We play the *Canticum* and *Vom Himmel hoch*, four hands, on the small muted piano in I.S.'s bedroom, he singing the solo parts in the former and talking about his added canons during the latter. A visit from Olga Koussevitzky, who asks I.S. to listen to a recording of her late husband's voice.

January 4. I.S. does not comment on Gretchaninov's obit in today's *Times*, though he knew him well. I.S. receives the Sibelius Medal (and no money) at the Finnish Consulate, a relief portrait that should be melted down immediately. Why did he accept it? Because he hopes to receive the cash prize in another year? The Consul reads a bombastic citation for the benefit of reporters.

January 5. During lunch, David Oppenheim hoists an assault on the whole of "modern art," including some of I.S.'s contributions, which upsets I.S., not for himself but because David is the sole arbiter of Columbia Records' new-music repertory. To the Museum of Modern Art afterward to see Monet's *Water Lilies*, then to dinner at Davidova's with Joseph Cotten and Moore Crossthwaite, and the premiere of Orson Welles's *Lear*.

January 7. With Deborah Ishlon to a screening of a technically very poor documentary of I.S. recording *Soldat*. At V.'s and Kallman's birthday party, Auden's friend Chuck Gerhardt is included in the sit-down-dinner group, with the S.s. Gold, Fizdale, Davidova, and Kyriena Siloti come later.

January 17. Apropos *Canticum Sacrum*, I.S. writes the tenor Richard Lewis complaining about Italian pococurantism: ". . .the trouble is that nobody knows the date. . . . They do not know . . . even the exact period in September. . . . It is always this way with the Biennale."

January 18. Ned Hertzstam, who proposes to make a 15-minute animated cartoon of *Petrushka*, comes with drawings for the film, a marked score of the sections to be used, and a not very subtle reminder that the film can be distributed in the U.S. without his permission. I give a lecture on Luigi Nono's *Incontri* at the Kantor Gallery in the evening and am very nervous because the S.s and Nono's mother-in-law, Trude Schoenberg, are present.

February 2. Hertzstam again. I.S. signs a contract for the *Petrushka* film **1956** for $10,000. Dinner with Gerald, Isherwood, and Don Bachardy at Frascati's on La Cienega near Pico, Gerald in top form and Christopher and Don beaming mutual affection; they are a perfect match, as if they had bought each other out of a catalog.

February 22. Visit from I.S.'s friend Pierre de Polignac of Monaco, who announces the forthcoming marriage of his son to Grace Kelly of Philadelphia. Prince Rainier comes at 5:30.

February 27. Edit tapes for four hours; the performance of Webern's Six Pieces is reasonably good. After dinner, with the S.s to "The Goldberg Variations," a public debate, supposedly between the Monday Evening Concert audience and supporters of Albert Goldberg's loyal opposition in the *Los Angeles Times*. But Goldberg does not speak, and the defenders of our new-music program policy have nothing to say. A non-event.

March 15. Gerald, for dinner, is even more fluent after champagne. Argues against precipitancy: "Moses was 80, Aaron 83 when they were sent to lead the Israelites out of Egypt, and Abraham was 100 when Isaac was born."

March 19. Rose de Haulleville telephones the news of Aldous's Yuma drive-in marriage to Laura Archera, a violinist from Turin. The S.s are slightly shocked, not for Hamlet's reason—it is more than a year—but because they suspect a long pre-arrangement. My Monday Concert: Mozart's Gran Partita, K. 361.

March 26. Joyce: "Sentimentality is unearned emotion."

March 27. A Red Letter Day: I.S. dedicates his *Vom Himmel hoch* recomposition to me, placing the first page of the score on my plate so that I see it when I come in for lunch.

April 12. To Jackie Horne's early morning performance of *La Cenerentola* in the Shrine Auditorium, the school-children audience making more noise at times than the orchestra. I find a curious instance of belief in predestination in Mme de Sévigné's *Letters*; when the Count of X is killed in battle, Mme de S., with a complete disregard of logic, remarks that the bullet had his name on it, "otherwise it would have hit one of the soldiers around him."

April 23. At Gerald's, Isherwood shows home movies, made on his last European trip, with some good sequences of E. M. Forster in Cambridge, and of Maugham at Cap Ferrat. Christopher says that as they went into dinner at Maugham's he heard him whisper to Alan Searle: "Who are these people?"

April 28. Hollywood. A note from Nadia Boulanger thanking me for the Gesualdo record: "Dear Bob, You don't know how touched I am! Such a recording shining of intelligence and *real* understanding. Hope we will once have an opportunity to talk, but what difference does it make for you—quite surely you go your way with this evidence of what one has thought and felt. It is such a priceless achievement. (The sforzandos are so

1956 enlightening.) Most affectionately."

June 17. Ogden, Utah. In the mountains, early afternoon, our train surprises a heavily antlered moose drinking from a stream. The animal lifts its head slowly for a look at us but, overweighted by its horns, does not move. Wyoming is greener than I have ever seen it, the vast sky pressing against the earth is more blue, and the ugly little towns for which I am so homesick in Europe are lonelier and uglier than ever. Small ponds, like mirrors or pieces of fallen sky, glitter on the prairies. A colt canters away from the train and a rabbit dives into a burrow. Toward evening, storms darken the distant sky, moving closer until one breaks over us, leaving a mescaline-bright rainbow.

June 18. The Mississippi is spilling into the lowlands beyond the levees. In Chicago, we celebrate I.S.'s birthday at the Pump Room with Philip Hart, then go to the Art Institute to see *La Grande Jatte*. In contrast with Seurat's sparsely peopled Sunday afternoon, the lake shore beaches are crowded. Back on the train, we darken our rooms to watch the lights along the Ohio River and the red glow over Pittsburgh, a vision of hell.

June 27. Joined by Lawrence Morton, we sail on the S.S. *Vulcania*. Our waiter, Gennaro Ombra, belongs in a De Sica film. Our next-table neighbor, General Carl (Tooey) Spaatz, receives cablegrams every few minutes. The ship is not air-conditioned.

July 4. Lisbon. Lunch at the Aviz Hotel, then through country smelling of curry, to Mafra, Byron's house in Moorish Sintra, and the pink palace of Amelia III in Queluz, which reminds the S.s of St. Petersburg.

July 5. Views of the African and Spanish coasts in early morning. At Gibraltar, dories surround us, each with an oarsman and a salesman. Pulleys are thrown over our deck rails, and baskets with shawls, hats, capes, and matador paraphernalia are winched up.

July 6. Lights on the Valencian coast are in view most of the night. Docking at Barcelona at 8 P.M., we are met by Eduardo Toldra, conductor of the local orchestra, who takes us to the Sagrada Familia, then to a fish restaurant. At 2 A.M. tugboats tow us out of the harbor, and we remain on deck in the warm night.

July 7. While we are breakfasting on the S.s' balcony, four porpoises leap in and out of the sea near our ship and as though racing it, like runners taking hurdles. After only an hour on the top deck, one understands the egoism of sailors—all that space and oneself the center of it—but how can anyone ever have looked all day at the sea and still have thought the world flat? V. says that whereas Atlantic waves collide and crash, Mediterranean waves fold and push. In the Straits of S. Bonifacio, the islands are closer together than expected from maps, and we can see churches, bell towers, and a small city on the Sardinian coast. At dinner, the ship's musicians, an accordionist and two violinists, followed by a waiter with a candle-sparkling cake, march into the dining room playing *Happy*

Birthday, but they fete four tables before finding the right one. Tonight being the last on board for most passengers, tensions about tipping can be felt all over the boat.

July 8. Ischia is fog-bound at 8 A.M., and we are in Naples before it begins to clear. A huge crowd at the dock, in which we make out and wave to Loredana and Adriana Panni, but wait to debark until the confetti has settled, and the weeping families of reunited Italians begin to disperse.

In the *pescheria*, near the Porta Capuana, the fish, heaped on tables, glisten like tinfoil. At Montevirgine, part of the road is blocked by a parade of flower-decked automobiles, a religious procession—the Whitsuntide veneration of the portrait of the Virgin painted by Saint Luke(!!)?—led by young-boy lampadephores in white suits with red sashes. The Convent of Loreto here, now the abbott's winter residence, has a stunningly beautiful rococo façade. The castle at Gesualdo is occupied by a family with a great many *bambini*. When Loredana explains to their papa who Carlo Gesualdo was (he had not heard), and who I.S. is (*ditto*), the man looks at I.S. with alarm, having momentarily confused the composers in her story and mistaken I.S. as the murderer of *his* wife. The Gesualdo coat-of-arms (lion rampant, dexter fore- and hind-legs raised) is emblazoned on the lintel of the gate. High on the wall above a cobblestone courtyard with a well in the center is the legend cut in the stone:

CAROLUS GESUALDUS EX GLORI ROGER II NORTH APULIAE ET CALABRIAE

One of the upstairs rooms has two chairs from the composer's period, but the other furniture is from an Italian equivalent of Montgomery Ward.

The altarpiece (*ca.* 1597) in Santa Maria delle Grazia is brighter, less faded, than expected, and one accepts the portrait of Gesualdo as lifelike if only because he looks so unlike anyone else. He wears a black robe with white, Spanish-style ruff and kneels at the lower left of the picture next to his uncle, Cardinal Borromeo, and opposite his second spouse, Leonora d'Este, at the lower right. The cloak of the figure above Borromeo is bright yellow, and the hell below orange-red, in clashing contrast to the Cardinal's magenta. One wonders what the musical reformer of the Council of Trent would have thought of his nephew's later music. What one cannot imagine are the madrigal singers, the church choir, the instrumental virtuosi, the printers and their presses, and the high musical culture that flourished 400 years ago on this forlorn hill.

A Father Cipriano suddenly materializes and leads us behind the chapel to the Capuchin monastery where he brings thimblesful of a berry liquor. As we leave, V. notices aloud that a corner of the front wall has been torn by bullets. Padre Cipriano blames *us* for this: "The American Army occupied the town near the end of the war."

We sail from Naples at 8 o'clock. Capri, hung with lights, glides by like

1956 a huge float.

July 9. Palermo. Red sunrise over the glassy sea. Debarking, we hail a taxi to Monreale, but as we start off a young man jumps into the seat next to the driver and informs him and us that he is our guide. A scuffle follows, the driver not wishing to share his prey, but we decide to keep them both.

Palermo is a city of wild flowers, garden flowers, flowers for sale, flower wreaths, flower garlands, flower pompons on donkeys and horses, flower displays in all the public squares; and a flamboyantly colored city, with rainbow-striped fishing boats, painted donkey carts, blue houses (blue repels flies), pink palaces and churches, and the scarlet stockings of school children. After two hours in the cool of the Monreale, we go to the Chinese Palace built by Ferdinand II for his mistress in 1799.

In the Capuchin catacomb 8,000 skeletons are displayed; or, rather, if they *were* skeletons, we would be less horrified. The trouble is that many of them are still remarkably fleshly and only slightly decomposed (are the walls made of limestone?), some have long hair, some are an off-putting pistachio color, while some, at least for my sensibilities, are simply too recently deceased. These corpses hang from the walls in a most macabre way, moreover, seeming at times to move, so that the visitor imagines the sound of scraping bones and the rustle of dried intestines. At one point the lights falter, as no doubt they are made to do for every tour group, after which we make our exit, though not before visiting the "Children's Corner," in which scores of infants are dolled up in their burial best, a sight so strongly lacking in appeal that I emerge into the daylight probably looking pistachio-colored myself. Lawrence is deeply shaken by the experience.

Back at the *Vulcania*, the haggling with the driver and guide starts with a demand for $50 and an offer of $12; but in five minutes and in spite of our resolutions, we are up to $35, which they accept. As we go aboard, they begin to quarrel about the division of the money, and a half-hour later, from our balcony on the boat, we see them still arguing. At lunch, over-hearing our talk, Gennaro says that we have given them at least double their highest hopes, and this episode, or the telling of it, we now realize, has weakened our own tip position with respect to the boat. At night, in the straits of Messina, which seem no wider than the Hudson at New York, we remain on deck watching the lights of the Calabrian coast under a canopy of stars.

July 10. Awakened somewhere in the southern Adriatic by the periodic moan of the ship's fog signals, I go to my porthole. But the sea is invisible, and the pulse of our engines is so feeble that we can hardly be moving at all. Just before noon a trajectory of clear atmosphere exposes a blue wall of mountains. Then Cephalonia and Zante appear, but in dense vapors, like fragile objects wrapped for shipment (Cephalonia in cellophane). At Patras, in mid-afternoon, we wait offshore for a welcoming deputation.

When at last it arrives, no doubt having been difficult to convoke, hospi- **1956** tality proves to be a lesser article on its agenda than propaganda. I.S. is asked to make a statement protesting British atrocities in Cyprus, but he complies only to the extent of condemning all atrocities everywhere and at any time. Finally stamped and ticketed for landing, we go to a sponson midship and transfer to a pinnace with canvas awning. The navigator, a leathery old Charon, guides the tiller with his bare feet and acknowledges his gadfly passengers by expectorating in the wind in our direction. A slow "put-put" to shore.

Photographs of indignities on Cyprus are displayed on the walls of the Customs shed, but the point of those in which soldiers are shown frisking priests is not clear: the real complaint would seem to be indecent assault. Prodigal sons returning from Chicago and the Bronx are evidently not trusted in the always corruptible Customs service, so none of the officials speaks a word of any language but Greek. Apart from the linguistic confusion, the declaration form requires that disparate commodities, a camera, a watch, a hundred cigarettes be counted together: total of 102.

We are rescued from the pandemonium by the dust-raising arrival of Mr. Spyrakis, our guide, whose authoritative manner in dealing with the officials and in paying one or two of a suddenly formed mob of porters suggests that he might be the mayor or chief of police. The Hotel Cecil, where he deposits us, is in great need of improvements. My seventh-floor room has neither lavatory nor sink, and to get there I must take a reluctant and quivering lift. Moreover, the "staff" is a single elderly man who becomes, in succession, registering clerk, porter, waiter, cashier.

Patras is a miserable city, a threat to preconceptions that several rounds of *mastikas*—Greek "redeye"—do not offset. At twilight we go to a restaurant north of the city on the Gulf shore, nearly running into, on the way, women with head bundles, bearded and stovepipe-hatted priests—some of them skillfully managing bicycles in spite of their skirts—and buses as crowded as hells in perspectiveless medieval pictures. The view at the water's edge—facing the mountains of Aetolia, with Calydon behind and Missolonghi to the west—is better than the food, which is limited to fried calamari and a nonresinated but thick-as-malmsey Achaian wine; in my case even the thought of calamari, like the thought of haggis, chitterlings, and whelks, will sustain a fast. I.S., on the contrary, eats so much that he complains later of having swallowed "too many spiders."

At nightfall, lights flicker like fireflies on the opposite shore, indicating an invisible city, or so we suppose until they move into the Gulf and are seen to come from fishing boats. The moth-like dazzling and clubbing of fish attracted to light is a method used by ancient anglers—"The fire-producing stone of night rowers" is Satyrius's periphrastic definition of flint—with the difference that pine torches are now replaced by flashlights and kerosene lanterns. Our pleasure in this spectacle is spoiled by the arrival of a passel of tourists from Council Bluffs, dumped from a bus for an *al fresco* banquet. After retreating to electrically bright Patras—an agreeable surprise in this sense, by comparison to low-watt and unfrosted Italian bedside lamps—we sit at an openair café embalming ourselves with more *mastikas*, although a single swallow can blur the power to distinguish whether the starry firmament is inside or out.

July 11. The scene from my window at 6 AM might have been copied by Chirico: a deserted square; an empty railway station; a large clock over the station door dividing the void into hours and fractions of hours. Directly below, men at sidewalk tables in the shade of the hotel are reading newspapers while their shoes are being shined. Beyond the station, fishermen are tying up at the docks: the Ionian Sea is already ablaze with the morning sun.

Bills paid, we pack into Mr. Spyrakis's "limousine." This expert driver, cicerone, and "nimble planner" reminds us of Mr. Eugenides, though the language in this case is demotic French. He also seems to be an able exchequer, dispensing the right perquisites, or so his manner, if not invariably that of the recipients, implies. His only evident failing is a national one, the too frequent use of his automobile's too-resonant horn.

East of Patras is a ferry slip, the reason for our early rising: crossings are infrequent and, after 8 o'clock, unscheduled. The vessel, a war-surplus LST, does not inspire confidence, but we embark, along with a tribe of goats, a donkey wagon, and some pedestrian *polloi*, to whom a ragged boy tries to sell cakes. The ferry plies between the castles of Morea and Roumeli, Venetian forts on facing promontories.

The road on the north shore is obstructed by a gypsy caravan preparing to depart from a squalid roadside bivouac. While the men corral donkeys, goats, chickens, and dogs, the women, wrapped in blankets and wearing headgear like that of the *très pauvres* peasant women in *Les Très Riches Heures du Duc de Berry*, wait by the wagons in the 100-degree sun. The S.s are as impressed by this encounter as I, a one-time fan of George Borrow, am disappointed. They believe in such arrant gypsy superstitions as the power to charm away warts. V.'s credulity is greater than I.S.'s, having been strengthened by an experience in the rue Passy in 1920, when a gypsy clairvoyant called to her in Russian, offering to tell her about Igor Stravinsky in her future; in Los Angeles, she regularly consults a gypsy palmist recommended by the Huxleys, and I.S. has also been influenced by the prophecies of this Azucena, in spite of his protestations that any knowledge of the future would make the present unbearable.

Lepanto, the first city on our route, is a pile of crumbling fortifications, a description that includes the harbor's sea walls and pincer, lobster-claws sea gates. It cannot have undergone much reconstruction since the famous battle, which actually took place south of Oxia, 50 miles to the west. After Lepanto, the narrow, bumpy, unpaved road—a dust cloud trails the car—

climbs steeply, and climbs and descends sheerly and precipitously all the way to Delphi. Two stretches are bedded with crushed rock, but these are the most dangerous of all; we stick fast in one of them and are obliged to appeal to a herdsman for help. During the entire seven-hour drive, we pass no automobile and no other vehicles except the mules and old women who transport the road's freight.

In spite of the shaping and reshaping of terraces on every arable slope, and the gathering and regathering of rocks into fences, the ground is barren. A thin-waisted Byzantine bridge spanning a gorge is the only remnant of an earlier culture. Near this, women are pounding stones to gravel, their faces partly veiled, but orientally, not for protection: their eyes are exposed.

In a mountain village still rubble-choked from the war, we sit under a chestnut tree eating *rahat loukouma* and drinking ouzos, chased by cold spring water. At another table three men with grizzled faces and wearing the Evzone costume—tasseled caps, pleated white kilts, fustanella, stockings, tufted slippers, handlebar mustaches—take only lateral and begrudging notice of us, being interested exclusively in Mr. Spyrakis's "limousine."

The road climbs again afterward to a point from which the Gulf is in view nearly as far back as Patras, so short a distance, crow-wise, compared with all the colonic miles we have come. From here to Amfissa the landscape is less bleak, and the sempiternal olive trees are relieved by eucalyptus and pepper, oleander and thistle, all in bloom. The inhabitants are less savagely aloof, too, and everyone, toothing toddlers to edentate beldams, screams at us begging cigarettes.

The Delphi Hotel is unfinished and our balconies, overlooking the valley of the Pleistos River, have not yet been enclosed. The sun is too strong for ruin climbing, and we do not venture out until 6 o'clock, though the heat is still fierce then, and only the Phaedriades are in shadow. The ruins—broken columns, shattered walls, crippled temples and treasuries— are disappointing. Nor does the superstitious, cruel, and opportunistic religion to which they are monuments inspire my awe: the oracle flattered the favored, told the powerful what they wanted to hear, and sold the equivalent of stock market tips to big investors. Worse still, guides are unavoidable. By 8 o'clock our side of the mountain is in shadow, the tourists are gone, and the empyrean is quiet.

July 12. To Athens, via Hosios Loukas, Levadia, Thebes. I.S., very grouchy because of the heat, dismisses the contents of the Delphi Museum as "breakage." As the sun mounts and we descend into ever hotter valleys, the shepherds' stone huts give way to thatched roofs and wood. We stop at a viewpoint of the Tridos, the intersection of the Delphi-Thebes and Daulis-Ambrysus roads. I.S. says that he had not pictured this landscape when composing his "*trivium*" music but would have supposed the area to be very small; in these wide and barren slopes, Laius and Oedipus would hardly have noticed each other let alone contested the right to pass.

A sudden blast nearly jolts us over the unrailed ledge and fills the road 50 yards ahead with a fountain of rocks and earth. When the debris settles, sending up colloidal suspensions of dust, a workman jumps down from a dugout in the hillside above, signals us to stop—we already have—and warns Mr. Spyrakis, or so I interpret the gesturing toward the abyss, that we could have been killed, as indeed we would have been if the departure of the ferry this morning had been a moment more punctual. Why are there no road blocks and no signs?

The road to Hosios Loukas is bumpier, the towns are more harshly destitute, than any we have seen, and the country, except for a few old women hoeing in the fields, is deserted. Mr. Spyrakis tells a horrifying story of the wartime murder of the entire male population of two villages in retaliation for the shooting of a Gauleiter. We stop at an outdoor restaurant in Hosios Loukas, but the thought of the murders has killed our appetites. Whereas the walls and ceilings in Luke-the-Stiriote's two churches are cracked and bruised, the dome frescoes are disturbingly new, spoiled by too much restoration. The buildings of the monastery are synthetic, compounded of Roman and Byzantine walls and modern bricks and cement. The most attractive features, the roofs with stone shingles and round, whitewashed chimneys, are found on every edifice, sacred and secular, in the region.

The Athens road descends spirally, and the countryside prospers with each downward loop. But so does the heat. I.S. knots the corners of a handkerchief and wears it like an English housemaid's bonnet. At Levadia, abode of the oracle of Triphonius, we dip our arms in the icy spring water until they turn blue, which makes the heat blister afterward. The sun is so powerful that we are hardly able to turn our heads in the directions of Thermopylae, Thebes, and Marathon. Compared to the mountain towns, Thebes, whose ruins could be carted off in a few trucks, has an almost hopeful look, and Marathon holds the promise of a breeze: "The mountain looks on Marathon and Marathon looks on the sea." But we do not feel the sea air before Eleusis. Athens, with Mount Lycabettus coming into view first, then the Parthenon, is a dusty-white city. Because of the undeclared war in Cyprus, our hotel, the Grande Bretagne, is now simply the Grande, and the statue of Byron across the street has been draped with a placard: "Aren't you ashamed to be an Englishman?"

July 13. Iolas, director of the New York gallery of that name, takes us to a shore restaurant south of the city. In the bead-curtained kitchen we choose our dinners from tubs of living cuttlefish and calamari, and from a display of fish laid out on a morgue-like marble slab, as if visual attractions were a clue to culinary ones.

Back in Athens, V., Lawrence, and I trudge steep paths and climb tall steps to the Acropolis, where sunburned and perspiring Teutons (dirndls,

Lederhosen) are photographing each other. The interior of the Parthenon is whiter, less wheatcolored than I expect, having been told as a child that it is beige. We spend the evening with Robert and Mildred Bliss, I.S.'s Dumbarton Oaks patrons.

July 14. Lunch by the sea, near Pikermi, with Iolas and Mrs. Ghika, wife of the painter.

July 15. To the Parthenon again. Candlelight dinner at Iolas's country home with Arda Mandikian, the singer.

July 16. With Lawrence to the Peloponnesus. In the valley below Mycenae, the only hotel is still the Belle Hélène, with Schliemann's name in the register. Excavations are under way outside the walls of Mycenae, but except for ghosts ("This house, if it had a voice . . ."), the citadel is deserted. The ascent is a cauldron, but the summit, under Prophet Elias Mountain and with a view over slopes of olive and cypress to Tiryns and Arcadia, is cooled by winds from Argos. Agamemnon's tomb, below the citadel, is hive-shaped. The stonework, unseen in the time of the incumbent, under gold, bronze, and jeweled lading, is as smoothly chamfered as an Inca wall. The actual tomb, in an adjoining room with no outside entrance of its own, is totally dark. Mr. Spyrakis sets a newspaper afire and thrusts it inside, to expose a possible snake, he says, adding that a woman was bitten here only a few days ago. However fitting as retribution for a despoiler of Agamemnon's grave, the story abruptly terminates my visit. We go to Epidaurus, where bee farms and pine woods provide relief. The amphitheater is surprisingly human-sized, after all the pictures that make it look like Hollywood Bowl. A photographer in an artist's smock ducks his head under a small black tent and emerges with a portrait of us.

By the time we reach Nauplia, the mountains are purple and the bay is rippling with boats. We climb Palomedes Rock, but the lions of St. Mark on the walls seem a glib emblem compared to the great Lion Gate at Mycenae. After dark, the quay becomes a *corso* for the whole population, ourselves included. Some small boys ferret us out, shouting "Stick-em-up!" and "Bang-bang!" followed by torrents of Greek that the cowboys and gangsters in American films do not know.

July 17. Part of the road to Nemea is bordered by bamboo. Green, mountain-girdled, with a temple to Zeus tumbled in a deep field, and the cave of Hercules-and-the-lion—a cave, in other religions, for Zarathustra, Milarepa, Jerome—Nemea, hereafter, will be my vision of the Valley of the Blest.

July 18. Athens. Letter from Marilyn Horne: her father, still in his early forties, has died from leukemia. Two dozen books from London. Also, a letter from Boulez about my Domaine Musical concert, saying it would help if I.S. could attend and that he is aware of what I have done for contemporary music and for him.

Sunion. Here on the windy cape, where Daedalus begat Icarus, is the

1956 Greece of our prejudices and, which comes to the same thing, child-picturebook imaginations: the Temple of Poseidon is white, comparatively intact—despite visitors' names, Byron's among them, scratched on most surfaces—and it stands above blue seas. Broken columns shine in the shallow water below the temple, where they have fallen.

At 6, a visit from John Pappaionou, who brings scores by Skalkottas.

July 19. To Istanbul in a nonpressurized and very shaky TAE airplane. Good views of Chios and Lesbos, of the Turkish coast and the sea of Marmora. Though the manager of the Hilton meets us at Customs, he has no rooms for Lawrence and myself, and we will be obliged to sleep in cabanas by the pool.

We enter the city via crumbling ancient walls and the Golden Horn bridge. The balcony of the S.s' rooms overlooks the Bosphorus and across to the Asian side, with the Tower of Leander, in the straits, directly in front. In the restaurant—shashlik and shishkebab—our waiter is a German who says he was captured at Stalingrad but escaped and made his way here from the Crimea. The local black market exchange, he tells us, is at least 10 times the official rate, which is virtually ignored.

July 20. Drive along the Bosphorus to the gates of the Symplegades, then back to see the remains of Constantine's palace and the pavement between palace and port entirely in mosaics.

July 21. I am awakened at 2 A.M. by Americans, black-market Turks, and girls in bikinis—one generation from the veil—splashing and shouting in the pool. Miss Betty Karp comes from the U.S. Consulate to change our dollars at the 9 lire rate, and to obtain my transfer from the poolside cubicle to a room.

July 23. The R. W. Blisses (I.S.'s former patrons) invite us to join their motor-launch excursion on the Bosphorus. Decaying villas and palaces line the shore the whole way. Some of them are architecturally inventive in a Rube Goldberg, Toonerville Gothic way, some, with Alpine roofs, look like Black Forest cottages, and some imitate Venice, approaching the water stepwise or standing to their ankles in it. Almost all are unpainted, and most have a large number of shuttered windows. The plainest of them remind us of the old clapboard frame houses now being razed in downtown Los Angeles.

We navigate close to the European side, then, at the cordon marking the channel to the Black Sea, cross to Asia and return along the far shore to the pink villa of Pierre Loti. As we enter the Golden Horn, the President of Pakistan is debarking from a Turkish battleship; a motorcade of Cadillacs awaits him on shore. Our route back to the hotel leads through a street called "Pig Alley" because of a shop selling pork to giaours.

July 24. Kariye Djami, near the Adrianople Gate, has been severely damaged by earthquakes, and as many as a third of the frescoes have been washed away in the resulting leaks. Muslim pargeting has preserved the others, most completely the anastasis in which the resurrected Christ joins hands with Adam and Eve in a jubilant dance. The Last Judgment, in the eastern domical vault, is partly obscured by bandage-like scaffolding, but not the Paradise, a cool white park abundantly stocked with birds and beasts and partitioned by small, easily fordable rivers; and not the Hell, a dark hole with a long funnel too small to receive the multitudes being driven there after their souls have been found wanting on the Simasis, which looks like a grocer's scales. A young restorer from Dumbarton Oaks tells us that this very morning, during the cleaning of one of the frescoes, a Simeon Stylites was discovered at the top of a column. The mosaics are even richer, especially the portraits of Christ's ancestors in the vestibule dome, the portraits of a leper with black sores, of a donor in oriental hat and costume, and a baptism scene in which a large fish swallows a white eel. The mosaic restorers work like dentists and in fact use dental tools.

July 25. To the archeological museum, Suleiman's Mosque, and the Bajazet Mosque, then across the Bosphorus in a ferry for a view of Istanbul from the other shore.

July 26. Another sleepless night, this time owing to bedbugs. I place the corpses of three of them in an envelope, which V. empties on the desk of the registering clerk in full view of a line-up of horrified tourists.

On the outside, where an old man in a tarboosh helps us into felt galoshes, the Blue Mosque is pearly gray, the color of the sacred pigeons in its yard. The inside is flooded with blue light from tiles in the direct aim of the dome and side windows. I.S. is impressed by the feeling of unity in the single large room, so different from a many-chapeled church, but he objects to the absence of iconography, adducing it as a sign of the "abstractness" of the religion. The legs of the Mosque are four great columns, sequoia trees in girth. Next to the two front ones are grandfathers' clocks, gifts from Queen Victoria. Though incongruous as furniture, the fact of them, of clock-time in a place of prayer, excites I.S.'s interest more than anything else. Some worshippers enter, carrying their shoes in their hands, then salaam, touching their heads to the rug-covered floor. The men congregate on a dais at what would be the place of the altar in a church, while the women, veiled and shawled, squat in a corner at the farthest remove from them. When an imam enters, shouting, everyone stands and a small boy diverts himself by running over the floor in his stockinged feet. Near the right wall is the hassock for the Koran reader, and in front of it the circle for the ulema, the exegetes and disputants—further evidence, I.S. says, of the religion's scholasticism. The minbar, a pulpit-shaped paladin, projects from the center wall. Next to it is a balcony enclosed by gold lattice—for the Sultan's wives, a hen-yard on stilts. As we leave, a muezzin is chanting from one of the minarets, and the faithful are washing their feet in stone troughs along the outer wall.

Hagia Sophia, in comparison, is an empty, dirty, stale-smelling turn-of-

1956 the-century railway station, except for large round plaques, green like the Prophet's robe and inscribed in gold with mottoes from the Koran, hanging like banners from the aisle columns. A flippant and familiar would-be guide attaches himself to us and becomes abusive when we fail to see the features of the Empress Theodora in the grain of a marble wall. Escaping him, we climb a dark ramp to the balconies. The upstairs floors seem to weave and sway, and the columns to thrust out from the center. The Seraglio is decaying, ill-kept, and reeking of dust and urine. A throne-seat extends over the pool like a cameraman's "dolly," presumably for the Sultan to watch his wives at their baths, but to imagine the place as Ingres populated it is impossible. The jewel collections are closed, and instead we are shown kilns for porcelain and glass manufacture and garish examples of the products of both.

July 27. An American Embassy car takes us to the airport, where photographs of the sinking *Andrea Doria* fill all newspapers. We fly over brown land, and, southeast of the Dardanelles, swamps and snaky rivers. Coastal Asia Minor is verdant, hilly, dotted with thatched-roof villages, and Lesbos is white and barren. In Athens, Dr. Doxiades is waiting for I.S. at the hotel.

July 28. I.S. tapes a message to be broadcast by the BBC in connection with the Hamburg Opera's Edinburgh performances of *Oedipus Rex* and *Mavra*. In the afternoon we sail from Piraeus on the S.S. *Mediterranean*, a small, decrepit, and overcrowded steamer, whose top deck is covered with the pitched tents of a troop of Boy Scouts. Two hours later, a tugboat siphons us through the deep narrow ditch of the Corinth Canal. The sides, just above the catwalks, are incised with the names of wartime guards. In the Gulf and the Adriatic sea, we watch the lights of boats all night long.

July 29. Brindisi harbor is dirty and its docks are piled with coal; difficult to imagine the Brindisium of *The Death of Virgil*. At tea time, in the lounge of our miserable boat, a banjo, accordion, and violin, the saddest orchestra I have ever heard, play "Dinah."

July 30. A breathless morning. Venice is a mirage of bell towers, then the green of S. Erasmo. A mustache of small boats escorts us into the Grand Canal and to a dock in the Canal of the Giudecca. On shore, the S.s count their 30 bags over and over, like rosary beads.

The city is hot and choked with tourists. At night we go to Pirandello's *Liola* at the Fenice. Letters for me from Darius Milhaud (about Satie's *Le Piège de Meduse*) and Dallapiccola, who says that he finds his

> signature and the date, March 18, 1921, on a collection of Gesualdo madrigals. I tell you this not to display my "advanced" mentality at the age of 17, but to thank you for having given me the first chance of my life (!!!!) to hear the *color* of Gesualdo. . . . I

congratulate you with all my heart for having accomplished a task **1956** which has always been at the limits of the possible. Two days ago I received a letter from our dear, lovely Magda Laszlo, who mentioned that you had done a fine job conducting two of my "Greek" works, so I must express my indebtedness for the second time. A day before the record came, I received the program of the Ojai Festival: there was no return address, but since *"non c'e il due senza il tre,"* I believe I should be thanking you for the third time. Please give my warm regards to the Maestro and Mme Stravinsky, and, most importantly, I hope your work goes well. Fondest regards.

July 31. The first joy of being in Venice is having it just outside the door. According to tradition, Fra'Mauro from the Island of San Michele had just finished his map of the world when a Venetian Senator saw the work and asked the cartographer: *"Dove Xella Venezia?"* *"La xe qua,"* Fra'Mauro answered, indicating a *puntino* on the map. "Why so small?" the Senator demanded, and Fra'Mauro explained that the point was in proportion to the whole world. "Then make the world smaller and Venice larger."

August 1. The Piazza tonight is an opera set, with soldiers, beggars, *raggazzi,* lovers, lovers-for-money, each in sufficient numbers to form a chorus. But musical quality is missing: whereas the gondoliers of the *cinquecento* improvised *giustiniani* to texts by Ariosto, their crooning, caterwauling descendants offer "Santa Lucia."

August 2. V. says that the façade of S. Francesco della Vigna, is "in Palladio's best First National Bank style," but I.S. defends it as "imposing." However this may be, it would look better in the large open space shown in Canaletto, being so encroached upon now that scarcely half can be seen from the end of the Campo. San Lorenzo, nearby, is no less rudely crowded by newer buildings, and would also benefit from wider dominion, except that its façade has long since been stripped of stone, and its brick underclothes have become a hanging garden of weeds. Still another neighborhood Palladian masterpiece dying of dilapidation is San Pietro di Castello, whose white, tipsy *torreloggia,* by Coducci, is one of the most beautiful in Venice. Yet these churches are in good condition compared to Santa Maria Maggiore, once praised by Burney for the quality of its music. The exterior is more than normally testudinarious—all Venetian churches suffer from skin diseases—and the interior is a rat-infested ruin. The Rio Terra di Santa Maria Maggiore leads to a prison, where the name of the filled-in canal changes, perhaps with didactic intent, to Rio Terra "of the thinkers." Lively radio music blares over the walls, but when we pause to listen, a dark-faced guard on the parapet scowls and motions us on.

August 3. We visit five churches at vesper hour: San Nicolò dei Mendicoli, where the Seven Swords of the Seven Sorrows stab Our Lady of the Dolors through her black evening frock and badge-like silver heart;

1956 San Polo, where the Madoneta wears a halo of silver stars; San Sebastian, where the white stone flesh of the statue on the pediment is pierced by green, oxidized arrows; the Misericordia, where the Abbazia is pockmarked with untenanted statue-sockets; and San Anzolo Raffaelo, in which the antiphonal responses between a young priest and a congregation of old women are so lullingly mechanical that when one of his sentences is unexpectedly longer than the others, the *"Ora pro nobis"* breaks in too soon.

August 4. An open-air *Tosca* in the Campo San Angelo. The Scarpia is a seasoned wobbler with a blubbery *crescendo* on almost every note, and the Tosca's vibrato spreads at times to a minor third. The better spectacle is not in front, but around: every window with a view of the Campo is a family-circle loge. Talking about theaters indoors and out, I.S. says that what most impressed him in Bayreuth was the weblike blend of the orchestra from under the stage. "The music was still a headache, but a headache with aspirin." This leads to a remark about Tristan and Isolde: "Of course such people have to swallow philters before they can *do* anything."

A letter from Dallapiccola: "We are looking forward with great friendship and admiration to being with you."

August 6. I.S.'s piano arrives. Trussed in canvas and hawsers, it is pulleyed from the canal to his second-floor room like a mule up the side of a ship. Faint sounds escape through his door thereafter, the same notes over and over, like piano tuning. (I.S.: "My brothers used to call me the 'piano tuner,' because I would repeat a note that I liked.") Later, the hotel staff seem much relieved. They had evidently expected him to compose as "Liszt" and "Chopin" do in films, with cascades of sound and stormy passages.

August 9. A windy morning. Sea-size waves beat against the Fondamenta, and the sky rumbles like an empty stomach. At noon, heavy rain turns the Grand Canal green, which makes the white face of San Giorgio seem even whiter. We spend part of the day in museums and churches, starting with the illuminated manuscripts in the Correr. One of these, *Marco Polo in Tartaria*, intended to inspire terror of the Turk, is opened to a scene showing Christians skewered through the extremes of their digestive systems. Antonello's *Christ Lamented by the Angels*, in the adjoining room, is a deeply affecting picture. The dead Christ at the center is surrounded by shadowy angels, one of whom, directly behind, seems to have transferred its wings to the corpse. But this Christ is an Adonis, and his beauty, the glowing *morbidezza*, too fleshly.

Some of the tapestries in the San Marco Museum are woven in toto with different tones of gold: gold angels threaded on faded gold backgrounds, gold lions of St. Mark on gold maps of Venice framed with purled ropes of gold. The most striking tapestry is one composed entirely of geometric swatches—a collage of squares, arcs, circles, half-moons—all differently dyed. In another, a resurrection woven at Arras, the pure white diaphanous light of the Christ dazzles the waking Roman soldiers whose motley provides a corrupt contrast. But the Venetian climate is unkind to color, and we remember how luminous in comparison are the tapestries in the dry, cold Escorial.

August 10. A courtesy visit to the Patriarch, Cardinal Roncalli,* to request permission to perform the *Canticum Sacrum* in the Basilica of San Marco. His gondola ferries us at noon to a tunnel on the Rio Palazzo, where a clerical secretary guides us through passageways and up flights of stairs. Ushered into the presence, I follow I.S. bowing and kissing the proffered ring hand, and try to adjust to scarlet: the scarlet skullcap on the Cardinal, the scarlet *galero* on a credenza by his chair, the scarlet watered silk cape, the scarlet-lined soutane with scarlet buttons, the scarlet stockings, the scarlet-bordered and scarlet-beaded slippers, the scarlet sash over the abdomen—the abdomen of a woman about to be rushed to a maternity hospital.

The Cardinal's French is fluent and his talk worldly wise, which I do not expect, having imagined such a man living in seclusion. Surprises are sprung, as when, recalling his years as Nuncio in Sofia and Istanbul, he remarks that "Orientals are more profoundly religious than we Catholics." Telling us that he officiated at vernacular Masses in these cities, he observes, clearly aiming at Rome, "Stupidity is always stubborn, intelligence should be resilient." I.S.'s Russian Orthodoxy interests him, and I think he would like to discuss the Filioque Clause and the Monophysite heresy; but I.S.'s own attitude toward the Eastern and Western churches is a mystery at present, perhaps even to himself. Turning to the matter of the meeting, the Cardinal asks I.S. why he has chosen a passage from the "Song of Solomon" for performance in a Christian church. I try to come to his help by providing a quick rundown of the Old Testament "sacred symphonies" in San Marco itself, but while I talk, His Eminence twiddles the gold cross dangling on his stomach and this epigastric play nearly distracts me from my subject. Still, the argument from precedents seems to satisfy him, for he hoists his large croup from the chair—it is another surprise that such a *basso buffo* figure, and all that tropical plumage, actually moves—and, standing, bestows his benisons on ourselves and the concert. We depart, again genuflecting and bussing the ring, then sidling and scraping *al rovescio*. Before we leave the palace, the Cardinal escorts us to the throne room, site of the Doges' ambassadorial dinners, to show us an unexpected view of San Marco's plain brick back.

To Torcello, stopping at San Michele to place a wreath on Diaghilev's grave, but I.S. waits in the boat, superstitiously refusing even to put his foot on the island. The church, so white from the lagoon, is the darkest sepulcher inside.

* Elevated to the Tiara two years later as John XXIII.

1956 The Laguna Morta is alive with birds and barges, and the rhythm of the boatmen levering their poles in the mud and walking from bow to stern is hypnotic to watch. Though following a channel marked by telephone poles and buoys, we are nevertheless obliged to stop from time to time to free our propeller from seaweed. The sky is a mass of Turner-like billowing movements, and at times the horizon seems to be high in the air and our boat to be sailing upward. Near Torcello we pass a sandolo whose only passenger is a goat, an Edward Lear image.

Going to bed, my thoughts return to the morning visit with the Patriarch. I was not invited, but I.S. insisted that I come, I think in order to have a record of the meeting.

August 12. Lunch with Berman at Carletto's near Treviso, then to Passariano and the Villa Manin,* a huge horseshoe-shaped court, smelling of new-mown grass and jumping with white butterflies. At Aquileia, the floor of the cathedral is a mosaic depiction of the Jonah story and of marine life, the aquarium of Paradise. Angel fishermen with water-wings lasso ducks in a seascape that includes large, white-bellied fish, eels, octopuses, giant sea snails and sea urchins, a whale, leviathans and other mythical sea monsters. Waves are outlined in black, and the surface itself undulates, though whether this is a planned effect I cannot say. As we depart, a storm explodes in the Dolomites, leaving a double rainbow over the Grado lagoon. The chimneys in the Latisana and Portogruaro (the *Castello di Fratta*) region are bi-funneled, like tuning forks.

August 17. A letter from Dallapiccola: *"Cher Maître et ami, . . .* tomorrow morning I will send you the *Piccola Musica Notturna,* a kind of sketch that I wrote at the request of Scherchen and that I have not yet heard. . . . I've just finished the Five Cantos for baritone and several instruments. . . ."

August 18. A festive night. Spectators fill most of the city's four hundred gondolas and canopied traghettos, to which green branches and colored lanterns have been attached. A procession of floats competing for a prize sails from the Rialto to the Dogana, one of them carrying a *tableau vivant* Venus-in-a-fountain, another a giant flowerpot with tin butterflies whirling above. The Communist entry is a long black scow with a grim white dove. The largest boat is that of the "Monteverdi Banda," a misnomer if ever there was one.

August 20. To the Villa Pisani at Stra. The furniture in Napoleon's bedroom includes a sunken tub with built-in steps and a portable sedan-chair WC. Outside are belvederes, loggias, and stables with, between the stalls, small busts of horses like chess pieces. We bumble through the pur-

---

* Mrs. Stravinsky took numerous photographs of the statuary, colonnades, and landscaping of the Villa. Months later, when developed and enlarged, one of the pictures was discovered to have a portrait of I.S. in the background. The Stravinskys reproduced this vignette on a screen that stood in their living room until her death.

suit-of-love hedge-maze, which has little nooks in which to withdraw when the lady has been caught, like the drive-off spaces for changing tires on modern turnpikes.

At the Villa Contarini at Piazzola, the upward view from the main floor beyond two balconies is of a ceiling of nudes à la Bouguereau. The music room is in the shape of a lute.

The statuary, parks and ponds of the Barberigo Palace at Valsanzibio would make a perfect set for *Figaro*, Act IV. The gardens are sloped, for water pressure: the Barberigi liked to play *giocchi d'acqua*, dousing their guests from spouts concealed in the shrubbery and remotely controlled by the practical-joking hosts.

At the Villa Venier Balbi, the caretaker of the chapel shows us a horrifying collection of 26 mummified saints, after which we retreat to a café in the town of Monselice and fortify our nerves with grappas.

August 21. Dallapiccola's *Piccolo Musica* arrives, inscribed *"en témoignage d'admiration et d'amitié."* Also a letter from Elliott Carter saying that Mitropoulos turned down his Orchestra Variations. And a letter from Boulez proposing the 1st and 2nd Cantatas of Webern for my Paris program. Says he has gone over the score of *Canticum Sacrum* and finds it moving and beautiful, especially the *Ad Tres Virtutes*.

August 22. To Longhena's Santa Maria dei Derelitto, one of the orphanages (the Casa de Ricovero) that supplied players for the female orchestras of the Vivaldi period. The grotesques on the façade are now thought to be portraits of victims of neurofibromatosis (Rechlinghausen's Disease), instead of, as formerly, grizzly barbarians, but they are a Venetian motif, found in the doorway arches of the belfries of Santa Maria in Formosa, San Bartolomeo, and the Ponte de le Guglie, where they are more leonine than human. The mustachioed mouths gnash sabre-like fangs, except for one, convulsive or drunk, in which the tongue curls to the side. Directly above these monster heads are four *Telamoni*, and above them, on the cornices, statues of the Virtues, one of them black, like the Virgin in the Scalzi, another ringing a schoolbell, and a third with foundling babies in her arms.

Venetian lacks the soft "j"; hence Zulian, Zan Anzelo, "zorno" for "giorno" and "ze ne peux pas," this from Alessandro Piovesan, whose French reminds I.S. of Manuel de Falla's, in that "h" is substituted for "j" and that Falla also could not begin a word with "st": *"Mon cher Estravinsky."* The Venetian vulgo generally shortens as well as softens, *"figlio,"* for example, becoming *"fio."* The sharp-edged "c" is avoided, too, *"portego"* replacing *"portico," "siguro" "sicuro,"* and *"Mi digo"* (the accusative) *"Io dico."* The word "Doge" is softened to "Dose," and the name of the architect "Coducci" to "Codussi." Unlike Italian, double "l's" are not pronounced; *"stelle"* comes out as a palatal *"ste-ye."* English "sh" and "ch" sounds are not natural here: Merzeria replaces Merceria, Greghi replaces Greci, and I.S.'s ballet is called *Petruska*. The "n"

1956 is dropped in certain positions, as in Fracesca da Rimini, and dropped altogether as a double consonant: the Venetians say "Madona," not "Madonna." But I do not know why they say "*dasseno*" instead of "*davvero*."

August 23. My vaporetto from the Piazzale Roma takes on a horde of U.S. tourists at the Railroad Station. As the boat chunters down the Grand Canal, not one of them within earshot exclaims on the beauty of any of the buildings, though all of them laugh about flooded basements.

August 24. Letter from Aldous, exactly the way he talks:

> Dear Bob, I hope you are now safely in Venice. Your postcards from Greece were rather disquieting—so much heat, with all the attendant ills that flesh is heir to. What one has to suffer in the name of Culture! My nearest approach to Greece this summer has been in a fascinating book by Professor Dodds of Oxford, called *The Greeks and the Irrational*. Immensely learned, but lively and very enlightening. Greece seems to have been rational for about 150 years, from 350 to 200 BC. Before and after, what extraordinary manifestations (in spite of the Parthenon and Socrates, in spite of Roman efficiency and engineering) of the irrational. Read this book if you can get hold of it. [The] letter about your visit to Gesualdo was very interesting. I hope the locked chamber in the castle will finally be opened. What bliss if it contains an archicembalo! Count Chigi has written to thank me for the record, and says he is making the pupils of his Academy listen to it as a perfect example of madrigal singing. Why not pop in to see him at Siena? Meanwhile I hope all goes well with St. Mark and rehearsals. . . . Work continues. The play will go on, I hope and believe, as soon as DeLiagre can find a goddess. But the species is scantily represented in New York. . . .

And a letter from Gerald, the way *he* talks:

> Dear Bob, I am delighted that Mykenae struck you as much as it did me. The amazing way megalithic building seems to emerge without break from the geological formation so that man's works and nature's mountain building seem to be an unbroken sequence. I remember being there when the yellow soil had just been replowed, the almond trees were in blossom, the sky intense blue and white, and in the spring sunlight the great fastness itself a pale yellow, while in the so-called "beehive tomb" of Clytemnestra the peaked vault was patinated with honey and the whole place boomed like a bell as the bee swarms went out. We were told they sometimes attacked the tourists.
>
> Vera sent me a photograph of the Byzantine mosque which

April 7, 1948. New York. During an intermission at the author's first rehearsal with the composer. Alexei Haieff, to the author's left, was a composer and one of Stravinsky's closest friends.

An Evening of

STRAVINSKY MUSIC

with

THE CHAMBER ART SOCIETY

ROBERT CRAFT, Musical Director

Guest of Honor

IGOR STRAVINSKY

conducting

Assisting Artist

ELLY KASSMAN, pianist

SUN. EVE. - APRIL 11 at 8:30

TOWN HALL

113 WEST 43rd STREET

Concert Management RAY HALMANS, 119 West 57th Street, New York 19, N. Y.

An Evening of

STRAVINSKY MUSIC

1. Symphonies d'Instruments à vent 1920-47
   First Concert Performance
   (will be played twice)

2. Danses Concertantes 1941
   Marche—Introduction
   Pas d'Action
   Thème varié
   Pas de deux
   Marche—Conclusion

   Conducted by MR. STRAVINSKY

Intermission

3. Capriccio for Piano and Orchestra 1929
   Presto
   Andante raposdico
   Allegro capriccioso ma tempo giùsto giùsto

4. Symphony in C 1940
   First New York Concert Performance
   Moderato alle breve
   Larghetto concertante
   Allegretto
   Adagio: Tempo giusto alle breve

   Conducted by ROBERT CRAFT

   Baldwin Piano

TICKETS AT TOWN HALL BOX OFFICE

Loge Seats (6 in Loge) $4.20   -:-   Orchestra $2.40 and $3.60
Balcony $3.00, $2.40 and $1.80, Tax Included

April 11, 1948. Program of the first concert jointly conducted by Stravinsky and the author.

SYMPHONIE
EN UT
POUR ORCHESTRE

PAR

IGOR STRAWINSKY

❋

Partition d'orchestre	Edition Schott 3840
Parties d'orchestre	en location
Partition de poche	Edition Schott 3536

[handwritten inscription:] To Robert Craft in remembrance of his noble and discriminated performance in April 1948 (Town Hall, NY) Cordially, I Stravinsky May/48

B. SCHOTT'S SÖHNE
MAINZ: Weihergarten 5
PARIS: Editions Max Eschig
46 Rue de Rome

SCHOTT & Co. Ltd.
LONDON W.1: 48 Great Marlborough Street
NEW-YORK: 25 West 45th Str.
Associated Music Publishers Inc.

Printed in Germany — Imprimé en Allemagne

May 1948. The score of Stravinsky's Symphony in C inscribed "To Robert Craft in remembrance of his noble and discriminated performance in April 1948 (Town Hall, New York). Cordially, I. Stravinsky May/48."

1950
A note in Schoenberg's hand discovered after his death. Item 2 reads: "Do not discourage people, friends. They will break the Schbg Clique. Encourage Craft."

November 4, 1950. Los Angeles. Canon (1928), inscribed by Schoenberg: "Dear Mr. Craft, news of your performances are very enjoyable.—I possess one copy of this canon. I want you to check whether the bass voice fits also to five parts. I cannot remember whether I planned it so. It seems to me it should only be added when all the others sing. With cordial greetings, yours, Arnold Schoenberg."

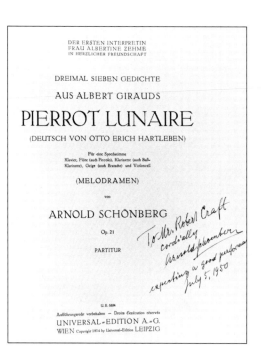

The score of *Pierrot Lunaire*, inscribed "To Mr. Robert Craft, Cordially, Arnold Schoenberg, expecting a good performance, July 5, 1950."

September 4, 1951. Arriving in Venice for the premiere of *The Rake's Progress*, with W. H. Auden and Chester Kallman, greeted by Ferdinando Ballo, Director of the Biennale's Fourteenth International Festival of Contemporary Music.

October 1951. Munich. Pause during a rehearsal of *Oedipus Rex*.

1952. Sketch for the Cantata, inscribed "To Bob whom I love. IStr, Easter/52."

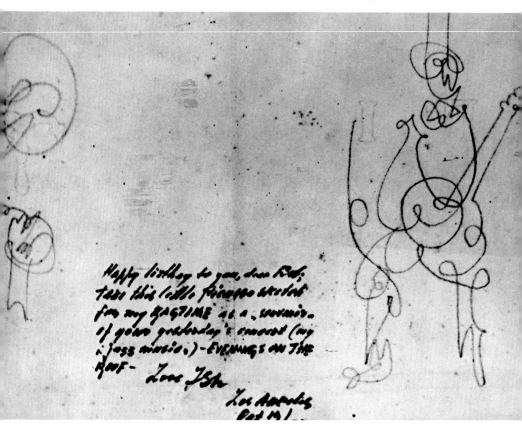

October 20, 1953. Picasso's one-line drawing for the cover of Stravinsky's *Ragtime*, inscribed "Happy birthday to you, dear Bob, take this little Picasso sketch from my RAGTIME as a 'souvenir' of your yesterday's concert (my 'jazz music')—EVENINGS ON THE ROOF—Love, IStr, Los Angeles, Oct 19/53."

September 2, 1957. Venice. With Giorgio di Chirico.

October 1954. Hollywood. With Aldous Huxley during a recording session of Gesualdo madrigals conducted by the author.

March 8, 1957. Royce Hall, UCLA. Left to right: Lucas Foss, Paul Des Marais, Pierre Boulez, Robert Craft.

October 16, 1955. Program of one of the Gesualdo concerts conducted by the author, which included a lecture by Aldous Huxley.

Music Society of Santa Barbara

October 16, 1955   -   Lobero Theatre

ALDOUS HUXLEY *and* THE GESUALDO MADRIGALISTS

Robert Craft, conductor

Grace-Lynn Martin, Marilyn Horne, sopranos
Cora Lauridsen, contralto
Richard Robinson, tenor
Charles Scharbach, bass

I. Four Madrigals by Carlo Gesualdo, Prince of Venosa
    Dolcissima mia vita   (c. 1560-1613)
    O dolorosa gioia
    Meraviglia d'amore
    Moro lasso

II. Mr. Huxley, speaking on "The Court of Ferrara and Gesualdo."

III. Four Madrigals by Gesualdo
    Ardo per te
    Tu piangi
    Ardita zanzaretta
    Luci serene e chiare

INTERMISSION

IV. A. Two Arias by Claudio Monteverdi (1567-1643)
    Lasciatemi morire
    Partenza amoroso
        Miss Horne

   B. Solo Ballata by Heinrich Isaac (c. 1450-1517)
    Mostrarsi adirata di fore
        Mr. Robinson

   C. Four Madrigals by Gesualdo
    Ecco moriro dunque
    Tu m'uccidi o crudele
    Io tacero
    Itene o miei sospiri

This program is produced by the Monday Evening Concerts of Los Angeles

March 9, 1957. Hollywood. In the control room at Radio Recorders during the author's recording session of Schoenberg's Serenade, with Pierre Boulez and Lawrence Morton.

December 3, 1958. London.
With the T. S. Eliots.

August 1959. Princeton. With Roger Sessions
(next to Stravinsky) and Edward T. Cone.

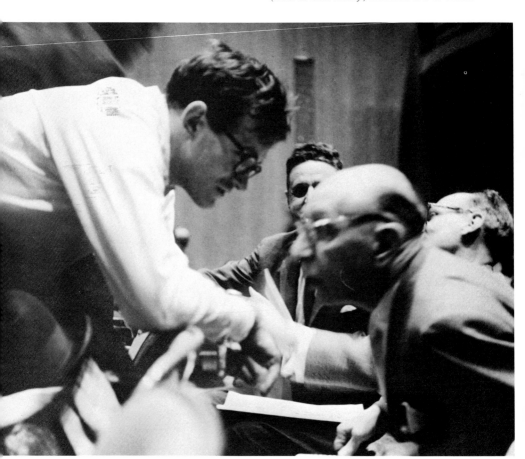

January 2, 1959. New York. Intermission during a rehearsal of *Threni* at the Metropolitan
Museum of Art. Milton Babbitt and Paul Fromm are seated to the composer's right.

Photo by Robert Emmet Bright.

October 15, 1959. In the courtyard of the Prince of Venosa's palace at Gesualdo.

October 14, 1959. Paestum. Stravinsky's signature is visible in the lower right.

tried to outspan Hagia Sophia and I have it on my desk. Byzantine **1956** history has a kind of ingrown self-sufficiency which didn't mask a great deal of sadistic punishment. I am particularly glad that you saw the little mosque by the wall which was used by the last Emperors for their orthodox worship. The mosaics there were a revelation as to what would have happened to that art had it been kept from becoming archaic and then revived as archaistic. Now, of course, you are on the run again and have ceased to be a private person. I look forward keenly to your triple return in January.

One is always finding out new things and seeing new correlates in this epileptic world. Somehow today I think aesthetics and philosophy plus psychotherapy are making a curious and almost agonized amalgam. Aldous, Bill Fortman, myself, all went with an electronics LSD medical friend to the huge exhibition yesterday. It was held in huge tents with the temperature somewhere in the nineties and smog at an almost record-breaking intensity. It was a strange experience and a kind of stretching of the mind to see our human incompetence, to understand our specialties and the incessant machines like steel insects building this comb of coordinated knowledge and spinning their webs of restricted reactions. . . . I am sure that kind of thing is an active extension of what William James advised as a necessary strenuous therapy—at least once a week to read for an hour something that is so much above one's head that one has only a ghost of what the whole thing is about. The mind is stretched, tolerance increased, and that flexibility of emotion called "humility," I think, is augmented. After which I was summoned off to a meeting with the chief of staff of Alcoholics Anonymous for the rest of the evening. Somehow I felt there was a connection between these apparently irrelevant interests.

Please give my love to Vera and the Maestro. I hope his strength has kept up during the tour and that he has enjoyed himself. . . . Take care of him in the awful isle of England. It is a gaunt climate and probably can be best endured by those who abandon all hope of any comfort in this life. . . . If you have time send me another note. . . . With best wishes to all you three. Affectionately, Gerald.

August 25. With Berman to Pomposa. The brick walls are inlaid with ornamented window-like circles containing high and low reliefs of Byzantine birds and animals, but the intricate motifs remind me of Celtic art. The church, with frescoes all the way around, is a whirl of color. I.S. sees a scorpion on the floor of the Abbey and, like Wotan with Brünnhilde, lights a fire around it. We spend the afternoon in Ferrara admiring the Schifanoia frescoes.

1956   August 26. Venetian night sounds: the lap of waves on stone; the plash of oars; their grating in the tholepins; the clatter of the *saracinesche* (the iron shutters on shop fronts) at sundown; the gondoliers' "OEI"— which seems louder at night probably because their black water-limousines glide by so quietly—and the voices of gondoliers arguing (what are they always arguing about?); the shouted numbers from a *tombola* on the Lido (*"tren-ta-du-e"*); the hooting of ships as they arrive and depart in the canal of the Giudecca; the singing of women in houses in the *calli*, strong and vibrant in the morning when they are spreading laundry, but quiet and gently palpitating at night; the bells of San Trovaso at nones, in two pitches and two speeds, and the bells of San Marco at midnight. At that hour I walk to the frieze of the drunken Noah at the bridge corner of the Doge's palace. Eyes closed in semi-slumber, the old man swoons and, for support, holds the trunk of the vine, in which I count twelve birds singing.

August 27. After dining at Harry's Bar with Berman and Mary McCarthy, we go to the Chiostro Verde and a Vivaldi concert by the Virtuosi di Roma. Seven concerti are played with no sense of style and no ornaments—the trills, turns, embellishments, appoggiaturas that the music requires. In passages for solo instruments and basso continuo, even the harmony is not filled in.

August 28. To the opening of the International Film Festival on the Lido. Seeing Serge Lifar in the seat next to the one reserved for I.S., V. quickly arranges a switch to avoid a confrontation. With the arrival of Lollobrigida, pandemonium breaks out, as reporters and cameramen shouting "Gina" converge on her in the seat directly in front of mine; I.S., and, in the row behind us, Artur Rubinstein and Maria Callas, have escaped unnoticed. The goddess, a peasant girl in manners and bearing, seems to be in a daze. Thanks to flash-bulbs, we are still seeing purple spots for the first half-hour of the film, *Der Hauptmann Von Koepenick*, after which we leave.

August 29. I try to invent a vocabulary of English words pronounceable as Italian, for use in shops and restaurants where both English and Italian are understood. A "bad one," for example, becomes the 3-syllable *"badone."*

We photograph the Rizzo statue on the canal side of the Palazzo Guaro ("Othello's House"); the acroterial angels on the pediment of S. Teodoro; the Hebrew inscriptions, faded but still visible, over doorways in the Ghetto; a persimmon tree in a walled garden near the Madona dal'Orto; and the Shakespearean name "Gobbo" over the door of a small hotel in the Campo S. Geremia. The shrines (*edicole*) on the corners of buildings, tawdry images in glass cubicles with iron gratings, are remembered with flowers by day, candles by night, and at both times passersby drop coins inside and cross themselves.

August 30. *Time*, August 27, reviews my Schoenberg record.

August 31. I.S. works on *Agon*, interrupted only by a brief visit from

Soulima and son at 4 and by Nuria Schoenberg and Luigi Nono at 6.

September 1. I.S. works on *Agon* all morning at the pink piano in the hotel nightclub, undeterred by ghosts of dance music and the stale odors of half-smoked cigars, but he complains of the difficulty in "composing my dry music in this humidity: to live in Venice is to live in a glass of water." Emerging for lunch, he remarks that "a series is a facet and serial composition is a crystallizing, a way of presenting several sides of the same idea." Enantiomorphs? A TV crew films I.S. throughout our rehearsal in the Fenice.

September 2. We drive to Urbino with Lucia Davidova. Tiberius' bridge still stands over the Rubicon, beyond the flat, sandy, umbrella-pine country south of Ravenna and the open stretches of sea. At the Tempio Malatestiano we are obliged to wait for a wedding before being admitted to Piero's *S. Sigismondo*. South of the San Marino mountain, the road turns from the coast and climbs through the landscape of the *quattrocento* painters, the terraces, and hairpin roads, the brown soil, the yoked pairs of oxen. The Pieros, Raphaels, and Uccello's *Profanation of the Host*, in which the Devil has been badly scratched by literal-minded zealots, are in the Ducal Palace's small upstairs rooms with brick floors, whitewashed ceilings and large fireplaces. To live here must have been cozy, if you were the Duke. The view from his bedroom window, to beyond the parapet, his mistress's private bridge, to the dry, whitening, Umbrian hills can scarcely have changed in five hundred years.

September 4. Venice. Nuria, Luigi Nono, and Vladimir Golschmann for lunch. With the Rubinsteins to Segovia's concert in the courtyard of the Palazzo Pisani.

September 5. At the Colomba Restaurant, Sacheverell Sitwell; and Lifar, whom I.S. ostentatiously snubs.

September 10. Our first rehearsal in St Mark's Basilica. An article in *Time*, "The Mad Madrigalist," refers to me as the "Young California conductor."

September 11. Virgil Thomson for lunch. He is quick and enviably lucid, and his fluency and control are the attributes of both a high intelligence and an enormous conceit. He works his bright blue eyes for all they are worth, now narrowing them as if to focus a subject more clearly, now popping them open as if to indicate the need for a larger point of view. More loquacious after wine, he takes even less trouble to conceal his vanity. Later, I.S. says that something about Virgil makes him think of a turtle. The chelonian gullet?

September 12. Rehearsal in the Basilica. Acoustical difficulties. I.S.: "We need blotting paper, not echo chambers." With I.S. to a concert to hear a piece dedicated to him by Nabokov.

September 13. At 8 P.M., the Biennale motoscaffo deposits us at an entrance to the Basilica from the Rio di Palazzo. The whole interior glows red from candles enclosed in red glass under the immense Greek cross sus-

1956 pended from the center ceiling. I enter from the chancel, bow to Cardinal Roncalli in the first row, and, before the *Canticum Sacrum*, begin the program with two pieces by Andrea Gabrieli, Giovanni Gabrieli's *In Ecclesiis*, Monteverdi's *Lauda Jerusalem* and *Pulchra es* (Marilyn Horne and Magda Laszlo), Schütz's *Es ging ein Sämann aus*. After about a minute into the first Gabrieli, a photographer's bulb drops from one of the balconies and explodes like a bomb; I fear that the audience will stampede, but instead it becomes less noisy. Twenty minutes after the conclusion of the concert, I.S. walks through the Piazza accompanied by the applause of hundreds of people who have heard the music there on loudspeakers. Late dinner at the Taverna with Nadia Boulanger and Nabokov.

September 15. I.S. gives me a jewelled gold wristwatch as a memento of the concert. Piovesan's *Musiche Religiosi di Stravinsky* is published. A letter from Boulez about my Paris program.

September 18. To Chioggia in the Biennale motoscaffo. Lunch at Sottomarina: a huge cake with, on the icing, a musical notation and "I.S." Back in Venice, we attend Balanchine's opening at La Fenice. Dinner at the Martini afterward with U.S. Ambassadors Charles Bohlen (Russia) and Llewellyn Thompson (Austria), two polylingual—the conversation is in Russian—as well as polished American gentlemen.

September 24. Turin. Letter from Boulez noting that the timings are much shorter than the publishers' estimates and proposing to add the *Japanese Lyrics* and Webern's Concerto for Nine Instruments to the program.

September 25. After recording Schoenberg's Five Pieces and the excerpts from *Le Martyre de St. Sébastien*, I go to the Palazzo Madama: Antonella's man in red and black, with grass-like brows, is skeptical of his portraitist. To the Risorgimento Palace, the Egyptian Museum (Galleria Sanauda), the church of the Consolata, where the sacristy walls are covered with ex votos commemorating the deaths of soldiers in the Ethiopian War, and San Giovanni, the repository of the Turin Shroud.

September 26. The 12:30 *rapido* to Milan, in rain all the way, the muddy Po overflowing into the rice fields. Stops at Vercelli and Novara, the two most enlightened cities of the mid 10th-century (Leo of Vercelli and Stephen and Gunso of Novara). A bumpy flight from Malpensa to Frankfurt and Berlin (Tempelhof), where I.S. meets me with Nabokov, Gerhard von Westermann, and Eric Winkler. On the way to the Kempinsky Hotel, I.S. says he is not feeling well and asks me to rehearse for him.

September 27. Wolfgang Stresemann presents me to the RIAS Orchestra, with which I work for six hours on both the 1940 and the 1945 symphonies. Most of the streets to and from the studio are bordered by empty, rubble-filled lots and bombed remnants of buildings.

September 28. Rehearsals 9–12 and 2–5, strings, then winds. After tea and schnapps with Balanchine, we go to the Städtische Oper for Busoni's

Faust, a stunning production. Staged as a series of *tableaux vivants*, four scenes are unforgettable: the Duchess of Parma, the Queen of Sheba, the Helen of Troy, and—the high point—the Lutherans, surrounded by Catholics, singing *Ein feste Burg*. Fischer-Dieskau is the Faust. The music—the organ part, choruses, waltzes, dances, harmonies—owes nearly everything to Liszt, but the beginning is too long, Philip Jarnach's contributions are feeble, and the staging is the chief element in the success, not the score.

Again to the Städtische Oper to see Henze's *König Hirsch*, or, rather, from a loge over the orchestra pit, to watch Scherchen conduct it. He is said to have had 58 rehearsals, which, because *I* could not bear to hear any of it twice, is difficult for me to believe. He comes to pay his respects to I.S.: good English, a high, piping voice.

October 1. In the fenced-off ruin of a synagogue, across the street from the hotel, bits of the tabernacle are visible even after the Nazis and the 1945 bombings. The entrance to the exhibition at the Hochschule für Kunst—where we see the huge but faded and ripped curtain of *Parade*—is flanked by posters with ponderous quotations from Heidegger. Dinner with Paulette Goddard and Erich Maria Remarque, longtime friends of the S.s; Remarque was in love with V. in the early Hollywood years.

October 2. I.S.'s concert (Sender Freies Berlin) in the Titania Palast: thunder and strong rain. The performances are agonizingly ragged because the players are used to me and not at all to him. Near the end of the first movement of the Symphony in C, he stops conducting and the orchestra plays the last measures by itself. The second movement begins after an unconscionable pause. During intermission, he tells us that he had blacked out. But he somehow manages to get through the long program.

October 3. I.S.'s speech is slurred and he has difficulty writing his name. Complaining of numbness on the right side of his body, he struggles to coordinate his movements but refuses to see a doctor and, instead, goes for a drive in Zehlendorf.

After six hours with the third-rate RIAS strings—their intonation is approximate, their rhythm inexact, their articulation unclear, their tone lusterless—I succeed in taping only the first movement of Berg's *Lyric Suite*. Mozart's C-minor Fugue goes better, but how could it not? Scherchen comes for a late supper of goose livers, strudel, sekt.

October 4. To Munich at noon, in an air corridor and at a low altitude. East German roads are virtually empty. Karl Amadeus Hartmann drives us to the Hotel Vier Jahreszeiten. I.S.'s numbness and loss of balance are worse; he complains of an excruciating headache. Yet this hypochondriac who will take his temperature and pulse several times a day when nothing is wrong with him still refuses to see a doctor. I insist that Hartmann call one anyway, and at 5 a Professor Diehl examines him, tells me that his reflexes are poor, that he has suffered a stroke, and that a "massive" one is a

1956 possibility within 24 hours. Returning in the evening, Diehl says that the blood pressure is still 200.

October 6. The blood preasure is down, but I.S.'s mouth droops at the left side and he is slow and weak. Hartmann announces the cancellation of the concert.

October 7. With the Hartmanns. He talks about Webern, with whom he studied for two years, much of that time in analyzing Webern's piano Variations from the manuscript, which, rolled and tied in ribbons, he would fetch from a bureau drawer and carefully unfold at the piano. Hartmann says that Webern's daughters refuse to believe even now that his music has any value and could possibly interest anyone. He also says that Webern's wife forbade him to hide David Bach, Schoenberg's Jewish pupil, on grounds that the family must be protected first. According to Hartmann, Webern was so frightened of his termagant spouse that "when I trekked some dirt on the rug, he hurried to sweep it up before she came into the room."

Walterspiel, the celebrated restaurateur, personally prepares a dinner for I.S.: shrimps on bread with a sauce, partridge, soufflé, Mosel and red wines—hardly a meal for a man who has had a stroke, but I.S. devours it. Afterward, Walterspiel brings a guestbook containing the signatures of, among others, Hermann Goering.

October 8. The two volumes of Henry Wotton's letters arrive. He describes dolphins in the canal of the Giudecca.

October 9. Dr. Maurice Gilbert comes from Geneva, consults with Diehl, tells us that another thrombosis could paralyze I.S.'s left side, and pleads that, if for no other reason, 10 years of composing should not be jeopardized by a concert appearance. Unfortunately, none of this is repeated to I.S. Telegrams pile up as a result of announcements about the stroke in the press. Balanchine calls from Frankfurt.

October 10. As should have happened six days ago, I.S. enters the Rote Kreuz Hospital on Nymphenburgstrasse. Diehl now openly discusses the thrombosis with us and the possibility of recurrence. We are at I.S.'s bedside all day.

October 11. "What happened to me?" I.S. asks when I enter his room this morning. He still has that fish-out-of-water look, is still slow, distant, and easily agitated. "One side feels as if it were on a different level from the other. I try to force my brain, but it is an effort for me to talk." He does talk, but self-recriminatingly, accusing his brain of being unclear. That he is unable to manage an orchestra rehearsal, let alone a concert, is obvious, yet Diehl has already given permission for him to conduct in Rome. A get-well telegram comes from the orchestra in, of all places, Dresden.

October 12. I.S. is livelier today, but perhaps artificially. V. and I go with the Hartmanns to Ilgen and Die Wies. Near Ilgen, overlooking the

Ammer, is the Schloss that had been picked for Mussolini's exile in 1944. The Ilgen church is white and gold, with silver candlesticks and a silver dove over the pulpit. In the balcony, above the organ pipes, angels blow trumpets and play psalters. Die Wies is larger and more ornate, the pulpit is borne aloft as if it were a chariot, and tritons gush water. The walls are covered by ex-votos for men captured at Stalingrad. High on the altar is a silver lamb.

A warm day. The grass is still green but snow has fallen on the lower Alps. In the Starnbergersee, a cross marks the place where Ludwig II and his physician drowned. A region of onion-domed baroque churches, white, gold, and silver inside and always full of music: organs in balconies or lofts, trumpeting angels, bells. But I am homesick today for the untidy landscapes of America, the less spectacular mountains, the wilderness, the green barns of Massachusetts. We stay with I.S. in the hospital on our return, then dine in the hotel, chatting afterward with Klemperer and daughter Lotte.

October 14. Signs of I.S.'s old strength. He tells us of his fears of paralysis during the past twelve days, of realizing that the decision to live or die was "in the power of my brain."

October 16. Train to Lausanne among passengers speaking Romansch. More painful even than the sound of that language are my feelings of guilt for having left the S.s in Munich. She is distraught, living on pills, and her own blood pressure is too high. They need me now, and since I do not want to leave, why do I?

October 17. Rehearse the Lausanne Radio Orchestra in Haydn No. 99. During lunch at the Centrale with Theodore and Denise Stravinsky, I decide to go to Munich with them in their car. Evening rehearsal: the *Begleitmusik*, which I like and the orchestra hates, and *Danses concertantes*, which the orchestra likes and I do not like very much.

October 18. Lunch with Dr. Gilbert, who drives me to the Klee show in Bern: 756 objects, including unknown-to-me sculptures and juvenilia.

I rehearse for two hours before and up to the hour-long broadcast, and after the concert drive with the Theodores to Morat, where we wake the doorman of the Hotel des Terrasses and spend the night in unheated rooms.

October 19. Lunch at the Kronenhalle, Zurich, where the walls are adorned by Picassos, Braques, Klees, Bonnards, and a photo of James Joyce inscribed to the owner. Winterthur, Lake Constance, and the ferry to Germany: fields, forests, orchards; Ravensberg, Waldsee, Ulm, and, on an Autobahn roadsign, the horrifying name "Buchenwald." In Munich we go directly to the hospital, where V. tells me that I.S. has been asking for me all day but does not want to see the Theodores—which they overhear.

October 20. Marilyn Horne comes for a birthday dinner, my second in, of all places, Munich. I.S., no longer confined to bed, would have been released from the hospital today except for the massages and other therapy

1956 administered there.

October 23. Diehl tells I.S. the whole truth about his condition, hoping to frighten him into giving up smoking, but the attempt is only partly successful: I.S. insists on five cigarettes a day. Why doesn't Diehl *order* him to stop? The death of Walter Gieseking, reported by a nurse, upsets I.S.

A letter from Boulez for I.S., who gives it to me to answer, concerning the organ for the *Canticum Sacrum*. The one in the Salle Gaveau has been dismantled, and no other Paris hall has a suitable one. He suggests the substitution of an electric instrument, an Alexander or a Hammond, and, for the recording, renting a Catholic or a Protestant church—except that most church organs, even good ones, are not tuned properly, and would not match the intonation of the wind instruments.

October 28. Two telephones from Boulez and a letter saying that he will be playing his *Structures* in Munich with Yvonne Loriod, but that he would prefer to have I.S. attend the performance of his own work in Paris than to hear his (Boulez's) in Munich.

October 29. Another letter from Boulez about the number of violas and basses required for *Vom Himmel hoch* and *Canticum Sacrum*. He has not yet seen the orchestra scores.

October 30. Lunch with Lotte Klemperer. Franz Waxman comes to ask for the concert premiere of *Agon* in a 75th anniversary concert for I.S. in Los Angeles. To the *pinacoteca*: Andrea del Castagno's marvelous portrait of a man with red turban; Lippo Memmi's *Ascension of Mary*, in which angels in a circle play a great variety of musical instruments; a picture of St. Julian murdering his parents in their bed at night.

October 31. A telegram from Boulez saying that the parts and scores for the *Canticum* have not yet come. Boris Blacher, drunk, flushed, hiccoughing, joins us in the hotel dining room.

November 1. With Lotte Klemperer, whose mother is expected to die at any moment.

November 2. The war scare is so great that the S.s are thinking of going to Geneva. Anti-British feeling is especially strong because, in the German view, Russia would not have dared to reenter Hungary, with the whole world cheering the Hungarians on, if Britain had not diverted attention to herself with the landings in Egypt. Bonfires are burning at several street corners, and crowds have gathered around them to protest the Soviet invasion.

November 3. The 12:47 "Mozart Express" for Paris, after a sad departure from the S.s. I finish Kitto's *The Greeks* before Strasbourg, where I have only three minutes in which to change trains. In the restaurant car of the crowded new one, Frenchmen with trenchermen's appetites slurp their soup, rain condiments on their food even before tasting it, mop plates with bread, and guzzle wines, cognacs, liquors. In Paris, the bomb-cratered factory cities of Germany seem a universe away. V. calls: Frau Klemperer is dead.

November 4. A gray Sunday. It is stamp-exchange day, and philatelists comparing their treasures huddle on the sidewalk of the Rond Point des Champs-Elysées across the street from my room. From my room, too, I hear the applause, boos, stomps, shouts of *"Oui!"* and *"Non!"* from children watching *guignol* in the park.

Boulez comes at noon, bringing his *Marteau* recording, and we eat downstairs in the Berkeley. He is balder, shorter, stockier, more solid in the solar plexus than I remember from 1952. Quick, precise, as lithe and springy as a bantam-weight boxer, and as sure of himself as if he were carrying an infallible plan of conquest in his pocket, he seems to me a mental creature primarily—this in contrast to I.S., a physical creature first, the rare escapee from what Nietzsche called the "violent severance from man's animal past." (In I.S., physical appetites and bodily gestures are often apparent before the mind comes out of hiding, for which reason, no doubt, the personality and self-identification of the physical gestures in the music are so immediate. Or, to put it differently, with I.S., "abstract thought"—for which he has an unlimited capacity, no matter how contemptuously he pretends to regard it—is never dissociated, or prescinded, from physical instinct.) Boulez's sexual nature is either neuter or very well hidden. He is charming, witty, and, in spite of a rapid nervous blink, even-keeled. The thought occurs to me—perhaps because he talks about *Un Coup de dés* ("Writers are in a worse way than composers, Mallarmé and Joyce already having done it all")—that with an eyeshade he would look like a croupier.

We speak our own languages, the arbitrary assignation of gender to every noun in French constituting an insurmountable obstacle for me, to say nothing of such problems of pronunciation as the proper palatalizing of the cacuminals. We seem about equally able to follow one another, too, except that the wines, which do not faze him, fuddle me.

His musical opinions having preceded him, we talk about my performance of his *Polyphonie X* in Los Angeles four years ago. He professes to be wholly immune from religious feelings, which tallies with his claim to be more interested in oriental than in Latin cultures, to the point of an aversion for all things Italian except spaghetti.

We go to his rue Beautreillis garret, not far from the Place de la Bastille on the street where Cézanne lived as a young man, climb four flights of stone stairs and two of wood. Every object and utility in this tiny lair conforms to the size of Boulez's script and musical detail: the small bed, desk, *salamandre*, reproduction of Klee's portrait of I.S., upright piano—on which he improvises a funny Brahmsian accompaniment to the beginning of the second movement of Schoenberg's Violin Concerto. His own manuscripts are rolled, tied like diplomas, and piled on the floor like logs.

At dinner with Françoise Stravinsky in the Milhaud apartment, 1 Blvd. Clichy, I learn that Tanaquil LeClerq has polio and is in a Copenhagen

1956 hospital. By the time I leave, the sidewalks teem with whores.

November 5. Lunch at the Sachs home with Marcelle de Manziarly, then to Mme Suzanne Tézenas, an attractive and hospitable woman, in striking contrast to the aggressive avant-garde paintings on her walls. From there I go to the Conservatoire to rehearse *"Surge, aquilo,"* and to the rue de la Visitation to rehearse the chorus, which is terrible and will not improve enough, then with Boulez to a restaurant near the Café Flore until 3 A.M. He is amusing about Messiaen (*"un bordel chrétien"*) and says that "the George Washington theme in *Ode to Napoleon* is pure César Franck."

November 7. Work with Ilona Steingruber at Boulez's: her pitch is perfect, her rhythm far from it, and she is often ahead of the beat.

Dinner with Boulez and Pierre Suvchinsky in a restaurant two Metro stops before the Pont de Neuilly: turbot and Sancerre; gigot and Richebourg; gateau St.-Honoré and raspberry liqueur.

Suvchinsky's hair is wintry; his handshake, in which the last two fingers do not engage, is limp; and his albino, tropical-disease complexion is mottled with patches of marchpane and pink. But these aspects are belying, for he is big-boned and *"robuste"* (a favorite word, near the top of the list after *"con"* and *"salaud"*), has a large appetite, and speaks in a loud (a Boanerges), though also a musical (a *viola pomposa*), voice. As if in compensation for the unhearty handshake, he crushes me with Russian bear hugs and smothers me with Russian-style, alternate-cheek kisses.

Despite 30 years in Paris, and Parisian modes of criticism formed before that, Suvchinsky is more Russian- than French-minded, and in some ways he reminds me of I.S. This Russianness—as I have come to think of it, for the qualities I have in mind are personal and individual first, Russian second—is characterized by an openness and volubility, a warmth formerly understood by the loaded word "aristocratic."

Suvchinsky is renowned for his talent in discovering talent, and his efforts to enlist support for it, entailing special difficulties in his case: he is penurious himself. He has been both champion and vindictive critic of I.S. and in the conversation about him tonight does not pull any punches because of I.S.'s illness. Friends before the war, the two compatriots were in communication only briefly after it—in 1945, during Suvchinsky's Sauguet phase. I.S. regarded Suvchinsky's derogation of his American-period music as the most heinous treachery, and when I encountered Suvchinsky at the 1952 Paris performance of *Erwartung*—on the staircase, leaving the theater before *Oedipus Rex*—I.S. received my report of the meeting in silence.

Suvchinsky leads off with questions about the Stravinsky children, expressing sympathy for the difficulties of life with a father who is a tyrant as well as a genius, and a special interest in Milene (whom Suvchinsky courted in 1937 and with whom he is still on *tutoyer* terms). He is rough on Theodore (a *"mouffle"*), whose ambidexterity, he thinks, may be an inverted, or left-over, manifestation of his father's gifts; perhaps the cerebral zones themselves were transposed. "In all fairness," he says, "to know that one has *those* genes is a burden." But his full contempt is reserved for Soulima ("A pianist? With *coupes St. Jacques* for hands?"), whom he denounces as a Nazi collaborator: "He provided music for Nazi UFA propaganda films, accompanied a German singer at the Opéra in music by the Nazi Egk, attempted, through Willy Strecker, to give concerts in wartime Germany, and was saved at the end only by helping Heinrich Strobel, who—with Auric, Sauguet, and his father's other friends—succeeded in clearing him."

Suvchinsky advances the all-too tenable theory that money is the root of all compromise in I.S.'s case. "Money was always too important to him. The lure of it led him away from composition and into concertizing. He hated to part with it, hated to pay the smallest tradesman's bill. But can you tell me what happened after *Noces?* The descent into *Mavra,* the Pergolesi *refacimenti,* the Tchaikovsky potpourri, the titivated echoes of operetta composers in *Jeu de cartes,* and the other *gaietés parisiennes?* Surely such a *bizarre metamorphose* must have some other explanation besides money? Wasn't the real trouble that he did not understand the general ideas of his time (Taine's sense), which is to say Schoenberg's ideas? After all, it was Stravinsky who turned the younger generation against Schoenberg. Not long ago Poulenc told me that the mere suggestion by anyone of his group that the music of Schoenberg or Berg might be worth examining would automatically have made them traitors in Stravinsky's eyes. At that time Stravinsky was dismissing *Wozzeck,* which he had not heard, as *une musique boche,* and Mahler, of whom he knew nothing, as '*Malheur.*'"

Here I put in my oar and protest that if Poulenc's version is accurate, he and the "Six" were as much at fault as I.S. and should not try to hang the blame on the older man and that, having belittled I.S. as "too old for the new hats he tries on in the *Canticum Sacrum,*" Poulenc should not mind being told that those new hats are part of the reason that I.S. is I.S. and Poulenc only Poulenc. But my interruption does not deflect the force of the indictment, and Suvchinsky continues with the charge that I.S. is "incapable of sustaining a reasoned and developed argument. He cannot go beyond doctrinaire aesthetics, *le gout, plaisanteries* and paradoxes!" This tempts me to interject that I would have thought *Sacre* and *Noces* highly reasoned and developed arguments, but Suvchinsky would agree; what he means are habits of verbal discourse more cultivated among professors of art than among artists.

He goes on to say that "Arthur Lourié, Olga Sudeikin's lover, was closer to Stravinsky in the Twenties and Thirties than anyone else and that between 1924 and 1930 the ascendancy was nearly total. Lourié should publish his memoirs; he was a kind of *valet de chambre* to Stravinsky, after all, and no one knows more about a man than his valet," though of course the

_1956_ sort of person who could be I.S.'s factotum, or _camerlingo_, would be unlikely to know much about him (which is Goethe's retort to the Prince de Condé's "No man is a hero to his valet": "Yes, not because a hero isn't a hero, but because a valet is only a valet"). "Having discovered that Stravinsky was a savage of genius—'_eine wilde Musik_' was Berg's description— Lourié set out to tame him, introducing him to Philosophy in the person of Maritain, and to Literature in various other persons; I remember seeing _Ulysses_ in Stravinsky's studio in 1926, brought there, of course, by Lourié." (Not necessarily; I.S. and Joyce had several friends in common, and Henrietta Hirschman, the sister of Joyce's business manager Paul Léon, was a very close friend of I.S. as far back as St. Petersburg.) "It was the old story of the man who _explains_ latching on to the man who _does_. Fortunately the genius was not tamed out of existence along with the savage, but there were portents, such as _Mavra_. What I do not understand is how Lourié could have had Stravinsky's musical esteem. But he did have it and was the first person to be shown each new work up to the time of _Perséphone_. Just how little progress was made at Lourié's _école_ is another, still almost unknown, subject. One of the ironies of contemporary music is that the savage of genius, the man who was all 'creative instinct' and 'natural talent,' came to be thought of as a fount of knowledge, an arbiter of taste pontificating about the glories of Gounod." It was Arthur Lourié, Suvchinsky might have added, who intrigued against V. before her marriage to I.S., for which reason Lourié's name is never mentioned in the S. household, and I cannot comment on him.

"If Stravinsky had not gone to America in 1939," Suvchinsky goes on, "he might have compromised himself politically. He was a frequent and welcome visitor to Blackshirt Italy during the Ethiopian and Spanish wars, and he conducted at the Maggio Fiorentino as late as 1939, by which time the festival had become a pro-Axis celebration. He even inscribed a copy of _Chroniques de ma vie_ to Mussolini. Was this because of pro-Fascist sentiment or because Mussolini's trains ran on time?" Certainly not the first alternative. Stravinsky was deeply afraid of Fascism, at least of the German kind, though these fears did not stop him from recording _Jeu de cartes_ in Berlin in 1938, by which time the orchestra had been purged of its Jews and of all good contemporary music, his own included. By 1938 all of his colleagues with a scrap of political, if not moral, sense, and not least among them Stravinsky himself, were protesting Nazism.

"Apart from the immediate excuse of money, the explanation lies in his even deeper dread of Stalin. The lecture on music in the USSR in the _Poétique Musicale_ convinces me that the fear of Communism would eventually have driven him into the arms of the Occupier. After all, Stravinsky was a White Russian. And his French friends, like T. S. Eliot's French friends, included Maurras and other former _Action Française_ writers, as well as Drieu la Rochelle and Lucien Daudet." Actually, I.S. and Daudet were acquaintances only at the time of *Petrushka*, when Daudet took him to visit the Empress Eugénie in her Riviera villa, and I doubt that I.S. knew the other two. "Klaus Mann noted the political tendency of these associations in his *Journal*, by the way, *his* good friend Gide having been well aware of them, and in truth the friction between the creators of *Perséphone* was more political than artistic. In Stravinsky's eyes Gide was a COMMUNIST; it was the time of Gide's first infatuation with the USSR—hence, *ni plus ni moins*, despicable and dangerous. From this alone you can see that Stravinsky was not a political animal. He did not have the remotest grasp of political facts, not the trace of a social concept. Which accounts, in part, for his turning to dogma, though of that, too, he understood precious little. 'I have no explanation of my own,' he used to say; 'Questions of that sort are for the Church to decide.' And he would quote Bossuet's 'The heretic is he who has an opinion.' What did the Church decide to do about Hitler? To keep very quiet while he murdered Communists and Jews."

This passionate recital has been well rehearsed and is not by any means having its maiden tryout. Clearly I am thought of as a plenipotentiary, rather than, as more often, a famulus, satellite, and the gray eminence who shanghaied I.S. into the "12-tone system." But Suvchinsky realizes that no one could lead *that* horse to water if it didn't want to go, let alone make it drink. The wording is for my benefit, too, though this hardly surprises me: anyone who has spent two minutes in the same room with I.S. has a theory about him, and a self-including story to put at the disposal of a potential biographer who knows the subject so much more intimately than anyone else. But even from my non-impersonating and compendious rather than complete translation, it is apparent that the arguments are the result of pent-up pressures. I.S.'s friendship was the central event of Suvchinsky's life. Bereft of it, Suvchinsky has naturally swung to a critical viewpoint in the opposite direction, the direction of the *enfant terrible* of the early 1950s, Boulez.

And the content? Some of the daggers are rubber and some are real, though I cannot comment on Suvchinsky's version of the Lourié influence but only continue to suspect from my observations of Lourié at Tanglewood 10 summers ago, and from what I know of his music and writings, that the evaluation is greatly exaggerated. Still, V. has always maintained that what Suvchinsky has been saying vis-à-vis Lourié is right and that I am wrong. As for the alleged perpendicular decline of I.S.'s music after the Russian period, that is the general view of postwar France. Nor will *Oedipus Rex* and the *Symphony of Psalms* be released from quarantine there until some daring antiquarian discovers that whether or not these masterpieces are "neo-classic" is beside the point.

The money issue is less easily disposed of. I.S. *is* aberrantly thrifty, and poor tradesmen, as well as luxury clothiers, *have* had to dun him for payment. He indulges in periodic splurges and can be as extravagant as a grand duke, and in consequence lives improvident for a time to the extent

1956 of being regularly overdrawn at the bank. Any photograph of his work-room shows that his possessiveness is all-powerful, but the possessions he most wants are people, and he has rarely succeeded in his friendships, demanding too great a sacrifice and a too exclusive loyalty. V. blames the money drive on the trauma of his loss of Russia in the 1914–1918 war, when his coffers were comparatively empty and he was forced to grub around; but it is more anal than that. Whatever the explanation, and how-ever formulated—Stirner persuasively argued over a century ago that in a society in which everybody uses everybody else for his or her own ends, all acts of charity are selfish—I.S. has supported a whole welfare depart-ment of relatives for most of their lives, and for as long as I have known him has kept destitute friends in funds.

The question of the imputed right-wing political sentiment is more vexed than this account allows. But prior religious questions require disen-tanglement and differentiations of a kind that, understanding little of that side of I.S. myself, I am not able to undertake. I would agree that his socio-political parts did not grow up to match his genius parts. But the real issue, it seems to me, is that the authoritarian mold of his mind is only spuriously related to politics. What it does relate to is the Church. And all that I can say for certain about his religiosity is that it is connected to his guilt feelings concerning his first wife. For certain, too, he has moved away from institutional religion since I have known him, which of course begs the question of my responsibility, to the extent that at present he is non-practicing. More important than his belief systems, however, are his inexhaustible intellectual curiosity and capacity for change and growth.

Finally, the "no mind" diagnosis, the gravamen of the argument concern-ing his failure to understand Schoenberg's "general ideas," is not even a fac-tor; nor, for that matter, is the Schoenberg antimony "true," which is not to go to the other extreme and claim that I.S. was one of the original 12-tone commandos. The real reasons for his musical attitudes, as described by Poulenc, were the circumstantial ones, his musical isolation and, which is both the cause and the result of it, his inability to communicate, to exchange views, with other composers. That no one dared contradict him can be blamed on the power of his personality. The mental equipment itself was, and is, up to any "idea," any complexity of understanding—though this is stupid beyond the need for rebuttal; the "mind" in *Sacre* is too subtle for such measurements. What Suvchinsky means by mind is simply a rhetorical discipline. Nor do I concede I.S.'s penchant for para-dox as an intellecual limitation. It is no more than a mannerism, a device of social rather than of intellectual behavior.

Still, this testimony is that of a man who was close to I.S. in the late 1930s and who understood the Russian background. By extension, I am able to recognize and confirm much in Suvchinsky's picture, however dif-ferent the I.S. of today. So, too, the I.S. *I* know would seem greatly transformed to Suvchinsky, though doubtless he could see by looking ahead, as I am able to see by looking back, the "continuity of personality." Precisely these differences lead me to wonder whether anyone has ever known more than one or another side of I.S. Even V., who can coordinate these views, is held apart from his deepest feelings by at least the length of each new composition.

November 9. Lunch at Nadia Boulanger's with Soulima. V. calls from Munich: I.S. is better, and Boulez, Stockhausen, and Nono have visited him in the hospital.

November 10. Boulez misses his return flight, and I am obliged to stage-manage as well as conduct the concert. Jean-Louis Barrault makes an amusing introductory speech to a packed Salle Gaveau, a modish audience, however, rather than a discriminating one, since each performance is received with equal enthusiasm and none has had adequate rehearsal. I talk briefly to Nabokov and Nadia Boulanger after the concert, and the Sachs chauffeur takes me to the Gare de l'Est for the night train to Munich.

November 15. With Katya (Mrs. Thomas) Mann and Erika Mann Auden, then to the hospital.

November 16. I record with the Munich Philharmonic in the Deutsche Museum, the hall in which I was photographed with I.S. in October 1951. Back at the hotel, a letter from Boulez in London: "You cannot know how annoyed I was to have missed the concert on the 10th. I arrived at Salle Gaveau at 8:15, just as you were boarding the train! In any case, I want to tell you how much I enjoyed meeting you, and how happy I was to have you conduct our concert. I hope that chances to collaborate will arise again. I will see you on December 3. I expect to be in Paris around the morning of the second, this time, I hope without complications!"

November 17. Hallelujah! I.S. is discharged from the hospital! We bring him back to the hotel. To transfer to my commonplace book:

> . . . God is glorified in the Sunne and Moon, in the rare fabric of the honeycomb, in the discipline of Bees, in the oeconomy of Pismires, in the little houses of birds, in the curiosity of an eye. (Jeremy Taylor)
>
> There is in rhyme a sense of return to exactly the same place. . . . Rhythm deals with similarity, but rhyme with identity. Now in the one word identity one involves perhaps the deepest and certainly the dearest human things. (Chesterton: *Fancies & Fads*)

November 18. To Vienna. Leave the train at Salzburg for passport control and Customs and wait 45 minutes for the express. A demonstration is in progress, with placards saying: "Hungarians die, America does nothing." The new train is overheated, shaky, crowded. In Vienna, I taxi to the Sacher Hotel; no message from Jackie Horne about rehearsals, and

1956 no answer from her telephone. Going to her address at 10 o'clock, I am permitted inside the portcullis, but the lights soon go out and the bastille is very dark. I have kept my taxi, fortunately, and in response to my banging and rattling the iron door, the driver rings the bell, the concierge appears, and, for a handsome bribe, shows me to Jackie's apartment, from which, after leaving a message, I escape. She comes to my uselessly large room in the Sacher at midnight, says that dreadful stories are being circulated by people who were in Hungary at the time of the invasion, but that life in Vienna is normal. All night long airplanes are overhead and trucks rumble in the streets.

November 19. The members of the Wiener Symphoniker, whom I rehearse in the Brahms Saal, are conceited in inverse proportion to their abilities, as I tell their conductor, Hans Swarowsky. Dinner with Jackie.

November 20. Record the Symphony in C, then to see my friend-through-correspondence, Hans Buchwald, who gives me a postcard in Webern's hand, 1942. With Jackie to see the Brueghels in the Kunsthistorisches Museum, and to an execrable German-language *La Bohème*.

November 21. Amalie Webern-Waller, who much resembles her father and speaks quite good English, comes to tea, after which I go to Friedrich Wildgans and Ilona Steingruber for dinner and an evening of examining Webern's notebooks from the Klagenfurt years (1900–1903).

November 22. Record the *Rake*, Act I, scene iii with Jackie, whose high C leaves no upper space to spare, as the sympathetic applause from the orchestra seems to appreciate. The train to Rome shunts at every stop all night long.

November 23. Change in Venice in mid-morning. Snow falls between Bologna and Florence, rain between Arezzo and Orvieto. A man in my compartment repeats passages over and over, *sotto voce*, that he is trying to commit to memory, not Dante or Leopardi but answers to a civil service exam. Roman Vlad is at the station in Rome and takes me directly to my rehearsal. Afterward, in the hotel, I.S. seems better than I had ever hoped possible.

November 24. Rehearse *Histoire* with Denise Bourgeois, a pretty *danseuse* from the Paris Opéra.

November 26. Duccio's *Maestà* is at the Istituto Restauro; the robe of the resurrected Christ shot with gold, suggests transparency.

November 27. Dr. Gilbert arrives for consultation with Dr. Gozzano. I.S. attends the evening rehearsal in the Foro, but is afraid to conduct.

November 28. At the afternoon rehearsal, I.S. conducts the *Canticum* straight through, a triumph for him, despite mistakes; he beams afterward and is in a peak mood all evening.

November 29. Letter from Boulez giving the time (Monday, December 3 from 3 P.M.) and place (Eglise de l'Etoile) for my *Canticum* recording, and promising a better harpist than the one who played the concert.

Dress rehearsal in the Teatro Eliseo. An American Embassy car fetches us for the concert. At the last minute, I.S., very nervous, asks me to conduct the Bach variations. When he begins the *Canticum*, his beat in the male duet looks like a fast 4—he rehearsed it in a slow 8—but I manage to signal the musicians from offstage. The concert has a wonderfully salutary effect on him, and he does not leave the reception, in a restaurant near the Palazzo Rospigliosi, until 3 A.M.

November 30. Dr. Gozzano warns I.S. that he should not conduct in New York, that his blood pressure is much higher today than the day before the concert, that he must stop smoking. The first page of Gozzano's report quotes I.S.'s description of the Berlin stroke: "I felt as if the left half of my face belonged to another man." I.S. writes in the margin next to this: "I never said face, but body."

December 1. Piovesan comes from Venice to discuss the commission for the Scuola di San Rocco.

December 3. Paris, the Gare de Lyon, 9 A.M. Boulez has two cars, owing to a taxi strike. Suvchinsky is with him, the first encounter with I.S. since 1939. V. goes to the Arthur Sachs apartment at the Ritz, while I.S. comes to my recording session. Tansman is there, but I.S., still offended by his letter about the Cantata three years ago, does not speak to him. Back in the Ritz, I sign a contract with Gerard Worms of Editions du Rocher to write two books. After a visit from Tchelichev, we leave on the night train for London.

December 4. 8 A.M.: "Behold the foggy mornings of the dead on Albion's cliffs." Bovril ads, red brick houses. The Savoy Hotel. I rehearse the Elizabethan Singers.

December 5. Rehearse from 2–5 at 14 South Audley Street. Scherchen is there; Leon Goossens is my oboist.

December 7. After examing I.S., Harley Street's Sir Charles Symonds says that the October 2 thrombosis was an ischaemic episode in the area of the basilar artery, *i.e.*, basilar stenosis. He performs the first of a series of venesections and brutally informs V. that a second stroke could occur at any time and would be fatal. To Wilson's *The Boy Friend*, later with Catherine Stravinsky, I.S.'s granddaughter, in the Savoy Grill.

December 8. Barrault and Boulez for lunch, after which William Glock drives the S.s and myself to Hampton Court, where the hedges, fountains, fir trees, and stone animals are wrapped in fog.

Back in the Savoy, T. S. Eliot comes for tea, accompanied by Stephen Spender, who disappears upstairs to fetch the S.s in their suite, leaving me alone in the lobby nervously trying to make bread-and-butter conversation with the great poet, who has not been introduced to me and does not know who I am. (Who am I?) When Spender returns with the S.s, we go to the almost deserted Grill and sit around a circular table, I.S. and V. across from Eliot, Spender between, to his right, next to V., myself to his left, next to I.S. After an inhibited, tentative, and soft-spoken beginning,

1956 during which Eliot's right-hand fingers tap a paradiddle on the table, I.S. orders Scotch and soda and Eliot sherry. Eliot says that from having seen I.S. on stages and concert podiums he expected a much taller man. I.S., whose height is a sensitive subject, does not respond, but he is obviously pleased when Eliot goes on to say that he had been much impressed by I.S.'s *Oedipus Rex* in Hamburg. In an attempt to forge a link to Eliot's art, I.S. says that he was introduced to it by Valéry, Maritain, and Jacques Rivière.

At the beginning of what promises to be deadening pause number four, V. shatters the formality by saying: "Mr. Eliot, my husband's most recent work owes something to you." When she adds, "Murder in the Cathedral," Eliot sits up, looks slightly alarmed, but, after she elucidates—"that was *Time* magazine's title for a review of the *Canticum Sacrum* in the Cathedral of St. Mark's"—laughs, a slow, head-back "ha, ha." V. goes on to say that Cardinal Roncalli, to make the concert available to everyone, had arranged for it to be broadcast in the Piazza San Marco, that a large crowd had gathered there and waited at the end for Stravinsky to emerge, and that when he finally did, he was warmly applauded, which greatly moved him.

Hunched, head bent forward and down from a lifetime of reading and writing, Eliot twists his neck along with his head when turning in Spender's direction and in mine. His speech is slow and measured—somewhat faster in French, in which, two or three times, I.S. seeks refuge—the voice weary, mournful, and as bleak as this December afternoon; when he speaks at all, that is, for I.S. does most of the talking and only Spender initiates subjects and adds chips of kindling wood under expiring ones. Of these, the *Rake* generates a few sparks, giving I.S. an opportunity to describe Auden's working behavior, how the librettist would start out each morning listening to the composer's ideas, asking questions about them, making notes, then trying to imagine a scene and a form and to fashion a plot. Auden went about this, I.S. says, "as effortlessly as anyone else would go about drafting a letter."

Spender proposes a subject for a play, outlining it to Eliot in a few sentences. "But you must write that yourself, Stephen," he says, in a tone that seems to carry the meaning "your sort of thing but not mine." Eliot very evidently likes him personally. Spender, not afraid of big topics, boldly broaches the question of Wagner's influence, apart from *Tristan* in *The Waste Land*. Eliot admits that Wagner's music once had a powerful effect on him, and though we wait with baited breath for more, the subject dies with the statement, having been made in a way that forbids continuation.

"Wagner" leads to Germany and the opportunity for I.S. to talk about his hospital experience in Munich. He does this partly to account for his considerable intake of liquids, the whiskey having been followed by a second and a third and by beer and tea. Unlike Eliot, I.S. gestures as he talks, and he uses his hands to illustrate the sludgelike texture of his blood. "The doctors say that my blood is so thick it could turn into crystals, like rubies, unless I drink a great deal," he says, molding the air in such a way that we see the jewels forming. Eliot's eyes indicate that he did not miss the brilliant image, but he responds with: "A doctor in Germany told me I had the thinnest blood he had ever tested."

Both men complain about autograph seekers and the demand for photographs. I.S. says that he ignores such letters unless the photo, envelope and stamps are enclosed, "because they cost money," a remark that embarrasses V. He goes on about publicity as a major nuisance in his life and says that this very morning he was awakened by a call from the BBC requesting a comment on a broadcast performance of one of his pieces. "I told them that we never listen to the radio," V. says, which brings on another relatively sustained laugh from Eliot. Then, just as Eliot is beginning to thaw and become almost convivial, I.S. excuses himself saying he has an appointment with his doctor. When we stand, I see that I.S. is at least two feet shorter than Spender and a foot-and-a-half shorter than the stooped Eliot.

To *Cymbeline* at the Old Vic in the evening; a Cecil B. De Mille ending.

December 9. Rehearsal at Morley College where Peter Racine Fricker introduces me. Then to a movie, *Bus Stop*.

December 10. Nabokov comes with Isaiah Berlin. Rehearse in St. Martin's-in-the-Fields. I.S.'s sixth venesection. Visit from Sir Gerard d'Erlanger, the Baroness's son.

December 11. Edward Clark shows me his letters from Webern. Dr. Symonds reports that the daily venesections have drawn 70 ounces of blood.

At 8:15, my concert in St. Martin's-in-the-Fields. I.S. sits in the first row next to Sir Ralph Vaughan Williams, but does not recognize him and the two do not speak. A reception afterward by Glock at 14 South Audley Street: Spender, Henry Reed, Michael Tippett, Edward Clark, Elisabeth Lutyens, Peter Heyworth.

December 12. Morning visits from Julian Huxley and Glock, who gives I.S. a volume of Thomas Tallis. While Glock is still with us, a message comes informing us that the voyage of the S.S. *Flandre* has been cancelled, and that we have been transferred to the S.S. *Mauritania*, leaving 48 hours later.

December 14. To Southampton and the boat. Alan Ladd and Dirk Bogard are in nearby rooms.

December 19. I win first prize—a clock—Janet Flanner second prize, in the ship's quiz.

December 21. New York, after a long wait for fog to clear. Gladstone Hotel.

&. **Postscript 1994.** 1956 was the crisis year of Stravinsky's later life. In January, on our return from New York to Hollywood, he began to complain of more severe, frequent and persistent headaches than ever before. His physician did not suspect polycythemia, or that a change in blood

1956 chemistry might be taking place, and continued with twice- or thrice-weekly injections of vitamin B12, to which he had been accustomed and on which he had depended since at least as long as I had known him. Sometime after the thrombosis on October 2, a hematologist told us that in cases of hypertension the vitamin is counter-indicated.

After completing his recomposition of the Bach variations, Stravinsky returned to *Agon*. This must have been difficult, his musical language having developed so much in the interim, but the coapting of the score's earlier and later parts could hardly be smoother. Work on *Agon* was interrupted again during the trip to Greece and Istanbul. Stravinsky was always extremely sensitive to weather, but though he had experienced 110-degree heat waves in Los Angeles, inland Greece, whatever the thermometer might have read, was less bearable. He was ill in Athens, but the decision to flee to Constantinople should be attributed more to Mrs. Stravinsky's nostalgia for the city she had not seen since the spring of 1920 than to the lure of the Bosphorus breezes.

The Stravinskys occupied the one habitable room on the small steamer that took us from the Piraeus to Venice, but it was not air-conditioned. (Neither was the *Vulcania*, but its staterooms had open balconies, and the Atlantic and western Mediterranian were cooler than the Adriatic.) Venice was quivering with heat, and on many afternoons we expected to deliquesce. But Venice offers compensations, and Stravinsky was able to continue work on *Agon*. During August and the first week of September we undertook more excursions to Palladian villas than my diary mentions, always accompanied by our dear friend and erudite guide Eugene Berman.

The *Canticum Sacrum* was beyond the abilities of the chorus and orchestra of La Fenice, but the main reason for the audience's failure to comprehend the music was the totally foreign idiom of the three central movements. Other obstacles were the reverberant acoustics of the Basilica and the dependence of the musicians on my beat, my cues, my tempos, to which they had become accustomed in rehearsals. When Stravinsky finally conducted himself, at the last minute—all of the photographs taken during rehearsals show him seated alone, and following his score—the performance sounded uneasy, as indeed it was.

I did not accompany Stravinsky on his concert tour in Switzerland—his elder son was with him—but after the thrombosis in Berlin, his Geneva doctor, Maurice Gilbert, who had dined with him in Montreux, told me that he realized Stravinsky was not well when he did not finish his Chateau Margaux.

From *Time*, October 1956: "The music world skipped a beat last week. . . ." Until his death fifteen years later, Stravinsky's health was international news. By November, after the anxious period in the Munich hospital, and with the Soviet invasion of Hungary and the Franco-British invasion of Egypt, both Stravinskys were impatient to return to New York.

๛ 1957

January 1. Lincoln Kirstein takes us to the Pollock memorial show at the Museum of Modern Art, but we spend most of our time in front of *The Street* in the Balthus show on the same floor. Then to *A Long Day's Journey*, which, for the S.s, who could hardly be expected to follow the play, is a long night's journey that never reaches day. At the Oak Room afterward: Judy Garland and I.S.'s old friend Edward G. Robinson.

January 10. Carnegie Hall. I.S.'s concert: *Perséphone* is very slow (58 minutes). Leonard Bernstein and Maria Callas come to the dressing room. I finish Musil's *Vereinigungen* late at night.

January 13. I.S.'s Philharmonic broadcast and V.'s exhibition at the Iolas Gallery. Elliott Carter remarks to I.S. that *Perséphone* owes a great deal to *L'Enfance du Christ*. I.S.: "No, but it owes something to Massenet."

January 14. I.S. records *Perséphone*. Milton Babbitt, Arthur Berger, Israel Citkowitz, Paco Lagerstrom, Leonide Massine are in the control room. It is the first time Vera Zorina, our Persephone, has seen Massine since the early 1930s.

January 15. After Menotti's *The Unicorn, the Gorgon and the Manticore* (the eunuch, the gorgonzola, and the maneater), we dine with Cartier-Bresson and Berman. Deep snow.

January 16. Lunch at the Pavillon with Arthur Judson, who tells us that Toscanini died this morning; I.S. is unexpectedly moved by this. Elliott Carter comes to listen to my Webern test pressings. With the S.s to Rattigan's mushy *Separate Tables*.

January 17. Lunch at the Brussels with two *Time* interviewers. "Why does the younger generation like your music?" I.S.: "It's a matter of biology."

January 23. Train from Grand Central for Los Angeles. I.S., reading Kawabata's *The Snow Country*, thinks that "it has everything European novels have except the point." the *New Yorker* has a good notice of V.'s show.

January 25. A whirling snow storm. The blue flames in the eastern Wyoming oilfields are infernal. Black fences compose snowscape draw-

1957 ings. We stop at Laramie, where my paternal great-grandfather and my father's two-year-old brother are buried, both of them having died on the return to New York after the 1905 earthquake in San Francisco. The station is surrounded by railroad barns, silos, ties and tracks piled criss-cross. Pigeons huddle under the parked livestock train next to us with a cargo of pigs and cattle; the pigs are asleep but the cattle moan restlessly in their cold, wet cages.

January 30. Hollywood. Letter from Boulez in the Hotel Plymouth, West 49th Street, New York. Editing the *Canticum* recording, he discovered that in measures 54–55 the tenor sang *"aromata inebrius"* instead of *"aromata illius,"* which "none of us noticed and which gives the *text* a flavor of Baudelaire."

February 3. Lunch with Aldous in his new house on the hillside beneath the huge "Hollywood" letters. He says that "two foxes walked by the back porch last evening, had a look in and departed." I try his new relaxing chair, but the vibrating agitates me. He gives us recordings of Byzantine music.

February 6. A cry from the garden: the Baroness has fainted. Revived, but still lying on the ground, the well-bred lady introduces the people standing around her to each other.

February 11. Letter from Boulez, outlining the three lectures he would like to give in Los Angeles: on interpretation, on the theory of sound today, and on the evolution of style. He asks for my advice on questions of English vocabulary. And he says that his Paris musicians were amused by Stockhausen's *Zeitmasse*, which they referred to as a jam-session.

March 8. A panel discussion at Royce Hall: Boulez and I vs. Lukas Foss and Paul Des Marais.

March 9. Record the 1st, 5th, 6th, and 7th movements of Schoenberg's Serenade, with I.S., Boulez, and Morton in the control room. Afterward David Raksin takes us to hear Oscar Peterson at the Peacock Club.

March 10. Dinner at the Luau with Marlene Dietrich, I.S.'s one long-time friend among the stars and nebulae of filmdom. She is apparently wrinkle-proof, but, then, she never smiles. Boulez says little but admits afterward that he was impressed by seeing *"l'ange bleu"* in the flesh.

March 11. At the Monday concert, I conduct both sets of Tallis's Lamentations, and Boulez conducts his *Marteau*.

March 28. Letter from Aldous:

> Dear Bob, Will you please give me some advice. I have made a dramatic adaptation of *Brave New World* in the form, not so much of a conventional musical as of a play with music—a ballet or two and some songs. Who would you advise me to approach for the score? Bernstein has been suggested, of course, and now someone of my acquaintance wants me to send it to Rodgers and

Hammerstein. What would be your suggestion? Needless to say, **1957**
if the maestro felt inclined to take some time off to do something
light—a little ballet music for brave new worlders and another
piece for the Indians on the reservation, plus half a dozen vocal
numbers, I would be only too happy. But I hesitate to ask him—
wouldn't want to do so before finding out what you think. I hope
all goes well with the family and with you.

April 26. I.S. completes *Agon*. Today is the fiftieth anniversary of the
first performance of his Symphony in E Flat and *The Faun and the Shepherdess*,
he says.

April 29. 2000-word letter from Boulez about the autumn concert in
Paris—program, publicity, recordings, participation of the Sudwestfunk
orchestra. He says that the extracts I have sent from my book are
"extremely interesting" (they are far from that). And he says my Webern
recordings are marvelous and will be a model for a long time to come, that
I should be truly gratified for having established this monument, which
does me the greatest honor.

May 1. With Aldous and Laura at the Beverly Wilshire, Aldous saying
that Francis Bacon's *Natural Historie* is worth reading for its language: "the
sperm of inebriates is unfruitful, because it wanteth spissitude." He gives
us recordings of Sweelinck and Lasso.

May 19. I.S. describes his father's death to me: "He was lying on a
couch when he called me and my brothers to his side. 'I feel well,' he said,
but the doctor, a young man, whispered, 'Your father will die now.' A
minute later he was dead. None of us knew exactly when he was on one
side and no longer on the other. Suddenly he had become a mere object.
Coins were placed on his eyelids. His death impressed me more than any
other I have ever witnessed."

I.S. says that every day, beginning in 1930, he has used a French prayer,
given to him by Eugenia Errazuriz, asking to know when his hour of death
is near. He tells me that while in Padua on Saint Anthony's 750th anniversary, after seeing the coffin and relics, he prayed to the Saint for a miracle,
and added the request that St. Anthony give him a sign that it was *his* miracle. He believes that both miracles occurred, referring to the "miraculous"
curing of his abscessed thumb in September 1925, the utter nonsense of
which, and I.S.'s sanctimony about, are impossible to swallow.

I.S. is amazingly well read in Russian and French hagiography. He says
that after the death of St. François de Sales, Marie de Medici had his gall-
stone removed from the body and set in her ring—"Plucked out to wear as
an ornament," as I.S. puts it. He believes that the stone was the result of
the aggravation of saintly restraints.

June 12. Dinner with Robert Graff, here to film I.S. for NBC's "Wisdom
Series." To prepare for the televising, canvas is wrapped around the entire

1957 S. house to insulate it, and all the furniture is rearranged.

June 13. Wetherly Drive is blocked from 9 to 4, to keep out noise, but Sunset Boulevard traffic is still audible. The "conversation" between I.S. and me becomes duller, more formal and forced as the hours drag on, but he enjoys being on camera as much as I detest it and is as natural and easy as I am tongue-tied and nervous. Precious little "Wisdom" is gleaned, and "my" questions are really NBC's.

June 16. With Balanchine to my *Agon* rehearsal. My "Stravinsky at 75," in today's *New York Times*, has been misguidedly edited: "On the whole, Stravinsky's creations appear to have been born, in his own phrase, 'tout habillé—full blown.'" "Fully *clothed*," surely, but who would need *habillé* translated? Two passages in the article arouse my nostalgia for an unrecapturable past, my account of how I read Mme Calderon de la Barca's *Life in Mexico* to him while he was orchestrating the *Rake*: "Episodes from the book remain vivid in his memory, though he absorbed them like phonograph lessons repeated during sleep or under hypnosis"; and my description of him playing something he has just composed at the piano: "If the music is vocal, Stravinsky sings the solo parts an octave or two below actual pitch and in a deep and tremulous non-voice. He also sings the purely instrumental music, groaning sometimes with impatience at his incapacity to realize the orchestra from the piano."

June 28. Boston. Telegram from I.S. for my concerts on Boston Common: *Greeting Prelude, Renard,* Capriccio (Soulima), Symphony in Three, *Petrushka*.

July 13. Santa Fe. I.S. rewrites some harpsichord passages in the *Rake* for piano and gives the manuscript to the player, Vernon Hammond, conductor at the Academy of Vocal Arts, Philadelphia.

July 31. New York. After lunch at the Brussels with three interviewers from *Life*, I go with Aldous to the Picasso show at the Museum of Modern Art. Of a picture containing both realistic female buttocks and a pair of sharp cones, he remarks: "We are attracted by the one and impaled on the other." Passing the brownstone Presbyterian Church at 55th and Fifth, and the skyscraper going up next to it: "God and Mammon in the usual proportion."

August 7. We debark from the S.S. *Liberté* at Plymouth, lowered to a tender in a choppy sea. At Customs, I.S. takes two pieces of someone else's luggage and leaves two of his own, whereupon the rest of the day is spent rectifying the error. Peter Cox drives us to Dartington and to Herrick's Dean Prior. I rent a car in Torquay and practice staying on the wrong side of the road. Dartington: old oaks and elms, flowers, thatched roofs, a 14th-century wall, yew tree in a cemetery, but the greatest attraction is our young cook, Judith Sutherland. Finish *Richmond Park*.

August 9. Letter from Boulez, at François-Michel's Le Clos Vert, Bretigny-Sur-Orge, with a full page of detailed information about automobile rentals. He asks me to settle the conflict between Columbia and Westminster over the release of their respective *Canticum* recordings. The S.s are bored and want to spend the weekend in London; we take the train from Newton Abbott.

August 10. To the Victoria and Albert: English tapestries and medieval weaving (chasubles); Byzantine ivories; Spanish Gothic—a retablo of martyrs being clouted, sawn in half, hacked, burned. I.S. comes to my afternoon rehearsal in a BBC studio.

August 12. Record *Dumbarton Oaks* and *Histoire* at the Maida Vale BBC studio and leave from Paddington Station for Newton Abbott. Letter from Boulez proposing to record the Webern Cantatas on the flip side of the *Canticum* record.

August 15. Letter from Boulez in Bretigny-sur-Orge saying he is translating my essays for the Editions du Rocher book, and working on his new sonata. He wants a score of *Agon*. With I.S. in Totnes, where we drink stout in a pub. He likes England, and the English.

August 19. With H. D. F. Kitto in Bath, but the great Greek scholar is proud of his ignorance about the Roman city, or even Shakespeare's

> I, sick withal, the help of Bath desired,
> And thither hied, a sad distemper'd guest;
>> But found no cure: the bath for my help lies
>> Where cupid got new fire—my mistress' eyes.

Return *via* Glastonbury and Wells.

August 25. Paris. Boulez meets us at the Gare du Nord. After lunch at the Café Tremouille, we climb the stairs to his Beautreillis apartment where he plays Stockhausen's Piano Piece No. 11 for us. Dinner with Giacometti at the Toscana, Avenue Matignon.

August 26. Lunch with Boulez. I.S. talks about Hans Richter in St. Petersburg: " 'Warum dieser Jungling?,' Richter said when he saw that I was to be his translator." Spend the afternoon with Boulez listening to *Zeitmasse*. The focus of Boulez's interest has switched from Webern to the Berg of the "Three Pieces for Orchestra." Dinner at La Pérouse with Nabokov and Jack Bornoff (UNESCO).

August 27. Lunch with François-Michel at Chez Joseph, and to Véga Records, where we listen to my Gesualdo test pressings. Nabokov and Boulez drive us to the Gare de Lyon for Venice.

August 28. We go directly to the outdoor restaurant at the Bauer. Thomas Beecham is there, but he does not see I.S. and I.S. does not make himself known. Sir T. is in mid-tantrum, evidently owing to an unsuccessful attempt to escape crème caramel. "I told you they have no tinned peaches in Italy," he reminds his wife (and everyone else); "the maitre d'hotel is a nincompoop." *Our* waiter complains about the sirocco. *"Tempo*

1957 *brutto*," he says, and, touching his parabolic, *commedia dell'arte* nose, reports that this infallible barometer forecasts rain. I.S. flenses and bones his trout like an ichthyologist dissecting a rare specimen. Afterward I go to familiar places first—to find my old self and see how and why the present edition is different?

August 31. Dinner with Countess Pecci-Blunt, the Pope's niece—Cardinal Pecci became Pope Leo the XIIIth—and mother-in-law of the current Prince of Venosa. She is fond of blasphemous stories à la Firbank and gossips about Zellerbach's debut as U.S. Ambassador in Rome: "High Society gave a large reception at which the Zellerbachs, completely ignorant of titles, protocol, and behavior went about slapping people on the back like Wyoming lodge keepers."

September 1. A regatta in the afternoon. Rival brass bands open up in the Piazza long before the races begin, while a concert of opera arias blasts forth simultaneously from a loudspeaker near the Bucintoro, which is Venetian antiphony of a sort. By mid-afternoon nearly every boat in Venice is in the Grand Canal, gaggles of gondolas and flotillas of sandolos, each bearing the standard of its patron saint and *sestiere*, and the boats of the police and fire departments, the latter spouting and spraying in a wide assortment of forms. Relics from the Arsenale Museum, including caravels with gold-leafed Tritons and baldachins on the poop decks trailing velvet canopies in the filthy water, head the water parade. The crews of these museum pieces carry arquebuses, halberds, culverines, and they wear tabards, doublet and hose, hauberks, piebald caps, and other antique garb in which they are as encumbered as an opera chorus at a first costume fitting. The races are an eternity in getting started and extremely dull when they *do*, except for a heat of swift, pod-shaped canoes.

September 2. At the Taverna with Giorgio de Chirico, large and bay-windowed, limp and amorphous, and with a built-in frown. He looks almost photographically like one or another of his innumerable *autoritratti*, the subtle brown eyes, the quiet, well-manicured fingers, the pale, womanish skin, the soft silver hair parted as it was in the pictures of 40 years ago—which, he says, is when he first met I.S.* Later in the day, Eugene Berman tells us that "in Chirico's case decadence seems to have begun a few minutes after birth. The great vision he had as a young man quickly lost its force and he devoted himself to technical studies. Canvas after canvas came out devoid of ideas but always displaying technical prowess. When I first knew him, 30 years ago, his notebooks were filled with drawings copied from old masters. He would copy anything that attracted him in anyone else's work, often fobbing it off without acknowledgment as his own. His own imagination had apparently dried up. Another reason for

---

* Chirico was Stravinsky's, but not Diaghilev's, first choice of painter for *Apollon Musagète*. He designed scenery and costumes for a later production of the ballet at La Scala.

the copying was his immense vanity. 'I can paint like Giotto or Raphael, or anyone else, even early Chirico,' he seemed to be saying. . . . I was with him in his studio in Paris one day in the thirties when 'Argyrol' Barnes dropped by to inquire if Chirico had a painting for sale similar to one from 1911 that Barnes admired. After calculating for a moment, Chirico answered that he did just happen to have another, similar one, which he could retrieve from such-and-such an exhibition in a month or so and sell to Barnes. When Barnes left, Chirico set to work copying the 1911 picture from a photograph, changing details, and signing and dating the result 1911. Chirico is a perfect subject for a Freudian biography. Consider all those self-portraits as Apollo, Don Giovanni, King Lear, a courtier to Louis Quatorze, and so on, and consider the tragedy of a man given a few years of lucidity during which he is a great painter, but after which, being unable to live with the knowledge, he denies he ever was the former person. Yet he is also aware of this. I remember an exhibition in Paris just before the war of his latest, most academic paintings. They were so bad that no one could find anything to say, and we all left the gallery silently shaking his hand. Chirico described this to me later: 'It was as if I were dead and the visitors were mourners who came to pay their respects but knew I couldn't hear.'" Still, at lunch today, Chirico sent up a few sparks from time to time that made us respect the remaining pile of ash.

September 9. Venetian washday. Clotheslines cross above the canals, and gondolas glide beneath sheets, shirts, dresses, tablecloths, trousers. A police boat patrols the Grand Canal against unsightly displays of laundry; no sooner does a pink undergarment appear in a window opposite ours than the water cops speed to the scene and excoriate the miscreant with that lowest of all imprecations, "*Napolitana!*"

September 10. To Mantua-the-melancholy across the Lombardian plain, my first experience of driving in Italy. The moats of the ghostly 500-room Palazzo Ducale are foully stagnant, and the gardens are "ruining along the illimitable inane," but the panorama from the balconies of the jousting courtyard and beyond the walls to the Mincio is the most romantic in the world. A wheeled divan or a stretcher would be the most suitable vehicle for a tour of the palace, since the painted ceilings, especially those with Giulio Romano's perspective tricks—the goddess whose raised finger seems to change position and to follow you in whichever direction you move—can be fully appreciated only by viewers on their backs. The dwarves' apartments are appropriately dwarf size, but the effect is macabre; inconsistently, no corresponding deformity is evident in the rooms of Federico and Guglielmo Gonzaga, both of them, like Rigoletto, hunchbacks. Male Gonzagas in paint and stone wear togas and laurel crowns, like Caesars. A more engaging portrait is that of Pico della Mirandola, a slender young man pointing a finger over an open book. At the other end of the palace from the *Camera degli sposi* is Isabella d'Este's music room, on

1957 the far wall of which Ockeghem's *Prennez sur moi votre exemple amoureux* is notated in blond and black intarsia marquetry.

In late afternoon we drive to Sabbioneta, the "little Athens of the Gonzagas," as the road signs say, though only the violent Vespasiano lived here. Some of the architecture—the Gallery of Antiques and Scamozzi's Olympian theater, which once had a fixed scene in perspective like Palladio's at Vicenza—is wonderfully elegant, but the decay—faded frescoes, chipped pillars, worm-eaten wood statues, ruined Pompeiian *grotteschi*, a mirrorless Hall of the Mirrors—and the contrast between the shabby, miserable population and the late-Renaissance grandeur are oppressive. A statue of Athena, the town's tutelary goddess, survives, and four of the original dozen life-sized equestrian figures carved in wood, Vespasiano's ancestors. Horse-breeding is still a local hobby, as it was in the time of the Gonzagas.

September 14. Venice. Visit from Marilyn Horne, en route to Rome. With Rolf Liebermann to Werner Egk's *Der Revisor* at the Fenice. Walking back to the hotel afterward, I.S. says nothing, then, suddenly: *"C'est très genant."*

September 15. To Bologna, where Gjon Mili photographs I.S. by the Nettuno, the Palazzo di Podestà, S. Petronio, S. Giacomo Maggiore, and the Liceo Musicale. Pheasant and a truffled risotto at Freddy's.

September 16. I.S. says he has named his lamentations *"Threni"*—from the Greek "mourning song," or threnody—*"Id est Lamentatio Jeremia Prophetae."* Its three parts represent Darkness, Hope, Consolation, and he describes an idea for a section in which "two tenors shout like two roosters."

September 18. From a new book about gondolas I learn that the comparatively flat, less crescent-shaped ones are older, and that today's new ones survive for no more than a few years, as compared to five or more decades in the past. Whereas gondolas were formerly built and launched from docks on the Grand Canal, they are fabricated in more obscure places now, near S. Trovaso, and on the canal of the Sensa.

With I.S. to S. Giovanni Decollato to see the newly-discovered frescoes, now thought to be the oldest in Venice. The elderly Sister Superior who chaperones us through the convent to the church is curious about us and would like to chat, and we, too, are more interested in her than in the few faded scraps of painting. Just before we leave, she goes ahead of us to the convent and rings a bell, whereupon the nuns flee upstairs from the tempting sight of ourselves.

September 20. I.S. is wakened at 1 A.M. by a telephone from Associated Press, Rome, asking for a statement on the death of Sibelius. He slams down the receiver.

September 21. Letter from Boulez about next year's Domaine Musical concert: he wants Gesualdo on the first half with I.S.'s *"Leçons de Ténèbres"* on the second. Says he is working "in colors and in cinemascope," and that this is more difficult than anything he has attempted before.

September 22. To the Villa Maser, where I would like to live and listen to madrigals. Drive from there to Gian Francesco Malipiero's home in Asolo. White-haired, squint-eyed, with a beautiful hooked-nose profile, Malipiero cackles and flutters about like an old woman—though he is very much a woman's man, said to entertain three mistresses even now. The house is pitch-dark, for the sake of his owls, nor does he offer to turn on a light until we reach a downstairs room, where the lamp is so gloomy that we wish he hadn't. Here he trains a flashlight on a cage with two owls, goes to his piano and plays E flat and D, after which the owls hoot the notes perfectly in tune. He then shows us a glass case containing what he calls "Stravinsky's rose," actually the flower that I gave to Piovesan for *his* button-hole on the night of Malipiero's concert, and that the well-meaning Piovesan placed on Malipiero's score. When Malipiero asked where the rose came from, Piovesan said "Stravinsky's loge" (which is true), where-upon Malipiero wrongly concluded that I.S. had sent it. Malipiero is intelligent, *méchant*, and totally without creative musical power.

Still in Asolo, we go to a luncheon with the owner of the Villa Browning, a Marchesa whose grandmother had invited the poet to live there. The garden here contains persimmon trees, 18th-century dwarf statues, and the ruins of a Roman amphitheater.

September 25. I.S. completes *Beth* (*Threni*). The exhibition of 18th-century musical instruments in the Goldoni show (Palazzo Grassi) includes open *cors de chasse*, curved oboes, viols with curved bows, short bassoons with metal bells.

September 30. By car to Vittorio Veneto and Cortina d'Ampezzo, where the restaurant proprietor brings a huge autograph book. Then Lienz, Heiligenblut—a stark place with a church clinging to a precipice—and, in snow and mists and on narrow mountain roads with no guide-rails, across the Grossglockner. After some 30 major turns and one-way traffic tunnels, we reach the green valleys of Austria. In Munich, dinner with Hindemith in the Hotel Vier Jahreszeiten.

October 5. To Baden-Baden on the Autobahn. The headwaiter in the Brenners Park Hotel restaurant asks I.S. if he is proud of the Russians because of Sputnik, launched last night. But I.S. is furious in equal measure with the Russians for having done it and with the Americans for not having done it.

October 8. A long letter from Boulez saying that he wrote a program note for I.S.'s 75th, but that some people have said he should show it to him before it is published. *"Qu'en pensez-vous?"* But I haven't read it. Asks about the Munich concert and wonders if Hartmann is still as *"globuleuse,"* as ever. *"Très amicalement."*

October 11. Paris, the Berkeley. My book *Avec Stravinsky* is published. With Nadia Boulanger to I.S.'s *Agon* rehearsal. A reception after the con-

1957 cert at the home of Mme Tézenas, with Cocteau, Giacometti, Nabokov, Mary McCarthy.

October 13. I.S. poses for Giacometti in our hotel room. Very vain about women, he allows Lucie Lambert to watch him. All his drawings are very bad, he says, but he clearly relishes each new failure.

November 12. New York. The local office of Radio Tokyo telephones requesting an interview at 2 P.M. I.S. refuses unequivocally. Promptly at 2, a television team arrives with cameras, tape recorders, photographic and stenographic equipment. I.S. is in a rage, the Japanese are very calm. As they leave, each one bids him "Melly Clismas." Train to Los Angeles.

November 15. Hollywood. Letter from Boulez, in Paris, apropos my plan to record *Marteau* for Columbia. Says he is curious to hear the piece in another version than his own, and would be *"enchanté"* if I do it, adding that my recordings of Webern give him complete confidence in me.

November 25. A letter from Alfred Schlee, Universal Edition, Vienna: "I got the record with the complete works of Webern—one of the greatest events of my life. I don't intend to tell you now which impression the complete work of this composer—to whom I had got a deep personal contact, especially during the war and the last years of his life—makes on me and on everyone who loves music. I only wanted to thank you for the love which made you create a very accomplished realization of this work and which is also evident in every word of the presentation. I am really grateful to you for it. What you have accomplished and professed here, is, I dare say, unique."

November 27. Sol Babitz comes for dinner with Kenneth Rexroth, who is tall and pot-bellied, and who wears a dirty brown suit, dirty shoes, a loud "artist's" tie. He tells jokes in an incomprehensible imitation Jewish accent. In his other talk, not many phrases are without four-letter expletives. He sloshes red wine all evening but is convivial.

November 28. Balanchine calls from New York announcing the great success of last night's *Agon* premiere.

ð **Postscript 1994.** Stravinsky's vitality, health, and spirits improved from the moment of his return to New York. Nervous about conducting the New York Philharmonic in January, though he had changed the program, substituting the less strenuous *Petrushka* for *The Rite of Spring*, he asked me to conduct all rehearsals except the last. But he led the concerts energetically, and the fear that we had seen in his eyes since October disappeared afterward. In January, too, he was the proud host at his wife's first New York exhibition.

Returning to Hollywood, he resumed the thrice-interrupted composition of *Agon* with new vigor, though he asked me to conduct the premiere, with the *Canticum*, on his 75th birthday, reserving the *Symphony of Psalms* for himself. June 18 was celebrated around the world, and the "living legend of Stravinsky," as Columbia Records began to market the product, dates **1957** from then. At the same time, ASCAP upgraded his royalty category, thereby boosting his income from the $35,000 range to something in six figures near the halfway mark to seven. He was also sought after for concert appearances all over the globe.

Stravinsky did not anticipate the success of *Agon*, either in Los Angeles or when he conducted it himself later in Paris, and he held out such poor prospects for the stage performance, in New York at the end of the year, that he did not stay to see it. But *Agon*, that wonderful amalgam of *Le Grand Siècle* (the Sarabande and Gaillarde), Webern (the Pas de deux), and Stravinsky's own Symphony in Three Movements (the Quasi Stretta) was to become his most popular ballet.

In 1957 the Stravinskys spent part of the summer in Santa Fe, where the opera company presented *The Rake's Progress*, the first and most enjoyable of their several visits to the city (they returned in 1959, 1960, 1961, 1962, and 1963); they met Paul Horgan on this occasion, and the friendship began that became closer over the years and lasted until the end—and beyond, for Horgan memorialized it in a book. From Santa Fe, the Stravinskys went to England, where they fell in love with the country of the western and southern coasts, as well as with the English musicians whose acquaintance they made at Dartington and in London. In Venice, Stravinsky worked on *Threni*.

One notable development in 1957 was the beginning of my collaboration with Stravinsky on the interviews that were to become books of "conversations." I would write up his answers to questions, or prefix questions to bits of his table and other talk, and ask him to edit, add or delete.

❧ *1958*

January 26. Dinner at Bel Air with Aldous, who reminisces about Eliot and Pound: "Even in the mid-Twenties, one could see that Ezra was mentally unbalanced. Still, he had a fabulous memory and great *joie de vivre*. I preferred his company to Joyce's, who was so rigid in his habits that he had to be served a certain white wine and no other; and to that of Yeats, though he could be amusing if steered away from Spiritualism and on to the antics of George Moore. An evening with Tom Eliot was the greatest strain, and a dinner at his apartment a form of hell, partly because the food was so bad but mainly because of apprehensions about what Vivienne might say next: her remarks were calculated to humiliate him. I remember him putting a record on the turntable and, with an indescribably sentimental expression, dancing with her slowly, cheek to cheek. What a strange creature he was, wearing a black satin chest protector and positively loving to dress up in evening clothes. A masochist, of course—living in those gloomy apartments in Edgware Road and off Baker Street, and working in the sub-basement of a bank. Think how after 20 years of a sterile marriage to Vivienne, he goes on to another one with John Hayward. I tried to portray Tom in *Those Barren Leaves*."

February 26. New York. Deborah Ishlon calls to say that Piovesan has died in Venice of pneumonia. After my St. Thomas choir rehearsal, one of its members, James Van Gaasbeek, hands me a letter from Robert Waldig, an NBC announcer now, 15 years ago a sergeant in Camp Pickett, Virginia, who used to play records in his office for me there, and who was in charge of a radio show in Richmond on which I appeared at a time when the U.S. Army was trying to make a case for the existence of "cultured" soldiers.

March 2. Elliott Carter for lunch. At 4, my St. Thomas concert: *Symphonies of Winds*, *Vom Himmel hoch*, Mass, *Symphony of Psalms*. Balanchine, Chavez, Alexis Saint-Léger come back after, then Lincoln Kirstein takes me to his apartment and to dinner with Auden. W.H.A. on Robert Graves: "Well he *is* eccentric, you know"; on Wilson Knight's Byron: "Quite looney but right about the sex. After all, there are only nine seductions in *Don Juan* and all nine are *of*, not *by*, Byron." Says he plans to write a libretto on *The Snow Queen*. When Lincoln says that Menotti wants a libretto on Gesualdo, Auden denies the possibility of dramatizing the life of a composer unless his music is used. But what about Pfitzner's *Palestrina?*

April 6. Hollywood. Gerald, for lunch, goes off like a geyser, and, like the one in Yellowstone Park, on schedule. Says he resembles Shaw in that "like all performing animals, I want applause."

April 11. Carmel, the Torres Inn. We spend the day at the San Carlo Borromeo and Santa Inez Missions. Women here wear Dutch-bun hairdos and knitted dresses, and the city is characterized by "quaint" shops, cottages, wine and cheese stores. "No bicycles, No dogs," a sign reads. On the drive to Point Lobos: mist, white dunes, and the pine trees that R. L. Stevenson likened to "ghosts fleeing."

April 26. Dinner at Isherwood's with the Huxleys and Rosamond (*The Ballad and the Source*) Lehmann, whose evening dress is too grand for mountainside Malibu and who combs her wig-like white hair all evening. Aldous and I.S. inhibit her.

May 3. To the Kreneks' for dinner. More suntanned than ever, he faithfully practices his heliolatry, however good he is as a Catholic. We drink two bottles of Aigle-les-Murailles, after which he becomes an engaging memoirist of Webern, Berg, Karl Kraus, Loos, and especially Busoni and his early 1920s Berlin soirées: "Busoni sat between a fortune-telling mystic and, for good luck, a hunchback. This odd trinity was sealed off from the guests by a row of empty chairs. Busoni, who did all of the talking, was seldom less than brilliant. He had great qualities of imagination, but his visionary powers far outstripped his powers as a composer. Coffee was served regularly. Once we were given sekt—though it had not been paid for and even as we were drinking it, the merchant pounded on the door asking for his money." Krenek himself is a man of impressive intellect, as he displays tonight in explaining the derivation of the time and density controls in his *Sestina* from the original 12-note structure by multiplying and dividing the number of the semitones of the intervals.

May 15. Interesting letter from Boulez about John Cage who "understood, even if badly, the problem of chance, the idea of a music *non fixée*, and the importance of acoustics. Unfortunately, he is naive and infantile, and he takes refuge in the innocence of Satie, a case very similar to Messiaen." On Stockhausen's *Gruppen*, he says that the style brings together disparate elements that are truly embarrassing. He wants to know the order of the contents for *Avec Stravinsky*, says he is working on the translation of the "Questions," but still does not know the instrumentation of *Threni*. The Cologne Radio Orchestra cannot be engaged for the Paris *Threni* because of a rivalry with the Hamburg Radio which had commissioned the piece.

May 18. Mike Wallace interviews Aldous on TV, not an ideal combination. During a party at La Rue with Isherwood, Don (*Bus Stop*) Murray,

1958 Hope Lange, and Marguerite Lamkin, *The Young Lions* is praised, and I argue that the "German" cast, Brando above all, and music (*Tristan*) is so superior to the "American" that the film boomerangs—not recognizing Montgomery Clift's girl friend in the film as Hope Lange, sitting next to me. Everyone pretends not to notice the *gaffe*.

June 12. Letter from Aldous with his translations for me of the crucial passages in Vatielli's *Gesualdo*; he has typed all of this himself, as the many mistakes testify. Typically, too, he gives alternate translations, however unnecessary in prose of this kind.

June 28. The sight and sound of myself in conversation with I.S. in the NBC Wisdom film are a shattering experience. My voice is too plaintive and at the same time embarrassingly tense. I have never been aware of gesturing while I speak and am therefore horrified to see that my hands and arms twitch nervously, that my legs are continually seeking new positions. The effect of this "objective" viewing has been to cripple whatever vanity I might have had.

July 29. New York. A letter from Boulez in Baden-Baden about the proofs of *Avec Stravinsky*. The Paris program is now set, he says: Webern's Passacaglia, Schoenberg's Variations, *Threni*. Henri Michaux is "enchanted" with my Gesualdo record, he goes on, and "*Je me réjouis de vous voir bientôt.*"

We sail for Genoa on the *Cristoforo Colombo*. Leaving the harbor, the smokestacks emit three mighty eructations, which I.S. likens to "An Alban Berg climax." Drink Strega with our fellow passengers the Fritz Reiners. "It is like furniture polish," I.S. says and, afterward: "I feel shiny inside now." He addresses Reiner as "*Amico* Fritz."

July 30. I.S. hides under his bed during life-boat drill. Whereas waiters on French boats convey the impression that they feel superior to their jobs, as if they ought to be running the government instead of bowing and scraping to ignorant Americans, the waiters on Italian boats appear to be happy to escape the farm and to find such easy berths in life.

August 1. A snapshot of my character, after La Rochefoucauld: I am feckless, irresolute, physically and mentally indolent, yet impulsive. As the resident critic at the S. house, I have become a scold. Good titles for some of my writings might be "Collected Carpings," "Cavils of a Curmudgeon," and "With Microscope and Tweezers." My imagination is preoccupied with sex, nor is my promiscuity only in the mind. I am sybaritic by temperament. The weakness that most annoys me, however, is my readiness to modify my views in the face of arguments that contradict them—sequaciousness. And, worst of all, I am suspended in the absolute middle between Horace Walpole's categories: intellectuals, who tend to see the world as comic, and feelers who tend to see it as tragic.

August 2. In the Azores. At about 10 A.M., the new volcanic island comes into view, almost hidden by seething steam, like dry ice ablating in water. We distinguish three fumaroles, ebullitions of lava boiling into the sea. I.S., invited to the bridge by the Captain to use his telescope, comes down to tell us about a maelstrom near the newborn island and to say that a neighboring island has had to be evacuated, its white village and terraced slopes now being shrouded in ashes. More than an hour later, a plume of white smoke from a water-level crater is still visible beyond the horizon.

August 4. Gibraltar. Even before we have dropped anchor, dinghies sail alongside selling shawls, wine, fruit, souvenirs, *bérets basques*. Whereas no boat had a motor a decade ago, all are equipped with engines now. And while the only language of the boatmen then was Spanish, transactions are now conducted in American: "Where's the money?," "Wanna buy a scarf?," "Five dollahs." Each boat carries a salesman-demonstrator and a winch-worker, who flings a rope over our deck rails, attaches a basket to it, and hoists his wares. Bargaining commences until the money is paid in the basket or the merchandise returned. We load passengers, fish, melons, cases of Johnny Walker.

August 6. Naples. The Principessa Doria escorts us to Capodimonte and on a tour of churches. Bulls' horns over doorways ward off the evil eye, she says, while rose corsages indicate childbirths. The façade of the Gesu Nuovo looks like a waffle-iron. A pigeon roosts on each nub.

August 7. Cannes. Footpedal boats skim out of the early morning fog like monster waterbugs. Two hours later, as we near Genoa, an elderly man and woman who have been eyeing I.S. all the way from New York are suddenly emboldened to address him. (All first-class passengers are elderly, which is part of the reason why we look longingly from our top deck to the progressively poorer and livelier decks of the cabin and tourist classes.) The man, rosewood walking stick and gardenia lapel apart, puts me in mind of a well-groomed Afghan hound, but his wife is that different kind of canine, the huntress of social big game. *She* does the talking, moreover, dropping into French at one point and then identifying the language in case I.S. might have taken it for Swahili. When eventually they move off, we overhear the Afghan barking at his bitch for "trying to catch *him*."

A dense fog in Genoa harbor, in and out of which small boats dart like phantoms. Gulls hover overhead as if to guide us, like the birds who guided Alexander across the sands to Siwa.

Italy after the United States: diesel fumes; windows that open out instead of up and down; unfrosted electric bulbs; large bath towels and push-buttons by the tub to summon the maid or valet; a cruet of olive oil on the restaurant table; storms of temperament from the clamorous, sweaty, melodramatic dining-room service, in contrast to the imperturbable routine on the boat: our waiter mumbles *"Mamma mia"* on each return from the kitchen, and the state of his nerves is such that he smites his breast and cries *"Mea culpa"* when we so much as point out the shortage of a spoon.

August 8. The Campo Santo—*"Il più bello cimitero del mondo,"* as the sou-

177

1958 venir hawkers claim—is now a major tourist stop, where *ciceroni* interpret and extol as if it were the Bargello. The monuments include sculptured family groups "taken" at the bedsides of the dying, husbands and sons with their hats in their hands, wives and daughters with their tears in their eyes. In one *tableau mourant*, the pose of a mother and child by the bedside might have been modeled on David's *Andromache Mourning Hector*. In another, a young wife pulls the bedclothes over her expired husband's face. And in still another, a newly widowed mother raises her infant son for a farewell *bacio* on his deceased papa's cheek. Almost as common are resurrection scenes in which the dead set out for Heaven with angels pointing the way like traffic policemen. The *fin de siècle* is marked by a trend to the nude, and especially to *pudicità*, in the persons of Eves and Niobes who hold their fig leaves to the forbidden place as coyly as stripteasers hold their fans; and a trend to Philosophy, rendered sculpturally as resignation: what horrible poses of resignation there are! Of the philosophers, Socrates—in an Inverness cape!—is a surprisingly popular saint for a Christian cemetery. Christ Himself is often made to look like a kind of Hegel, a Hegel surrounded by brooding, pinions-folded, philosophy-student angels.

I.S. recalls a monument in another 3-D illustrated cemetery at Padua, a sculptured reconstruction of the actual automobile accident in which the entombed family was killed. A careening lifesize automobile was carved on the grave, with a goggled chauffeur inside and a woman screaming through her veil. "It was as real as Madame Tussaud's," I.S. says, adding: "Surely Taste is a moral category." Of the many hundreds of figures on these sarcophagi, none—I am thinking of those serenely smiling Etruscans on their tombs—expresses repose.

August 9. With our 20 bags in the trunk and tied to the roof of a large Cadillac, we cross the Apennines to Piacenza, Parma, Cremona, Brescia, Verona, Venice. A sign at the entrance to the Cremona cathedral: "Women dressed like men will not be admitted." Chimneys north of Cremona are shaped like curling smoke. At Riva-Garda, I.S. says that Rimsky-Korsakov sent him postcards from here during summer vacations, "and once, on his return, he gave me 25 pages of the orchestra score of *The Snow Maiden*—left, alas, with many letters from him, in Ustilug."

August 10. Venice. I.S. in the Piazza: "This year the pederasts outnumber the pigeons." Byron: "Gehenna of the waves, Thou sea Sodom!"

August 14. We are awakened by a Sousa march, played by the band on the deck of the U.S. cruiser *Des Moines*. Later, U.S. sailors, their eyes on every woman, mix with the odd parade in the Calle Largo XXII Marzo: a German with a monocle trying to look like Eric Stroheim; girls trying to look like Brigitte Bardot; beat generation types successfully looking beat; an elderly English woman with blue-rinse hair; a husky black U.S. sailor followed by a small, fascinated Venetian boy: the sailor, turning, sees the boy, smiles, pats him on the head, gives him a dollar.

August 16. Reading Bembo's *Gli Asolani* and attracted by the romantic Queen of Cyprus, I go to the Academy to see her portrait in the *Miracle of the True Cross of S. Lorenzo;* and to S. Salvator to look for her tomb. Next to the latter is a confessional with a doorbell, and, as a mouthpiece, a perforated ivory cross—dirty, as if from the descriptions of sins.

In 1438 the Catalonian traveler Pero Tafur wrote that no four-legged animals were permitted in Venice (no cats!) and that perfumed bonfires burned perpetually to fumigate the streets and deodorize the canals—history's first operation aerosol.

August 17. To San Lazzaro degli Armeni. A French-speaking monk escorts us from the dock as bells peal and bearded brethren emerge from every direction and converge on the church. The service, that of the third day of Assumption, includes a grape-eating ritual. But if the sense of taste is satisfied, the others are not: the incense chokes, the chanting is out of tune, the floor punishes the knees, and the pyrotechnical effect of a crescendo of candle-lighting is spoiled at the climax by supplementing electric beams. We go to "Byron's Room" for tea and rose marmalade, served by a femininely fussy monk who assures us that the scandalous poet's writings are safely banned from the island. The windows look over gardens toward the casino on the Lido, a short stretch of water but many long centuries away, where Byron used to ride tantivy on the deserted dunes. Opening the door to leave, I.S. finds the entire brotherhood lined up to collect his autograph. Reputedly very learned, they are also prepubertally childlike.

From San Lazzaro to San Francesco del Deserto, more aptly named now than ever: only 15 friars remain. And no wonder. The island is an aviary, and the squawks, trills, twitters, hoots, warbles, boul-bouls (nightingales), together with, offshore, the jobations of gulls, are deafening. Most of these noisemakers are unseen, but a peacock parades the main pathway, and pigeons and plovers, swallows and "lecherous sparrows," owls and ouzels (?—I am no birdwatcher!) are visible in the trees, gardens, cloisters and eaves of the church. Lizards dart across the church floor, their orange gullets inflating like bubblegum.

In the shallows around the island, men in boots are gathering mollusks. Buoys double as shrines here, and some are carved like *rimmonim;* the fishermen replace the candles and adorn the shrines with flowers.

In the Campo San Bartolomeo tonight our thoughts are with Alessandro Piovesan, whose haunt this used to be. Piovesan, ever late on his way to a crisis—underarm briefcase never containing the papers for which he was always searching—is now too soon dead. At last year's farewell dinner, when he proposed a toast "To next year," my thoughts went to I.S. But it is Piovesan we are mourning, and whom we now remember, and always will, by his own favorite word, "*Spirituale.*"

August 19. The 29th anniversary of Diaghilev's death. I.S. and Lifar

1958 see each other in the hotel lobby but do not speak.

August 25. An excursion with Piovesan's widow to Pomposa, Mesola, Comacchio, Ferrara, Mirandola. Mesola, the Xanadu (hunting lodge) of Alfonso II of Ferrara, celebrated in Tasso's *"Mesola, il Po da lato"* and set to music by Giaches de Wert, is now a dreary Palazzo Municipale. We rest in a café and eat hot *cornetti coppia*, rolls shaped like pairs of bulls' horns placed back to back; the Ferrarese name for them is "married couples." Comacchio, famous for eels, is a city of colonnades, canals, and cobblestone streets loud with the clatter of wooden shoes.

Ferrara: the frescoes of the Zodiac in the Palazzo Schifanoia contain no Christian image or symbol. The road to Mirandola lies between fields of straw stacked conically, like teepees. Almost everything in Mirandola is named for its philosopher-son—"Castello Pico," "Drogherie Pico," "Caffè Pico." Like Sanguinetto, San Felice, and other towns in the region, it is a miniature Ferrara, with a small Castello Estense, and the bases of buildings slanting outward.

August 27. Venice. Nina Kandinsky, in the Piazza tonight, tells us that Mondrian "hated nature. Our house in Neuilly was surrounded by chestnut trees, but Mondrian always asked us to 'close the window. I cannot bear trees.' When we went together to see *Boris Godunov*, Mondrian left the theater because the Boyars' beards made him nervous. He liked thickly-made-up women." Switching to Klee, she says that "the most curious thing about him was his relationship with his cat, a mysterious and, as Klee believed, psychic creature who seemed to understand everything about him, as *he* did about the cat, who watched him paint. Once when Klee was visiting us in Paris—I think it was in 1934—he decided to call on Picasso. Kandinsky did not go with him—Kandinsky and Picasso never met—and Klee came back from the meeting much humiliated, saying that Picasso had kept him waiting and treated him in a superior manner."

August 28. To Magliano (Treviso) and the Villa Condulmer where 30 or so huge black barrels are lined up in the wine caves. The piano in the upstairs ballroom belonged to Verdi. At the Villa Emo, Fanzolo, a horse ramp replaces the front stairs. The gardener will not admit us, probably because the present Count Emo still resides here, but the housekeeper has heard of I.S. and overrules.

September 15. Brussels. With André Souris and Robert Wangermée to Huy, on the right bank of the Meuse, for my concert in the huge Gothic church of Notre Dame. My performances of the Masses of Machaut and I.S. are applauded by an audience of musicologists. With Jeanne Déroubaix afterward to Liège and then the train to Cologne, where at 11:30 P.M. we change for Milan and Venice.

September 16. In Venice, I go with Auden and Spender to V.'s vernissage at the Cavallino Gallery. A convention of philosophers is being hosted in the city by the Cini Foundation, and I pass Jean Wahl and A. J.

Ayer in the Frezzeria, and, in the Piazza, E. M. Forster, who walks with his feet turned out, trousers hitched high, hands folded behind his back, forward-thrusting head looking only at the pavement.

September 17. Lunch with the Lamberts, Spenders, and Nabokov. After the Hamburg Orchestra concert in the Fenice, I collide in a side street with Auden, wearing espadrilles cut to accommodate his corns. He is rushing back to his hotel, "because I've just learned that Leopardi wasn't born in the South." To the Piazza with Isaiah Berlin, who speaks in sudden, rapid spurts and is very droll.

September 18. Auden, for lunch at the Bauer, gives me his Cini lecture, *The Pattern and the Way,* and the typescript of his introduction to Valéry's *Analects.* I ask if he knows that Nathalie Sarraute's essay on Valéry in *Les Temps modernes* calls the poems "imitation classicism, pretentious and platitudinous." Auden: "Well, that says something about frogs, nothing about Valéry." But Sarraute is Russian!

I.S. is five minutes late and Auden, fussing obsessively about punctuality, predicts that "the Russians won't win the war because they won't be there on time. 'Dieses warten,' as Tristan says." Now in his German period, Auden says his translation of Goethe's *Italian Journey* "will make him sound like a limey." Less annoyed by untidiness than by unpunctuality, he suggests that the Augean cleaning was a mistake. When I.S. finally arrives, Auden, openly skeptical of the pill bottles being lined up on the table, whispers to me, "The steadiest business in the world would be a pharmacy next door to Stravinsky." At one point, Auden observes that "true creators are always ashamed of most of their past work. Are you ashamed, Igor?" "No. I would do many things differently but I am not ashamed." The poet's next assertion is that Tolstoy had a great sense of humor: "I'm sure that even in his late years if you had said, 'Now come off that old plow,' he would have laughed." I.S. thinks he would have died of apoplexy. Talking about *"l'esprit de con* in literature," Auden calls the work of a famous male writer "a *connerie bien élégante,*" but says that certain female writers, and especially Virginia Woolf, lacked this spirit. The "female" difference, he says, is "the *vas deferens.*" One of his critical yardsticks is "people one would like to be with at dinner. No character in Dostoyevsky would have made an amusing dinner companion, whereas most of Dickens's characters, including many who were evil, would have been fascinating company at table." He also proposes as a category of literary classification, "Great masterpieces of boredom," and nominates Dostoyevsky as "a major bore. He cannot stop talking about his soul. I cannot bear the Russians' total lack of reticence."

The O.E.D. missed "unkiss," he says, a word he found in Aubrey, but his vocabulary today—*hyssop, dittany, pennyroyal*—suggests that he has been reading a treatise on herbs. He shows us his new poem, "Farewell to Mezzogiorno," which explains his panic on discovery that Leopardi was not born in the south. When I.S. complains of intestinal unrest, saying he

1958 has swallowed so much bismuth that he feels like a weir, Auden sings the Methodist hymn: . . ."every bowel of our God / With soft compassion rolls." Auden's paws are pudgy, milk-white, hairless, the fingers stained with nicotine, the nails nibbled halfway to the moons.

In the evening we go with him to a concert at the Fenice, for which he grimly prepares by reminding himself of Nietzsche's "We possess art lest we perish of the truth." At intermission, in the street café in front, he engages I.S. in a discussion about an opera and suggests that "one should study it." "No, one should just steal from it," I.S. replies, not inappropriately in view of the peculations in the *Rake*. When I point out that the second half of the concert begins in two minutes, Auden's response is: "Cyril [Connolly] would say, 'Just time to eat a lobster.'" Back in the theater, Auden remarks that the women's chorus "looks like a bed of petunias."

September 21. After tonight's *Threni* rehearsal, the S.s, Auden, Lucie Lambert, and I go to the Colombo restaurant where a graphologist approaches our table and asks I.S. to write a line on a piece of paper. Auden thinks that this would be foolish, "quite obviously the man knows who Igor is," and writes five lines himself. The character reader then proceeds to draw circles, parallel lines, and mysterious symbols, which even Auden cannot explain. When we are alone again Auden puts on his "dog-collar" and digresses on Biblical symbolisms (*e.g.*, the moon as the Old Testament, the sun as the New); on the argument of *sui generis* (*e.g.*, that man's image is God-like because the image of every man is unique); and on angelogy, much of which sounds like a put-on, except that Auden is fond of scholastic exercitation. Though he and I.S. are equally keen on ritual, dogmas, and faith in the redemptive death, Auden has arrived at his beliefs through theology, I.S. through "mystical" and "miraculous" experience (however diligently he may have applied himself at one time to the *Grammar of Assent*). As a Patripassionist heretic, Auden naturally accepts the Filioque Clause.

September 22. Card from Isaiah Berlin, at the railroad station. He has sent a fan letter to I.S. about the moving experience of meeting him, then immediately regretted this pomposity, as he calls it. Says he is too anglicized to be able to write such things simply.

October 1. Venezia *sub aqua*, the wind raising whitecaps. A duckboard bridge crosses the Piazza, but the café orchestras continue to play under the arcades, like bands on a sinking ship, and crew-cut Americans sit at the tables writing postcards.

October 4. Brussels, the Lamberts', 4 Square de Meeus. Liveried footmen carry my nicked and battered, handleless, and roped-together bags from the street to my room where, to my horror, a valet and two maids unpack the contents, painfully displaying my ragged pajamas and worn-out "dressing gown" on the bed, placing the laundry in a hamper too good for it, folding my "clean" undergarments and placing them in drawers (where I will probably forget them), removing my ancient and disgraceful shoes and belt for polishing and my tuxedo for pressing. Though these people will never be the same again, their professionalism deserves the highest praise: not one of them has snickered over the quality of my clothing and the mess in my bag.

Two hours before dinner a gold-embossed menu and notice of dinner attire are brought to my room (and to those of the 17 other house guests). Service at table is white-gloved, and the voice in which the wine stewards announce the Chateau and vintage before tipping the decanter is so quiet and discreet that neighbors do not overhear. Igor Markevitch, sitting across from me and incomparably better adjusted socially, knows my recording of Schoenberg's Variations and wants to talk about the piece, which he admires but which intimidates him as a conductor.

The conversation of the rich, to generalize, is insular and confined to received opinions. After port, I walk in the Square beyond the line-up of Rollses and their chauffeurs. A tray awaits me in my room with cold breast of pheasant, tarts, wine, and a printed card with a request not to tip the staff. Even the Kleenex on the bed table seems to have been freshly pressed.

October 6. Conduct *Threni* and Webern's Symphony, Variations, and Second Cantata in the large auditorium of the Exposition Universelle.

October 11. Hamburg. With I.S. and Rolf Liebermann to Lübeck, "the world capital of marzipan" and the city of Buxtehude, Bach, *bernstein* (amber stone), and Buddenbrooks (the family home is now a beauty salon). After herring and carafes of green Mosel in the Schabbelhaus, we visit the Heiligen Geist, a 12th-century hospice (like the one in Beaune), still inhabited by old men who live in small cottage-like cubicles, each with flowerpot and mailbox. These residents sit before their doors, some puffing meerschaums, nearly all wearing seamen's caps, which they doff for I.S.

In the tall Marienkirche, built in 1251, we try the partially rebuilt organ once played by Johann Sebastian Bach. On Palm Sunday 1942, British bombs struck the church, dislodging two two-ton bells that crashed sixty meters to the floor where they are still embedded, frozen in a molten state that resembles running, over-ripe Brie.

October 18. To Donaueschingen, ourselves in Prinz Furstenberg's car, the S.s' 20 bags in a truck. The rebuilt 18th-century Schloss is set in an attractive park with gardens, a swan lake, fountains, tall trees turning seasonal yellow. At the entrance, one of several concierges leads us to a shuddering lift and from it, on the third floor, through galleries of royal portraits and a cannon armory capable of sustaining a turn-of-the-century Central American revolution. After a 5-minute walk we reach the Kaiser's suite in the east wing, where the S.s stay, and the Crown Prince's suite, where I stay. The furniture includes cheval glasses, consoles, eiderdown beds, dressing tables. Propped on one of the latter, next to the intra-castle

1958 104-number telephone directory, are seating charts for luncheon and dinner guests: Prinzen (Schwarzenberg, descendant of Beethoven's patron),
and Prinzessen (the Princess of Bavaria), an Erzherzog, an Altgraf, and so
many Grafen (I shall have to look them up in the *Grafliches Taschenbuch*) that
my "Mr." looks distinguished. From this list I learn that Lucie Lambert is a
Baroness.

At 1 o'clock, we go to a luncheon in one of Prince Max Egon von
Furstenberg's smaller houses, a half-mile hike from the cruelty-to-old-
machines elevator through corridors gory with battle paintings, bristling
with antlers of slaughtered stags, and overweighted with sofas and cabinets
in German Empire style; Prince Max Egon is addressed as *"Durchlaucht"*
("serenity"). Because strict protocol obtains at table, I am seated next to
the similarly untitled Olivier Messiaen, a limp, humorless man with profound eyes and no small talk. Later I try to convince I.S. that a part of
Messiaen's mind and emotions would be more at home in the century of
Francis of Assisi, and that the composer is a mystic and a Holy Roller
rather than a *naïf*, which is I.S.'s epithet. But I.S. really does dislike the sentiment, the repetition, the mechanical phrasing, the bird calls, the bom-
bast, and the blockbusting volume of what he knows of Messiaen's music,
besides which he will never forgive Messiaen's criticisms of the *Rake*. Back
to the conciergerie for a guide to lead us through the labyrinth to our
rooms. (A letter there, forwarded from 6 cities, from Patricia Delaney, the
pretty blonde on the *Cristoforo Colombo*, with a *molle à la fesse* and an annoying
Eskimo-style nose-rubbing kiss.)

The baggage van has arrived while we were at lunch, and the contents
of all 20 pieces of luggage, carefully packed by I.S. in Venice and not to be
opened until Hollywood, have been neatly arranged in closets and drawers. His hundreds of pill and medicine bottles are set out on night tables,
and his summer clothes suspended in lockers. After a tantrum that includes
the smithereening of a lamp, he summons valets and maids to repack.

The blonde *Mädchen* who comes to prepare my bath says that one of her
duties is to go through the castle every morning changing the date on the
desk calendars.

October 28. Hamburg. I have a high fever. Several telephone calls
from Glenn Gould, also ill, in the next room.

October 29. Vienna. Dinner at Lucie Lambert's, Wenzgasse 18,
Hietzing. She is the best of whatever may be good about being an "aristocrat," but I am no match for her. Worse, while I have more or less gotten
cold feet, she hasn't. And she has not been discreet. Nabokov now calls
me Count Bob de Rothschild, and the other day Count Salm embraced and
kissed me on both cheeks.

November 1. When I meet the S.s' at the station, they excitedly tell me
about changing trains in Venice yesterday just as every bell in the city
began to ring in jubilation for the election of Cardinal Roncalli as Pope.

Dinner with Hans Popper, a stiff evening, since we know him only through **1958** correspondence. Owner of the Western Steel and Metals Corporation in San Francisco, with which he made a fortune at the end of the War collecting scrap metal on Okinawa, he has come to us at Boulez's suggestion as someone who can help I.S. with currency exchanges in Japan next spring.

November 4. I.S. conducts *Oedipus* at the Vienna State Opera, staged by Oskar Fritz Schuh, scenery and costumes by Caspar Neher. A letter to I.S. from T. S. Eliot: *"Cher maître . . .* we were very much pleased to hear that you are willing to accept the cocktail party. . . ."

November 15. Paris. Alberto and Annette Giacometti for lunch, except that he eats nothing, being unable to take his eyes from the coffee girl whose face he would like to model. Talking about wives, he asks his if she would mind adding the coffee girl to the family: "Three wives would be perfect, two preferable to the tyranny of one. *Tu veux avoir de petites companions?"* He orders and drinks about 20 cups of coffee.

November 22. Rome. *Crostini tartuffati* at Il Buccho with Orson Welles, then to Gasparo del Corso's Palazzo Torlonia to see his Monsù Desiderios. In two large ones, thick, almost *relievo*, white figures rush about on architecturally fantastic sets, which tends to support Berman's theory that one artist painted the architecture, another the figures.* With del Corso to V.'s vernissage in his gallery, then to a reception with Moravia, Morante, Chirico, and Carlo Levi.

November 26. A 10 A.M. telephone from the Vatican summons I.S. to a private audience with the new Pope.** I.S.: "I have no evening clothes here." The Vatican: "Come as you are." I.S.: "I *are* in my pajamas." But he consents, calls Adriana Panni to drive him there, swallows a tooth tumbler of Scotch.

December 3. London. Party at Faber and Faber. Many photos of the S.s with the Eliots, who take us to "their" restaurant, L'Ecu de France.

December 4. To David Astor's lunch at the Connaught, I.S. opposite Harold Nicolson, V. between Nicolson and Isaiah Berlin, myself with Spender and Edward Crankshaw. V. makes a hit with the novelist Henry Green.

December 5. Michel St. Denis comes to discuss the staging of *Oedipus*. Lunch at the Berlins' in Oxford with Edgar Wind, Stuart Hampshire (Wind's wife's lover), John Sparrow (who has deduced, from evidence in the novel, that Lady Chatterley's lover sodomized her), Maurice Bowra, David Cecil, Spender. To the Ashmolean in the afternoon.

---

* Félix Sluys's book *Monsu Desiderio* was the first to identify the two painters as Didier Barra and François de Nomé of Metz.

** The account of this visit in Paul Horgan's *Encounters with Stravinsky* tallies with the one told to me by Stravinsky immediately afterward, except that Horgan mistakenly describes Stravinsky receiving the invitation at a rehearsal.

1958   December 6. Lunch with Sir Campbell Stuart and Lady Crossfield at Anthony Gishford's on Highgate Road. Sir C.S., toothy and tweedy, said to be a descendant of Charles II by one of his French mistresses, enlists me as a member of the Hudson Bay Society. Dinner at Henry Green's, after having been warned not to mention his writing. He is very deaf, and his wife, Adelaide, daughter of the 2nd Lord Biddulph, midwifes the conversation, in spite of which the S.s understand him only when he tries out some pidgin Russian, picked up in Moscow during the War, where he was selling machinery. He is quite informal, and after dinner lifts one of his pants legs to the knee. He says that Waugh's bar is a false-front bookshelf whose titles are "Spender by Isherwood," "Auden by Spender," "Isherwood by Auden."

December 7. Dinner at the Spenders' with Graham Greene, who is so much taller than I.S. that a distant onlooker, not already aware of the diminutive height of the one, might take the other to be a former basketball center. Greene says he had been told that I.S. was in the audience at a New York preview of *The Potting Shed*, and regrets are exchanged that they had not met then. But conversation-making is not easy and lulls are frequent. He lends no support to the infrequent moments of not exactly doubling-up general amusement, nor quite reveals how he regards our own participation in them. And he intimidates the S.s. They have read all his books, beginning with *The Power and the Glory* because of their fascination with Mexico, and they are attracted in advance to the author of them, if not always by his obsessions with pity, fear, self-destruction, failure, the need to run away, the hollowness of physical love, the problem of Pelagian moral arguments. Yet they do not know how to say *"Bonjour"* to him in a way to make him talk; and though not shy as a rule, they cannot bridge the shyness of the other along with their own. And Greene *is* shy; if he were aware of how much the S.s admire him, he would freeze altogether.

His talk is topical, which is not unlooked-for, but the S.s are unaware of the Wolfenden debate, concerning which Greene suggests that T. S. Eliot and John Hayward should be induced to address a letter to the *Times* on the respectableness of two men keeping house together; except that T.S.E. and J.H. are no longer on speaking terms. When Greene's transparent blue eyes focus on one of us, they seem to be seeing something else. As the evening wears on, his brows knit, his jowls weigh down, and his saggy face sags a little more. It is a sad, wise, fanatical face, the mask of a man who has seen a great deal and knows the worst.

Greene talks about the difficulties of unblocking royalties in bamboo-curtain countries, where *The Quiet American* is immensely popular: "It looks as if I will have to spend the rest of my days in China."

December 8. Dinner with the Eliots in their Kensington Court Gardens ground floor flat. The name does not appear on the tenants' roster, but the T.S.E.s are holding hands in the open door when we arrive.

The walls of the apartment are bare except for bookshelves, and most of these are in the dining room, "which is where arguments come up," Eliot says, "and the reason that dictionaries and reference books should be kept there." As if to illustrate the remark, and in response to some speculations by I.S. concerning the word "paraclete," T.S.E. fetches a well-worn Liddell and Scott from behind his own chair but offers a synonym ("the comforter") himself before opening it. He helps again, when I.S. cannot recall the name of the monastic order on San Lazzaro degli Armeni. "The Mechitarist Fathers," Eliot says, and he tells a curious tale about their history. He also provides lapidary translations for his wife of the foreign expressions that occur regularly in I.S.'s talk but denies ever having been a linguist: "I only pretended to be one in order to get a job in a bank." He is a quiet man, slow in formulating his remarks, which trail off in *diminuendo*, and the life in him is not in his voice, but in his clear, piercingly intelligent gray eyes. He breathes heavily, wheezes, and harrumphs a great deal, "Hm, hmm, hmmm," deepening the significance, it seems, with each lengthening "m." His high ha, ha, ha laugh is too slow, but we cannot sustain our own laughter long enough to cover his. His fingers are constantly folding and unfolding, or touching tip to tip, which suddenly makes me realize that I.S.'s hands, otherwise remarkable for the large spread between the knuckles, are the least nervous I have ever seen.

Eliot carves and serves the meat and, to fill our glasses, walks around the table like a wine steward. His manner is formal, reserved, parsonical, and his every comment deliberated. When pressed to adjudicate, he restricts himself to implications. I.S., in comparison, seems to think with the tip of his tongue. Asked about his public readings, Eliot says, "I cannot recite my poetry by memory because it was rewritten so many times that I forget which version was final." Most of his stories are self-deprecating: "One day in a New York taxi with Djuna Barnes, I noticed that the driver had become engrossed in our conversation. After she left, he asked me whether 'that *woman* was a writer.' On one occasion when my airplane was grounded at Gander, I became aware of a young, academic-type woman watching me and hovering ever closer. I invited her for tea and escorted her to a counter, fearing the worst—what had I *really* meant in such and such a poem. Then it came: she was preparing a thesis on Virginia Woolf and, since I had known her, what did I think of her novels?" When the talk turns to mutual French friends, Eliot is interested above all in I.S.'s recollections of Jacques Rivière and brother-in-law, Alain-Fournier. "Cocteau was very brilliant when I saw him last," Eliot says, "but I had the impression he was rehearsing for a more important occasion." During a tense interval I mention Hugh Kenner's *The Invisible Poet*. T.S.E., who seems not to have read it, fidgets nervously, but when I praise Kenner and say that he is good on the plays, he cannot conceal his relief. I.S., in a similar situation, is always fortified with killing comebacks.

_1958_ Table talk, otherwise, is about taxes (I.S. says that he feels guilty on learning that tonight's dinner is not deductible) and about Dylan Thomas. "He had the richest gift of humor of any contemporary poet," Eliot says. "He might have written a good comedy, too, though whether he could have fashioned a libretto I am unable to say." Walter Scott's best verse, he remarks, is in _The Heart of Midlothian_, and he recommends Lockhart's biography to I.S.

We drink sherry before, claret during, whiskey after dinner, at which time Eliot brings a scrapbook bulging with photographs and clippings and invites I.S. to compose something for it, saying that he writes in it himself every night.

> "A time for the evening under lamplight
> (The evening with the photograph album)"

I.S., on the return to Claridge's: "He is not the most exuberant man I have ever known, but he may be the purest."

December 28. New York. The Gladstone Hotel. I.S. poses for the sculptor Berthold Müller-Oerlinghausen. Auden for dinner; martinis before, wine during, and, a change in diet, Drambuie after. When I.S. tells him that we hope to see _The Seven Deadly Sins_, for which he and Kallman have composed the English-version lyrics, he says, "Better hurry and get tickets or you will never get in. _Vanessa_ is on at the Met that night."

December 29. I.S., telephoning the G. Wittenberg Surgical Appliances Company: "This is Mr. Stravinsky, S-T-R-A-. . . ." He spells it loudly and deliberately, as he does when dictating a telegram. "Two years ago you fitted me for a truss. I want an appointment to have it repaired." He has dialed a wrong number, however, and the other party has apparently had to hear the entire speech without finding an opportunity to interrupt. I.S. ill-humoredly cradles the receiver, then carefully dials again. "This is Mr. Stravinsky, S-T-. . . . You made a. . . ." The same party answers, very annoyed. Annoyed now himself, I.S. double-checks the number in his address book, finds it correct, still believes he has misdialed, tries again. "This is Mr. . . ." This time the man on the other end, no doubt believing himself the victim of a raving lunatic, slams down the receiver. At this point V. discovers from the telephone directory that I.S. has miscopied the number. The foregoing is a typical I.S. "scene." At least one such occurs daily.

੩ Postscript 1994. I did not accompany the Stravinskys to Houston at the beginning of 1958 for his concerts and her exhibition there, but Edward James, who was still trying to commission Stravinsky to set one of his poems, was with them, and Paul Horgan, whose honorable book _Encounters with Stravinsky_ includes a detailed chronicle of the sojourn.

A new medical crisis occurred in 1958. The regular, often weekly, phlebotomizing that since 1956 had supposedly "contained" Stravinsky's polycythemia was no longer considered safe. After the return from Texas, Stravinsky's visits to his doctor, Sigfrid Knauer, were increasingly frequent and, finally, daily. (I was Knauer's patient at the time as well and could do some of the driving.) Knauer, together with his Russian-born and Indian-bred wife, Indra Devi, deserves a place in any biography of Stravinsky in the Hollywood years; by age, cultural background—he spoke Russian as well as German—and holistic medical philosophy, he was closer to Stravinsky than any of his other American-period physicians. Knauer broke Stravinsky's vitamin-injection dependency, treating him instead with calcium, "Hepato Alpha," homeopathic medicines and, for the bursitis, acupuncture. But at the end of May Stravinsky was hospitalized for 10 days with a bleeding ulcer. Two new doctors were consulted, Hans Schiff, cardiologist, and Henry Jaffe, hematologist, and Stravinsky was given an intravenous injection of radioactive phosphorus ("phosphorus 32"). The long-range effects of P32 therapy were still unknown and this was an anxious time for him; if the dosage happened to be too strong would the polycythemia vera (the full name of the disease, a family joke) turn into leukemia? Thirteen years and as many masterpieces later, Stravinsky died not of polycythyemia but of pneumonia, and kidney and heart failure; but in 1958 the risk and uncertainties were a constant concern. Still, Stravinsky amused himself and us by pretending that he was radioactive and might light up like a firefly. By the middle of July he had received radio phosphorus for the fourth time, administered now in liquid form. The ulcers had long since healed.

I was in Santa Fe later in July to conduct, of all things, the *Eroica* Symphony. The day after the concert I joined the Stravinskys' Los Angeles-to-Chicago train in Lamy. In Chicago, between stations and after transferring to the one for New York, we dined with Paul Fromm, the patron of modern music, who had invited me to conduct a program in New York at the beginning of January to include the American premiere of *Threni*.

The crossing on the *Cristoforo Colombo* was smooth and, compared to the *Vulcania* two years before, luxurious. The ship's hostess, Principessa Doria-Pamphili, was especially attentive to the Stravinskys, and during the five-hour stop in Naples she graciously accompanied us to churches and museums. In Venice, on August 11, a piano was installed in Stravinsky's room at the Hotel Bauer, and he began work on the composition that was to become the Movements for piano and orchestra.

In the autumn of 1958, I was in Hamburg three times, the first of them to rehearse the pieces Stravinsky was to conduct with the North German Radio Orchestra and Chorus in Venice in mid-September—*Threni*, *Oedipus Rex*, and *The Rite of Spring* (my first experience conducting the work)—the

1958 second for a concert of my own, and the third with Stravinsky for his concert. These first of many visits to the city were made enjoyable by the generous hospitality of Rolf Liebermann, then the director of the Norddeutscher Rundfunk, in which capacity he had commissioned *Threni*, later the Intendent of the Hamburg Opera.

Brussels, following the first stay in Hamburg, was much less agreeable. The city was overcrowded with World's Fair tourists, and the only room I could find, closet-sized and with no bath, was in a private apartment. At the end of September Stravinsky conducted *Threni* in Geneva, Basel, Zurich (twice), and Bern. By the time he returned to Venice at the beginning of October, I was back in Brussels, in more comfortable circumstances, to conduct *Threni* and Webern in a concert sponsored by the World's Fair. I spent a wonderful week with the Stravinskys in Florence in October and a much less pleasant one with them in Vienna, a city they had always and intensely disliked: the inhabitants, the Imperial architecture, the food, the ingrained 19th-century performance style of the orchestras. But they were happy in Rome, from whence we traveled to London by train and on to New York by sea, Stravinsky's doctors having advised him not to fly.

1959

January 11. New York. To Pennsylvania Station for New Orleans and Los Angeles.

January 12. South of Atlanta: pine woods, corn fields, whitewashed wood-frame churches, unpainted cabins on brick legs (no house has a foundation), swamps, ponds with thin panes of ice, muddy roads, black women wearing red kerchiefs, billboards with Southern names (Ida Cason Callaway), a Civil War cemetery (in La Grange; an iron fence enclosing a field of white headstones). We leave the train in Montgomery for a walk in the warm, fragrant air. A sign directs us to a "General Waiting Room." Another, less conspicuous one, points to a "Colored Lunch Counter."

Mobile. Sea smells, gulls, rusty tankers. In New Orleans, after dark, we go to "Hyp Guinle's Bar" to hear Dixieland jazz, then walk in Jackson Square. River odors and molasses. (My mind goes back to 1943—June 18, of all days—and my first, and only, experience with a *putain*. A pretty young woman knocked on the door of my cheap hotel room here, said "Do you want me?" and when I gulped out "yes," told me to take off my clothes, including my dog tags. She inspected me, sheathed me, threw up her dress, took a position on the bed, where I mounted her awkwardly and where the elapse "between the desire and the spasm" was far too brief.) At midnight the *Sunset Limited* climbs slowly over the Huey Long Bridge. Oil wells rise out of the swamps, bright as Christmas trees.

January 13. Three hours after a walk in warm, rain-fresh San Antonio, we go out again in Del Rio, where a loudspeaker in a café across from the station blares lively Mexican music and invitations to try its hot tamales. The Rio Grande is a thin brown trickle in a low gorge. Sanderson, at sundown, is a grim adobe town beneath a shelf of smooth, black mountains.

January 15. Los Angeles. Letter from my inimitable mother: "The review in *Time* is just absolutely great." I.S. receives a letter, not the first, from his former landlady in Bad Wildungen. Since he did not answer the last one, received some six years ago and addressed "*Lieber* Professor Stravinsky," the new one, to his irritation, adds the nobiliary particle:

1959 "Dear Mr. Igor Von Stravinsky: It was in 1902 that you were living in my home, "Johanna," with your brother Gury and your parents. Your father told me that he was at the Imperial Opera in St. Petersburg, and he showed me a gold watch, a present from the Tsar. . . . Maybe one day you will come here. . . ."

February 6. A letter from Isaiah, containing his essay on Montesquieu and saying that with Nabokov's help he managed to retrieve and destroy his fan letter to I.S. Apropos our upcoming concerts in Japan, he calls *The Tale of Genji* "a splendid dull masterpiece." Says that he does not like *Lolita*, but signed a letter to the *Times* in favor of its publication in Britain. From his *Montesquieu*, a typical Isaiahan comment on a letter by the philosopher to Madame du Deffand: "the pleasure of watching grave and dignified theologians not thrown roughly on the ground but sliding gently into the abyss."

February 10. The Danish Ambassador calls from Washington to tell I.S. that he has won the Sonning Prize. Letter from Auden:

> Dear Bob: Many thanks for your letter. By all means make use of any correspondence that you have (I agree that Ebert should be omitted). As there is a double question of interest about collaboration
>
> a) Composer-Librettist
> b) *Librettist-Librettist*
>
> it might be worthwhile introducing some of the discussions between Chester and myself. For instance, though of course 2 librettists are not 2 people but a composite personality, I have been amused at the way in which critics, trying to decide who wrote what, have guessed wrong. The actual facts are:
>
> *Act I*
> Scene 1. Down to end of Tom's aria . . . "This beggar shall ride." W.H.A. From there to end of scene. C.K.
> Scene 2. W.H.A.
> Scene 3. C.K.
> *Act II* (C.K.).
> Scene 1. Down to end of Tom's aria ". . . in my heart the dark." C.K. From there to the end of scene. W.H.A.
> Scene 2. C.K.
> Scene 3. W.H.A.
> *Act III*
> Scene 1. C.K. (except for lyrics sung off-stage by Tom and Shadow).
> Scene 2. Baba's [i.e., Shadow's] verses at beginning and end of scene. W.H.A. middle (card-guessing game). C.K.
> Scene 3 and Epilogue. W.H.A.

Do you have a copy of the original draft scenario at which we *1959* had arrived when I left Hollywood in Nov 1947? If you do, we would very much like a copy to refresh our memories on the exact steps by which we arrived at a final version. Love to all, Wystan

February 25. Telegram from David Oppenheim at Columbia Records: "Varèse trusts you completely and prefers not to send metronome markings."

February 27. Gerald says that stepping stones were placed in running water in ancient Greece because spirits were not supposed to leap over water. Though terrified, I conduct a live "dialogue" with him on television.

March 13. To open a ball at the Beverly Hilton for the Los Angeles Music Festival, V. and Vincent Price dance in a spotlight. Harpo Marx joins us at our table.

March 19. Lunch at Huxleys' with Romain Gary and Lesley Blanch. Aldous, dominating and correcting Gary, rather too obviously prefers her to him.

March 24. Long letter from Boulez about the irremediable misunderstanding with I.S. Says he has still not seen Goléa's article in *Das Musikleben*, and, *"Vous êtes très amis, et je ne supporte pas longtemps que l'on attaque mes amis."* He promises to follow my suggestion about seeing I.S. in Copenhagen May 25. Says that his performance of *Threni* in Munich went very well except for the flugelhorn.

March 25. Honolulu. We leave the plane in a sudden, warm rain, as clouds break over Diamond Head, but the orchid and frangipani leis, thrown by natives wearing yellow muu-muus and warriors' helmets, are strangulation threats. After settling in the Princess Kaiulani Hotel, we swim, just before sunset, in the slow Waikiki surf. R. L. Stevenson's hut, given him by Princess Kaiulani, has recently been moved from the beach to a nearby lot.

March 26. Island flora: African tulip trees; bougainvilleas; ear pods and monkey pods; crawling cactus and Mexican creepers; creeping philodendrons; night-blooming Cereus (a sinister, tentacular plant); blood-red caliphers; jade vines; picoma trees; pink shower trees; banyans with aerial roots. The Hawaiian language contains pure vowel words—*aiea*—in which each letter is pronounced as a separate syllable. "H" is a vowel, too, as in mahi-mahi, a delectable dolphin or *mahi-tahi*, which means cravat (a corruption of "my tie"?). Muu-muus, the head-to-toe *sac* dress, are known as Mother Hubbards, the New England missionaries having concealed the native charms with this garment. The homes of missionaries' descendants are among the most prosperous on the island.

March 27. The Royal Hawaiian Cemetery. To keep defilers away, the graves of Kings and Queens are marked by taboo poles with gold balls.

At Pearl Harbor, the sight of the flag above the superstructure of the

1959 sunken *Arizona* jolts me back to the unforgettable afternoon when the news of the bombing was broadcast over the loudspeaker in the football stadium on Long Island where I was watching a game that did not come to a stop.

March 28–29. On Wake Island, a shadowless solarium. After nine hours of empty ocean, we scuff through pink coral dust to an open-air canteen. Another plane, eastbound, lands soon after ours, and one of its passengers, a Swiss, approaches and says: "I want to thank you for your Webern records." On Wake Island! The Filipinos in the work crew who watch our take-off are charcoal black, like figures in an underexposed negative. Guam, at midnight, is bathed in moonlight, and a hot wind rustles the palm trees.

March 30. Manila Airport, 5 A.M. The S.s count their baggage—*ras, dva, tri, chetyri*—over and over. Mr. Morris, the U.S. cultural attaché, drives us to the Manila Hotel, where a dozen eager porters pack us into our rooms. Old Manila, what we see of it on the way, is miserable except for pretty lattices and grilles and the translucent mother-of-pearl clamshell windows. The bay shores are lined with Coca-Cola carts and hundreds of "nightclubs," actually tiny, two- or three-customer booths. They are a squalid sight now, at daybreak, but in comparison to the clusters of orange-crate dwellings inside the old walls, they seem almost hopeful.

Mr. Morris accompanies us on an excursion to Taytay and Lake Taal, stopping on the way at the Church of Las Piñas to hear the bamboo organ. Built in 1824 by Diego Cera, a Spanish friar who had no metal, the entire organ—keys, pedals, 901 pipes—is made of bamboo. To make the pipes termite-proof, Cera buried them in beach sand for a year, but the pipes replaced since his time have succumbed to the pest.* Gounod's *Ave Maria*, played by a monk for our alms, sounds like a choir of recorders: sweet, weak in volume, out of tune.

The road leaving Manila crosses salt flats, and the roadside is heaped with bags marked ASIN, the dialect word for salt. Another common sign is SARI-SARI, the local word for "sundries"; but all directions and most billboards are in English, no progress having been made toward consolidation of the eight major Philippine dialects. Beyond the flats, at the edge of the jungle, a police roadblock warns of banditry in the neighborhood, but this encourages rather than alarms the S.s. The road is hemmed in by canebrakes and is at times entirely canopied by liana. The only human habitations are bamboo huts on stilts, in the midst of coconut and banana groves, and the only people on the road are two men carrying red-shakoed cocks. Halfway to Taytay a carabao herd crosses in front of us.

---

* In 1973, the organ was dismantled and shipped to the workshop of the Bonn organ builder, Hans Gerd Klais, where it was wrapped in a plastic cocoon reproducing Manila's tropical heat and humidity. A year later, the organ was reinstalled at Las Piñas with 129 metal pipes in addition to the 901 made of bamboo.

Taytay is treeless and the townspeople carry large black umbrellas against the torrid sun. On the main street is a parked bus full of sleeping passengers; it is siesta time, Mr. Morris says. All wide-awake Taytayans clamor to be photographed and to sell us fruit. Some of them say "Happy New Year," but the only other English they know is "Coca-Cola," the product being the economic index to the whole community, to judge by the stacks of empty cases everywhere. The terrace of the Taal View Lodge provides a panorama of the great volcanic lake thousands of feet below.

Dinner at the U.S. Embassy with the "Chip" Bohlens, who obviously enjoy exercising their Russian, which they speak with an attractive American drawl. They show color slides of Russian churches taken during their Moscow incumbency and slides of the Banawe country in northern Luzon, where a week ago two geologists were decapitated—for the probable reason, the Ambassador says, that they had asked indiscreet questions. In one frightening photograph, a Banawe warrior charges toward the camera brandishing a spear, though *his* intention, Mrs. Bohlen says, was not to throw but to sell it. I ask about José Rizal, "the Philippine Goethe," whose statues embellish Manila's parks and whose biography fills its bookstores; but the Ambassador says that Rizal's *Noli Me Tangere* is "no more than competent literature."

According to the Bohlens, dog meat is a delicacy here, served in the highest society, and markets exist in which the buyer may select the canine still in the quick. So great is the native appetite, and the danger from dognappers, that the Bohlens keep their own poodle under guard. When at one point the Ambassador opens the screen doors for more ventilation, a large rat leaps inside and up the stairs; it is not found by the time we leave.

I try to sleep with the lights on, hoping that they may discourage the musical geckos on the wall, and the cockroaches on the floor, from joining me in my bed.

March 31. The great rice fields of Antipolo and Morong are parched and brown, and the whole island world is waiting for the rains. In one town a draughts contest is in progress in the middle of the street, and in another a game of billiards. Water carriers trot along the road in a swinging caracole, holding their shoulder poles with the right hand and balancing themselves with the extended left, like football players running interference. Planting has already begun in one irrigated paddy near Morong, and, nearby, a circle of women winnow the rice with flails. Morong itself is draped from end to end with fishing nets, and its church, a cross of pagoda and baroque, is inhabited solely by pigs.

April 1. A turboprop to Kowloon, where a travel agent escorts us from the airport to the ferry and, across the water, in Hong Kong, to the Repulse Bay Hotel. As the boat starts to move, a BBC voice, through a loudspeaker, warns us not to smoke. Repeated in Chinese, the warning lasts 10 times as long and swoops up and down a whole xylophone of inflection. Among the foot passengers, the coolies slough their shoulder poles and baskets to the deck. Small boys go from car to car peddling Wrigley's chewing gum.

The Repulse Bay might have been built by the Canadian Pacific Railroad for a Chinese settlement in Saskatchewan. We sit by a stained-glass peacock window in the restaurant, then move to a terrace overlooking the jade sea, the purple sampans, and the sugar-loaf islands. The waiter inquires whether we "want eat egg first or fiss" (fish), but the food is British. The *salon de thé* orchestra makes a Rossini overture sound like "Chopsticks." In the lobby we meet the Conroys, our next-door North Wetherly Drive neighbors!!

April 2. Today's *South China Morning Post* publishes a photo of I.S. at the airport, along with the story of the Chinese annexation of Tibet and flight of the Dalai Llama. At William McGee's, in Gloucester Road, 15 tailors take turns speaking to us through the English of one boy who, as they measure and fit us, translates a stream of questions about life "stateside." The McGees are Shanghai Chinese, he says, and they do not understand the Cantonese and other dialects of Hong Kong. He adds that while few boys of his age can do brush calligraphy, older people are nonetheless contemptuous of penmanship. But, then, according to him only a few Hong Kong Chinese can write at all or remember enough characters to be able to read a newspaper. His own English is a language of lallations (the unpronounceable "r"). He says "fóul dollas" but means "four dollars," not "filthy lucre." Why, if he singsongs his native tongue, is his English so monotone? When we leave, V. asks the Chinese for "good-bye," but he says " 'Bye-bye' is all we know."

We hire three rickshaws and bump alongside buses, trolleys, automobiles, and pedestrians—Chinese, Indians, British civil servants, tourists, beggars, porters with yokes, women with head-loads. Our runners, who are barefoot and who carry towels in their belts to mop perspiration, deposit us at a pier where we watch a junk unloading crates marked "Made in Japan." In addition to the cargo, the small vessel carries a family of seven and is an ark of domestic animals as well. At sunset, Hong Kong is curtained in mist. I go to sleep with the hoot of harboring boats in my ears.

April 4. At the Kowloon Resettlement Area, concrete apartments housing half a million refugees, children swarm around us but superstitiously turn away from V.'s, and everyone else's, camera, because that instrument steals a piece of your soul. At one place we are delayed by a wedding and at another by a funeral, the former with red, the latter with white flowers. In the silver-plated, glass-sided hearse, six men in Western-style business suits but Chinese ceremonial headdress sit around the coffin.

Lunch at Shatin on a terrace overlooking the valley of the Kowloon-Canton railroad. Farther inland are walled cities, temples, pagodas. Today is Chinese All Souls', and the road is crowded with processions. Buddhist dead are exhumed after seven years and reburied in blue urns, leaving, in the first place of burial, cenotaphs that look like concrete armchairs. On the road to Taipo, caged pigs are carried on bicycle handlebars. At Taipo our driver promises to show us a "model poetry farm," meaning chickens, not a group of aspiring versifiers attending a lecture by Stephen Spender. A little farther, at the border of the People's Republic, women come up to the wire fence to be photographed, demanding "one Melican dolla" for the service. They wear loose black trousers, high-collared jackets slit at the sides, and lampshade hats. At Castle Peak, on the return to Kowloon, junks with black sails fill the bay.

April 5. To Tokyo, over Okinawa, a violently rattling and bumpy flight during which even the stewardesses are sick. Photographers meet us, as well as Jones, the Pan Am representative, who takes us to dinner at the Hananoki Restaurant with a beautiful girl, Kaoru Kanetaka. Afterward we sit at low tables in the Ginza where girls in tight toreador pants bring tea.

April 6. The city is preparing for the royal wedding. Railings are being built around the moats of the Imperial Palace to keep the crowds from falling in. Because the cherry blossom season is over, celluloid and paper imitations have been fixed to street poles and trees. Throughout the city, colored balloons float messages of what I take to be felicitation, until Jones tells us that they are business-as-usual advertisements.

At I.S.'s press conference this morning, the translations of his interpreter, Hans Pringsheim, nephew of Frau Thomas Mann, are generally rapid, but occasionally a short phrase of I.S.'s—"No, I don't like it"—lasts a full minute in Japanese. Cameras grind throughout the hour-long interview, but the faces behind them betray no interest in their target. The questions, too, are very far from the subject.

The sea at Kamakura today is the gray of Whistler's Pacific in the Frick, and the beaches are obsidian black. We sit cross-legged and numb at the knees in a Chinese restaurant eating shrimps in scrambled eggs, our first meal negotiated entirely with chopsticks.

The Great Buddha of Kamakura seems smaller at three yards than at 300, from which greater distance, moreover, the eyes appear to be closed. People wait in long lines to kneel before it, pray quickly when their turns come, and clap their hands as they rise. I.S. thinks "it is full of electricity." The crowds at the nearby toy-stalls seem equally rapt, but some of the playthings, magnetic cylinders and so forth, look like mechanical aptitude tests.

Complaining of pyloric spasms during the return to Tokyo, I.S. wonders why no one has written a book about toilets and travel, with chapter headings on WCs in Greece, the lack of them in India, and Spain from the bathroom window: the subject is so extensive that a two-volume compendium is needed. Our intestines regulate our travels and are our upper-

1959 most worry, and the uppermost emotion of all those tourists at Persepolis and the Taj Mahal is anal anxiety. But travel literature never mentions the subject, and of major authors only Voltaire gave due importance to *la chaise percée*.

April 7. Reception at the Fukudaya, a 17th-century farmhouse converted to a restaurant of *chambres privées*. After exchanging shoes for slippers in what was formerly a stall for massaging steers—to distribute the fat evenly—we dangle our legs over a brazier deep in the floor beneath a low table; here geishas bring hot saki, kneel at our elbows, and replenish our cups after each sip. Tonight's special hors d'oeuvre is a spoon-size tennis racket made of fried kelp, in honor of the first meeting, on a tennis court, of the Prince and Princess-to-be. Successive courses—tempura, *unagi* (eel), and too many other seafoods to remember let alone eat—are served in a larger room, in which we squat around an open firepit. After dinner, the geishas perform some very boring folk dances to scratchy phonograph records.

April 8. Arriving at the Kabukiza Theater during an interval between plays, we are shown the offstage music room, the costume and prop rooms, and the mechanism of the revolving stage (invented by the Japanese four centuries ago), then introduced to an 11-year-old actor, sword carrier to Togashi, the Keeper of the Barrier Gate in *Kanjincho*, the next play. Behind the curtain an even younger actor is being readied for presentation in a formal initiation rite, a kind of Thespian Bar Mitzvah that proves to be as moving and theatrical as the play itself. Both children glisten with greasepaint.

Back in the foyer we buy boxes of sushi and *maguro* (raw tuna) to eat during the play, which is announced by the clapping together of two wooden blocks. As we reach our seats, an attendant runs across the wide stage-front, pulling the curtain open with him. The child debutante and six adult actors march onstage and kneel on mats facing the audience. One of the elders then makes a speech, every few words of which are punctuated by heads-to-floor bows from the other five.

What most impresses us in the melodrama *Kanjincho* is the unity of sound and gesture, for the actors are no less accomplished musically—in the art of *Sprechgesang*—than they are plastically, as actors and dancers. In fact, *Kanjincho* might be described as a *Sprechgesang* opera, with *Sprechgesang* arias, recitatives, dialogues, ensembles. And to us the musical element is primary: the grunts, groans, strangulated falsettos; the *glissando* on the hourglass drum; the wheezy native wood-notes wild of the flute. When the hero, Benkei, prevents the villain, Togashi, from seeing that the scroll from which he has pretended to be reading is blank, and when, to indicate extreme tension, Benkei crosses his eyes, audience shouts approvals. Prolonged shouts meaning "Take your time," "Do it well," "Olé," burst out again later as Benkei, again escaping Togashi's suspicions, performs the series of leaps known as *Tobiroppo*.

Kaoru K. takes me to the Benibasha, a loud and crowded nightclub. "Ladies and gentlemen, winter is over," the host proclaims. "Spring is of most comfortable climate and every creature begins. We should be happy if you would be able to smell real Japanese Nation." This is by way of introducing some deodorized folk dances to an almost exclusively American clientele. All announcements are in American, too, and in fact the only non-American feature is the herd of about 50 girls standing behind a grille, an over-made-up, totally expressionless harem-for-hire.

From the *Asahi Evening News*'s report of I.S.'s press conference:

> "What is modern music anyway?" Stravinsky asked. "I don't care a damn about so-called modern music. You ask whether my style is modern. My style is my style, that's all. . . ." As the three best conductors of his music he picked Pierre Monteux and Fritz Reiner—adding that they had both become "lazy"—and Robert Craft, whom he called a very good and active conductor of his works, "the old ones, the new ones, and even those not yet written."

April 9. From today's *Mainichi*, the English language newspaper:

> Stravinsky said he has had an "old contact" with Japan through his composition on an old Japanese "Waka" poem. . . . He produced, in 1913, three pieces on a Russian version of the Japanese poem[s]. . . . The maestro . . . had been interested in Japanese wood block prints . . . .his "two-dimensional" music met with severe criticism at that time. Critics of the time were idiots, he said. . . . Asked to name works of his own that he would like to recommend: "I would recommend all my works. . . ." He explained that the best works are those which can be felt in his heart and ears, just as in the case of an expectant mother. "Are you expecting a baby?" came a question. "Yes, I am, but I am interrupted by this visit to Japan. May I interrupt you to take my lunch?"

Classical Japanese pornography has an antiseptic effect on Western, or at least my, sensibilities; or so I feel after an inspection of improper prints surreptitiously shown today in a bookshop. Instead of voluptuous postures of idealized naked females, inert people are portrayed and always fully and elaborately clothed. While the point of many of the illustrations is obscure, others confront the viewer with grossly exaggerated sexual organs. Like the best European erotica, this is largely 18th-century.

The landscape outside Tokyo is more beautiful in the rain, and farmers still wear the straw raincoats pictured by Hokusai, but the spectacle of so many bicyclists holding umbrellas, which are part of hotel room equipment, is too acrobatic and nervous-making.   During a thunderstorm on the drive to Hakone, we take refuge in a hotel in Miyanoshita. South of Kamakura, concrete fortifications from 1945 still defend the beaches, but it seems to me that a more formidable obstacle to an invading army would have been the roads; indeed, one wonders how a country so highly industrialized can afford such narrow and imperfectly paved ones. Near Hakone we encounter a funeral procession, its colored-paper wreathes wilting in the downpour.

On the return to Tokyo, I count seven major traffic accidents. "Kamikaze drivers," says "Slim"-san, *our* driver, adding that they come down the wrong side of the road attempting to bluff the counter-traffic into the ditch. Motorcycle drivers are even more reckless and aggressive. Like many pedestrians, they wear surgeons' bandages over their noses and mouths.

April 10. Cannonades proclaiming the royal wedding day jolt us out of bed at 6 A.M. Having been warned to remain indoors and avoid the crowds, we watch the parade on television. Whereas the horse guards gallop almost into the screen, and the banzai-ing mobs are shown at close range, the Prince and Princess are kept at a great distance.

From my notebook: "Japanese eyesight is not poor, or at any rate spectacles are less endemic than wartime caricatures have led us to expect, but teeth are worse. Japanese men and women belong to different races. The latter pursue a cult of quintessential femininity—shyness and modesty, high, hushed voices and doll-like make-up—in opposition to a blustering, bellicose masculinity. But this exaggeration of sexual characteristics is in no sense chivalric, the Japanese woman being the parfit servant of her knight."

Other entries observe that the Japanese say "Yes" when they don't understand, hoping you will forget; and that the women giggle without apparent provocation, yet fail to react in any situation we regard as humorous. That I.S. is enjoying himself here more than V. can be attributed partly to his Japanese height; whereas my knees press the wall of the WC and my head is a foot above the mirror when I shave, these utilities are exactly tailored to him. Another reason is the absence of tipping, of the fumbling for money, the nuisance and embarrassment suffered at arrivals and departures everywhere else in the world.

April 11. With Donald Richie to red and gold Nikko, through windswept and comparatively barren country, in which hay mounds have been thatched to poles and saplings. Nikko is untouched by spring, and snow begins to fall in late afternoon. The temples are as gaudy as Grauman's Chinese Theatre in Hollywood. We approach them through a gateway guarded by freshly lacquered green and vermilion gods, and inside we park our shoes at the door and pad about on cold, straw-matted floors. Priests in black hats and green and white robes are purveying religious trinkets, but most of the visitors crowding the corridors are schoolchildren. The hills beyond the compound are overgrown with groves of mausoleums.

Back in Tokyo, I.S. receives a visit from Mrs. Noemi Perressian Raymond and her husband, whom he knew in Morges in 1918 and 1919 but has not seen since 1942, at a dinner in New York at Fernand Léger's. Mr. Raymond was U.S. Attaché in Switzerland during World War One, and the money collected for I.S. in America at that time, most of it from Mrs. Raymond's mother, passed through his hands. In New York in the early 1920s, Noemi Raymond had acted as intermediary between I.S. and Pierre Monteux.

April 12. The crowd on the station platform awaiting the early train to Kyoto consists largely of young women with puffy cheeks and flat profiles carrying babies in back-pouches; old men with wispy white beards; and old women in kerchiefs, smocks, boots, accompanied by children dressed like Eskimos. In spite of the crush, everyone queues up in an orderly manner, and when the train arrives, no one pushes. The Osaka Festival officials who help us to our seats say "Thank you very muts," and "If you pease, if you pease," in response to no matter what *we* say or do. Our fellow passengers in the caboose are camera fanatics who spend the entire journey photographing exits from tunnels. This so-called observation car is equipped with a bar—"Scotch" whiskey, both Japanese and imported—and two WCs, respectively identified on the doors as "Western Style Lavatory" and "Japanese Style Lavatory"; the latter, a hole in the floor, attests to the superior strength and flexibility of Japanese knees.

Waiters canvass the train for luncheon orders hours in advance so that the meal may be served at appointed times and without delay, but at noon the smell of sushi in the third-class carriages makes us regret not having ordered the Japanese-style meal ourselves. In the European *wagon-restaurant*, the division of labor is so minute that one person sets the table with knives, another with forks, and yet another with spoons. *Oshibori* (hot towels) are distributed before and after each course, as they are every hour or so in the caboose.

The landscape is industrial as far as Atami, where we reach the sea. After that, neatly rounded rows of tea bushes cover mile after hilly mile, then give way to flat land growing rice. At Kyoto, photographers and geishas meet us, the latter, in full costume and clacking on high wooden shoes, as embarrassed as we are, perhaps, though faces under so much white flour betray nothing.

April 13. Kyoto. The temple of Sanjusangen-do is a forest of 1,001 lifesize wood-and-gold-leaf images of Kannon, Goddess of Mercy, each with 11 faces and a prodigious number of hands. The long, straight ranks of this graven assembly occupy the largest room in Japan. The other rooms contain other wood sculptures, diabolical figures chiefly—demons,

1959 demiurges, winged Beelzebubs—along with a few ascetics and contempla-
tives and Sivas playing cymbals and a lute. The proliferation of the
Kannons, the literalness of the multiplication, appalls I.S.

The long avenue entering Osaka, where we go for a *Figaro* by the
Vienna State Opera, is choked by side-street rivulets debouching dense
and perpetual traffic. The Japanese orchestra and chorus in the opera are
good enough, if never quite in tune, but the dramatic action disappoints:
we want more Kabuki. At intermission, a Japanese musician approaches
I.S., addressing him in, so it seems, English, but I.S. says that he sounded
"like Donald Duck." After Act Two, we escape 10 flights up in the same
building to the Alaska Restaurant. From this elevation the neon advertisements are like abstract paintings. What luck not to be able to read them!

April 14. From today's Osaka *Mainichi*: "Stravinsky, speaking before a
news conference here, said he had been inspired by Kabuki music and indicated strongly that several musical ideas already are forming in his head.
He said he has been impressed by the 'rhythmical orderliness.' He said
that [Kyoto] was a city of 'great character,' and that it made a deep impression on him, in contrast to Tokyo."

Kyoto is rectilinear, like a Chinese city; a city of wooden buildings,
whose survival must be attributed to miraculous rains and efficient fire
departments; a city of black houses with black slate roofs; of permanent
rush-hour-size crowds in gray and black kimonos; of black-robed monks
and priests with shaven heads; of swarming bicycles; of bamboo television
antennas; of tourists, predominantly Japanese, who pour in and out of temples and shrines like gusts from Aeolus's bag. Kyoto is not conspicuously
clean, except in the residential districts where piles of firewood are tidily
stacked against each immaculately proper house.

The lake of Ryoan-ji is girdled by a carpet of moss, red camellias, and
trees as holy as the temples. Never destroyed and apparently never
pruned, many of the limbs are supported by systems of Dali-like crutches.
The spiky ginkgos with strips of white cloth tied to their branches, the
equivalent of ex-voto messages, are like women in curlers. We rest on the
Temple porch, regarding, if not contemplating, the furrowed sand and its
famous islands of rock.

The twin images of the Deva kings, under the eaves of the Ishiyama-
Tera gate, are worm-browsed and whitewashed with bird droppings.
Inside, novitiates and lay brethren gently whisk the grass with besoms.
The temple itself is half-hidden by tall cryptomerias. As we enter, by way
of a porch hung with huge paper lanterns, a priest is kneeling before an
altar piled with oranges and bread and performing ceremonious hand flour-
ishes accompanied by animalian guttural noises. According to tradition,
the *Tale of Genji* was written in the adytum's "Murasaki Room," for which the
author paid the rent by copying a sutra—now on display and said to be
indubitably in her hand. Two beautiful scroll portraits of her are also pre-

served here, "Murasaki Looking at the Moon" and "Murasaki at Her Writing Table." In the first, the writer stands gazing out of a window, long hair covering her shoulders and back. In the second, the hair is braided and a pleated kimono billows behind her like a tent.

April 15. The treasure of the Shugakuin Palace is a fragment of a painting on the walls of the Middle Tea House, a picture of a fish escaping through a torn net. Shugakuin is also famed for its cherry trees, on which late blossoms look like popped popcorn; and for its gardens, the tidiest imaginable, thanks to a task force of old women in white smocks and caps who tiptoe about dusting the moss.

The woodland temple at Kozan-ji is the repository of the great animal-cartoon scrolls by the eleventh-century priest Kakuyu. Houses in the area are moss-thatched, and the roofs are held down at the gable ends by sawhorse braces. At the temple, on the edge of a ravine, a priest and his wife welcome us with low bows, green tea, meringues, candy butterflies, candy blades of grass; temple tea cannot be sipped or gulped, but must be swallowed over the meringues in three draughts and held in the mouth like Communion wafers. Our signatures in the guest book are apparently the first in Western script.

At tonight's Kyoto Geisha review, a caricature of posturing Kabuki actors, I.S. marvels most at the instant changes of scenery. Every prop turns upside down or inside out, and the winter scene becomes the cherry blossom scene in 10 seconds flat. The final tableau, a sunrise over the rocky Japanese coast, is a tawdry but breathtaking spectacle that wins prolonged applause. I.S.: "*C'est très Mikado.*"

April 16. The Katsura Detached Palace disappoints, perhaps because we have heard too many expressions of rapture about the architecture. But our visit is spoiled by showers that muddy the paths and by the guide to whom we are leashed and who lectures us on the "Mondrians in three dimensions," the "modular coordination" of the paperbox rooms. I.S. likes the idea, the formality, of the "Moon-Viewing Platform."

The walls of Sambo-in are covered with paintings of golden clouds, bamboo and pine branches, gold-flecked chrysanthemums, willows lightly trembling in the wind. Auden: "One knows from the Japanese what a leaf must feel." The black hats of the horsemen winding in procession through one series of panels are a Zen picture in themselves. In the last pavilion, a fat Buddha statue gazes without appetite at a tray of fresh fruit.

As we enter the temple of Byodo-in, in the center of a small lake and with a bronze phoenix on top, like a weathercock, a bell booms. The Amida-Butsu inside is attended by *putti* playing zithers and dancing for joy, each on a private cloud. We stop at a roadside restaurant in Uji and drink saki and eat candied fish, finally persuading the proprietor to leave his television long enough to serve us. In the street an old man sells cinnamon cakes from a cart harnessed to three monkeys.

1959   Go with Nicolas Nabokov, just arrived from Tokyo, for a massage, an hour of steel-fingered female, not to say androphobic musculature—at one stage the masseuses jump up and down on our backs—without a moment's pause and at a cost of only 300 yen. Just before leaving, one of them asks us, "Want empty the gland for hundred more yen?" Nicolas has gone whiter and shaggier since we saw him last, and he looks more and more like Turgenev. He is like a big lapdog with the S.s, smooching, hugging, and cuddling them with animal affection. The corners of his mouth have turned down, for the reason, I.S. thinks, that having so often imitated American speech out of the sides of it, he is beginning to talk that way naturally. But his culture and sex talk, droll as ever, helps the S.s forget Kyoto for a moment, and his impersonations are brilliant. Once he has been heard in such set pieces as "The Parents of the American Fulbright Student in Florence," to say nothing of improvisations like the hilarious "Noh" play put on for us tonight, the butt of the mimicry can never again be seen in the same, pre-Nabokov way. We walk in the paper-lantern district of the Gion, which I.S. likens to "a dainty Broadway."

April 17. The rooms of Nijo Castle are peopled with life-sized mannequins, posed and costumed to illustrate scenes from the Shogun's court. The floorboards outside the Shogun's bedroom chirp like birds as we trod on them—on purpose, to betray would-be assassins.

The paintings in Nanzen-ji include scenes of a hunter wearing a decoy deerskin and antlers, a jungle full of brightly burning tigers, and a Bosch-like fantasy picture of a man on a crane's back high in the sky. The temple collection of percussion instruments features a *mo kugyo*, a fish-shaped wood block with a flat mouth. Struck by a sponge mallet, it emits a long, low moan, like a seashell.

April 18. The temple of Konju-ji smells nauseatingly of sandalwood, and the Buddha in the half-lotus position on a dais strewn with lilies seems to me over-refined. Our guide, a young monk, is annoyed about equally with us and with his job, and to show that we are wasting both his and our time, he deliberately Baedekerizes in Japanese. When V. films a game of ring-around-the-rosy in front of the temple, children come running from all directions to be in the picture, graciously bowing to her afterward.

April 19. On the road to Osaka this morning we pass two pilgrims, dressed in white robes, white hats, white leggings, and carrying wooden staves. The Osaka Noh Theater is a square room half filled by the elevated stage and the long, wide *hanamichi* (ramp). The audience faces the acting areas from two sides, but during the whole of our nearly five hours here, not more than half of the two hundred or so seats are occupied, while about two-thirds of the occupying half are always asleep, in rotation, as in the system of elected terms in the United States Senate. The audience eats continuously, and the knitting of chopsticks provides a steady accompaniment to the plays. A few stalwarts, elderly men, follow the texts in score books—from back to front, like rabbis reading the Bible.

The first play, with three white-faced actors as ghosts, is a riddle to me. A chorus of eight men in black cassocks and gray-blue aprons chants somberly, I have no idea what about, for a *mauvais quart d'heure*. In the next piece, a kind of *entr'acte* called *Futari-Daimyo*, a peasant boy outwits two pompous Samurai, defeating them in duels and stripping them of their finery, a *Don Quixote*-type satire, but the ballet of dueling fans is so exciting, comparatively, that about half the audience wakes up to watch.

In the third piece, the back row of the chorus chants while the front row dances, one performer at a time. Now and then the dancers brandish their fans as if for momentous action, but nothing happens, and the play is inhumanly slow and boring. A foot is poised in the air for so long that we forget about it and are startled when the actor stomps it down with a crash. The actors wear *tabi*, the two-compartmented white footgloves, sliding their feet as they walk and raising their toes first. The dancers chant, too, alone at first, then in dialogue with the chorus. When the chant rises a diminished fifth toward the end of the play, the effect is earthquaking.

The next piece, *Hanagatami*, is an oriental *opera seria* slower than *Parsifal*. Five musicians and eight choristers enter the stage like burglars, through a half-height butler's pantry window in the right rear corner. The choristers hold their fans in front of their heads during this infiltration, then conceal them in the sleeves of their surplices. The drama is concerned with a maiden who wishes to present a basket of flowers to a Prince, but who does it improperly and is rebuked; the first two hours, at any rate, are a lesson in floral presentations to princes, though at the end of the play, when she again offers her bouquet and it is accepted, I fail to perceive any difference in method. The Prince, a child of eight or nine, wears an orange costume with white pants, and a black *Kammurai* hat with a tail. He neither speaks nor acts, except to exit, but he wiggles and looks worried, as if he had neglected to relieve his bladder.

Near the beginning, an old man enters carrying a flower basket, followed by a girl, dressed like Pocahontas, carrying another of the same. The "girl" is a man, of course, but the mask is small, and the man's gullet wobbles beneath it. The "girl's" voice, moreover, is deeper than any of the men's voices, besides which the mask distorts "her" words acoustically—though we have no reason to complain about that. For about 30 minutes the old man and the flower girl stand motionless while the chorus mumbles a low dim chant. Then the Pocahontas exits, and for a hope-raising moment the end seems near. Instead, the music, a duet of wolf cries and howls accompanied by clicks and taps from the drums, grows more dramatic until she reappears with a twin sister, for whose benefit the whole lesson is repeated.

The musical element is always paramount, from the ritual untying of the cords around the percussion instruments at the beginning to the last note of the offstage flute. The Prince is heralded by a fanfare for flute and drum, almost the only occasion when the drummer is not licking his thumb and moistening his drum head. The vocal noises—gravel-filled gargles, slow slurs in falsetto—are as astringent as the instrumental. (Abé, the author of a classic book about Noh, had studied with Schoenberg in Berlin shortly before *Pierrot Lunaire,* which allows for the possibility that Schoenberg had heard something concerning Japanese *Sprechgesang* from him.)

Hanagatami is followed by an offstage concert of flute and drum, then by another chant play in which each member of the chorus executes a solo dance, in effect a walk punctuated by loud stomping, except that some of the dances conclude with comparatively spectacular leaps.

The final play is named for the god of fencing, whose abode is Mount Matengu. The god himself, Kuramatengu, makes an appearance toward the end, and his entrance, with the *hanamichi* curtain raised straight out and up, forming a canopy, and not, as ordinarily, rolled or drawn, is its most impressive moment. Five- and seven-syllable verse patterns are easily distinguished here, owing to the higher pitch of what I take to be the tonic accent; but the drum also measures the beat of the verse, and provides the play, as I.S. says, with its "pulse." The story describes young Prince Yoshitsune's education in swordsmanship; at any rate, the first part of the drama exposes his lack of skill in that art, for which reason the old god is summoned. Kuramatengu wears a gorgeous purple, white, and gold coat and, to distinguish him as a god, a mask several times larger than those of humans. He moves by leapfrogging, perhaps to indicate the eccentricity of a god as imagined by earthlings.

April 20. The Osaka Bunraku theater surprises us at first, the puppets being so much larger than we expect, and the stage many times the size of a European marionette booth. Four puppeteers, one bare-faced and three black-hooded, like Elizabethan stage-keepers, manipulate a single doll. By an optical deception, the three hooded figures, and their three distractingly spider-like pairs of legs, appear to be following the puppets. However that may be, this controlling crew is so apparent that a sustained effort is required to focus attention away from it; and though to disregard it becomes easier as the play unfolds, we can never give ourselves entirely to the reality of the dolls. The puppeteers move in waist-deep trenches except during duels, battles and other crowd scenes, for which they emerge full height on the open stage. With characteristic Japanese fidelity to scale, the child puppets are manipulated by children.

The musical element, the *joruri,* interests us more than the play, and the performances of the narrators, who read, sing, and ventriloquize for as long as an hour at a time, are *tours de force.* Not surprisingly, given the demand for realism, the range of the vocal gesticulation is far wider than that of Kabuki and Noh. The narrative style of today's play, a talky tear-jerker full of murders and kidnappings, provides corresponding swagger and exaggerated pathos. The plot seems to glorify a peasant woman who has sacrificed her son that the son of a nobleman may live. We follow it vaguely through three brief, action-filled scenes, but the fourth goes on for nearly three hours and is all narration, accompanied by a single samisen.

The audience, largely old women, is both noisier and hungrier than Kabuki and Noh audiences, and the theater smells sickeningly of sushi and hard-boiled eggs. Each act is announced by the offstage clapping of two wooden blocks, *tsuke-uchi*, and by accelerating beats of an offstage drum. A drum roll fills the pauses between scenes, exactly as in *Petrushka*. Before the curtain parts, the musicians are swung in, stage left, on a revolving shelf. They kneel rigidly behind a row of lecterns, the narrators on the audience side, the samisen players toward the stage. Before beginning to read, they hold their books to their heads with both hands, and, at the end of the play, drop their heads to the lectern, woodenly, like the puppets, remaining in this position until the musicians' platform is revolved out of sight. The audience never watches the readers, which we do most of the time.

April 21. Lunch in Kobe at the home of the Muriyamas, the principal patrons of the Osaka Festival and the owners of a celebrated collection of silk-screen portraits of haiku poets. The meal, served in the garden, is barbecued American style, but served orientally, men first. Madame Muriyama listens attentively to I.S.'s every word, at one point questioning him about his use of "conservative." "I dislike the idea of conserving, of keeping in cans," he says. "The conservative offends us when he tries to stop new things from growing, the radical when he shouts, 'Look here, see how radical I am!'"

April 22. To Nara. The rice fields are guarded by scarecrows with noisemakers that clap loudly in the wind, but the ruse is unsuccessful and flocks are feasting everywhere. Architectural geriatricians are rejuvenating the temple of Horyu-ji, board by board. This great pagoda, the oldest temple in Japan, is a sparrows' nest, for which reason it whistles like a colossal flute. The most striking objects in the museum are a Neptune-like figure holding a trident and riding the back of a frog (Amanojako), a black horse with white glass eyes, and a portable shrine, a kind of traveling-salesman's sample case of Buddha dolls.

The forest of the Kasuga Shrine is full of overfed but still greedy deer, and the Great Buddha is not only the largest in Japan, but also, surely, one of the ugliest images in the world. Women wait in line to touch another, smaller Buddha against baldness.

April 23. On the train to Tokyo, Fujiyama is in view for most of three hours.

April 25. After conducting two rehearsals for I.S., I go with him to a private concert at University House. A flutist demonstrates a throat trill and a slow *portamento*, and a kotoist, wearing clawlike picks on his right thumb and first two fingers, shows us the uses of his instrument in a variety

1959 of music from 16th-century polyphony to 20th-century Hawaiian guitar. When our host observes that the new koto music is "at least sincere," I.S. snaps back with "that is no excuse." And when a young composer asks I.S. the trick question of whether he would change the order of a series if he came to a place where he "heard" it in a different order, the answer is: "I would find a way to 'hear' the notes in the proper order." In reply to a question about "melody," he says that the word is restricted by usage to a fairly recent genre of music. "What is the melody in a piece of 16th-century koto music, or in a *virelai* by Machaut? 'Contour' may have some meaning, but not our 'melody.'"

May 4. An afternoon of Gagaku at the Imperial Palace. According to the program, the first piece, *Etenraku*, "has been source of inspiration for creation of Japanese folk songs as well as having been set for Western symphony orchestra." The choreography, for male dancers, is without event or interest, and our attentions are confined strictly to the music. The dance stage, in a gravel court, looks like a boxing ring. The musicians are seated outside and behind, between two *taiko*, 25-foot-tall, and 600-year-old, drums, struck by men on ladders. The other instruments are mouth organs; kotos; flutes; small cymbals; deep, thudding theorbos; and the *hichiniki*, which resembles a shawm. Of these, the mouth organs and the *hichiniki* are the most curious. The former, held like periscopes with the pipes pointing up, sustain harmonic clusters, and in most of the pieces are the first and last instruments to sound. The *hichiniki* produces a sloping, siren-like wail in which all intermediate step-wise pitch is dissolved. (I.S.: "We cannot describe a sound, but neither can we forget it.") No more than a handspread long, the instrument has a large double-reed mouthpiece through which the player seems to breathe in as he blows out, as if performing a Yoga exercise. One of the dances tells the story of Ch'ang Kung of the Ch'i Dynasty, a Prince so fair of face that he was obliged to wear a grotesque mask in battle. The music is alternatively monophonic and polyphonic, but no matter, since it is so much more attractive as sonority than as composition. Ch'ang Kung's mask is the head of a mythical beast.

Hans Popper takes us to visit Suma-san, the retired diplomat, and his collection of Chinese art, one of the richest still in private hands. Suma-san himself greets us at his garden gate wearing a kimono and wooden shoes, which surprises us because heretofore we have seen him only in American-style business suits. Among his treasures are Wei Buddhas, Middle Chou bronzes, Han terra cottas, and innumerable steles, porcelains, jades, screen paintings, scrolls, each of which he shows with the same phrase: "A very singular piece, don't you think?" This is invariably true, but the most singular piece of all is the bald, powerfully built and barrel-chested—like one of his Buddhas or an ex-wrestler—Suma-san himself. But what we will remember above all is his vaingloriousness, the scale of which is so grand as to be forgivable. He can hardly finish a remark without complimenting himself: "My watercolors are very attractive, very well done, don't you think?" Nor does the fluency of his English stop him from regretting that today's conversation fails to make use of his other two dozen languages. (In truth, he *has* served widely in the diplomatic corps, last and least fortunately, except for the growth of his collection, as Ambassador to China during the Japanese occupation.) The new Crown Princess is his niece, a fact that does not have to be prised out of him, and the royal wedding has puffed him up even more, though his account of it is interrupted by Madame Suma's summons to tea. Later, as we prepare to leave, the self-confessed connoisseur endears himself to us by gathering 20 or so of his children and grandchildren to line up with I.S. for a photograph.

Dinner tonight, in a geisha restaurant by the Tokyo River, consists of fried bees, tentacle soup, and cold, candied, undecapitated fish. The geishas are uncommunicative. After disrobing us, our suits, anyway, and helping us into kimonos, they kneel at our elbows like guards.

May 7. In Yokohama after I.S.'s concert tonight, Kaoru suddenly complains that a particle of some kind has blown into her eye. I escort her to a hospital, ring the emergency night bell for 20 minutes before a nurse appears, and, inside, wait another 20 for a doctor. Cockroaches swarm over the floor—which would bother me less had we not been obliged to leave our shoes at the entrance—but the doctor, when he comes, seems not to notice them. (He certainly *sees* them.) Without washing his hands, he lifts Kaoru's eyelid between bare thumb and finger. No mote is found and no remedy prescribed. I pay 100 yen, and we depart, Kaoru not relieved.

May 8. A final, matinee visit to the Kabukiza, to see a play about an Emperor who is remembered for having treated his animal subjects more kindly than his human ones. It is remarkable chiefly for the acting of three "dogs" and for a ballet of demons. We fly at night to Anchorage.

May 10. About an hour before landing in Los Angeles, on our flight from Seattle, a motor on the left side fails. We fasten seat belts, remove ties and shoes, and begin to review our lives. The airport near the runway is covered with white foam and firetrucks are parked just beyond, but the touchdown is without incident.

A letter from Henry Cowell: "I have often admired your concerts from the audience and am delighted that important new music has so good a champion."

May 11. A letter from Edgard Varèse:

> Dear Mr. Craft: All of us who love Webern's music and have far too little opportunity of hearing it are very much indebted to you for your Webern album. I was the first to introduce him to this country at concerts of the International Composers Guild, a soci-

ety of modern music I founded and directed from 1921 to 1927. The ICG gave: Six Bagatellen for string quartet; Five Pieces for string quartet; Three Pieces for cello and piano; Three Pieces for violin and piano, and the *Geistliche Lieder*. I have just had copies made for the ICG files of two letters Webern wrote me at the time, and thinking you might be interested am enclosing copies for you. With thanks for making this unique composer available.

June 24. Santa Fe. Leaving the theater after my *Anna Bolena* dress rehearsal, I try to jump the rope at the entrance, miscalculate the weight of the orchestra score that I am carrying, and fall on the concrete with, in consequence, an excruciating pain in my right arm, which is loose at the elbow and profusely bleeding. John Moriarty and Bliss Hebert drive me to St. Vincent's Hospital, where I lift the dangling limb to a counter and try to fill out admission forms with my left hand. Minutes later I am wheeled into the operating room and injected with sodium pentathol.

June 29. The surgery has relocated the dislocated right elbow, but chips of bone have been left in the arm. The S.s arrive from Los Angeles and come directly to the hospital.

July 12. Our concert in the Cathedral. I.S. conducts *Threni* (I sing in the chorus), and I conduct the *Trauer-Ode*—with my left arm, which is difficult. A dinner party at La Fonda by Paul Horgan.

July 17. Hollywood. When Dr. Edel removes the cast from my sore, swollen, and black-and-blue arm, I swoon and can scarcely remain standing. I am unable to straighten it beyond the 90-degree angle, moreover, and must make every move with great care. But what a relief to be out of that hot, heavy, itching cast. Balneotherapy begins tomorrow.

August 28. Princeton. The S.s arrive at the Princeton Inn and, after lunch with Roger Sessions, visit Robert Oppenheimer.

August 29. Princeton. I.S. talks to the contemporary music seminarists in the morning. I have never been so proud of him: sensible, concrete, practical, witty, wise, informed, inventive, positive, modest. The young people, in contrast, are pretentious, abstract, negative, dull, uncertain. Oh, the aridity, the poverty of purely analytical discussions about music! Still another contrast: he is polite and gracious, as if he had not noticed that no one stood up when he entered the room, and that some of the students lay sprawled on the floor throughout. (He tells me later that he was deeply shocked.) We return to New York in a limousine provided by Columbia Records.

September 6. London. The Eliots for dinner at Claridge's. T.S.E. looks younger and *is* livelier than last year, though he seems to think of himself as a hoary ancient with little time left. Social obligations are the bane of his existence, he says. "I cannot accept lectures because the people who pay for them expect me to attend cocktail parties at which I am caught between someone wanting to know what I think of existentialism and someone asking what I *really* meant by this or that line." When Mrs. Eliot asks if we have read "Edmund Wilson's attack on my husband," T.S.E. describes Wilson as "a brainpicker. I know, because he once tried to get me drunk and pick mine. He is insanely jealous of all creative writers, and his only good line must have come from personal experience or been told to him by someone else. In one of his stories, a man stroking a woman's back remarks on how soft it is. She says: 'What the hell did you expect, scales?' "

Eliot observes that in Pound's new *Cantos*, "There are more Chinese characters than ever; Ezra is becoming the best Chinese poet in English." When I.S. talks about his impressions of the Japanese theater, Eliot says he once watched a Noh dancer in Yeats's *The Hawk's Well* and was very moved by the performance: "One really could believe that the dancer had become a bird." He asks I.S. about Japanese tastes in Western theater: "Ionesco, I suppose, and Tennessee Williams?" When Büchner is mentioned, Eliot observes that "*Wozzeck* is too simple for a play, just simple enough for an opera."

He gazes at each of us in rotation, and beams affection toward his wife each time around. He drinks a gin and tonic before, claret during, and whiskey after his partridge dinner, for while it is evident that he enjoys sniffing the cheese platter, after some deliberation and a final moment of indecision, he does not actually choose one. When Aldous's name is mentioned, Eliot says, "I don't read him, of course; I am much too fond of him for that. He was very pessimistic when we saw him last. Too many people in the world and more all the time. So there are indeed, indeed." One looks for a hidden twist or irony in the echoed word.

Eliot enjoys talking about the weather—"Isn't it unusual? Why last year at this time. . . ." Telling us about his plans to visit his Missouri birthplace, he says that the house doesn't exist any more. "If a plaque were to be erected, it would surely go to one of the neighbors."

September 7. To Stratford for Olivier's *Coriolanus*. I have never before been so struck by the soldiers' amatory language—though it is not that, of course, but the Neo-Platonic, Renaissance idealization of friendship. Still, in the case of such up-to-date lines as Menenius's "I tell thee, my fellows, thy general is my lover," the contemporary audience can hardly be expected to keep in mind that the Elizabethan "lover" is synonymous with "chum." Coriolanus himself seems to prefer his officers to his wife, and his mother to everyone, though the remark "There's no man in the world / More bound to's mother" is unbelievable, partly because of his exaggerating rhetoric about her (*e.g.*, "The honored mould / Wherein this trunk was formed"). And the performance must be faulted on this point: Olivier's Coriolanus overpowers the Volumnia, who is far from a Lupine matriarch. And his staging does not distinguish Romans and Volsces at all clearly, the

1959 final scene being richly confusing, Coriolanus dying not in Corioli or Actium but, apparently, on the Tarpeian rock—which hardly accords with his "Cut me to pieces, Volsces; men and lads/Strain all your edges on me. . . ."

Stephen Spender drives us back to London in his Jaguar, but stops to pick up a young hitchhiker, which makes I.S. nervous. At 3 A.M., drinking claret at the Spender house, I.S. mentions Eliot's remark at dinner yesterday that Shakespeare was more interested in *Coriolanus* the play than in its poetry. Yet the weaknesses of the play, foremost among them its unlikable hero, nearly sink it. Consider, on the other hand, the line "Break ope the locks o' the Senate and bring in/The crows to peck the eagles."

September 9. Train to Edinburgh, Hotel Caledonia. In contrast to the bumpy ride, Fischer-Dieskau's *Die Schöne Müllerin* is too smooth, and the pianissimos are too precious.

September 10. Drums and the skirl of bagpipes wake us. A few minutes later 16 Highlanders in kilts with sporrans parade below our window, ruddy types looking as if they had stepped off the labels of whiskey bottles. With Spender in the evening to a terrible performance of *Wozzeck*.

September 15. Venice. The canals smell of sulfur and feculence, the lagoons of stagnation, especially at low tide. The city's most pervasive odors are of *vaporetto* and *motoscafo* exhausts (like a World War I gas attack); urine (especially acrid in dark alleys in early morning); canine excrement (an impasto on crowded pavements); the reek of drying fishnets in front of the Arsenale (one of them ignominiously draping a stone lion, part of Morosini's Greek booty already desecrated six centuries earlier by grafitti, supposedly Harald of Norway's); and the stench from the refineries at Mestre. Cooking odors are saturated by *frittura di pesce*, while the Erberia stinks preponderantly of cabbage, the Merceria of coffee, the Fondamenta del Vin of vinegar. Interiors exude dankness (even clean bed linen is dank-smelling), mustiness, decay, and churches are redolent of incense, altar flowers (sickly-sweet tuberoses), and, just possibly—it is the rarest of emanations—the odor of sanctity.

Venetians themselves are strongly aromatic, some because of infrequent bathing, some from perfumes (patchouli, favored by elderly females, barbers' pomades by elderly males), some from garlic and Chianti—a halitosis corrosive enough to peel paint: perhaps these noxious, acetylene-like exhalations *are* inflammable, and the more grossly afflicted might ignite and breathe fire like demons in Dante.

Colors cannot be described, of course, or even precisely compared. Thus one could say that when the tide is out, the "ring" of the city—in the sense of the "ring" in an emptied bathtub—is spinach green, but it would be better to say algae green in the first place, and that changes with every passing cloud.

Venice is an ingrown, self-reflecting city, a city of mirrors (the *"calle dei specchieri"*), of which the largest is the lagoon. It is also a maker of glass, and of all of its glasswares—blown, cut, incised, engraved, frosted, gilded, **1959** tinted—the most beautiful are two azure *candelabri* in the Scalzi and the violet ampulla-shaped ceiling lamps in the arcade at Florian's.

Venetian occupations are no less ingrown. Women in tiny island worlds still make point lace, as centuries ago men carved quatrefoil. And Venetian love is ingrown: Venice is a world capital of pederasty.

October 12. Fly with I.S. from Treviso to Rome, where we join Berman and Robert Bright and drive to Naples *via* Sperlonga, a cave on the beach, with the sound of the sea breaking outside. The grotto encloses an artificial pool shimmering with eels, and an adjoining room in which workmen are trying to piece together mutilated statues whose torsos, detached limbs, and incomplete bodies suspended by ropes and appliances look like exhibits in a surgical museum.

October 13. In Acerra, a very poor city rich in courtyards and staircases, we stop for a funeral procession—a brass band, a troop of schoolgirls carrying floral wreaths, a baroque hearse drawn by two glistening black horses with black plumes, mourners, heads lowered and wheeling their bicycles by their sides. We stop at a trattoria in Benevento, a dreary city, still rubbled from the war; the house wines are a yellow fluid from Pantelleria and a *vino nero*. Flies circle a mangy dog sleeping on the floor, a scene from Norman Douglas's *Old Calabria*. In Gesualdo, Bright takes dozens of photographs for Columbia Records.

October 14. To Paestum. More photographs, but I.S. and I cannot look toward the camera because of the lizards swarming underfoot.

October 18. Our Teatro San Carlo concert: I conduct Haydn and Berg's *Three Pieces*. A party at Henze's afterward, and after that the midnight train for Bologna.

October 19. I go directly from the Bologna station to a morning rehearsal. The orchestra is better as well as better-behaved than the Neapolitan. I.S., not feeling well, complains of a dizzy spell.

October 20. V. arrives from Venice bringing a letter from Spender and his *Rasputin* libretto for Nabokov.

October 22. I conduct Mozart's No. 29 and Schoenberg's Opus 34. After the concert: Adriana Panni from Rome, Lawrence Moss from Los Angeles.

October 23. Drive from Bologna to Milan, stopping at the Este Library at Reggio Emilia. We leave the main road near Parma and wind up a perilous one to the castle ruins at Canossa, where in 1077 Henry IV, the Holy Roman Emperor, received absolution from Pope Gregory VII: a romantic, desolate landscape with snow patches. In Milan, at Biffi Scala, we meet Leonard Elmhirst from Dartington. Night train to Paris.

November 6. London. With Isaiah Berlin and Lord Boothby in the Royal Box at Covent Garden for *Un Ballo in Maschera*, intelligently and sensitively conducted by Rudolf Kempe. During intermissions a sit-down din-

1959 ner is served just outside the loge.

November 7. Letter from Berman: "I do appreciate your writing to me. You are the only person in the S. family who shares my view that letter writing is an integral part of a civilized (and civil) person's daily life and not something one does when one has time on his or her hands. And who has time to spend anyway? You and I are both extremely busy people. . . ."

December 11. New York. A letter for I.S. from T. S. Eliot: "I hope that you have read THE DELUGE (of which, as I said, a text appears in the Everyman volume in the Everyman Library). . . . I hope that you will not be overworking while in New York. . . . Your programme of travel and work while in Europe astounded me. . . ."

After our *Noces* rehearsal, Auden, Kallman, and Kirstein for dinner.

December 15. A telegram from John Walsh informs us of the death, in Paris, of Catherine d'Erlanger, Lady in Waiting to Queen Victoria and I.S.'s friend since Diaghilev days; she was in Venice when Diaghilev died and, no one else coming forward, paid for his funeral and interment. She claimed a genealogy from the time of the First Crusade, and an Avignon Pope had granted her ancestors a dispensation permitting them to eat meat on Fridays. Prodigally rich at one time, her tangible fortunes had dwindled in the course of a long lifetime shared with profligate paramours, and she was obliged to dispose of her homes in London (Byron's house in Piccadilly), Paris, Venice, and on the Brenta (Palladio's Villa Malcontenta, which went to Bertie Landsberg). Her Hollywood home was disappearing, too, by parceling and desuetude. Toward the end, it had become a kind of flea market in which practically all the contents were for sale; even the ash trays had price tags on them.

The Baroness was my landlady from April 1952, and my part-time employer, as a reader, during the next four years. I think of the prodigious amount of print we devoured together, entire shelves of books and some authors *in toto*; moreover, I still recall much of the reading matter, probably from having pronounced it aloud. What these sessions meant to her, apart from a pastime, I do not know, but the book that made the strongest impression on her was *Obermann*, from which she borrowed a motto: "Let us perish resisting, and if it is nothingness that awaits us, do not let us act as if that is a just fate." The motto she lived by was "never complain, never explain."

My most vivid memories of the Baroness are of those readings. A chronic toper by then, she would sip Benedictine while lounging in regal deshabille on a sofa that was moth-eaten and worse: my occupational hazards were pruritis, and the bites and stings of centipedalians and creatures black and hairy. Her snobbish, unruly cats, Sita and Terra Cotta, used to join her, plumping themselves on each side like courtiers, jealous of each other and of every caller. Cole Porter was a sometime caller, a man of charm and intelligence whom I.S. liked and admired. (Callers of better times and places, the Sitwells, Michael Arlen, Cocteau, her son-in-law Prince Jean-Louis de Fauçigny-Luçinge, were caricatured on the walls in the Baroness's own, genre Marie Laurencin, portraits.) On some days a tiara adorned her hair, which was inconsistently orange; on other days, metal curlers. But her clothing was less varied. At any rate I seem to remember her most often wearing an inside-out maroon flannel sack and woolen socks, one of them halfway to the knee, the other all the way down, like Hogarth's Bedlamite, except that the Baroness's preferences were French: she used to refer to herself as *"La Folle de Chaillot."*

My recollections of her dinners are no less clear, especially of drinking wine from silver goblets tasting of tarnish. I see I.S. on one occasion shoving his empty plate in her direction and the Baroness pushing it back. He used to refer to her as *"Notre dame des tapettes,"* and she *was* a patroness of interior decorators, being dependent on them in her commerce in *bric-à-brac.* During all the years that I knew her, she was continually dispossessing herself of her rummage-sale surroundings.

Toward the end, her memory failures were more frequent and her attempts to hide them undisguisable. She would break off in mid-sentence with "No matter," pretending she had suddenly realized that to go on was not worthwhile. At the end, too, she grew corpulent and seldom ventured out. Finally it became apparent that she could no longer live alone, yet she would tolerate no companion except the Russian girl who came in the afternoons to paste newspaper cuttings in scrapbooks, a futile task that reminded us of Bouvard and Pecuchet. When she suffered a fall, we had to call the Police to help lift her into bed. The last time I saw her was on the day she learned of the cruel but unavoidable arrangements for her abduction to her son's home in Paris; she would have preferred to die in her own home. By this time she had been bedridden for months. John Walsh, her *beau-idéal* of many years, came to tell her of the trip, promising: "You will soon be up again and then we'll have fun." At this, during no more than three or four seconds and conceivably for the first and last time in her life, the stoic old lady started to cry.

Postscript 1994. 1959 was the first of four globe-trotting years. Nicolas Nabokov had been urging Stravinsky to participate in a Tokyo festival, similar to those in Paris in 1952 and Rome in 1954, and, eager to go, Stravinsky signed contracts for Japanese engagements in the Spring of 1959 before learning that Nabokov's fete had been postponed. But no matter; or, rather, all the better, since Nabokov himself accompanied us during most of our visit and provided its liveliest, most amusing, and congenial moments.

At this remote date the reader will hardly believe the extent of the American appetite in 1959 for everything Japanese, from Zen Buddhism and archery to film and theater, *Genji* and Mishima, sushi, flower arrangement and tea ceremony. But at that time, Japanese hotels, restaurants, and services of all kinds were immeasurably less efficient than they are now. Nor did Stravinsky's VIP status count for much: the pampering to which he was accustomed in Europe was unknown here, or known in unrecognizable forms.

Stravinsky was fascinated by Kabuki, Noh, Gagaku—the court music that continued to attract him back in Los Angeles, from recordings given him by Japanese musicians. He was especially drawn to Japanese percussion and plucked instruments, the modes of attack as well as the sonorities, and traces of influence can be heard in his own music of the time, Movements and *Epitaphium*.

Stravinsky's concerts were received warmly but not with the wild enthusiasm they would have inspired in other world capitals. Did Hans Christian Andersen's joke at the expense of the Japanese in *Song of the Nightingale* misfire? Was the audience even aware of it? Our German-refugee hosts, the Korns, Poppers, and Pringsheims explained that Japan's European musical culture was predominantly Viennese, and that the Tokyo and Osaka audiences had not been exposed to contemporary music. In fact, the first performance there in Japanese of Stravinsky's *Three Japanese Lyrics* took place in August 1991.

My accident in July, in Santa Fe, resulting in multiple fractures in my right elbow, would have been interpreted by Groddeck as proof that my "it" was protesting my desire to conduct. Whatever the truth of that, I was out of the hospital for only a week when I conducted Bach's *Trauer-Ode* with my left hand—an athletic feat of sorts in that the pattern of the second beat in the four-in-a-bar measures was unnatural, that between beats I had to turn pages with the same left hand, and that to maintain balance with the heavy cast on my right side was difficult.

The Santa Fe Opera's publicist, Lillian Libman, wrote up the elbow incident for the *New York Times*. She had interviewed me and quoted me accurately, and when the Stravinskys arrived from Los Angeles, I introduced her to them. I liked her, initially, and sympathized with her vocal handicap, what today would be called a voice-box voice. Later in the summer, we decided to retain her to manage some New York concerts planned for December and January, to be sponsored partly by Columbia Records and partly by Karl Weber, a Swiss Businessman who had commissioned the Movements for his young pianist wife.

Back in Los Angeles, the injured elbow was a nuisance for weeks to come, especially the hot and heavy cast and the itching of the arm inside. Many nights were sleepless, and the frustration of not being able to play the piano and write was extreme. When finally the plaster was removed, the therapies employed to straighten the arm—I could not lower my hand beneath the sternum—were ineffective. Eventually Dr. Knauer restored the action of the arm by acupuncture.

I had agreed to participate in symposia on the state of contemporary music, at Princeton in August, and though not in a condition to do so, I did attend. Whereas a year before I had recorded Stockhausen's *Zeitmasse* and Boulez's *Marteau sans maître* and had generally followed the carryings-on of the avant-garde, I now found most of its products pretentious and puerile, and while Milton Babbitt's lectures on serial analyses interested me, they were far over my head. (Instead of music theory that summer week I read the Memoirs of Madame Vigée-Lebrun.) Stravinsky came to my rescue, as he had done many times before and was to do again, speaking in my place. At a time when our "conversations" books were being calumniated by those whose achievements they failed to appreciate, a description of Stravinsky's visit, in the British magazine the *Score*, remarked that the Stravinsky of the books was evident in every word of his talk. During my stay at Princeton, Roger Sessions and Edward T. Cone were extraordinarily kind to me.

In Venice, in September and early October, we received daily calls from New York. Deborah Ishlon of Columbia Records, and Lillian Libman, whom I had not sized-up at all accurately, were at odds concerning the organization and promotion of the December and January concerts. In mid-October Stravinsky and I went to Rome, Naples, Paestum, and Bologna, where Vera Stravinsky joined us, coming from Venice on my birthday.

❧ *1960*

January 10. New York. I.S. conducts the premiere of Movements, and I conduct Schütz, Gesualdo, Monteverdi, and Bach (*"Aus der tiefe"*).

January 20. I.S. videotapes *Firebird* for a Bernstein concert. Glenn Gould, Bernstein's soloist in Bach's D minor Concerto, drops a plumb line to measure the elevation of the piano stool from the floor, beats time as he plays, tongue striking his cheek like a metronome, mouth trembling as if from a voodoo seizure. Until the actual filming, this old man of 27 is wrapped in scarves, sweaters, and blankets. But he removes his gloves to shake hands with I.S.

February 1. Hollywood. Letter from Nadia B. about the Monday Evening Concerts: "You give your entire life to the preparation of these superb programs to render so many things true which would only seem unthinkable dreams. . . . Believe, dear Bob, in my deep appreciation."

February 3. Letter from Isaiah on the Sadler's Wells production of *Oedipus*, which Isaiah considers "one of the greatest works of the twentieth century in any art."

February 25. I.S. writes to the Royal Theater, Copenhagen, answering a question about the possible reduction of the orchestra of the *Sacre*: "a technical impossibility. When we performed this work with Diaghilev in London, where the orchestra pit was smaller than in Paris, we added to the orchestra space two boxes taken from the public at the right and the left over the orchestra pit. . . . I am very sorry not to be able to help you in this, especially as I am a very sincere admirer of Jerome Robbins, and I would be happy to have him staging the *Sacre*. . . ."

March 5. Letter from Milton Babbitt:

> I am delighted to hear about your book; you are the person to do it, which would normally disqualify you automatically. Really, I am overjoyed, particularly since I have just undergone an evening's interview by Joseph Machlis, who is writing an undergraduate

textbook on contemporary music for McGraw-Hill. He refers to himself happily and proudly as a "packager," and revels in his non-professionalism, while reminding you of the fundamental validity of his attitude in the form of a royalty of 20 grand a year from his monumental contribution entitled *The Enjoyment of Music*. The enjoyment is all his. The outcome of the interview was that the "specialized nature" of my music and my refusal to describe it in more "accessible" terms disqualified me from significant inclusion in his volume to come. I am very happy to hear that Mr. Stravinsky is so well, and so well at work. My deepest love to both of them.

April 27. Toronto, Westbury Hotel. Rehearsals and concert with the CBC. I conduct Tchaikovsky's Second Symphony.

May 3. New York. Balanchine comes to my room at the Gladstone and I go over the *Monumentum* with him, convincing him to choreograph it.

May 14. Hollywood. Letter from Glenn Gould:

I was terribly sorry not to have been able to work with you in April and, to make matters worse, to have to miss seeing you and welcoming you to Toronto. Is it possible, do you think, that we are jinxed—perhaps fated never to work together? After all, this is the third time in a row and that doesn't augur very well.

I am dictating this letter by telephone from Philadelphia where I am still ensconced in a full cast and will be for sometime to come. The temporary improvement during March, which enabled me to play some concerts, turned out to have been due to the taking of cortisone but it was a temporary improvement only and the trouble came back full force.

I am sorry to hear about your hepatitis. We do manage to keep in step with ailments! Please do take good care of yourself.

I understand that the concert with the CBC Symphony was a great success. I have heard nothing but enthusiastic reports and I understand that the orchestra took to you famously, which, believe me, with that crusty group of side-men, is not always the case. They were greatly impressed, as well they should be. . . .

August 1. During our flight to Mexico, I.S. talks about Maximilian and Juárez as an ideal subject for Verdi in his *Don Carlos* period: "Imagine the scene with Maximilian tipping the soldiers who are about to shoot him, and the scene with Carlotta going mad in the Vatican." These thoughts are interrupted by an announcement from the steward that "men and women may use the lavatory indistinctly."

1960   At the airport, I.S. is greeted by a committee of composers,* a detachment of soldiers, and several busloads of schoolchildren. To the Bamer Hotel in a "crocodile" cab, so called because of a black sawtooth necklace painted around its perimeter, but the taxi's tactics are far more jagged and dangerous than the emblem suggests. The driver contests the center of the road against buses whose destinations are long Aztec names knotted with "tl's," "tz's," and "xt's"—Ixtapalapa, Tlalnepantla, Azcapotzalco.

August 2. The Bellas Artes is half filled with students for our rehearsal this morning. One of them approaches I.S., saying, "We are too many to meet you, and I have been chosen to shake your hand for all"; I.S. thanks them from the stage for this delegated handshake. During intermission, following my read-through of the *Lulu* Suite, he remarks that "Berg is a thematic composer primarily; how he loves to caress his themes, to turn them this way and that. But the vibraphone goes on urinating in the ear a little too long." The Bal y Gays are there, friends of the S.s from 1940, who in 40 years of marriage have grown as alike as twins. Refugees from Franco Spain, they own a small gallery on the Paseo de la Reforma. Introduced to them, I try to make conversation in a gabble of Italian and Spanish, and they let me go on and on before saying, in excellent English, that they do not understand a word, whereupon we laugh and are instant friends. Edward James turns up, too. His laugh, like a hornbill in the jungle, sounds even more mad here than in Hollywood.

At Guadalupe the two main buildings tilt so radically away from each other that from the front portal of either the toppling of the other seems imminent. The plaza is crowded with Indians lurching toward the church on their knees, inching forward in evident pain, sometimes with long waits between moves, like birds changing position on a beach. A young woman leans on the shoulder of her small son, also on his knees and carrying a baby in his arms. I.S. is impressed by this and offended, later, by James's mock prayer, "Dear God, forgive us our outlets." I.S. kneels before the Image of the Virgin, touches his forehead to its glass case, and burns a candle at Her shrine.

But the Guadalupe pilgrimage does not increase I.S.'s charity at this afternoon's press conference. He dismisses a New York music critic as "a crab; he even walks sideways"; and he describes an opera by one of "Les Six" as "*Les Mamelles de ma Tante.*" His kindest words are reserved for his

---

* The *Mexico, D.F. News* reported: "Newspapermen, photographers, radio announcers quickly crowded around to record every word of the distinguished visitor. Jack McDermott and Horace Edwards, Counselor for Public Affairs and Cultural Attaché, respectively, for the American Embassy, helped in interpreting for the Mexican reporters. Robert Craft . . . and Mrs. Stravinsky stood to one side as newsmen bombarded [Stravinsky] with questions. . . . The great maestro slowly made his way to the airport building, flashbulbs continued to pop incessantly . . . at least 100 persons surrounded him continuously. As he neared the airport waiting room, uniformed students from the National Conservatory let out a cheer."

friend the Mexican poet Alfonso Reyes, whom he first met in Argentina in 1936: "Reyes was a small man with a large wife. Facially he resembled Burl Ives, but his wife looked more like the rest of Ives. In spite of their sizes, Reyes tried to fulfill the abduction rite and carry his bride over the doorstep. I did not see him do this, but will picture him doing it as long as I remember him at all."

August 3. A "Museum of the Revolution" is under construction in Chapultepec Park, but the engineering is *ancien régime*, the workmen passing their buckets of cement hand to hand, like an 18th-century fire brigade. The driver who takes us from here to the astronomical pyramid at Tenayuca has no idea of how to find it. We stop every few minutes for fresh supplies of information and always turn in radically different directions afterwards. In the town of Tenayuca, women are the only creatures, including mules, actually at work: grandmothers haul heavy bags past staglines of idling young men, while great-grandmothers collect laundry from the limbs of cactus plants. The pyramid itself seems disproportionately small for the stone serpents, weighing several tons each, coiled in its yard. I.S. compares it to a *paskha*, but it is flatter than that and its lines are melted or blurred, as if it had been under water for a long time. We scale the walls and burrow through the catacombs at the base. I loathe the pre-Columbian world with its slave-state, priest-ridden, god-ridden societies, and its unspeakable cruelties: even the greatest heroes might have their hearts torn out. Since suicides went directly to Heaven, the mystery is that Aztec civilization did not disappear by its own hand.

August 4. Mexico City. At our concert tonight, V. sits in the silk-and-feather audience, flanked by the President's wife and Don Celestino Gorostiza, the director of the Bellas Artes. The orchestra plays the "Viva Mexico" for I.S. at the end, and the "Diana," the salute accorded, very rarely, to the bravest matador.

August 8. 8 A.M. The airport. A wrangle with an immigration official who insists that I.S.'s first name is really George. On the plane, the man next to me crosses himself frantically as we speed down the runway, then sits calmly back and reads *El Universal*. Beyond Antigua, we fly low over volcanoes, some red-lipped and still steaming, others filled with pools or sealed with vegetation. The terminal at San José is full of progressive frescoes and reactionary guards. At Panama, where we land again, with views of both oceans, a gathering of musicians awaits I.S. who, bathed in steam, receives a beautifully embroidered native fabric and listens to their spokesman introduce himself as an "electronic composer." Cameramen appear, too, and as we make our way to the plane for Bogotá, joined by a Panamanian woman wearing a feather shako, this touching, humid scene is filmed.

The new plane, a Braniff jet, roars and flexes, then rises like a rocket over bay and canal and into the sudden, equatorial night. The lower

1960 Andean slopes are bright with orange fires—milpas, I think. At Bogotá, where we need heavy coats, the path to the terminal is thick with dead *cucarrones* (beetles). Olav Roots, the Russian-speaking conductor of the orchestra, drives us to the Tequendama Hotel.

August 9. We awake breathless and lightheaded, and I.S., complaining of vertigo and fluttering heart, sends for an oxygen mask, which he clasps to his nose for periodic inhalations. The furnishings of the Teatro Colón, where I rehearse, were brought from Europe a century ago by boat and mule train, a journey of many months. More than half of the orchestra is European, too, and I.S., switching from Italian to French to German to Russian, is always understood by at least one faction. The theater is cold and most of the musicians wear ponchos throughout the rehearsal. We still do not know whether our second concert is to take place the day after tomorrow or not until Saturday, but I.S. says that this is simply *mañana*-ism and that we must adjust to it.

On a late-afternoon tour, the driver shakes hands with us as we enter his cab and thanks us again and again for hiring him. The city is a mixture of ugly new international-style buildings and pretty and old local ones: green balconies and white walls, all with "*Cuba sí, gringos no.*" The eaves of hillside houses project over and, in some cases, almost completely cover the narrow streets. Whereas the Indian women in the market place carry loads of pineapple on headtrays the size of card tables, here they wear bowler hats, do their hair in long braids, and stack their burdens on their backs. Mules do not, in most neighborhoods, distinguish between street and sidewalk.

For no apparent reason we are taken to a cemetery above the city, a desolate place with cows pasturing in the streets and buzzards banking overhead like airplanes unable to land. Our driver says that his daughter is buried here, after having been "killed in a hospital." An Indian family, kneeling with lighted candles by the cemetery gate, reminds us of a Holy Family by Georges de la Tour. Back at the Tequendama, we receive more handshakes, innumerable "*muchas gracias,*" and other signs of untold gratitude.

Linguistic ambiguities add to the confusion in the Tequendama restaurant. Thus I.S. asks for a side order of ham, but receives jam, the waiter mistaking Spanish for English. A party of *norteamericanos* arrives next to us, the men pushing the chairs of their seated women to the table like lawn mowers. Compared to the Colombians, the *norteamericanos* talk and laugh too loudly and too much. The dinner music begins with "A Song of India," which makes I.S. feel very old. "I remember the day Rimsky composed it. How surprised he would be to know that his opera is remembered by this piece alone!" Our dinner guest, a Bogotano, is interested in Albert Schweitzer, whom I.S. describes as he knew him in the mid-1930s: "He came to a concert of mine in Strasbourg and we dined together afterward. His clothes—the frock coat and the wing collar—were those of a provincial pastor, but he made me think of Maxim Gorky. One could see that he had charisma, and anyone who had talked with him would readily believe stories of the sort I heard at Aspen, after his visit there, of animals coming out of the woods to eat out of his hand. But already that night in Strasbourg, the poor man was surrounded by idiotic adulators."

August 10. The collection of pre-Columbian gold cached in the basement of the Banco de la República is the richest in the world, and its gleam is so great that only a little electric lighting is required. Some of the gold is alloyed with copper and platinum, but most is pure and bright yellow. All the Andean cultures are represented, though my impression is of a preponderance of Chibcha objects. These include disc-shaped diadems, doughnut-shaped earrings, heart-shaped pectorals, crescent-shaped crowns, gold breastplates, armlets, penile ornaments, greaves, goldfoil bangles, ear spools, lip pendants, and nose ornaments like epaulettes of Napoleon III. The largest part of the trove consists of death raiments— laminated funeral masks—burial talismans, and funerary urns, the most common of which are shaped like whiskey flasks. Another large part is from the boudoir—gold tweezers for eyebrow depilation, gold hairpins and safety pins, gold male utensils and body ornaments. I remember gold canes and cane finials, and gold scepters, gold aspergillums, gold flutes, a gold *boca marina*, gold fish hooks, gold animal figures—alligators, sad-eyed frogs, abstract snakes and gold-wire Klee-like cacique figures strung together in necklaces like paper cutouts.

Bogotá's bookstores are well stocked, and the city's literary reputation, Humboldt's "Athens of South America," is borne out in the people we meet. Our new friend Edgardo Salazar de Santa Columa says that *El Espectador* publishes book reviews of the caliber of those in *Les Arts* and the *TLS*, adding that "Bogotanos read only because they have no place to go and nothing else to do." One of the customers in the first store we visit is a hunchback. As soon as the S.s see him they want to touch his hump for good luck. I ridicule this Russian superstition, as I have before, comparing it to scrofula and the royal touch, and I protest the indignity to the afflicted, stigmatized man. But they are perfectly serious, and deeply disappointed when he departs before they have time to push near him.

Today's reception for I.S. at the U.S. Embassy is attended by many mustachioed *señores* and large, bosomy *señoras*, who fit perfectly Hazlitt's description, "plump, florid viragos." Most of the conversation is about a language congress, now in session in Bogotá, whose aims are the elimination of silent letters from written Spanish and the expunging of anti-Semitic definitions from the dictionary of the Spanish Academy in Madrid.

From a visit to an emerald dealer I learn that the valuable stones are the deep-green, perfectly homogeneous ones, rather than the pale ones with gardens inside. We also visit a souvenir shop selling boa constrictor and ocelot skins, as well as stuffed adult alligators and live—puffing, glaucous-

1960 eyed—baby alligators. The proprietor says that jungle Indians employ poisonous but tamed snakes to *protect* their young children and that these babysitter reptiles are not only trained to guard the hearth from animals and other snakes but that, as a rule, they refrain from stinging their keepers.

From V.'s memo book on Bogotano behavior: "Bogotanos drink large quantities of post-prandial coffee, then retire for long siestas; a Bogotano says *gracias* and *con mucho gusto* an average of a hundred times a day; in spite of the altitude, Bogotanos are long-winded, and their largest expenditure of word air is about politics; Bogotanos commit a fair number of the nearly two hundred murders that occur in Colombia every month."

August 12. I.S., or a part of him, is monumentalized. Early this morning three women come to make a cast of his left hand, which they place on a wet towel and cover with a gray pudding. This takes 20 minutes to dry, after which one of them cracks the plaster with a hammer and piles the artifacts into a pail.

During my part of the concert tonight I.S. reads Simenon. But he listens, too, and after the Bach-Schoenberg Chorale-Preludes remarks: "It is *Farben* and *Dynamik* music and so rich in both that one must hear it a dozen times to hear it all. Nevertheless, I regret the final harp arpeggio in *Schmücke Dich* and the last cymbal crash in *Komm Gott.*" At intermission he discovers a spider on the lavatory wall, reaches for one of his scores, says, "I will kill it with *Firebird.*" Just before bed, though still terrified of cholera and dysentery, he says: "I am getting very bored brushing my teeth in ginger ale."

August 14. To the Salt Mine Cathedral at Zipaquira, a pre-Columbian excavation now expanded and impregnated—like a ship in a bottle—with a church. During the first part of the drive, rain pulses against the car like surf, but at Chía, where a beautiful colonial-period bridge still spans the muddy Rio Bogotá, all is clear. Thereafter the architecture in the villages, enhanced by windowsill geraniums, is predominantly Swiss. A farmers' fair is in mid-celebration along the road, but most pedestrians have had too much *aguardiente* and are unsteady on their feet.

The tunnel into the mine envelops the car very closely, and the claustrophobia bothers, especially after some confusing turns and a few hundred yards of Lascaux-like obscurity, but not as much as the suffocating salinity. The sodium-chloride Chartres is about a quarter of a mile inside its mountain, and from the subterranean parking lot to the eerie lead-and-blue church is a considerable trek. Today being Sunday, the place is crowded with Indians. The priests, in green robes, might belong to a heretical sect, Adamites or Albigensians, but are definitely part of an underground movement. The church was built for the convenience of the miners, who regard it, as do Colombians generally, as the eighth wonder of the world. At the inaugural service, half of the congregation fainted in the thin, salt-flavored air. Fearing to do the same, we hurry to leave, but our car lacks air, too, stalls, and has to be pushed.

After returning to Bogotá, we continue in a different direction to Tequendama Falls and the *"tierra caliente,"* a corkscrew descent of 3,000 feet. At each downward coil, the tangle of vines, flowers, and fronds is thicker and more richly tropical in color; we peel overcoats, jackets, and eventually shirts. Only 20 or so miles from Bogotá the air is 40° warmer.

Tequendama Falls is "twice as high as Niagara," a souvenir-hawking Indian shouts, near the precipice, but the bottom is invisible in mists. In the absence of retaining walls, a Madonna statue is the only deterrent to suicides, the latest of which took place only a few days ago, an Indian woman throwing herself into the cataract and pulling her screaming son with her, all in view of a horrified crowd.

From the Falls to Santandercito, at the edge of the jungle, the road is a narrow, fenceless shelf overlooking a 2,000-foot drop. It is also unpaved, riddled with cavities, in places all but sealed off by fallen rocks; the threat of a landslide is as unnerving as the threat of the abyss. We cower close to the mountain and crawl ahead, on the theory that forward movement, to no matter where, is less of a risk than a "U" turn. Slips over the side are marked by shrines and crosses. At one point, while I am in the throes of a swooning, Icarus-like moment, a bus with the name Jesús María Pizarro roars by us, wheels bulging over the brink, horn blaring contempt. (Colombian drivers pass or stop anywhere without signaling, nor can they be trusted to obey traffic lights, for which reason the Bogotá police stand on tall podiums—and under awnings of tinted glass—*au-dessus de la mêlée.*) Finally, at the jungle level, and before starting back, we eat a fritanga and drink a nerve-steadying herb tea in the Hostería de los Andes.

August 15. The air route to Quito follows the Magdalena River to the Cauca River (the *tierra adentro* of the archeologists); it also follows the ups and downs of air pockets, in which we are violently buffeted much of the way. Ecuador is a cracked, reddish crust carved with rhomboid villages. Quito has a new terminal, newly splashed with murals, newly stocked with Indian wares, but in the street, at a tenth of the price, nonfranchised Indians sell the same things—silver buckles, blankets, Panama hats, shrunken heads mounted on short poles. Taking off again, we skim red-tiled adobe houses and mountain shelves on which clouds droop like partly deflated balloons. At Guayaquil, a riverain city and the junction of sea, jungle, and desert, small boats cross the bay, leaving spirochete-like tails of water. In the excavation sites of Trujillo and Chan-Chan, the sand is imprinted with mysterious mounds, higher than the waves of the sea.

At Lima, after dropping through several layers of bad weather, I.S. is received like a film star. The night is cold and damp, as is the Country Club, a gloomy Manueline hotel with rooms a lonely half-mile from the lobby. We transfer to the no less palatial but centrally located and heated Gran Hotel Bolivar, where we leave our within-walking-distance accom-

1960 modations long enough to try three kinds of fish—*corvina, liza,* and *pejerrey*—all delectable.

August 16. I attribute my dizziness and the bends this morning to the powerful black coffee taken to be alert for an 8 A.M. rehearsal, rather than to the abrupt change of altitude. The orchestra, except for a pretty flutist from Boston, Eleanor Preble, is the worst ever. The players cannot keep a tempo, their tuning is vaguely Pythagorean, they read slowly and forget immediately, and each direction has to be repeated three times. Moreover, the Indians do not, on principle, admit to mistakes: either the player wasn't ready, or his instrument was at fault, or he hadn't understood where we were beginning, or one of the *gringos* in the orchestra had said something to confuse him. According to their regular conductor, however, the Indians are dependable in the concerts, the *gringos* nervous and erratic.

We spend the greater part of the afternoon in the Museum of Anthropology and Archeology looking at textiles—above all, laces from the necropolis of Paracas. The life of an ancient Andean was a purgatory of weaving. The Chimu ceramics feature owls, turtles, monkeys, cats carrying litters, a vicuña giving birth. One room displays ceramic models of legless, armless, and otherwise mutilated people, as well as skeletons evidencing surgery—skulls with copper or bronze trepanning—and some 200 pre-Columbian surgical instruments. Other exhibits include *repoussé* gold masks; objects carved in nacre set with precious stones; a yard full of Tiahuanaco steles as large as the sarsens of Stonehenge; a *sub rosa* collection of phallic objects (including jugs whose spouts whistle when poured through) and depictions of sexual activities; whether from preference or birth-control laws, sodomy was the pre-Columbian norm. At the end is a vast collection of mummies in flexed position, knees to chins, hands and feet bound by hemp-of-byssus, and with bamboo tubes, through which the corpses were fed chicle from above ground, still in their mouths. Eternity symbols—cornucopias, crowing roosters—embellish each coffin.

We drive from the museum to a corral of llamas (a Quechua word) and alpacas, snooty beasts who spit spitefully in our direction.

August 18. Marmosets are sold on the streets in Lima, from cages resembling hand-organs. But, then, almost everything is available out of doors here, and in this and other respects, Lima reminds us of Naples. The cafés, the street noise, the boys who clean the windshields of cars stopped at traffic signals, and our favorite restaurant: all are Neapolitan. But the resemblance breaks down with the architecture, the statuary, and the thick gray sky. Driving in Lima is like driving in the Lincoln Tunnel: the visibility is about the same, the lights are phosphorescent in both cases, and the air is equally foul.

The ruins of Pachacamac are an hour's drive from Lima, between the sea and pink-brown sand dunes. The better road, as solidly paved as the Appian Way, is in the disinterred city itself, on a hill facing the sea and

Pachacamac Island, which is white with guano, like a frosted cake. The **1960** dead city and the architecture of its afternoon shadows are severely geometrical, and the stillness is pierced by the cries of guano birds echoed in the moaning seaward wind. Behind us are the Andes, vague, blue, illusory, perhaps not there at all but known to be from maps.

Back in Lima, the Music Club's cocktail party takes place in a home that could qualify as a museum of Cuzco primitives and colonial-period soapstone carvings. The language of Society, here and elsewhere in Lima, is French, and much of the talk is about events and mutual acquaintances in Paris. Another subject is servants. "Peru is the only country left where servants are still inexpensive," someone informs me, as if this were my most pressing problem. But Lima *is* feudally class-stratified, as well as race-stratified; the only Indians at this party *are* servants.

August 19. Pizarro's cadaver, in Lima Cathedral, is contained in a yellowish, viscous sack lying in a glass case to the right of the door. Kika, the Peruvian girl who accompanies us there, will not look at it. "That is the man who destroyed our culture," she says. After 400 years!

I go with V. to the Cemetery of the Presbyterian Master, where the dead are stacked in long rows of granite filing cabinets. We search unsuccessfully for the grave of her uncle, the Marquis Théodore de Bosset, hero of the Russian Navy in the 1905 war against Japan, and later the Admiral in charge of the Tsar's private fleet.

Shortly before the concert tonight, Manuel Prado, President of Peru, comes backstage, where Señora Prado tells I.S. that she saw him "conduct something or other" in Venice in 1951, when she "went over for Carlos de Beistegui's Ball." (*"Elle a du chien,"* V. says later, but I remind her that this classic expression can be translated as "She's a bitch.") Unfairly, no doubt, but by the end of the interview I have formed a prejudice in favor of a revolution in Peru. Some satisfaction comes sooner than I expect. Entering his loge, the praxicopomatic President is greeted by hisses and boos from the dress circle, and by still ruder noises from the upper balconies, all in the greatest possible contrast to the stomping, cheering, and bravoing a minute later for I.S.

August 20. Ascending over roofless hovels—it never rains!—and the white-rimmed, beryl-green sea, we fly to Antofagasta and Santiago. The airfield at Antofagasta, where we walk in a warm sun and cold, dry wind, is in a featureless desert, but the Chilean police warn us not to take photographs. From here to Santiago the earth is a spilled chemistry set of cobalt, laterite, copper, sodium, and sulphur, the Andes an almond-white wall rising out of a bed of dirty cotton-wool clouds. Dry rivers wind down the mountains and spread into alluvial fans, but at Santiago the rain is so strong that we circle above the airport for nearly an hour before landing. Claudio Spies meets us at the airport and accompanies us to the Carrera Hotel where we eat filet of *congrio*.

1960   August 21. Jolted out of bed at 7 A.M. by a brass band playing the national anthem in the plaza in front of our rooms, we go to our windows and watch a platoon of goose-stepping soldiers at a flag-raising ceremony. Above them and behind is the cordillera, white, gleaming in the sun, and higher than anything in the world.

To Las Vertientes in the afternoon, with a group of Chilean musicians. Mimosa and wild peach blossom whiten the hills, and the trees, including pines, poplars, and willows, are refreshingly green and varied. The party at Las Vertientes is a feast of pies, cakes—a delicious *loukouma*—and remarks by I.S., one of which is that "Palestrina was a great bureaucrat of counterpoint." He describes Santiago, from his drive through, as a "used car lot of statues and monuments. The smaller the national history, the larger the commemorating stones." During the return to Santiago a light rain falls and black ponchos appear everywhere. At the hotel we eat *chirimoya*, the sweet, white, mushy fruit with black-almond pips, scooped out of hard, avocado-like shells.

August 22. V. receives a visit from Fabian Fedorov who describes her father's funeral in Santiago 25 years ago. Other visitors include Delia del Carril (former wife of Pablo Neruda); a sister of Paul Thévenaz, who drew I.S.'s portrait in Leysin in 1914; and, most interestingly, because she had an affair with I.S. in London in June 1921, Juanita Gandarillas, the separated wife of I.S.'s friend Tony Gandarillas, nephew of Eugenia Errazuriz, whose death Juanita describes to us. But if these people and associations from the remote past have had a disturbing effect on the S.s, they betray no sign of it.

I.S. is brilliant chatting with a musician after my rehearsal this morning, saying that he has a sense of his material long before he begins to work, and that this must be the same with all composers. (Hume: "It is impossible for us to think of anything which we have not antecedently felt.") "But," I.S. goes on, "I am always surprised by the suddenness with which my material comes to an end. I feel like a satisfied animal then." When the inevitable question comes up about his borrowings from the 18th century, he answers simply, "Let's say that I was a kind of bird and that the 18th century was a kind of bird's nest in which I felt cozy laying my eggs." The standard question about electronic music provokes the answer that he is afraid of having involuntary physical reactions to it.

August 24. Our concert. I.S. conducts *Ode* and *Firebird*, and I conduct Webern's *Marcia funebre* and Debussy's *El Martirio de San Sebastian*. The Webern goes more smoothly than expected, although the orchestra has no idea of attack, phrasing, anacrusis. In the last movement of *Firebird*, the horn comes in on F instead of F sharp, which, I.S. says, coming offstage, is "like salt when you expect sugar."

August 25. The cordillera turns to fire in the setting sun and, for a time, as our plane bumps and drops between the mountains, we are afraid of turning to the same thing. Buenos Aires at midnight feels like January in

New York, but in spite of the cold and the hour, I.S. manages some affable remarks for television. "BIENVENIDO STRAVINSKY," a big banner reads at the airport entrance. Reaching the Plaza Hotel at 1 A.M., we start to unpack, but at 2 A.M. I.S. complains about his bed, and we resettle on another floor.

August 26. The Teatro Colón is a perfect sound box, and Webern's *ponticello* whispers are clearer here than I have ever heard them. The musicians, whose foreign languages are German and Italian, not French and English, are the quickest and ablest we have encountered on the tour (no great compliment), but they are sour, humorless, and unwilling to be corrected. After a run-through of *Firebird*, an elderly gentleman introduces himself to I.S. as a fellow pupil of Rimsky-Korsakov. (I.S. to me: "Not true, but even if it were, what right does that give him to disturb me now?") Rimsky apart, he wishes to commission a piece "of major proportions" for the opening of a new hall. (I.S. to me: "Why doesn't he ask some Elgar specializing in that sort of thing? 'Of major proportions' means 'pompous.' ")

Buenos Aires is a city of beautiful trees: jacarandas, Japanese magnolias, hydra-headed ombus, aguaribays. And a city of absurd statues and monuments. I.S.: "A lifesize statue of a man in an open place is ridiculous. Size suggests the heroic, as in Michelangelo's 'David,' and why bother to carve the man next door?"

White-collar complaints in Buenos Aires, from race hatreds to the plumbing, are scapegoated to Perón, whereas the walls of blue-collar neighborhoods are scrawled with the slogans "*Vuelve Perón*" and "*Obra de Perón.*" According to our silk-collar host at dinner tonight, the people are divided, bitter, without hope. "The true *obra de Perón* is that *nous ne sommes pas les nouveaux riches mais les nouveaux pauvres.*" This conversation takes place in the La Cabaña restaurant, where the photographs of prize steers on the walls and the stuffed steer in the lobby inhibit my appetite.

August 29. Our Teatro Colón concert. I conduct Bach-Schoenberg, Webern's Six, and fragments from the *Martyr.*

"Señor Stravinsky, what does South America mean to you?" a reporter asks, and the answer could hardly be more candid: "Hotel rooms, first of all, some too old, some too new. And wildernesses, deserts and jungles, with their extremes of climate. And faces in symphony orchestras that might have come from Inca tombs. And nationalism: each country hates its neighbor. And racism: I saw swastikas in Santiago and have been told that they can be found here. Above all, I learned that South America is culturally colonial to Europe, having few ties to the United States and no vital ones, meaning religion and language; from here, the Monroe Doctrine does seem a purely *yanqui* idea. Finally—you will not like this, but I will say it anyway—my general impression of South America is of a *triste* continent." They do *not* like it, but I.S. is not now and never was one

1960 to withhold his mind for that reason, or to curry favor with the press for *any* reason. He is chafing today because of a 26 percent service charge on his hotel bill.

We spend the day with Victoria and Angelica Ocampo at San Isidro, Victoria's book-filled house, with gardens of giant philodendrons overlooking the Rio de la Plata. Warming ourselves beside a *quebracho* fire, we eat *empanadas* (a beef and raisin *pirozhki*) and flick through photograph albums of such former house guests as I.S., Tagore, Count Keyserling, Isherwood, St.-John Perse. (Victoria on Perse's wife: "She's a 100 percent American, but nice in spite of that.") Afterwards Victoria takes us to Algarrobo, where, in 1818, Juan Martín y Pueyrredón planned the wars of Chilean and Peruvian liberation; but she is wearing slacks, and on that account is admitted only after a terrific row. Not slacks, of course, but blue stockings are her normal garb, and though hosiery of that color rarely carries attractive connotations, Victoria is a beauty, with a young girl's fresh pink complexion. She is also very proud—the portraits of her grandparents in her living room were painted by Pueyrredon *père*—and contemptuous of her new Thyssen neighbors, with their protective electric fences.

Victoria has invited a group of Argentine musicians to meet I.S. at teatime. Among the questions discussed are the problem of trying to teach both an "integrated-traditional" and a "mathematical-experimental" approach to composition (no conclusions); and the faults of *avant-gardisme*, which are its dependence on an absurd competition—the need to outdo—and its ignorance of music in the pre-electronic era (no remedies). When something is said about the "power" of Beethoven, I.S. jumps on the word: "I don't like it because it really means 'use of power.' Say 'might,' rather." This exchange makes me realize how little my published colloquies with I.S. show his cunning with words, his many-sided apprehension of them, and his sense of their aptness and weight. I also realize that I have nowhere recorded one of his favorite and most characteristic expressions, "Who needs it?" This is employed in a variety of circumstances, though never more frequently than at concerts of modern music, when he will listen quietly for a minute or so to a new string quartet by Professor Q, then grow restless and start to squirm, turn to me and stage-whisper: "But who needs it?"

In the car to Buenos Aires, a Russian woman, friend of the S.s', diverts us by reciting virtually the whole of *Old Possum's Book of Practical Cats*. Night traffic is even more dangerous in Argentina than day traffic. The intersections of the long suburban avenues are without signals or lights, and the only law appears to be every man for himself. Headlights, moreover, are turned on only at the *suspected* approach of another vehicle.

August 30. Our second concert. I.S. stops conducting after the beginning of the chaotically played Fourth Tableau of *Petrushka* and, after a fearful pause, starts it over again. "Such are the humiliations of fame," he says later: "The notes should be articulated like *petits pois*, but they come out like pease porridge and the public applauds all the same."

August 31. Spend the afternoon with Jorge Luis Borges at Angelica Ocampo's apartment. Nervous and shy as a ferret, he continually folds and unfolds his napkin, realigns the silverware, traces the creases in his trousers. Nearly blind—his lenses are as thick as piano-leg casters—he fixes each of us in turn with one eye, but says he cannot see anyway, and he compares himself to the captain in *The End of the Tether.* He teaches a course in advanced English at the University of Buenos Aires, "for which a mere eight months were allotted formerly, but which the clever people now in control have reduced to four." His range of reading in English from O. Henry to Henry James, and in five other languages, leaves us far behind, and we sit around a centerpiece of purple anemones listening to him—and eating *dulce de leche*, which I.S. later fears will make him ill.

September 1. Dinner at Mme Erize's with the Swiss Ambassador and Alberto Ginastero.

September 3. I.S. receives the Order of Maya from Dr. Diogenes Taboada, in the Gold Room of the Palacio San Martín. Our concert for the Mozarteum (Mme Erize). I conduct the *Lulu* Suite.

September 4. At 6:30 A.M. we fly over the long causeway and the muddy river; both shores are in view from the middle. Montevideo is a city of red rooftops and beaches, and the earth beyond looks as if it had been churned by whirlpools. Nearer São Paulo, where we put down just long enough to learn that our concert has been canceled, the land has been turned into dark green *fazendas.* Before Rio, the ground is split into canyons shaped like streak lightning.

The Ouro Verde is a small Copacabana hotel with a terrace on the wave-patterned mosaic sidewalk. As we sit there before bed, drinking thimble-sized cups of blue, sugary coffee, a huge yellow moon appears, and a host of dark-complexioned girls in tight pants and sweaters soliciting every man on the walk.

September 5. 6 A.M. A canine chase, two terriers running pell-mell to the surf and back as fast as possible. The earliest bather is a fat man exercising with a fat rubber ball. Watermelon carts appear next, stands selling fresh crabs, and boys with condor kites. The beach is soon crowded— chocolate skins, *pousse-café* skins, and pale skins in about equal numbers. Later, an American in the bar tells us that "integration is more apparent than real, and apparent only on the beach."

Rio is a city of iron balconies, iron grilles, iron shutters; a city shaded by beautiful trees; a city of new buildings on stilts and old buildings *made* of stilts; a city of curvaceous wooden churches. The road to the Paneiras Corcovado is partly canopied with vines, like a tunnel, and alternately washed away and blocked by landslides. From the Corcovado at moonrise, Rio is indeed a "*Cidade Maravilhosa.*"

1960   September 6. An American in the bar says that he lives by borrowing at 6 percent in the United States and lending at 28 percent here, "But it's risky." I.S., back from a sundown stroll, says he was solicited by one of the *poules* patrolling the hotel area. "I was touched by her suggestion; and tempted: you could dial a telephone with her nipples." The beach, at midnight, is littered with lovers.

September 7. Brasilia, Port-of-Spain, New York. The pilot for the first lap is an I.S. "fan," a fact that once cost him a job, he says, the staff psychiatrist of a U.S. airline having rejected him because his reply to "What are your favorite books and favorite pieces of music?" was "Nietzsche's *Zarathustra* and Stravinsky's *Rite of Spring*." I.S. and I stand behind him in the cockpit during take-off and an unscheduled tour of the bay. To the west of Rio are jagged mountains, cities hugging the fringes of winding dirt roads, and eroded and sun-calcined plains. Beyond the agglomeration of new buildings at Belo Horizonte are clumps of jungle, dried-up water holes, coiling black rivers with sand islands, like spotted snakes. From the air, Brasilia is a large-scale map with future streets traced in and circular perforations for future trees. From the ground, the few lonely skyscrapers suggest a partly undenticulated comb.

Three hours after changing planes, we cross the Amazon at Santarem, where the great brown river is swollen by transfusions from large blue tributaries. From here to the Orinoco, storm detonations leave smoke-like puffs of clouds over the thick green jungle. Trinidad seems exaggeratedly British, what with the BBC accents on the loudspeaker, the pith helmets, the Bermuda shorts, and the Crown insignia of the airport employees. In the waiting room, I.S., watching a baby's unsteady walk, says: "Just like me." A native village, come to see someone off, forms a quilt of color as we lift into the air.

September 16. On my return to New York from Kingston, V. says that I.S. was annoyed because I said that I slept well at home: "He doesn't sleep well with us?"

September 17. New York. Lunch with Aldous, who talks about Nixon: "No resemblance to the human race whatever. His jowls remind me of those monkeys who store chewed bananas. A Musée Grevin figure."

September 18. Rome. To avoid the crowds for the Olympic Games, we drive directly from the Rome airport to Perugia.

September 19. To Borgo San Sepolcro, Gubbio, and Venice, arriving too late to hear Schumann's *Paradise and the Peri*.

September 20. Letter from Isaiah on *Roots of Revolution*, for which he has written an introduction. A dull book, he says, but useful for those who want to know where such and such obscure revolutionary was born, when he was imprisoned, or hanged, or eaten by Siberian wolves.

September 24. With I.S. to the John Cage-Merce Cunningham evening at the Fenice, but we leave after a few minutes.

September 27. Our concert in the Palazzo Ducale, Sala Dello Scrutinio. I conduct Berg's *Preludium* and *Reigen*, *Der Wein*, the *Altenberg Lieder*, and I.S. conducts *Monumentum* and *Orpheus.*

October 14. Brilliant letter from Isaiah on Russian messianism, and the self-preoccupation of Russian literature, even in the Western and aesthetically pure novels of Turgenev. An antique shop near Santa Maria in Formosa displays three 18th-century human-lattice pictures of the kind V. copied for the Baroness d'Erlanger, carnival acrobats forming four, five, and six pyramidal tiers.

October 15. Venice is submerging. The water in the hotel lobby this morning is 30 inches deep. Barelegged porters provide a piggyback ferrying service between the stairs and an elevated plank-board highway leading to the Piazza, itself a boat basin where gondolas and drowned rats float in the filthy water of a long-needed street-cleaning. A few tables are above water in the center arcade at Florian's, and near them the café orchestra bravely plays on, like the band on a sinking ship. On the Piazzetta side, pigeons flutter nervously overhead as booted boys wade excitedly in the mounting tide. But a cold Bora blowing whitecaps on the Grand Canal sends us back to our rooms, back over the single-file bridge on which we join other refugees gingerly walking with shoes and stockings in hand.

October 21. Thoughts about the eventual evacuation of Venice—eviction, in the case of the last Homo sap. on the last garbage scow—and the final gurgle of the scuttled city as San Marco sinks, a *Cathédrale engloutie.* Libraries, paintings, and other art can be saved, but I am thinking about the unrecoupable losses, the decorated ceilings in the great palazzi; the *cortilli*; the loggias; the bridges and their iron railings (all of them different); the iron window grilles; the muzzled well-heads; the chimneys; the escutcheons; the street lamps and votive lamps; the calvaries and shrines; the canal-side—as distinguished from the *campi- calli- salizzade*-side—façades; and the relief sculpture: the angels, the lions, the dromedaries (the wall of the Palazzo del Cammello), and, in spite of Michaels and Georges aplenty to kill them off, the dragons.

Venice is, or was, a city of music, of choirs and organs, of brass instruments sounding in stone churches, of madrigals sung in palazzi, of operas, and of bells, which still regulate life here: people still set their watches by the *nona*, still start and stop work by the *marangona*, and the bells toll not only the hours but also the character and remembrances of the hours, including our mortality. The music of the three-tone bells—San Marco's five and the Frari's four are too many—with the constantly changing positions between the three isorhythmic parts, is mesmerizing. The bells of Santa Maria del Giglio begin with *"mi,"* followed by *"re,"* which limps after the higher part in ever shorter steps, then passes it, whereupon the *"mi"* becomes the gimpy one. Then the *"do"* enters, seems to take sides with the *"re"* against the *"mi,"* and is the last to sound, trailing off, like an *ejaculatio,*

1960 with ever longer pauses after each ever fainter peel. The whole performance, moreover, lasts less than two minutes (an *ejaculatio praecox*, then.)

Venice is a city of birds. The drone of them on San Francesco del
Deserto is as loud as an electric generator. Venetians still predict weather
from the altitude of swallows: low-flying ones spell rain. Canaries still
chirp in window cages all over the city, and pigeons "coo" in the Piazza,
these last despised, partly, I think, because they do not hop but walk one
foot after the other, like overfed businessmen.

And Venice is a city of angels, dancing (on the Salute), trumpeting (on
the corner of the Zobenigo and under the cupola of the "Ascension" in San
Marco), floating (on the Riva del Vin side of the Rialto Bridge), and simply
exposing their celestial forms (the Scuola di San Teodoro, where one of
them looks slightly bat-like—a bat out of Heaven, then?).

November 13. Genoa. I.S. writes to Giuseppe Galletta, Filarmonica
Antonio Laudamo, Messina: "I am very sorry that my decision to cancel
my trip to Sicily has deprived you of the participation of Robert Craft for
your concert in Messina. R. Craft is one of my closest friends and associates on concert tours; he could not leave me when I made the decision to
return (November 25th) to New York for a blood treatment."

November 27. Paris. "Lunch" at the Boule d'Or with Suvchinsky and
François-Michel. At other tables: baby-faced North Americans, oily-faced
South Americans, brewer's-bloom-faced (telangiectatic) Gauls. The tempo
of François-Michel's talk is too fast for me, and with the exception of my
meager contributions to his *Encyclopédie*, I know too little of what it is about
(literary *mesquineries*, Saussure's distinction between *langue* and *parole*, and
Claudel, whom I.S. describes as a *"cochon incontestable,"* despite François-
Michel's *"Oui, mais un grand poète"*). His gourmet talk, what I manage to
digest of it, contains useful knowledge on such matters as *perdreau* basting,
the wisdom of asking for the less exercised left *patte* of the *poulet*, and of
choosing the Gruyère close to the *croûte*—while of course avoiding any
cheese at the slightest whiff of ammonia. He complains that our first wick-
er-cradled bottle of wine has not been sufficiently aerated, though the
glasses are the size of small goldfish bowls. This leads to a discussion of
pre-phylloxera clarets, after which everyone begins to sniff, sip, debate the
merits of body and bouquet, and report the reception of the palate, as if
that abused organ, after a flagon of vodka, could differentiate between
Lafite-Rothschild and plonk. Yet, after all, perhaps François-Michel's can.

All told, we soak up, or down, two bottles of vodka, three of claret—as
if in obedience to Spenser's "Pour out the wine without restraint or stay"—
and two of champagne, this in addition to several slugs of Calvados. In
consequence, of course, we are stupefied, the worst of which is that we
have an appointment at five with Chagall, who has come expressly for it
from Rouen. Fortunately, V., finding herself in conversation with the
South Americans at the adjoining table, and realizing early on that she is

on the brink of inebriety herself, takes no more, and is therefore able to *1960* guide her debauched and reeling menfolk back to the hotel. (As I test one leg, then the other, the thought strikes me that I might turn to stone—on the analogy that certain chemical elements convert from one to another until stability is reached, at which point they become lead.)

It is already 4 o'clock by the time we arrive and steer I.S. to his bed, on which, after replying to V.'s "Are you drunk?"—"And how!"—he goes out like a light. Trying to sober me up for the meeting, Suvchinsky and V. work me over as if I were a K.O.-ed boxer, Suvchinsky holding ice-filled compresses to my forehead in spite of my protestations on behalf of my sinuses and my insistence that the real trouble is with the medulla oblongata.

> They played him a sonata — let me see!
> "Medulla oblongata" — key of G.

At 5 o'clock, I.S. being beyond communication, I venture forth with V. But though I go with her as far as Nicolas Nabokov's apartment, where the meeting is to take place, I am too queasy to enter and can only truckle ignominiously, as well as headswimmingly, back to the hotel. An hour later, with the return of the valiant V., we learn that Rolf Liebermann,* who had flown from Hamburg for the meeting, took the story as a great joke—"for which I will always love him," V. says, adding with a feline scratch that "Chagall couldn't have behaved more pompously, and his wife looked at me as if I were depraved, or had come from a Roman orgy. Wasn't *her* husband ever drunk? I wanted to ask. What about all those upside-down roosters?"

٭ Postscript 1994. Stravinsky's Movements for piano and orchestra baffled the audience at the premiere (New York, January 10), but Balanchine's ballet based on it three years later was quickly recognized as breaking new musico-choreographic ground.

Back in Hollywood, the Stravinskys decided to add a sun room to their house by extending the library over the front terrace. The new room increased bookshelf space by about four times and included built-in cabinets designed to store Stravinsky's manuscripts—but in the wrong place, since they were not protected from the desiccating afternoon heat. The room was quieter and more comfortable than my apartment, and I began to work there late at night, in the purring company of Celeste, the Stravinsky cat.

The South American tour had been proposed by the composer's longtime Argentine friend Victoria Ocampo, the editor of the magazine *Sur*, who had helped to organize his appearances in Buenos Aires and Rio de

---

* Liebermann's memoirs mistakenly say that I was present.

1960 Janeiro in 1936. Mme Ocampo was an accomplished récitante in Stravinsky's *Perséphone*, as well as the publisher of the Spanish edition of his autobiography. She introduced him to the works of her writer friends Ortega y Gasset and Jorge Luis Borges, and, in London in the summer of 1934, she effected a meeting between the composer and another of her friends, Aldous Huxley, that marked the beginning of the happy relationship that developed in Los Angeles a decade later.

Our most enjoyable hours in Buenos Aires were spent with Victoria in her San Isidro home, and with Vera Stravinsky's stepmother, who had moved there from Santiago in the late 1930s, after the death of Vera's father. The one flaw in the arrangements at San Isidro was Victoria's intolerant blue-law teetotalism: wine, at her table, was served only to Stravinsky (a decanter of Bordeaux placed in front of his plate, which must have been the rule in 1936 as well). Christopher Isherwood, a onetime house guest there, had warned us of this inconvenience, describing how he had smuggled gin and Scotch into his room until caught out one day when a maid discovered a cache of the merchandise in a bag under his bed.

The South American expedition was less than gratifying musically owing to orchestra strikes, the non-arrival of the players' parts, and sudden shortages of funds. The tour was unprofitable as well; almost as many concerts were canceled (São Paulo, Rio de Janeiro, Caracas) as took place (only six in all). I was responsible for all of the rehearsing, which was onerous work because the orchestras were somewhat primitive and my Spanish very primitive.

Not long after our arrival in Venice, the annual inundations (aqua alta) began. The most severe of them inspired *The Flood*, Stravinsky's main work of 1961–62. Our concert in the Doge's Palace included the first public performance of *Monumentum*, Stravinsky's translation for instruments—and more than that, a transformation of vocal music into instrumental music without precedent—of three Gesualdo madrigals composed in about 1600. Matching 17th-century-style transportation was provided for the rehearsals and concert in that Stravinsky was borne up and down the Golden Staircase in a sedan chair. A portable sedan chair toilet had been installed in a screened-off corner of the huge salon that served as our dressing room, and shortly before the concert, in response to an emergency call to the Ospedale Civile, a motor boat, siren clearing the way, brought some urgently-needed paregoric.

Our sojourn in Genoa was enjoyable both musically and socially, thanks to a good orchestra and a gracious lady Intendent. In Rome I became involved with a glamorous divorcée, slightly older than I was but very much more experienced. Complications developed when she came to New York in late December and accompanied the Stravinskys and me to Washington. The affair ended badly, but also much to my relief; which is called *Schadenfreude*.

❧ *1961*

January 5. While I.S. records his Octet at Manhattan Center, Paul Horgan, V., and I go to the 92nd Street "Y" to hear Eliot read his poems. Robert Lowell, though more than just noticeably "tight," as became evident in his easy jokes at Carl Sandburg's expense, introduces the poet. Eliot, short of breath, hoicking and clearing his throat, introduces each poem with a slightly self-deprecating remark: "'Portrait of a Lady' is said to be slighter than 'Prufrock,' which, I daresay, is true." An anecdote about an undiscourageable correspondent on the subject of Whitman's influence draws laughter. Responding to applause, Eliot reads two encores. Lowell invites us to join Eliot afterward at e.e. cummings's in the Village, but we go instead to the last hour of I.S.'s recording session.

January 20. Massey Hall, Toronto. About halfway through the recording session of Schoenberg's Piano Concerto, Glenn Gould arrives, removes his mittens, soaks his hands in milk, dries and inserts them in fingerless gloves, and begins to practice as if he were alone on stage. Pleading fatigue, he says he does not want to rehearse with the orchestra at all, but only to record. Though far from ready, we run through the first movement, after which, despite many places not in sync with the orchestra, he pronounces the result "very good." I protest that we are not covered in measures, etc., etc., until finally he agrees to play it again. The remaining movements, in which the orchestra is sight-reading, are also taped nonstop, with insert patching-up afterward. Then Gould's bundling-up process begins—the sweaters, coat, scarves, cap, and mittens—and off he goes with several minutes of recording time to spare. Howard Scott, the emcee, says that I have been extremely lucky in getting this much playing time out of the great pianist.

January 23–25. Los Angeles. I.S. records *Firebird* in three evening sessions in the American Legion Hall. His knowledge of the score, which he has not conducted in its entirety since, I think, 1915 (if then), is astonishing, but he has been studying it carefully, correcting errors, making

237

1961 changes, replacing the tenor and bass tuba parts with trumpet parts, etc.

February 25. Letter from Gould: "Dear Bob: I think that we have turned out a fairly distinguished result and I think it has much more spirit and magnetism than most recordings of this period of Schoenberg. . . ."

March 17. Telegram from Varèse: ". . . sending scores and material of *Arcana, Deserts,* and tape two channels with instructions on back. The [Koussevitzky] Foundation lawyer told [Schuyler] Chapin he expected favorable answer from [Musicians'] Union tomorrow. Please give my best regards and sincere regrets to the Stravinskys. Sorry can't be present good luck and warm greetings from us both Edgard Varèse."

March 31. Cuernavaca. Lunch at Las Mañanitas, joined at the end by Edward James. The lawns here are an aviary: black herons with gold combs; pigeons with shuttlecock fantails and leggings that remind me of the long-underwear tights of pugilists in the '90s; parrots screeching in the surrounding plumbago bushes; peacocks, strutting like Ziegfield girls but emitting a strident cry that sounds like "Help!" I.S. says that in the Russia of his youth, to see a peacock outside one's window meant bad luck (a death in the family), but could this have been a common occurrence?

At 3 o'clock, the death of Christ—it is Good Friday—is commemorated in the plaza by acolytes in white dalmatics shaking rattles and turning ratchet wheels. We reach the Borda Hotel in Taxco by nightfall, when the moon, rising like a World War I observation balloon, is the signal for the dogs on the adjacent hills to begin a nonstop barking contest; and for the start of a candlelight parade that for three hours winds out of the hills and weaves through the dark town below, moving in spreads and bunches like a concertina. Virtually the whole population takes part in this procession, which disbands in the streets below Santa Prisca, but reconverges at midnight at the Convent of San Bernardino for the final act of the day-long Passion Play.

We go to Santa Prisca ourselves at about 11, chauffeured through packed streets by Vicente, a powerfully-built man who might have had a successful career as a bandit. The church—Vicente: "This is Santa Prisca, you see what I mean?"—is empty except for two boys polishing the gold columns of the altar (*"No toquen el dorado"*), which look as if they had been squeezed from giant tubes of toothpaste, and Indian women kneeling on the bare aisle stones and saying their orisons beneath a crucifix draped with a transparent purple veil. The walls are covered with silver hearts, mandorlas, and ex-voto pictures of lost pigs and cows.

At midnight the crowd outside the entrance to the convent is motionless and silent. Inside, a few steps from the door, is an unshrouded Christ image with silver angel wings and a black cross roped to the lacerated and bleeding back. Beyond, in front of the altar in the main room, is a hill of Calvary, with three lifesize crosses. The one in the center is empty, but the ladder used for the descent leans against it, and strips of embalming linen hang from the cross-bar; effigies of dead bodies are nailed to the other two crosses. On the floor is a solid mass of kneeling Indians, every face, except those of children tottering on the brink of sleep, transfixed. Suddenly, a somber, strange wail goes up from an unseen organ, and at this a narrow path is cleared from the door to the center cross, to which a teenage boy makes his way, black-hooded and bare to the waist, with a heavy cactus cross on his back and lighted candles tied to the wrists of his spread-eagled arms. With great effort, in evident pain, and with the support of four other boys, he kneels. As his knees touch the floor, the organ stops and he begins a long, slow chant that is gradually taken up by the whole congregation.

The absence of clerical vestments—for all outward signs, the officiating priests could be plainclothes detectives—makes the ceremony all the more real: so far from being an embodiment of virtues and ideals, or projection of the wish for a higher humanity, the god of this drama is the Ecce Homo, man who suffers and dies, and whose death redeems the lives of the kneeling people. An hour or so after the drama in the convent, a platoon of young Indians, wearing the helmets and tunics of Roman legionaries, gathers in the plaza to stand guard over the sepulcher. At dawn an air-raid siren screams the end of their vigil. On our return to the hotel, an incongruous scene: Edward James runs by, chased by half a dozen boys pummeling him with fists and sticks. No doubt he has tried to buy one of them on the wrong night. We go to bed under clouds that look like curdled milk.

April 1. Helping us to check out of the hotel this morning, Vicente asks: "Have you enough [i.e., more] bags?" On the road to Acapulco, boulders and barns bear the legend *"Muera Apurto"* ("Kill Apurto") in white paint. "Apurto is the Governor of the Province," Vicente explains. "Mexicans are funny people, señor. You see what I mean?" Crosses stud the shoulders of the steep road *bajando* to the hot country, marking the fatal plunges of the careless or unlucky, and at one perilous turn a stone coffin stands at the place where a fence would have done more good. Automobiles are rarer than donkeys, which the Indians ride not on the withers, like gringos, but to the rear. We pass an old mule with five small boys astride its deeply ridged back.

In the valleys, the arid cactus *barrancas* are relieved by maize, the husks, cobs and stalks of which are stored in trees, like huge birds' nests. Pigs and cows roam at large, attended by vultures. And the farther *bajando*, the more fragmentary the clothing. Vicente: "It is hot, señor. You see what I mean?" Near Iguala, the Indians along the roadside are selling ceramics, baskets, guavas, chicle, lovebirds, and pulque, swinging pots of the latter toward our speeding car like priests with censers. We stop at a thatched-roof roadside stand and, surrounded by dark-eyed children, drink coconut milk spiked with gin, a combination that, back on the road, puts us to sleep until Vicente announces: "There's Acapulco. You see what I mean." Dinner with Agnes deMille. Red sunset. We watch the cliff divers.

April 7. Mexico City. Our concert in the Palacio de Bellas Artes: I conduct Beethoven's Eighth and the Mexican premiere of 3 Pieces from *Wozzeck;* I.S. conducts *Sacre* (televised).

April 8. Coyoacan. A breakfast of "Virgin's milk cheese," which we buy in the market, and the sweet cheese of Oaxaca, which is peeled or unraveled from a white ball. Watch a wedding in the church of San Diego Churubusco, which includes a rendition of "None But the Lonely Heart" by a tenor, violin, and organ in three different versions of unison, after which the priest extends the bride's veil over the groom's head and anoints them from an ampulla. The beggar who pushes his cup to us as we leave has the face and beard of the Christ image inside the door.

To Tepozotlan and the Churrugueresque church, which the S.s first saw in 1940 and which impressed them then, they say, more than any other in the world. The rose-colored stone and glittering gold interiors *are* alluring, even beyond their description, as we come to them from the maguey desert. The aisle columns are wrapped in red velvet and the angels are white—ghostlike in the frame of so much color—but the unforgettable feature is the chapel of the Virgin of Loreto, in which a narrowing funnel looks up a hundred feet to a blindingly white Dove of the Eucharist, reflecting an older god, the sun. As I.S. observes, "It is a womb, mirror-lined like all places of love, like a brothel."

May 11. Letter from Glenn Gould: the edited Schoenberg Concerto has a "wonderfully analytical clarity. I am very proud of it and my congratulations to you."

May 12. To Ingmar Bergman's *Virgin Spring.* Leaving the theater three hours later, we discover that the hill with the "HOLLYWOOD" sign is in flames, and that all streets in the vicinity are blocked. After a wide detour east and south, we reach home to learn that Aldous's house and its contents have burned to the ground.

May 13. After worrying all day about the safety of the Huxleys, a call from Mrs. Nys informs us that they are safe in a hotel.

May 18. The Huxleys for dinner. "Well, it *is* rather inconvenient, losing all your notes, annotated books, correspondence, library, accounting, addresses and telephone numbers," Aldous says. But he is badly shaken and cannot conceal it.

June 11. To be polite, I.S. goes to Royce Hall to hear Shostakovich's Symphony No. 11 and Khrennikov's Violin Concerto, but he squirms, fidgets, groans, makes denigrating remarks in a loud voice, and finally, even before intermission, bolts from his back-row seat.

June 30. Letter from Spender in London: "Dear Bob, I have spoken to

Francis Bacon and he would be thrilled to do a portrait of Stravinsky. There is one very definite condition—that Francis can destroy the painting if he does not like it. Apart from this there is the question of who has [owns] the painting. Marlborough Fine Arts might wish to give it to a public collection (perhaps the Tate). Francis would require 5 or 6 sittings, at the least. Love to the Stravinskys and you. We see a lot of Chester and Wystan. *Elegy for Young Lovers* is July 13. Perhaps you should send a cable to Glyndebourne? "

July 2. Santa Fe. La Fonda Hotel. Letter from Berman about I.S.'s decision to go to Russia:

I do realize that for the Maestro this is a final vindication. . . . He has a hawk's eye and his mind is as acute as ever, so I would like to have a chance to listen to his devastating impressions.

July 19. Letter from Isaiah, not looking forward to Auden-Henze at Glyndebourne.

August 25. New York. Balanchine comes and is obviously attracted by my friend the Met dancer Judith Chazin, a voluptuous specimen of his "type"; he offers to audition her.

August 27. Dinner with the S.s and Judith at the Varèses', 188 Sullivan Street. I.S. and Varèse are unprintable on most contemporary musicians, but the invective is first-rate. Varèse on a much overrated conductor: "The *con* thinks that Marc-Antoine Charpentier is the imbecile who wrote *Louise*."

August 31. Varèse and Elliott Carter for lunch at the Pierre Hotel. Since I.S. is not ready on time, I go downstairs first, but find myself in the elevator with the Hindemiths. Recovering from the surprise of seeing me emerge with the wrong composer, Varèse asks me to introduce him, but by this time Hindemith is halfway down the corridor in the direction of the restaurant. When I catch up and convey the request, Frau Hindemith says "no" a split second before Herr Hindemith says "yes." As Varèse watches them hurrying away, I can think of no other excuse than that Hindemith isn't feeling well—which can hardly accord with Varèse's impression of him a few minutes later in the hotel restaurant indulging a huge appetite and, when at length I.S. arrives, positively leaping from his seat to greet him. Almost all the talk at our table is generated by I.S., no doubt because, unlike him, Varèse and Carter are not accustomed to large draughts of Scotch at noontime.

Afterward I go with I.S. and Varèse to a tape-editing cubicle at 52nd Street and Seventh Avenue to listen to my *Deserts* recording. Varèse wants everything as loud as possible, I.S. as soft; but, then, I.S. does not like the piece. On the way back to the hotel, he says: "The wiggle of the tambourine in the electronic music section sounds like a rattlesnake."

September 9. Göteborg. When a reporter asks V. if I.S. belongs to any clubs (Lions, Kiwanis, presumably), she answers: "No, but he could join

1961 Alcoholics Anonymous." On the train to Stockholm, I.S. reminisces about his trip on the Gotha Canal with his brother Gury, in May 1905*. In the Stockholm railroad station, Gereon Brodin and other nice people from Sveriges Radio meet us, drive us to the airport, and spend nearly three hours with us while we wait for the flight to Helsinki.

A shaky ride, landing in Helsinki at midnight. Having swallowed too much schnapps on the plane, I.S., in a brief television interview, says "ish" for "is," but the Finns cannot have noticed, their language being so clotted with diphthongs anyway. The ride through moonlit forests to the sound-asleep city is "romantic." The hotel occupies only one floor, the ninth, of an office building; the Finnish word for elevator is *hissi*, the Swedish *hiss*, and the words appear side by side, without English, German, Russian, or French translation.

September 10. The view from our rooms of the gull-busy boat basin and the wooded islands makes the S.s nostalgic for St. Petersburg. We go to Järvenpää, where Sibelius's white-haired daughter meets us at the pathway to the composer's house and walks with us between tall birch and pine to his woodland grave, a large granite slab with a nameplate on which I.S., bending a knee, places a bouquet that has been thrust in his hand. In that instant a photographer emerges from the forest, snaps a picture, disappears, all as fast as a cuckoo in a clock. Sibelius's over-ninety widow welcomes us at the door of the house, a cozy residence with a tile stove in each room, wood floors scrubbed white and smooth, and no aura of Beethovenizing; Sibelius's works, recordings and bound volumes of scores, are tucked away half-hidden in a cabinet. On the return I.S. tells me that he had heard Sibelius's First or Second Symphony with Rimsky-Korsakov, whose comment was, "I suppose that is also possible." I learn from this anecdote that Rimsky called I.S. "Guimochka, as everyone did who loved me." I.S. claims that he is fond of some of Sibelius's Italianate music: "I like Italian-melody-gone-north. Tchaikovsky did, too, of course, and through him the taste became an important and attractive part of St. Petersburg culture." A thick fog has settled over Helsinki harbor and all night long we hear the cries of lost boats.

September 11. While rehearsing, I count in Russian and explain in German. At intermission, one of the few English-speaking players says to me: "You have humor way of thinking." The violin section includes the

---

* In August 1985, the Swedish Radio, Stockholm, kindly sent me photocopies of the captain's passenger list, May 28, 1905, trip No. 7, for the Gotha Canal steamer *Motalastrom*, Stockholm to Göteborg. Igor and Gury Stravinsky were passengers, and Igor inscribed a brief message in Russian, signing (in Latin letters), "Igor Stravinsky, *komponist*." Gury, writing in German, describes himself as a "student." Johann Virke, a stage director with Swedish Television and a descendant of the *Motalastrom*'s captain, provided these documents through the kindness of Mrs. Lisbeth Holm of the Swedish Radio.

most distractingly beautiful girl I have ever seen: red hair, brown eyes, *1961*
ivory skin: Helena Lehtela. Unfortunately she speaks no word of any language but Finnish.

September 12. The center of the old city is a white square with a statue of Tsar Alexander II; the new city, it goes without saying, is a mass of gray stone apartment buildings that could have come from, and be shipped to, anywhere in the world. While I.S. is interviewed by the Finnish radio and the newspaper *Helsingen Sanomet*, V. looks for, but does not find, a hotel that she remembers from her childhood. The markets with their heaps of mushrooms, berries, fish, flowers, and food stalls managed by old women who speak Russian have made V. homesick for St. Petersburg. We eat roast reindeer for lunch, pickled reindeer tongue for dinner.

We will remember our Helsinki concert above all for the large number of bouquets received. At a party in the hotel afterward, the speeches are short, the speakers hospitable, grateful, shy, and kind. Mlle Lehtela is there, and I learn through an interpreter that besides playing the violin she is a well-known film actress who regularly makes movies in the USSR. Probably I won't kill myself.

September 13. Stockholm, the Grand Hotel. A letter from Ingmar Bergman: "The *Psalm Symphony* has, during many years, been a source of spiritual power in my life." But Bergman does not attend tonight's special performance of *En Rucklares Vag* (*The Rake's Progress*), for which he is the stage director, at the Royal Opera; his absence is attributed to a skeptical remark about his movies by I.S. to a reporter in Göteborg. As we enter a loge on the left side of the theater facing the stage, I.S. receives a prolonged standing ovation.

The stage apron has been extended over the orchestra pit, neutralizing the proscenium arch. Moreover, the deepest stage depth is exploited throughout, most effectively at the end of the brothel scene, where the actors freeze in silhouette in the far background. A Brechtian poster, "*En Rucklares Vag,*" is used as a between-scenes drop, replacing the curtain and emphasizing the episodes as a progress of pictures in Hogarth's sense. The groupings are Hogarthian, too, and in some of the pictorializations, especially in the earlier episodes, Hogarth is openly imitated, most effectively in the scene where Mother Goose, bottle in hand, falls backward on her couch, a veritable *tableau vivant* of the original. The sets are changed not in the dark but before the eyes of the audience and as a coordinated element in the movement of the play. Thus "London" is lowered from the sky and populated with tradesmen and townspeople during the trumpet solo introducing the street scene. This is the most attractive set but it is also the last that can be described as English in color and style of decor. After it, the costumes become more Swedish, gray and black gradually predominating over pink and orange, but this more muted and somber palette also follows the tenor of the play.

1961   In spite of egregious musical cuts, wrong tempi, and a few places where Bergman is at loggerheads with the book, I.S. is more moved than I have ever seen him by any performance of any of his theater works, though, in truth, he is seldom not angry. "Tom's decision to marry Baba is convincing," he says, "and I want to thank Bergman for that. And for so much more besides. When Tom leaves for London, Anne weeps, Tom starts to go to her, and Trulove motions him back and goes to her himself: I believed in Trulove's gesture. Another thing: in the auction scene, the singing of Tom and Shadow from different places in the audience *does* bolster the idea that they are 'at large.' These small points, and many more, help to establish the credibility of the play." Best of all, Bergman's groupings are "natural" without infracting the conventions of opera: the arias and the actionless ensembles, such as the quartet and trio in the first scene, are sung *to* the audience, stage front. The difference is that Bergman's singers act, move their bodies and use their eyes, as singers are rarely trained to do.

The most novel aspect of the musical performance is that the harpsichord is elevated from the orchestra pit to slightly below stage level, where it is equidistant from, and serves as a transition between, singers and orchestra. One result of this is that *secco* recitatives can be and are performed *sotto voce*. Another is that the card game, played as a crescendo on stage, is all the more effective in contrast to the dynamically static harpsichord accompaniment.

At the end of the opera, I.S. receives a long standing ovation. I am bursting with pride for him myself and thinking of all those terrible performances of the opera in Geneva, New York, etc.

September 14. A bibulous luncheon in the Bernes Restaurant as guests of the Union of Swedish Composers, then to the Radiohusel to listen to tapes.

September 16. Uppsala. Ochre and red buildings, windmills, farmhouses roofed with sod. The old church on the Royal Ridge occupies the site of a temple to Odin and, still earlier, of a circle of sacred trees. The pews, pillars, and pulpit are as worn as driftwood. A row of hourglasses still stands on the rostrum, each with a 15-minute measure of sand as guarantor against ecclesiastical filibuster. The church was frequented by professors and prebendaries, some of whom, including Anders Celsius, are buried in the floor. Outside and separated from the church is the *klockstapel*, a wooden belfry laced from the waist up with rounded shingles, like a coat of mail.

Our driver takes us to the home of Linnaeus, the tomb of Swedenborg, the statue of the Arctic explorer Finn Malmgren (V.'s distant cousin), the gold casket of St. Erik, the 18th-century Teatrum Anatomicum, and the Carolina Rediviva Library, which has the part-books of Schütz's *Christmas Oratorio*, some organ entablatures in Buxtehude's hand dated 1680 and signed "*Membra Jesu Nostri, Organista S. Maria Virgines, Lübeck*," and a collection of drawings by Swedish kings, of which the best, by Gustavus IV, might have been inspired (at least) by Goya.

Dinner in the country home of Set Svanholm, director of the Royal Opera, with Ingmar Bergman—tall, nose like a clasp, deep-set eyes, a mole on the right cheek—and Keti Larabei, the Estonian pianist and his newest wife. His English, resourceful if not flawless, is abetted by hand movements that become livelier and increasingly expressive the more he speaks. Everything he says, moreover, is clear, formed by a well-tailored mind, and nothing about him is tentative. He is passionate, too, and when he declares, "The artist has only to discover what to do and with all his strength to purify the doing," I want to discover something right away, rush out, and do it myself. I.S. asks what initially attracted him to *The Rake*. "A bad performance," Bergman says, which opens the door to a discussion of *his* performance.

The Bedlam and Brothel scenes were overpopulated, I.S. suggests: "A few characters can be memorable, never a crowd of them." Bergman agrees: "I invented a name for each person in the chorus, but my work was destroyed when the ensemble had to be enlarged for more vocal volume." His first idea was that "the stage should be sufficiently long and deep to permit the actors to appear and disappear in darkness, instead of through doors." His second was that "the opera should be divided into two acts of five and four scenes each, principally because Act Two, as published, does not have a strong beginning-middle-end structure. As I see it, the play up to the unveiling of Baba's beard is one line; and not only the play but also the music: this is the protasis, the rest is the peripeteia. I was more concerned about connecting the episodes along these two lines than with rounded act-structures. I thought, too, that especially in this opera the audience's attention must not be lost for a single moment, which accounts for—please forgive me—the cuts." Bergman has abbreviated the orchestral march introducing the brothel scene, and excised the whole of Tom's aria at the beginning of the Bedlam scene, two places where other directors have complained of I.S.'s misapplied musical thrift and introduced pauses "necessitated" by insufficient musical time.

"Another reason for the two-act division," Bergman goes on, "was that I did not want the intermission to come after the bread machine and allow the audience to go out confused. This is the most difficult scene in the opera both to believe in and to stage." I.S. agrees, adding that: "The waltz music—hurdy-gurdy music, and in that sense mechanical—is deliberately indifferent." Bergman dreamed that the machine had a lion's mouth. "I dream about everything I do," he says. "Dreams purify my ideas." This delights I.S., who often solves compositional problems in his dream life.

Bergman's greatest achievement, I interject, is in having made Baba believable—which, I add, is not easy: to reverse a remark by somebody in Henry James, "She was perhaps a lady but never a woman." Baba recog-

1961 nizes Shadow for what he is, and though she enters the drama as a monstrosity from nowhere, she leaves it as a sympathetic personality. Bergman: "Baba cost me more thought than anyone else. She is the artist in all of us, not merely a circus artist, and this is the reason why she represents such a great advance over the original idea of the Ugly Duchess. Her beard must be beautiful, too, not grotesque; the audience must believe in the reality of what it sees no matter how fantastic. Besides, the point of the marriage, at least by the time of the breakfast scene, is not its exoticism but its conventionality. Tom is bored with her because she is shallow." Bergman expresses this in the breakfast scene by having Baba and Tom lie far apart on a ludicrously large bed.

The climax of the opera for Bergman is the confrontation of Tom, Baba, and Anne in the street. "That is where Shadow's work is shown in the open, and the reason I bring him on stage. He must look on gloatingly." I.S. remarks that "The silent movement of people in the street at the beginning of this scene is the most beautiful tableau in the opera. You have a deep feeling for music." Bergman: "The question for the opera director should always be, 'How much does the music tell us already?' In this scene it tells us that they are not people at all but shadows."

I.S. expands on his impression that the second act was more Swedish than the first, more like a Bergman film. The freaks at the auction, and again in Bedlam—a medieval madhouse, more Brueghel than Hogarth— were especially Bergmanesque, and so was the solitary dummy-fool at the end of the brothel scene. Bergman says he had spent so much time on the first part of the opera that too little remained for the rest. "Moreover, I became wary of following Hogarth, who is dangerous because too attractive in himself."

I.S. says that the Epilogue succeeds, as it has not in other productions, "because it did not come as a shock: the audience never loses track of the 'fable' aspect." This was managed like a Brecht *Verfremdungseffekt*, though Bergman's illusion of reality, cave-of-shadows reality, is precisely what Brecht tried to dispel. Bergman: "The Epilogue is a question of preparation, for which reason I also begin each act with it, to create a frame for the whole work." (He staged a dumb show during, and even before, the Prelude to Act One, and again before Baba's inventory recitative, which is the overture to "his" Act Two; but these devices serve to fix audience attention as much as to prepare for the Epilogue.) "The Epilogue should mean that 'Now the play is over and you can go home and talk about the singer's high C.'"

In the graveyard scene, Shadow enters, as well as exits, through the ground, and I.S. thinks the appearance weakens the effect of the disappearance. But he likes the way Shadow sits on the tombstone at the beginning of the scene, and likes the silhouette of three Gothic steeples, whose presence is more and more strongly felt as the action develops. Bergman: "At

246

first the audience is aware of the three spires only as ominous presences, but by the end of the scene it knows that they are Golgotha, and the meaning of the play."

I.S. also says that the Bedlamites respond too quickly, stand up too fast, after Anne's first strophe with flute duet, and that, after her exit, Tom, for a dying man, gets up too abruptly. Bergman: "Mistakes like these are part of the charm of opera. And probably they are necessary: they seduce us into trying again."

September 17. We spend the day at the country home of Karl-Birge Blomdahl and in the evening see his opera, *Aniara*, from which I.S. departs rather too quickly.

September 18. The Royal Theater at Drottningholm possesses more than twenty 18th-century sets, which include not only backboards but also perspectival systems of sliding side-scenery as well. The intendant works the antique machinery for us, displaying movements of clouds and waves, demonstrating thunder from a drop of rocks in a net, and the ascent of a plaster god—a "real" deus ex machina. When officially present, the King and Queen sat on red thrones in the front center of the audience, but when incognito and with a paramour, the King remained sequestered in a latticed loge to the side. Plaques still designate the seats for *"cavalieri," "friseurs," "valets."* Forty or so actors' rooms surround the stage, each equipped with a fireplace, pewter *lavabo*, clothes block, wig dummy, dressing table, mirror. The corridors have been made into galleries displaying actors' portraits, handbills for such popular plays of the time as Voltaire's *Tancrède*, and theater designs, including many by Bibiena and the originals for Cesti's *Il pomo d'oro*. The wallpaper is a hand-sewn painted parchment.

September 20. I.S. gives an interview, answering typed questions. He pencils-in answers to some of them in spite of having written at the top: "These questions were collectively composed and I am a person who does not think collectively."

September 21. A few days ago we saw the first act (only) of a very bad performance of *Rigoletto*. This morning, when I unthinkingly whistle one of the tunes

I.S. asks whether it is *Rigoletto* or *Traviata*. What he means, of course, is the *Traviata* melody:

1961   This is one of a thousand examples that he hears intervalically first, as he claims, rather than rhythmically: intervals are connecting roots, rhythms mere elaboration.

September 24. Our concert. I conduct the *Symphonies of Winds*, the Etudes, and the Symphony in C. I.S. conducts *Sacre*.

September 25. More talk with Bergman about the *Rake*, in a large room on the first floor of the hotel: waitresses keep appearing with unordered trays of tea and cakes—to catch a glimpse of Bergman and try not to faint.

Why is the clock in the Brothel scene not shown? Bergman: "Because it is obvious in the music. I prefer to see the eyes of the actors watching something unmistakably heard as a clock, and to make the actual audience believe through the eyes of the stage audience." He contends that "Shadow should be a kind of lawyer, the *advocatus diaboli*, but critics only understand typecasting. They complained that my Devil was not demonic, and that Tom pouts and mopes more than he roisters. The progress of the Rake is accounted for in the sets, don't you think? Tom really does look like a millionaire in the fourth scene."

Why is the auction crowd dressed in black? This struck us as Hyperborean and reminded us of the black-robed oarsmen in wood-carvings of toy scullers for sale everywhere in Stockholm. Bergman says that black *is* worn in the parish boat races in his native north, but that he had not thought of this while staging the scene: "My reason for choosing black was simply to focus attention on Baba and Anne by giving color only to them." I.S.'s last suggestion is that the auctioneer should be removed still farther from the bidders, who sit—and this is wonderfully effective—with their backs to the audience.

At the mention of I.S.'s *Oedipus Rex*, Bergman says he would stage it without masks. "A mask may be beautiful, and it can be a useful façade for all sorts of things, but the price, loss of contact, is too great." As we part, he asks me to keep in touch with him, I think because he wants to film the opera.

September 29. Berlin. A tour of *"Die Mauer"* in Mayor Willy Brandt's car, starting at the Brandenburger Tor, where the barricades, land mines, and other death traps are partly, and cruelly and cynically, concealed by flowers. I.S. points to what was once the Adlon Hotel on the other side, saying that this was where he met Schoenberg in 1912. In between are policemen with bloodhounds, binoculars, walkie-talkies, and submachine guns at the ready. In the French sector, *"Die Mauer"* is still low enough so that East and West German neighbors may converse over it. Old place names survive here, some of them, such as *"Bellevuestrasse,"* now brutally ironic: *"Dem deutschen Volk,"* says a sign above the door of a huge building still gutted from the war. Crosses with wreaths and bouquets commemorating fatal East-to-West leaps mark the sidewalk next to the boundary at many places. Every house bordering the wall is sealed, the windows and doors bricked up and boarded like a set for *No Exit*.

Someone has scrawled *"Wir sind alle Bruder"* on the door of a blockaded church, where even the crucifix is barb-wired, a *real* crown of thorns on a wooden effigy. In a field beyond an area not yet walled but patrolled by tanks, old men and women labor at gun point. Several times during this heart-sickening tour we close the windows of our car against the stench from buildings rubbled and derelicted in the carnage of 1945.

September 30. Belgrade. Our passports and currency declarations are collected and processed, and our baggage is examined, before we are allowed to leave the plane. Then I.S. discovers that his briefcase, containing the only manuscript of the first part of *The Flood*, is missing. Apparently it was not transferred when we changed planes in Frankfurt, but a member of the Santa Fe Opera staff will return for it tomorrow. The night is hot and windy and the streets are crowded with pedestrians. Our rooms at the Metropole face the Sava River where it curves to meet the Danube. The site of Roman Singidunum makes me think of Trajan's Column—the sculptural scroll of the Dacian Wars—which, in turn, makes me homesick for Rome.

October 2. At a seedy performance of *Eugene Onegin* in the tiny and nonventilated National Theater, we learn that success here is gauged by the quantity of flowers trundled on stage afterward, the applause swelling with each bouquet, as if the bouquets were the singers themselves. The stage must look like a flower show for every artist who can afford it. These nosegays are stored in the artists' large but weakly illuminated dressing rooms during the performance.

October 4. The Metropole's telephones have been disconnected, the lights are constantly failing, the handles of doors and bureaus fall off at the slightest tug, and room service takes between two hours and never. But the most serious problem is the water, which works for only a few unpredictable moments each day and is always scalding. We hoard it, using our bathtubs as rain-catchers, and improvising runnels to flush the toilets, burning fingers and drenching clothes in the process. The hotel's only guests, ourselves apart, are the personnel of French, Italian, and American film companies on location. The "stars" among the Americans—Gregory Peck, Mel Ferrer, Jeanne Crain, Akim Tamiroff, John Barrymore, Jr.—seldom leave the bar and its skiffle band, presumably because of language difficulties and the lack of indigenous entertainment elsewhere worth the while.

Language. Maids, waiters, porters know a few words of German or Italian, but most officials we meet speak only the local language. The S.s are able to follow the drift of this through words with common Slavic roots, but they complain that these "etymological conversations" are tedious.

1961 *People*. The women are bulky and blond, the men, in caps and dunga-rees, large-boned and heavy-set, like Marshal Tito. Everyone to whom we are introduced, musicians, dancers, theater employees, culture officials, is hospitable and grateful for our (*i.e.*, I.S.'s) visit.

Politics. No American or Western European publication is available at any kiosk. Italy, a short sea-change away, seems as remote as Bhutan, but we are always aware of Russia. The name of the principal hotel in the commercial district is "The Moscow," that of the principal square, "Marx and Engels." As in other East Bloc countries, tips are rumored to be refused; the saying here is that "tips are not given, but they are taken."

Money. The official exchange is 600 dinars to the dollar, but the U.S. Embassy gives us 850. Yugoslav currency is "soft," meaning worthless any-where else.

Food. Some of the dishes could be edible if less grossly cooked. The local wines and cheeses are coarse. We subsist principally on almonds, baklava, Turkish coffee, and a salty Serbian *chèvre*. Slivovitz, the plum liqueur, imbibed everywhere and at all hours, is the most enduring and endearing of Yugoslav institutions.

Music. The orchestra is obviously enjoying its discovery of *Kral Edyp* by Igora Stravinskog i Zana Koktoa, and it is sad that such excellent musicians are totally unaware of this and practically every other contemporary clas-sic. Photographs of Tito are on the walls and desks of every room in the Music Academy, but the only likeness of a musician is a portrait of Liszt.

Architecture. All government buildings and the newer apartment houses are in a severely unornamented one-party style, ugly to the point of comi-cality. Because most churches and mosques are also new, large, and ugly, perhaps we overrate, in contrast, the attractiveness of the old, steep-gabled shops and houses around the market place. Like Athens, Belgrade is elec-trically bright—when the lights work. Like the Greek city, too, Belgrade is prettier at night, thanks to the Cyrillic signs in neon.

The country. A late afternoon drive to Oplenac, the Escorial of the last Serbian kings. Traffic in this land of poplars and plane trees, tobacco fields and vineyards, white-washed farmhouses with thatched roofs is limited to bullock carts and canvas-covered gypsy wagons. The women wear black shawls, the men black hussars' hats, leggings, handlebar mustaches. The Oplenac mosaics, manufactured in Germany about 40 years ago, exemplify the bad taste of our parents—which I say knowing that our own good taste will last an even shorter time.

The dressing room, where we wait before conducting *Oedipus* and *Perséphone*, is so full of flowers that when U.S. Ambassador George Kennan comes to greet us, I.S. compares the visit to that of "a diplomat at a state funeral."

October 6. At the Belgrade airport, I.S. to a culture official who wants his summation of the visit: "*A la longue* we got rather bored with the hot water."

October 7. Zurich. After one night in the quiet and comfortable Eden-au-lac, we are transferred to the Baur-au-lac, where I find three letters from Boulez. He talks about his courses at Basel, analyzing Webern's Second Cantata and Debussy's piano Etudes *"dans le dernier détail."* Also, *"J'espère qu'on pourra arranger quelques jours ensemble."* In the second letter:

> I'm in the throes of preparing a new book of *Structures*, which is to be done at Donaueschingen. Since your card from Stockholm, things are moving quickly concerning the taping of *Pli selon pli*. I'm making two essential corrections for this version: 1) the first piece, *"Don,"* is now for a large ensemble and no longer has anything to do with the piano piece; 2) Improvisation 1 will also be orchestrated and expanded; I've begun the new version. As soon as the definitive version is performed, I'll tear myself away to get a copy to you (by the beginning of next July, let's say, in Amsterdam). One other thing: can you tell Stravinsky that, if everything goes well, I'll conduct three evenings (14, 15, 18 of next August) at the Festspielhaus in Salzburg in honor of his 80th birthday, with the *Sacre* and *Les Noces*. Massine will be in charge of the choreography for these performances and the orchestra will be the Berlin Philharmonic. I don't know which chorus yet, or which soloists. But I'm very happy about doing it, especially under such conditions: I think we'll get some musical results of high quality. What a shame that I have so much work, and that it is so urgent, just when you will be passing nearby! I very much hope we'll see each other next year, perhaps at Salzburg? In the meantime, fond thoughts of you and my very best regards to Igor and Vera.

October 8. A visit from Paul Sacher, after which I.S. is examined by Dr. Niehans, the celebrated cell-injector (from minced foetuses), and the model for the Nazi doctor in Dürrenmatt's play.

October 12. The exhibition of Hittite art in the Kunsthaus includes marvelous orthostat reliefs of jugglers, lutenists, hand-clapping dancers, a fierce griffin with an absurd pussy-cat mustache, a warrior with an Assyrian beard, a weather god with hammer and tongs. The ceramics include pitchers with pommel handles; rhytons; half-sieve strainers; fertility idols (as if made with matchsticks, and as abstract as Arp); curled-toe babouches, reminders of Janissary-period Turkey; figurines of dancing gods with stilts and horned caps, or the tall, conical caps like those of medieval jesters or 19th-century schoolboy dunces. Hittite gold, in statuettes of steers, is dandelion yellow, but some bronze and gold objects are striped with silver or electrum. Hittite cuneiform, on clay writing tablets, looks like the beach tracks of a flock of birds.

1961   I.S. says that the decor of the Zurich Opera's *Nightingale* is more African than Chinese: "'Death' himself—herself—is an African liban rather than a Chinese shaman, and the Bonze looks like a Barbary Captain Kidd." I am more disturbed by other aspects of the staging. Why does the palace of the Emperor of China look like a coolie's hut, and the mechanical nightingale like a pterodactyl? And why do the Japanese emissaries have green faces? A bad crossing? Too much tea?

October 14. With I.S. to Klemperer's *Fidelio* at the Opera. I stay up all night with Berman, who has come from Rome to convince me that I must never leave the Stravinskys. Of all the Stravinsky Old Guard, he has always been the most sympathetic to *my* problems vis-à-vis the S.s.

October 15. Letter from Boulez saying he was very touched by my letter, wishing me good luck for the rest of our tour, and sending regards to Vera and Igor—names I have never used in all my 13 years with them.

I.S. conducts his *Soldat* at the Opera on a double bill with *Nightingale*, conducted by Victor Reinshagen and beautifully sung by Reri Grist.

October 16. Zurich to London, on the same delayed plane with Klemperer and his daughter, arriving in time at the Savoy Hotel to keep our dinner appointment with the Eliots. More hunched than when we last saw him, the poet leans forward when he stands, as if from a yoke, or like a skier ready to start down a slope. His coloring has changed, too—the lips and large ears are damson—and the lines of his face are leaner and sharper, reminding me of one of those Hittite ceramic birds.

He complains of the nuisance of repeatedly having to refuse invitations to the Tagore centenary. "I took a volume from the library the other day, to be certain that I had not made a mistake, but I could make nothing of it. Difficult to tell that to the Indians, though, or to admit that one does not put their man with Dante and Shakespeare. Bill Yeats claimed to like Tagore, but he was making a case for the 'the East' at the time. . . . I receive regular shipments of the works of new Indian poets, together with letters inviting my comments. Once I replied, ripping the thing apart, only to find my by-no-means-complimentary letter appearing as a preface to the published poems!" (which is not an unheard of response: Gauguin printed a half-critical letter from Strindberg in an exhibition catalog). "In payment I received a Kashmir shawl, which I returned. Soon after, another and much better shawl came with a note agreeing that the first one had not been worthy of me."

Tonight's dinner has been arranged to discuss a proposal that I.S. set "two lyrical stanzas," as Eliot describes them, from *Little Gidding*, though Eliot himself expresses doubt "that they can be set." Nothing is said about this, however, and instead the poet and the musician talk about favorite *romans policiers* and about plays of Voltaire they have not read. "I knocked down a complete Voltaire at auction when I first came to England," Eliot confesses, "but never went to pick it up. That has been on my conscience ever since." Both men are Simenon addicts. I.S. estimates that he must have read at least sixty, and Eliot avows that "I can read about Maigret when I can read nothing else." Another mutually admired sleuth is Perry Mason, partly because "the author knows California law"—this from Eliot—"but Chandler was a better writer." Concerning the debate in the recent *TLS* on mistranslations in the *New English Bible*, Eliot admits to "enjoying this sort of thing, when I know, as I do now, that I have the right end of the stick." Pound's name comes up, and Eliot confides that "Ezra was always a poor judge of people, and indeed of most things except poetry. He really did believe that his monetary ideas would change the world. And weren't we all tarred by that brush? But he had great gifts, and I owe more to him than to anyone else. Which reminds me that I also owe him a letter; hm, hm, difficult to know what to say."

A noncommittal "Yes?" escapes Eliot's lips during each pause in the conversation, until V. recounts some of our Yugoslavian adventures, and at the same time voices some criticisms of Switzerland, including Rilke's "Switzerland is a waiting room on the walls of which Swiss views have been hung up." At this Eliot interposes a whole sentence: "I see what you mean, but I like it because more than any other country it resembles what it used to be."

October 17. A letter from Elliott Carter:

> Do you think it would be possible for me to get a performance at the Domaine Musical during the 62–63 season when Helen and I will be in Rome and Paris? The Double Concerto was recorded just after the concert for Epic—Fromm series—and all went a great deal better than at the concert. . . . I would have liked it to have been in your "new directions" series. I hope this will reach you in Belgrade, if it does, do look up Milko Kelemen whom we met in Japan and liked very much. He is the hope of Yugoslavia as far as I know. Helen joins me in sending our love to you and the Stravinskys. We hope that all is going well, that you were able to answer the sphinx and question the oracle. This year I am giving a class on the *Sacre* at Yale, and find that I have always loved it so that I have never really thought too much about what was happening in it—and what does is remarkable I now find on analysis— and all this is only another cause to be thankful for all the wonderful music Stravinsky has written. All best, Elliott.

October 18. *Oedipus* at Sadler's Wells, conducted by Colin Davis and staged by Michel St. Denis. Afterward, I.S. goes through the score with Davis, asking him to change several tempos.

October 20. Oxford. Lunch at Isaiah's with Robert Graves, who is tall and military in bearing, large-eared, and, today anyway, for his inaugural

1961 lecture as Professor of Poetry, neatly shorn. Because of the nose, which, like Michelangelo's, has been broken, one thinks of a pugilist, and—doubtless as with the sculptor, too—the fingernails are rinded with dirt. When I.S. asks about his present work, Graves says: "I am disguised as a professor, implausibly." When Graves asks the same question, I.S. tries to explain that he is engaged in "serial versification," to which Graves replies, "Poetry is less purely genial than that and more demonstrably linked to moral questions." He begins a story: "I started down the street this morning thinking about a woman when suddenly my breast pocket burst into flames. . . ." But whether the fire was merely allegorical or actually incendiary we never find out, for he switches to "hallucinatory psilocybin mushrooms," claiming that they "can induce a state of grace." He also reports on a conversation with David Ben-Gurion, who told him that "Israelis are less good taxpayers than the citizens of Protestant countries, but rather better than those of Catholic countries." On Paul of Tarsus: "He was not a Jew, of course, but a Syrian; you remember the Ebionite Epistle?" And Plato: "He did more harm than any one man before Freud." And Aristotle, "a thoroughly unpleasant character." And Alexander the Great: "Shall I tell you my new idea about him? It will take just three minutes." (He actually glances at his watch.) "That legend of the Priest's serpent at Siwa is nonsense. Alexander decided to conquer the world entirely out of the jealous desire to surpass Dionysus. Like Dionysus, he had himself declared 'Son of Zeus.'" Graves puffs on his cheroot while this is allowed to sink in.

Composing a "tonal row" and accompanying words of dedication for the Berlins' guestbook, I.S. asks for an English equivalent to the Russian "*kanitel.*" Literally, the word means a silver or gold skein, Isaiah says, but, commonly, a long, entangled argument—whereupon someone quotes "or ever the silver cord be loosed." Graves lobs this back—he is faster with words than anyone I have ever encountered—with "The Yiddish is '*magillah,*' and the Greek and Latin are. . . ." Nicolas Nabokov to I.S. in Russian: "Do you suppose he knows the Etruscan, too?" Watching Graves listen enviously to the Russians, I ask which of his languages he would most readily exchange for it. "German," he says, without hesitation. After he has left for his lecture, Isaiah remarks that he would do anything to depose Jesus and crown the White Goddess, but he is a true poet.

Isaiah reads passages from the Bible for us in Hebrew, translating word for word and explaining, *El, Elim,* and *Elohim:* "*Elohim* is used to denote the lords of the others, the Hammurabis, the 'After Strange Gods'"—he seems to be aware that Eliot's title is not Biblical and not a quotation.* He promises to prepare a properly accented copy in Russian transliteration of the story of Abraham and Isaac, if this is the episode I.S. chooses for his

---

* The title comes from Kipling's story "On the City Wall" (". . . go whoring after strange gods").

cantata. But Isaiah urges him to consider the first and seventh days of the Creation, a suggestion that fails to attract I.S. because of the length: "The music would be longer than a British weekend."

October 23. London. Dinner in honor of I.S. at the Institute of Contemporary Arts: Cyril Connolly, Spender, Herbert Read, Isaiah, *et al.* I sit next to E. H. Gombrich, who talks measurement psychology. When someone solicits his opinion of a picture, he says—black eyes shining, long, blunt chin looking more of both—: "I don't know. I am a historian and therefore prefer sitting on fences." At another table, Henry Moore chats with I.S. about the pigeon hazard and outdoor sculpture. I.S. tells him that what he remembers most clearly about Rodin's atelier is "The *démodé* furniture: it had no connection with what Rodin was doing."

October 27. Tea with E. M. Forster in his rooms at King's College. Natasha Spender and I knock on the inner door—the outer has been opened to expose the nameplate "Mr. Forster"—exactly as a campus clock strikes four, a punctuality that visibly pleases Mr. Forster. His cranial index, nose, and fingers are long, and his legs are too long for his torso, which partly accounts for his floating walk. Shocks of gray-brown hair still cover the crown of his head, and his mustache, which wiggles pleasantly during toothy grins, is still tinged with the same color.

Most of the room is lined with bookshelves, and piles of books stand on tables and the floor. Forster sits on a divan with ourselves in flanking arm-chairs, which leads to talk about his furniture and his claim to have "few possessions, including heirlooms, I would mind losing. That mantelpiece was made by my father, but I could do without it." One wonders if he would part as painlessly with the framed embroidery, next to it, of his mother's name.

Again and again the conversation grinds to a stop, each of them agonizing because Forster's silences are so acutely critical. Worse still, the questions with which he artificially resuscitates the talk instantly dissolve it again by requiring only monosyllabic answers: "Did you come on the 2:36 train?" When Tolkien's name comes up, he says, "I dislike whimsicality and I cannot bear 'good' and 'evil' on such a scale. . . . To my surprise, I liked Thomas Mann's *The Holy Sinner.* Mann always *knew* a great deal, of course, but his other books are so heavy." Mentioning *Don Quixote,* Forster says, "I never reached the end of it did you?," and though obviously I did not, would I admit it if I had? He talks about meeting Tagore in 1910 and about a trip to Uganda, this prompted by a question of mine concerning an object on his table, a smooth white box with wires attached to the base, like a jew's harp: "The natives played these instruments as they worked on the roads, cutting pieces of telephone wire for the strings."

He refers to his Harvard lecture on music and the arts with evident pleasure: "Someone had seen from my work how much I cared; I accepted the invitation within an hour of receiving it." Musing on the question of why

1961 "humanists" are intimidated by scientists, he says, marvelously: "We fear that we cannot tell them anything, and we are self-consciously aware of the nontechnical nature of our language." A glint shows in his blue eyes and in everything he says, though he rarely looks at us, watching instead the glowing briquettes in his fireplace—unseeingly, like King Alfred and the burning cakes, or so I suspect until he stands to poke the coals. Because he does not say anything louder than *mezzo-piano*, I fear that his requests for me to repeat some of my remarks are a consequence not of deafness but of my savage American accent—that or the incredibility, or abject absurdity, of the content. One naturally regards the man as a judge. Even the weather is a subject for adjudication: when I wonder aloud whether the rain has stopped, he settles silver-rimmed spectacles on his nose, goes to the window, says, "I will try to *decide*."

Back in London, Cyril Connolly comes for dinner at the Savoy. He is an amusing raconteur but a bored listener, in which role, however, he relaxes his "gimlet glare," as he calls it. "The latest complaint of psychoanalysts," he says, is that "Nowadays women want to go back not simply to the womb but all the way to papa's penis." He describes a pre-lunch conversation today with the President of Senegal on the merits of certain French wines, "then when the meal was served, I discovered that he was a strict Mohammedan." Connolly has the head of a Bacchus, a flat profile with Pekingese nose, and flat ears growing sprigs of hair—"earbrows," I.S. says.

October 29. I.S.'s *Perséphone* performance in Festival Hall.

October 30. At midnight we fly to Cairo with Lucia Davidova.

October 31. Even at sunrise, the road from the airport to the city is jammed with wooden donkey carts. After a nap—our rooms at Shepherd's (808 and 809) are directly above the Nile—we drive to the Pyramids, but are held up, on the way, by a flock of women in black cerements squatting in the road at the entrance to a hospital and loudly and dismally wailing. This open-air requiem fascinates I.S., the idea of professional mourners as much as the din they make. A leper-like pall hangs over them, as if they themselves might be from the Kingdom of Death.

At Cheops, now with television aerial, progress is obstructed by another female mob, except that this time the girls are from Transatlantis and a little inland. They cling for dear life to the red-tassled saddles of kneeling camels and bravely try to look happy for a barrage of tripod cameras— their own cameras, inactive for once, apparently growing from their stomachs like umbilical tumors. Although posing tourists this way is an ancient routine for the camels, and their thin shanks and shaggy skins show them to be unfit for less humiliating work, they yawp and whine most ungraciously. When the head drover shouts the order to rise, they dip backward and kick their forelegs outward like dancers, whereupon the air is rent with a chorus of "Ohio"-accented screams. Moments later the dismounted ladies, feeling immensely relieved, exhilarated, and proud of their American moxie, no doubt tip accordingly. Some of them, in turn, prepare to photograph their guides, but, like the Chinese, the Arabs believe, surely with justification, that the camera steals your soul. I.S. dislikes the pyramids. *"Francmaçonnerie,"* he says, and back we go across the Nile.

Each street and alley in the bazaar is a stage for hundreds of small events, but the stercoral stench prevents us from watching any of them for long. Goldsmiths and silversmiths, brass founders and ironmongers, potters, treadle-loom weavers, dyers and cosmeticists, jewelers with loupes, leather-workers with awls: all work *en plein air.* The shopkeepers greatly outnumber these artisans, but the largest population of all is that of the ineluctable interlopers, the unshakable scavengers, cadgers and "baksheesh"-crying beggars.

We stop at the "Nile Vally Perfumes" shop, having been steered there about as casually as tracer bullets by a driver whose preliminary parley with the proprietor has clearly concluded in the promise of a mutually satisfying division of the spoils. Though empty on our arrival, the establishment is rapidly infiltrated by other people, a well-coordinated team, we deduce, some of whose members simply pose as contented customers, while others try to wheedle us into buying or help to display such commodities as sandalwood and musk, attars and sachet powders, mascara, antimony, kohl. The main salesmanship techniques are to flatter the buyer's taste and to insinuate that "Nile Vally Perfumes" maintains a secret pipeline to Chanel.

In the opening phase, the proprietor stands benignly apart chewing cachous. But when V. orders a hundred amber cigarettes—probably at four to five times the list price, if one existed—he glides into action. Confident of recovering the investment, he even switches on the lights (we had not realized there were any), the better to display a dozen rare but resistible products including an "aphrodisiac amberpaste" for I.S., "a blood-warming concoction, sir, very good for elderly gentlemen wishing to reenter the portals of youth; yes, sir, an Open Sesame." When at last we escape—which is not that easy—he thrusts a booklet into our pockets. It warns that: "Owing to the great number of designing merchants who vainly try to imitate my wares, an impossibility owing to their excellence, and, furthermore, use a name similar to mine in order to deceive, I have registered in the Courts of Law to obviate entirely. I therefore advise my clients to take great care that my full name is printed on each article that comes out of my store Nile Vally Perfumes." No doubt some vain imitator gave himself away by spelling it "Valley."

Still in the bazaar, we drink arrack and ﻛﻮﻛﺎ ﻛﻮﻻ (Coca-Cola) at a sidewalk café. Within a radius of a few yards from our table a man is tooling a piece of metal, a boy honing a knife on a whetstone, a woman suckling a baby from her mud-caked bosom, a donkey staling in the dust, and an old man, to whom no one pays the slightest attention, apparently dying in the gutter. At the next table two turbaned Arabs share a nargileh, passing the stem back and forth without wiping the mouthpiece. We are hardly seated before peddlers besiege us with nougat and sesame-seed cakes, pomegranates and yellow guavas, sandals (at least 50 draped on cords around the salesman's neck), and parrots and lovebirds in cages strapped to the Papageno's back. "O.K.? O.K.?" they say, as who in Cairo does not? Knowing that we cannot refuse them a few piastres, they are not easy to elude. Some suffer from trachoma and the dread bilharzia, and some are blind. They are a scratching lot, too, with especially itchy pubic regions, unless this is for reassurance that the instrument of their gender is still there.

None of the objectives on our after-dinner taxi itinerary is half as engaging as the driver himself. His get-up is part Arab, the djellaba, and part Chicago-gangster-in-the-'twenties—a bevel-brimmed fedora worn at a menacing tilt. But if a gangster, he is the most bonhomous imaginable. Like all Cairo cabbies, his goal is to deposit us at a commission-paying nightclub. To enlist my compliance in this aim, he talks luringly of the pectoral attributes of the houris and odalisques at the Arabi Hasha Club. "We go to Arabi Hasha, Egyptian place, lovely." As it turns out, everything Egyptian is "lovely," just as everything American—pronounced as two words, "Emery Cain"—is "verygoodverynice" (one word). Would we like to visit the Hilton Hotel and hear Emery Cain's music? Is verygoodverynice.

Well, actually, we wouldn't. What I.S. wants, of all things, is a wedge of halvah. So off we go, only to find that Mr. Verygoodverynice's recommended store, Aly Hassan El Hati, in spite of being "Egyptian" and "lovely," as well as very far away and expensive on the meter, stocks nothing even remotely near that line. Each of his excursions into "English" is followed by an explosion of self-appreciative laughter and a soliloquy in Arabic. But as a guide and source of information, he is not without shortcomings. One of them is that he snobbishly reproves our interest in neighborhoods that he calls "very cheap parts, strictly for wogs." Another, more serious, is that he cannot read. "Who is that?," I.S. asks, pointing to a statue of Ramses the Second. "Oh, a statue." "Of whom?," I.S. persists, lowering the aim of his finger to the inscription on the base. "Very famous man." "What man, what is his name?" "Oh, Egyptians never put *names*." But we end up liking this verygoodverynice fellah to the extent that we almost swallow his parting bait: "'Bye. See you tomorrow. What time?"

At night the streets look as if a Shriners' convention had been roused from sleep and, perhaps because of a fire, only just had time to grab its fezzes and run: a city in pajamas, then, some sleeveless like chasubles, and some striped, as if there had been a jail break. Some of the men also wear colored Kufayah scarves, and some a lace skullcap that seems distinctly an article of bedroom apparel. But the street noise—radios blaring from cafés,

automobile horns tooting without let-up, as they do at American weddings—is in no way nocturnal. Nor is the tempo of street life. The waiters
hustle their hookahs and coffee trays at a more rapid pace than they do in
the daytime, and at one place the pedestrians actually hurry out of the path
of the murderous Mr. Verygoodverynice, holding up their nighties as they
run, like Carpaccio's monks lifting their soutanes while fleeing the lion of
St. Jerome.

November 1. At sun-up the river is flagged with sails, the upstream
traffic, like inbound New York commuters, scarcely moving, the down-
stream racing out of sight as if propelled by nuclear power. A felucca with
"FLY TWA" on its sail cruises slowly up and rapidly down the stretch of
hotel-fronted river, over and over, like a streetwalker.

We are three hours in the Museum of Egyptian Art and another half-
hour dodging a dragoman at the entrance. The building is hideous, the
overcrowding of the contents is suffocating, and a high portion of them
are macabre—inevitably, Pharonic culture being known almost exclusively
from tombs. The entire first floor is a mummy morgue, and the other
floors are abundantly stocked with mummies' rope-wigs, which look like
clumps of discolored seaweed, as well as eviscerated organs, exhibited
together with their resin-soaked wrappings and canopic jars. Even so, the
mortuary aspect and the monotony of the funerary artifacts are less stultifying than the sameness, the same deities, postures and patterns, sculptural
motives, repeated in iron-clad traditions through dozens of dynasties and
thousands of years. Most of the objects, moreover, are mutilated and
defaced, and at least half of the statues are decapitated or dismembered—a
succession of fractured Pharaohs, with or without pschent, torsos held
together by orthopedic appliances and the plaster filler used for surgical
models. Anyone feeling the need to "escape from freedom" should spend a
few hours here contemplating the other extreme.

What does give pleasure are the representations of birds, fish, and animals, the lions, leopards, monkeys, anubises, horses, rams, and dappled
cows; the Nubian rooms where, uniquely, the statues of women are the
same height as those of men; and some of the jewelry, among the acres of
turquoise and coraline amulets, scarab seals, sigil and signet rings long
since copied and mass-manufactured. Some of the furniture is attractive,
too, though not, to our taste, the nouveau-riche rococo from the
Tutankhamen tomb, that 18th-Dynasty Forest Lawn. And some objects
attract simply by virtue of their contemporaneity to us: a Las Vegas gam-
ing board, for instance; and a carpenter's kit complete with levelers, plumb
lines, T squares, rules.

We hobble out of the museum on wooden legs, and, stepping through
the gates, are nearly run over by a truck of the "Nefertiti Laundry Service."

On the road to Sakkara, in the cooler part of the afternoon, we overtake
a flock of sheep being driven into a slaughterhouse, each doomed animal

daubed on its neck with blood-like dye. And a wedding procession, in which the betrothed is enthroned with her maids in a tall donkey cart; this is not an especially arresting sight, however, for the reason that the male Arab's dress is so much like a bride's anyway. No two donkey carts are the same size, but the wheels of most are so large that the linchpin is above the height of the animal. They carry fruit, copra, tuns of water, palm baskets, and loads of workmen, like prisoners in tumbrils en route to the guillotine.

A canal borders the road, bathtub and laundry, fish pond and sewage system for a million human beings. On the other side is the Nile, not always in view but inferable from the masts of dhows and feluccas rising above the levee. The rich land between the road and the river grows maize and cane sugar. Many of the tall stalks of the latter are further elevated by ibises, under which the plant bends when the birds come in, landing like ski-jumpers, or, tucking in their legs at the last moment, like hydroplanes. What infinite pleasure to behold this biblical landscape: the fertile fields, the carriage of women with amphorae on their heads, the buffaloes slowly turning the water wheels goaded by officious dogs—the landscape, except for our automobile, of Joseph's Egypt!

At Memphis we wait for the passage of a trainload of apparently disconnected dromedary heads and humps, these features alone protruding above the frames of the flat cars. "Modern" Memphis is a cluster of duplex mud huts with indented upper levels like the adobe houses in Taos pueblo, connected to the lower levels by ladders—another reminder of Taos and of Amerindian cliff dwellings. Beggars, even more numerous than in Cairo, ambush our automobile while it is still moving, virtually forcing us off the road while demanding to be photographed for money. For money, too, young hispid-headed boys (the hair of adult men is greased and matted) shimmy up the tallest palm trees, barefoot but as fast as monkeys. A short way beyond Memphis, I.S. describes a black goat, tethered by the roadside, as "a color sounding-board: just as an orchestra tunes to 'A,' so would a painter tune the landscape to this black."

At Sakkara, a row of the feet of otherwise demolished statues might be a prop from a Surrealist movie. In the tomb of Mera, the tinted low reliefs of birds and fish, of gazelles, mongooses, ibexes, porcupines, hippos, and crocodiles are worth all the pyramids of Egypt and other countries in which this dullest of forms has flourished. Mera himself is portrayed in various guises, one of them as a decoy on a hunting expedition, wearing the skin, claws, and tail of a leopard. On another occasion, wrapped in a robe, he listens to his wife play the harp, and, on still another, reclines on a high divan while his musical spouse sniffs a lotus. The colors are vivid even through a fine patina of blown sand.

The inland road to Cairo is congested with men and animals returning from the fields, the men shouldering hoes and flails exactly like those in the Mera friezes. We come to a Bedouin camp where the atmosphere is blue with smoke from cooking fires. The women, carrying jugs single-file to and from a roadside well, are uniformly black-robed, their faces uniformly covered by sequined veils. Some wear amber necklaces as well, and silver anklets. The evening air is silky, and the only sound in the villages is the murmur of nesting birds.

In the Kumais Restaurant with our new Copt friend, Fares Sarapheem, we squat on low leather cushions around a taller center one set with a round brass tray; the walls are covered with damascenes woven with epigraphs from the Koran. As soon as we are seated, and in the speed with which chlorinated icewater is served in American restaurants, a busboy deposits a handful of bullet-shaped incense pellets in our tray. He and all low-level waiters are dusky Nubians with embossed, tattoo-marked foreheads, while his superiors are light-bronze Arabs, and the head waiter is "white." In short, a hierarchy of pigmentation obtains here, the masters being identified by lightness of skin, the sutlers and underservants by progressively darker shades. We hear again tonight from brown and khaki-colored people, or at any rate not conspicuously pale ones, that so-and-so "works like a nigger."

The meal begins with prawns and stuffed grape leaves (*warak-enap*), moves on to *dorad*, *karouss*, and *fateh*, the main dish, a spicy stew of rice and boiled meat. The Western palate—mine, anyway—takes more readily to oriental sweetmeats, and tonight's is the delicious *puri*, a kind of Shredded Wheat cooked in honey. As we eat, Fares Sarapheem holds forth on the Copts, "the true Egyptians, the Christian inheritors of Pharaonic Egypt. The Coptic language," he goes on, "is a rendering of hieroglyphic Egyptian in the Greek alphabet, with seven additional letters to signify sounds that do not exist in Greek. But it is a dead dialect, surviving only in the Mass." Switching to politics, he says that Nasser's dissolution of the latifundia system has robbed the Copts of their wealth and supremacy. Yet they support his foreign policy because it has kept Egypt free from foreign intervention and foreign commercial domination, the bogey of the British cotton-wallah. "Egypt was a subject country from Cleopatra until 1917," he adds, "and for six hundred years our khedive was the puppet of Istanbul." But I am summarizing and hence deflavoring Fares Sarapheem's highly original English, whose felicities include many honorifics for ourselves, and little introductions of the sort: "Perhaps it would be interesting to mention. . . ."

Walking from the restaurant to the Kasr el Nil we come upon a blind man singing for alms in a beautifully floriated style, musical *passementerie*.

November 2. The Delta road to Alexandria is divided most of the way and in good condition. Police checkpoints, like toll booths on American turnpikes, are numerous, and we are obliged to stop and be counted at each one; invariably they display photographs of a smiling, toothpaste-ad Colonel Nasser. Of beasts of burden on the road, women outnumber both

1961   the donkeys and the camels, and *no* woman is empty-handed. They carry head-trays with round loaves of *rayesh*, backloads of panniers and heavy bales, and, not infrequently, babes-in-arms. Woman's uniform is black—otherwise how, in this transvestite society, would we tell them from the men?—with exceptions in Alexandria, where a handful of Europeanized rebels (or fallen creatures?) flaunt themselves in washed blues, pink, and orange.

The donkey and camel traffic, if it were not so cruel, would be marvelous to watch. Very small donkeys carrying huge sacks with a passenger atop, like a garnishing, are a common sight, albeit a less enjoyable one than when the animal is otherwise freightless and the rider jogs along, legs out in a wide "V" and dangling sandals from toes. *No* load can make a camel look less supercilious, but the creature's long, knock-kneed, foreleg-amble reminds us of Max Beerbohm's drawing of Aldous Huxley, and if only on that account we are bound to regard it with fondness and respect. Never again, though, will I use the expression "camel-colored" (have I ever?). They are a thousand shades of pink, puce, fawn, bistre, black, and even white.

The mast tips of otherwise unseen feluccas, in altogether unseen canals, move through the flat land like periscopes, but the boats themselves are visible only from bridges. Road-repairing is women's work, and the lot of the oldest and weakest is to carry the heaviest scuttles of gravel and stone. At one place, a man wearing a white djallaba with shiny brass buttons rides by a squad of these laboring women, shading himself from them with a parasol; and whereas he is mounted on an impeccably groomed Arabian horse, the purple-veiled daughter or wife following him, at presumably the proper number of paces, bestrides a mangy mule.

By noon the roadside world is asleep. Even the chickens stop their scratching while men sprawl on the ground, in doorways, in mule carts, in rope nets under mule carts, and perhaps even in the houses, which become prettier and more prosperous-looking the deeper we are in the Delta. At Tanta, capital of Lower Egypt, the yashmaks are mere bikinis, concealing the face below the nose only, and no doubt marking a triumph of emancipation, compared with the full masks worn by the women of Cairo. In the next village, Damanhur, a skinned water buffalo has been suspended by its tail in the middle of the main street, where it centers the flies.

Of a sudden, the air is fresher, cooler, more moist, and the vegetation changes abruptly; banyans are common now, and the date palms are pregnant with udder-shaped yellow-red fruit. At Alexandria, the riparian side of the road becomes a quay, and because the longshoremen are bent too low under their quintals to see their way, old men lead them across the teeming highway by the hand. Feazings by each tied-up boat suggest that the sailors perform Arabian Nights rope tricks.

The dress of most Alexandrians on the Mediterranean side of the city is

European. So are many of their names: along with the common "Fawzi" and "Ali Ibrahim" are the "Banco Donizetto," "Rosenthal Brothers," and "Socrates & Co." French is the first foreign language, to judge from the notices on postal boxes as well as from conversations in the Union Restaurant, where we dine on grilled *crevettes, loup de mer*, a compote of dates in warm buffalo milk, and a bottle of white Clos de Pharaoh. Afterward we hire a Hantur to go to the column of Pompey, but stop en route by the gates of a cemetery to listen to the keening of a band of professional *pleureuses*: squatting on their haunches with black shawls over their heads, they might be imitating a flock of ravens.

In early afternoon the city is emptied as if by a plague, and except for some fishermen caulking their caïque, even the beaches are deserted. Our new, English-speaking driver is indignant about Lawrence Durrell's "misrepresentation of Alexandria," though it seems to us that the novelist's crime, in this regard, was in having made the city so much more exotic than it is. The Royal Palace, now a museum, and Samalek, the Royal harem, now a hotel, would be prize exhibits in any collection of freak architecture. Except for its Gothic gargoyles and keyhole-style Arabic windows, the palace would go unnoticed in flamboyant and crenellated Boca Raton. Since each new king added new monstrosities, the fall of the monarchy could be regretted as the frustrating of architectural curiosity. The lawns are the greenest in Egypt, and the gardens, smelling like hair tonic, the best kept.

When we reenter the city, the sun is low, and life has returned to the streets. And not only life: in the Greek quarter we are delayed by a gilded eight-horse hearse. Elsewhere, Muslims are spreading prayer mats on the sidewalks or already praying, in fetal position and turned magnetically toward Mecca (as white ants are magnetically sensitized to the north). As we start across the salt flats of Maryot, the rim of the sun is still afloat, but it disappears in a sudden dive, like the keel of the *Titanic*. Ducks and other birds are profuse along the lake shore, and pole-propelled fishing boats (the *tarada*) knife through the dense reeds. Farther south, in the shallows, a herd of buffalo oozes to the neck in the mud. Yeats's adjective is "true":

> O what a sweetness strayed
> By the Mareotic sea. . . .

Liberation Province begins with signs of hope, in new houses and newly irrigated patches of land, but these quickly disappear in spinifex and scrub desert. We come to a vast nomad encampment, the men huddled around fires in front of large flat tents, the camels foddering or squatting on the ground like a domed oriental city. Otherwise the only habitations all the way to Ghizeh are a gas station at the halfway point and some tattered British barracks from 1942. All through the black night our headlights flash on Arabs walking along the road, their white robes billowing ghost-like in the rising wind.

November 4. On our way to the Coptic Museum this morning, I count nine chandelier stores, including the "El Ismail Youssef Mohammed Chandelier Company." Chandeliers seem to rank just below tourism as a major industry, and every sizable home is reputed to possess several of them.

The Museum lies within a Roman redoubt whose walls are three thicknesses of brick and five of stone. The interior is cool and clean, and the contents, in agreeable contrast to the Museum of Egyptian Art, are intelligently displayed. My difficulty here is in identifying the Coptic in the absence of obvious iconographic clues: camels, Angk talismans, black-faced saints, and the Cross with the three-step standard (representing the three days before the Resurrection). The animal and bird motifs of early Coptic art—the lions, donkeys, rabbits, eagles, and doves—could be Byzantine as well, while much of the later art of Byzantium is distinguishable from that of Islam only in having been stamped, and not prominently, with Christian symbols: the Muslims took over the forms intact. Cufic copies of the Gospels are on exhibit, and parchment lectionaries in which Coptic and the beautiful right-angular Cufic script are on facing pages. The building itself, with its honeycombed, sunlight-tempering window grilles and *moucharbieha* (shuttered bay windows), is Islamic. Readily recognizable as Coptic, of course, are the Ethiopian treasures, the barbaric crown of Menelik II, and the fruits of the loom, wonderfully animated figures in many-colored threads.

A monk with a sextant-shaped beard, like Tintoretto's Nicolò Priuli, escorts us through the adjoining Church of St. Sergius, which is so Moorish that without our monk we would not believe it is a church. A spidery old woman in black rags sits on the outside doorstep nibbling nettles.

We eat incomparably better than that ourselves at the home of Victor Simaika, son of the founder of the Museum and Fares Sarapheem's cousin. To judge from his references to polo games with the Duke of Edinburgh, from the display of photographs with Barbara Hutton and the stengah-drinking set, and from the blizzard of so many other society-column names that hardly any gaps occur between, Mr. Simaika is very *mondain*. He has just returned from the airport and the dispatching of a favorite Persian cat to Zurich for medical attention (Niehans and Jung, no doubt). But he is a great charmer, too; indeed, somewhat more than that, for without so much as letting his monocle drop on its black silk-tether, he confesses to the truth of his reputation as a "big ladies' killer"—which leaves one wondering as much about the large, mysterious females as about Mr. Simaika's methods, whether strangulations or what. Otherwise the conversation touches on Evelyn White's *The Curse of the Copts*, some Copts still believing in the ancient malediction; on the Coptic paintings at Faras, on the Nubian Nile, recently uncovered by the expedition of the Polish Academy of Sciences; on the monachism of Cairo's Bektashi Moslem sect; and on the Coptic addition of Love to the Paulist trinity of Faith, Hope, and Charity.

The Simaika apartment faces the Nile above a garden of sycamores and jasmine. As we dine, sails glide by the window like giant moths.

My smallpox certificate having been filched yesterday, along with an otherwise empty wallet, I go to a hospital to be revaccinated: admission to Australia without the document is impossible. The operation is performed in a forbiddingly filthy and malodorous room, where I roll up my sleeve with no confidence and, indeed, am not given any cleansing daub of alcohol. Has the needle been sterilized? Too late to think about that now or to pray to American gods of hygiene. The nurse jabs me as if I were personally responsible for Suez. By dinnertime I have a fever and a festering lump on my arm.

The Mosque of Ibn Tulun is one of the great buildings of the world, yet our Copt driver has no idea how to find it. According to maps, we cannot be more than three blocks away when he stops to take soundings from pedestrians, none of whom has heard of it. (Everyone knows all about *us*, of course: "American?" "Money, please." "O.K.") One urchin offers to guide us, climbs aboard uninvited, and directs the driver over a wide area before we realize that he has merely chosen us to be the sponsors of his first automobile ride. Another waif, this one with a book under arm, volunteers and actually fulfills the service, though when at last we reach the great dun-colored walls, he reviles us because of the size of our—extra large, as it happens—baksheesh.

Leaving our shoes with the shoe-minder, who chalks numbers on the soles, gives us shoe-checks and helps us swaddle our feet in felt, we cross the ambulatory and enter a courtyard the size of a piazza in an Italian city. In the right portico, women in head-to-toe chadors pray in purdah, behind a fence of rugs suspended from a wire. In the *liwan*, to the left, the men kneel in groups of six to recite their prayers, one member of each unit slightly to the fore. Clergymen and sacramental middlemen are nowhere in sight.

November 5. To untrained and infidel eyes, a day in the Museum of Islamic Art is either several hours too long or several years too short. "Taste," in the absence of religio-historico-cultural blinkers, becomes an imperative, and we force our simple prejudice in favor of things Persian to a point at which we begin to dislike things Egyptian, above all the brassware and polychrome lustres. Islamic art, Persian included, is an art of ambages, of meshing and interlacing, of fretting, filigreeing, foliating, lozenging, lobing, and its patterns are too complex for our unaccustomed eyes. Even the water jets in the fountains coil like cobras.

From the outside, the Mohammed Ali Mosque conjures comparison with a colossal crustacean, partly because of its mustache of minarets—

1961 around one of which, when we arrive, three ravens are wheeling like a propeller. From the inside, where the many-colored lamps are shaped like alembics and retorts, the mosque might be a laboratory. Saladin's citadel, nearby, is a walled, medieval city, with pennants and oriflammes on its towers. The atmosphere is thick with dust, and it reeks of urine and the nauseating stench of abattoirs. Worst of all are the flies—especially the circumvolant nimbuses of them that attach to us the moment we leave the car—and the beggars who swarm about us *like* flies, many of them maimed, eyes red and vitreous, or covered with white film, faces pitted and scrobiculated, coughs coming from the deepest catacombs of the lungs. In Cairo, sickness, disease, and death are never far away. Funerals are held in the streets, in large, carpeted and furnished tents; we have yet to traverse the city without encountering at least one of them. And I am forgetting the vast necropolitan suburbs with, over the tombs, hutches in which the survivors spend their holy days in proximity to the remains of the departed.

In the river villages this is marketing as well as wash day, to judge from the spread of wares on the canal bridges, and the laundry and copper ewers on the canal banks. South of Aiyat, the road signs are in Arabic only, and life is abruptly more primitive: we pass two men hacking a still-bleeding buffalo in the middle of the road, and going about their grisly work as nonchalantly as if they were chopping a log. But while the *condition humaine* in the villages appalls us, the same is not true of the pastoral life and the life of toil in the fields, which cannot be very much better. Is this because of a romanticizing notion that tending goats and growing vegetables are more "natural" modes of existence, meaning that we see no barrier and little difference between a man and his animals, and that "soul" is rooted in "soil"? I had better not pursue the thought, in any case, lest my own prejudices be traced back to illustrations on date boxes that were daydream-inducing in me as a child. During *kayf*, the noon siesta, the verges are strewn with exanimate Arabs who, the burnous covering their faces, might be cadavers.

After the turn from the river to the desert, forsaking the parasols of eucalyptus and Australian pine for the open sun and sand, we swelter in a 15-degree leap in temperature. The world of Mobil Oil gasoline pumps is left behind, too, exchanged for nomad gas stations, mule carts that roam the desert roads carrying tanks the size of puncheons, or Porto wine barrels, siphons hanging from their bungholes like umbilical cords. The guards at a desert post greet us with straight-arm Nazi salutes and the password "Nasser." (Police camels are white, like some state-trooper cars in America.) A few miles farther, near a walled city with dovecotes on every roof, a caravan crosses the road, each camel loaded with hay, through which their humps show like turrets of partly camouflaged tanks.

Desert people are evidently accustomed to great privacy. Men, naked except for their turbans, are cooling themselves in the roadside culverts, and we surprise a Bedouin woman, who has failed to gauge the swift approach of our car, without her veil. An ancient Packard packed with a **1961** dozen Arabs nearly collides with us, automobiles being so rare that confrontations involve crises as to which vehicle shall pass on which side.

At El Fayum, lo and behold, a new red Cadillac convertible, an oil sheik's bauble, shines in the restaurant parking lot as if it had been newly-minted this morning and flown in minutes ago from Michigan. A Bedouin woman with a ring through her nose stands staring at it in awe, until she notices our interest in *her*, shakes her fists at us and struts off like a peahen. In the restaurant, we consume a lunch of water buffalo scaloppini, under a plaque commemorating a banquet given here by Churchill for King Ibn Saud, February 17, 1945. Outside, a snow of ibises has settled on the shore of the lake.

November 8. We spend part of the 40-hour delay "for engine repairs" at the airport, part back at the hotel. Apologizing for the "inconvenience," a Qantas official adds that it is also "the reason our planes are so safe." I.S.: "Naturally. They are on the ground more than in the air." Eventually we rise over Cairo and the pyramids, over the Monastery of St. Catherine in Sinai, over Aqaba, and the walled cities and emptiness of Arabia. Halfway across the Persian Gulf the bar is locked, like the bar of the Super Chief as the train approached Kansas. At Karachi, a Sikh policeman—jodhpurs, blue turban with white feather, neatly-twirled black mustache, lathi— comes aboard. "Just like *Firebird*," I.S. says. Five hours later, at Calcutta, the clothing of the boarding officials and maintenance squad is reduced to dhotis; here and in Bangkok these crews bring mosquitoes and heat with them. Over the Gulf of Siam, the plane shivers as if from a tropical ague— "turbulence," the pilot says, unnecessarily—and the landing at Singapore, where blue-black Malays empty ashtrays and primp pillows, is rough.

November 9. Day breaks over the South China Sea. The landing strip at Darwin is a platter of red earth on a jungle promontory. In the terminal, we pass a rigorous health inspection, breakfast on gin and orange juice, then fly three more hours, over desert, black hills, and, finally, red-roofed cottages on sand dunes. Sydney, from the air, looks like impetigo. At Kingsford Smith Airport, I.S. protests to a mob of reporters and against their barrage of cameras that he has had no sleep during the 36-hour flight and cannot give a press conference. In the Chevron Hilton, we telephone Los Angeles for news of the Bel-Air fire and learn with relief that the area of the conflagration is not near North Wetherly Drive.

November 11. In the airport again, for the flight to New Zealand, I.S. assures an official who has been explaining why he must pay overweight that he "understands the *logic* of it. What I am objecting to is the money." One of our fellow passengers on the bumpy turbo-prop is Field Marshal Lord Alexander, with whom we chat in a V.I.P. waiting room. He reads a Perry Mason during the flight and is greeted in Auckland by hundreds of hip-hip-hooraying schoolgirls in kilts. Our first view of the island is a rim

1961 of white sand between light green sea and dark green hills. The Rodean, where we stay, is a boardinghouse with a view of the bay and not much else.

November 12. (Sunday) As we tour the harbor, mussel-gatherers follow the ebbing tide, and Maoris with cockney accents pick the pools for periwinkles and haul in nets spangled with shellfish. England is closer here than in Sydney, in cricket fields, bowling lawns, church spires, tall oaks, Constable-like clouds, Marvell-like shadows and greens, Empire names like Khyber Pass Road. Each house has its "tidy plot" of flower and vegetable gardens, and—the ultimate Englishness—everyone is a gardener. "That hedge'd take a bit of cutting," our driver remarks, indignantly, and though a moment later disclaiming that he is a "horticulturist," the sight of some yellow gorse, "that noxious weed," puts him out of sorts.

He pronounces "Maori" with the German "*au*" ("Mauree"), and his "Yes" might have an umlaut ("Yoess")—when he uses the word at all, that is, for he prefers to say "righto." His "r" is a combination of Dixie and Kennedy Bostonian: we are in an English cah, in a land of flowhs, whose seat of Pahlamint is Wellington. The pronunciations of the waitress at the Rodean are more remote: breakfast consists of braid and eegs, unless one prefers scones (rhymes with prawns); small hills are hillies; and she translates I.S.'s whiskey orders to "nips"—the furtiveness suggested by the word being appropriate to the restrictive conditions under which the article is acquired and consumed. Road signs warn the motorist to "Tip No Rubbish," and cockney expressions occur even in the language of the law.

Pride in New Zealand's natural beauty dominates most conversations, and little curiosity is evinced, however strongly it may be felt, about other lands. The tone of this talk is that of an appeal to prospective settlers, but the lure—which includes such benefits as free hospitalization—is offset in my case by a bachelor tax. Another favorite topic is the rivalry with, and superiority over, Australia: "Our horses are better racers. We have better lobsters." The Australian view was most succinctly put by a baggage porter at Sydney Airport: "Going to New Zealand for a few days? That'd be enough, I should think."

This afternoon's tour is accompanied by a steady discourse on New Zealand history and local lore, during which I.S., in the back seat, falls asleep. After 20 minutes or so, he wakes with a start, exclaiming "The street!" Then, after a strenuous pause, he manages to say, "What is the street of our hotel?"—confessing later that he had dreamed he was in Paris and was directing a taxi to his old apartment there. Dinner at the Rodean consists of cockle fritters, steamed *hapuka*, and bread served with about a pound of butter per person.

November 14. From today's *Auckland Star*:

Igor Stravinsky, in a fawn cardigan, walking with the aid of a stick, eyes shielded against the morning glare by dark glasses . . . placed his music in perspective this morning. . . . He feels that it is his duty to let people hear his works as he himself conceived them. "There are many conductors, but not many good ones, and even if they are good ones they cannot know exactly what is in my mind. . . .Children accept without quite knowing the reasons. That is, until they are, say, eleven. Then they change. They want to know the reasons. Sometimes they become a bore. . . . Critics usually praise in such a way that I am not flattered at all, because I can see they do not understand. Sometimes I am not very happy about some passages in a work. I would like some help. But the critics miss these passages and take exceptions to others. . . . A good Parisian orchestra under a competent conductor who knew the score [Referring to Monteux and *The Rite of Spring*] and also understood my intentions took sixteen rehearsals to learn the work. The other day I conducted it with a good orchestra in Stockholm after two. . . ." Stravinsky refused to say whether he had been amused by seeing his critics discomfited by time: "they could have found out a lot earlier."

Our concert tonight starts at 8 P.M., which is 8 A.M. on our circadian clocks.

November 15. The flight to Wellington offers good views of Mount Ruapehu, its smooth flanks covered with a mantle of snow, and of the still smoking Ngauruhoe volcano. The landing is in strong winds, and we soon discover that Wellington is almost always wet with spindrift blowing from the straits in a semipermanent gale. The city is more Victorian than Auckland, but its most attractive Victorian buildings, with Gothic windows, iron railings, and iron awnings, are being demolished. I ask to see the home of Mary Taylor, Charlotte Brontë's pen-pal who had a shop here in 1845, but our hosts know nothing about this. As we pass a statue of Victoria Regina herself, I.S. remarks: "She looks like a policeman."

Among the hundred hands I.S. is obliged to shake at United States Ambassador Akers's reception are those of other ambassadors, of the Prime Minister of New Zealand, and of many members of Pahlamint. Large N.Z. lady to I.S.: "Frankly, Mr. Stravinsky, I like *Firebird* best of all your works." I.S.: "And what a charming hat you have." Small N.Z. gent to I.S.: "People here are very fond of modern music. We had half a program of your works once" (I.S., later: "My *Sheherazade*, no doubt"), "and we've heard pieces by Shostakovitch and Ache [Egk]." Wife of high N.Z. dignitary to I.S.: "Do you like architecture, Mr. Stravinsky?" I.S.: "Let me think about it."

November 16. Today's *Dominion* contains photographs of I.S.'s arrival, and an accurate report:

Not only pop singers rate welcome cheers and banners. The same greetings were given to the world's most famous living composer, Igor Stravinsky, as he stepped from an aircraft at Wellington airport yesterday morning. Looking small and frail as he braced himself against the boisterous wind, the 79-year-old Stravinsky waved an acknowledgment and moved across to shake the hand of a little girl standing amid a band of students from Victoria University. "Victoria University Music Society welcomes her patron, Igor Stravinsky," the banners read. "We Dig Ig," "Vic Digs Ig," "We All Dig Ig." Undaunted, Stravinsky smiled broadly before being shepherded through the airport building.

From the *Wellington Evening Post*:

Stravinsky says that he left Russia in 1910 "because of health reasons." . . . Asked if America . . . is an artistically stimulating country, he said he felt no country was more stimulating than others. . . . His health is obviously good, judging by today's interview. . . . Stravinsky spoke . . . with the mental agility and energy of a much younger man, despite having been kept awake much of last night by the noise of the wind. . . . The famous composer speaks with enthusiasm about the operatic work he is now composing under commission to American television. He said it did not concern him that the work was being done for TV: "I don't know what TV is."

On jazz: "I am not interested in jazz today though I was in the early 20s." He predicted a revival of "Romantic music. . . . I mean the music immediately after Beethoven," and he mentioned Schubert and Weber. But of electronic music he said: "I don't like it at all." He gave as his reason for conducting: "I want the music to reach the public as I wrote it."

November 17. From today's *Dominion*:

Stravinsky on his own early works: "My attitude to them is just to leave them alone. I am moving. They are probably not moving. . . ." "I compose under the influence of ideas, and climate cannot change my ideas and my technique. . . ."

On his wife: "A painter of today and not yesterday." [Mrs. Stravinsky looked] very elegant in a black woolen dress. . . . A special bracelet with the letters "I L O V E Y O U" linked together encircled her left wrist, a birthday present from her husband. A gold and pearl chain with a turquoise cross, and a large pearl and aquamarine cocktail ring completed her ensemble.

November 18. Our concert in Wellington Town Hall is televised. I conduct *Pulcinella* and the Symphony in Three.

From the *Wellington Evening Post*:

> Igor Stravinsky's rehearsal of the National Orchestra at the Town Hall today became an added attraction for many who had attended the Christmas parade. When the parade finished at the Town Hall they went inside to listen to the orchestra. In a carnival atmosphere, a couple of hundred people listened to the rehearsal, but were not lucky enough to see Stravinsky conducting. He contented himself with following the score from a front seat, while his young associate conductor, Robert Craft, directed the orchestra. Although Stravinsky did not step onto the rostrum, he was the conductor in empathy from his seat in the stalls and he had numerous comments for Robert Craft as they went along. Craft knows the maestro so well, having worked with him for 14 years, not only in music but in books, that he can translate his desires with little need for prompting.

We drive along the straits to an igloo-like concrete fortress at the harbor entrance, a reminder of the war. The roadside colors are marigold, foxglove, wild sweet peas, wild daisies, golden wattles, pale lupines, roses, and geraniums the size of peonies.

A visit from Doris MacFarlane, a friend of my sister, married to a sheep rancher in Parnassus, a railway junction in Samuel Butler country on the South Island. Except for a trip to Wellington 22 years ago, Mrs. MacFarlane has never traveled, and the journey here was her first in an airplane. Since our concert is also her first with a live symphony orchestra, this is an exciting weekend for her, but tomorrow morning is shearing day in Parnassus and she must be there by 4:30 A.M., before the musterers take to the hills and the dawn birds can give the alarm to the sheep. She talks to us of sheep-tending: of lambing, docking, and dipping; of the crutching of ewes, the eyeclipping of heavy fleeces, the care of the hoggets and the fate of the culls.

Doris's hands are scarred from crayfish, which she hunts in snorkel and fins, but without gloves. Another of her seaside pastimes is making earrings from surf-polished marl. She says that during a drive along the beach not long ago, she heard what sounded like a woman sobbing. Running to the water's edge, she found a dolphin dying from a propeller wound, "Tears rolling from its eyes, and its cries terribly human." She talks about the blue ducks and the mutton birds, the wedge-tailed shearwaters, that migrate from the south of South Island to Siberia, and that only Maoris are licensed to hunt. Cold mutton bird rates as a great delicacy, she says, but is indigestibly rich.

No danger, in the St. George Hotel, of our stomachs being put to the test. The fare is indigestibly poor, and an intolerably puritanical code is enforced whereby wine, available in none of the city restaurants, *can* be obtained, but only by registered guests ready to be regarded as depraved. As rule-ridden as a boarding school, or reformatory, the St. George admits visitors at prescribed times only and subjects them to suspicious looks. Coffee is not available at dinner, but only tea, and vice versa at noon. Guests who forget to affix a special notice to their doors are inundated at daybreak with a clattering service of compulsory tea.

November 19. In the airport waiting room, I.S. draws a man sitting cross-legged next to us with the sole of his shoe sticking in our faces. Marinated in Scotch by the time the pilot makes his rounds, I.S. tells him: "I feel like a planet." Sunset is a blue, red, and black flag above a precipice of cold white light.

November 20. Sydney. During a tea break in our initial rehearsal this morning, I.S. shocks some of the players by asking for beer. "I am struggling with my global image," he tells a reporter. "I feel upside down and way down there. We have a geography of the spirit, after all, and in it, a Great Barrier Reef of the soul."

November 21. At I.S.'s press conference, someone asks whether he has had "any ideas" since his arrival in Australia. "I have 'ideas' all my life," he snaps back, "and neither more nor less in Australia than anywhere else."

Dinner at Lady Lloyd-Jones's attractive 1840s plantation house, which has fine gardens and gazebos. Lady L.-J. is high-spirited and much less tame than her lions, who include Patrick White as well as I.S. A tall figure with a craggy jaw and hard stare, White laments "the unofficial censorship in Australia, the provincialism that patronizes second-rate imports, and the many intellectual deprivations of life in the antipodes." But he prefers to talk about ballet, books, the music of Mahler. When he talks at all, that is, for he has a silent temperament, the only nonbuoyant Australian so far, a lonely artist who has probably been groaning inside all evening. He promises to attend our concert, even though it is to take place, as we discovered at today's rehearsal, in a vast Victorian cavern with an opulent echo.

November 22. Reminders of Empire: a statue of Captain Cook, Victorian brownstone houses, names like Hotel Castlereagh, the zoning by trades: Macquaries Street is a surgeons' row like Harley Street. But England vanishes after a little below-the-surface scratching. Nor is the physiognomy of the city predominantly English, certainly not its amusing architecture, the tiny houses with tall steeples, polychrome houses with valentine-lace ironwork, and the cottages with names that D. H. Lawrence ridiculed. The most attractive buildings, with broad verandas and white columns, are the work of Francis Greenway, the convict architect ostracized by the free settlers even after he had built the best of their city.

The Taronga Zoo. Malayan otters have kind faces with Edwardian whiskers; they squeal like pinched schoolgirls. Kangaroos and wallabies in the mass are a distressing sight: they limp like cripples and spend most of their time picking each other's fleas. Koalas are marsupials, too, but nocturnal; when a keeper plucks one from the bole of a tree and plumps it in my arms, it turns away from the light. As we approach the gorilla cage, the yellow-eyed tenant flings an armful of sawdust in our direction. The birds, red-headed lorikeets, red-eyed manucodes, gaudy macaws, cassowaries, are gorgeous and noisy, except the kiwi, which is not only apteryx but also agoraphobic, seldom leaving its hut, as if to cooperate and speed up the process of its approaching extinction. "Satin birds" fill their nests with bits of anything blue. Some of the birds of paradise have opal eyes and scissor-tails five times the length of their chassis; some, black velvet, have even longer antennae, no doubt for jaded lovers. Kookaburras, with recessive lower mandibles and hearty, knowing laughs, are revoltingly complacent.

November 24. From yesterday's *Morning Herald*: "Igor Stravinsky sat like a broody eagle in a corner of a shabby ABC rehearsal studio at King's Cross yesterday during the third of four rehearsals for tonight's concert. His associate conductor, the American, Robert Craft, patiently took the orchestra through some of the most important music of this century.

[Quotes V]: 'He often buys me presents and is very nice when he thinks not about music.'"

Evening flight to Melbourne, the Menzies Hotel.

November 25. Today's *Melbourne Sun* quotes I.S.:

"I am not a teacher who tells you what to do. I am a composer who does what he thinks, and if people don't feel my music they can go to hell. . . . It has been so long I don't think of Russia as 'mother Russia' any more. . . . I am very loyal to my American citizenship. All Europe has sadness for me. My first wife and daughter died there of consumption, and I said good-bye to Europe. I will never live there again. Next year I am 80 and still everybody invites me all around the world. . . . When I die, I leave you my music. . . ."

November 26. After an hour of listening and waiting for a lyrebird in Sherbrook Forest, a tinkly bell-bird appears. The woods smell pleasingly of gum leaf and moss, and the fern forest looks like an illustration for Humboldt. "Each tree is an individual," V. says—Dylan Thomas's "gardener" says "always pray to a tree"—but the deeper I wander among the tall eucalyptus, the more I feel the absence of individuality in the loneliness of Australia, and in the silence of the wilderness defined by the cry of a bird.

November 27. Melbourne, a city of stately trees—silver-green eucalyptus, willows, casuarinas—is more Victorian than Sydney and less colorful,

1961 even when, as now, decked out for Christmas. Six very nice Russian refugees give a lunch for the S.s. Vodka and *pirozhki*, in quantity. I.S. is very drunk.

Larry Adler, who has heard part of I.S.'s Sydney concert, wants to commission a harmonica concerto. His letter says that he plays the *Chanson Russe* and had to encore it in a concert in Copenhagen: "My deepest respects to you for your gesture in bringing your music . . . to Australia."

November 28. At the Palais Theater, St. Kilda, I.S. conducts the Victorian Symphony Orchestra in an odd pairing of *God Save the Queen* and *Le Baiser de la fée.* I conduct *Jeu de cartes.*

November 29. Melbourne to Tahiti, with a change of planes in Sydney. Numerous photographers record the transfer, but our new fellow passengers are annoyed because their flight has been delayed two hours for us. New Caledonia, three hours from Sydney, consists of a ring of white coral around an emerald lagoon, hills striped like tigers, a runway scratched in the livid earth like a vaccination. We walk to the Nouméa terminal in sapping heat. Inside are dusky Dominicans wearing white shirts, rope belts, fedoras; French marines with red pompon berets; *"flics"* in khaki and kepis; Oriental women with slit Chinese skirts and faces like statues at Angkor; giggling, half-naked native boys, to whom I say *"Bonjour,"* thereby provoking an explosion of laughter.

Nandi, a few hours later, is a sauna bath. As soon as we land, over rice terraces and watery valleys, a Sulu in a white apron charges through the plane spraying DDT in our faces. The terminal is new, air-conditioned even on the half-open outside ramps, and equipped with numerous shower rooms, all with electric dryers. Fijians, sponge-haired, wearing white skirts with sawtooth serrations at the hem, are gentle and well-mannered. We buy batik from them, and drink spiked pineapple juice at tables strewn with purple hibiscus. Rousseau was right, I.S. says, if by "natural people" he could have meant the Sulus.

November 29. (*Sic:* we have crossed the International Date Line): 2 A.M. Tahiti. The tarmac, on a short, narrow, crushed-coral dyke, is lighted not by hurricane lamps but by naked flame torches in iron sconces. Our plane turns gingerly around at the end of the runway, wings wobbling over the water like the balancing bar of a man on a tightrope. A reception of Tahitian belles in blue sarongs and redolent gardenia leis awaits I.S. An elderly U.S. tourist to one of the *Taïtiennes:* "Say, young woman, what's that flower in your hair?" "Tahiti flower." "Oh, I see."

The Hotel Tahiti is a cluster of thatched bamboo cottages on the edge of the lagoon. A perpetual light wind, like the sound of rain, ventilates the inside, but I hear other, less romantic noises as well, including the "chirp, chirp" of amorous geckos and the scuttle of small, unidentified (rodent?) feet.

A rooster debate at 4 A.M. Unable to sleep, I walk in the soft silver morning. Across the open sea, beyond the spray of waves on the outer coral crown, is Moorea, newborn and lovely in the amethyst dawn.

I say "*Maruru*" ("Thank you"—my entire vocabulary) to the girl who brings breakfast, then show her that the faucets of the wash-basin produce no water but only a kind of orange pekoe tea, leaves and all. Giggling, she explains in verb-less but gestureful *tutoyer* French that this is a result of the rains. Am I alone, she asks, looking around the room? When I admit that, regrettably, this is the case, she disappears and returns with six other giggling girls who employ the pretext of examining the faucets, but hardly trouble to conceal that the real object of curiosity is me. They wear flower-patterned gingham sarongs and gardenias over the left ear. All have long hair, braided or loose, and all are barefoot. Gauguin was an accurate observer of *Taïtienne* toes, as well as of the large flat feet, thick calves, shapes of heads and of eyes; but thanks to the later admixture of Chinese, these girls are prettier than any *jeune fille* in Gauguin.

Papeete is not pretty, apart from a few picturesque colonial buildings with colonnades and open balconies peeling white paint. Chinese shops, with advertisements in ideograms and girls leaning over sewing machines, seem to outnumber the French, but the stores are less interesting than the traffic, especially the motor scooters, driven by girls in sarongs trailing long hair, and the buses, with benches along the sides and open at the rear to admit domestic animals. On the sidewalks, French priests and officials mix with Polynesians of a thousand complexions. Small steamers, yachts, and ketches fill the harbor. We spend the afternoon on the beach at Fautaua (pronounce five syllables), a cove of sable sand.

At night, while I watch the orange flares from fishing canoes, two "hostesses" join me on the hotel terrace. One of them is a quarter-caste, she says, the other a pure Tahitian. Communication is confined to bar-room, *bêche-de-mer* French and to the English names for a few of the less complicated drinks. At midnight some American businessmen arrive and attempt to dance the twist. They wear flower-patterned Truman shirts and crowns of gardenias awry like Bacchus's girdle of grapes and from the same cause. Neither of my companions has any idea where America is, or, for that matter, Europe. Within minutes the superannuated American adolescents have paired off with the mature child *Taïtiennes*. The whole island is a vulva, ready and willing.

November 30. A marital squabble in the other half of my hut wakes me in the middle of the night, the wall between being a thin, resonant tympanum. "So you think I married you for your money?" the man shouts. (Not until morning do I see that this may well have been the case, but what can have been *her* reason?) Switching on the bed lamp, I am vaguely aware, on the floor by my slippers, of a hairy object, which, putting on my spectacles, I identify as a spider about the size of my fist. (Later I try to recall whether I actually screamed, but a totally paralyzed person is incapable of that.) The fright is mutual, evidently, for the monster flies under my bed, on which I huddle in the center, shivering. Suddenly I remember the bug bomb in the bathroom, and, at length, overcome my abhorrence long enough to leap from the bed to fetch it—my flight and arrival causing infinite confusion among the cockroaches and lizards night-basking there. Spraying the area under my bed, I nearly asphyxiate myself before the creature emerges and climbs to my night table, where I blow the poison at it like an open fire hydrant. Retreating to the wall, now somewhat groggily, the arachnid dodges me there like a PT boat in an air raid until finally falling to the floor, where it lands on its back with a sickening thud. The legs twitch horribly for a moment, then draw in as, tremblingly, and no doubt cowardly and cruelly, I bear down with the spray can.

In the morning, the hotel maids laugh at my pallor as they sweep out the corpse and its crab-size legs. The spiders are harmless, they say, but "beware of the centipedes." I resolve henceforth to spray every surface of the hut before going to bed, and to sleep sitting up, bathrobe over my head, and all lights on.

Still shaky in the afternoon, I call on the Chilean Consul at Punavia, in the district of FAA (pronounce three stutters, like a bleating lamb: the Tahitian alphabet has only 13 letters), whose beach is reputedly the best on the island. The women of Punavia, combing their long hair on the steps of their Napier huts, are so perfectly Gauguinesque that I am not surprised by the sign near the little church of St.-Etienne: "Paul Gauguin lived here 1896–1901."

The Consul, a white-haired hidalgo with gentle brown eyes, fondles the hackles of a parrot while telling me of his love for Tahiti. Unshaven and sloppily dressed, he is somewhat embarrassed thereof, but lonely, too, and happy to talk to a foreigner. His *"vahine"* ("wife"—a corruption of "vagina"?) is a teenage girl with long braids, long fingers, a long—too long—animal laugh. The Consulate yard is cluttered with idols from Easter Island, assorted refuse, pigs, monkeys, chickens, mynah birds, cats. I swim with the *vahine* in the warm lagoon as far as the coral reef, on which I cut my leg. She squeezes lemon juice on the wound, and laughs (too long) when I wince.

At dinner, V. talks about the first Christmas she remembers. "I received a newborn black lamb with a blue bow, and lambs and Christmas trees have reminded me of each other ever since." I.S. cannot remember his first Christmas, but only "a reminder of it: I was a baby sitting naked on the sands of a Baltic beach—how agreeable to feel the hot sand on one's bare behind! My mother gave me a bottle, and I filled it with sand, and emptied, refilled, and emptied it again and again. A pine twig fell beside me and I grasped it and tried to push it into the bottle—without success, whereupon I began to study the twig, and to think how similar it was to our Christmas tree." This memory leads to the recollection of a childhood schoolmate pointing out a cat to him and saying that the cat was skillful in catching fish. "The word 'skill' impressed me, and I have paid attention to it ever since."

I.S. goes to the Hopital de Papeete for a prothrombin test with Dr. Georges Thooris.

December 1. Tahiti is tandem-shaped. We circle the larger (210 kilometers) of the two wheels, stopping first at Faratea, a restaurant near the entrance to the smaller wheel. Almost everywhere the ground is littered with bald, skull-like coconuts, whose husks have been gathered into pyres; the coconut trees have shiny metal armbands, shields against rats. Other trees include the breadfruit; the mango, which bears purple fruit; the chestnut, whose hard, straight wood is used in making pirogues; and the kapok, whose fibers provide stuffing for pillows. The plants and flowers include elephants' ears, wurra lilies, red ginger bushes, flamboyant pink acacias, yellow hibiscus, and pandanus (aerial roots and leaves with "joints" like spiders' legs, which shows what is on my mind).

Every few kilometers is a church, most of them Catholic and looking as if borrowed from French villages; but some are Protestant, Mormon, and Seventh-Day Adventist. The one architectural oddity worth remarking is none of these but the tomb of King Pomare V. It resembles a bottle of Benedictine, red-capped dome and all—intentionally, it is said, to memorialize the monarch's favorite fluid and cause of his demise. The only other buildings of interest are a lazaret, whose lepers sit or stroll on a wide, roofless porch; and, on a hillside facing the sea, the ruins of the temple of Arahurahu, in which smiling, toothy, pregnant-baby idols stand in a rectangle of volcanic stones.

Spend the evening with Henri-Georges Clouzot. Fox-eyed, hirsute, and a lively conversationalist about actresses (Monroe, Bardot) and painters— the reason for his retreat here is to study painting himself—he convinces I.S. that Nicolas de Stael killed himself "because he failed to find the rules and limits of his art." Returning to Papeete in Clouzot's jeep, in the drenching, straight-down monsoon, we pass coatless, umbrellaless people walking in the dark, one of them an old man playing a guitar.

December 7. Los Angeles. I.S. sends a telegram to Mrs. J. F. Kennedy: "I have just returned from a concert tour in Australia and only today received your thoughtful invitation. I am touched and honored. Deeply upset that I must keep concert engagements in June. Respectfully."

December 10. Visit from Bruno Walter on behalf of the Vienna Philharmonic to invite I.S. to conduct there.

December 17. Mexico City. *"Feliz Navidad,"* the neon signs say, and the lamp posts along the Avenida are thatched with Christmas evergreens. The Alameda, from our hotel rooms, is a child's sugarplum dream of gold, sapphire, and ruby lights, but the wonder of wonders is an electric bird of paradise that changes colors and tail positions three times a minute. A hurdy-gurdy grinds in the street. The balloon vendor next to it has either lost his stock or found a spendthrift customer: a varicolored cluster floats

1961 past our window. Somewhere in the outskirts is a ferris wheel of exploding fireworks.

"Mexican people have much *revolución*, señor, but they very happy people. You see what I mean?" This of course is from Vicente, happy himself to see us again as we are to see him. Driving by a cinema with a queue five blocks long, he remarks: "The people stand many hours, señor. Mexicans have much time, señor."

December 18. Today, marking the end of the two-week celebrations of the miraculous appearances at Guadalupe, countless pilgrims parade to the shrine from starting places miles away. At the head of each of these processions is a band of cornets, violins, guitars, cymbals, tubas playing very lively tunes. Behind the musicians come the banners with the image of the Virgin carried by boys in the black suits of an order of hyperdulia, and behind them the ordinary marchers—braided Indian women, for the most part, with babies on their backs and gladioli in their hands.

At Guadalupe we stand next to a family of kneeling Indians, their lips moving in prayer; one of them, a small girl, holds her white Communion dress an inch above the floor, as if to curtsy, while her brother, a ragged infant, feet calloused and caked with dirt, clutches a green plastic whistle as if it were his only possession. A busload of U.S. tourists empties into the church where, next to the Mexicans, they look as pale as pernicious anemia. "Hold on to your wallets, everybody," their gringo guide says, as they hurry nervously past the boy with the whistle. They hardly seem to breathe for fear of the germs and the superstition.

One of the chapels displays a glass coffin containing an embalmed, brown-frocked saint with skin like Parian. Coins and paper money have been piled on the body, and letters, photographs, wax flowers, and babies' shoes are pinned to the wall behind. In another chapel, I.S. buys candles to place on the altar table, though the ones already there are melting together. The Indians plant their candles, then lie procumbent to pray, or with heads to the floor like Muslims.

December 19. The church of Santiago, built on ruined revetments of Tenochtitlán, is white inside, with black spandrels, now looped and twined with ropes of Christmas evergreen. The monk in the glass case to the left of the altar must have died by drowning, to judge by the adipocere. Another preserved corpse looks like a statue carved in marzipan. The treasure of the church is a wood sculpture of a captive Christ in a pure white robe with a golden hem.

Vicente takes us to the Plaza de Garibaldi to hear *mariachi* music, but the players, friends of his, have to be corralled from several cafés. They wear black velvet jackets and wide-brimmed forward-tilting sombreros, and their instruments are a clarinet, a cornet, and several sizes of guitar, tiny *vihuela* to big bass. For 10 pesos, the vocalist sings the "*Corrida de Pancho Villa*," the "*Corrida de Emiliano Zapata*," and "*Guadalajara*." While we listen to this street concert, a one-legged beggar polishes our car.

Vicente's next stops are the pink palace of Porfirio Díaz; a ramshackle house, nearby, where Zapata lived in 1914—"Zapata no fancy man, señor"—and the Zócalo: "Seventy Aztec temples stood here, señor. I never know how they move so many stones, but I think they have very strong religion."

December 20. Our first concert in the Bellas Artes. I conduct *Scènes de ballet* and I.S.'s 1921 Tango in his arrangement for wind instruments.

December 21. To Toluca, on a steep route marked with *"curva peligrosa"* warnings. The slopes are thickly wooded, as they were when Doña Fanny Calderón de la Barca made the trip, at which time the country was infested with bandits. The Nevada de Toluca, with brow of black clouds, is in view long before the city. The Plaza is a park of ahehuete trees, which, according to Vicente, is the wrong name, the Spaniards simply being unable to pronounce *"agua"*; we see what he means when he describes a group of buildings as part of a housing "proyect." The sidewalks are spread with ceramics, blankets, baskets, Christmas *juguetes* (toys).

In the Toluca market, the older the Indian women the more they seem to carry. One poor crone, bare feet purple with cold, is bent double with a bale of moss that would balk a mule. The more prosperous and younger female peddlers wear bright blue wool stockings, matching blue ponchos, straw hats, and ladder-like racks strapped to their backs. The men wear cheverel leggings, carry nothing, and knit as they walk. The specialties of the food market are *churros* (chocolate cake coiled like rope), hot pigs' knuckles, plucked turkeys for Christmas, piles of dried *frijoles*, purple peppers, *pescado frito*.

Toluca is still Aztec, according to Vicente, and the mountain people still believe in Tlaloc, Huitzilopochtli, Quetzalcoatl. Whatever the truth of this, an indelible and uninterrupted ancient life survives in this harsh, mountainous *ciudad de los tigres*, as the Spaniards called it because the Indian braves wore wildcats' heads and skins.

On the return, Vicente discourses on bullfighting: "The bull he no cry because he real man, señor. And the bull is the only one in *corrida* who doesn't want fight, señor. The crowd want fight. And the matador. Then why all the people cry so loud when the matador is caught, señor, but they no cry when bull is caught?"

December 23. Los Angeles. A letter from Isaiah: "Dear Robert, Herewith the text. I have adopted a fairly home-made method of transcription and there are no mysterious orientalisms of pronunciation, etc."

And a note from Boulez: "Cher ami, . . . the retrospective went very well, and I think we will record the program in April, as soon as I have a little free time. Suzanne Tézenas will certainly send you the program, including a brief text I wrote for the occasion. . . . More news later, when I know that you have returned to Hollywood. Warm wishes to you, and

1961 fondest regards to Igor and Vera."

December 31. A card from Nabokov, in Paris: "Dearest Bob, Happy New Year! Were you well met in Bangkok?* I'm doing a festival in Brazil in Aug.–Sept. 1963. Then another in Israel in Sept-Oct. of that same year. Must see you about it. When? *Please* ask I.S. to write again to Mrs. Kennedy and offer an alternative."

And a letter from Isaiah warning that the food in Israel is abominable, partly because of theological reasons. Apropos the London staging of *Perséphone*, he says that he likes the music very much, the text not at all.

ᵇ **Postscript 1994.** I quoted Australian and New Zealand newspaper descriptions of Stravinsky in the diary for the reason that they struck me as ingenuous and fresh in a way that was no longer possible in Europe and America. The people of those countries did appreciate his visit, and he himself was pleased with his reception there and with the realization that his music was known and performed down under. He had been wanting to visit Australia since 1932 and had decided against it then only because of the long travel time. In Melbourne, of all places, he was the luncheon guest of a group of Russian refugees, youngish working-men who knew little of his music and simply wanted to meet him. After the customary exchanges of given names and patronymics, and the ingestion of caviar blini and vodka, he answered questions about their native land with an openness that I had never observed before. An outing of this kind was unimaginable in Hollywood's White Russian community which, in any case, he shunned (snubbed, some said); during my years in Hollywood, I remember him attending only one social function organized by his compatriots-in-exile, an amateur performance of a play by Ostrovsky, and that was because one of the actors was his gardener, Varzhinsky.

The Mexican trip in the spring showed that Stravinsky's religious fervor had been dormant but not dead when in the mid-1950s he boycotted Hollywood's Russian churches, complaining that he had scarcely finished confession when the priest who had shriven him asked for his autograph. (Pope John XXIII, at the end of the private audience with Stravinsky in November 1958, also requested an autograph.) Stravinsky was no less deeply moved than the Indians by the Good Friday observances in Taxco.

Our return to Mexico in December was ill-advised, not only because the potential concert audience had vacated the city for the holidays and the performances took place in an empty hall, but also because we had been traveling since September and had had enough of it. The concert was so ineptly managed that we left Mexico with a distaste and never returned.

---

* We had planned a side-trip to Angkor in November, on our way to Australia, and Nabokov had arranged a reception in Bangkok by the Royal family.

1962

January 6. Hollywood. A note from Varèse concerning our recording session next month of *Renard* and his *Ecuatorial*: "Dear Mr. Craft . . . looking forward to seeing you and the Stravinskys. . . . Happy to hear *Renard* again."

January 13. Toronto. I.S., at the taping session for my broadcast, is intrigued by Sibelius's *Canzonetta* for strings, the theme music for the program. To Buffalo by car, then a plane to Rochester and Washington.

January 15. Luncheon at Mildred Bliss's with St.-John Perse (Alexis Léger). I.S. receives the key to the City of Washington from District Commissioner Walter N. Tobriner. Just before the ceremony, V. asks what the key will open. "Our hearts," Tobriner answers. I.S., no mean diplomat himself: "The hearts are already opened."

January 16. St.-John Perse for lunch, bringing a copy of his *Anabasis* inscribed, "A Igor Stravinsky, *honneur de notre temps, qui sait ce qu'il y a d'action et de solitude secrète dans la création. Affectueusement.*" He says that after reading his Nobel address, "Some young Swedish physicists told me that they were weary of hearing about the opium of the irrational, and they asked if I thought a scientific explanation could be found for the *germination poétique*. I suggested that they substitute 'experimental' for 'opium,'—the experimental irrational, but I said that poetry can only begin in the inconsequence of the absurd. The application can be scientized in the logic of the word, of course, though I have not attempted to do this myself, or anything along those lines: I am too busy trying to develop my own intellectual *maîtrise*."

He defends Heidegger's theory of the beginnings of poetry, quoting him on Hölderlin and Trakl; and attacks the "canalization into logic" by English and American "university philosophers." I.S. interjects that "Universities today are department stores. Worst of all, they no longer allow art itself to be the teacher, but promote instead 'the art of teaching' and even 'the teacher as artist.'" Moving on to *"le hasard,"* and to Einstein's "God does not

1962 throw dice," Perse says that the idea of a chance universe is giddying.*
Here I.S. protests that he does not understand chance in art: "One has a
nose, the nose scents and it chooses, and the artist is simply a kind of pig
snouting truffles."

The mention of Joseph Conrad inspires Perse's highest flight of eloquence. "He was the most perfect aristocrat and the truest friend I have
ever known. . . . Valéry and Claudel, in comparison, were my intellectual
friends, but hardly more than that." He agrees with I.S.'s remarks on
Valéry in the Bollingen volume of Valéry's plays, and goes on to tell the
story, which we have heard from Aldous, of finding the author of *Monsieur
Teste* on a street bench one night, head in hands and the picture of despair:
"My wife is going to have a baby," he explained, "hence I shall need money,
and have to write again, which of course means the Academy."

"Conrad would never judge a friend either morally or intellectually,"
Perse continues. "He regarded friendship as sacred. Obviously he did not
love the sea—he chose to live forty-two miles inland—but man-against-
the-sea, and ships. He could never understand me when I talked about the
sea itself. I think he must have disliked my poems. Yet the only literature
that I am certain he positively detested was Dostoyevsky. Describing a
dinner somewhere in the country with Shaw, Wells, and Bennett, he told
me that These *savants cyniques* of the literary industry talked about writing
as action,' which so horrified poor Conrad that he left the table pretending
he had to catch an earlier train. Describing the scene—in *épouvantable*
French, except for one English word I shall never forget—he said that
'Writing, for me, is an act of faith; they made me feel so *dowdy.'* "

Switching to the subject of his travels in Patagonia and Tierra del Fuego,
Perse sounds like a page from his own *Amers*—"The wind, the ocean, the
cold, the earth and sky unspoiled by the detritus of man." "*La Poésie est une
façon de vivre,*" he says, "*c'est pourquoi je déteste même parler de 'la litterature.'* The
rationalists invented 'literature' and killed poetry—almost."

He tells the story of his experience as special envoy of the French government to the Kremlin in 1935. "Litvinov translated for me but adjusted
everything I said. Each evening the dinner table was heaped as if for an
orgy, and an orgy of toasting did take place, glasses of vodka being
downed, one after the other, in honor of each of the commissars present,
with a final toast for Comrade Stalin. I managed to switch carafes and
drink only water. Then I noticed that although Stalin drank, it did not
affect him. I assumed he had received water, too, and was certain of it
when I saw that he ate only goat cheese and fruit. Eventually the commissars found me out. But when they questioned me, I replied that, like

---

* For the philosophy of the nonintentional universe, *cf.* Jacques Monod's *Le Hasard et la
necessité* (Paris, 1970). Monod concludes, "Man knows at last that he is alone in the indifferent immensity of the universe, whence he has emerged by chance."

Comrade Stalin, I did not drink. This was greeted with an explosion of silence, Stalin's water-drinking apparently being an open secret. He looked at me fiercely for a moment, then started to laugh. I had a better opinion of him after that, as I know he had of me, but in the Kremlin Museum next day, I was followed by police. When I asked why, Stalin said: 'I wanted to know what interested you most.' " Perse clearly believes that the pendulum of Stalin's reputation has swung too far toward the Khrushchev view. "Stalin was a man of extraordinary good sense," he says, "and I refuse to believe the stories about him as a table-tapping mystic. He was not vain, moreover, and he was never an actor."

Perse recalls that he met I.S. after the premiere of *Firebird*, but that they began to know each other well only in 1921, when I.S. was arranging the three movements from *Petrushka*, and the two of them were often together at Marguerite Bassiano's at Versailles. He says that at the premiere of *Sacre* he saw men swinging their canes at each other and opening and shutting umbrellas. "I was with Debussy both shortly before and shortly after that evening, and I remember how excited he was by the music at first, and how he changed when he saw that it had taken the attention of the younger generation away from him. He felt abandoned, and he began to criticize the work."

Perse also recalls I.S. in Boston just before his marriage, "Registering in a very proper hotel and asking the clerk in slow, loud, and *épouvantable* English, 'May I have with me a female companion?' Some adoring old-maid disciples of yours overheard and were nearly overcome with embarrassment."

Full-face, Perse bears some resemblance to Poe, albeit a neat and very sane version, while in profile he reminds me of E. M. Forster. He is dapper—a striped suit, vest, and bow tie—and he stands, a head taller than I.S., like a ramrod. I.S. asks his advice about what to say when he receives a medal from the Secretary of State this afternoon, complaining: "I do not want to be decorated like a general; I want to be *méchant*." To which Perse, the professional diplomat, replies, "Courtesy can be the nastiest thing of all." At 5 P.M. we go to the Benjamin Franklin Room, eighth floor, State Department, 21st and "C" Streets, where Dean Rusk gives I.S. a medal.

January 18. Dinner at the White House. The presidential limousine calls for us at the Jefferson Hotel at 8 o'clock. Our arrival is timed via the driver's two-way radio, and we are checked at the gate. The White House lawn is covered with a light snow, and the ice-covered trees are like crystal chandeliers. TV lights flood the porch, around which a mob of cameramen is poised like a football team for the tackle. The Kennedys—taller than we expect, she more slender and he more Palm Beach color—emerge a moment before we do. He greets us in a public-address voice, she in a Marilyn Monroe pant. Meanwhile the photographers push, shout—"Hey, Jackie, look this way"—and even roll on the ground like the paparazzi in

1962 *La Dolce Vita.* Accompanying us through the foyer to an elevator, and from there to an upstairs reception room, the President inquires about Mr. Rusk's medal-pinning ceremony, and the progress of rehearsals for I.S.'s upcoming performances of *Oedipus Rex*.

The other guests are the Arthur Schlesingers, Pierre Salinger, Lee Radziwill and her friend Helen Chavchavadze, a beauty, whom JFK monopolizes during the pre-dinner conversation, the Leonard Bernsteins, Marshall Fields, Goddard Liebersons, Nicolas Nabokov, Max Freedman—in other words, more of a Kennedy-circle dinner, with political payoffs, than an I.S. dinner (Balanchine, Aldous, Auden, Perse, Isaiah Berlin, Kirstein, Paul Horgan).

The women sit on sofas by the fireplace while the men huddle around the President—until he pairs off with Chavchavadze; I.S. stays alone with Radziwill. For my own part, ignoring the obvious strategy of dulling minds and memories, I drain two Scotches too rapidly and can't get enough caviar, bad as that combination is, to help absorb them. Even so, talk is self-conscious and makeshift. One tries to appear blasé and not to look two steps away to the President or to "Jackie," who sits with V. Jackie's light gray eyes are prettier than in photographs, which in any case makes them dark brown, and the thin haggard look that female America is imitating is nonexistent. Afterward I remember nothing about the room, but a glimpse of the painting of a Western Plains Indian on the corridor wall facing the door gives me an unexpectedly patriotic shiver.

V. descends the staircase on the President's arm, I.S. and Jackie take the elevator, and I walk with Nabokov, who is droll and unprintable about the portraits of Taft and Harding on the walls. As we enter the State Dining Room, ushers lead us to our places, V. to the center with the President on her left, Jackie opposite with I.S. on her right, myself between Salinger and Mrs. Schlesinger, who talks about the novels of Anthony Powell—to my considerable relief, since I am politically up-to-date only on the Australian election. On the third round of champagne and near the end of the meal—*sole mousse*, *gigot* (V., later: "A perfect dinner for concierges")—the President toasts I.S., and at two shaky moments in her spouse's speech, Jackie's eyes show twinges of anxiety. "We have been honored to have two great artists with us in recent months," he begins, and I wonder if I.S. realizes that Casals is meant by the other. "When my wife was a student in Paris, she wrote an essay on Baudelaire, Oscar Wilde, and Diaghilev." (I.S., later: "I was afraid he was going to say that his wife had made a study of homosexuality.") "Now, I understand that you, Mr. Stravinsky, were a friend of Diaghilev's. And I have just been told that rocks and tomatoes were thrown at you in your youth." This is based on V.'s briefing during dinner, when the story of the *Sacre* premiere amazed the President and made him laugh aloud. I explain to I.S. later that "rocks and tomatoes" is an American rendering—they are thrown at baseball umpires—because he understood the statement literally. But the speech is short and, because an American President is honoring a great *creative* artist—an event unprecedented in American history—it is moving. As I.S. thanks him, the anxiety passes, quite unnecessarily, from Jackie's eyes to V.'s.

Afterward the men gather at one end of the table and the women retire to the Red Room. Forgetting, and anyway loathing, this barbaric British custom, I.S., wanting to be with V. and being dependent on the Russian words with which she puts him on track for what he fails to hear, starts to follow her. But Nabokov shepherds him back and seats him on the President's right. Cognac and cigars are passed around, and with them the character of the President's talk grows manifestly more masculine in terms of the frequent use of Anglo-Saxon tetragrams. "How do you feel now, Mr. Stravinsky?" he asks, and the answer is "Quite drunk, thank you, Mr. President." Marshall Field puts a question to I.S. about Prokofiev and the USSR. Seeing that I.S. does not understand, Leonard Bernstein comes to the rescue, though instead of stopping there, goes on to describe the reception of I.S.'s music in the new Russia: "I saw tears in people's eyes and not only for the *Sacre* but also for the Piano Concerto, which, after all, is an astringent piece." (I.S. *does* understand this and, talking to me later, is skeptical about the shedding of much lachrymal liquid over his Piano Concerto.) Duty done, the President's talk turns to politics, wherein he shows skill as a debater and an ability to bring arguments to a head. He even displays some evidence of reading, describing Sebastian Haffner's article on the Berlin crisis in *Encounter* as "playing to the gallery." His attention never wanders from other speakers when they have the floor, but this may be defensive, since he knows that every eye is trained on him. And he does seem to be saying what he thinks. Item: "We are essentially a conservative country, the liberal element always having been a small minority, and by liberal I mean, simply, open to new ideas." When at one point the discussion turns to syndicated columnists, he voices his opinions about each of them in unguarded and unminced terms. He even talks about Cuba without apologetics.

The Kennedys accompany us downstairs to the door and wait with us there for 15 minutes until the chauffeur, not anticipating our early retreat, is found. Here, alone with us, they are gracious, warm, and totally disarming. I.S., in the car: "Nice kids."

Back in the lobby of the Jefferson, V. is attacked by a scrimmage of newshens. Upstairs, I.S. remarks to her: *"Le président me rapelle un jeune homme de football qui ne peut pas jouer à cause de son mauvais dos."* But V. is not listening, being only immensely relieved that he did not try to engage the President in a tete-à-tete about having his taxes reduced.

January 19. The *Washington Post* this morning:

Dinner began with a filet of sole mousse instead of a soup course.

1962

Next came a shoulder of lamb with green beans prepared with almonds and cold stuffed hearts of artichoke. A French cheese was served with a green salad. Dessert was a parfait with fresh strawberries and little cakes.

Mrs. Kennedy's sister, Lee, the Princess Radziwill of London, was there, with a friend, Princess Char-Cha-Vadze. Mr. and Mrs. Marshall Field had come from Chicago. From New York came noted composer-conductor Leonard Bernstein and his lovely wife. Special Assistant to the President and Mrs. Arthur Schlesinger, Jr., and Mrs. Salinger were in the group. The Stravinskys came with the composer's co-conductor Robert Craft.

After dinner, Mrs. Kennedy led the women into the newly decorated Red Room and the President took the men into the Green Room—all except Igor Stravinsky. A devoted husband, he followed right along after his handsome wife into the Red Room. But an attendant came and escorted him to the President in the Green Room.

The men stayed briefly by themselves. As soon as they joined the ladies, Stravinsky went up to Mrs. Kennedy and made his excuses. She graciously insisted that he leave since she knew he had a difficult day ahead of him.

. . . Everyone admired the handsome long, two-piece gown in which Mrs. Kennedy received the Stravinskys in the cold and chilly night outdoors. She and the President walked outside the door of the Diplomatic Room and stood in the cold without wraps as the Stravinskys got out of the White House car sent to conduct them to the party.

Lunch at Perse's with Auden, who is wearing not merely dark, but black glasses, like a blind beggar. The poets sit side by side, but since neither wishes to speak the other's language, Auden comes through on my side during most of the meal. His opener to Perse seems a little odd—"By the way, what is the French for *Hühneraugen?*"—but since his most recent poem begins with this word (corns), we wonder if the question is really concerned with French translation or with Auden's podiatric problems. In any case, V. advises him to try space shoes; the footwear he has on looks as if it had been borrowed from a peasant out of Brueghel.

Auden is still in his epigram-aphorism phase. For general enlightenment, he distinguishes the two in his characteristic (a) . . . (b) . . . form: "An aphorism must apply to everyone, past and present, but an epigram need apply only to particular cases and to a single person. Wilde's description of fox hunting, 'The pursuit of the uneatable by the unspeakable,' is an epigram because it would be understood only by certain people at a certain time. On the other hand, his 'A cynic is a person who knows the price of everything and the value of nothing,' is an aphorism because it is universally comprehensible." French examples are cited first, probably in deference to Perse, except that Auden assures me: "La Rochefoucauld's are inferior to the Marquis of Halifax's, and Flaubert is only a provincial manufacturer of them." His favorite French example is Proust's "In matters of love it is easier to overcome a deep feeling than to renounce a habit." Asking I.S. for Russian examples, and being told that the best are in Turgenev and Herzen, Auden goes on to say, "I became rather wary of the Russians after the first sentence of *Anna Karenina*, which, obviously, should be the other way around. Now, if you are going to do aphorisms, surely the first thing is to get them right."

He offers a string of instances from Karl Kraus, whom he calls "one of the great people of the century." I quote the Kraus-ism about how, in 1919, he proposed to have the Austrian national anthem changed from "God Save the King" to "Thank God for saving us *from* the King"; but since this does not contribute to the quotient of aphorisms, Auden only frowns. Although the crest of his Teutonic period must soon be due, he tells us that his cablegram to Robert Graves on the occasion of the latter's inaugural Poetry Professor lecture at Oxford was in German.

Switching to operas, Auden declares *Die Frau ohne Schatten* "Hofmannsthal's best, except for the M-G-M ending." Commenting on Karajan's *Ring*, he remarks on the conductor's "extraordinary devotion to the dark. Most of it took place in a blackout, presumably for an audience of owls, and with Brünnhilde singing about *'Die Sonne'* the whole time. Nor did we have all of the *Ring*! The stagehands struck after *Siegfried*."

Talking about *The Flood*, I.S. says that the visual representation of the Devil puzzles him: "My first idea was to photograph a mobile red spot. But the flood itself is very clear in my mind. I do not want waves, or any back-and-forth movement. I have an idea instead for a single dancer turning this way and that and bobbing like a piece of wood, always in the same place. I saw an underwater film of the Red Sea not long ago and was impressed by the way the fish came right up to the bathysphere. They were exceedingly confident monsters!"

Auden's best remark is: "Narcissus was a hydrocephalic idiot who thought 'on me it looks good.' " He pronounces a certain novel "the best queer book of the year," and he maintains that its author, "who is as ambidextrous as a polyp, uses his wife more as a shield than as a resource." Later, apropos of I no longer remember what, Perse remarks that *"La justice est une invention suisse."* Auden doesn't hear this, but when we all laugh, he springs to attention, afraid he may have missed a new aphorism (or was it an epigram?). He departs early, saying he is on his way to attend a Mass for black Africans. "Heaven knows they need it, poor things. The world has had enough of Uncle Tshombe's Cabin."

In the evening, I.S. conducts *Oedipus Rex* and I conduct *L'Heure espagnole*.

1962   **February 4.** Hollywood. Letter from Julian Faigan in Auckland: "I hope that you remember who I am; I met you at the rehearsal here on the night before the concert of Stravinsky's works. After the concert, I didn't get a chance to tell you how much I enjoyed it. It was really wonderful—a great experience to see the composer himself and to hear our orchestra play so well. I have spoken with many members of the orchestra since that concert and they all say that they liked working under you."

February 23. Letter from George Dreyfus of the Melbourne orchestra: "Most of the orchestra realized that we played disastrously and we're very disappointed, seeing all the hard work you had put into rehearsals. Don't think of us too badly—we tried—but are definitely not used to the precision, tension, call it what you will, of your music making. But after all, you did come to Melbourne and did conduct our orchestra and, like many others, I won't forget it for a very long time."

March 15. Work with I.S. and Balanchine on *The Flood* staging. Letter from Spender at the University of Virginia: "Dear Bob, Thank you most tremendously for the typescript. It certainly is fascinating—the most interesting section of this masterpiece I have read. It is quite miserable here. Dingy, stuffy, dark rooms, in this godawful town, miles from anywhere, frightful weather, and no company. The business about Southern hospitality doesn't apply to the university. . . . It was lovely seeing you in California, and you were most kind to us. Thank you very much. Yours affectionately, Stephen."

March 28. Record *The Flood* in the new CBS studio on Sunset Boulevard, spending most of the time correcting errors in the parts. Miraculous music. I.S. has fully understood film time, that it can be slowed down and speeded up, that images can follow each other without transition.

May 5. New York. At CBS, 485 Madison Avenue, Balanchine, Bernstein, the S.s, and I attend a private screening of Bernstein's New York Philharmonic performance of *Oedipus*, which I.S. likes. During lunch with the Bernsteins at The Four Seasons, Felicia spills a Bloody Mary in, of all places, the lap of her white dress. Bernstein, amazingly, remembers the very British translation of *Noces* in I.S.'s 1934 recording, and sings passages of it for us.

May 8. Sail to Le Havre on the S.S. *Flandre*.

May 14. Because of a railroad strike, François-Michel meets us at Le Havre with three automobiles, one for the baggage, one for the Russian-speaking passengers (Suvchinsky), and one for the French. We stop at the cathedral in Rouen, then on to Paris and the Berkeley.

May 15. Visit from Isaiah. Many of his sentences conclude with upsets belied by the preceding adjectives, *e.g.*: X. is "intelligent, charming, capable, and a complete crook." On *New Yorker* short stories: "Their best feature is that you don't actually have to read them." He describes a meeting with an Italian impresario to discuss a proposed visit to Israel by the San Carlo Opera: The Israelis wanted to omit the "San" and have the company appear as the "Carlo" Opera, to which the Italian response was: "I suppose you want us to perform *La Clemenza di Tito*." Isaiah says that while he was strolling with Auden one afternoon, they were startled by a thunderclap, after which Auden exclaimed, "Oh dear, the headmaster must be angry."

Dinner at Beatrice Rothschild's with Giacometti.

May 16. Lunch at the Plaza-Athénée with Samuel Beckett, a tall, thin man with furrowed forehead, wrinkled and aggrieved face, long fingers, much potential silver-mining in his teeth, and the modesty and retiring manners of an oblate. His startlingly blue, deep-set eyes and bristling straight-up hair remind me of a bluejay. "I have motored in from my country house in a sardine can," he says, in a soft, light, musical voice, and from his description of the vehicle, we are surprised, seeing it later, not to find the tires wrapped in rags.

"I first met Yeats in Dublin, in 1934. W.B. never gave the impression that he had any sense of humor, but that was far from the case. I knew Jack Yeats better than I knew W.B. Their father considered Jack the more gifted son. I don't agree, do you?" At one point V. says that critics should be ignored, this for I.S.'s benefit, since he is quarreling with one at the moment. "Yes," Beckett replies, "but some of them live such a long time." He expresses interest in the possibilities of notating the tempo of the performance of a play, and of exactly timing the pauses. Not surprisingly, I.S. likes the idea of such controls* but thinks that circumstances are too variable. When de Gaulle is mentioned, Beckett remarks that he is "beginning to sound like Péguy."

The most common artifacts at the "Ancient Art of the Tchad" exhibition in the Grand Palais are labrets of shell and bone, cow masks, and bolas with stone weights shaped and carved for traction like hand grenades. The show is rich in figurines of cows, hippos, crocodiles, "fretful porpentines"; and in statuettes of dancers with distended lips, and other sanctuary idols from the necropolis of Butte de Medigué.

I.S. and I go to visit Cocteau. He is not at home, but a young friend, in the shower when we arrive, dresses quickly and chases after him to a café a few blocks away. At length, worryingly pale and breathless from the exertion of running and climbing the stairs, the *enfant terrible devenu monstre sacré* arrives and is a prince of hospitality, affectionate, simple, and genuinely moved by I.S.'s act of attention. When we leave, he gives I.S. a copy of *Cérémonial espagnol*, drawing a head on the flyleaf. Dinner at Chez Laurent

---

* This is not all that the two men believed in common. I.S.: "Music is powerless to express anything at all." S.B.: "There is nothing to express, nothing with which to express, nothing from which to express, no power to express. . . ."

1962 (Rond Point des Champs-Elysées) with Boulez, Spender,* *et al.*

May 17. A visit from Spender.** An early evening flight from Le Bourget to Nice, then over the Sahara.

May 18. Brazzaville. 6 A.M. A salmon sky streaked with violet and mother-of-pearl. We come in low over the swirling Congo and its plumes of mist, tilting toward the runway above tin roofs surrounded by green the color of frozen peas. Our spectacles smear with moisture as we step out into the sodden heat. I.S. pretends to be concerned that the natives might be anthropophagous.

Breakfast in the terminal's open air restaurant is served by French-speaking waiters wearing the billowing black trousers of women in Turkish harems. The walls groan with the heads of big game, but these trophies inhibit my appetite less than the numerous giant cockroaches promenading about and the smell of cooking in palm oil. The clothing of some of the souvenir sellers at the entrance is skimpy; while some are in standard European dress, some are wrapped in blankets, and some sport skullcaps and ankle-length robes with blue or green stripes. Most people are remarkably short in stature.

Leopoldville, from the air, is a mixture of Le Corbusier and thatched huts. Thereafter, the Congo basin is covered with a film of blue smoke. We cross the Zambesi, loops of bronze foil, not far east of Victoria Falls. The red Rhodesian desert is marked by lonely, island-like clumps of trees, by jebels—monument-like formations of black boulders—and a dirt track on which a car raises a dust cloud a mile high. The guards in Salisbury terminal—stovepipe tarbooshes, long white robes, shoulder-to-waist sword sashes, cummerbunds—might be soldiers of Toussaint l'Ouverture.

Near Johannesburg the khaki desert is broken by trees, evidently planted only recently against erosion, and the sky is full of slowly dissipating funnels of smoke. The slag heaps of the gold mines, gray-white, sulphur-colored mounds, are like giant cake molds, or Chichen Itzas.

White Johannesburg is a bilingual city, like Brussels and Montreal, and English is the minority language; and a new city: I.S. remarks that he is older by a decade; and predominantly white: room service in our hotel, the Carlton, and all "higher" types of domestic service, is provided by East

---

* Spender describes the dinner in his Journals: "About a dozen people there, including Simone Signoret and husband. I sat far away from Stravinsky. When the party broke up, Stravinsky was still very lively, violently denouncing to the head of French Radio the attitudes of French wrters to him in 1922."

** According to Spender's Journals, he "Called at Berkeley Hotel to say goodbye to Stravinsky and Bob Craft. Stravinsky was sitting up in his chair with bright eyes like some creature in a Beatrix Potter drawing. He was excited about going to Africa, and showed me Alan Moorehead's books, especially a photo of a rhino. 'I want to see that animal,' he said, 'it's like this. . . .' Suddenly he was on all fours, his stick with hook turned up like a horn, his eyes stared—a rhinoceros."

Indians, while lift boys, porters, and menial workers generally are Bantu. **1962** When V. asks our Afrikaans driver if the churches are segregated, the reassuring tone of his "Yes" explains his confusion over her further question: "Is Heaven segregated, too?" The Bantu live in special districts, as do, but apart from them, the "coloreds," meaning Muslims, half-castes, or anyone neither white—Chinese and Japanese are legally white—nor Bantu. The character of the city, nevertheless, derives from the customs and occupations—rickshaw taxi-ing, head-bundle toting (women only)—of the Bantu. After dark many of them squat on the curb, huddling by gutter fires: the night is cool at this altitude (6000 feet), and we wear top coats.

Johannesburg is one of World War II's major refugee cities, and all European and many other countries are represented in the orchestra. A Budapest-born cellist tells me that he was a prisoner of the Japanese in Indonesia and came to South Africa after the war because of its opportunities. A Yugoslav woman describes how, four years ago, she and her mother and daughter abandoned their automobile on a highway near the Austrian border, fled through the woods to Austria and eventual asylum here. A violinist from Amsterdam says she survived the Occupation there by living like Anne Frank. From the other side of the political fence, our Italian headwaiter tells us that he was interned in Ethiopia, where he learned Amharic and Gheez; our elderly German room maid is the widow of a Berlin archeologist who was working in Tanganyika at the outbreak of the war and who was taken by the British to a camp in Rhodesia, where he died. South Africa welcomes these people because they are "white," and because, probably wishing to forget the injustices they have suffered abroad, few of them recognize and protest the same things here.

The orchestra and chorus are entirely "white." This provokes I.S. to ask whether both mightn't be improved if the personnel were not drawn exclusively from the ruling minority. "Isn't it likely," he asks an Afrikaans musician, "that in so large a country some 'nonwhite' might learn to play the bass drum even better than the 'white' musician now in charge of that instrument? Or, if that seems improbable, certainly you will agree that some nonwhites must be blessed with voices that could improve or at least swell the chorus." The Afrikaans musician's answer is that the nonwhites have their own chorus, and that it is much better than the white one. In this case, I.S. says, *he* should have the nonwhite chorus because his goal is the best possible performance of his music—the segregationist argument the other way around, except that "best possible" means "regardless of color," which is not a logical argument in South Africa, though, of course, no one pretends that logic has anything to do with racism.

The Dutch-descended Afrikaans we meet are courteous and hospitable in various ways imputed to Southern "colonels" in the United States. Because they anticipate criticism of apartheid, conversation is always straying guiltily toward it. Their argument is that they have developed the

1962   country and achieved the highest living standards for all the people in all of Africa. Now they are being asked to grant a vote that would reduce them to a powerless minority and force them to abandon everything they have labored so hard to build. They claim to be victims of the colonial inheritance as much as the nonwhites, and complain that world publicity has never dared to state that side of the case. Their main emphasis is that the nonwhite population is incomparably better off now than a decade ago, and, materially speaking, this is true, however incomplete the argument. Finally, "The nonwhites do not want integration and are not ready for equality"—nothing is said about whose fault it might be that after all this time they still aren't—"whereas apartheid is a tradition as old as European South Africa, indeed, the basis of the culture." These arguments are familiar in the southern United States, of course, for which reason American criticism is regarded as hypocritical: "In the United States, integration exists on statute books," they say, "but from the White House down, American Negroes are a servant class and a zoned people." To which I can only reply, lamely, that we are at least trying, and, well, three cheers for those statute books.

May 20. On our way to the Western Areas Gold Mine to watch tribal dances, we pass Diepkloof, of *Cry the Beloved Country*, and Carletonville, a mining city of 50,000 inhabitants that was an empty plateau only a few years ago. The road follows the great reef of auriferous conglomerates, and the country is humped and pyramided all the way by gray, beige, white, and—from the cyanide used in placer processing—green-blue slag heaps. It is also marked by power stations and corset-shaped hoist towers, from which shafts are sunk 7,000 feet to below sea level.

The Bantu on the roadside sell oranges and watermelons, or simply loll in the grass, or prop themselves against trees. When ambling along the highway they tend to group around someone playing a musical instrument, which induces shuffling dance movements. The most popular of these improvised instruments is a two-string tabor with a flattened-petrol-can sounding-box and a piece of railing for the backboard. The men shade themselves with color-striped parasols, the women with head bundles. Nearing the mines, we reduce our speed, for the sake of newly-arrived tribesmen so unaccustomed to automobiles that they have been known to run out in front of them, like headlight-blinded animals.

The dances are held in the compound of Blyvooruitzicht— "*Blyvoraussicht*," or "Happy Prospects," an Orwell-inspired name, surely, since the workers live like paid prisoners, or at any rate look like them as they stand in queues and hold out their mess tins to receive dollops of gruel. The miners serve a term of six months, then return rich to their villages. They come from tribes as far away as Rhodesia, Mozambique, and Bechuanaland, as well as from the Swaziland and Basutoland protectorates.

The ambit of the dance area is a circular grandstand filled with Basuto and "blanket people"—men in blue-violet karosses and tightly wrapped pink or khaki blankets. The Basuto wear straw hats with pagoda-like knobs, and European trousers artistically patched, *not* necessarily because worn or frayed but because the wearer likes the pattern. Ears, ankles, and upper arms are adorned with metal rings, but never in a uniform way. Indeed, individuality to this extent is never apparent in any crowd of comparable size in Europe or America, and more wit is manifest in the costumes of the dancers than in the creations of Europe's most expensive couturiers (which may not be a great compliment). Here, moreover, everything is improvised from no other source materials than can be found in dustbins. Nonconformist, too, is the audience participation. A man in front of me sways to the sound of his jew's harp without a regard for the arena, while others laugh and heckle. Spectators come and go throughout the performances. From time to time, the wind raises scarves of dust and a sickish, ammoniac smell of perspiration.

Each dance group moves around the arena, completing a circle. At about the halfway point, the next team, noisily revving up outside like the next bronco in a rodeo, begins to agitate for its turn, with a rally of singing and hand-clapping. When these preliminaries become unduly protracted, the leader hectors his company forward with a whistle, assisted by uniformed policemen, who, to the delight of the audience, do not resist dancing along and otherwise getting into the act themselves.

The music is not intended as a concert for the grandstand but is directed exclusively to the dancers; the guitars and concertinas are inaudible to us. The clapping and the stomping precipitate dust storms, increased by the feats, inspired by the Swazi drumming, of rolling, leaping, kicking, and high-jumping among spectators as well as dancers. The musical instruments, like the dancers' costumes, have been put together from crude and improbable materials. An orchestra of reed flutes, each player contributing a single note, like carillons or Webern, provides the subtlest music. The loudest is a charivari of jingles, rattles, and bells attached to automobile tire inner tubes wrapped around the dancers' legs. It accompanies a Xosa ritual in which the dancers shimmy, shiver, squat, crouch, and fling their arms up like praying mantises.

One performer wears a miner's aluminum helmet, a belt strung with a dozen neckties, and a flossy mophead tied to each knee. The entire garb of another, a would-be comedian—catcalls drown the laughter—is a grass hula skirt and a large comb stuck like a cockade in his stubble hair. More amusing for onlookers are the "in drag" antics of a great muscular creature in a green beret and a woman's fur boa.

The last dance, by a dozen men from the Machupi tribe of the Limpopo River, is the most spectacular, and so is the dress: white skirts and ankle feathers; purple, blue, black, and green tail feathers; deerskin headgear and shield covers. At the climax of this dangerous-looking ballet, after a

1962 tremendous gust of sound, the music stops suddenly, as if truncated by an invisible force, and the dancers plunge their hatchets into the earth in blood-freezing silence, hurling their shields to the ground afterward and savagely somersaulting over them. In spite of assurances to us from the manager of the mine that "it is not a war dance," the action can only have intended the extinction of the receiving parties. This time, the musicians, wearing winglike ostrich feathers, are separated from the dancers—for safety's sake. They play ratchets and a battery of marimbas made of scrap-metal slats placed on a trestle of empty barrels. The melody is repeated over and over, in crescendo, and in several ranges simultaneously, the larger barrels in augmentation against the smaller ones.

May 22. I.S. receives a letter from a woman in Durban who says she knew him in the Hotel des Crêtes, Clarens, in 1913, and who wants to be certain he is "the same Russian composer who used to pound the piano there all day long." Our concert tonight draws pickets with placards reading: "Only the Moor is not admitted." But how many people will recognize the *Petrushka* reference?

May 26. The Ndebeli (Mapok) kraal is in an olive-and-yellow landscape stretching to a pink desert horizon. Near the gate, a monument to "the pioneers who broke the Zulu nation" reminds us of similar piles of stone in the American West commemorating slaughters of Indians. Inside the kraal, Bantu men, with dogs and long-tailed Persian sheep, raise their hats and wave their knobkerries in friendly greeting. The land is sadly desiccated, and the streams—with names like "Sand River" and, more optimistically, "Fountain" this or "Fountain" that—are all dry.

The kraal huts stand behind a long white wall on which "windows," "shutters," "doors"—in the form of diamonds and squares, none of which is exactly straight and whose symmetry is quite drunk—have been painted in bright green, purple, and orange. Below and in front of these glittering designs is a sun deck on which the Ndebeli women sit like queens at court, in heavy raiment. The Ndebelis are a matrilineal society, and a visit to their village quickly quashes any belief in the universality of the Oedipus complex. The power of continuing the culture resides exclusively with the female. While wives are bought with biblical numbers of cattle, husbands are sunk in mortgages and denied access to the purchase until paid for in full. The female remains in command after marriage, too, which is less unusual, and she determines whether her spouse shares the hut or sleeps outside. One disadvantage, however, quite literally outweighs all the wife's advantages: these Amazonians are so heavily shackled in brass bracelets from wrist to elbow and from ankle to knee that they are scarcely able to move.

Ndebeli women wear necklaces of woven grass encased in beads and, like the bracelets, welded on and permanent. The women are also wrapped in colored blankets and their sex, even of the youngest baby, is concealed by beaded aprons and a beaded G-string. Male children, in *1962* contrast, are naked except for flies, which nobody heeds, though they are whisked away from their sisters. Unmarried adolescent girls are naked from their aprons up, which enables us to see that from a mammary point of view the female is in decline, in an exact sense, from about the age of 13. Not so their meridional proportions. The staple millet is swilled in such bulk that abdomens are as distended as they would be a week or so before an accouchement. The coiffures of these Ndebeli belles feature four small tufts, like phylacteries, on skulls otherwise smoothly mown and glistening with pomatum of lamb fat.

The interiors of the huts are painted in the same style as the wall. We buy admittance with gifts of snuff to giggling female elders, purchased near the entrance, along with beaded figurines. The whole kraal is busily beading to fill a Christmas order for Macy's.

May 27. We drive to Springs, a mining city surrounded by piles of yellow slag, to give a concert for the Bantus there. The houses are tin-roofed shanties, but new communities are pointed out to us, with expressions of regret that the people are "not yet ready to live in such dwellings," the old argument against housing developments in U.S. slums. At sunset, thousands of women appear, balancing tins of water on their heads.

Much more than the concert itself, the audience enjoys the demonstrations of instruments preceding it, especially the percussion, the trombone when it "slides," and the tuba when it suggests gastroenteritis. At the conclusion of the program, appreciation is expressed by the singing of a dolorous Protestant hymn, as if on purpose to remind us of the cultural confusion wrought by colonialism. Why should a people with its own rich and varied music greet us with this dismal specimen of the captors' art? The Afrikaans' answer is that city Bantu despise their own "Kaffir culture." But the Afrikaans have been disingenuous in their reasons for scheduling the concert in the first place, since it was transparently a demonstration, for our benefit, that the benighted blacks are not yet ready for European culture and that the Bantu really are savages. Isn't it just conceivable, however, that the Bantu might resent a concert given uniquely for them, in their compound, a white orchestra and a black audience? *"Bantu"* means men, and *"Muntu"* man. But how were the ancestors of these poor people to know, when they created the words, that other Bantu existed in the world and that they were "white"?

On our return at night to Pretoria, a fire raging on the veldt is like a prehistoric tableau.

May 28. Our hotel, the Union, is Victorian in physique, style of service, and meals, which include copious breakfasts and teas. Our Bantu room waiter has heard that I am American, yet seems surprised to find that I speak something more or less resembling English. He asks if I know "the American Negro orchestra conductor, Dean Dixon?" I say I do, and I laud

Dixon, adding that I enjoyed playing under him in my student days in New York (which is true), but failing to mention that Dixon was unable to find a conducting post in the United States for the racist reason.

Pretoria is a city of pillared porches, Dutch-colonial gingerbread, and some bronze, most notably in the statue of President Kruger, glowering on a pedestal in the plaza. Our concert is in City Hall.

May 29. An early departure for Kruger Park, in two cars, with the Anton Hartmanns and Johann Van Der Meer. On the roadside: Bantu boys carrying calabashes and bags of oranges on their heads; metal-collared Bantu women, as melonous and protuberant as fertility idols, with baskets and rolled-up sleeping mats on their heads; Bantu men sleeping comfortably on two-wheeled bullock carts. All Bantu heads are covered, all white ones are bare-headed.

The fields near Witbank, a coal and carbide city at the beginning of the carboniferous beds of the eastern Transvaal, grow sunflowers—the seed oil is a major export—gerberas, yellow wattles, arums, aloes. This is Swazi country, with domed Zulu-style huts, in front of which tall native women stand erect and motionless, selling watermelons.

Belfast, the highest point of the upper veldt, is in a region of salt lakes, which look saltier than they are because of white birds on the shores, like the salt crystals on the rim of a Margarita cocktail glass. The landscape a little farther along is weird, owing partly to the vegetation—scrubby, black-stemmed proteas, milk-white eucalyptus, blue gum trees—but mainly to the anthills. Small, mump-like papilli, until now, they are eight or nine feet tall here, and parched and porous, like Gaudí's stucco towers. Machadodorp, a city of willows and lime-colored mimosas, is warmer, and, soon after, the climate is fully tropical; the natives carry umbrellas and live in straw and grass tukals. We stop at a picnic site in which the garbage disposal is left to scavenger baboons.

At the entrance to Kruger Park, we are required to sign sworn affidavits that we do not have firearms or other weapons. The road inside the Numbi gate is dusty, tortuous, narrow, but immediately rich with signs of spoor: tracks, ordure, munched and trampled bushes. The shapes of trees are sinister: the flat-crowned thorn trees with wizened trunks, the wild figs, the baobabs, the cassias with pendant pods, the white bougainvilleas, the flame of Africa, the red-flowered Kaffir plum trees with hanging finch nests, and the tall fever trees—so-called because they are the complexion of a man with yellow fever. The dry season has begun, and except for riverbanks the park is brown.

Suddenly, about 20 feet from the road, we see a waterbuck in a glade, black horns, violently twitching ears, and on the rump a white circle like a brand. He watches us over his shoulder, poised to run, but does not move until we do. We should expect to find two cows nearby, but the girls do not appear and we drive on. This encounter turns the park into a spell, and we go forward—I do, anyway—with clenched nerves.

Two bends in the road beyond, we come upon an impala herd: brown backs beautifully sheened, beige stomachs, black grill-striped behinds, pinched tails, dainty white feet, black ankles like Russian ladies' fur-lined boots. The antlered leader, in the center of the pack, wiggles his ears and grunts a warning that frightens a young doe and causes it to leap like Pavlova. Impala travel in safari, like a cavalcade of camels, but group when they graze.

A duiker appears next, picking its way in a henlike head-first pecking movement. Then a family of koodoo, the women and children feeding; nor do they interrupt on our account, though the mandarin-bearded buck lifts his streamlined horns and watches us with distrust. Koodoo are identified by large ears, white lipstick, white forelegs tufted at the knees like the evzone costume, lightly striped coats, long black flyswatter tails, and white tickbirds riding perkily on their backs.

At the Pretorius Kop entrepot we go out to see a pair of West African rhinoceros soon to be released into the park; full of tranquilizers—phencyclidine, chlordiszepoxide—they doze like barrels of wet dynamite. At Skurukwan we walk from the road to the hippo pool accompanied by armed rangers, the only place in the park where visitors, if protected by guards, are permitted to leave their cars; not long ago a man was mauled to death here by a lion. Hippos, submerged on a shoal near the opposite shore, are invisible except for their conning-tower nostrils and eyes, with which the surface of the river bristles. Suddenly one of the great graminivorous brutes raises his keel, yawns—a vast, obscene red maw—and snorts—a truck stripping gears—whereupon the whole otiose herd surfaces with an ear-cracking detonation and proceeds to blow, bellow, gargle, and spout like any gang of beach bullies. Because of this we do not hear, but luckily chance to see, a mother hippo slip out of the foliage on the mudbank a few feet from us, where she has been bolting branches and fouling the river. The sight of the young one sheltering between her hind legs makes me ashamed of the foregoing unkind epithets.

Back on the road are purple-gray wildebeests, timorous creatures with black eyes or mascara. And baboons, who sit like stumps in the center of the road, then leap to our hood, fenders, rear window, and ride along with us, making us feel like politicians in a parade. I fetch a candy in the glove compartment, open a slit of window, pass it through, and in an instant the receiving baboon is on the windshield pointing to the compartment and demanding more. Soon they will be saying, "Go home, Yank!"

It is now animal rush hour by the river. A sable antelope crosses the road, running with an end-to-end, rocking-horse movement; a hyena, with a sloped, gargoyle-like back; a steenbok fawn; a bush-buck lamb; and a warthog that, seeing us, charges into the woods with tail straight up like a flag. Elephant defecations and devastations—wide swaths of broken branches—have been increasingly evident, but they do not prepare us for the sight of a huge bull of the species bursting into the road 20 feet ahead. Taller than the trees and far larger than I remember the proboscideans in circuses and zoos, he thrashes about as if greatly agitated, ears flapping like sails. We fear that a herd may follow him, or, if he is a rogue elephant feeling trapped by our presence, that he may charge us. Neither contingency develops, and he simply turns and re-enters the forest, but an elephant in the wild is an awesome thing, and we hold our breaths passing his point of exit.

Skukuza Kamp, the largest in the park, billets 500 people in rondavels, and as many more in a tented bivouac area. The dining-room decor—animal trophies, witch doctors' mantic objects, Zulu shields and assegais— offers no respite from the park, and neither does tonight's outdoor film on African arachnids. The flashlight of the ranger who guides me to my rondavel discovers hyena and baboons on our side of the Kamp's low wire fence. He says that they are waiting to burgle citrus fruit and leather shoes, and that they are adept at opening the doors of huts and automobiles. Several times during the night a lion roars nearby.

May 30. At 5 A.M., after a breakfast of Skukuza *pirozhki*, we drive along the Sabie River in elephant and lion country. Shortly after, the sun rises orange, but turns white in seven minutes. Our first animal is a baboon sitting at a fork in the road like a traffic cop. Soon other baboons appear, scratching themselves, nursing pink offspring, clamoring for and receiving tourists' handouts—a defection to the welfare state bound to disturb the ecological dependencies, except that in the abundance of Kruger Park, the chain must overlap as well as interlock; impalas are so plentiful that a lion has merely to reach out as they go by, like grabbing a sandwich in a cafeteria.

Only yards away we see two great glistening elephants nonchalantly consuming a tree. They take no notice of us, and go on crunching their morning lumber with as much noise, in scale, as any American at his crackle-and-pop cereal. As we drive away, a monkey jumps from a tree, grasps our radio aerial, and rides on the fender like a straphanger in a subway. Its face is black, its body gray-white, its testicles billiard-chalk blue, and its tail, in contrast to the baboon's, which loops cheekily upward like a girl's pony tail, drops down straight away. Rounding a turn, we encounter eight lions in the road ahead, the elders prowling leisurely in our direction, the youngsters playfully pummeling each other. They must have had their *petit déjeuner* by now, since an antelope, on the wrong side of the wind, has crossed the road only a few yards back, perhaps knowing, however, that the lions were sated. The lions ignore us, yet give no ground to our car, as if, like Berkeleians, they could deny its existence simply by refusing to look. But the true explanation is Ortega y Gasset's "The animal fears man, who has been created by Nature, but he does not fear the unnatural artifact of human fabrication."

When one of the lions pads by my window only inches away, the glare from its cold yellow eyes crosses my heartbeat like a shadow of ice. The thought occurs that the lion may be using the car to cover its scent, but it lopes into a thicket, where it yawns as harmlessly as an actor in a summer theater during an intermission in Shaw's *Androcles*. The young gambol into the bush, too, and have soon melted without trace into the landscape. Who would now suspect this undergrowth to be part lion, and who, thus initiated, would trust the appearance of the jungle?

Birds are everywhere: glossy starlings; blue-casqued guinea fowl; red-beaked honey birds; yellow, waddling hornbills; purple-crested lories; violet troupands; black butcher-bird birdcallers, who impale the victims of their dissembling on thorns; a black bird with a prima donna breast, long flappy wings, and a tail like a ray fish—of such length, in fact, that the creature seems to float from tree to tree like a glider. A single bird in a tree always seems to perch on the topmost branch, like a hatpin, or on the tip of the most extended side limb. Vultures, appropriately, seem to prefer dead or totally bare trees, but whirlpools of them are always present in the sky.

Near lower Sabie, the road, running along an expanse of river, exposes a crocodile on the far bank, its jaws half open in a depraved grin. As we watch, a second crocodile climbs to a rock, midstream, where a kingfisher loops over it like a stunt flyer, alighting on the reptile's dripping back to look for encrusted edibles, and, finding none, stands there in a daredevil pose, vainly preening.

The roadside is dense with impala, their coats, in the early morning cold, a frizzy, goose-flesh fur. The sight of two impala rams fighting inside a widely scattered circle of ewes and charging each other like jousting knights—the ferocity of the combat and the ugly grunting noises—would forever destroy, for movie-bred children, the sentimental Disney image of the doe in a dingle.

About a mile from lower Sabie we espy a leopard couchant in a copse only a few feet from the road. It sniffs the air and twitches its whiskers like any house cat and with incomparably greater felinity than a lioness. Birds scream when it walks, a movement of such litheness that the lion is a hobbler in comparison. Walking, it displays a sleek white throat, a lustrous rosetted back, and a slowly sloping tail with upsweep at the end, compared to which the lion's tail is a mere knout. It wants to cross the road to the riverside but can find no egress in the suddenly formed barricade of tourists' cars.

Returning to Skukuza on the northern river road, reputedly a good one on which to see zebra, we sight giraffe first, pruning treetops. They are a pure fantasy animal, more so here, in their habitat, than in a zoo: unicorns would be less surprising. A moment later a dozen or more come into view

1962 at the riverbank. They have white earflaps, are cornuted like Michelangelo's *Moses*, and they cross necks like French generals embracing. To drink the water, they must spread and sprawl, a posture so clumsy and vulnerable that one marvels at the survival of the freak at all. Finding itself discovered, another giraffe, peering at us over the top of a tree like a gardener over a hedge, ambles away in a long side-to-side roller-skating movement, the hind leg of each side touching the ground first, then the longer front leg.

Zebras are even less trusting. We surprise 20 to 30 of them prancing nervously in a field. Despite their considerable distance from us, the mares cautiously shield the foals. Every surface is striped, from dewlap to fetlock, whorled nose to Cathedral-of-Siena legs. Some koodoo are grazing nearby, pooling their more powerful auditory radar with the zebra's more acute olfactory sense. "An *entente cordiale*," I.S. says.

The chief game warden, our host at tonight's Skukuza campfire dinner—of *polenta* and *sosatie* (haslets spitted like shashlik)—says that a close count is kept of elephants in the park and a reasonable estimate of the lion population, but all other censuses, and especially of impala, which must fluctuate radically at lion lunchtime, are unknown.* The warden says that he once saw a crocodile catch and kill an impala at the riverbank and hide the cadaver in a cave: "A 'croc' does not eat fresh meat but stores it until it gets 'high.' " He also tells us about the discovery of a cannibals' ossuary in the Limpopo mountain region of the park: and imparts fascinating information about a variety of creatures including the edible lizard (the dthub), the fennec, the rhim, and the nearly extinct oryx, which is being imported from Arabia to breed here. But the most appealing of his stories is about a baboon in a tree suddenly seeing a lion directly below and fainting. Henceforth we will feel more sympathetic toward baboons.

May 31. The sun rises from a lavender sky, matches every shade on the color chart from blood red to white and turns the river mist into a cataract of gold dust.

Just outside the Kamp we meet three lions, a "triangle," evidently, with monsieur trying to growl away *le gigolo*. And a crapulous trio, to judge by the vultures overhead. Farther on, two more lions, young ones with incipient manes, bound across the road only four or five yards in front of the car.

A driver from the opposite direction tells us of a large herd of elephants around the next bend, on the far bank of the Sabie, almost hidden by reeds and palms and visible only through binoculars. Information of this sort is exchanged everywhere in the park—"Beyond the bridge about 30 yards to the left we saw an ostrich"—and without it we would have missed a great deal.

---

* According to Cuvier, "*Les espèces sont nécessaires, les unes comme proies, les autres comme destructeurs et moderateurs de propagation.*"

The road between Mbyamite and the southern gate is the wildest and loneliest of all, and the animals seem doubly alert, perhaps because of the tall, lion-concealing grass. A saddle-backed jackal, silver with red-clay-colored belly, runs zigzag from us like a professional fugitive; or, as *Venus and Adonis* puts it:

> . . . to overshoot his troubles,
> How he outruns the wind, and with what care
> He counts and crosses with a thousand doubles.

The country is more weird at each turn, and the anthills suggest the chimneys of H.G. Wells's Morlocks, or of subterranean survivors of the next war. Leaving the park, I.S. remarks: "Animals do not have to *do*, they just *are*," which sounds like his "A nose is" philosophy.

June 1. From Pretoria to Johannesburg and the flight to Capetown. For our benefit, the pilot circles Table Mountain, the Twelve Apostles, and the Bay area, which obligingly lights up as we land. It is a Côte d'Azur climate, with palms and umbrella pines, but the white houses with black shutters and brick houses with iron balconies and tin roofs are remote from anything Mediterranean. Political resistance slogans on the road from the airport, FREEDOM'S GOING, REMEMBER SHARPVILLE, STOP THE VORSTER NAZI BILL, are as numerous as roadside advertisements in the United States. We drive past rugby fields and through the market place—Dutch flower stalls, two-wheeled Bantu handcarts—to the Mount Nelson Hotel, which, for liveliness, would compare unfavorably with a sanatorium for paralytics.

June 2. The manor house at Groot Constantia, the estate of an early governor, whose vineyards established the wine industry, is a handsome white building with looped Dutch-style gables. It is also a museum of colonial furniture, including teakwood bidets, stinkwood tub seats, armchairs with fan-shaped splats and cabriole legs, Delft celadon wine vessels, and a library—a volume of voyages dated Venice 1520, opened to Vasco da Gama's description of the Cape. Returning to Capetown, we overtake a column of "nonwhite" boys who, it is later explained, are from "a kind of Borstal unit for recidivists." Recidivists at 14?

A large reception for I.S. in the City Hall, with speeches and petits-fours. The Mayor, gold chain of office around his neck, looks like a sommelier in a pretentious restaurant. Someone tells us that he is Jewish and that a "Jewish bloc" exists in Parliament, as if this testified to a liberal regime. V. shocks this person by telling him that her own main interest in South Africa is the Crosopterygian—the armored fish, twice captured in South African waters, from which, some scientists argue, the amphibian emerged. At dinner we try more ordinary fish: hake, kingklip, snook, steenbras.

1962   **June 3.** A final excursion, to Muizenberg, False Bay, Kalk Bay, Chapman's Peak Drive, where a fog rolls in on the surface of the sea like a tidal wave. The sandy lowlands that we mistook for snow from the airplane at night are fringed with yellow heath flowers, blue hydrangeas, pink Watsonia.

June 4. Our concert, I.S. in *Le Baiser*, myself in *Firebird*.

June 5. Fly to Rome via Kimberly, Johannesburg, Salisbury, Brazzaville. A sign at Kimberly airport advertises the diamond mine as "The Largest Man-Made Hole in the World," which sounds indecent. The hole is surrounded by scrub desert, mounds of gray slag, strip farms, ponds shaped like boomerangs. After takeoff, the man next to me spills his coffee in my lap. "So sorry."

June 6. Rome. At 5 P.M. we go to Tivoli with Adriana Panni.

June 11. Two reminders of Africa: the elephant with the obelisk, in front of the Chiesa di Minerva—is this Milton's "elephants endorsed with towers"?—and, in the Campo dei Fiori, the legend "LUMUMBA ASSASSINATO" white-washed on the statue of Giordano Bruno that marks the site of the philosopher's pyre.

Call on Giacomo Manzù in his Latino Malabranca studio, where he is at work on the bronze "Doors of Death" for St. Peter's. His nose is notched, his forehead furrowed, and his hair would seem to have been transplanted from the crown to the back of the head and neck, where it curls between his shirt and ears in classical maestro style. Throughout the visit, his eyes study I.S.'s head professionally, even greedily.

The studio is built against an alcove of ancient Roman bricks only slightly higher than the doors themselves, a full-scale model of which, with a Death-on-the-Cross blocked out in gold paper in the upper right panel, stands in the center of the room. The three walls have been covered with tapestries, the only furnishings, the studio being cluttered with easels, cavalettes, and clay casts of the sculptured reliefs for the doors.

Manzù says that the upper left panel will contain a Death of the Virgin, and that the two smaller spaces beneath will be filled with *natures mortes*. Below that, the deaths of Abel, Moses, and Saints Joseph and Gregory the Great will be depicted, and, next underneath, representations of deaths by earth, air (in space), water, violence (war). The war tableau is envisioned as the hanging of a partisan, with the victim's mother at his side. These central panels are to be executed in low relief, the *natures mortes*, and six squares at the bottom with animals symbolizing death, in full relief—like the efts, insects, and shells on the lid of Jamnitzer's silver box in Vienna. The animals are a porcupine, a serpent, a tortoise turned on its back, an owl, a crow, and a *guira*. When I confess that I do not know this word, the artist quickly draws a squirrel.

The only completed panel is the Death of Gregory, which Manzù and a helper carry outside into the light, to enable us to see it clearly. The Angel

January 19, 1962. Washington, D.C. After a rehearsal of *Oedipus Rex.* Cartoon by René Bouché.

September 13, 1961. Stockholm. A conversation with Stravinsky, backstage at the Royal Opera during an intermission in a performance of Ingmar Bergman's staging of *The Rake's Progress.*

HOTEL HASSLER
ROMA

[Handwritten note on Hotel Hassler letterhead, in Stravinsky's hand, French, largely illegible:]

Vous avez fait nos comptes
avec Bob Craft
le 15 novembre 1960

Bauer hotel bill   L. 199.700
    " portier "   28.500
Rome–Paris Billet de
    chem. de fer (W.L) 44.300
Rome–Venise (Podillac) 60.000
Venise–Genova " | 40.000
Genova Rome (ch. de fer) 5.900
Colombia Excelsior Hotel 102.960
    dernier breakfast —— 880
                    ─────────
                    482.240 Argent que Bob
m'a payé en dollars (chèque sur Bank of Am.)
$ 777.00 le 15 nov 1960
─────────

                Moi, j'ai payé à Bob $ 908 somme
que je lui devais pour avoir répoli avec
l'arch. de Genova les parties que je diri-
geais le 12 et 13 nov. soit $150.00 et
le ⅓ des 1.400.00 Lires italiennes que j'avais
reçu pour ces 2 concerts soit $758.00

                    JStr

November 15, 1960.
Rome. Example of
Stravinsky's
bookkeeping.

November 22, 1961.
Sydney. Cartoon by
C. Kahan.

December 1966. Hollywood. Recording a sound track for a United Airlines promotional film.

March 29, 1962. Hollywood. Recording *The Flood*. Stravinsky is in the control room.

October 4, 1962. Leningrad. With Vladimir Rimsky-Korsakov.

October 5, 1962. Leningrad. An exhibition of Stravinskyana.

October 8, 1962. Leningrad. Conducting *Le Baiser de la fée* in Philharmonia Hall.

Photo by Robert Cato (CBS)

August 26, 1964.
New York. Editing a
recording.

May 1963. Hamburg.
Rehearsing *The Flood*.

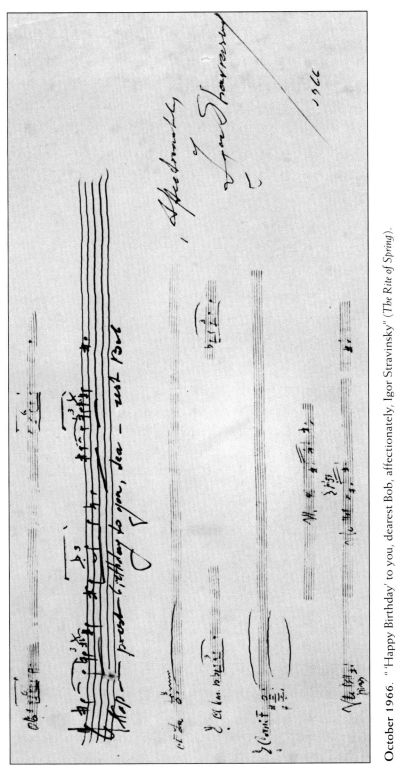

October 1966. "'Happy Birthday' to you, dearest Bob, affectionately, Igor Stravinsky" (*The Rite of Spring*).

June 14, 1964. During a flight from Denver to New York, Stravinsky notated the first themes of his Symphony in C and Tchaikovsky's First Symphony on a soiled paper napkin.

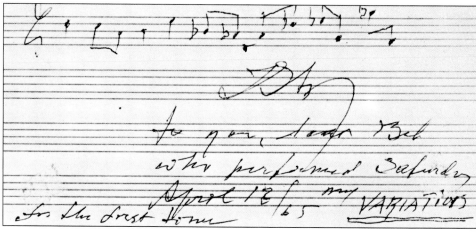

April 13, 1965. Chicago. Memento of the first performance of Variations with the Chicago Symphony, inscribed "To you, dear Bob, who performed Saturday April 13/65 my Variations for the first time."

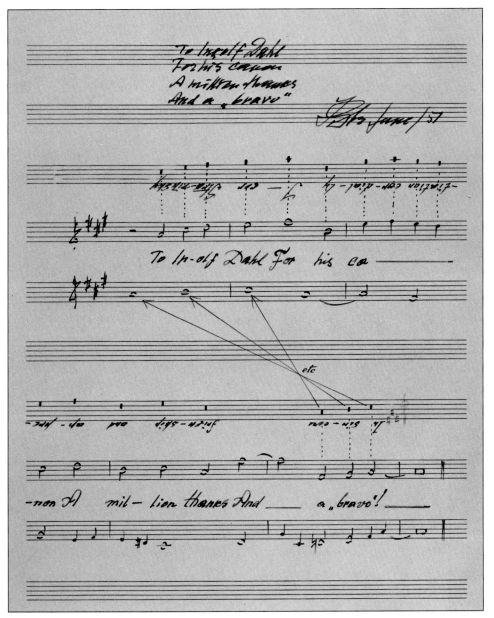

Hollywood. "To Ingolf Dahl / For his canon / A million thanks / And a 'bravo.' IStr June/57 "
Stravinsky added an accompaniment, a mirror image, to a canon by Ingolf Dahl , which was
composed for Stravinsky's 75th birthday. The intersecting and dotted lines indicate the musical
relationships.

December 1989. Elliott Carter and the author with score of the former's Double Concerto for a performance in New York.

of Death, helmet visor thrust back, points from the left to the slumped but still-mitred head of the enthroned Gregory, whose long papal cope, the focusing feature of the composition, flows from the head to below the body, which it dwarfs. Rubbing the patina to show the true tincture of the bronze, the sculptor says that, in spite of the risk, he prefers to work directly in bronze, to feel that the form is entirely his. He makes only a few sketches and a few cloth and paper maquettes, whereas he may try as many as 10 castings; pinned to the table is a laundry list of trial moldings for the animals of death, on which several scratches follow the name of each animal, more for the aciculums of the rodent than for any of the others. He claims to make no more than a single copy, saying that "Two is already mass production," and says that he refused the Vatican's request to include the Resurrection: "Resurrections are baroque, too baroque for me, in any case, and their drama is diluted; but death is purely dramatic."

The only other opus in the studio is the head of a cabaret girl; a striptease artiste with an unforgettable twist of *je m'en fiche*-ism in her lips.

The yard of Manzù's larger studio, in an industrial outskirt, guarded by high walls and hounds, is crammed with sculpture, as is the three-room atelier, which, because of the many figures and busts wrapped in canvas cloaks and hoods, might be a morgue. The shelves of the main room are stacked with unfinished figurines, puddings of gesso, and a hardware store of hammers, hatchets, picks, pestles, spatulas, chisels, drills, saws. A plaster bust of Kokoschka lies in a corner next to a terracotta head of a boxer, and, in the center of the room, two otherwise nude bronze ballerinas stand tautly on their slippered toes tying ribbons in their hair. As we admire them, Manzù pats their behinds with pride, but also, I think, concupiscence.

His sculpted chairs piled with vegetables and fruit are so real that we want to touch them—and do: a cold, macabre sensation—but these technical exercises, as Manzù calls them, shrugging his shoulders—disturb us in the same way as the statues in the Campo Santo at Genoa. Is it because a still-life in three dimensions and actual proportions is as morbid as Madame Tussaud's? Or because a *real* chair in bronze seems a waste of the metal as well as of artistic talent?

At one point he remarks, "Unlike the poet and the painter when they complete their work, I, when I finish mine, must still endure the suspense of the *fusione*." One is reminded of Strindberg's "The art of the future will, like nature, leave a lot more to chance."

Manzù's palms (thenars) are itching to do I.S.'s head, but he says: "I cannot just begin; I have to study photographs, think for a long time, and be inspired. I.S.: "In my case, the 'necessary angel' appears only when I am already working, and then sometimes the lady takes a lot of nudging before her wings begin to flap."

June 14. Piero's *Misericordia* polyptych, now in the Istituto Restauro, is

1962 surrounded by detailed photographs of every stage of its cleaning. One of the restorers, our longtime friend Licia Vlad, explains that an oil emulsion was used for the cape that the Queen of Heaven spreads above an apse of kneeling worshipers but that her other garments are in pure tempera, which may indicate that they were painted at different periods. One of the kneeling figures wears a black hood, as members of Tuscan *Misericordia* societies still do. Popular tradition identifies the man on his left, with the most arresting face in the group, as the artist's self-portrait. To my eyes, the Sebastian in the left panel is more a Masaccio creation than a Piero, and more a dumb, brutalized peasant than the disappointed lover of stereotyped Sebastians. Daubs of Piero's trial color mixtures survive on the marginal surfaces of the wood beneath the picture.

Also in the Istituto is an icon from Santa Maria in Trastevere, a toile already once restored—transferred to cedar boards—a millennium ago; the discovery of this earlier effort at preservation has excited the workers, who think it may be one of the oldest icons extant. The face is in the Fayum tradition, but the remainder of the picture is full of movement, the Madonna dandling the Infant as if she were giving Him a walking lesson. The pedestal for her left foot is, or appears to be—there are many lacunae—the prostrate person of a pope.

To me the most affecting of the to-be-restored treasures is a chipped and candle-blackened *Ecce Homo* inscribed, in a banner painted on the frame, "*Antonellus Messinius pixit.*" The eyes of Antonello's young redheaded model are bloodshot, as if from conjunctivitis, and a noose and its shadow hang around his neck. The flesh is flecked with tears of blood and transparent perspiration, and if the picture has a fault, it is that the painter prided himself too much on this pearly perspiration.

June 17. Fly to Hamburg, where Balanchine, Rolf Liebermann, the Spenders, and a large crowd greet I.S. at the airport. Scores of cables, telegrams, and letters await I.S. at the Hotel Vier Jahreszeiten, where we talk in the S.s' rooms until after midnight.

June 18. At a public reception in City Hall, the Burgermeister presents I.S. with the City of Hamburg's 80th-birthday gift, a first edition of Lessing.

June 24. First performance of the three Greek ballets, beginning at 10 A.M. I conduct *Agon*, Leopold Ludwig conducts *Orpheus*, and I.S. conducts *Apollo*.

July 13. New York. Finally wading through the two-month accumulation of mail, we find a piece in the June 10 *Times* by Martin Mayer. After the *Rake*, he says, I.S. "looked to the young. Specifically, he looked to a pale, slim, nervous yet strong young man named Robert Craft. Perhaps he saw in Craft some of the monstrous intensity of his own youth." *My* monstrous intensity?

August 29. Lod Airport, Tel Aviv. As we leave the plane, a chorus of schoolgirls welcomes I.S. with songs; or so we suppose, looking at their open mouths and thrusting bosoms, but a jet is revving up in the vicinity and we hear nothing. When we move within range, the girls pelt us with carnations, some of which I.S. gathers from the ground to form a bouquet that he waves in a return salute. This is the warmest reception ever, from people, photographers' bulbs, the still-sweltering sun. "Shalom! Shalom!" everyone is saying, and the cordiality flows around us like a warm bath.

At the Dan Hotel the room clerk speaks Russian, the receptionist Spanish, Italian, and Greek, the maitre d'hotel German, the telephone operator English, the chambermaid French, the elevator boy—a *sabra*—Hebrew only. Vigorous handshakes are exchanged with all of them, and all of them greet us like long-lost relatives. "Welcome home," the room waiter says, with an enthusiasm befitting the return of the *juif errant*, except that his confidence in me seems to wane rather quickly, for by the end of the meal he is procuring illicit cream for my coffee. The delicacy of the dinner is a kosher red caviar on unleavened bread.

Tel Aviv, on the south side of our rooms, is a cliff of balconied apartment houses, like dressers with the drawers open. From the west windows, under a planetarium sky, the Mediterranean is sprinkled with lights from fishing boats. Except for the surf, the only sound is a wail from an Arab café somewhere down the beach.

August 31. Awakened by shouting, I hurry to the window in time to see a dozen not-that-young women, sufferers from nothing more serious (I hope) than obesity, drilling on the beach like a squad of recruits in the Marines. The instructor shouts and the ladies salaam; or, arms akimbo, then folded behind their fleshy backs, twist and bend their trunks; or roll on the ground, apparently trying to bounce; or lie as nice ladies should not, kicking their legs like overturned beetles. They droop a bit after the workout, but no one is noticeably more svelte. Perhaps the simpler solution would be to cut down on the curds and whey. On another part of the beach, two young girls are displaying about all that legally *can* be displayed of precisely the flesh that these elders of the sex would like to be reduced to, and doing it for the benefit of two bald but otherwise hairy men too absorbed in conversation to look.

I begin this morning's rehearsal in the Mann Auditorium with misgivings, having been told that nearly everyone in the orchestra once was, and in most cases still considers himself to be, a conductor. But the players are as cooperative and as adult—orchestral musicians often being remarkably childish—as any with whom I have worked. They are quick, too, which is not surprising, except that we had anticipated a show of resistance to our modern program: the stalwarts reputedly are not merely conservative but Viennese-conservative, and my very first beat shows me that the mold of their style *is* the sentimental tradition, that their first love is Old, but not

1962 old-enough, Vienna. In any case, their musical performance is less remarkable than their linguistic one. I.S. addresses the players in Russian, French, Italian, German, English, and in no instance is translation required. After hearing their own exchanges in other tongues, we conclude that *any* language would be understood, if not by the triangle player, then by the trumpeter or the harpist.

During intermission a joke goes the rounds, one of many sparked by the recent visit of Willy Brandt. It seems that Herr Brandt had expressed his pleasure to Mr. Ben-Gurion that the Mann Auditorium had been named for a "great German writer" (author of *Buddenbrooks*). "But it is named for an American writer," the Prime Minister reportedly answered. Herr Brandt: "Really? I do not think I have heard of him. What did he write?" Mr. Ben-Gurion: "A check." One imagines this example of the patriarchal powers of repartee traveling throughout the country, and the family pride left in its wake.

After the rehearsal we go to Jaffa, "for purposes of sightseeing" in our driver's words. But the truly impressive sights are people, most memorably of an ancient rabbi—corkscrew side curls, gabardine coat, a black hat over his yarmulke—being led by a small boy who holds his left hand, the other hand tapping the pavement with the white cane of the blind. In the same neighborhood, the narrow streets near the harbor, another religious venerable wears the Daniel Boone cap with the 12 peltries representing the 12 tribes. That these people have transplanted themselves with no modification in clothing from the Vitebsk of Chagall to the heat and humidity of a Florida climate seems impracticable and unnecessarily uncomfortable, and our friend, the Haganah veteran Ahron Propes, agrees: "The wardrobe is a survival from a mystic way of life, and it should be adjusted." But no one will say how, or venture to introduce a rabbinical summer style. This ambivalence toward religious orthodoxy, and indeed every kind of hereditary religious dispensation, is one of Israel's profoundest problems, both individually and at the government level. "I am not a believer," an American acquaintance tells me, "yet when I am here I put on my hat and tallith and go to the synagogue; and though I have long since drifted away from any semblance of the dietary observances, in Israel I follow them strictly." The statement is typical. One wonders how long these traditions will last when they are no longer needed to preserve identity.

Our driver is a refugee from Germany—except that "refugee" is never used here; Israel is "home," and today's refugees are "newcomers." A hitch with the British Army during the war left him with an odd brand of English. He refers to "Christ's crucification," for instance, and though he can supply Biblical references for everything we see, they are scarcely recognizable to anyone brought up on the King James Version. Fortunately, he has other lore, especially a bag of stories about the 1956 campaign. "Arabs run better without their footwear," he says, "and since they were

always running, the Sinai Desert, when we got there, was a harvest of old *1962*
shoes."

Tonight is the eve of the Sabbath, hence the two candles and two loaves of bread in a napkin on the table by the dining room door. The headwaiter, taking us for "newcomers," bids us "welcome home." And rightly, I am beginning to think, for we do feel at home here. As if to convert feeling to fact, a letter awaits me in my room from a kibbutz woman who, seeing my name (Kraft) in a newspaper, claims kinship, and substantiates the connection with a long list of wrong relatives. So much for "Jewish names."

September 1. *"Shabbat Shalom,"* the room waiter says this morning, and the greeting explains the frugality of the breakfast, the creation of fire being forbidden on the Sabbath. Another, more welcome, consequence of holy writ is the suspension of rehearsals: my body is still functioning on Pacific Standard Time, a discrepancy of 11 hours that leaves me with a diagonal feeling and in need of a time pill. One unforeseen complication resulting from the obeisances of the Sabbath is that no laboratory technician will take I.S.'s blood, and his weekly examination is due today. A doctor comes instead, and after punctiliously fulfilling the Greek (Hippocratic) part of his duties, he no less strictly follows the Hebrew part by refusing to sign I.S.'s medical logbook and defile himself with a pen.

Public transportation services, including some international airplane flights, are halted until sundown, and automobile traffic is thin—in some areas virtually at a standstill: "Sunday driver" would have a different meaning here. En route to the Weizmann Institute ourselves, we imagine that bystanders are thinking us flagrantly sacrilegious. Recalling that the interdiction against travel on the Sabbath does not apply to journeys by water, I.S. says that the younger Jews of Ustilug used to sit on water bottles in railway coaches; since his arrival in Israel, I.S. has been repeatedly reminded of Ustilug, at first simply by scraps of conversation with elderly settlers from Russia, then by a quality of "coziness" which he holds to be peculiar to Russian Jews. I have rarely seen him so moved as he was yesterday when presented with a history of the Jewish community of Ustilug compiled by descendants of families from there.

Meyer Weisgal, director of the Institute, is a refreshingly unorthodox academic dignitary. His favorite expletive is "Jesus Christ," and his imagery tends to be earthy, "bald as a camel's ass," for example, being his description of a colleague's tonsorial problem. During lunch at his home, with Abba Eban, the Minister of Education, a discussion develops about anti-Semitism in the Soviet Union and recent Soviet newspaper attacks on "the philosophy of the Bible," though on evidence few of the attackers can have read "The Book," which has been on the Soviet *index librorum prohibitorum* these 40 years. Eban attributes the Soviet refusal to allow their "Jewish" musicians to perform in Israel to "fear of defection." At this juncture, the S.s, meaning only to keep the discussion afloat, nearly sink it with

1962 some testimony of exactly the wrong kind. They say that a waiter at the Dan, a newcomer from the USSR, has told them that in his experience racism did not exist in the Red Army, whereas in Israel, peoples from different countries and with different shades of skin are constantly waging disputes of a prejudicial kind.

We visit Ashkelon, birthplace of Herod the paranoid, and a nearby kibbutz of exotically dressed newcomers from Algeria. Sections of pipeline for the rerouting of the River Jordan, large enough to be a tunnel for a small automobile, have been rolled to the side of one stretch of the road.

September 2. Caesarea. Our French-speaking guide is a fluent quoter of Josephus and a learned commentator on such subjects as Roman castramentation and the origins of the cunei, the diazoma, and the skene. A stone has been uncovered in the amphitheater, incised with the name of the procurator Pontius Pilate. On him, as on many Roman officials, Christians took iconoclastic revenge, decapitating every Imperial Roman image in the country except a statue of a woman in Ashkelon, which may prove the rule, its resemblance to an early representation of the Madonna very likely being the reason for its escape.

Reaching Haifa at dusk, we drive directly to a lookout, near the gold dome of the Bahaists, for the view of Acre lighting up across the harbor. Many Druses are in the streets, mysterious people trailing long veils from white turbans.

Our Haifa concert takes place in a cinema between screenings of *A Streetcar Named Desire* in what may be the hottest room in the world. The slightest exertion induces a flood of perspiration, and when I conduct, my spectacles steam over like frosted glass. I am soon swaddled in my clothes as if I had fallen into a swimming pool, and after the first movement of the Symphony, I remove my tie and unbutton the upper part of my shirt. At the end of the piece, I peel my jacket as well, which greatly amuses the audience, and the prolonged applause may be less an expression of enthusiasm for the music—which they may suspect of having been the *Istar* Variations—than of curiosity to see what will come off next. No wonder that after the Violin Concerto, when I pull a bath towel from under my score and pass it to the soloist, Zvi Zeitlin, whose handkerchiefs and hand towels are waterlogged, and when he mops and then I mop, this humid scene wins a thundering ovation.

September 3. Life along the road to Nazareth and Tiberias is pastoral, with little evidence of husbandry; Arabs wearing aquals and kaffiyehs are more numerous than on any of our other routes. The economy of Nazareth, a hideous city, seems to depend entirely on souvenir-selling; and since the water of "Mary's Well"—"Where Jesus drank"—is bottled and sold, so, perhaps, are the local earth and air. A church "as large as St. Peter's" is promised for the city a few years hence, and, indeed, size would be the only attribute in which any confidence could be placed. An hour beyond Nazareth, the Sea of Galilee comes into view, and the purple-and-beige mountains of Syria. Our ears crackle as we descend.

Tiberias, a stone village with iron balconies, is forlorn and oppressive: the only life is in the Sea, where the fish leap and the bathers are both human and goat. We are admitted to the grounds at Capernaum by a Franciscan friar, lonely as a lighthouse keeper and so pleased to have visitors to whom he can speak Italian that he may never be able to stop. He wants to talk about the arts, rather than about the years of Christ's nemoricole here and the quarry of old stones—Roman olive-oil presses, largely—of which he is the custodian. For I.S., the dereliction of Capernaum, coming after the tawdriness of Nazareth, is a shock. The traditional site of Christ's first miracles is marked by a chapel so dingy that even the Nazareth city fathers might have dumped it as surplus goods. And instead of an elite guard of one of the holy brotherhoods, the place is inhabited solely by this garrulous monk, the unique survivor, who falls on us, half crazed from the solitude and the heat, like the last defender of the fort in *Under Two Flags*; or, rather, Capernaum being some 600 feet below sea level, the solitude, the heat, and the bends. But much of the shock is also due to conditioning by Art, the Holy Land of our imaginations having been formed in large measure by Tuscan and Umbrian landscapes in quattrocento paintings.

September 4. Prejudices of art raise no obstacles to biblical visions on the road to Jerusalem, this in spite of wrecked trucks and tanks left by the roadside as memorials to the blockade-runners of 1948. On the contrary, in the Judean hills biblical mirages are conjured up at every turn, a man on a ladder picking a fruit tree, for instance, becoming a picture of Absalom suspended by his hair. At times the territory of Israel narrows to a defile not much wider than the road, which means that we are only a bull's eye from barbed-wired Jordan. The higher we climb, the more barren the brown, terraced hills, until suddenly looming before us like a white crown is the city of the mellifluous name.

From our rooms in the King David Hotel, Jerusalem is a white wall turreted in front and machicolated to the west, and for these and other features it bears a remarkable resemblance to the city of Carpaccio's imagination in the *"Prédication de Saint-Etienne"* in the Louvre. Below the wall is the gulch of Gehenna, a dry moat, and beyond it are round Turkish towers, square Gothic towers, the Tower of David, cross-topped cupolas of Eastern churches, Muslim orbs. The Jordan frontier is marked by a row of carrot-shaped cypresses and shrubberies hollowed like bagels, beyond which is a no-man's-land of rubble and desert. From the angle of another hill, a short walk east of the hotel, we can see the Mount of Olives, Gethsemane, the Valley of Moloch, and Golgotha.

Seeking more views, we drive along the border as far as Manhat, which, lying directly on the line, has been evacuated, a dead city under the eyes

1962 of a ghostly Ottoman tower. At sunset the desert is violet, and its cities—Moab, Gilead, Bethlehem—turn salt white. Back in Jerusalem in the blue light of evening, we leave for our concert under a barrage of church bells from the Old City as discordant as the different versions of the Only Veracity they advertise.

President Ben-Zvi's presence at the concert obliges I.S. to lead the *Hatikva*, a dreadful dirge in D minor (the Sanhedrin Blues) reminding us of *Má Vlast*. I.S. is nervous about this, and after an uncertain first beat, when he finds the orchestra quite capable of sustaining the mournful melody on its own, the relief is so great that he swerves into the remainder with blood, schmaltz, tears, and a final Bernstein lunge.*

September 5. A morning tour, starting at Mandelbaum Gate, where buildings are sandbagged and a détente seems to be as far away as ever. This neighborhood contains another borderline, less violent, if at times hardly less troublesome, entirely within Israeli territory: the ghetto of the extremist Neturi Karta sect, the Me'a She'Arim zealots who live only for the Sabbath, measuring the hour and the day in terms of the remaining time to it. Rabidly opposed to the Erastian state of the Zionists, on the unarguable grounds that it was created not by the Messiah but by men, they are a considerable nuisance to the government, refusing to pay its taxes and to serve in its defense. Nevertheless, they are the atavistic conscience of the whole country. What most impresses us about them is that they have successfully marooned themselves and their gnostic way of life, or way of waiting for God, in the heart of a modern city. The fathers and husbands go about in sackcloth and cover their wives and daughters in long dresses, coarse black stockings, and, lest they tempt other men, woolen wigs, while half a block away *Lolita* is playing at the cinema.

The Dead Sea scrolls, at Hebrew University, look suspiciously new. The black script on the clean white parchment sheets, sewn together like frames in spools of film, is easily legible and can be read by school children. To me, this preservation of the language is more remarkable than the preservation of the scrolls. A commentary on Habakkuk is on exhibit, as well as a copy of the Book of Isaiah, and the Essene text "The Sons of Darkness and the Sons of Light." Each scroll is displayed with the jar in which it was found, together with photographs of the jars in the caves at the time of their discovery.

In the presidential "Log Cabin," which, together with its incumbents, is a national symbol of pioneer Israel, an adjutant reads citations for I.S. and myself, after which Mr. Ben-Zvi presents I.S. with an antique vase, and me with a medal and standard. The ceremony over, the President switches

---

* Newspaper notices cited the discernment of the interpretation, but what they said about the remainder of the program provoked I.S. to remark on the still active Talmudic tradition in music criticism.

from Hebrew to Russian, which appears to be the domestic language of elderly officials—white-haired cabinet ministers, octogenarian social planners, and such. It develops that Mr. Ben-Zvi and I.S. had been in Poltava at approximately the same date, and as they exchange recollections of it, other guests join in. At one point a game gets underway of renaming Russian writers as Jews: Pushkinson, Gogolman, Lermontovich. When we leave, Mrs. Ben-Zvi beseeches I.S. to "say a good word for Israel when you are in the Soviet Union."

Back in Tel Aviv we dine with Theodore Kollek, who is said to typify the new Israel, and who does present a striking contrast to the Russians of the morning meeting. Husky, hard-drinking, cigar-smoking, Teddy Kollek is a man of action, as well as an intellectual whose off-duty passion is archaeology. He shows me a Luristan chariot ornament, addorsed heads of mythical animals in bronze, found on a dig not long ago, and when I admire it too much, gives it to me.

September 6. From today's *Jerusalem Post*:

> Hundreds of persons crowded round the entrance of the Tel Aviv Museum (Beit Dizengoff) yesterday afternoon to greet Mrs. Vera Stravinsky as she arrived with her husband, the composer-conductor, for the opening of an exhibition of her paintings. The show comprises 34 oils, mainly abstracts. It will be on display three weeks. Mr. and Mrs. Stravinsky were yesterday received by the President and Mrs. Ben-Zvi at Beit Hanassi in Jerusalem. They were accompanied by Mr. Robert Craft and Mr. and Mrs. Zvi Zeitlin. The artists were introduced to the President by the Director-General of the Prime Minister's Office, Mr. Teddy Kollek, and the manager of the Music and Drama Festival, Mr. Ahron Propes. Mr. and Mrs. Stravinsky also visited the Hebrew University and were received by the President, Mr. Eliahu Elath.

September 7. One of I.S.'s callers this morning, the parent, she says, of a new Mozart, is proof that the traditions of chutzpah are alive and well, for she plainly implies that it is high time I.S. renounce his own footless activities and dedicate himself full-scale to teaching her whiz-kid, certain-to-be-world-changing genius. Another caller, this one evidently *meshugah*, wants to commission a concerto for shofar and orchestra.

The director of the Haaretz Glass Museum in Ramat-Aviv, an attractive new circular building, discourses, as he leads us through, on glassmaking techniques: the discovery of the sand-core method, the method of coloring by cobalt and manganese oxides, and the marvering and crizzling of the parison, which is the glass in its bubble-gum state. Like other chronologically arranged museums, the Haaretz constitutes a strong argument for the decline of culture. In glass manufacture, moreover, the downgrade is

1962 noticeable as early as the Late Bronze Age. The gradient is not always even, to be sure, and individual objects of beauty were produced in all periods, but the direction of the slope, as it courses through the Persian, Phoenician, Sidonian, Hellenistic, Roman, Byzantine, and Islamic periods, is unmistakable. Furthermore, the decline is characterized by the same process in every culture; it is always a matter of more bulk and volume, more gilding and incrustation, MORE. Almost always, too, it is marked by a turning away from the functional toward the purely decorative, and by a final stage that descends from the baroque to the merely bizarre. The Haaretz, in sum, presents the case for "old bottles" (leaving aside the question of wines), of which the very oldest—cosmetic phials, finger bowls, an aryballos—are small and simple in form and color. In the Roman period, which is already a long way downhill, the stock of utilities expands to include such instruments as the strigil. But the old forms have been vulgarized, meanwhile, and pure colors have given way to color effects, including iridescences and rainbow patinas. Ancient Hebrew glasswares are identified by ashtaroths, menorahs, corn sheaves, clusters of grapes.

Leave-taking at the airport is misty-eyed and smothering. Another departing passenger, observing the fuss made over I.S., asks me if I know "who the old guy is," but without waiting for my reply goes on to remark, "On second thought, whoever it is must be an old goy or they wouldn't pay that much attention." We are in Rome at 3, in Venice at 11.

September 8. Venice, the Bauer Grunwald. Lunch at Villa Cipriani with Adriana Panni and Massimo Bogianckino, the manager of the Filarmonica Romana.* Italian cuisine is so much more calorific than Israeli that we are logy all afternoon.

September 9. Telephone from Ralph Parker, Hurok's representative in Moscow, discussing our programs there. The Russians have turned down my proposal to play Schoenberg's Five Pieces, even at the risk of having us cancel the trip.

September 10. I.S. works on *Abraham and Isaac*, picking up from his Santa Fe stopping point. After dinner we watch a group of German tourists pile into gondolas for a crepuscular ride, then take a gondola ourselves to see Tiepolo's *Abraham and Isaac* in Santa Maria dei Derelitti, but the building is closed. The Cardinal's Palace, from the Rio di Palazzo, shows that many more *diamanti* have been dislodged since we were here in August 1956. Return by the Greek church, whose minacious bell tower seems likely at any minute to topple into the canal.

September 16. Across the meres and minches to Torcello, in the Biennale motor boat.

September 17. Paris, the Berkeley Hotel. Letter from Glenn Gould: "We would dearly love to have you come to Stratford and participate in as

---

* Later Mayor of Florence.

wide a sampling of our enterprises as you feel your time would afford."

September 21. Bringing 15 months of uncertainty to an end, we fly from Le Bourget to Moscow in a Soviet TU-104, which does not have seatbelts because, the stewardess tells us, they are not needed in Russian airplanes. Neither are lunches, evidently, though hostesses who have not been to charm school and have no camera smiles bring us vodka and *zakousky*—sprats, herring, caviar. Nearing Moscow, the airplane dips low over forests turning yellow, meadows still green, lakes, canals, and boat-busy rivers. The landscape is rich and tidy; I have been picturing a muddy, sprawling country on the lines of the Russia I.S. characterizes as a combination of "caviar and *merde*."

I.S., straining to see, is excited and open-mouthed, and V. is choked with emotion. Aground, we taxi past airplanes, unseen in our world, from Poland, Bulgaria, China, and halt near the terminal. A reception committee pushes to the foot of the staircase that is wheeled to the door of the plane, and at the same time I.S. emerges, bowing deeply, a gesture out of another era as his dark glasses are glaringly symbolic of another kind of life (Hollywood, I regret to say). We move toward television lights, blinded like moths.

Among those steering us to the waiting room are the familiar faces of Tikhon Khrennikov and Kara Karayev; and the familiar-by-resemblance face of a woman with the slant Tartar eyes Picasso saw in I.S., who sings to me in a high voice, *"Je suis la nièce de Monsieur Stravinsky."* A short, stout woman, who could be a stand-in for Jacob Epstein, says *"Ich bin Yudina"* and plants a wet kiss. Another woman, telling me in English that she is the daughter of the poet Konstantin Balmont, hands me a birch-bark basket containing a twig, a leaf, a blade of wheat, an acorn, some moss, and other souvenirs of the Russian earth that I do not greatly need at the moment.

Inside the terminal, hand-shaking is almost continual, and so are the repetitions, from large, round, smiling faces, of *"Dobro pozhalovat."* Most of these people have waited a seesawing year for this moment, and some have been hoping or fearing far longer: for Maria Yudina, a lifelong dream is being fulfilled. The atmosphere is like a child's birthday party and everyone, not least among them I.S. himself, is bursting with relief. A neat, bright-eyed young woman introduces herself as Alexandra Alexandrovna, my interpreter, and we pack into a limousine.

The divided highway—through birch and pine woods, in a cold pink sunset with an Edvard Munch feeling—has much less traffic than any major road in the United States, but, more than anticipated, this is a thought that suddenly makes me aware of my cold-war conditioning. Moscow is lighting up as we enter, and V. studies the miles of new apartment buildings on Leningrad Prospekt for landmarks, without success. At the National Hotel, on Red Square, the airport committee, slightly diminished, awaits us all over again, but this time seals its welcoming with vodka

1962 and sweet champagne. We are witnessing the event of modern Russian musical history, some say, and others tell me they are still rubbing their eyes, never having believed it would happen. When I.S. reads a telegram from Shostakovitch, nationalist sentiment flows with the national champagne and gets even thicker.

We escape to the restaurant with Xenia Yurievna, the new-found niece, who says that 30,000 people have queued up for the Leningrad concerts, and says it so earnestly that I fear she may have arrived at the tally by her own footwork. The restaurant seems to have ambitions as a nightclub—moldy jazz-type noises come from a band in a far corner—which may explain why single men are relegated to a small adjoining room. The waitresses are blond, uncorseted, and unhurrying, and the customers—among them Indians in saris, a party of Italians very happy to find espresso on the menu, and Chinese, who are the "best-dressed" people in the room—appear to have all the time in the world.

The Chinese are "conditioned," too, as much as we are, V. says, a conclusion reached after watching them cut their food into tiny, chopstick-size pieces. Except for the portrait of Lenin on the wall and the absence of neckties, the restaurant is not unlike many in the East 14th Street Manhattan neighborhood that I frequented in my college years.

The hotel lobby is the place of embarcation for a pair of dilapidated elevators and a staircase with Atlases who appear to be holding up the second floor; nothing is holding up the drapery over the Atlases' private parts, however, for which reason, probably, they look as if they are about to drop the building. At the front desk we receive tourist folders for the "Lenin-Stalin Mausoleum" on which an unsuccessful attempt has been made to cancel the name "Stalin"; it is still distinctly legible through the blacking out. At the second-floor desk, a concierge wearing a white *kokoshnik*, like those of the nurses in *Petrushka*, leads us to our rooms, at the end of a long corridor in which cuspidors have been placed at several convenient points, possibly with a view to serious service owing to a nauseating smell of fish glue.

The S.s' suite, vacated by the Prime Minister of Singapore minutes before, might be called the Napoleon Room (to commemorate the visit of 1812): the ceiling fresco is a "Lancret" (peacock and nude femme fatale); the draperies are in Empire-style crushed velvet; the furniture includes chairs with fasces arm rests; and the "Sèvres" vase, on a pedestal in the corner, is adorned with Imperial gold eagles and a likeness of the Corsican himself. The principal clashes with those appointments are provided by a sub-Landseer portrait of a heroic dog and a five-pronged modern lamp. All our meals are to be served in this medium-sized ballroom, Alexandra Alexandrovna says, and waiters and maids soon come to take our breakfast orders (caviar and coffee). These people are as curious to talk with the S.s—returning White Russian celebrities are rare—as the S.s are to talk with them. They work and rest in 24-hour shifts, which can hardly make for the greatest efficiency, but which they claim to prefer. One girl, telling V. that her vacation begins in a few days, is rewarded with a gift of rouge.

Before bed, I walk in Red Square, which is empty except for a few trucks and a few pedestrians. The night is crisp and crystal clear, and the red stars on the Kremlin towers burn like beacons.

September 22. The glossily resonant Tchaikovsky Hall, where I rehearse the Moscow National Orchestra this morning, doubles as a portrait gallery of the great composers. Ivanov, the conductor—yellow hair and the face of a good woodsman in a Russian fairy tale—introduces I.S. to the orchestra, which receives him with applause and bow-tapping. The greeting seems restrained, but Alexandra, to whom I confide this impression, answers, "We do not have cults of personality here, and do not glamorize artists as you do in America, where Ulanova's claques are an embarrassment to the Bolshoi Ballet." Not since Stalin, perhaps, I want to say, and also to protest that the cases of Ulanova and I.S., returning after 50 years, at age 80, and as a Russian-born world immortal, are hardly analogous. But, in truth, I like the refreshing absence of the *"Sehr-geehrter-Herr-Professor-Doktor"* protocol; and I like seeing my name in the *affiches*, when I recognize it, in the same type as everyone else's, instead of, as for my concerts with I.S. in Europe and America, in the pica otherwise reserved for piano tuners.

The orchestral ensemble is good, quick to adopt my alien demands of phrasing and articulation, and harder-working than European orchestras in general. The *Sacre*, played with an emotion I can describe only as non-Gallic and un-Teutonic, is an entirely different piece. The sound does not glitter as it does with American orchestras, and it is less loud, though still deafening in this very live room. The musicians obviously prefer the lyric dances to the rhythmic ones, but even in the broadest *cantabile* they do not chew into the visceral fat or weave their torsos with passion as Russian violinists are wont to do abroad. This sobriety is very much to I.S.'s taste, and his only criticisms are that no one is attentive to tuning—they consider our own concern with it exaggerated—and that the harp, in *Orpheus*, is honeyed and weak in volume: although two players share the part, it is less penetrating than ever before. Another satisfying oddity is the bass drum, which is open on one side as if sawed in two; the clear, *secco* articulation from the single head makes the beginning of the *Danse de la terre* sound like the stampede I.S. says he had in mind. He also likes the *rape guero*, heard above the din of the whole orchestra like a giant locust rubbing its appendages together. I.S. notes that the bassoon timbre is different than in America, and that "The five *fagotti* at the end of the *Evocation des ancêtres* sound like the *cinq vieillards* I had imagined." But in every respect the music is radically unlike the conductors' showpiece it has become in the West.

Following a reception at the Composers' Union, with Khrennikov,

1962 Shaporin, Dankovich, and Kabalevsky, we make a tour, starting at turbaned St. Basil's and the Kremlin. Alexandra, my interpreter, and Karen Khachaturian, nephew of the composer and our escort from the Union, use the pre-1917 names that the S.s are likely to recognize, and we drive about being told anachronistically that the green building on our left is "the Hall of the Nobles," the rose-colored building on our right "the English Club, which you know from *War and Peace*." The colors of the old city, of the low, flat 19th-century houses with double windows and circular archways, are pastels—peach and pink contrasted with strong blues, ochers, greens. But these attractive houses survive only helter-skelter among mammoth gray apartment and office buildings. At Sparrow Hills, on the south bank of the Moscow River, the site of Napoleon's first view of Moscow, we leave the car for a walk. The afternoon is russet and gold, and a gauze of blue smoke hangs over the city. The S.s are silent and more moved than I have ever seen them.

Nor does the mood change back across the river at the Novodevichy Monastery (which means "New Maidens," a redundancy unless the place was intended for repentant fallen women, new maidens in heart). This excursion, at V.'s insistence, is obviously against the wishes, unspoken, of Alexandra and Karen, for the Novodevichy, decaying behind ancient walls, is an island of the Old Russia. In the gardens, women in black kerchiefs, tattered coats, and lifetime shoes are kneeling and praying before graves with crosses and statues of angels. In the church, a priest in a white cassock is officiating before an elderly congregation, some of whose more fervent members lie kow-tow, in the totally prostrate position that I.S. used to assume during his own devotions in the Russian Church in Hollywood.

This unexpected look behind the door has driven a wedge, however slight and transparent, between the S.s and their escorts, though the visit has not been outwardly opposed and though I could be overstating the feeling of their silent resistance. (*I* have felt it more strongly than the S.s, in any case, but then, 24 hours in the Soviet Union have helped me to realize how much farther advanced is the disease of self-consciousness in my generation than in theirs.) Inside the church, nevertheless, we are all three aware of an anxiety in our chaperones, attributable less, I think, to the large number of people there than to the fact of the direness of their all too evident poverty.

The conversation in the car, later, is inhibited. Karen talks about "the *new* Soviet life," the free education, the free medical care and free medicine, the free utilities, the nine-rubles-a-month rent, the wonders of the Metro and of the street automats, where a kopeck in a slot procures not only a sandwich but also a spray of perfume. Alexandra, taking another tack, uses the Novodevichy as an example of religious toleration—"Why even my own mother knows a priest"—and talks about the church as a relic of an older generation soon to die a natural death, and hence of no consequence.

As for the S.s, they are disturbed not for any religious or political reason but simply because the Novodevichy is the Russia they knew, the Russia that is a part of them.

Tonight, exchanging impressions, the first time we have been alone long enough to do so, I am conscious of a need to push into black or white, and aware of a need, for the first time in my 15 years with the S.s, to feel some coordination between my impressions and theirs, a confirmation that in some measure our experience has been the same. We agree that the foreign picture of the Soviet Union is absurdly misleading, even concerning such uncomplicated questions as the condition of consumer goods; V. has come with trinkets, as Peter Stuyvesant came to the Manhattan Indians, except that she is now ashamed to distribute them. The S.s are indignant, too, at having suffered so many months of worry; and they are ashamed of their suspicions, as recently as two days ago, about "being taken in by flowers and flattery." Moscow is not "grim," they say, and the people do not appear more "oppressed," "happier" or "unhappier," than people do elsewhere. Suffering and pride go well together, of course, but the pride encountered here is of an altogether different order. Furthermore, the S.s say that the disappearance of servility and *nichivo*-ism is "hardly believable." As V. puts it, after a trip to the post office: "Servility has been replaced by civility." The man who drives our limousine is not a "chauffeur," the girl who cleans the room is not a "maid," the woman who checks our coats is not an "attendant," the man who operates the elevator is not the "lift boy." (What they *are* I do not know, but the most common greeting is still "*Tovarich*.") All of which only indicates how overwhelmingly "pro" is the judgment at the end of day one.

Yet the S.s do not share my feeling that in spite of all the similarities slightly transposed, and in spite of admirations aroused by so many things that we see, and sympathies for the people we meet, intellectually speaking we are on a different planet from the France that is only a long Parisian lunchtime away. And they do not feel as I do, for the simple and natural reason that they are home. For them the U.S./USSR schizophrenia has suddenly disappeared. Their abiding emotion now is a deep love of, and pride in, everything Russian. (How sensible, if unjust, of immigration departments to have put the birthplace question first, the citizenship question second.) Only two days ago, in Paris, I would have denied that I.S., and to a lesser extent V., could ever be at home here again, meaning by "here" not the political Soviet Union (though even that could be arranged), but in "Russia." Now I see that half a century of expatriation can be, whether or not it has been, forgotten in a night.

September 23. The passersby in front of the Conservatory at 9 A.M. include women in boots and kerchiefs and men in leather jackets, some with berets and some with Lenin beards. Nobody looks like Marx or Castro.

1962   I note many solid improvements in the orchestra this morning, above all toward rhythmic steadiness in the strings. I also note further transformations in I.S. At breakfast, V. sarcastically attributes at least part of the change to the removal of "money and taxes" as subjects of conversation, thereby freeing about 40 percent of his talk for other topics. Another reason is that I.S., speaking his own language, was always a different person; now—speaking it with musicians, who call him "Igor Fyodorovich," which quickly establishes that family feeling peculiar to Russians—he is more buoyant than I can remember him. But, then, this is the first time in his life that he has conducted a Russian-speaking orchestra. That none of the players speaks a word of any other language makes me feel the isolation of the USSR more strongly than anything else, orchestras usually being so polyglot. I.S. remains outside the family only by virtue of his elegant manners, typified by that courtly bow from the door of the airplane.

Returning to the hotel, we find V. tearful. Her cousin Valodya has brought a packet of family photographs and told her about her mother's death during the war, the first news of her in 25 years. This is the moment V. has dreaded ever since the trip became a possibility, though she has also sought the certainty. She spent the earlier morning looking for the home of her first marriage and quickly found the street, on which no building had been destroyed or changed, but failed to recognize the house. This has been almost as upsetting.

In the evening we go to *Boris* at the Bolshoi Theater, whose plush, gilt, and glittering chandelier are monuments to the ancien régime. Our loge, directly over the orchestra pit, is half shrouded by a red canopy, but I.S.'s presence is known and creates a stir. The conductor, on the other hand, is not acknowledged on his entrance, for the reason, Alexandra says, that "he hasn't done anything yet," though even when he has, and the singers, too, audience appreciation strikes me as remarkably restrained. But the visual aspect of the performance is superior to the musical. The sets could be *tableaux vivants* in the Kremlin Museum, and actors more richly robed would be difficult to imagine. I.S., who has not heard the music in 20 years, is both moved and—by Rimsky-Korsakov—annoyed. "Mussorgsky accompanied Pimen's act of writing by a single bassoon; but Rimsky, to be certain that everyone got the point, added other instruments and reduced an original idea to a commonplace. Rimsky not only deformed Mussorgsky but also tried to export him." I.S. remarks that the music of the Coronation Scene "must have" inspired the death march in his own *Nightingale*, as the Tsarina's unaccompanied song at the beginning of Act Two obviously inspired Mélisande's *"Mes longs cheveux."* I.S. likes the revelry of the Polish scene above all, but deplores the way it "turns to marmalade at the end." During intermission, he is feeling almost compassionate about the Poles: "What a history! But then, if you pitch your tent in the middle of Fifth Avenue, it is quite likely that you will be run over by a bus."

Another late-night séance, in which the S.s again complain of the misinformation of other visitors, conveniently forgetting that few others have enjoyed red carpet visits such as theirs. I.S.'s volte-face has now reached the point at which I would hardly be surprised to find him appearing in the role of defender of the faith (Lenin's). His defense of Russia, in any case, is virtually complete. "What a beautiful factory. *Chudny* apartment house." In Hollywood, when dinner is five minutes late, heads roll, but a two-hour wait here is commended as "excellent service," which it is, compared with the even longer delays. Perhaps this change is also caused by the resumption of that Russian time-scale according to which a visitor arrives for tea and stays to talk until midnight. When the dinner finally does appear, moreover, he will comment on "the marvelous salt!" but fail to mention that the pièce de résistance would effectively resist an electric saw. If tonight's meal had been served to him in France, De Gaulle himself would have received a telegram about the decline of civilization, while here it was "*vkusno*" ("very tasty"), a judgment not based on any sustained attempt to eat it.

Ralph Parker, to whom I confide some of this transformation, asks whether I think I am now seeing "the true Stravinsky." All I.S.s are true enough, I answer, but my picture of him is finally being given its background, which does wash out a great deal of what I had heretofore supposed to be "traits of character" or personal idiosyncrasies. Furthermore, I can now understand the Soviet view of I.S.'s expatriate years as a pillar-to-post course from circus ballet to Roman Catholic Mass to Hebrew canticle, a view that leaves out of account the value question of how perfectly fluted I.S.'s pillars are and with what exquisite capitals he has adorned those posts. In future, I will try harder to listen to his music from their *sub specie patris* perspective.*

V. says that I.S. is slipping into diminutives, a tendency he affects to scorn in Russians abroad, and she adds that, contrary to experts abroad, diminutive forms are not more endemic than they were 50 years ago. Tonight, for example, he asked the waiter for a spoon-*chik*, a "petit-bourgeois solecism of a revealing kind," V. says, though she has always held that I.S. is a 100 percent Russian, whose international sophistication was invented by, and is to some extent an imitation of, Diaghilev. I.S. has also begun to address his niece Xenia as "Xenechka," which seems remarkably inapposite. Xenia, a courageous and good-hearted woman, appears to regard her uncle as something a new Soviet invention has retrieved from the moon.

September 24. An interview with I.S. in this morning's *Pravda* con-

---

* After our return from the USSR, I began to hear Russianisms even in *Pulcinella*—the horn counter-melody at No. 65, for example, and the D-minor tenor aria, titled "*Troika*" in the original manuscript.

cludes with a spurious quotation: "I salute the noble Soviet Union." Ralph Parker calls, says that this stock phrase is tacked on to every interview, advises us to ignore it. The difficulty in I.S.'s case is that he has annoyed the Western press by receiving *Pravda* and refusing *Time*, and the latter will call for his denial of the statement and be well aware that he cannot give it without insulting his hosts. Parker succeeds in pacifying the principal foreign newspapers with the argument that I.S. is not a United States cultural exchange artist, but a guest of the Soviet Government. "USA" appears only after *my* name on placards and programs, but *could* it have been put after I.S.'s name? His confidence is a little undermined by this breach of faith, as he calls it, but he does not mention the matter to Alexandra and Karen, both of whom behave rather sheepishly when they appear.

Among the surprise visitors at the rehearsal today are Carlos Prieto, the elder son of our Mexican banker-friend, and Lily Brik, Mayakovsky's amour, whom V. last saw in Petrograd before the Revolution. Lina Prokofiev, not encountered since 1938, in Paris, is also there, though Russians in Paris have advised us that even to inquire about her could do her harm: she spent eight years in Siberia during and shortly after the Stalin era, on unfounded suspicions of spying, a result of consorting too much with British and Americans—she speaks excellent English—in the embassies. Madame Prokofiev is accompanied by her son Sviatoslav, a gangling, grosser image of his father.

At this same rehearsal, the conductor Rozhdestvensky makes a present to I.S. of a cover of Debussy's *Préludes*, Volume II, on which, after the printed words *"pour piano,"* the composer has written, *"et surtout pour amuser mon ami Igor Stravinsky, ton ami Claude Debussy, juin 1913."* Rozhdestvensky says that he purchased the page for a few kopecks at a Moscow bookstall, where it may have been for years, passed over by people who could not read Latin letters. The gift provides me with an opportunity to make inquiries concerning I.S.'s house in Ustilug, whence it must have come, but only Xenia Yurievna has heard of the place, and she knows nothing except that in 1914 I.S.'s Beliankin cousins moved his possessions from there to a warehouse in Poltava. Xenia has a photograph of the Ustilug house with her, though, and one of the neighboring *shtetl*. Since I.S. feels more strongly about this happy home than about his comparatively unhappy childhood one in St. Petersburg, he looks at the picture reluctantly: Ustilug is a subject he will not discuss. The surfacing of the Debussy autograph most likely indicates that his possessions there—manuscripts, paintings, books— were looted after the Germans destroyed the place in World War I.

In the Oruzheinaya Palata (Kremlin Armory Museum) this afternoon, we find ourselves looking less intently at the exhibits than at the other visitors: Tartars, Mongolians, Chinese, Red Army soldiers, kerchiefed Russian women, Uzbeks wearing black-and-white hexagonal caps. Shod in felt overshoes, and in tow of female lecturers, these people glide awkwardly over the polished wood floors, like tyros on a skating rink. An ecclesiastical museum, first of all, it is rich in crosses, Bibles, and clerical garments, all lustrously jeweled: a gold surplice brocaded with 150,000 pearls (*Henry V*: "The intertissued robe of gold and pearl"); a Bible encrusted with a tutti-frutti of rubies, diamonds, emeralds; another Bible set with tear-shaped amethysts. The Imperial jewels—an orb and scepter, throne seats, baldrics, fur-trimmed crowns and ermine-lined robes—are no less rich, and the Tsars' horse equipages (saddles, bridles, halters, cavessons, stirrups, whip handles, harnesses, pommels, cantles, a horse's bit with a topaz stud the size of a bird's egg) are the most extravagantly bejeweled objects of all. One of the horse blankets, the tribute of a shah, is made of the feathers of 500 yellow parrots. The Oruzheinaya is a museum of fabrics and needlework, too, of winding sheets and palls in gold and silver thread, of silks and satins, taffetas and velvets, of sleigh rugs with cloisonné spangles. And a museum of Imperial utensils, silver plate with niello tracery or appliqué gold.

Lermontov's *Masquerade* at the Maly Theater tonight is well acted and so lavishly decorated that the stage picture could be a collective dream-wish of upper-class elegance. The S.s have been told abroad of a shortage of actors with convincing "aristocratic" accents and "refined" intonation, but they deny any evidence of that lack tonight. The mise-en-scène, whose rapid pace depends upon ingenious uses of a revolving stage, seems to follow the old Meyerhold production. The long evening is relieved, if not shortened, by some incidental dancing to a well-chosen potpourri of Prokofiev. But what an odd play! While the first two acts are in some ways hardly less powerful than *Othello*, to which the plot contains a not over-strained parallel, the third act is unmitigated bathos. Evidently unable to provide a dramatic solution, Lermontov simply pops an "evil genius" out of the bag and lays the tragedy to a forgotten vengeance-seeker of long ago.

The most brilliant performance of the evening does not take place on stage, however, but in the seat next to mine where, line for line and for four-and-a-half hours, Alexandra pipes a resourceful translation of this difficult verse play into my ear. (She apologizes in advance to our neighbors, but no one pays us the slightest attention.) In the intermissions we drink tea with the stage director and scene painter and talk theater with Alexandra. Her passion, and largest source of income, is in translating plays, and she asks me to recommend new English ones, stipulating that they be "something like Wesker."

September 25. Ekaterina Furtseva, the Minister of Culture, an attractive blonde with abundant *charme slave*, is said to be Khrushchev's mistress and referred to privately as Catherine the Third. During our official visit this morning she talks exclusively about the future, giving poetical recitations of production statistics and enticing descriptions of new orchestras and new ballet schools in Tashkent and Siberia, which she graciously invites us to visit.

At the Lenin Mausoleum we jump the queue, a caterpillar of booted and bundled, capped and kerchiefed humanity winding a half mile around the north corner of the Kremlin. I feel guilty about doing this, to be sure, but we *couldn't* have waited six hours, and those who *have* waited seem so long-suffering. Inside, we join a double file and descend a staircase in pious silence. In front of us are turbaned heads from the Southeast, fur-covered heads from the far North, dark faces, light faces, yellow faces, square faces, slant-eyed faces. Soldiers keep the traffic moving in the marble corridor below, and soldiers face the glass catafalque from each side, standing at near rigor mortis themselves. The hair and brows of the small recumbent figure in the black suit are red, not black as in photographs. But surely the figure is not an embalmed body but a wax doll. Nor does this make any difference. Seeing is believing, whether Mohammed's toenail, a splinter of the True Cross, or the "real" remains of Lenin. I.S., later (is he changing back?): "The religion of Lenin is the opiate of the masses."

The Leningrad Ballet performs *Orpheus*, *Petrushka*, and *Firebird* tonight in the Kremlin Theater, a new auditorium with seats for 6,000 and devices for radioed translations at every one. The theater is also equipped with escalators, lounges, bars, through which we are guided by Khrennikov's daughter Natasha. The composer Dmitri Kabalevsky sits behind us, and though reputedly opposed to I.S.'s visit, he weeps at the end of *Firebird*—which, come to think of it, is not incompatible with anti-Stravinskyism. At times, the music and the staging are hardly recognizable, especially in *Petrushka*, which seems much less "Russian" to us than the Fokine-Benois version. *Firebird* is the best performed and received of the three, but not surprisingly, since in some respects, including length and sentiment, it is the prototype of the Soviet story-ballet.

Shortly before the lights are lowered for *Firebird*, the audience applauds I.S., who acknowledges it with a bow. A moment later, Khrushchev, accompanied by four members of his cabinet, enters the loge directly across the hall from ours, whereupon the whole audience stands and applauds. Then, soon after the music begins, or seems to—the tempo is strange and the sound unbalanced—someone directly below shouts "Viva Khrushchev!" The cry is taken up by other voices and an attempt made to turn it into a rhythmic chant, but shushing noises are also heard, and are soon in the majority. Still, the demonstration is quelled only after the lights are momentarily turned up. "Cubans," Alexandra says, in a voice lacking sympathy: "It happens all the time." At the end, Khrushchev stands and applauds in I.S.'s direction, but vanishes before the first curtain call.

September 26. Kolya K., a self-declared poet, aged 26, has haunted the hotel lobby for three days in the hope of interviewing I.S. This afternoon he is partly placated by being allowed to talk unofficially with V., who deeply offends him at first by referring to his hero, Yevtushenko, as "a tribune who might have been a poet in another time and place." But V. says the same of Mayakovsky, an even more unpopular verdict. Whereas Brecht is a Kolya idol, Rilke is unknown to him even by name, and Edna St. Vincent Millay is his favorite twentieth-century English language poet. His pantheon of painters is even more curious in that it contains no Renaissance master, but only such "moderns" as Cézanne and Renoir, whom K. champions as avant-garde causes. Confessing an inability to appreciate more recent art, K. tells V. that at an exhibition in Paris he saw "a clump of barbed wire that was called 'Dream.' Now what has barbed wire to do with dreaming?"

On the question of the arts under Stalin, he says that the dictator is supposed to have remarked, apropos some poems by Simenov to his mistress, "Just two copies should be printed, one for him and one for her." On the new climate of "liberalism" toward the arts, K. feels that "the most dangerous enemy is the foreign press. Many government officials want to support the so-called rebel poets, composers, painters, but as soon as they are published, performed, exhibited, the foreign press exploits their 'defiance of the regime,' which is patently not the case with Yevtushenko." The essence of K.'s political argument is that "The Russian people have risen from a terrible history to the highest place. They have never known what you call prosperity, but that will come, and as they go ahead, the United States will become increasingly bitter. We do not want war, if only, to obviate other arguments, because we have so much to develop here. We think Americans should realize that as long as Khrushchev is in power, war is not likely, and that they should help him against the militarists and the Stalinists. But is it true that Americans have bomb shelters? Surely they can't be *that* silly?" This is the first time that the cold war has been referred to. Later, V. repeats the gist of this conversation to I.S., who says that Stalin is historically important for the reason that "he attempted to, and for a time did, prove that people do not matter."

Tonight's concert in Tchaikovsky Hall is a moving experience, but the applause is obviously directed more to the returning prodigal son than to his music. *Orpheus,* in any case, is attended with much reading of program notes, coughing, and other signs of restlessness in every section of an audience as stratified as any in the West, from eager youth in the balcony to apathetic age parterre. As an encore, I.S. conducts his wind-band arrangement of the *Volga Boat Song,* but the music refers to the wrong Russia and the wrong past, and the severity of the instrumentation—the audience has waited in vain for the strings to play on the second time around—reduces the ovation and hebetates the mood. Still, the applause, in rhythmic unison, goes on and on until I.S. appears in his overcoat, holds up his hand for silence, and tells the audience, "You see a very happy man." Afterward, in the dressing room, the orchestra players bring gifts, for me a lacquered box

1962 with a firebird on the cover.

September 27. The former Yusupov estate at Archangelskoye, one of the great *podmoskovnaya* (suburban villas), is now a showcase of 19th-century country life. Geese waddle on the lawns, and drays are on the roads, the horses with the large surcingles and horseshoe-shaped shaft-bows (*doogah*) familiar from old illustrations. The villa is a heavy, ocher building whose tall, untapered, dome like an ocean liner smokestack, becomes on the inside the crown for eight Corinthian columns supporting a white cornice. The room itself is barren, whereas the side rooms are galleries of pictures and furniture, including cabinets and chairs of Karelian birch, and rugs woven in the Yusupov mills at Poltava. The ceilings in the bedrooms are low, to concentrate the warmth.

A party of Cameroons is visiting the grounds, accompanied by an Intourist guide who lectures them in Arabic. When one of them recognizes I.S. from the photograph in today's *Pravda*, all of them gather around for autographs—to the ill-concealed fury of the abandoned lecturer, who is obliged to stand dumbly by while the S.s talk to her charges in French and English, and to each other in Russian. Would the Cameroons, who seem to be regarding the excursion as a lesson in medieval history, believe that I.S. went to school with, and that V. was a friend of, the man whose home this once was? "Yusupov was such a perfect gentleman," V. says, in the car. "When he called on us in the Crimea during the Revolution, we were living in a single room, with no furniture, yet he did not look around for a chair, but unhesitatingly sat on the floor, as if this were the most natural thing in the world to do."

Returning to Moscow on a different, less rural road, we pass log-cabin *izbas* with fancy wooden-lace window frames; even the tiniest *izbushka* is equipped with television antennae. We also pass the enshrined hut that was the scene of Kutuzov's council before Moscow. Parker explains, later, that Kutuzov is no longer merely the hero of strategic retreats but a newly rehabilitated symbol of aggression and that the grounds of Borodino have been adjusted to this revisionist interpretation.

Prokofiev's *War and Peace* tonight helps to confirm this, for while Napoleon appears in it as a small-time fascist neurotic, Kutuzov, the solitary, is a genius as big as Russia and rather larger than history. The opera is a succession of friezes similar to museum panoramas, all of them good to look at as pictures. But the book cannot be parceled out or reduced to operatic mold, and even if Prokofiev had limited himself to three or four tableaux, Tolstoy's characters would still be too roomy for him. Nevertheless, the music is more pleasing, especially in the long first-act cotillion, than I.S. makes out, and the performances, most memorably of a soldier in black boots dancing a mazurka, are excellent. We sit in the Imperial Loge (or whatever it is now called) above a group of Kazakhis wearing skullcaps, beards, and caftans cut like Victorian frock coats. In the intervals, the cast greets us in a private room where we feed on *pirozhki* and sugary champagne. I.S., later, feeling tipsy, complains that the champagne "had the wrong nuance."

From the opera, we are whisked to Moscow Television Studios for a late-night interview. Answering a question about his next composition, I.S. lays an egg as large as, but less magical than, Kastchei's. When he says, "I am writing a biblical cantata, in Hebrew, for the people of Israel," faces fall and, after an awkward pause, the program limps to an end. Parker attributes the stony reaction to the Soviet attitude to the Bible, to the feeling that Israel is the 51st state, and primarily to a wish that I.S. would choose a text in his mother tongue. A newscast immediately before our appearance shows Khrushchev being cheered along the route of his Turkestan tour, and, after this, the arrival at the Moscow airport of the new United States Ambassador, Foy Kohler, who looks as grim and unfriendly as Gromyko is made to look on American television.

September 28. The Scriabin Museum, in the composer's former apartment, No. 11 Vakhtangov Street, Arbat district, cannot have changed very much since his time. Madame Blavatsky is still a presence, along with the *clavier à lumières*, which looks like a harmonium and seems an unlikely instrument for the realization of Scriabin's visions of a synesthesia and the *"déroulement de tous les sens."* The caretakers, two elderly ladies madly in love with "Vanya Cleebourne," introduce us to a young "electronic composer" who plays his "tape filter" for a film, *Cosmic Space*, the techniques for which are mysteriously purported to have been developed from Scriabin's ideas concerning the *clavier à lumières*. We also hear a recording of Scriabin's "Black Mass" Sonata, played by the late white, or red, hope of Soviet pianists, Safronitski. The museum possesses a letter to Scriabin from I.S., expressing enthusiasm for one of the later sonatas.

After the Chekhov House, a red brick fin-de-siècle eyesore, we go to the Kamerny Theater—on Kikitski Boulevard, the "bark" of the old city, on the analogy that Moscow grew in concentric rings, like a tree—where V. played in Beaumarchais's *Svadba;* and to the Tolstoy House, which is in a neighborhood of attractive lime-colored buildings with white, arched window frames, and a tall dovecote at a nearby street corner.

During intermission in tonight's concert, a repeat of the first one, I.S., pale and perspiring, complains of nausea but refuses to see a doctor. I ask Alexandra to fetch one anyway, and she returns with an elderly woman who tells me that I.S. was a legend to her in her childhood. She finds his pulse weak and refuses to sanction any more conducting, at which I.S. angrily drinks brandy and coffee, stalks on stage, and does better than two days ago. But the delay has put the foreign press on the trail, and when we return to the hotel, newsmen are perched there like carrion crows. The medicos who come to examine I.S. are dumbfounded at the extent of his private pharmacy—the pills and powders, ointments and unguents, liquid medicines, thermometers, syringes, suppositories—and incredulous at the (true) story that just before the concert he swallowed 10 drops of an opium paregoric and washed it down with two tumblers of whiskey.

September 29. The morning is spent answering cables about I.S.'s "stroke" and denying press reports that anything of the kind occurred. At night the three of us go to the Obratzsov Puppet Theater's parody program of music and musicians. Child prodigies are mocked by an infant in a perambulator howling for its bottle and babbling baby talk, then smashing into the Rachmaninov Second Concerto. Gypsy-style "dark" singing is lampooned by a teen-age girl with a bass-baritone bray; and American-style tap dancing, Hope-Crosby comedy acts, and "sexy"—"sex-appeala," the Russians call it—adolescent crooning are all adroitly spoofed. What interests me in these burlesques is the typifying of American physical characteristics, "how the Russians see us." The drollest of these gently anti-American satires is a take-off on television commercials, an elaborately developed choral fugue about vitamin pills "that keep you alive until you die," and though by no means the highlight of the show, it wins the most vigorous applause—from an audience that, to judge by the UN switchboard of languages in the lobby, is more than half foreign. The performance can be followed without knowledge of Russian, though at certain points the spectator must at least be able to recognize it, as in the skit with a French poodle that growls angrily when its pretentious mistress bids it "*Bonjour*" but barks with pleasure when she says "*Zdravstvuyte.*"

The prize of the evening is a take-off on young-generation poetry readings. Invariably the poets have huge mouths, terrible grammar, and atrocious manners, rudely clearing their throats and spitting on the floor. One of them, after affectedly announcing "the first chapter of my new novel," utters a few obscure and disconnected words, then says, "I will skip the next 16 chapters since they are concerned entirely with the psychological development of Chapter One." The word "psychology" takes a severe beating, and not only here, as we have learned in conversations.

September 30. Today, V.'s name day, occasions festivities on the part of our hosts that would shame the church-going White Russian regulars in Hollywood. Gifts are brought: broadloom linens, an electric samovar, lacquered trays (recalling the old arts of Palekh and Mstera), wood and terra-cotta miniature animals. A new conviviality is apparent, too, in which all trace of the official manner of a week ago has vanished.

October 1. Today's *Pravda* features a photographic spread of hate-ugly faces with captions about "the racial war in Mississippi," and our new friends ask us, with genuine incredulity, how such things are possible "in a country as advanced as *Amerika*."

Along with several high-level Russians, we attend a lunch given by Ambassador Kohler at the United States Embassy. He proposes a toast in Russian but switches midstream to English, asking an aide to translate the latter part. What he says, in substance, is that as a Russian-American, I.S. is a unique link in cultural relations. But Madame Furtseva, Khrennikov, and Krilov from the Soviet Embassy in Washington listen with blank faces, do not reply, and do not applaud. Their attitude is that I.S. is here not as a representative of the United States but as a guest of the Soviet Union. All the same, his position *is* extraordinary: as the one Russian-born creative artist of the century to have attained the highest level of world prestige, he has, until now, been *persona super non grata* only in Russia. After lunch, privately, he makes the point that the cultural exports of the United States and the Soviet Union are essentially the same: pianists, orchestras, ballets, "not creative talent but performing talent, which, I suppose, is all that *can* be exported, though the prospect of more and more *Wunderkinder* playing Tchaikovsky concertos is not my idea of a musical Eden." He observes, too, that whereas the artist in the United States complains of the government's rejection of responsibility to support the arts, in the Soviet Union he might decide that the duty of government is to leave them alone.

The evening reception by Madame Furtseva and selected Soviet musicians, in a private room at the Metropole, turns into the most extraordinary event of the trip, a kind of Last Supper for nondisciples during which I.S. reveals his Russianness more completely than at any time in the 15 years I have known him. Nor is it any wee supper, either, but an excellent dinner of white veal and *Kievsky kotleti*, proving that good food exists when ordered by the right people. Madame Furtseva presides at the center of the table, with I.S. to her right and Shostakovitch to her left; to see the two Petersburg-born composers together is to be struck, above all, by the similarity of their complexions and sandy hair. V. sits across from Furtseva, between Aram Khachaturian and Kara Karayev, and I sit between Karayev and my earphones, Alexandra, who translates word for often unbelievable word.

Shostakovitch's face is the most sensitive and intelligent so far encountered in the USSR. Otherwise, he is thinner, taller, more boyish-looking than expected. He is also the shyest, most nervous human being I have ever met, chain-smoking, chewing not merely his nails but also his fingers, twitching his pouty mouth and chin, wiggling his nose in constant adjustment of his spectacles, looking querulous one moment and ready to cry the next. He stutters, too, and his hands tremble—when he shakes hands, his whole frame wobbles, which reminds me of Auden—and when he speaks, at which time the others look at him anxiously, as indeed they might, his knees knock audibly. He has a habit of staring, then of guiltily turning away when caught: all evening long he peeks illicitly at I.S. around Madame Furtseva's nicely rounded corners. The thoughts behind those frightened, intelligent eyes are never betrayed; or at least *I* cannot read them. His new wife sits beside him, an adoring pupil, one would guess, but by age, looks, and an equally shy, serious, and distant manner, a daughter.

Then it starts. *Confiteor me.* Each composer proposes a toast—"*Na zdorovie*"—which in effect is an invitation to return to the fold; and each begins by baring his soul, confessing to some shortcoming of his own, some misunderstanding about I.S., some prejudice or lack of sympathy. (*I* confess, too, but only in this parenthesis, that whether or not the nature of these revelations is biologically "Russian," and the answer is surely that one man's "lack of reticence" is another's "candor," the propensity to confess certainly seems to be; Oblomov may have disappeared in the Revolution, but Stavrogin is still very much around.) Not much of this is needed to turn the room into a Finnish bath, in whose vapors everyone, proclaiming and acclaiming each other's Russianness, says almost the same thing. I.S.'s human qualities—Russian qualities, after all—are lauded and the man, well, all who have met the man have seen how genuine he is. (No one says a word about the composer, and only Shostakovitch toasts future music by him—though, to be fair, none of them has or could have any notion of I.S.'s real stature as a composer.) Again and again, each one abases himself before the mystery of their Russianness, and so, I realize with a shock, does I.S., whose replies are soon overtaking the toasts. In a perfectly sober speech—he is the least alcoholically elevated of anyone in the room—I hear that "the smell of the Russian earth is different, and such things are impossible to forget"; they are, and so far so good. But he goes on to tell Khachaturian and Khrennikov of his desire to know more of their music, which is a polite untruth but disturbing in that they have expressed no curiosity about his music. All that Khachaturian says is that I.S. "has been a 'legend' to me all my life, but now that I have seen the man I am greatly moved by his sincerity" (cheers), a non sequitur that leaves little doubt about the nature of the myth.

I.S.'s most serious confessing gets under way in his reply to Madame Furtseva, whose patriotic preamble advances the dubious proposition that "All really great men are optimists." Here is I.S., not "in effect," but in actual quotes: "A man has one birthplace, one fatherland, one country—he *can* have only one country—and the place of his birth is the most important factor in his life. I regret that circumstances separated me from my fatherland, that I did not give birth to my works here and, above all, that I was not here to help the new Soviet Union create its new music. I did not leave Russia of my own will, even though I disliked much in my Russia and in Russia generally. Yet the right to criticize Russia is mine, because Russia is mine and because I love it, and I do not give any foreigner that right" (*bolshoi* applause). It is an astonishing speech to at least *this* criticizing foreigner, who is beginning to feel more foreign every moment, so astonishing that, as I see when we are back in the hotel, the S.s are embarrassed to have had it overheard by me. But it *is* believable, and so is every word he says tonight except the professed interest in the music of the two K.s.

I.S. does regret his uprooting and exile more than anything else in his life, which I say not only because of these emotional speeches—though they have come from the depths—but mainly because of the change in his whole nature here. Now, looking back at Hollywood, the perspective *from* Russia, I can see that his domesticity is still entirely Russian; in fact, he will eat his soup only from the same spoon with which he was fed by his *babushka* 75 years ago. And in Hollywood, or anywhere, he will go through the day, if possible, speaking only his mother tongue. Just five years ago, in Baden-Baden, he flew into a rage on hearing the news of Sputnik, forbidding us even to mention the Russian achievement. Was the power of this jealous hatred, the result of the Mother Country's deprived love, responsible for his at times too conspicuous "Western sophistication," in the sense that the latter became a weapon to prove his superiority, and that of other cultures, to the Russia which failed to recognize his genius? I am certain of only one thing: that to be recognized and acclaimed as a Russian in Russia, and to be performed here, has meant more to him than anything else in the years I have known him. And when Mother Russia restores her love, 48 years are forgiven with one suck at the breast—several sucks of vodka, in fact—at this amazingly Dostoyevskyan dinner.

October 2. A reception at the Canadian Embassy. Stalin, paying a visit here once, saw a photograph of King George V, mistook it for one of the Tsar, thought he was being insulted, and fled. So the Ambassador says, anyway, and he tells another, currently popular, story about the child who asks its *babushka* if Lenin was a great man. The answer, of course, is "Yes." The child then asks the same question about Stalin. A very bad man, says the *babushka*. "And, *babushka*, Khrushchev?" "Hush, my child, he is still alive." The Ambassador has a collection of abstract paintings by Karitnikov and other artists not exhibited publicly. Seeing I.S.'s interest in them, he takes us to the Kostaki "gallery," which is Kostaki's own three-room flat in a huge apartment house several versts from the center of the city. This is well worth the trip: the icons are masterpieces and there are important paintings by the avant-garde, early Kandinsky—an especially fine one on glass—Gabo, and Larionov. But we want to see the Sergei Shchukin collection, if time permits.

The musicians in Kiril Kondrashin's orchestra are younger than those in the Moscow State, which means, as it would anywhere in the world, that the ensemble is more exact, the varnish on the sound less thick. After conducting the Capriccio with them tonight, I receive a presentation copy, inscribed by about 50 of the players, of their new recording of Shostakovitch's Fourth Symphony. I also receive flowers from the *New Statesman*, whose Moscow correspondent is Ralph Parker, and flowers from the soloist, Tatiana Nicolayevna, who is the least asthenic pianist imaginable.*

---

* She died of a cerebral hemorrhage in San Francisco in 1993.

1962 Rehearsing the Capriccio has been the oddest musical experience of the trip. The orchestra parts, copied from a pirated score, are full of mistakes—missing accidentals, wrong clefs—some of them grotesque solecisms, as in the case of several lugubriously flatted sevenths in the finale of this jolly piece.

October 3. A farewell buffet for I.S. and the plutocrat performers Rostropovich, Gilels, Kogan, Oistrakh, given by Parker, who has become unofficial liaison officer between our hosts and ourselves, as well as our chief outside source of information, relaying the tenor of the Soviet reaction. A British correspondent in India before the war, Parker, who had married an Indian woman, came to the USSR to escape race prejudice against his family. Through the Soviet government, obviously, he seems to know that I had been a member of the American Labor Party and has correctly assumed that my "leftist" politics are in large measure responsible for I.S.'s Russian trip. Parker has a gently mordant manner and is well-read. Over the years, now 21 in the Soviet Union, he has developed discretionary habits. He will sweep into a room as if to shout "Eureka," then, seeing Alexandra there, or other possible informers, sidle up and softly whisper his tidings in our ears instead. I.S. refers to him as *"Signor Sotto Voce."*

October 4. Fog obscures the towers of the Kremlin but does not delay our flight to Leningrad—after a snack at the airport, ordering from a menu in Russian and Chinese. In the one-class plane, Alexandra engages me on the subject of psychoanalysis. "Self-indulgence," she says. "People should be taught to master themselves with willpower and to solve their own problems." I try to argue from utility, namely that capitalist psychotherapy, with its bourgeois-objectivist rationalizations, has helped many people to lead useful lives, and I suggest that this soft science will appear in the Soviet Union pari passu with the rise of a cultural elite. But when I talk about the Freud-Marx synthesis of such Western Marxists as Marcuse (who?), she regards me as a blasphemer. "Society," she says, is simply a question of "What is good for the people." I agree, but imprudently ask who decides what that good is and am accused of "Philosophy, which is only putting the world in parenthesis; the good is better living conditions and the freedom to pursue one's inner life." With this she moves on to "the parasitism of the bourgeoisie," and to the question of whether the United States is "a common denominator society, using 'individualism' as a slogan." Alexandra has read more widely in pre-twentieth-century English, French, and German literature than I have, but has never heard of Joyce, Eliot, Proust, Kafka.

The Leningrad welcoming committee is smaller, older, poorer than the Muscovite. A pale elderly gentleman wearing a hearing aid greets I.S. and starts to weep. It is Vladimir Rimsky-Korsakov, and I.S. has failed to recognize him, for the given reason that he has a mustache instead of, as when last seen (1910), a beard; but the real reason, I.S. tells me later, is that "He said 'Igor Fyodorovich' instead of 'Gima.' He always called us, me and my brother, 'Gury and Gima'." Vladimir lives in the apartment house on the English Prospekt in which I.S. wrote *Firebird*. Relatives of I.S.'s friend and co-librettist Stepan Mitussov are present, too; and a nephew of Diaghilev, a man with old-fashioned and most unproletarian manners, who speaks English and French; and a daughter of M.K. Ciurlionis, the Lithuanian verticalist painter (ziggurats, ladders), musician, follower of Wundt and Rudolf Steiner; and again the daughter of Balmont, with another basket of posies and moss, as well as a photograph of her father with goatee and shoulder-length, Buffalo Bill hair. The Leningraders, *these* Leningraders at any rate, are more cosmopolite and European than the Muscovites. They bow, kiss hands, and do not shy from foreign, especially German, expressions.

After a long drive through postwar suburbs, I.S. recognizes the Imperial Riding School, and from there on he is home. To right and left, every building is *"chudno"* and *"krasivo,"* and he has a story to tell about each one. We drive along the Neva to the green-and-white Winter Palace—rose-and-white, when the S.s last saw it—and down the Nevsky Prospekt to the Yevropaisky Hotel. V., who lived here on visits to St. Petersburg in her student years, says that the furnishings, the German piano, Louis Seize clocks, Empire ormolu beds, desks, chairs, are unchanged (in spite of reports that the furniture had been used as firewood when the Yevropaisky was a hospital during the war; or has everything been restored?). In the evening we go to Tolstoy's *The Living Dead*, in the spectacularly beautiful Alexandrinko Theater. But the title is also a description of the performance. As our first-row seats tip uncomfortably forward toward the orchestra pit, and as the gypsy singing, in Romany, is a Himalayan bore, we leave after the first act.

A late-night floorshow is in progress as I enter the hotel's roof restaurant, a magician sawing a woman in half to the accompaniment of rhythmic unison clapping and cries of "VI-VA KHRUSHCHEV!" from a party of, evidently, vivisectionist Cubans.

October 5. A drive to Peterhof, now Petrodvorets, and Oranienbaum, now Lomonosov, the city of I.S.'s birth. The road is deserted except for peasant women shouldering large nets of cabbages that, Alexandra says, they are taking home to salt. The Gulf of Finland is in view at times, and the derricks of the Kronstadt shipyards. War scars are everywhere, in charred buildings, in woods cropped by artillery fire, and Petrodvorets itself, the object of a systematic German attempt at demolition, was severely shot up, but has been admirably restored. A Russian tank stands as a monument to mark the point where the German advance was stopped.

The principal Petrodvorets palace is rated as Rastrelli's magnum opus, but the romantic rusticating of nature, as arranged by Rastrelli and others,

1962 is as great an attraction. We roam in bosquets, in Peter III's Dutch tulip garden, where Lermontov conceived *The White Sail*, and on poplar avenues where the leaves have fallen or blown on the fir trees like yellow snow. We walk by fountains, cascades, statuary—the mighty Russian Samson destroying the Swedish lion—and a pool in which, two centuries before Pavlov, fish swam to be fed at the sound of a bell.

Except for the forest of TV poles, the long rows of unpainted wooden *dachkis* in nearby Lomonosov, which was not captured by the invader, can have changed but little since the time of I.S.'s birth. But I.S. says he never saw the city again after his first few days there, if he saw it then, and he has no clue as to the location of this first home. For fanciers of rococo, Lomonosov is an *embarras de richesses*, what with Catherine the Great's pale-rose Chinese palace, her delectable *"palais des montagnes russes,"* Menshikov's palace, domed like a grand duke's crown, and the low, long, flat, and colonnaded Peter-period palaces. Near the last of these is an artificial lake on which the Tsar fought mock naval battles.

Dinner is in Monferrand House, now the Leningrad Composers' Union. We sit with about 30 guests at a "T" table, I.S. presiding at the intersection, directly under a portrait of Glazunov. From this ironic position issues what surely must be the Union's first monologue on serialism, and it is received by an audience incomparably better informed than any so far. In comparison with their Moscow colleagues, the younger people here are *frondeurs*, even though the atmosphere is that of a provincial club welcoming the hometown hero. And clearly the hometown boy has never enjoyed himself more. Only Glazunov seems not to be having a good time.

One of the "12-tone" apaches is Dmitri Tolstoy, son of Alexei, the turncoat Stalinist writer. A young, stately, Pierre Bezuhov pyknic-cyclothymic type, he gives I.S. and me short piano pieces written for and dedicated to us. After proclaiming himself an admirer of I.S.'s music, he begs him, touchingly and ludicrously, to send him "a score of *Firebird*, and anything else you have written."

As we return to the hotel at midnight, a hundred people are waiting on the pavement in front of Philharmonic Hall, each one representing a large block of seats; according to Parker, this or another hundred—every watch may be divided into several reliefs—will remain there all night. Parker says that the queue is a year old, that each place in it has had to be checked every month, then every week, and finally, as the date nears, twice a day, before and after working hours. An 84-year-old cousin of I.S.'s has told Parker that since her number is 5001, she will have to watch the concert on television.

October 6. The collection of Scythian gold in the Hermitage basement includes art and artifacts from the whole Russian geography, history, and prehistory. Early Sarmatian culture is represented, treasures from the Chaltamlik burial sites, works of Greek-period craftsmanship from

Theodosia on the Bosphorus, and objects from Peter the Great's Siberian collection. The gold is light in color and the forms, whether of ornaments or utilities, rarely tend to the geometric and abstract. The principal objects are harness buckles, scabbards, goblets (one with a relief showing a tooth extraction, not unlike backwoods dentistry in pioneer America), laurel leaves—a surprising number of them—carcanets, crowns. The vast display of bibelots includes tiny gold flowers, acorns, sheaves of wheat (for prehistoric Miss Balmonts), sea urchins, dancing humans, birds in flight. Some of these are totems, like the bulls, eagles, serpents, and winged humans that our young girl guide reproves me for comparing to angels. (They are "geniuses," she insists.) Tsarist-era gold, in clocks, snuffboxes, toys, has this in common: it is useless, too richly jeweled—a gold-lion paperweight with diamonds for teeth—and it looks as though made by Fabergé. The visit to this Scythian Fort Knox entails a mile hike through corridors stuffed with grotesquely large bowls—the largest, a jasper punchbowl, would do in a Beverly Hills kindergarten as a swimming pool—made of purple agate, lapis lazuli, malachite. Stored here, too, are bathtub-size tureens for cooling jeroboams and rehoboams of champagne.

By the time we arrive at the Composers' Union for a concert of I.S.'s Septet and Octet and an exhibition of Stravinskyana, some 500 people are gathered in the paneled oak library under likenesses of Tchaikovsky, Mussorgsky, Glinka, Glazunov, and Lenin. The student instrumentalists are excellent, but the tempi are erratic, and the finale of the Octet is played faster than I had ever supposed possible. The music stops exactly where the sides come to an end in somebody's 78 rpm recording, even when a phrase is in mid-career. For the Septet, Professor Maria Yudina herself steps to the piano, which she plays with skill and control, though the music, the Gigue anyway, makes little sense and cannot have pleased the audience, no matter how earnest the applause.

Madame Yudina, in her night of glory, escorts I.S. through the exhibition, sitting at his side during the Octet and receiving him on stage after the Septet. Some of her stage behavior might have been learned from Klemperer, which is to say that she does not bow or smile, and even the most energetic applause is acknowledged with no more than a trifling nod. She has been known to cross herself with passionate ostentation before playing, which can scarcely ingratiate her with Soviet audiences. She has also read impromptu lectures to them and poems by Pasternak. Once, too, she reputedly stopped in the middle of a Prokofiev sonata, saying, "I simply cannot continue with *this* after Beethoven!" Yudina has carried I.S.'s banner in the Soviet Union longer than anyone else. Unsurprisingly, she is not popular with the powers of the Composers' Union, and when, at their luncheon party today, she popped a book from under the table and attempted to make them listen to her read religious philosophy, the expressions of dislike exchanged on both sides nearly degenerated into an open squabble.

Yudina's Stravinsky collection fills walls and glass cases in several rooms and includes photographs of Schoenberg, Berg, Webern. Indefatigable in I.S.'s cause, she will fly to Moscow late tonight to play his Piano Concerto, then return here for a second performance Monday. In profile, playing, she looks like my idea of Bach without his wig. Full face, in the street, with her cane and handbag—from which she is forever pulling books, jars of honey, sweets, poems by Pasternak—she looks like (and is) a Doctor of Philosophy. She is famous for having played private command performances of Mozart for Stalin.

October 7. At the Composers' Union, I.S. listens to tapes of four new Soviet compositions. The first, a triptych cantata employing texts by Essenin, Blok, Mayakovsky is by Sviridov, a pupil of Shostakovitch, and the music is steady, solid, unhurried (all euphemisms for "boring"). It does not venture beyond a primitive triadic scheme, and the most novel instrumental idea, the octaves between piccolo and contrabassoon, is more effective in *Alexander Nevsky*. In this context the second piece, a quartet by Salmanov, qualifies as experimental music, though it does little more than naively repeat a Bartok or Gnessin *pizzicato-glissando*. The third piece, a sonata for violin and piano by Ustvolskaya, another Shostakovitch student, also shows exposure to Bartok's sad, falling minor-thirds. Mirzoyan is the composer of the final piece, a symphony for strings and timpani that starts with a steppe-like Largo, goes on to some *Schelomo* (and is equally profound), and concludes in a fast movement that is half rhapsody, half Moscow two-step, and all kitsch.

After these samplers, chosen to please good old radical us, how can I.S. continue to proselytize for the Schoenberg school, whose thought is light-years away and whose emotional world is on the other side of the galactic field? But *he* has had the same reactions, telling me afterward that he had been writhing inside and: "That was the real *rideau de fer.*"

In his reminiscences, spoken and written, I.S. hardly mentions the Nikolsky Sobor, an architectural marvel even for Leningrad. This is all the more surprising in that the Nikolsky is only a long block from his childhood home, while the belfry, a separate building, is visible from the street in front of his house; not to mention that belfry—he never has—is like living near, but not mentioning, the Taj Mahal. The Nikolsky is a double-decker church, the upper part a sun-filled but now otherwise empty room, the lower a sanctuary for old women. The low-arched lower floor is dimly lighted by oil-wick lamps suspended from the ceiling, and by the tallow candles of votaries. V. buys a candle herself and is charged four times more than anyone else, which may be social justice of a sort (Robin Hood), but which leaves her with the inference that in the new Russia this kind of experience occurs only in churches. Xenia's husband, and his son-in-law, accompany us on this expedition, albeit with an air of derring-do. Both have lived a block away most of their lives, both are architectural engineers, but neither has been inside the church before. They look on with amazement as I.S. dips his fingers in the stoup, crosses himself, genuflects. Not far from the Nikolsky, we pass a synagogue, bulb-domed like a church. A sizable group of bearded and black-hatted men is gathered in the street outside.

I.S.'s other descriptions of the neighborhood of his early years have also been wildly misleading as to size. The Krukov Canal, in front of his old apartment, is about 25 feet wide. He says that all the buildings on the other side are new to him, but that the iron railings are the same, the cobblestone street, the wooden footbridge at the corner, and tramcars, which still skid loudly by on their rails. A plaque commemorates the residence of "the composer and conductor" Napravnik in the house next door to the blank wall commemorating the 24-year residence there of the composer of *Le Sacre du printemps*. I.S. says nothing as he looks at the door I have so often heard him describe—it opens directly on the street—and he shows no trace of emotion.* Contrast this with his reaction, around the corner, to the Conservatory and the Maryinsky Theater. In the instant in which he recognizes the former, an involuntary "Glazunov" escapes him (after 50 years!), whereas, looking the other way, at the green-and-white Maryinsky, his face ripples with pleasure. Anyone who had seen this could not doubt that he had learned to hate music at the one address and to love it at the other.

Xenia Yurievna, at home, 72 Ulitsa Glinka, tells us that I.S.'s old apartment, next door, at 66, is identical to hers, a statement that drastically reduces the scale of I.S.'s published recollections of it. During dinner at her home, she describes her life under the siege, serving in an *opolchenie* at first and then with a burial battalion: at least a third of the city's civilian population died from starvation.** Her husband fought at Stalingrad, and from there to the end of the war, which came for him near Magdeburg. Xenia's children and their spouses are attractive, shy, cheerful, scientific-minded people in their twenties, with a smattering of English. Her Stravinsky collection includes many ancestral portraits, medallions, and photographs—most remarkably a daguerreotype of I.S.'s great-grandfather, Ignatievitch, a mutton-whiskered gentleman here aged 110. (According to legend, Ignatievitch's death at 111 was the result of a fall suffered while climbing over a fence on his way to a forbidden outing, a doctor having ordered the old tomcat to stay home and the family having locked the gate.) Many of the photographs of I.S.'s father show him in the costumes of his most popular basso roles, such as Holofernes and Sparafucile.

---

* "But I could not let myself," he said, characteristically, when reading this diary in January 1963.

** See Leon Goure, *The Siege of Leningrad* (Stanford University Press), 1962.

1962   One would have thought that such an evening would be a deeply disturbing occasion for I.S. I see no sign of it, but V. says that several times during dinner he reverted to childhood expressions.

From Xenia's, we go to the Maryinsky Theater—to see *it*, and not *Lohengrin*, which is in the way. (I.S. had wanted to attend a performance of *Kitezyh*, but the Composers' Union resisted the request with mysterious excuses until a susurration from Parker explained that the production is famously bad.) Once again, I.S. is radically wrong on scale. The beautiful theater, light blue and gold, blue ceiling, chandelier, is less than half the size of his description. When he was a child, the hem of the curtain was embroidered with medallion portraits of singers, one of them his father's. According to the intendant, the *Lohengrin* production was mounted in honor of Ribbentrop's visit in August 1939 and, by coincidence, scheduled for performance again on the day of the German invasion. (I am misquoting him, though, for he will not say "German," but only "fascist.") Tonight's is the first revival since then, he says. We would have been happier with the ban.

Upstairs in the foyer, a bust of Lenin stands where I.S., as a boy, saw Tchaikovsky.

October 8. I.S. talks informally to a group of young musicians following our morning rehearsal, but today's questions are of a different stamp: "Doesn't serialism constrain inspiration?" "Isn't it a new dogmatism?" I.S.: "Certainly it is a dogma, but don't dismiss it because of that. So was 'the old system' constricting and dogmatic—to bad composers." Then, turning to Khrennikov, he says, "You, too, Tikhon Nikolayevitch, will be trying it soon." Everyone laughs at this, including, most magnanimously, Tikhon Nikolayevitch himself, who recently informed a composer's conference that "the 12-tone system has no place in Soviet music," and to whom, therefore, the joke must have had a cutting edge. All the same, I.S.'s colonizing has gone about as far as it can go on a verbal level, except that he could still recommend pieces to be performed. My own feeling is that to the custodians of this outward-growing, big-statistic society, Webern's music can only seem like the nervous tics of a moribund culture. *I* feel no need for it here, in any case, and no correspondence between it and what I have seen of Soviet life, while on the other hand a Stravinsky-shaped vacuum did at least exist.

The turquoise palace of Tsarskoe-Selo, now renamed Pushkin, was gutted by the retreating German army, but the cupolas again gleam as though newly splashed with gold, and the wing containing Cameron's Chinese Room, Peacock Room, Blue Drawing Room, with intarsia woods from North Vietnam, as well as the bedroom and green dining room of Catherine II, are triumphs of restoration. The satellite buildings in the surrounding parks were inspired by French *dix-huitième* examples—a trianon, an *orangerie*, a monopteral pavilion—and so, perhaps, were the groves of sycamores and the gardens trimmed like canapés. In the tall birch forests, children are making sport of gathering leaves.

A stone marks each verst on the royal road from Tsarskoe-Selo back to Leningrad, where, at Nevsky Prospekt, we are held up as a ski team on two-wheel roller skates poles along in snow-country clothes: practicing for the Olympic Games, Alexandra says, and no wonder if they win.

Shortly before tonight's concert, I.S. receives a last-minute request for tickets from some teen-age members of the "Stravinsky Club of Kharkov," and he arranges to get them in. Parker finds a seat, too, for I.S.'s 84-year-old relative.

Mounting the podium, I.S. turns around and tells the audience that he attended his first concert in this hall: "Sixty-nine years ago I sat with my mother in that corner"—he points to it—"and heard the Symphonie *Pathétique*, conducted by Napravnik to mourn the death of Tchaikovsky. Now I am conducting in the same hall. I am very happy." This moving little speech is even more of a success than the music, which, after all, and as I.S. quips, "was half Tchaikovsky" (*Le Baiser de la fée*) "and half Rimsky-Korsakov" (*Fireworks* and *Firebird*). He had asked the Composers' Union to invite Nadiezhda Rimsky-Korsakov, the composer's daughter, to the concert, *Fireworks* having been composed to celebrate her marriage, but Parker tells us that the old lady declined because she had always known that I.S. detested her husband, the composer Maximilian Steinberg.

October 9. We walk from the Hermitage Bridge, where punts and kayaks are racing in the Moyka River, to the Pushkin Museum. The relics here include the poet's vest, worn in the fatal duel; his death mask, which emphasizes the large brow, flaring nostrils, small mouth; and his library, about half of which is in foreign languages. From Pushkin's former residence we go to one of V.'s, at the Moyka corner of the Champs de Mars, a sand-graded parade ground when she knew it, now a garden with a mammoth war memorial; then to Aptekarsky Ostrov, the island where she was born* (but which would have been a more appropriate address for I.S.: "*Aptekarsky*" means apothecary); to Kammenoi Ostrov, where a tree planted by Peter the Great is now in the middle of a street; to the Peter and Paul Fortress; to a corvette, the first to mutiny in 1917 and now a naval museum; and to the pink Kshesinskoi Palace, former home of the ballerina and mistress of the Grand Duke, where a plaque on the balcony commemorates Lenin's first speech after his arrival at the Finland Station. V. shows us where she crossed the ice in 1917 to hear Gorky speak.

According to Alexandra, our tour of the Hermitage this afternoon has covered 14 kilometers. I slog through in constant surprise at the dimensions of familiar pictures—the *Madonna Conestabile*, for instance, is so small that it might be circumscribed by the hands of a pianist. But nothing I can

---

* At Pesochnaya Ulitsa, 4.

1962 say about the Hermitage will satisfy me.

Leningrad is tall, regular, Western, straight—in contrast to circular, haphazard, oriental Moscow. And in Leningrad, the royal city, the people look more drab, partly because the buildings are so sumptuous, than they do in proletarian Moscow. I.S.: "The most beautiful thing about Leningrad is St. Petersburg," a city of romantic bridges and islands, and of small cobblestone streets and byways not yet macadamized, unlike the largest thoroughfares. The ugliest buildings in St. Petersburg are churches: the Issaksky, a heavy, black roost for imperial eagles that deserves to be in Berlin; the Kazansky, which imitates St. Peter's and deserves to be in Rome, Georgia; the Spassa Nakrovee, which consecrates, or desecrates, the site of Alexander II's assassination; and the Gastiny Dvor, the "upside-down trousers," as I.S. calls it. St. Petersburg is a polychrome city: the Dance Academy, a building the size of a California aircraft factory, is ocher; the Gorky Theater is green; the Anichkov Palace is red; the stables by the Champs de Mars are peach-color; and the Yusupov Palace, in which the first few stages of Rasputin's murder took place, is yellow. It is a city of classical angles and perspectives, and of planned space—I am thinking of the semicircular space cut back from the corners of streets contiguous to the Fantanky River. But at night, St. Petersburg is a lonely, melancholy city, like Venice in the winter. After 6 o'clock, I.S.'s old neighborhood is all but deserted as well as very dark, street lamps being far apart. At midnight, romantic mists hang low over the canals, and a ghostly gloom envelops the city. One imagines the Yusupov Palace full of light and gaiety, as it once was, but the beautiful old building is empty, dark, and dead.

Tempting generalizations I will never pronounce in public: Russians are hospitable; sentimental; "optimistic"; patient (an amazing capacity to stand in queues, though Parker says that some of this is laziness: "They would rather take a place on a line than work"); voluble (heavy artillery wouldn't interrupt most of them, but the voices and the language are less grating at great length than French and German); direct—the compliments, not to say encomia they address to us and each other in their toasts—but not frank (they will hide the real reason for anything they do not wish to reveal, like dogs burying bones); fundamentally friendly (they are friendlier to Americans than vice-versa, certainly); generous ("You like it? Here, take it," vs. the spirit of *"Klein aber mein"*). Their manners are not "good," but their ready affection more than makes up for this. I, at any rate, have never known a more affectionate friendship in so short a time than I have had with Karen Khachaturian, though we are able to converse only very haltingly. Russians have no commercial spirit—our venal pursuit of money—and no wasteful competition, even in the arts. Thus, if Russian composers dislike each other as intensely as do European and American composers—some of them ought to, for sure—the Russians nevertheless cooperate and function as a political entity in a way that their Western counterparts might envy. Lastly, "sophisticated" conversation—meaning, I suppose, a certain range of reference to modish mental bric-a-brac—is in short supply. It is replaced by "enthusiasm."

After tonight's concert, we rush to the midnight train for Moscow, carrying bouquets along with our bags. As we pull out of the station, a Diaghilev, a Tolstoy, a Rimsky-Korsakov, and a Balmont run alongside for a moment, like another era trying to catch up.

October 10. The sun rises through green forests touched with autumn gold, and from Klin to Moscow we press our noses to the corridor windows, watching people in shawls, caps, and boots going about their work in a land of brightly colored barns and *izbas*, the world of I.S.'s *Pribaoutki*, and of the Kandinsky, Jawlensky, and Chagall of half a century ago.

At the National Hotel, a letter awaits I.S. from a Polish branch of Stravinskys living in Danzig, complete with genealogical tree. At noon, Khrennikov and Khachaturian arrive laden with farewell gifts, samovars, gold spoons, silver tea glass holders, inscribed scores.

The farewell banquet at the Metropole is a happy occasion, free of speeches and of formality—indeed, somewhat too relaxed: pellets of bread and even apples are flung about the room. At these affairs, spouses sit next to each other and are not separated as they would be at protocol dinners in the West: the wives we meet are all professional women, chemists, archaeologists, physicians, scientists. Shostakovitch, at I.S.'s side this time, seems even more frightened and tortured than at the first conclave, perhaps fearing that a speech is expected of him. He converses neutrally, at first, then like a bashful schoolboy blurts out that the *Symphony of Psalms* overwhelmed him when he first heard it and that he made his own piano score of it, which he would like to present to I.S. Seeking to return the compliment, I.S. says that he shares some of Shostakovitch's high regard for Mahler, at which Shostakovitch starts to melt, but quickly freezes up again as I.S. continues with: "But you should go beyond Mahler. The Viennese troika adored him, you know, and both Schoenberg and Webern conducted his music." Toward the end of the evening, and after several *zubrovkas*, Shostakovitch touchingly tells me that he would like to follow I.S.'s example and conduct his own music, "But I don't know how not to be afraid."

I.S., going to bed, says he has been imagining a conversation on the other side:

"The Russians have skyscrapers."

"Yes, but they are built on mud and will soon collapse."

"Well, they do have very good roads."

"Of course, but they are the work of slaves."

October 11. A telephone call at noon fixes an appointment with Khrushchev, returned only yesterday from a 12-day tour. We enter the Kremlin by the Bashnya Borovitskaya gate at 1:30, after our driver says

1962 "Nikita Sergeyitch" to a guard who asks for no identification. Passing St. Ivan's, gleaming white and gold, we stop at the Council of Ministers Building, from which Suslov, the Marxist ideologist, on his way out, waves a greeting but walks by, which seems to surprise Khrennikov, who may have been expecting him to be present at the meeting. A solitary soldier stands at the door, and a civilian secretary who leads the S.s to a tiny elevator and climbs the two flights with me. We pass a large cloakroom and walk through a long corridor to a waiting room that resembles a doctor's office, with a table of foreign-language magazines and a portrait of Marx on the wall, like the doctor's old professor. After five minutes, the same secretary ushers us to a long room with a long conference table covered in green billiard cloth. Khrushchev, behind a desk at the far end, sees I.S.'s limp and hurries to his side. I.S., addressing him as "Nikita Sergeyitch," apologizes "for taking time that must be doubly crowded after your absence." Khrushchev, only slightly taller than I.S., with small, brown, swivel eyes (you would not be able to look if they were larger), gives us short, energetic handshakes with a pudgy, short-fingered paw, and says, "I wanted very much to meet you." We sit at the far end of the billiard table, I.S. and V. facing Khrushchev, myself and Khrennikov next to him. Lenin is present, too, in a photograph on the wall behind Khrushchev's desk, as well as in a frame on his blotter next to a file marked *"Tass,"* and Marx, over the door, beyond several racks of pull-out maps.

Resting his rimless spectacles on the green felt and asserting his elbows there, Khrushchev talks about his trip. "I had been promising to visit Turkestan and the Aral Sea region for a long time, and though I was too busy to do it now, I felt it could not be postponed. What I saw impressed me so much that I returned by train, to give myself time to think about it." He describes the irrigation of the "Hungry Desert," in which "skeletons of camels have been found, though human beings have never been able to exist there. We have built a 1,300-kilometer canal and redirected the once-dried-up Amu-Darya. Rice and cotton are already growing, and in a few years the whole region will flourish." Anticipating the future, and not only of those regions, Khrushchev beams with pleasure and becomes even more energetic. He smiles, too, exposing a gallery of dental gold, but does not smile *all* the time, which is one's impression of him from newspapers. "The world's largest and fastest supersonic jets are being built in Tashkent," he goes on, glowing at the prospect of the Soviet lead in "inertial navigation." And he describes a territory, near Samarkand, in which "the English found gold—mere gold—but where we have discovered fountains of naphtha and inexhaustible deposits of copper. The gold is still mined, but as a quaint sideline industry. The women in these regions like to show off their wealth by wearing heavy red velvet, even in that oppressive heat, but they live in squalid houses and will not improve them because of an old fear of being taxed. When refrigerators, television sets, and laundry machines first reached the stores there, everything was sold in an instant and paid for from, literally, barrels of money." Elaborating on the good living conditions, in contrast to the misery on the Indian side of the border, his tone becomes aggressive and boastful. (I.S., later: "I think he wants India.") I.S. asks if the people in these regions speak Russian or if he used a translator. Khrushchev: "All *my* republics speak Russian; I have never had a translator in our country."

I.S. translates for me, this being the only occasion at which Alexandra has not been present, although a speech studded with statistics and geographical names is easy enough to follow, besides which the speaker could hardly be more concrete. (Afterward, the S.s remark on his "very correct Russian.") Khrushchev is acutely sensitive to whatever we say, and even more sensitive, I think, to whatever we might say; clearly, he does not want I.S. to talk about music. (But what *are* his thoughts about this emissary from the Tsarist past?) He does most of the talking, in any case, and as he can scarcely contain himself on the subject of his trip, nearly all of the 40 minutes are devoted to that. When we exchange observations about Moscow and the S.s tell him how beautiful they find the city, Khrushchev says: "Yes, not long ago I drove around really looking at it myself, and I was impressed; but it was a pigsty for 800 years." As we leave, he repeats Khrennikov's invitation to stay in a *dacha* in the Crimea, carefully including myself.. I say *"Bolshoe spasibo,"* and he, graciously, *"Priezzhayte opyat"* ("Come back"). I.S., in the car: "He is like a composer showing you the score on which he is working, and of which he is very full and very proud."

Sheremetievo Airport is an obstacle course of reporters, tape recorders, television cameras. An American reporter to V.: "I understand you had an interview with Khrushchev." V.: "Oh no. It was a visit, not an interview. *This* is an interview." Reporter: "Well, did you talk about music?" V.: "Mr. Khrushchev is not a musician. We did not exchange banalities about music, but listened to him relate fascinating things about his trip." * Reporter to I.S.: "Will you say something about the beauties of Russia, Mr. Stravinsky?" I.S.: "Beauties are to be loved, not talked about." "Mr. Stravinsky, what was your impression of Khrushchev?" I.S.: "Palace eunuchs are not running his affairs."

A hundred new friends and now familiar faces crowd around, stuffing our arms and pockets with presents (bottles of vodka, tar-like lumps of pressed caviar, photographs, flowers) and our hearts with kisses, embraces, tears.

The four-hour flight to Paris in an Air France Caravelle is memorable because of the rediscovery of food: *saumon fumé, crabe à la russe,* veal. When

---

* Next day in the Western press: "As Khrushchev is ignorant of music, he talked banalities about his trip."

1962 we land, at about 10 P.M., I.S. is surrounded by reporters, the news of his meeting with Khrushchev having been broadcast. To avoid an interview, I.S. protests that he needs time to sort out his impressions, but he does say, "One must be very gentle with the Russian public and talk to them as one talks to children." Late night dinner with François-Michel and Suvchinsky. We stay in the Hotel Windsor-Reynolds.

October 13. After a visit from Nabokov, dinner chez Tézenas with Giacometti.

October 14. Jean Genet for lunch, a small man—for some reason I had expected a bigger one—and in spite of the leather jacket, open shirt, necktie slack like a noose, unexpectedly soft-boiled. His gray-brown eyes are frightened but at the same time as impertinent as a stethoscope. He likes or doesn't like, and he lays it down short and sharp, frequently with "*Ça m'emmerde*," or "*Ça m'embête*," but after a round or two this is predictably perverse. When Dostoyevsky's name comes up, he says "*Tout ça m'emmerde beaucoup*," and his reaction to "Tolstoy" is "*Connais pas.*" He was unable to finish Kafka's *The Trial*, he says, "*parce qu'on a trop parlé de ça.*" From time to time he laughs with us, but then looks dangerous again and ready to bite. And when the punch line of someone else's joke has already been delivered, he has a prickly way of following it with "*Eh, alors?*" He contradicts, when an actor is described as handsome—"*Même à dix-sept ans il était très moche*"—and when we speak well of a film, he finds it "*Abominable.*" He flatters I.S., or tries to, telling him that his voice is "like the sound of the percussion instruments in *Histoire du Soldat*." (Actually, it is an acute remark.) When I.S. asks him, innocently, "Do you like to read at night?," he pretends to think deeply before coming back wickedly with "*Oui, peut-être.*"

October 18. Rome. Our concert at the Teatro Eliseo, I.S. conducting his arrangement of Beethoven's *Song of the Flea* for the first time. Dinner with Roman Vlad, Henze, and Ingeborg Bachmann.

October 28. Caracas. Because the principal hotel has just been bombed by terrorists, we stay in the Circo Militar (Círcolo de las Fuerzas Armadas), an officers' club that amounts to a private village. "Erected in the great days of the dictatorship," the Circo is an example of the corruption of the "in" party. The officers' entertainments include a cinema, a stadium, swimming pools, and a perpetual concert piped into every room, hall, and even into outdoor space. Guards with submachine guns stand at the gates, and though the marble bars, ballrooms, restaurants are empty except for us, every table is fully set at every meal.

October 29. Caracas resembles Los Angeles in the freeways on which traffic regulates itself by threat, and in the glass elevators, like thermometers, on the outsides of buildings. But the political graffiti here are more outspoken: "*Vivan las guerrillas,*" "*Muera Fidel,*" "*Romulistos Asesinos,*" and so on, back and forth. Unlike Los Angeles is the mountain range between the city and the sea. The peaks, like elderly courtesans, lift their veils only at night. *1962*

The United States Embassy, where we attend a reception, looks over the city from a hill. "It is like San Francisco without the bay," the Ambassador observes to me, but what with the ring of armed guards, it *feels* more like Alcatraz without any San Francisco. A time bomb exploded in the Embassy laundry chute a week ago, and the Ambassador himself will not attend our concert because the police cannot guarantee to protect him in the University auditorium.

October 30. The lisp and elimination of the "s" are more marked here than I have ever heard; the musicians address I.S. as "Maetro Travithky," and when I announce Debussy's *Gigues* for rehearsal, it is repronounced "*Heeg.*" During my *Petrushka* rehearsal, I.S. tells the pianist to open the lid all the way, use the left pedal only, and play *forte* and *secco*; and since I have heard these directions a dozen times, I should record them as definitive. He also instructs the strings to play the triplet in the *Cantique* (Four Etudes), including the augmentation in the first and last measures, with three up-bows on one bow.

The hills across the highway from the Circo swarm with shacks, their walls made out of billboards with parts of the advertised products—a woman drinking Pepsi-Cola—still showing. Rich people tell us that the indigent people who have drifted here from the jungle consider themselves better off than ever before, no matter what, which means no plumbing, no water, no latrine but the street, no electricity except by filching from other people's outlets during the night. Though warned against strolling here—the dirty labyrinths are impassable to automobiles—we do so for as long as we can stand the stench, which is long enough to discover a Russian church. Nor are we attacked or threatened except by some girls of nursery-school age who turn toy submachine guns in our direction.

Commenting on the extremes of poverty and wealth, Federico Schlesinger, late of Vienna and now proprietor of a local hotel, says, "Venezuela does not spend its money but throws it away." Federico's own greatest treasure is a tooled morocco guestbook inscribed by every celebrity who has dared to come within the three-mile limit. Ernest Hemingway, perhaps irritated by the fulsome testimonial of a previous signer, has written, I suspect with malice, "To Federico, may his luck continue."

October 31. Marcel Roche, director of the Institute of Scientific Research, several thousand feet above the city, takes me through the buildings and describes the work being done to combat the *schizotrypanum cruzi*. This is transmitted by cockroaches and, he says, has already caused cardiac damage to at least a tenth of the population.

At a late-night farewell party in the garden of Rios Reyna, president of the orchestra, girls with tall, spun-sugar coiffures sing attractive Creole songs, but my own attention is held by giant moths alighting on the walls, and grasshoppers with chassis the size of large peapods.

1962   **November 17.** New York. Auden for dinner, in the Pierre restaurant. His face now hangs in loose folds, like an elephant's behind, and in marked contrast to his extremely tight trousers, the cuffs of which are as much as 10 inches above his flat, platypus-like feet. He says that in the train club car on his way to lecture at Yale, some students sent him a note: "We can't stand it a minute longer: are you Carl Sandburg?" He wrote back: "You have spoiled mother's day."

After asking the waiter to bring him a "veg," he remarks that "Cardinal Newman could have become a saint but thought it too fruity to do a miracle." Then, greatly amused by I.S.'s story of a U.S. Immigration Official in 1939 asking if he wanted to change his name, Auden says that when *he* was examined for United States citizenship, "It didn't look too good because I admitted I was a writer, whereupon the interviewer told his secretary to put down 'Can read.' One of the questions, incidentally, was 'Do you intend to kill the president?,' and I am certain that if I had answered 'Yes,' no one would have noticed."

Talking about his ideas for a libretto on the *Bacchae*, he reveals that "The *Elegy* was our version of *Arabella*." Switching to other operas, he describes the beginning of the second act of *Die Walküre* as "a Victorian breakfast scene, Wotan meekly cracking his morning egg behind the *Times* while Fricka furiously rattles the teacups. *Pelléas*," he says, "is an underwater opera. Nobody can be that refined; it succeeds only because it flatters the audience. Imagine devoting an opera to people with manias for losing things!" Apropos a line in *Vanessa*, he wonders "where the author had seen 'weeping deer,' " and, in defending opera against other types of music, he remarks, "People who attend chamber music concerts are like Englishmen who go to church when abroad."

His literary references nowadays are exclusively German. "Lichtenberg's notes on Hogarth contain a better translation for 'The Rake' than 'Der Wüstling,' but I can't remember what it is." "The Germans tend to regard one of their classic authors as Jesus Kleist," he says, and he proposes a new classification for a whole category of females: "the Rilke-girlfriend type." He loses his way on a trip to the "loo," however, and this must have given him an unpleasant turn—"*schwarze Gedanken*," he would probably prefer to say—for shortly afterward he announces: "When my time is up I'll want Siegfried's Funeral Music and not a dry eye in the house."

November 20. My American Opera Society performance of the *Rake* in Carnegie Hall: Ansermet is there, but I.S. avoids him.

November 29. Toronto. I rehearse and I.S. records *Babel*. Is it a coincidence that this arch-enemy of *Francmaçonnerie*—he slyly omits the cedilla when pronouncing the word—should have chosen the text, since Masons were supposedly ordained at the building of the Tower of Babel? Hearing the work live for the first time, I am struck by the beautiful wind chords at the end, but the choral music lacks pulsation.

੩ Postscript 1994. Stravinsky's 80th birthday year was the fullest of his **1962** later life, and the diary, exceptionally, provides a nearly complete outline of it. Moreover, the narrative of the Russian trip introduces a different perspective from that of the book as a whole in that Stravinsky was part of the landscape instead of, as everywhere else, my fellow observer. To see him in an approximation of his cultural background, even an updated one, was the most memorable part of the experience for me, far more so than the glimpses of Soviet cultural politicians during the Cuban missile crisis, and of the continuing dominance in music, as in painting, of academic socialist realism.

I should have emphasized that Mrs. Stravinsky was much less ambivalent about the "new" Russia than her husband, as well as less apparently charmed by the Soviet officials and musicians with whom they associated. But Stravinsky's blatant volte face on our arrival in Paris, his *Retour de l'U.R.S.S.*, belittling the country and people he had just left, troubled me: was his display of Komradery during the trip entirely false? He was said to resemble his father, an operatic basso renowned for his impersonations. But back in Hollywood, Stravinsky quickly immersed himself in new projects, and the Russian trip, if not forgotten, was seldom mentioned.

My Russian diary attracted considerable attention when it appeared in *Encounter* (London) in 1963. Private views of the inside of Khrushchev's Kremlin were rare, and the meeting between the ex-miner Communist boss and the famous Tsarist-period artist going home after 50 years was dramatic. Oddly, many readers seemed to think that Stravinsky had written the article. When we dined with Luigi (*The Italians*) Barzini in New York shortly afterward, he congratulated Stravinsky on it—to my astonishment; obviously Stravinsky could not have said what I said about him. A new twist, then: up to this point I had been accused of ghost-writing Stravinsky and now he was assumed to be ghost-writing me.

I am still struck by the contrast between the reception at the White House, the Presidential limousine, the walkie-talkie security guards, the in-honor-of dinner that was also a political pay-off, and the arrival at the Kremlin, where no sentry was in sight and we were escorted into Khrushchev's inner sanctum by a plainclothes secretary.

Stravinsky's first year as an octogenarian was marked by more public exposure than he had ever had, in South Africa, Israel, Italy, Germany, Canada, Venezuela, as well as the United States; even to read the itinerary fatigues me now. But in spite of the globetrotting, he finished *The Flood*, that still undiscovered masterpiece, and wrote a considerable portion of the new and very different music of *Abraham and Isaac*.

✒ 1963

February 1. Hollywood. Party at George Cukor's with Bette Davis, Katharine Hepburn, Groucho Marx. Coarse language from all except Hepburn.

February 6. Dinner with the Renoirs and Madame Slade, Auguste Renoir's model.

March 4. From Glenn Gould: "This is by way of being a fan letter for *Erwartung*—absolutely one of the most marvelous things you have ever done! In fact, the whole record is tremendous."

March 7. To a performance of Mahler's Seventh by the Los Angeles Philharmonic superbly conducted by William Steinberg. A chat with Anna Mahler backstage.

April 20. Hamburg. To *Mahagonny* at the Staatsoper, the first evening in our two-week "theater cure." The staging, by a Brecht pupil, is admirably severe, especially in the groupings of the chorus, but after applauding the director, I.S. turns to the composer; "There are interesting things everywhere in the score, but it is not everywhere interesting." And the musical substance has been lavished on a flimsy play. (Berg must have known *Mahagonny*: Lulu has a touch of Jenny, Berg's Athlete more than a touch of Weill's, and the choice of instruments in Berg's "*Garderobe*" scene owes something to the sax and banjo in Weill's jazz band and the zither in his glutton scene.) Whatever the quality of the music, the piece is dispiriting, a lively beginning followed by a three-hour downward plunge with no upward swerve; we leave the theater in the dumps. No doubt, too, this long decline has a deleterious effect on my judgment, so that most of what I remember as good seems to have occurred comparatively near the beginning: the boxer's death, the brothel scene ("*Erst wasch die Hände*" and "*Jungens macht rascher*"), and the scene with the glutton (an "*Er ist tot*," a "hats off," and a "that's that").

Hamburg is no Berlin-in-the-20s. Risqué lines and situations provoke uncertain titters, and all over the theater Herr and Frau Schmidt exchange whispers and knowing nudges. The audience sits back as if it were enjoying a musical or operetta, even if a strangely depressing example of either.

The scene in the Vier Jahreszeiten restaurant later might be a continuation of the last scene of the opera. The final abasement of society is represented in the opera by pickets with placards saying *FÜR GELD!*, while in the restaurant, bellhops in floor-length aprons march about carrying the same kind of signs summoning people to telephones: *BITTE HERR STOLZ!*

April 25. Grundgens's staging of Schlegel's *Hamlet* at the Deutsches Schauspielhaus provides a language lesson, if little else. The English lines leap into the mind like subtitles in a foreign film, if one catches the German trigger words that release the springs. This involuntary translation mechanism gives many of the German phrases an unbecomingly comic sound: *"Ein Meisterwerk ist der Mensch,"* for example, and *"Hat der Kerl kein Gefühl für seine Arbeit?"* Even the forms of address, *"Gnädiger Herr"* this and *"Gnädige Frau"* that, strike me as droll, partly because they are used here in Hamburg for the S.s. The German vocabulary is so much smaller, too— like a translation of Lamb rather than of Shakespeare—that we are aware of repetitions of phrasing. But what can any translator do with a succession of words like the Ghost's "unhousel'd, disappointed, unanel'd"? Another, unexpected impression is that the language, though Germanic only, is softer than the combination of Latin and Germanic in the English.

Exactly how close to the meaning the translation might be I am unable to say, but the action often seems to indicate that any connection is tenuous. "Who's there?" Bernardo asks, and the other guard counters, "Nay, stand and unfold thy self." But the Bernardo in this performance is long since unfolded and, even allowing for poor visibility, stands less than a foot away. Nor does Hamlet himself take any pains to act in reasonable conformity with what he is saying, or what one remembers him saying in English. To begin with, he is wholly devoid of a poetic or intellectual temperament, while being a great one for leaping and somersaulting, playfully wrestling with and knocking Rosencrantz about, half throttling his mother, prematurely practicing balestras on Laertes—the loudest Laertes in theater history. Hamlet, in fact, is faster-moving than anyone else on the stage, which contradicts not only the usual picture of the character but also the specific suggestion in his mother's speech during the duel that (like Aeneas) he is heavy-set. In one scene he rolls and squats as if he might be preparing for a performance elsewhere as Puck, and in the *prie-dieu* scene he comes tearing in like a professional sprinter or as if he were following a canine interpretation of "a Great Dane." In short, no indecision, no pale cast of thought, but a great deal of roistering and rapidly translated action, for which reason, in part, the play feels so prosaic.

The decorative and atmospheric aspects of the production are no less odd. Several series of abstract panels are imposed as backdrops or subliminal advertisements. Unobtrusive at first, they become less abstract with each scene and more expressionistically involved, eventually forming an intolerable symbolic accompaniment to the play. Thus a great deal of gray is exhibited when the outlook for Hamlet seems to be taking that complexion, and of red when we should sense that blood is about to be shed. In the graveyard scene the panels are smeared in a way that might be understood as posing a riddle, thus focusing attention on the solution of the symbolic conundrum rather than on what is otherwise the most successful scene of the evening, which the gravediggers play like contemporary Berlin wits. But whatever *do* those panels mean? Dirty laundry? That the cemetery is not in a posh neighborhood?

As for the costumes, Horatio looks like an orchestra conductor or maitre d'hotel, Polonius like an idiot Wilhelm II, Fortinbras like a space-traffic policeman, the Norwegian army—green leather uniforms and crash helmets—like shock troops of the future. Still other periods are suggested by the music and the choreography. The former consists of spurts of pseudo-Handel on an organ (which seems preferable to rancid sackbut sennets), the latter of modern-dance ballet—in the dumb show, during which Hamlet never so much as slyly glances at the King. It remains to be said that this action thriller takes place in two dramatically shapeless divisions, separated by an intermission just long enough for philosophers to read Karl Jaspers's program notes, "*Hamlets Wissen.*"

After the performance, I.S. remarks, "The play is like a turkey which nobody knows how to cut because Hamlet himself is developed so far out of proportion to the other characters." I wonder if "philosophical" passages seem to stand out more because of the German language, Ophelia's "We know what we are but not what we may be," for instance, which makes off, centuries ahead with the cake of Existentialism and the belief beyond appearances ("There is a special providence"). I had never before noticed to what extent Polonius's boringness is a family disease, both children being afflicted with it as well, and I had quite forgotten Hamlet's generosity to artists, *i.e.*, when Polonius orders the actors to be treated "according to their desert," and the Prince counters with the order, "Use them after your own honour and dignity: the less they deserve, the more merit is in your bounty."

April 28. To *Don Carlos* at the Opera. Here the staging lacks action, while some of the little there is goes wrong, such as the sword-drawing in the street scene, a weak curtain-closer that marks the breakdown of credibility in the work as a whole. Nor do the sets offer compensations, their main feature being a row of overgrown asparagus meant to represent trees. The drama falls off so sharply after the Grand Inquisitor scene, in any case, that the rest is hardly more than a costume concert. To make matters worse, the Inquisitor is miscast, a feeble elder rather than a holy terror; and the orchestra does the casting, implacably setting the scene for a more powerful person and voice than King Philip's. Despite the shortcomings, I.S. is rapturous. "What scope and vitality Verdi had, and with what scale he could endow his people! How I would like to have known him! His was the true spirit of *libertà*, and he, not Wagner, was the true progressive, not merely the Verdi of the Risorgimento and Cavour's parliament, but the composer of the *Don Carlos* duet: which is so much more likable than the *Blütbruderschaft* music that fat people in horns and hides howl at each other by the hour."

April 29. To *Wozzeck* at the Oper and dinner at Lemke's.

May 2. When I.S. takes his seat in the middle of the third row of the Staatsoper, a moment before the lights dim for *Der Rosenkavalier*, the audience applauds him. He acknowledges this with a deep bow, but whispers to me: "It is because everybody is happy to see me sit through four hours without syncopation." But he *doesn't* sit, or, at any rate, doesn't sit still. "Strauss holds his breath too long," he says, and "How long can this false counterpoint go on?" all this in a *voce* not *sotto* enough, and, "How can anybody swallow all that *Schlagsahne*?" Prurience, he remarks at intermission, is tolerable only in Mozart.

May 5. We fly to Amsterdam and from there to Prague and Budapest in an Ilyushin turbo-prop. At the empty and ominous Prague Airport, two policemen enter the cabin just before take-off and check every face against a photograph. Budapest airport, a half-hour later, is totally dark and—except for our welcoming party, a press photographer, and three Italian women from a concert agency, one of them, Toti del Monte, a diva of yesteryear whom the S.s had known in the 1930s—likewise deserted.

The city might still be under a wartime curfew. The streets are very dimly lighted and virtually without traffic, vehicular or pedestrian. But shell holes and other damage from the fighting of seven years ago are visible even in the gloom.

The Grand Hotel, on Margit Sziget—Margaret Island, in the Danube—hides behind a levee in a park of chestnut trees, now in blossom. No renovation appears to have disturbed the Grand since the great days of Hapsburg decline. The turn-of-the-century bedroom furniture is imitation rosewood; the landscapes and portraits are framed in gold guilloche; the beds are covered by eiderdown dumplings; the windows are draped with velvet curtains large enough to conceal the modesty of a small operatic stage. Less charming, for nonantiquarians, is the plumbing. The water, both "cold" and "hot," dribbles out lukewarm and sulphurous, and the toilet gurgles vindictively for an hour or so after use. (So does our neighbor's, as we are forcibly informed because of a high transom permanently open to the adjoining apartment.) But the first clue that some ill may have befallen the old Empire is in the WC. In the morning, a dirty paper band is laid across the toilet seat. It says "Sterile," *in Russian.*

May 6. The contrast between the faded Franz Josef appointments and

1963 the clientele in the hotel dining room is bizarre. Most of the guests are
political missionaries, a description that includes several delegations of
Africans; a party of Frenchmen who, when we pass them, seem to be mut-
tering something against General de Gaulle; and a sizable contingent of
Chinese. The latter, wearing stiff-collared Mao tunics, share an endless
speech-making dinner with Hungarian officials—in, so I.S. says, very correct Russian. Nor are the entertainments of this aggregation less odd than
its appearance. At about 6 o'clock, in an adjoining dance pavilion, an
eight-man jazz combo starts through a repertory of American hit tunes of
the thirties featuring "Stars Fell on Alabama" and "Smoke Gets in Your
Eyes." The floor then rapidly fills and color-integrates, except for the
Chinese, who do not participate and, on the contrary, clearly regard their
western allies as puerile offenders against intellectual dignity. The crowd is
vivacious, and the Hungarian girls wear their hair like nests, in the
American way. (Or is it the Thracian way? Cf. Archilochus: ". . . the ungodly
Thracians with their hair done up in a fright on top of their heads. . . .")

The food, except for *caffè espresso*—coffee bars are two and three to the
block in Budapest—is ostentatiously bad. A few imports are available,
including Scotch whiskey, English gin, French sardines, French champagne, French wines (Hungarian wines, according to I.S., taste "like shel-
lac"), Icelandic caviar (*sic*, not "outlandish," though it is that, too); since the
USSR is both the largest exporter of caviar in the world and Hungary's
biggest brother, the promotion of an Icelandic brand seems spectacularly
eccentric. Is it protest, penance, or both? Surely no one could *prefer* it to
the Russian, as the S.s perhaps too openly indicate by clamping their noses
against its repellently ichthyoid odor. I.S. notes that despite the rumors of
famine, everyone looks remarkably fat, but V., after observing the bolting
and guzzling, gorging and swilling at neighboring tables, says that the fat
is emotional and the crapulousness a sign of deprivation.

The Hungarian National Radio Orchestra is rich in tone and precise and
fluent in rhythm, and the concert is the most satisfying on our tour, as well
as the most warmly and, I think, discriminatingly received. But the
rehearsals, because they take place in the small, acoustically perfect Franz
Liszt Hall, are more gratifying than the concert. The players' first foreign
language is a grudging German, with English a close second, French a poor
third. Hardly anyone speaks Russian, and in spite of the parity with
Hungarian on toilet seats, the language of the Occupier is certainly not
popular. The few Hungarians who talk to us about the USSR are far from
enthusiastic, in any case, and those who have traveled there are openly dis-
paraging.

May 7. Although the director of the Hungarian National Ballet apologizes for "the very tired orchestra," the *Sacre*, in the Hungarian State Opera
House, is musically accurate and the group-calisthenic choreography well
done. Moreover, I.S. says that the *temenos*—the magic circle—and the

Elue's descent into the cave were in the original libretto. This season's repertory, the director goes on, totals 60 operas: "In a city as small as Budapest, an opera can be given only a few times, whereas in a city the size of New York, a very few operas can be played again and again. Still, our ballet has performed *Sacre* 40 times this year, which, I think, is as good a record as New York." He is incredulous when I.S. tells him that the work has never been fully staged by an American company.

From the ballet, we go to a restaurant in Buda to hear an ensemble of cimbalom, clarinet, and strings. All the pieces begin with moody cadenzas and eventually turn into rhapsodies. The players wear muzhiks' blouses, and during their vodka "breaks" they stand, click their heels, and raise their glasses to I.S.

May 8. The Union of Composers is a well-informed multilingual group that includes an alarmingly pretty girl who, it is said (though that is beside the point) has written a highly successful opera. Delegates from the Union of Soviet Composers attend a reception there for us, bringing recordings of our Moscow concerts last year. Zoltán Kodály has promised to come, but since he is I.S.'s age and has only recently taken a bride of 20—following the death of a first wife 30 years *his* senior—his absence is accountable.

May 9. As we leave the hotel for the drive to Zagreb, a girl hands I.S. a note: "Dear Mr. Stravinszki! I please one autogram because I very like *Petruska* and you, Podmaniczky, Judith." He signs in the Hungarian manner: "Stravinszki, Igor." Travel fever shows in the eyes of the people who come to see us off, which makes us feel like departing prison visitors.

A long avenue with ocher churches and ocher trams leads to fields of black loam in which stooks of straw are stacked like tepees. Here, and all the way, most agricultural workers are women. From time to time a red star on the gate of a collective farm reminds the motorist of who is in charge, but crucifixes and shrines are a far more common sight. A plaque on one of the low, thatched-roof houses of Martonvasar commemorates Beethoven's stay there in 1808; at least that is what it seems to say, but when I try to read it, or pronounce any Hungarian aloud, our driver is seized with such fits of laughter that I fear we may land in a ditch. A catastrophe of the sort is only narrowly averted when we come to Szekesfehervar (say-cash-fe-hair-var), a city with Roman and Byzantine ruins and a turquoise-and-marigold rococo square. By the time we reach Nagykanizsa (nadg-caneezha) and Siofok, where we eat in a "bisztro" on Fout Street—a name, we have learned from experience, that will not sound as Chinese as it looks—I have learned to hold my tongue.

Lake Balaton is half hidden by a blizzard of dandelion fluff. The fields and forests to the south are richer and larger, but the farmers work with primitive hand implements, including hand barrows, and they seed the earth from aprons, as their ancestors must have done a thousand years ago. At the frontier, gun-toting guards, barbed wire, and a double barricade on

1963 the bridge explain the claustral look in the eyes of the people who came to see us off this morning.

The road on the Yugoslav side is unpaved as far as Cakovec, and thereafter, in the mountains of Illyria, worse than anything the word "unpaved" can suggest. The land is poor, too, and the few strips that have been plowed on the steep hills are not much wider than toboggan slides. The people, almost without exception, wear gray or black clothes, as if in mourning for some national disaster, which indeed seems to be the case, and though the houses in Cakovec itself bristle with TV antennae, this does not inspire confidence in the local prosperity. A work crew, idling in the yard of a derelict factory, looks as if it had given up and was simply waiting in the hope of being rescued by helicopters.

Our Hungarian driver pronounces "Cakovec" Aristophanically, "Ka-ko-kek," but the Yugoslavs to whom he appeals for directions fail to associate any part of their geography with this word. Nor are the "aids to pronunciation" in our guidebook any help in this case, or in any case but the most desperate. Thus *"Gdje je najblizi restoran?"* is the Croatian for "Where is the nearest restaurant?" (Nearest? A question of starvation?). "Could you recommend me to a good hotel?" is *"Mozete li mi preporuciti jedan dobar hotel?"* We will remember the Croatian for "restaurant" and "hotel," at least, however we manage the anterior matter.

The megalithic new city of Zagreb, entered via the "Square of the Victims of Fascism," is a cruel contrast to the Strossmajer Gardens and the vined and turreted old city. Hundreds of vanguard musicians, here for the Biennial of Contemporary Music, are billeted in our hotel, and electronic composers, microtonalists, and old-time 12-toners mill about the lobby and bar.

May 9, 10, 12. I like the "Jugs," but could not live in their East-West, North-South, Latin-Slav, Catholic-Orthodox cruciform culture. And I admire their guts. They were criminally underrated and neglected by Churchill and Roosevelt in the war, at one time holding down more German divisions than the British and Americans in Italy, but we still patronize and neglect them, in spite of which they are full of good will. I note one national idiosyncrasy: whereas they can be relied on to follow instructions to the letter, they will not extend the *principle* of them a step beyond, to unspecifiable eventualities. Thus the ushers at the late-night far-out concerts are strict about keeping people from entering the hall during the performance, but when a young man jumps to the stage from a nearby loge, like John Wilkes Booth, and begins to strangle an *avant-gardiste* making a jejune noise on a clarinet mouthpiece, they do nothing to restrain *him*. Or are they way ahead?

May 12. The Zagreb musicians have learned I.S.'s Movements in less time than any orchestra heretofore, and their reading of it, with the excellent local pianist Jurica Murai, is music-making of a high order. After the concert, in which I conduct the Symphony in Three as well as Movements, I.S. remarks, apropos the *Monumentum*, that transferring the music from voices to instruments short-changes the harmonic tension: "What is radical to sing sounds tame and archaic when played."

May 16. Paris. A journalist calls asking I.S. to tape-record a get-well message to Cocteau, as Braque and Picasso have already done. But he refuses, and so firmly that parts of the telephone fly off as he recradles the receiver. At lunch, with all ears to him, he says: *"Cocteau ne peut pas mourir sans faire réclame."* The remark is partly a reversion to type, for just as he became more Russian in Russia, so in Paris he quickly returns to and fulfills the expectations of a society whose smartest applause is reserved for the most barbed bons mots. Yet his feelings about Cocteau *have* changed. Only two weeks ago the news of the heart attack (and the thought of the subtraction and the narrowing circle) upset him. But on learning that his old friend had begun to recover, signs of annoyance appeared, as though, having already written off the account, it was a nuisance to reopen the books. I.S.'s feelings about Cocteau have always puzzled me, and though V. attributes them to a pernicious influence of Diaghilev, surely I.S. must have known Cocteau on independent terms at least at the time of the *Oedipus* collaboration. I have heard only sharp remarks about him, nevertheless, in all my 15 years with I.S., and the last time the two of them were together, in Paris last May, I.S. jibbed at keeping the appointment. When I.S.'s daughter-in-law, Françoise, sent him a copy of Cocteau's self-portrait (drawing) in a coffin and as if dead, I.S. wrote under it: *"Quel horreur!"* meaning what bad taste. At about that time, too, and after repeatedly prompting himself to "put something about Cocteau in one of our books," I.S. produced for that purpose a thousand or so partly libelous words, later blue-penciled and edulcorated under pressure from V. to the two paragraphs that he considers high praise, published in *Dialogues and a Diary* .

One of today's luncheon guests is a biologist who talks about the possibility of life on other planets, based on noncarbon elements. How I wish I could follow even the half of what he says concerning the chemistry of carbon compounds and the red shift, but I am a scientific illiterate, understanding less of the world around me than a three-year-old Eskimo.

Dinner with Ionesco, Giacometti, Nathalie Sarraute. My first impression of Ionesco is of a Chinese actor—the slightly slant-eyed mask, with remnants of hair tucked about the ears and lower cranium by a skillful make-up artist. Behind the mask is a permanently worried face, with a deep frown and sulky eyes. No smile escapes him all evening, but after watching him pan through a few jokes, one wonders whether his zygomatic muscles are still capable of pulling out of the pout and into such unfamiliar directions. Would he be less cross if his striped serge suit and checkered shirt were in less strident conflict? I think not, for on second glance one sees that this is the actor's costume, exactly what the well-dressed

1963 Berenger would wear, besides which, sharp or too noticeable clothes help to mortify shyness and punish self-consciousness, as well as to shield by advertising how well guarded we are. "*Ça dépend*," he says, again and again, fiddling with his fork, molding and unmolding bread crumbs and restricting the conversation to inhibited artificialities.

When the New York production of his *Rhinoceros* is mentioned, Ionesco condemns it, "except for the freak virtuoso performance of Zero Mostel." He greatly dislikes Broadway, of course, and New York even more. "It is a *chien ville*. Most cities can be classified as either dogs or cats. Naples and Venice are cat cities, London and New York are dogs, and Paris is both." (I think of how Auden, to whom classification games of this kind are old sport, would relish this feline-canine form, and with what a priori certainty he would set about categorizing the cities of Central Asia; nor would Auden miss the point of Ionesco's preference for a Paris he considers ambivalent.)

We switch from New York to the Soviet Union, but it, too, is unloved; or, rather, so virulently hated that Ionesco strikes at it blindly, like a boxer stung to the quick. The Russians buy and read more books than any other people, V. says. "You see them reading in buses, on benches, in queues, during intermission at concerts." "Yes," Ionesco agrees, "but such bad literature." V. mews back at this with, "True, it *is* likely to be only Pushkin or Gogol, and no one would claim Parisian sophistication for the Russians. Still, masses of people read poetry there as masses of people here do not." Ionesco: "But such bad poetry. Yevtushenko." This time, remonstrance comes from Sarraute, who has just returned from Moscow and has been talking with I.S. about her experiences there (she speaks perfect Russian); but rather than let the argument get farther out of hand, Ionesco simply dismisses the USSR as a "*révolution technocratique.*"

He is guiltily talkative, though, about his recent house-call on de Gaulle, describing it as an act of courage on his part, "for the reason that French intellectuals are one hundred percent against De Gaulle, and I am what people call a Saint-Germain-des-Près intellectual." Whether or not he feels that his motives may appear shaky, or that "courage" does not have the right ring, he tries to cover his tracks to the General's door by calling it an anti-conformist gesture—which is like Cocteau's attempt to justify his standing for the Academy on the ground that, since the honor is no longer honorable, to receive it constitutes an act of rebellion.

We come away yearning for the raw technocratic materialism of the *chiens villes* and complaining about Parisian insularity and, at the same time, its pretense to be the seat of the planet's acutest criticism. Michel Butor, who walks back to the Berkeley with us, explains that Ionesco must have felt intimidated; "he is not really like that." (I.S.: "Fewer and fewer people are what they seem.") "He can be five different characters in an afternoon, and the whole gamut from morbid to high. His politics are mixed up simply because he has suffered alike from failure and success and is afraid in equal measure of both the avant-garde and the reaction." I.S.: "How interesting to be five different people! And, after all, if you have the talent to create a variety of *personnages* for the stage, why not also create them for yourself?"

May 24. Bergen, Norway. My concert, *Perséphone* with Brigitta Lieberson (as the *diseuse*), a terrible tenor, an amateur chorus, and the Beethoven Violin Concerto. The violinist, Joseph Suk (Antonin Dvorak's great-grandson) arrives only minutes before, and we have no time even to set tempos, let alone rehearse the piece. I conduct a fanfare for the King's entrance, then the national anthem. I.S. was wise not to come—a 12-hour trip, with waits in Copenhagen and Oslo, and poor musical standards—but he has put me on the spot, substituting for him at a gala opening with the King and Parliament in attendance.

May 25. H.M. King Olav V's luncheon party in the Royal Lodge at Gamlehaugen. The hotel maids have been squealing *"Kongen, Kongen"* all week at the sight of the invitation on my dressing table and, since yesterday, when H.M. appeared at the concert, thus obliging me to conduct "God Save the Kong," their attention to me has improved to a point where they re-mop my floor every 10 minutes. The Gamlehaugen lodge, a 30-minute drive from Bergen by forest and fjord, is out of an Osbert Lancaster cartoon, complete with widow's walk, sentinels' bases at the main gate, and the royal colors flying from the roof.

A protocol officer ushers me from the door to the main room, presents me to the monarch, a pleasant and ruddy, not to say alcoholically florid, gentleman whose graciousness conceals every hint of the intense boredom he reputedly suffers at all concerts, hence no less at mine. (When, after the Beethoven, the audience began to applaud in rhythmic unison, His Majesty rose to leave, which meant that the audience had to rise, too, and the applause to freeze in mid-reverberation.) From H.M., I am handed along to admirals and generals with ever-diminishing clusters of medals and braids, to high clergymen, M.P.s, millionaire shipbuilders, Sonja Henie.

At table I sit between a bishop and a knight and feel like a pawn. Solitary drinking is not permitted; instead, one must fix one's eyes on those of a partner during the whole draught, as if in a state of hypnotic fascination. The vintages are excellent; and, since a non-Norwegian-speaking guest is naturally inclined to fortify himself on such occasions, and since he may never again succeed in drawing the attention of another pair of eyes, small wonder if he drains his glass at each opportunity. The Kong himself drinks the health of each guest individually, starting on his left around the three-pronged table from his position at meridian. Each of us, as his turn approaches, watches for the royal nod, hoists himself and his glass, and locks H.M. in the eye-to-eye embrace, this time omitting the *"Skol."* None

1963 of this is as stiff as I am making it sound, and the excellent *"Lunsj"* (lunch) of *"Sprosteke Kylling"* (crisp chicken) is expeditiously served and happily uninterrupted by testimonials. Afterward, teetering from the toasts, we move to a verandah for cognac and liqueurs. Here are tasseled cushions, frilled armchairs, chintzes, *Jugendstil* tapestries of Norse mythology: blond goddesses, lilies and swans, krakens, *Yggdrasil*.

The conversation of the shipbuilders centers on the inauguration of the Munch Museum in Oslo next week. "It has been determined," one of them says, "that 66.5^0 Fahrenheit is the optimum room temperature for the oils. Now I remember Munch's studio with paintings strewn all over the floor, and if they were in his way he would walk on them or stack them outside in the snow. Now, too, we pay $50,000 for the kind of picture he would give to the grocer in settlement of a bill. In fact, those grocers are, so to speak, sitting on their Munchs and waiting for us to buy them, just as American farmers wait to sell their land to builders of turnpikes."

Back in Bergen, and having missed today's installment of the perpetual Grieg concert, I walk by the quay, the gabled houses, and the statue of Bjornsen—the most vigorous stride, living or graven, I have ever seen—at the head of Ole Bull Street.

May 26. Fly to London at 1 A.M. Letter in the Savoy from Isaiah: "Dear Bob, I have asked Gilbert Ryle, partly in order to see what you and the Stravinskys think at the end of it all. He was not in the least surprised to be asked (he should have been), as he is rather a vain man; but he is very distinguished, though you will find, I think, a fairly militant lowbrow, albeit disguised."

May 28. The T. S. Eliots for dinner. Apropos my Russian diary in *Encounter*, he says that the British Arts Council asked him to receive Yevtushenko, but that the meeting was not a success: "I am unable to speak through a translator unless I know him. . . . Incidentally, Igor, one of your Russian 'r's' reminds me of the variety of 'r' sounds in Sanskrit that Indians do not recognize as differentiations but nevertheless they pronounce."

May 29. Oxford. Lunch at Isaiah Berlin's with John Sparrow and Professor Gilbert Ryle, a big-boned, major-in-mufti type, with bald, brindled cranium, thrusting jaw, and "intellectual" brow; one feels that without further make-up—he arrives in a parka, tweeds, specs, pipe ("Damn the dottle, let's get our teeth into the problem")—he could take to the stage playing a private eye (Bulldog Drummond). About two minutes of conversation make clear that the Professor is a purely British phenomenon, deeply suspicious of "continental intellectuals," and, indeed, of anyone from "abroad." If he were to make an exception, moreover, it would undoubtedly favor a lean, outdoor-type Australian pragmatist, say, over some pasty-faced Middle European logical positivist, even if the ideas of the latter on how to "do" philosophy were closer to those of the Professor.

"Why are your chaps always bringing up Dewey and James?" he asks me. "The world would have been so much better off without those Great American Bores." No answer is expected, of course, and the impossibility of expostulation has already been conceded. Besides, more seriously offending countries have yet to be dealt with. (When they have been, one sees to what extent philosophy is a national and school bias. "Steeped in port and prejudice among the monks of Oxford," Gibbon wrote, escaping the fate.) Noncompetitive philosophers such as those of the USSR rate only indulgent amusement, and, for open laughs, a Soviet philosophical journal is quoted on the Professor himself, cited as a "bashful materialist" and "creeping empiricist." Stronger medicine is reserved for closer trans-Channel targets. "One of my greatest satisfactions as an editor was in publishing a review of the works of one Teilhard de Chardin, then rumored to be a biologist. What a lot of lemon juice we poured on *that* old teleological pancake." Merleau-Ponty fares no better: "French *clarté*, indeed. And, by the way, have you noticed how many French intellectuals have become retroactive heroes of the *maquis?*" Mention of Karl Popper provokes the remark, "The first person pronoun, found twice in Aristotle, occurs 17 times in one of Herr P.'s shorter footnotes; he can hardly bear to use any other word." Two Israeli philosophers are dismissed with the comment, "Neither is actually very good at listening," and an over-enterprising British colleague is swept aside as a "literary civil servant. One wonders about these people who try to take the pulse of every new movement. Where do they get all the fingers?"

But the acid tickles more than it burns. On the subject of "philosophers' jamborees," he says, "The *real* philosophers are the translators. Picture two thousand of us in an auditorium in Brussels with Professor Gorgonzola on the rostrum being translated line for line: 'The ontological postulate of the, and . . . oh, pardon me, Professor, but I didn't get the last phrase.' Well, *I* got it. Rubbish, of course." Telling us of an invitation to a similar picnic "somewhere in the Great American West," he remarks that "they wanted me to 'express my views on philosophy,' as they put it, in a five-minute television interview, to which I replied that I doubted if I could make anything clear to anyone out there in less than five years."

Talking about the difficulty of trying to keep up with new publications, I.S. cites the case of a friend who has learned to read while he walks, even though he looks like the absent-minded professor, or the last eccentric. The notion of crossing the quad with a book to one's nose delights Professor Ryle—"Oh, jolly good, very impressive indeed, splendid, splendid"—but he does not agree that eccentrics are disappearing, "at least not when I look around at my colleagues in the common room." An aroma, unmistakably of that location, is twice uncorked, first when he replies to one of our queries with "That's a further question which I will answer when you have answered mine," and again when he illustrates a limitation of the

1963 word "correct," in the sense of behavior, with the example of Lord X, "who when told that his wife had been killed, responded with 'What a pity.' This, you see, is perfectly 'correct,' but most people would probably agree that something is missing." Once or twice I wonder whether the best of his *aperçus* ("Every generation or so philosophical progress is set back by the appearance of a 'genius' ") roll off somewhat too readily, undermining confidence in their hundred-percent spontaneity, and arousing suspicion that a repertory is being worked off, in the manner of Tchichikov or Mr. Jingle. After lunch, a bowl of cherries is handed round. (The Professor's appetite is commensurate with his frame, and when the main course is finally being cleared, he resists three attempts by the butler to remove his bread plate.) "I have a cherry tree of my own," he says—to my surprise, as I had pictured him in landless bachelor's digs—"but have not yet tasted its fruit because the birds get there first." V. recommends a new kind of protective net, but the Professor's answer is that "The tree is 30 feet tall and I'm not," which is empirically verifiable, to be sure, as well as, one fears, an example of more than a little philosophical activity.

The only real mishap occurs when the word "music" slips out. The Professor glums thereat and is soon beating a retreat back to, as he says on the way out, "academe." (But when did he leave it? Can he have regarded the visit as an excursion into "real life," as he defines that concept in his new lecture, *A Rational Animal?*) When he has gone, I.S. compares him to "a very brilliant schoolboy who, without meaning to, has made us feel like very dull schoolboys." The truth is that whereas the Professor has enlightened and exhilarated us, we have failed to provide him with good cutting matter for his wit.

Our evening in London is divided between a new *Figaro* at Covent Garden and a fiftieth-anniversary *Sacre* at Albert Hall. The *Figaro* is a gala performance in the presence of the Queen Mother, whose loge we stand and face during the national anthem. But the glittering, bedizened audience is in striking contrast to the set for Act I, which might be a suite in the Dorchester Hotel and doubtless is applauded for the reason that most people are pleased to recognize it. Solti's performance is souped up, overmolded, too pushed and high-powered, with a scale of dynamics more appropriate to Varèse. I.S.: "Mozart is poorer than that."

Arriving at Albert Hall during the *Danse de la terre*, we find half of the orchestra following Maitre Monteux's actual beat, and the other half following what the players, and no doubt *le maître*, too, know the beat should be. In I.S.'s loge after the *Danse sacrale*, the two tiny gentlemen pose together as if for an advertisement on the longevity value of modern music: "Why we didn't retire at 60." "Monteux is shrinking," I.S. observes to me afterward. "He seems only half as heavy as when I saw him last," at another *Sacre* blowout in Paris 11 years ago. And the question of the old maestro's reduction seems to disturb I.S. all evening, in spite of V.'s reassuring "*multum in parvo.*" I.S. seems not to have been touched by the occasion and is loudly critical of the performance, but late at night, re-entering the Savoy, he simmers down about the wrong tempi long enough to call *le maître "un très brave homme."*

From Albert Hall we go to the Eliots', nearby, for late-night cheese, apples, and Scotch. They have heard the performance "on the wireless" and applaud the composer as he enters. Comparing tonight's ovation with the reception of the ballet in London in 1921, Eliot observes, "The English think it is polite to laugh when confronted with something serious that they do not understand." The conversation turns to this afternoon's Derby: "I used to wager in the Calcutta Sweepstakes," Eliot says, "but I never drew a horse. During a visit to Stockholm in 1948 I put some money on a long shot called Queen Mary—out of loyalty, of course, not because of a hunch—but we came in last." When I ask Eliot to inscribe his new pamphlet on George Herbert, he says, "Herbert is one of the very few poets whom I can still read and read again. Mallarmé is another, and, hm, so is Edward Lear. . . ."

May 31. Stephen Spender drives us to Canterbury and Saltwood Castle for lunch with Sir Kenneth and Lady Clark. The Kentish woods are carpeted with bluebells, and pink hydrangeas are blooming in country gardens. The hops fields near Canterbury are honey-colored like the newly scrubbed sandstone of the cathedral itself.

To go from the cathedral to Saltwood is to go from the scene of Becket's murder to the scene of the hatching of the plot, or the pledging to it, for it was at Saltwood that the villainous conspiring knights met, afterwards extinguishing their candles to avoid each other's eyes—according to Tennyson, who was imbuing the murderers with a degree of conscience they do not seem likely to have had. Turning to more recent Saltwoodiana, Stephen says that one prospective caller rapped at the portcullis but was turned away with the explanation that "Lady Clark is busy weeding the battlements." According to another anecdote, the chatelaine once reproved a serving wench for having "fingered the tulips just before the Kents came to dinner." In the best of this Firbankian anthology, a story about some gentlewomen at a court ball complaining to each other about the nuisance of being obliged to send to the bank once or twice a year to fetch their tiaras, Lady C. remarks that *her* tiara has become terribly worn. But to visit Saltwood is to see that the battlements *would* need weeding.

Except for a television aerial on a parapet, and a scullion's or varlet's flivver parked by the moat, the picture of the castle could be titled "Saltwood as Becket knew it." The collection of narwhals' horns in the entranceway is second only to that of the Musée Cluny, and the masterpieces of perfect pedigree displayed in every room and corridor qualify the castle as one of the great private museums of the world. Even in the "loo,"

1963 the wallpaper is by William Morris, who may also have been responsible for the plumbing: "Only the Queen Mother knows how to use our WC," Lady C. says, unwittingly adding to Saltwood lore.

From those weedy battlements, Sir K. can survey his demesne over the milky haze of the downs to the sea, the sea of Turner's *Storm at Folkestone*, which hangs in the library. Sir K. waxes eloquent on the painting, but I can render no more than the gist of his talk: "Turner was always living in houses along the River Thames, you see, and getting up at dawn to study morning light on water. Now look at that light. And at this circular movement. He thought in circles, you see; I doubt that his hand could have moved at all if it had had to do classical symmetries. Perhaps we should call him the arch anti-classicist."

At table, and for I.S.'s sake, Sir K. puts forth the notion that "instead of trying to suppress modern painting, the Russians might reasonably have claimed to be its discoverers, what with Jawlensky, Malevich, Gabo, Archipenko, Soutine, Chagall, El Lissitzky, Tatlin, Kandinsky, De Stael, Poliakov, Berman, Tchelichev, Goncharova, and Larionov. The difficulty for the Soviet Union is that they all became refugees. Kandinsky's case is the most curious because he was potentially, if not in fact, a *great* painter, at least up to the time when he went back home and became a commissar. I'm sure he liked that, for a time anyway, but after his experience in politics, reality went underground and he painted only squares, circles, abstractions, all very dead. *There* is a clue to 'modern art.'"

The lunch being heady, I recall only one other remark: "Real gourmets always take red wine with salmon." And in rapid succession I feel that I am (a) an unreal gourmet, (b) no gourmet at all, (c) anti-gourmet. Having shown the highest appreciation of Sir K.'s Scotch, a specially-bottled private stock, I.S. is rewarded with the gift of a bottle when we leave; at this, Lady C. gasps, "Oh, no," and Sir K., not succumbing to embarrassment, says: "Don't worry, dear, there is enough left for you."

Back in London we dine at the Garrick Club with Henry Moore, an open and immediately likable man with clarion opinions and an appealing, debonair giggle. At one point the talk drifts toward the quagmires of "taste," which, I.S. says, "is for pederasts. For most other people it is simply a matter of familiarity. Other people's toes are ugly; ours are not because we grew up with them and got to know them in the piggly-wiggly stage." Here Moore supervenes: "But there is something much bigger than taste, and that is the sense of terrible importance." I ask which sculptors have this sense, and he comes down with finality and without hesitation on each of the names I propose: Rodin was "a sculptor," Brancusi was "only and totally a sculptor," Matisse was "a sculptor," Picasso is "a sculptor," Wotruba is "a sculptor," Giacometti is "a great *artist*," Marini is "a bit of a sculptor," Manzù is "a real sculptor, but a bad one." Later, describing a Cycladic vase he has just acquired, words fail him and he takes a pen, draws the object for us with a few swift strokes, says: "Well, as you can see, that's not a ceramic at all but a sculpture."

June 1. With Stephen Spender to visit David Jones in his bed-sitting room on the second floor of a lodging house in Harrow-on-the-Hill. The residence is more cocoon than room, and even as silkworms go, the tenant is delicate and withdrawn. Jones's face is boyish, an impression created in part by bangs and a glabrous skin, in part by a grin—that vanishes suddenly, however, leaving us aware of how deeply troubled his expression was before. His shyness and lack of animal confidence retreat somewhat with each link in a chain of cigarettes, yet never to the extent that our presence can be made to appear as less than a great burden on him (the cocoon is so close). Then, too, we are all the more conscious of our intrusion in that his solitary confinement is so obviously self-willed.

Paintings, drawings, manuscripts, books are scattered everywhere, and he complains of having to unpile his bed every night and to pile it up again in the morning. This afternoon it is strewn with sheets of foolscap, on each of which the calligraphic hand trails off to the lower right, as if the writer were unable to follow the shape of the paper or confine his thoughts to it.

Since the first picture he shows us is of a lion that he drew at the age of six, we wonder if he has ever willingly parted with any of his work. Whatever the answer, the most potent pictorial image in the room is a colored drawing of a woman's head, faintly reminiscent of a Henry Moore. The recent *Tristram and Yseult Aboard Ship* is more pre-Raphaelite, and more than faintly. "I know only a little about ships," he says, "enough for a little ship, perhaps, but you must know a lot to do a big ship." The latest picture, a labyrinthine but still unfinished "Annunciation," recalls Blake. I.S. likes it, and very gently remarks that it seems complete to him now, but might, with more elaboration, become too complex. Jones acknowledges the danger, but says he wants to add a bit more color, "If, at the same time, I can keep it a drawing. Of course," he subjoins in a more cheerful voice, "I don't much like anything I do."

At one point his distress in trying to remember the word "wire," the which broke on one of his pictures, seems inordinate, and at another, when he counts on his fingers, eyes closed, in an effort to recall whether he is a Capricorn or a Scorpio, he has evidently lost any quotidian count of time.

His mood changes again when exhibiting one of his plaques of Latin lettering *à la* Eric Gill and telling us: "I posted it to a convent in Wales, from which, after a great delay, it was returned with the explanation, 'No one has any use for Welsh in Wales any more.' Evidently even fewer people have any use for Latin," he adds, and a seraphic smile forms, this time fading very slowly. We turn about the room, examining long undusted books, a majolica angel, a cross of palm. Why? And why have we come? Out of admiration for a writer of genius and a man who has attained a life of purity, in the midst of so many lives of pastiche.

He makes a beachhead on his thickly littered table and puts a spirit ring ashore, a small mound of sugar, a punctured can of evaporated milk, and a meager assortment of other comestibles. It is teatime, and a kettle hangs from an andiron, but we trump up a pressing reason to depart. As we go, Jones tells us that he has been ordered to pay back-taxes on some long-since-spent award money from an American foundation, and that he does not know what to do, being penniless, which he does not say, and unable to deal with the forms to be filled out and the bureaucracy.

On the return to London, we feel haunted, but also lifted, by his aloneness. At what point does the self-consciousness of the solitary man—"Sisyphus was a bachelor," Kafka said—and the pedantry, the paranoia, and the overdeveloped sensibilities that are his commonest forms of hypochondria, at what point do they begin to shut him off from the outside? When did David Jones begin to believe in his illness, and is it agoraphobia, that typological disease of the inward-turning? Or is he a *malade imaginaire*? Real or imaginary, is the malady traceable to the war, to experiences shared with men that could never afterward be recalled with women, let alone shared with them, therefore resulting in a withdrawal from their society? That great dramatic monologue, *In Parenthesis*, is no withdrawal, in any case, but an affirmation of the world, while the *Anathemata is* a retreat, behind language, symbols, obscurity, and behind the window panes of his room; and it is as much a breakdown in communication as *Finnegans Wake* after *Ulysses*. To *me*, that is, for the breakdown in communication may well be on my end only, and my judgment Philistine.

Back at the Savoy, a telegram for I.S. from Oxford: "Much tenderness from your admirers Robert and Kitty Oppenheimer and George Kennan."

June 2. Ath Cleath. The "center of paralysis," Joyce called it, and, more indulgently, for it is dirtier than Chicago, "dear dirty Dublin." In the crowd at the airport are many sunburned and freckled priests and a flock of Sisters of St. Vincent de Paul in swan-like *chapeaux à corne*. How musical their voices, in contrast to the flat, pinched, and only slightly varied vowel sounds of the London bloke! Nor is there any reluctance to speak. "Now would that be Mr. Eyegore Strawinsky?" a bystander asks me, half singing the question. The Hibernian lilt is less noticeable in our driver, but he quotes Yeats in describing parts of the Ould Sod that he thinks we should visit, an itinerary that does not include North Ireland for the reason that "it is still Occupied."

June 3. The Joyceana in the Sandycove martello, now "James Joyce Tower," is more modest than that of more than one American university, but at least *Ulysses* is on sale here, as it is nowhere else in Dublin. We climb to the small bleak room on a spiral fire escape in an appropriately spinning wind, shivering in our topcoats, too, though bathers, turned purple-blue, are plentiful on the beaches beneath the tower.

Residential Dublin, rich and poor neighborhoods alike, consists of rows of identical brick houses, each with clusters of chimneys like sows' teats. The rich homes of Merrion Square—Yeats's, Sheridan Le Fanu's, Wilde's among them—have rounded-arch portals, white pilasters, brass door knobs and knockers. A plaque on the poor, Synge Street birthplace of G.B. Shaw describes him as the "author of many plays," but the slightly richer brick childhood home of James Joyce, in the still poorer purlieu of Rathmines, is unmarked. On our way there, V. wonders aloud whether any other modern city of the size can have spawned so many major writers, and at once the driver advises her: "To be a writer here, lady, all you have to do is keep your ears open," and as if to prove his point, he is soon giving us a vivid story, in steep b'jayses brogue, of how Brendan Behan, having had one jar too many, started a brawl with some famous bowsies and ended up in the pokey. I.S. wonders why, of all the writers Dublin born and bred, so few have been buttered here. (Paronomasia is a contagious disease in Dublin, thanks to the emphasis on the music of the language; puns are homonyms and musical accidents first, after all, the words bumping together by the attraction of their similarities of sound, the connecting coincidence of sense discovered only after the musical event.) The driver is unbudgeably convinced that Shaw, Wilde, Beckett, and the others evacuated the homeland for no other reason than to escape the climate.

June 4. The illuminated books in Trinity College Library are a fantasy world of birds and beasts both fabulous and real, and the mandala-like mazes of ornament and the script itself are not less marvelous, above all the minuscules in the Book of Armagh, whose syllabic flags (accents? ligature signs?) remind me of Cufic. The books' first attraction, nevertheless, is color, including that of the bindings, many of them madder-stained pigskin with linen cord and iron hasps. Compared with these Celtic manuscripts, the oldest paleographic treasure in the Library, a Ptolemaic stone with parallel texts in hieroglyphs, enchorials, and Greek, is drab and disappointing.

June 5. The treasures of the National Museum, hardly less rich in spoliation of the monasteries, are jeweled crucifixes, croziers, missal cases, pricket candlesticks, and hundreds of other ecclesiastical utilities and adornments. Yet the collection of Bronze Age gold interests us more. The most common objects are torques, gorgets (for wimples), and posy rings with bezels carved in the shape of clasped hands, or *ouroboros*. Otherwise, lunular and penanular forms predominate, as they do in Nigerian art.

June 7. Visit to Eamon de Valera, after a lunch at the U.S. Embassy in Phoenix Park with Ambassador McCloskey and some intellectual priests, all of them mourning, as is I.S., the death of Pope John. The fate of our concert is in doubt, since all public entertainments are likely to be suspended.

A drive to "Howth [Hoath] Castle and Environs," where the seaward slopes are gorse-golden, returning through Phoenix Park, Chapelizoid

1963 (Chapel-is-id), and Summer Hill, Sean O'Casey's slum, where we attract some Unsmiling Irish Eyes. The tide is out, leaving the swans stranded in the sulphurous Liffey mud.

June 8. A drive to Clonmacnoise via Athlone and, on the return, ivy-covered Clonony Castle and Kildare. The road leaving Dublin is shaded by beeches and elms, and on each side are stone-walled lanes, stone bridges, hems of stone fence enclosing fields and dells. Most roadside cottages are stuck together and repeated, as if by multiple mirrors, individuated only by their flowers, especially lilacs and whitethorn. In the main street of Mullingar, four men are dancing a reel to the accompaniment of a fiddle and hand-clapping onlookers. South of Athlone, the scutch grass has been shaved from the peat bogs, which are ready for cutting. This is generally done by machines today, but at one point we overtake a mob who, shouldering the old double-edged sleans, look like the rabble on the way to the Revolution of 1789.

At Clonmacnoise, seven ruined churches and a cemetery of old Celtic crosses sleep on a hill by a bend in the Shannon. The smallest churches are simple biliths, walls slanted together corbelwise, but the one called Ui Ceallaigh (O'Kelly) has a vaulted roof. Hand querns and other stone implements of the destroyed monastery are scattered on the grass, but the best-preserved of the ruins is a crannog tower with a cap shaped like the nose cone of an ICBM. I wander in the sweet air, thinking Clonmacnoise one of the sacred places of the earth.

June 9. Our concert with the Radio Eireann Symphony Orchestra in the Adelphi Cinema.

June 23. Milan. Like the sacristan in *Tosca*, the custodian of the crypt of St. Ambrose jangles his keys from time to time, but in this case to remind us of the need for fresh boosts to his economy. Ambrose's skeleton lies in a glass catafalque, flanked, at a slightly lower elevation, as befits subordinates, by the skeletons of Protasius and Gervase. The Ambrosian skull is mitered, those of his two escorts are gold-crowned. The tightly clamped teeth of all three are stained as if they had been lifelong betel chewers. The royal purpure, the scapulars, the jeweled slippers, the branches of silver palm are a dramatic contrast to the skeletons they accouter: the picture seems more an allegory of medieval kings illustrating the temporality of earthly treasures than a triptych of Christian martyrs. A gold phoenix perches like a vane on the top of the catafalque, ready to crow the Resurrection.

In the *mostra* of Iranian art at the Palazzo Reale, Islamic Luristan is richly represented, but the Hittite section is disappointing, except for two gold tablets covered with thornlike script, and a pair of gold *mitènes*—fingerless gloves, with a gauze of gold mail on the back of the hand fastened to gold rings at the hilt of each finger; Glenn Gould would be attracted to them for piano exercises.

We spend the drowsy afternoon at the Certosa di Pavia. Soft, foamy summer clouds. Bronzed fields of wheat. Wild poppies and wild sweet peas. Ilex. The scent of lime trees by Leonardo's canal, of mint-like privet in the Certosa grounds, and of new-mown grass everywhere.

Each time the door of the church opens, drafts of cold air are exhaled, but apart from the air conditioning, I do not like the interior: an angel has been packed into every archivolt, an ornament squeezed into every squinch. A party of tourists is marauding the quiet, among them a woman whose automatic "What?" after every remark of the guide so resembles the bark of a dog that one would like to offer her a bone.

The only sounds in the cloister are the buzzing of flies and the turning of gravel by a hand shovel, an old-fashioned noise that agreeably defines the surrounding peace. The cloister comprises 24 duplex cells topped by a fence of 24 Gothic chimneys. Each cell is equipped with a revolving dumbwaiter for meal trays (like the MacDowell Colony), a strapontine table and bed, a garden, a well, and a leafy pergola in the community vineyards. In sum, the Certosa was a meditators' co-op ruled by ascetic disciplines that kept its exclusively noble-born inmates in trim condition for *this* life, in fact establishing records for longevity, whatever it did for them in the next. Why, then, do *I* shudder at it? After all, symmetrically balanced space such as this is supposed to generate a sense of euphoria in the laterally symmetrical bodies of chimpanzees and humans. Is it because I doubt my power to summon the positive, favorable images necessary for prolonged solitude? Or that even though my life is a chaos of distractions, I do not believe that I can resist them by the method of prayer reading, of the Hindu endlessly reciting his *japa?*

The late-night rehearsal at La Scala of the Hamburg Opera's productions of *Oedipus Rex* and *The Flood* is a demonstration of how the Axis must have worked. The German stagehands take to their tasks like an army on the Blitzkrieg, and a Panzer army to boot, for they have two-way radios and closed-circuit television. The smoothest, most impressive performance of the evening occurs when Dr. Rennert, the stage director, exasperated to breaking point by the misfocused lighting, orders the entire *Oedipus* set dismantled and rebuilt to the reach of the beams, a job that the German crew completes in a mere 18 minutes, but one that would have defeated the Italians for a season or two. The Italians, of course, are in charge of the lighting, and, as noted, they do about as well with it as, two decades ago, they did with other matters in North Africa. Throughout the rehearsal, a *"maestro direttore"* shouts and begs through his telephone: "Luigi . . . la luce . . . per piacere, Luigi, pronto, la luce . . . si, la luce, ma adesso, adesso . . . la luce . . . L-U-I-G-I." The impatience of the Germans shows more openly by the minute, until we expect them to seize the apparatus, as once they took over the Italian army and eventually confiscated Italy itself. Whereas the Italians only pretend, and unconvincingly, to crumble and fawn before their supe-

1963 riors, the Germans reply smartly to theirs with *"Jawohl, Herr Doktor"* and even click their heels. (I.S.: "People are born *'Herr Doktor'* in Germany.") The standby Italian stagehands squat on the floor, huddled together like prisoners of war and displaying the bewildered expressions with which they were often seen in wartime newsreels. The one apparent difference from 1945 is that they are able to desert their German masters and disappear for long espresso breaks.

Oedipus is creditably staged, though the goriness of the eye-gouging would be more appropriate to *The Cabinet of Dr. Caligari*, and the cardboard effigies—exposing heads only, like old-fashioned photographers' dummies—give the impression that the chorus is in mud-baths. The one musical failure is that the Shepherd is miscast, the singer being both vocally heavy (a mere Bo-Peep is required) and addicted to bleating, as though he had taken to the language of his flock.

The Hamburg Opera deserves great credit for its staging of I.S.'s latest problem opus. *The Flood*, as Herr Rennert perfectly understands, is a resumé of I.S.'s theatrical forms. The precedent for pantomine goes as far back as *Renard*, the arias of Lucifer-Satan represent the element of pure opera, and *The Building of the Ark* that of pure ballet. The narrator is a Stravinskyan device as old as the *Soldat, Oedipus, Perséphone, Babel*, and as new as *A Sermon, A Narrative and A Prayer*.

Herr Rennert has some capital ideas. One of them is to have the voice of God broadcast from various parts of the hall, like an electronic concert, and at the same time to lower His words from Heaven on plaques like the Tables of the Law. The difficulty with this in so large a theater as La Scala is that the electronic God is too portentous for the modest frame of the music. Tonight, moreover, the plaques either do not appear on time or else disappear too quickly, before anyone has read them through, for no other apparent reason than to prove that the hand is quicker than the eye. Add to this the lateness of the lighting (*"Luigi . . . L-U-I-G-I . . ."*) during the bass drum introductions to God's speeches (I.S. says that the player should use a wooden stick, depress the center of the head with the flat of his left hand, and strike close to the taut edge of the vellum), and spectator frustration is comprehensible.

It is also a good idea, dramatically, to keep Lucifer-Satan on hand throughout, as Rennert does even during the flood itself. But the Lucifer must move, dance as he sings, as the music tells him, and not simply plant himself to the side of the stage. Still, the failure can be blamed only partly on this diabolical paralysis. Another factor is the lack of any transformation in Satan after the Fall. He switches masks, it is true, but the new one bears an unfortunate resemblance to Papa Katzenjammer, and the comic touch at this point is disastrous. Furthermore, the Melodrama should be an inset, separated from the action before and after, at least by lighting, and Satan must do something to indicate the change of scene, even if only to step into a telephone booth to say "Eve."

The parting curtains reveal a solitary bench, stage right, and behind it a cloakroom rack with the masks of Satan and the Noah family. The actors, shawls partly covering their street clothes, enter before the Prelude, followed by the chorus, not costumed and walking like factory hands when work lets out after an exceptionally fatiguing day. When they halt, unmilitarily, at stage center, the music begins. Their *Te Deum* over, they fan out to stage aprons on each side of the orchestra pit and watch from there as a part of the audience. The final *Te Deum* is sung there, too, after which they "exeunt severally" in the most disorderly sense. While these arrangements solve the problem of disposing of the chorus, the interruption of the music to gain time for ferrying the singers across the proscenium and into the bleachers is fatal.

Another, no less mortal, disadvantage in this tonight-we-improvise beginning is that it contradicts the music. The Prelude must be played before a closed curtain, in darkness, and free of all visual associations. Essential, too, is the opening of the curtain in synchronicity with the 12-note harp ladder (which requires an expressive *ritenuto*). In fact, all four 12-note ladders were intended to accompany curtains, either of material or of light. The bassoon version of the ladder, the dissolve from Eden, should be synchronized with a crescendo of light from deep darkness to the equivalent, in wattage, of a mezzo piano; the stage remains murky and shadowed afterward in correspondence with the new, minatory note in God's music, that masterstroke which adds a storm cloud of *ponticello* violins and violas to God's voice and doubles, equiponderously with piano and harp, the two lines of the voice itself (the Eastern and Western Churches?),* like the two unaccompanied priestly basses in *Noces*. The third musical ladder should follow a small ray or spot of red light from a total blackout to the Devil,** while the fourth is coordinated with the slow final curtain, whose cue is the cello and bass chord. But in the Hamburg production no visual connection is established with any of these musical staircases, nor is it made apparent that they are the frame of the work.

If the *Te Deum* is sung as a concert piece, ignoring the enlarging movement (composed with television in mind) *in* the music, then it would be better to hear, and not see, the angels—Local 27 angels, at any rate. But I should also note that the Hamburg staging stops the music before the return of the *Te Deum* to allow more time for the narration, and that this pause is another fatal one. The fault here is partly I.S.'s; the music *is* per-

---

* The change in color and the restoration of the octave in God's music *after* the flood are no less simple and subtle inspirations, and the accretion of a few flute, harp, and celesta notes during Noah's line, "The earth is overflowed with flood," instantly and magically transforms the atmosphere.

** One critic shrewdly described the work as anti-clerical, the music associated with the idea of sin being decidedly nasty in contrast to the innocent paterfamilias music of Noah.

1963 ilously short, and as a bridge it is too pat, in the same way as the reprise of the opening of *Agon*. (I remember I.S., stopwatch in hand, asking me to read the narration "in a brisk tempo," after which he said he was pleased, since he would "only have to compose 10 more seconds of music.") Is the whole of *The Flood* too abbreviated? Not for the cinematography I.S. had in mind, even though he cut both the text and the ballets to less than half of what the television producer had calculated as acceptable minimum timings. A short piece is not made longer by adding pauses, in any case, and some of the impression of scrappiness in the Hamburg interpretation could be overcome simply by not stopping so long between each bit and piece.

The Hamburg Narrator is wrong, too, as narrators generally are. (It seems to me that dramatic authors must regard narrators as "natural" children, *i.e.*, reminders of weakness.) He is, after all, and in principle, *only* a voice, yet for want of cinematography, this all-too-embodied voice too often receives the full burden of visual attention, which is the case with the entire Genesis speech. More imaginative use is made of him in the Catalogue of the Animals, where he becomes an on-the-spot television news reporter swiveling, microphone in hand, from Ark to audience and reeling off the names of arriving couples as if they were movie stars at a Hollywood opening. Still, the Comedy is the most serious failure of the Hamburg production, or uncomic failure. The music demands action— running, slapstick—yet no one moves, and a half-minute of silence has to be inserted to get the Noahs aboard, though, once there, they stand frozen, looking as tragic in their deadpan masks as anybody in *Oedipus Rex*.

The ballets are better conceived than executed. Both are costume pieces. The builders of the Ark (hammer-and-nail male sex symbolism) wear space-cadet jumpsuits, and the girls who dance the flood (reversing Balanchine's identification of the beleaguered and beleaguering sexes) dress like waterdrops (female sex symbolism). The Ark itself is an all-purpose galleon suspiciously resembling the titular vessel in last week's *Flying Dutchman*. At the first bolt of lightning, a solo waterdrop splashes in from the wings, followed in a trice by a cloudburst of her colleagues who proceed to enchafe the Ark. The picture here, of the 80 or so animals—supernumeraries in street clothes but with papier-maché animal heads, horns, tusks, trunks, bills, manes—crowded together like refugees and riding out the storm, is so touching that it nearly rescues the whole performance.

June 24. After tonight's performance, we dine at Biffi Scala with Luciano Berio, Umberto Eco, Berman, and Adriana Panni.

August 2. Santa Fe. With Catherine C., who, soon after our initial conjugation, is inquiring how long it will take me to rally, and whether I may be expected to hold the fort any longer next time. She addresses me as "sport" and "killer," remarkably inapposite endearments in my case, however vividly they suggest the panurgical powers of my predecessors. The

second embrace is less concentrated, in any case, because of a distracting
thought comparing this activity to a smelting process, the heat of the bodies furnishing the flux that will separate the metal.

August 7. My first performance of *Lulu*.

August 30. Rio de Janeiro, the Copacabana Hotel. The afternoon sun
turns the fog to mica. In an eerie, apocalyptic moment, the Corcovado
Christ looms through the dispelling vapors like the airborne Christ-statue
in *La Dolce Vita.*

I have increased my Portuguese by 10 words today, raising the total to
11, but progress, even on this scale, is a questionable asset. For one thing,
our driver takes too much heart from it. Supposing us to have been sham-
ming until now, he fires away with such speed that I am at a loss to interject even a punctuational *"Sim"* ("Yes") or *"Espere um instante"* ("Wait a
minute"); and as nothing else in my vocabulary will turn him off, I switch
in desperation to an equally unresourceful Spanish *("Caramba").* Searching
for a store in which to buy whiskey for I.S., I learn that sign language can
reduce even the most garrulous direction-giver to the same means. When
at length the whiskey store is found, after several tryingly Trappist scenes,
I rehearse my pronunciation of *"Não"*—a less nasally feline noise than the
one Brazilians make—until the clerk holds up a bottle of one of I.S.'s
brands *("Sim").*

In the evening, all Rio seems to be holding hands and, when the darkness deepens, more than hands: the beach is strewn with twining couples.
Surveying this sabulous Agapemone, the spectator must acknowledge the
influence of topography—the sugarloaf phalloi—the sensual sound and
scent, the loneliness and timelessness, the continual caress of the sea. But
the human topography, the ballooning bosoms and thrusting *labia majora*
of the Copacabana professionals is the most actively conducive landscape.

At night, the city's huge mendicant population takes to outdoor cubby-
holes and crevasses while the utterly destitute coil up on the open ground,
protected only by newspapers or rags. When we park for a moment on a
hill above the bay, a bundle shifts position in the gutter—an old woman, as
we see when the poor creature raises her blanket of sacking as if to ask us
why we have disturbed her sleep. But she disturbs mine, too, returning
again and again in a procession of people remembered: the black laborers
with bare backs, bare feet, and fanciful folded-newspaper hats; the black
belles in percale and dimity dresses and with orange-rust hair; the girls in a
street-side lace factory manipulating their bobbins with, for Rio, unwonted
dexterity and speed; the cariocas in stand-up street bars drinking round
after round of coffee (do they ever work?); the near-naked waifs stealing
precarious rides on the wide running boards of the *bondes* (open trolleys).

August 31. All Rio is rebuilding, which means that the regional and
characteristic are being replaced by the international and indifferent. It

1963 seems, too, that the few doomed remnants of colonial styles still extant are always found side-by-threatening-side with the newest opus Niemeyer. This is the case with laundry-blueing Santa Luzia, now hedged around by skyscrapers; and the case with a score of old frame houses nearby, all with tall shutters, wrought-iron railings, walls of pellagrous paint. A popular local irony is that the most graceful of the surviving old structures, the Casa de Saudi, was until recently an asylum for lunatics.

The façades of the best colonial church architecture are elegantly simple, but the interiors are tropical tangles. São Bento is a case in point. Its walls crawl with *rocaille* and creep with vegetal ornaments, so that only after long peering do we discover the human figures in the lush carvings, like hidden faces in Henri Rousseau jungles. The exceptional church, with an interior no more complex than the exterior promises, is the white, octagonal Outeiro da Gloria, which sits like a coronet on one of the older city's highest hills.

September 1. The Zoological Gardens are also, if only incidentally, a *jardin des plantes*, the walks being shaded by banyans and colored by hibiscus and bougainvillea. The sight of animals from northern habitats suffering from the heat upsets V., and she tries to comfort one old bruin with compatriotic feeling—"*Vy govorite po-russki?*—though at the same time, and perhaps for the same reason, she refuses to speak German to a seal that looks like Bismarck and seems even unhappier than the bear. I.S., observing the anthropoids, wonders what it would be like "to go about on all fours with one's behind in the air and a plaque on one's cage containing a Latin binomial and a paragraph of false and irrelevant information, like concert program notes. Nowadays, I suppose, the animals are sexually attached to the keepers." Near the exit a flamingo stands immobile in a pool covered with pea-green scum, like a fixture on a Miami lawn.

Today's rehearsal of our concert of sacred music in the beautiful Igreja de Candelaria is scheduled for 2 o'clock, but at 2:30 the doors are still closed, and the musicians do not appear until 3, at which hour it is discovered that the orchestra librarian has neglected to bring the corrected parts. Half of the players never turn up, moreover, while those who *do* eventually present themselves allow us a mere 30 minutes' working time, the union foreman having decreed that no matter how late in starting, the rehearsal must end punctually. Our complaints are met with amiable shrugs but are thrown out of court (the foreman's) with the argument, "This is not a factory"—as if anyone who had spent as much as a day in Rio could believe in a stop-watch rule even in factories. The rehearsal, such as it is, nevertheless pleases, if only in the Latin diction of the chorus. The Brazilian pronunciation, a squall of sibilants, softens every edge ("*genite,*" for example, becomes "*zhenite*") and smooths all "k" and "ch" sounds with gently hissing cedillas (as in *pacem*).

To a jeweler friend of Jocy de Oliveira's to see a display of stones from

Minas Gerais. They range from common aquamarines, tourmalines, and chrysoprases to imperial topazes, pink and green diamonds, and emeralds and rubies both cut and cabochon. I borrow the lapidary's loupe for a look at a rare, water-clear Brazilian sapphire, and watch him measure a refractive index, work the alloy wheel, on which the stones are faceted, and the carborundum and emery wheels, on which they are polished.

We stop at a *favela*, a hillside Casbah smelling of carrion, cooking-in-oil, *merde*. A political entity virtually outside the jurisdiction of the police, the *favela's* physical density, no less than its secret customs and codes—including kangaroo courts—is well-nigh impenetrable. Not far along, our path is barricaded by a sow and her farrow; but we have no wish to continue. Later, discussing the experience with Brazilian acquaintances, I am surprised not so much by the absence in them of a moralizing tone—such as some affluent North Americans use in berating *their* slum dwellers for laziness and lack of ambition—as by their ill-disguised disapproval of V.'s readiness with a *cruzeiro* for every beggar and by their lack of sympathy with her remark, "The only question is why we should deserve to have anything to give." At the same time, neither V. nor I.S. would ever think of questioning the political and social conditions responsible for the *favela*, whose Cubistic superimpositions of basketwork huts they are able to regard as beautiful.

With Jocy de Carvalho to the C. restaurant, which affects the Regency style of Dom João: tall mirrors and high ceilings, gaitered and liveried waiters. The first and last courses—the *cachaça* (cane-sugar alcohol) cocktails and the coconut entremets—are the best of the dinner. The best of the conversation is Jocy's about Euclides da Cunha, though I.S.'s talk on another subject is so typical that this is what I will record. To the maitre d'hotel taking our salad orders, he explains that a "paregoric dressing" would be the only safe kind for him, then goes on to report the intestinal news of the day. When I first knew him, his matutinal salutations almost invariably included an inquiry about my "regularity," as well as a full description of his morning fears, even when already flushed. It is characteristic of I.S. that where bowels are concerned, total strangers are chosen for the frankest confidences, and if attentive enough on such favorite topics as diverticulitis, pyloric spasms, enema dreams, and log-jam nightmares—as tonight's maitre d'hotel pretends to be, though his understanding of French is obviously limited to the menu—they are generally found to be, like this waiter, *"muito simpático."* Dining rooms are I.S.'s preferred setting, too, and the mere mention of prunes, *crudité*, or "roughage" during a meal can lead to some extremely unappetizing digressions. I have often wondered whether this *Tisch-Gesprache* owes anything to his German nurse, Bertha, but in any case it shows the identification of "pre-napkin" and "prelapsarian" in his mind, and indicates a traumatic toilet training.

September 2. Not surprisingly, our concert at the Teatro Municipal

1963 begins an hour late, a time spent in a sweltering greenroom under a portrait of Gomes, the composer of *Il Guarany*. The audience is loudly, even vocally, appreciative, and the performances are good, my own failure of nerve when sharing concerts with I.S. not, for this once, having "frozen me up." I.S. is besieged by admirers backstage afterward, Governor Carlos Lacerda among them, Sir John Barbirolli, and Heitor Villa-Lobos's widow, who bestows an *abraço* and reminds I.S. of her husband's visit to him in Hollywood many years ago. At a reception following the concert, an American doctor, here for an International Congress on Tropical Medicine, fills me with sleep-destroying information about the local forms of filariasis, the "snail vectors" of which are a principal item on the Congress's agenda. He believes that Darwin suffered from a form of this disease.

September 3. A visit to the niece of Machado de Assis, in Tijuca, near the base of a steep mountain, appropriately called—it is climbed almost continually by a file of black women with head loads—"the *favela* of the ants;" we never learn whether the name is metaphorical (for the laboring female safaris) or a description of actual entomological activity. Rimsky-Korsakov visited Tijuca several times during his four-month stay in Rio in 1864. No sooner have we made the acquaintance of Machado's niece than her husband hustles us off to see an Order of Merit awarded him by President Roosevelt in 1944 and a photograph of himself in San Francisco among the Brazilian signatories to the United Nations Charter.

The descendants of "Machadasi," as they refer to the author, are not conspicuously conversant with the writings of the founder of their fame, and they seem slightly nervous that his spreading reputation may oblige them to read him. One of Machado's books has lately been published in Moscow, they tell us, in a tone blending pride and alarm.

Machado's injunction to burn his manuscripts having been less ambivalent than Kafka's, the quantity of his literary leftovers is small. But a batch of family letters survives. Showing us one of these, in a neat, clerk's hand, from the novelist to his fiancée, the niece blurts out that her uncle was "not white" and that his fiancée's family opposed the marriage *"parce qu'il avait de couleur."* A few photographs have been preserved, too, but the only one worth the mention is a too-sweet portrait of a young but motherly woman that had held Machado in a state of trance, his niece says—onanistic trance, I would say, to judge by the poem he addressed to it, with its fixation on the woman's gloves, and by comparing the sentiments of these verses with the sentiments in his classic of disguised onanism, *A Woman's Arms.*

When these relics are removed, whiskey, tobacco, and salvers of sandwiches are passed around. When I light a cigarette for the niece's daughter, I notice her staring at my matchbook, from a Hollywood restaurant, as covetously as a Conquistador eyeing a gold ornament on a savage. She is a phillumenist, it develops, who has collected three thousand of these folders. We promise additions.

September 5. Shortly before midnight we drive to a secret rendezvous in the hills where a *macumba* ceremony, a mixture of Catholic and African rituals, is to take place. The trail to this eyrie is marked at each turn in the road by candles, and at major intersections by piles of poultry eviscerations. The actual entrance, at the foot of a hill mounted by 60 steep stairs, is designated by a whole galaxy of candles and a portable shrine. At the top, two women, white-robed like Sisters of Father Divine, lead us to a grotto of holy images, black-faced Josephs and Marys, St. Sebastians and St. Georges (known here as Ogoun). Leaving the grotto and taking us to the *heiru*, a rolled-dirt compound slightly larger than a tennis court, our guides stop every few steps to chalk crosses on the ground in front of us. Inside the *heiru*, we are installed on a bench near the center sidelines, where the extremely rich insect life—its stridulations remind us of a Cuban percussion orchestra—loses no time in finding our bearings. V. is afraid of caterpillars, but I.S., hearing a snort from something unseen in the woods, only hopes that nothing bigger than bugs decides to fraternize.

One end of the *heiru* is formed by a candle-decked altar with a painted backcloth of an austral moon and stars. At the other end is the circle of the dead, a cairnlike pile of stones enclosing a wooden cross marcelled with white ribbons; everyone gives this the widest berth. Three or four hundred people stand beyond the fenced sides of the *heiru*, men and women segregated, as are the score or so white-robed celebrants gathered within; presently V. is led to the women's side. Meanwhile, a man in a white suit stenciled with insignia on the sleeves comes to warn us not to cross our arms or legs lest the spell (*candomblé?*) be broken. This is said in utmost earnest. But when V. asks whether the women in white organdy dresses and silver neck crosses, in center court, are the vestal virgins, he breaks into profligate laughter, assuring us, after catching his breath, that "*Ça n'existe pas ici*"). And, in truth, these necklaced women *are* matronly in their proportions, or at least far from wraithlike, which for some reason reduces my never-bounteous faith in them as spiritual agents. Are they in fact the exact opposite of V.'s suspicions, namely, instruments of what anthropologists call sexual hospitality? Among the spectators almost all the men and some of the women smoke cigars, and everyone except ourselves is "black."

Tonight's ritual is that of *ubanda*, or white magic. We never learn how this has been determined—phases of the moon? haruspication of those roadside entrails?—but it is for this reason that the celebrants are continually touching the ground: the gesture signifies the burial of black magic, victory over Echou, the African god and spirit of evil. Tonight's principal celebrant, greeted by a stingy drum roll as he proceeds to the center of the *heiru*, is a bearded, turbaned, darker-in-hue Billy Graham; which is to say that the manner of his delivery is partly evangelical, partly heart-to-heart sex talk. I cannot follow the matter of it, but the gist, to judge by repeated Latin-root words, seems to favor the "spiritual" over the "material." It fills an hour, in any case, and survives more false endings than Beethoven's Fifth.

Yet because of the audience, the avian audience especially, we are never bored. Flocks of doves that had been fluttering about the *heiru* before the sermon now settle in the surrounding sapodillas like baseball fans in the bleachers, except that they listen with Sunday attention and quiet. When, at about the halfway point, one of them flies to the Billy Graham's head, and perches there, as if bringing him a message, we are almost prepared to believe in metempsychosis. And to suspect preternatural influence or ESP is practically unavoidable in the perfect timing of a chanticleer's bugle notes at two major pauses in the prolix speech, in the transfixed expressions and maudlin nuzzling of a pair of heretofore ferocious dogs, and, above all, in the behavior of two geese—"One spiritual, one material," I.S. says. Whereas these geese have claxoned without pause before the sermon, during it they lie silent and rapt at the Billy Graham's feet. Then in the moment that he finishes, making the sign of the cross, they waddle a yard or two from him and consecrate the matrimonial rite, the gander rowing his wings over the goose like a *premier danseur* in a ballet about a boat. The act inevitably appears to have been sponsored by the Billy Graham, who watches conspiratorially, in any case, as a *cri de coeur* heralds the climax and as excited flapping and postcoital cooing confirm it.

One of the Father Divine girls now replaces the Billy Graham, whose retiring tattoo is as niggling as the fanfare hailing his entrance. Three men join her, then dress each other in scarlet mantles and nightcaps that resemble the tasseled nuptial hats of Mohammedan brides in the *nichau* ceremony. They plant candles in the ground at the center of the *heiru*, and light cigars, the incense and lustral smoke from which nearly asphyxiates us but is a great tonic to the mosquitoes. At this point everyone kneels to sing a litany, which clots with passion as it grows louder. A chant, "Jesus, Mary," follows,

accompanied by clapping, drumming, stepped-up earth-touching, and it lasts until the Father Divine girl rings a plantation-type dinner bell. This cue for a hag, heavily strung with beads, to become possessed—the descent of the god into her—also sets the becalmed geese honking plangently enough to save Rome. The beaded hag, after a wind-up like whooping cough, emits an eldritch scream, then throws herself to the ground panting, "Ya, ya, ya, ya, ya," and puffs her cigar to a blaze. It is not a convincing performance, and when the others in her coven enter their trances, fling themselves earthward, lie prostrate, and follow suit through the rest of the mummery, we depart. These seizures take place against a chant in which the word "Negro"—"*Nay-gro*"—is repeated monotonously. As we stumble back down the mountain on the candle path, another litany has begun. I go to bed at 5 A.M. humming both the solo

and the response

, etc.

September 7. Brazilian Independence Day. Another midnight drive, this time to a samba ceremony, alleged, like the *macumba*, to be clandestine, though one wonders how a corroboree of three thousand people can be a secret. Again, we are the only "whites," but tonight's tumult, unlike last night's, portends the Black Revolution. In order to penetrate the crowd, we link hands like mountain climbers, and are therefore unable to clamp our noses against the acridity; every sebaceous gland in the steaming room seems to be hyperactive. And what a room! The far wall is covered with a backdrop representing the black-and-white mosaic waves of the Copacabana sidewalk. On a platform in front of it about 20 musicians are playing both standard and native instruments, most of them percussive; the percussion section, in any case, throbs like a migraine at the core of every piece and even causes the brick walls to vibrate. Nor does the dancing afford relief. One expects so much sizzling flesh to ignite into something saturnalian, but nothing happens except the weaving and swaying of the samba line—the memory of portages and the coffle?—always the same, endlessly repeated. Pulling each other outside again, to the ozone of the street, we ask the direction to Rio from an old man sitting on the curb, piping on a penny fife and singing a melancholy *saudade*.

November 3. Hollywood. Gerald comes at 5, pixilated as always but subdued, not once spreading his long, tapering fingers. He brings his new book, *The Five Ages of Man*, and tells us that Aldous will be dead before our return from Italy. "Aldous was unable to believe in a personal god," he says; "his religion was always abstract." But isn't Gerald's the same?

1963   **November 16.** Palermo. In some areas of the city, so many bombed buildings are still unrestored and even uncleared that the war might have ended yesterday. In one narrow street near the market, struts and wooden soffits have been inserted between buildings to keep them from caving in. Though heavily damaged, too, the market itself is thriving, and must be the liveliest center on the island. And the most deafening, beginning at the entrance, where the fiacre drivers solicit fares with whipcracks as loud as the revolvers of on-the-town cowboys. The market is powerfully vocal, the contents of every booth, table, trundle, costermonger's barrow being advertised by stentorian voices sustained by bellows-like lungs; we hold our ears while a rapscallion a few steps away cries his produce in a great high-to-low arc of impressive resonance and duration. The fruit and vegetable stalls are first: strings of red peppers, pyramids of tomatoes and artichokes, clusters of grapes, mounds of melons, prickly pears, purple eggplants, persimmons, lemons, figs, and pairs of pendant, testicular squash. The displays of sponge-like *funghi* are striking, too, and of mortadella loaves, spherical cheeses, heaps of polenta, grains in turned-down burlap bags, and towers of tangerines: the perfume of tangerines saturates even this stew of odors.

The butchers' shops are in the center of the market. Here are hares and lambs still in their skins; ropes of black sausages; flitches of bacon; slimy messes of gizzards, tripe, entrails; and trussed and gibbeted poultry, plucked and red as if flayed. At the fish stalls surrounding the Church of Santa Eulalia of the Catalans are sardines, wet and glistening like tinfoil; tubs of turtle claws, black mussels, pink langoustines, squid, calamari; and countless shades of glazed-eye blue, gold, and bronze fish. We watch a fishwife flip a mullet on the scales, then let go with a great Santuzza cry of passion, which, however, does not distract the customer, who follows the dip of the beam with distrust and begins to haggle with her as a matter of course.

Each booth displays a Madonna with a tiara of candles, a wedding or family photograph, an oilcloth backdrop depicting a harvesting scene, or one of fruit-picking and of loading mule carts, labors invariably supervised and assisted by low-flying angelic hosts.

We drive from the markets to the baroque, buttock-fixated Oratorio of the Knights of Malta and the Oratorio of San Lorenzo, Serpotta's masterpiece, a wedding-white confection whose treasure is Caravaggio's *Nativity*. But the sight of a donkey with mountainous bales strapped to its sides and shackled to a curbstone—all Sicily depends on a cruel system of donkey slavery—makes the S.s forget about Caravaggio, buy lumps of sugar in a nearby store, and fetch a pan of water for the overburdened beast.

No public performance is scheduled today at Maestro Giacomo Cuticchio's marionette theater, but we rap on the door anyway—in a bomb-made alley doubling as a chicken coop—hoping to induce the famed puppeteer to favor us with a private one. He invites us to see his *fantoccini* in their backstage cupboards, where they hang from racks like the poultry in the market, and, showing us how they work, is soon treating us to a full performance. When a small doe-eyed girl with large earrings begins to crank a mechanical piano, we move to one of the audience's backless benches.

The picture in the frame of the tiny stage is a curtain advertising Maestro Giacomo's motto and formula:

ARTE — MORALE — DILETTO

As soon as this curtain is rolled—like a windowshade—we are deceived by scale. The marionettes seem to be from one to two feet tall, rather than, as D. H. Lawrence described them, two-thirds of human height. They are manipulated by wires, instead of directly, digitally, which accounts for their jaunty, hip-swinging, bowling walk. All of them wear shining armature, silver in the case of the hero knights, Rinaldo, Tancred, Orlando, and burnished bronze for "Papa Leone" and the ladies, whose cuirasses are accommodatingly bosomy. The armor and plume of the traitor knight are black, and, reversing David and Goliath, he and his fellow villains are small and thin (Ibsen's Lean Person): the most generous hearts are found in the burliest brutes. The coats of mail and turbans of the Saracens are black, and so, of course, are their Stalin mustaches. The Spanish knights, though hardly less swarthy or more sympathetic, are allowed to wear red kirtles and boleros. But then, the painted donkey carts on every road in Sicily today depict the same warriors in the same scenes from the same *Orlando Furioso.*

Maestro Giacomo begs off the strenuous work of a battle scene, but when some children join us, gives in and puts on a ferocious fracas. The story seems to compound an episode from the Crusades with one from Charlemagne—*which* ones I cannot say, nor is Giacomo's thundering dialect narration any help. A dragon identifies St. George, as the crown, scepter, and red Frankish beard identify Carlo Magno; and the horns and cleft feet betray the Devil—a very human creature who, at the end, is brought to book fettered like a felon, then hauled away by angels armed like the hero knights, though less heavily, as befits an aerial unit.

Each of the four changes of scene exposes a deeper interior stage. The final one, representing a plain before Jerusalem, is reserved for the most spectacular carnage. This ultimate battle begins with solo combats and ends in a general clash, after which the lopped limbs and other severed parts—the marionettes are built in sections like cuts of meat on butchers' charts—darken the stage horizon. The most impressive aspect of this Armageddon is the noise, the clatter of swords, shields, visors; the neighing of steeds; the stomping and shouting, the Japanese-movie grunting and

1963 groaning. The slaughter over, the death rattle of the tinny piano stops, the lights go on, and Maestro Giacomo emerges like a conductor from a hidden orchestra pit, mopping perspiration, bowing to our applause, then piecing the sauteed Paladins together again and racking them up in their closet.

Tonight's dinner at the Circolo Unione concludes with a gigantic *cassata siciliana*. Barone Agnello, our host, and the principal patron of the local orchestra, is famous for having been kidnapped a few years ago and held by brigands in a mountain fortress. His sister, our hostess, might have modeled for a Francesco Laurana queen. As represented in the Circolo, Palermitan society is insular and separatist, regarding Rome as remote, and a trip there as something of an undertaking. Palermo is literary-minded: people read much and go *north* in the winter. Table talk is in heavily accented French, a lifesaver for me, since Italian here is more rapid than on the peninsula, except the Barone's, whose diction is as deliberate—the word *"contento"* rolls out *"cone-taint-toe"*—as if he were giving a speech lesson. Among themselves they speak a parody dialect which is not to be confused with the parody dialect of the *"borghese,"* yet resembles it in that both lack the future tense. Their speaking voices are musical but weary, as if oppressed by the long catalog—Greek, Roman, Carthaginian, Byzantine, Saracen, Norman, Catalonian, Hohenstauffen, Hapsburg, Bourbon, U.S. Army—of their cultural surfeits and depredations. The Barone positively drones through words like *quattrocentesco*.

November 17. The long corridors of the Villa Igiea, our hotel just below Mount Pellegrino, have been exploited photographically in Antonioni's *L'Avventura*, but the hotel's most promising future in films is as a background for ghost and murder stories. Some passageways are not merely penumbral but as dark as a tunnel of love, and it is possible to be permanently lost between lobby and bar and momentarily lost in one's own room; small wonder that a number of distinguished suicides, Raymond Roussel's among them, occurred here. All is forgiven, however, in the morning view, that first slot of sun on the smooth, metallic sea, and the soft, still morning air broken only by the vascular put-put of a fishing boat.

The Villas Valguarnera and Palagonia, both in Bagheria, are dying of deturpation and indifference, those endemic Sicilian diseases. But while Valguarnera is a still-sumptuous ruin, Palagonia, unless a rescue squad acts immediately, will soon disintegrate altogether. It may be described, without shedding much light, as a later cousin of Bomarzo, yet it is odder than that because surrounded by ordinary buildings, a reason that accounts for much of the oddity of the Rodia Towers in Los Angeles. Goethe, whose augustness left no room for unwholesomeness, was shocked and exasperated by it, and to think that he had seen, and avoided meeting, the Prince who created it! If only the great poet had been able to put aside his passion for progress and good works and turn his powers of observation to abnormal psychology!* The Prince was a bimetallist, of course, with interesting complications: those hundreds of mirrors inside the Villa and all that perverse statuary on the garden walls, of goblins, dwarfs, hunchbacks, Moors, animals with human heads, winged fauns, griffins, misshapen and disfigured classical divinities, obscene goats—in short, an All Hallows' Eve. A musical one, albeit, for the strange assembly is playing cymbals, zithers, flutes, guitars, long-necked cellos and basses, all as if modeled from engravings in Bonanni's *Gabinetto armonico* and carved in black tufa.

From Bagheria we drive to Cefalù, stopping in a spooky *trattoria* on the way. On the return, we encounter a funeral procession, an immense hearse, carrying only flowers, drawn by a team of glistening black horses with black pompons and black panaches. The coffin follows on the shoulders of four elderly pallbearers and behind it, wailing alone, the widow, thickly veiled. Girls in convent uniforms follow her, praying aloud, after which come the solitary mourners, the men curiously gotten up with leather buskins and guns slung on their backs: it is *cacciatore* season. The next village has turned out in force to salute the procession, and the windows of most houses are draped with quilts and bunting as brightly colored as Joseph's coat. Automobile headlamps are lighted in respect.

November 18. The *Trionfo della Morte* fresco in the Palazzo Abatellis is as powerful as the Angers tapestry of Death on his green horse. Here Death, screaming mouth in an ovoid rictus, rides an elongated, half-skeletal animal, forehooves in the air, like the horse in Leonardo's "Study for the Battle of Anghiara." For a change, this Death shoots his arrows through lords of wealth and power, princes and popes, instead of peasants; the picture could be called "Death-the-archer strikes high society."

Minutes after leaving the Abatellis, we encounter a brutal reality. An old woman, only a few steps ahead of us, starts across the street without looking and is crushed beneath a bus—a shocking, sickening, horrifying sight toward which a crowd is soon pushing for a better view; the police are obliged to fight their way through to cover the body with newspapers and, until an ambulance comes, stand guard by this gutterside *cappella ardente*.

Why does this incident apparently upset me so much more than it does Adriana and the S.s? I cannot speak for them, obviously, but I do know that there is too much careless, callous, violent, and unnecessary death in Sicily. And that death here seems very close, an impression caused in part by the sight of so much misery and poverty, a sight that beautiful buildings

---

* "The cornices slant this way and that so that our sense of hydrostatic balance and the perpendicular, which is primarily what makes us human beings . . . is upset." Elsewhere, writing of a monastery, Goethe remarks that "a celibate group can create the greatest of works. . .but one old bachelor—witness the case of Palagonia—has rarely produced anything sensible."

1963 and noble landscapes only mock. For in view of the ragged *ragazzi* of Palermo, the pampering of aesthetic emotions, or of any emotions except pity and indignation, is indecent. And to answer the suffering of these people with such complacencies as "not by bread alone" (as if anyone has a right to say *that* before everyone has bread) is criminal negligence—American no less than Italian, our own government apparently not yet having understood that there are no longer any "standards of living" to be protected, for the simple reason that there is no longer any place to hide.

November 19. To Segesta and Selinunte, with a driver more interested in showing the sacred sites associated with Salvatore Giuliano. One of these is the scene of the bandit hero's murder, "not in Castelvetrano, whatever history and the police may have established, but right here in Monreale." The driver says that when the film about Giuliano was shown in Montelepre, the hero's native village, the *contadini*, judging the presentation insufficiently epic, pelted the screen with eggs. Going from Montelepre to Partenico—from the violent to the non-violent reformer—the arguments are all loaded the other way. Danilo Dolce's balloon must be pricked. I mention an evening with Dolce and Margaret Mead at Auden's in New York and he says, "You foreigners have all been duped. Dolce is only a great *filibustero*. He has a dozen illegitimate children and lives with a married woman who has a dozen more of her own. He is trying to populate Partenico all by himself." Dolce's real sin, as the next remark indicates, has been in offending Sicilian pride. "He has been successful enough in exposing our poverty abroad but has failed to make our rich Sicilians aware of it, and we have more millionaire *principi* now than ever."

From 50 yards away, the temple at Segesta looks as if it were made of cork. Closer still, the surfaces prove to be pitted and eroded like the barks of old olive or camphor trees. A flock of swallows scuds sway as we approach the ruin, but the only other sound during our visit is the distant glitter of a goat's bell. Inside the temple, in the full sun, some of the columns are iridescent, with lustrous veins of red, orange, and gold. Goethe found more profitable matter for contemplation in the structure of the wild fennel growing near the temple than in the dead building itself, concerning which he drew a moral similar to the one about the friability of the tufa at Palagonia; but he did not like the countryside, describing it as brooding in a "melancholy fertility." We climb from the temple to the amphitheater, which overlooks the sea, and where lint-like pieces of clouds tuft the surrounding peaks.

The foliage south of Segesta is turning autumn colors, muted as yet, fuscous and tawny except for the flame-red pear trees and bright yellow aspens. The fields have been plowed, but the soil is poor and pock-marked with cacti. In the town of Vita, the "life" can only refer to chickens and mules, the latter, pulling carts, plumed like Theda Bara. Santa Ninfa, on a knoll, is livelier, and its agglomeration of angles forms an attractive Cubist picture.

Whereas the skeleton of the temple at Segesta is gnawed but still standing, every bone of Selinunte has been violently and as if systematically broken. For me it is haunted by the noise that must have followed the exertions of the sundering Samson, when discobolus-shaped capitals and giant salami-slices of columns crashed into the earth like flying saucers. "Psst. Psst." *That*, at any rate, is not an imagined sound. It comes from a man of unprepossessing aspect—what appears of him, for he remains largely concealed behind a cracked stylobate. He extends a cupped hand containing, we suppose from his manner, a lubricious photograph, but it proves to be a figurine that he claims to have excavated and wishes to sell. His story may be true: ·tomb robbers are employed nowadays for their expertise despite the risk to the archeological petty cash. These scavengers are obliged to accept the work, moreover, since they cannot make off with anything as major as a metope, and receivers are likely to be government agents in disguise. The scamp will not give up, and he pops out at us at intervals along the path (*"Psst, Psst, professore"*), even following our car on a bicycle for a time when we leave.

At Gibellina, on the return to Palermo, the land, in color and texture, looks like elephant hide. Alcamo, just beyond, is said to be the "heart" of the Mafia country, but "arsenal" might be a better word. The driver will not talk about the Mafia; perhaps he has taken the *omertà*, the oath of silence, himself.

In the evening, calling on the Principessa di Lampedusa, the formidable Alessandra Wolff, in her Via Butera palace, we narrowly escape dismemberment by a giant Cerberus at the porte cochere and, inside, are nearly turned back by her concierge's built-in look of disapproval. A vehement, peremptory, not to say blunt woman, the Principessa receives us on the *piano nobile* attired like a doge: coif, mink shoulder rug, black robe, velvet slippers, jeweled hoops on both forefingers. The daughter of a singer, and herself blessed with a round, uvular, bass-clarinet voice, the Principessa vocalizes her vowels so that *"vuole,"* for instance, comes out *"voo-oh-lay,"* in three warbled syllables. An impressive linguist, she converses with V. in Russian and moves smoothly through the major European languages while loftily implying that she can as easily manage the minor ones too.

Even more doge-like in her salon, she plumps herself into a curule and assigns us to smaller chairs on each side of this throne, as if intending to hold court. Save for one dim lamp, the room, book-lined from floor to very high ceiling, concedes nothing to the last hundred years, nor does it appear to have been disturbed in that time by the enterprise of dustcloth or mop.

A framed photograph of Prince Giuseppe Tomasi, her late spouse, stands on a console to her right, next to a pile of foreign language editions

1963 of his book. The conversation is confined to the book, and on this subject the Principessa is an indefatigable monologist. *"Ah, Lampedusa, quel homme!"* she croons. *"Il avait des sentiments si fins. Comme je suis triste et seule sans lui."* In fact, and as literary Palermitans are aware, they did not even live together most of the time, seeing each other only twice a year and then briefly. But she goes on: *"Imaginez-vous ce que c'était la vie avec lui."* We cannot do so, of course, and need not try since she is soon giving us her own very substantial account. Yet the story of the publication of the *Gattopardo* is as good as the novel itself.

Autocratic with her guests, the Principessa is positively despotic with her servants. She interrupts herself to rap out some sharp commands to a rheumy-eyed old codger, resembling Max Beerbohm and standing slump-shouldered in the doorway, and she ruthlessly orders a no less browbeaten footman in a long-unlaundered white jacket to fetch another cognac— after harshly admonishing him for failing to pass the hors d'oeuvres. Otherwise she keeps to the main path of her narrative, stepping out of it only now and then to dispose of an imperceptive critic or anyone who has stood in the way of her husband's book. And, in truth, we cannot but admire the swift, clean strokes of her axe as "whish" goes the head of Enrico Falqui, whose criticism is *"tutto falso,"* and "wham" goes that of Leonardo Sciascia, an incompetent for the reason that "he did not even know Lampedusa." We are relieved not to hear her opinions on other, especially political, matters; during World War Two she chose to live in her homes in German occupied Riga and Stomersee.

November 20. Palermitan audiences are permitted to smoke, and the air, by the intermission of our concert, is as dense and blue as a *fumerie,* or the club car on the *Super Chief.* "Agnus Dei" sings the chorus, and "scratch" goes the response of someone lighting up in the first row.

After the performance of *Vom Himmel hoch,* I.S. remarks that the chorale melody was too obtrusive, that "instead of a point d'appui," it lumbered along in clumsy contrast to the lightfooted artifices of the variations. A no less serious fault was the lack of articulation, the unwillingness or inability to play "off the string." Left to themselves, the violists would execute every line for "tone," which is to say not merely legato but portamento; and the harpist, instead of attacking each note *smorzato,* would glue them together.

November 21. The Gancia is virtually the only large Palermitan palazzo to have escaped the bombs of 1943, for which reason, and because of the railway-station proportions of its main *salone,* it was chosen for the ballroom scene in the film of *The Leopard.* In the wall by the main entrance, where an umbrella stand would be found in a Victorian mansion, is the rounded indentation, like a piece of well-worn billiard chalk, used for snuffing torches. We are shown through by the present owner, Prince Wolff-Stomersee, who hangs on I.S.'s every word as if he intended to have them carved in marble. (Which is the reason I.S. sidesteps every trap laid for his opinion; he seldom pops when put on a griddle and expected to do so.)

November 22. To Agrigento by way of Mussomeli, where loaves of hay, hollowed like tents, are pitched between black, wheat-soil hills; and Castello Diana, which the *Guide Bleu* describes as "an impregnable fortress," though it seems reasonably pregnable to me. The muleteers in this region wear long archiepiscopal purple capes, which cover their heads, cowl-like, and flow over the flanks of their animals. These people seem more African than Italian, but are in any case a reminder that whereas the coastal cities of Sicily may belong to Italy, the harsh, half-savage interior is an altogether different land.

The interior of Agrigento Cathedral might be Mexican, except that the columns have been quarried from the temples of older religions. Workmen are repairing the coffered ceiling, held up to it on a tall wheeled tower, like a mangonel. As we watch, a cataract of wood and plaster crashes around our feet.

The Museum of Archeology is safer. To judge by the profusion of Demeters with breasts like brioches, *in*fertility must have been a problem; but the fault may have been a corrupt bachelordom, penises commonly being represented as curled, like anchovies on hors d'oeuvres. The Silenuses bear a striking facial resemblance to Cyril Connolly.

The temples of Agrigento have not suffered destruction on anything like the scale of Selinunte, though the roof of Juno appears to have been swept off in a tornado, and Concordia has been made to swallow, though it has not digested, the church of "St. Gregory of the Turnips." (The lack of romance in these names—"Our Lady of the Asparagus" is another, and "Selinunte" means celery—is not compensated for by gastronomic anticipation.) Violence of a personal kind seems to have befallen the Telamon statue, which lies on the ground fractured into armillary layers like the *Guide Michelin's pneu* figure.

The land near the Lampedusa town of Palma di Montechiaro is parched and white. Thereafter it flattens toward the beaches and dunes west of Gela, which are still studded with German "pillboxes" and *chevaux de frise*. Seeing these fortifications, our driver recalls the news of the American landing here as it affected him as a child in Palermo: "The Germans acted as if we had betrayed them; they kicked anyone who came near them. The GI's, for their part, were friendly and generous, but the first one I approached gave me chewing gum when I had asked for *caramella*, and, not knowing what it was, I swallowed it." (I, too, remember the news of the landing at Gela; or, rather, the eye of my memory funnels back to that long dead and buried day, and I see myself, dog-tag 32748830, standing in an endless line outside the mess hall in the New Orleans Staging Area, while newsboys on bicycles ride by shouting "*Times-Picayune, Times-Picayune;*

1963 Landing in Sicily"; except that *"Je suis un autre,"* and I can no longer enter that other mind.)

A half-hour north of Gela, Etna comes into view, with a plume of smoke like a *bersagliere's* feather. Soon more smoke appears, this time ominously because much nearer home, in fact from the hood of our car. We stop halfway up a hill, and the driver steps out, to look, listen, and wait. Nothing happens, of course, nor after a dozen tries does the motor show any signs of "turning over." Instead, *we* turn the car around, aim it downhill, push it, jump aboard, and in a few seconds are at the bottom, without having coaxed even the faintest tracheal cough from the engine. Here, for the first time, we notice the loneliness of the surroundings and the rapidly descending dark. So, apparently, does the driver, because his looking and listening are agitated now. Then luckily, providentially, two motorcycle policemen, the first ones I have seen in Sicily, come cruising by. What is the trouble with the car, they ask, and aren't we wary of stopping in these bandit-infested hills? Mirabile dictu, they have just heard an announcement on their radios of our concert in Catania tomorrow, thanks to which they requisition the next passing automobile to take our driver to the nearest town likely to have a mechanic.

Some 30 minutes later, during which interval a number of other drivers stop to survey our situation—no doubt attracted by the possibility of seeing a mangled body, or at least some spilled *sangue*—a mechanic actually does materialize, a short, dark, highly excitable man in a beret and very roomy overalls. He sets about his business by looking, listening, waiting, some not very energetic pushing, and finally by inclining his ear to the hood, like a doctor with a man who seems to have suffered cardiac arrest. The result is a decision to operate, a very grave step, evidently, calling for no end of shrugging and arm-waving. At long last the car *is* actually opened up, and a large and frightening array of tools flourished, among them a giant monkey wrench, which, if accidentally dropped into the now-exposed viscera, would undoubtedly justify several months of repairs at a garage. At length the beret and upper half of the overalls disappear into the nether regions of the unhooded area, accompanied, to a lesser extent, by *la polizia*. A long time later the beret and overalls emerge, rather blacker than before, and make for the front seat of the car, where knobs, gears, clutches are poked, pressed, pulled, pushed, pedaled—to no effect and without a churr in response. At last the partly submerged *polizia* surface as well, also try the driver's seat, and perform there in the same way and with the same result.

Finally it is decided to commandeer one of the kibitzing bystanders to take us to the next town, for which eventuality, miracle of miracles, beret-and-overalls actually has a rope. When at long last a towline is secured, the *"ciaos,"* the *"grazies,"* and the hand-waving at the breakup of the party would befit a departure for the moon; and, indeed, the last-minute debate that develops about the signaling system to be adopted during the voyage would seem to imply that some monumental feat of engineering really is about to be assayed. Off we go, at long last. Or rather, off *they* go, for the rope slips loose at the first tug by the other car, thereby provoking a tremendous expenditure of oaths and accusations between beret-and-overalls and the indentured other driver. A 15-minute *pausa* ensues while new knots are tied, this time of Gordian complexity and security. And, strange to tell, this time we move.

Our new driver, declaring himself delighted to have us aboard, is evidently *molto contento* with the whole adventure. He speaks a few words of "Inglis," for he was captured on the second day of the war, then taken to Cairo and later Palestine, where he married. "*Certo,*" those were the times. And what do we think of it all now, of "*la Roosia*" and the "*Cinesi*"?

At Caltagirone we hire a taxi, and this driver, too, as it happens, speaks *un poco inglese,* having spent the war—ah, those were the days!—in Glasgow after managing to be taken prisoner in Algeria. "*E molto bello, Glazgo, ma freddo, freddo.*" And what do we think of Mussolini? He wasn't all bad, you know. And the Americans, who have all the money? Well, America is better than "*la Roosia,*" anyway, because of "*la democrazia.*"

We reach the hotel in Catania at 10 o'clock and are thunderstruck with the news that "*Il presidente Kennedy e morto, assassinato!*" Stunned and unbelieving, we sit by the radio most of the night.

November 23. Black-bordered photographs of the late President are on walls all over the city, the flags on every public building are at half-mast, and the line of black, empty *carrozze* at the hack stand in front of the hotel looks more than ever like a funeral train. I drive to Siracusa with Berman and wander through museums and churches, climbing a wobbly ladder for a closeup of Caravaggio's *Death of Santa Lucia,* burrowing in "The Ear of Dionysus," a cave with freakish acoustics: in one place, the sound of a Kleenex tearing seems to have the decibel level of an express train. Back in Catania, after our concert, I.S. composes a cablegram to Mrs. Kennedy. Seeing him mark it "night letter," V. says "at a time of personal and national tragedy you cannot show you have thought of saving money." I.S. insists that parsimony is not his motive, but good sense. "Furthermore, I do not see why I shouldn't always use good sense, and especially during national disasters." We leave for Rome on the night train.

November 24. During our train stop at Naples, we see a newspaper headline: "*E morto il piccolo maestro, Aldous Huxley.*" So it has happened, and at the predicted time. I mourn him; and mourn myself; his death is the death of a part of me. At one time, during a period of five years, we met at least once, and more commonly several times, a week. Then, after Maria's death, his remarriage and his and our travels separated us. Lately he

1963 seemed to belong to an already completed past. Can those past feelings be articulated today, while avoiding today's pictorial edition of them? Is it possible to revive a memory without memorializing it? Or possible to deny that essential part of the origin of valedictions, the *need* to mourn?

All recent memories of Aldous are vividly clear, in any case, and the picture they form is heartbreaking. The last years of his life, from the discovery of Maria's cancer, were never free from the mental cruelty of incurable illness, for hardly had he watched the end of her struggle when he entered the same lists himself. Call it "his way" that no one ever heard him complain, that he "guarded his grief" and kept others from touching his wounds. This very brave man, alone and nearly blind, went on working, supporting a host of dependents. He *had* to produce a book a year, *had* to and did lecture until three months before his death, which was that of Pirandello's *"L'uomo dal fiore in bocca."* Nor was mortal illness the only specter. The failure and critical drubbing of a play on Broadway, the waste of time and mind on film projects, the generally belittling reception of his writings: these were hard knocks, the more so for an author who had been so popular. At the time of McCarthyism he was subjected to an official indignity. "Would you refuse to take arms against an enemy of the United States?" he was asked. And Aldous Huxley, a man far more deeply responsible to Society,* human as well as American, than most of the citizenry he honored by living in their midst, was actually denied American citizenship because of the pacifist clause.

As Maria's health declined, Aldous, struggling to save her, tried everything from hypnotism and acupuncture to the newest "expander-of-consciousness" drugs.** He even took her to Lebanon to see the magician Tara Bey, whose American tour, a few years before, the Huxleys had underwritten by their intellectual and financial support. Since Aldous did not tell us when the cancer had entered the cobalt stage, her death came as a shock. What an agonizing sight he was then, so miserable and so alone. I see him at the funeral, groping his way down the aisle, his bowed head still a head taller than that of anyone else in the church. I see him at the graveside, giving his arm to Maria's sturdy, dry-eyed mother, who did not need it. Maria, who shared so little of the world of his imagination, who was bored by the music he loved, who read to him hours at a time without lis-

---

* At least twice he took the trouble to testify in Sacramento against power-lobby legislation, defending the battery-propelled automobile against the vested oil interests and taking up the cause of the importer of his perforated-celluloid eye-focusers, after the manufacturers of optical instruments had successfully banned them.

** He had urged I.S. to take mescaline and LSD in the interests of science, to see what effect they might have on a creative musical mind, but to I.S., music, as he heard it in his chemically normal mind, was enough; to have taken mescaline would have been to him like Keats putting cayenne pepper on his tongue to "hop up" the taste of claret.

tening: this same Maria was his seeing eye, the eye of all his affection, and
without her he was as helpless as an unfledged bird.

In the lonely weeks after her death, we kept him company as often as he
would allow. Painful slips would occur, including that sign of delayed
shock, the solecism of the present tense: "As Maria tells . . . I mean, used
to tell me." Because we tried to avoid her memory in our own remarks,
conversation was both ghost-ridden and leadenly self-conscious. We and
all his other friends worried about him alone in that empty house, where,
when I took him home at night, he would let me walk with him to the
door and fit the key in the lock, but would otherwise resist boy-scouting.
His refusal to accept help crossing the streets was a great anxiety, and we
would watch, or not watch, these passages, fearing the worst. He entrusted himself to his hearing and memory on his afternoon walks, but in Los
Angeles even those acute faculties were inadequate. In the last years he
suffered one serious fall.

Memories of the early 1950s return, but helter-skelter. I see him at the
cinema, though apart from documentaries—I remember taking him to an
Italian film on Bosch, to an anthropologist's film on a Central American
Indian tribe—he loathed "the movies." He cut a bizarre figure in
Hollywood theaters, sitting by himself in the front row and moaning
"Inconceivable tripe," "Monstrous oafs," "Semi-minus epsilons." Ordinarily
his Chinese perforations served him at films, but he would switch to a
magnifying glass for a better view of . . . well, the charms of *The Blue Angel*,
which we saw together in a seedy cinema on Wilshire Boulevard. Aldous
also braved the movies for the sake of I.S., who, like Wittgenstein and for
relaxation, would go to almost anything, no matter how bad, and on as
many nights of the week as I would take him.

A sheaf of pictures comes back, too, of Aldous listening to music, which
was one of the delights of his life. On this subject, though, I can tell his
story only by intruding my own. From 1952, he regularly attended
rehearsals and concerts of the pre-classical music—Monteverdi, Schütz,
Couperin, Bach—that I was performing. I should add that he was interested in, but did not love, new music, or indeed much music of any kind after
Beethoven, with the exception of Verdi's *Falstaff*. In 1954 he fell under the
spell of Gesualdo di Venosa, whose madrigal scorebooks I had transcribed
and whose texts he translated for me; in fact he twice introduced my concerts of this music with racy public lectures on life in the North Italian
courts of the time.

Another picture now reappearing is of Aldous the museum-goer, his
lanky, elastic-vertebrae back bent toward an object which he studies, like a
bacteriologist, through a pocket glass. The place might be Pasadena's
Huntington Library, where I remember turning the pages of a Shakespeare
folio with him, or the Museum of Modern Art in New York, where he
hated most of the pictures but would return again and again to Monet's

1963 "Water Lilies." Monet's sight, when he painted the picture, was almost as weak as Aldous's, hence it seemed to have been composed to Aldous's scale, and in any case he did not use his glass when looking at it.* The amount of reading, writing, manuscript-correcting, proofreading he could get through with that glass was astonishing; he did not use dictaphones or tape recorders until the final years.

In another glimpse, I see him elbowing his way through the thick of a Hollywood party at Glenn Ford's. He winces at the voices, yet fastens like an anthropologist to the film moguls and the actors with pink shirts and bare feet. (My own conversation with him that night was about insomnia, and I remember being advised to "eat a stalk of nerve-relaxing celery just before going to bed.") Aldous was surrounded at these affairs by flocks of adoring females, elderly women in saris to culture-struck nymphets for whom the initial attraction may have been the unfamiliar charm of the English language, versus the "beat" talk of their boyfriends. Everyone felt the magnetism of this shy soft-spoken man with the noble head and cameo features.

I should note, too, that Aldous was anthropologically interested in other juvenile delinquents than the luminaries of filmdom, and that he was actually rescued from the fire that destroyed his home by a gang of boys. As he described it later, "The gang came to warn me a good 15 minutes before the arrival of the television trucks, which, in turn, were half an hour ahead of the fire engines that could have saved the house. After the boys had led me to safety, through the one open street, I noticed that some familiar faces among them were missing. When I expressed concern about them, the leader told me not to worry because they were out starting more fires."

"*E morto il piccolo maestro*," says the newspaper. And even before his long, drawling body is cold, the reputation industry will have decided just how "*piccolo*" he was, done its summing up, which is obituarese for hatcheting down, the failures being so much easier to see than the enduring value. How predictable the whole process, being so exactly in accord with the birth dates of the clerks who practice it. Aldous Huxley, a good and gentle man, a better writer than those who will bury him in their columns, dear Aldous will be patted on the head and put away as an "era."

Well, I, too, am a clerk with a birthday, and as an obituarist am even unholier than thou. I will not be able to read him soon again, for I would hear the voice, which would measure the void.

November 25. Our concert in Santa Maria Sopra Minerva, for an audi-

---

* Monet's spectacles, exhibited in the Musée Marmottan in August 1971, were as thick as Aldous's, and the lens on one side was almost opaque from what looked like brown paint, which may have been an effect of time, except that both lenses had light green tint. What pleasure Aldous would have had from these Marmottan pictures of *nymphéas* and *nénuphars*, which compose differently at different distances but would compose close up for him!

ence of cardinals and priests, is televised in its entirety by RAI. I.S.'s rhythms, spare instrumentation, and sharp chords do not suit the shocked atmosphere following the assassination.

December 11. New York. We call for the Eliots at the River Club on East 52nd, New York's most convenient street, he says, "Because it is a dead end." On the way to the Pavillon, he glimpses the United Nations building and denounces it as "the center of an anti-European conspiracy." He drinks and eats almost nothing but from time to time sits upright and focuses his piercingly intelligent gray eyes on each of us in turn. "I am rereading *Nostromo*," he says, adding, "After reading Conrad it was a terrible shock to hear him talk. He had a very guttural accent." "Like mine?" I.S. asks, but Eliot deflects the question: "Yours, Igor, is easier to understand." I interject the unneeded information that Conrad's and I.S.'s fathers were born a few miles apart, that the novelist and the composer came to English as their third culture, via French, that both were patricians who hated the regimes from which they had exiled themselves, that both remained aloof from Western politics, and that neither of them ever voted.

On the subject of languages, Eliot says: "My Italian was quite fluent when I was at Lloyds, but Dante's Italian is not the most suitable instrument for modern business phraseology. I had a smattering of Roumanian, too, and of modern Greek, and for this reason the manager of the bank insisted that I must also know Polish, indeed, that not to know Polish was illogical." When we leave, Stravinsky and Eliot walk arm in arm to the *vestiaire*, where the headwaiter remarks to the attendant: "There you see together the greatest living composer and the greatest living poet." But V. saves the two men from embarrassment by remarking, in exactly the right tone, "Well, they do their best."

December 23. Visit from Isaiah Berlin, on his return from a tour of inspection of British scholarship students at Western U.S. universities. "Los Angeles is a very gloomy place. Even Fresno is preferable, for a night, if only because one can believe that people are actually born, live, and die there." At Las Vegas, "The men shove their big silver dollars into the gambling machines as though they were Tibetan prayer wheels."

After expressing annoyance over some inaccurate references to himself in Bernard Berenson's recently published journal, Isaiah sidetracks himself into an anecdote about Berenson and A. J. Ayer: "Ayer had been talking to B.B. for a certain time when the old gentleman suddenly stood up and left the room saying, 'I'm sorry, but I simply cannot listen to this any longer.' I understand exactly how Berenson felt. Still, it is unpleasant to have that said to one."

Talking about the Eichmann trial, Isaiah says, "It was unnecessary and horrible; I agree totally with Martin Buber. It was, moreover, quite German; everyone seemed to be a German Jew, and they were all speaking German. Eichmann was writing all the time in his glass cage—what I sup-

1963 pose Kennedy should have had in Dallas. He looked like a trapped animal, and a trapped animal is upsetting to see. I am not pleading for him, but merely telling you how one felt looking at him." While relating this, he removes and cleans his glasses, and we see that his wonderfully intelligent eyes are also very gentle. Suddenly deciding to depart, he does so promptly, bidding softspoken, polite *adieux.*

&. **Postscript 1994.** This was the last of the five years of travel beyond Europe that had begun with our visit to the Far East in the Spring of 1959. In 1963 we spent less than six months home in Hollywood. Stravinsky had been concert-touring since 1924, and, though more than twice my age, he bore the strain of moving from hotel to airport to hotel better than I did, though of course all the rehearsing fell to me.

The diary is silent about the Canadian documentary film covering the period from the end of March in Toronto to the beginning of May in Hamburg. Because of stormy seas during most of the crossing between New York and Bremen, it includes only one scene on board ship. Moreover, precious footage of the Hamburg Opera's staging of *The Flood,* taken from the orchestra pit during a performance, was unaccountably not included in the final edit. These losses were partly offset, however, by a wonderfully animated conversation, caught by the camera and soundtrack, between Stravinsky and Nicolas Nabokov. Here is Stravinsky in the process of translating—an almost constant activity in his case—speaking Russian, French, and English, and finding the mot juste in all three.

The two weeks in Rio de Janeiro were more enjoyable than Mrs. Stravinsky's diary suggests, but the Sicilian trip, which started so propitiously, ended in grief. The deaths, in rapid succession, of the conductor Fritz Reiner, President Kennedy, Aldous Huxley, and, soon after our return to New York, Paul Hindemith, came as profound shocks for Stravinsky; his next compositions were memorial pieces. My diary neglects to say that the Stravinskys went by train from Palermo to Catania and that I went by car because I had wanted to see the Roman mosaics at Piazza Armerina. The Stravinskys were in the Catania hotel when I arrived, but they had not yet heard the cataclysmic news of the assassination.

❧ 1964

January 5. I.S. and I by car to Philadelphia, the Bellevue-Stratford, for our rehearsals with the Philadelphia Orchestra. V., staying in New York, goes to a dinner party at Thomas Messer's with Marcel Duchamp and Hans Hoffman.

January 7. Letter to I.S. from Eugene Ormandy in Bermuda: "Please convey my best wishes to Mr. Craft for his success and I look forward to meeting him in person."

January 10. Our matinee concert in the Academy of Music. I.S. conducts *Perséphone* and I conduct his Symphony in C and Schoenberg's Five. Dinner at Claudio Spies's.

January 11. After the evening concert, I.S. and I return by car to New York.

January 13. Blizzard. After we wait for two hours in Pennsylvania Station, all trains are cancelled. We find a limousine driver willing to risk the half-plowed roads and leave with him for Philadelphia at 5, arriving at the Academy of Music three minutes before downbeat time. The entire orchestra is on stage, but the hall is empty except for Ormandy and three others. Return to New York after the concert.

January 14. Our concert with the Philadelphia Orchestra in Philharmonic Hall.

January 18. Dinner with Spender at La Caravelle.

January 20. I.S. and I by train to Washington for our Constitution Hall concert with the Philadelphia Orchestra. Visit with Mrs. Robert Woods Bliss afterward.

January 21. Train to New York. Auden for dinner. He drinks a jug of Gibsons before, a bottle of champagne during, and a bottle (*sic*) of Cherry Heering (did he think it was Chianti?) after. The different qualities for delectation in these fluids hardly seem to count in comparison to their effect as a means of conveyance—supersonic—to the alcoholic Eden. Despite the menu of intoxicants, he remains not only unblurred, but also performs some mental pirouettes, as if the mixture of liquids had formed an intellectual ichor. But V. believes instead in a physiological separation, that Auden must have multiple stomachs, like a cow, the gin going to the omasum, the wine stopping in the reticulum, the kerosene in the rumen. I.S., for his part, is impressed by the display of liver power, "though livers learn, of course, and Wystan's would naturally be the most intelligent in town." My own fascination with *homo bibulus*, to round out the appreciation, is with the capaciousness of the plumbing: not a trip to the "loo" all evening. Labial difficulties occur, to be sure, but they are overcome by a sort of isometric exercise, a screwing up of the rugosities of the nobly corrugated face, and by bursts of music, including some very melodious singing of bits of Rossini's *Petite Messe solennelle*. Otherwise the only sign of tipsiness is an initial lurch at departure, after which a gyroscope seems to take over.

I.S. wants to compose an elegy to the memory of President Kennedy, "either six or nine stanzas of two long lines and one short. I have a choral piece in mind, low in tessitura. Probably I will use a male choir, though whether or not with instruments, I cannot say." * Auden is tickled by these carpenter-like measurements—"I'm an old hand at this sort of thing"—and decides then and there to "do a double octet and a quartet. I'll throw in a bit of 'Grant Us Thy Peace,' of course, and I won't forget that 'his name was John.' " (I.S. later: "Wystan is wholly indifferent to J.F.K.; what he cares about is the form. It is the same with his religion. What his intellect and gifts require of Christianity is its form—even, to go further, its uniform.")

Having just written a talk on the Sonnets for the BBC, the poet vents some opinions about scholars: "Hotson is frightfully learned but all wrong. Rowse is good on the background, quite dotty on Shakespeare." The work of another authority is dismissed as belles-lettres. But the main difficulty is that "it won't do just yet to admit that the top Bard belonged to the homintern. Too soon after the recognition that Beethoven was queer."

After mentioning a public reading on his agenda, he forbids us to attend: "I never allow anyone I know to come to those things. First, I want to keep my tricks to myself; second, I'm always afraid that someone in the back of the hall is going to shout: 'We've heard all that before,' or 'Get *her*!' "

Hammerskjöld's *Diaries*, for which he is writing a foreword, reveal an early belief in a mission and a tragic end, Wystan says, and the subject of Hammerskjöld's death leads to the story of the suicide of an Austrian poet—"he was a bit late in seeing that Hitler wouldn't do"—whose house

---

* This suggests the combination of the *Introitus*, composed over a year later. As soon as the *Elegy for J.F.K.* arrived, March 3, 1964, Stravinsky decided that the words better suited a solo voice. The association of solemnity with a low-tessitura male-voice choir is at least as old as Compère's *Quis numerare queat*.

Auden now owns and inhabits. ("Won't do" is his hardest-worked expression.) Switching to the English scene, he remarks of certain writers that "the Lord should hurry and take them now that their time is up," but he reprieves Compton Mackenzie because "he still has to do his book on the great liars, T. E. Lawrence and so on." Wystan contends that a doctor who conceals the gravity of a patient's condition from him is guilty of great wickedness: "The Psalm says, 'Lord, make me to know the measure of my days.' After all, we need time to make peace with our competitive friends." He says that when called to his father's deathbed, he greeted the expiring parent with: "Well, Dad, you're dying, you know." And he adds: "Ideally one should die upstairs, like Falstaff, with a party in full swing below, and people saying things like, 'Now why doesn't the old boy get on with it?'"

Turning to music, he offers an estimate of the influence of Max Bruch on Elgar, and, speaking of Britten's *A Midsummer Night's Dream*, suggests that "it is a mistake to conclude each act with people going to sleep." Referring to *Rasputin* and Nabokov—"A composer who will never realize his talent because he cannot bear to be long enough alone"—he declares, "The idea should have been rejected out of hand for the simple reason that the *true* subject is hidden, as the audience is aware and quid pro quo. What *Rasputin* is *really* about, of course, is a prodigious penis."

Getting on to historians, he says that if a certain professor "has missed the whole point of a small event like the General Strike—which, as a witness, I know he did—we can hardly be expected to trust him with the Middle Ages or the Russian Revolution. The reason for the strike, obviously, was the middle-class English boy's desire to drive a bus or train." On Hannah Arendt's *Eichmann in Jerusalem*: "I would have defended the book myself except for the automatic answer that *goys* like it."

He bemoans an upcoming dinner party by "a social register bluestocking who addresses me either in words of six syllables or Greek, and, worse, quotes my poetry at me." He claims to be able to recognize every line of his verse but says he often fails to identify excerpts from his prose. His German quotations tonight—the Teutonic period is still at high tide—are all from Qualtzinger. At one point we are told that Rilke is "the greatest lesbian poet since Sappho." Yevtushenko is dismissed as "the poor man's *Howl.*"

February 6. I join the S.s' train in Buffalo in the middle of the night, following my Toronto recording of the Gesualdo Tenebrae (responsories, Miserere, and Benedictus) with the remainder of the service in plainsong.

February 8. Los Angeles. Letter from Isaiah saying that Auden has no feeling for J.F.K., but, then, neither, in all probability, did Tennyson for the Duke of Wellington, yet the poem is good.

March 8. We fly to Cleveland. A welcoming telegram from George Szell, now in New York. (Would he remember auditioning me in 1946 for an assistant conductor's job? I remember *him* all too well. I arrived at

1964 Severance Hall directly from an overnight train and was met by three other applicants who told me that the auditions were a sham, that the position had already been filled by Theodore Bloomfield, a Cleveland native from an influential family. Szell, frostily and without the least semblance of graciousness, told me to be seated at the piano and play the introduction to Mozart's K. 465, the "Dissonant" Quartet, the full score of which he placed on the music rack—a bad choice, obviously intended as a surprise but familiar to everyone of my generation. He then put up the score of Beethoven's Second and asked me to conduct the first movement from memory, after which his only comment was to propound the view that the opening chords are the beginning of the melody that follows and must not be separated from it.)

April 6. Hollywood. I conduct the *Elegy for J.F.K.*, after a brief backstage rehearsal. Richard Robinson sings, reliable as always.

April 25. Telegram from Balanchine and Kirstein about the premiere of the Fanfare.

April 29. To Detroit and Ann Arbor. After seeing our rooms in a city hotel, we move outside to the Inn America Motor Hotel.

May 3. Russian Easter. After our Philadelphia Orchestra matinee, we leave for Toronto, the S.s in a limousine, myself with Glenn Watkins in his car, which soon comes to a stop with a flat tire, thereby separating us from the S.s until we catch up with them, parked in front of a restaurant in Kitchner, Ontario.

May 12. New York. To Richard Burton's *Hamlet*. All streets near the theater are blocked by the 25,000 people who have come for a glimpse of Elizabeth Taylor.

May 16. London, the Savoy. The first *Rake* recording session, in the Abbey Road studio, St. John's Wood. The singers have never performed together, the orchestra is sight-reading, and nobody has slept.

August 20. Lod Airport, Israel. Isaiah meets us, and I go directly to an *Abraham and Isaac* rehearsal in Jerusalem.

August 24. We leave Jerusalem in the morning and stay in a resort hotel near the sea. During the intermission of our Caesarea concert—same program as yesterday in Jerusalem, I.S. conducting Bach-Stravinsky and *Symphony of Psalms*, myself *A. and I.* and the Capriccio—the President of Israel presents I.S. with a gold medal, to which he responds with a written, deeply-felt speech.

August 25. Before take-off, sitting on our El-Al plane for New York, I.S. signs 100 programs for Massada excavators who have heard the broadcast of the concert. At the Regency in New York, we share the penthouse floor with Burton and Taylor. The Beatles are next door in the Delmonico, and, in consequence, Park Avenue is blocked with adolescents of all ages.

September 10. Letter from Isaiah on the Jerusalem concert, contrasting the sincere, touching, but less than sophisticated audience, with its open-

shirt, populist types, and I.S., a porcelain figure, with his egg-like head, **1964**
wholly removed from the world of the last quarter of a century, an 18th-
century figure conducting before an audience that Isaiah compares to one
of American frontiersmen somewhere in the 1840s.

September 12. Los Angeles. I.S. receives a clipping of an article by
Nicole Hirsch, in the *Paris Express*, the only accurate report of his interview
about *Abraham and Isaac* in Jerusalem last month:

> It all began three years ago. Stravinsky was at Oxford at the home
> of his friend, the philosopher Isaiah Berlin, who read some pas-
> sages from the Bible for him in Hebrew and with ancient scansion.
> Deeply impressed by the musical quality of the language,
> Stravinsky dreamed of using Hebrew in a vocal work. In 1962,
> invited by the Festival of Israel, Stravinsky made a memorable tour,
> and at that time the commission was proffered. . . . Stravinsky
> later refused the money and gave it to the fund for the restoration
> of Massada. "I wanted the Hebrew to be sung in a different man-
> ner than in the religious tradition, which is fixed," Stravinsky said. .
> . . "I did the same thing in Russian. My *Noces* is not sung like
> Tchaikovsky or Rachmaninov, after all. . . . The *baryton* has a dou-
> ble role, that of a narrator, who tells the story, and that of a singer,
> who comments. . . . The language led me to employ appoggia-
> turas, as in Arab chant. . . . As for the serialism, that is perfectly
> natural; it is the *other* way which is exhausted. I cannot do other-
> wise. . . . Schoenberg understood this."

September 22. Berlin. I.S. conducts *Renard* and Capriccio (Nikita
Magaloff), and I conduct *Noces* and *Abraham and Isaac* (Fischer-Dieskau).
Afterward, with Auden, Spender, Nadia Boulanger, Nabokov to a reception
for I.S. in the Hotel Kempinsky. To bed with Dagmar Hader between the
concert and the party—too rapidly—and again after—too slowly! Nicolas
telephones at 2 A.M., and Dagmar answers—deliberately, to provoke a
scandal.

September 23. Auden for dinner, in his "unacknowledged legislator"
manner, but easily defending his title as top wit. He is here at Ford
Foundation expense for a Congress of African and European writers, but he
confesses to being "unable to follow nigritude." Nor does he share our
enthusiasm for the tribal dances of Dahomey, which we have just seen at
the Berlin Opera House. Did none of that beautiful bird-mummery—the
dancers are like grounded birds—impress him? Nor the way the dancers
run about like birds plucked of their feathers and climb to the tops of
poles, where they flap like birds who have lost the secret of flight? Nor the
scene in which the male dancer's ruffs vibrate like a cock's wattles, while
the female, hair like a willow tree, waits for him to regain his vigor as the

young males hover ever nearer, threatening to understudy him?

On the subject of this afternoon's session at the Congress, the poet's loneliness, Auden holds that "in spite of all that *einsam* rubbish, poets are no lonelier than other people. Poetry itself is lonely, in the sense that few people read it. But why bother about that when we know that the few really care? And anyway, who would want to be read by the cinema-novel public? After all, it's rather a privilege amid all the affluent traffic to serve this unpopular art."

His main pique against the Congress is that its meetings are conducted in French. "Why should I be compelled to listen for hours at a time to Pierre Emmanuel's rhetorical frog effusions?" Antibatrachian remarks of the sort flow unabated all evening, and at one point he says that "Rimbaud, Baudelaire, and Proust would be much better if they had written in English. As for Mallarmé, well, *chic* nonsense is the most appalling kind."

He says that he came to our concert last night with a raincoat over his arm, was stopped by an usherette and ordered to check the coat. "I protested, of course—*Krieg* is the only language *Krauts* understand—and told the Waltraute that the right to hold one's coat in one's lap is surely not legally *verboten* even in Deutschland. An *ober* Waltraute intervened and, fearing a scuffle, said I could take it with me but would have to wear it, which I did. A very hot concert."

He talks about a film that the Austrians are making of his life in Kirchstetten. "One scene is in church—not terribly appropriate, perhaps; a naughty bar might have been more suitable—but you can hear me singing. Besides, the priest loved being photographed and got all dolled up for it. You can also hear me speaking *Kraut*, ungrammatical but chatty, and I get in some *echt* expressions."

Switching to poets, he expresses admiration for Robert Frost, "in spite of his mean character, for he was jealous of every other, and especially every younger, poet. So was Yeats a jealous old man who behaved abominably to younger poets. But Yeats was untruthful, too, for which reason I dislike his poetry more and more. Why can't people grow dotty gracefully? Robert Graves is aging well, by the way, except that he has become boastful, implying he's the oldest poet still fucking. Now obviously it is normal to think of oneself as younger than one is, but fatal to want to *be* younger."

Shelley, "a thoroughly uninviting character," is condemned for shareholding in cotton mills, but Auden may be seeing him in the light of Dickens's "Merdle," since he condones Wordsworth's similar investments in railroad stocks because "I'm fond of trains." Byron was "a master not of language but of speed. Goethe, had he been able to understand him in English, wouldn't have liked him at all." Goethe's love-life, he goes on, "shocks and bores me. He moves along smoothly, then every once in a while along comes one of those awful outbursts of '*Mein Liebchen.*'" He would like to translate the *Römische Elegien*, but says that so far the task has seemed impossible. "I also want to do a poem explaining why photography isn't an art; and of course any claim that the cinema is an art is rubbish. For the moment I have a medieval anthem in the works, one of those the-latter-half-is-the-mirror-of-the-first-half things. I promised it to Willie Walton at a party when I was in my cups."

Is he in his cups now? He chews out a waiter for bringing him a glass of water: "I haven't had any of that for 30 years and don't propose to start now." When Stephen Spender joins us and I.S. asks him what he would like to drink, Auden whispers to me, "Cocoa, I should think, or sarsparilla." There is no mental fuzziness, in any case, though diction is less distinct with the ebb and flow of *alcools*, as "frogs" say, and conversation becomes more and more a one-way street. His memory for poetry is unfailing, and he spouts it as if he had been struck by the hoof of Pegasus. When he is obliged to rummage for a name or date, the signs of the throes of thought that appear are a contracting of his twill-weave facial integument (with a wiggly wen), and a stirring, with his right hand, of what might be an unseen pancake batter.

Inevitably moving on to Wagner, he remarks that "Mrs. Hunding didn't keep a very proper hearth for the old dear. Incidentally, the most unfortunate instance of stage-timing I have ever seen occurred in a performance of *Siegfried*: the anvil broke in half just as the hero was raising his sword to strike it."

On the subject of the forthcoming American election, he thinks we should bear in mind that "it might be better to be governed by a crook than by a fool." He plans to visit East Berlin tomorrow, in spite of the ordeal of the border police, who wheel reflectors under every car, like the mirrors that dentists use for upper teeth. When Spender remarks, "It is like a genteel prison over there," Auden rebounds with: "All that can be said about a genteel prison is that it would appear to be better than a boorish one."

His departure is heralded by some fresh abuse of "the frogs," whose "famous *clarté* is thicker than the thickest *Wiener* treacle. The French, my dear, are hardly white." Tomorrow's conference is foreseen as "a day among the Laestrygones. If the subject of literary criticism comes up, I will bolt. After all, we were put on this earth to *make* things."

November 5. Letter from Isaiah, very amusing about Adorno, whom he knew well in Oxford and considers a marvelously comical figure. On the dispute about whether Covent Garden will be allowed to call Aron *"Aaron"* in its staging of *Moses und Aron*, because the 12 letters of the German title are said to reflect the 12-tone system of the score, Isaiah says that he has asked Adorno to contribute a note to the program booklet, not a single word of which will be understood, thereby confusing matters still further.

December 13. Leroy Aarons's interview with I.S. in the *New York Journal American:*

1964

The interview is over, Igor Stravinsky, stooped and small under the weight of his 82 years, picks up his cane, lifts himself out of his chair and limps slowly and carefully toward the bathroom of his Hotel Pierre suite. Suddenly he pauses. He turns to an end table on which stands a leather-covered flask. Stravinsky picks up the flask, draws a glass from a tray on another table, and continues out of the room. . . .

"How do you do?" he asks in a most cordial Russo-French accent. . . . He speaks slowly, quietly. He talked about the *Elegy for J.F.K.*: "The Elegy is in memory of somebody I knew, and whose loss I infinitely regret. We were at a concert in Sicily when it [the assassination] happened," he recalls. "I was conducting my Mass there. I told the Italian audience I would play this Mass in memory of Kennedy. I never saw such sympathy for strangers as in Italy. All the walls were covered with his portrait. . . . The day of his burial I repeated my concert in the Cathedral [of Santa Maria Sopra Minerva, Rome]. It was the only open building in the city. . . . The *Abraham and Isaac* is a very different question. . . . In the Christian religion, the Abraham sacrifice is the greatest sacrifice, other than Jesus, of course, but we are talking of the Old Testament. It seems to me to be very close to the philosophy of Kierkegaard which I esteem very highly.

ॐ Postscript 1994. At the beginning of March the Stravinskys purchased the home of the late Baroness d'Erlanger at 1218 North Wetherly Drive, and, after six months of extensive renovations, moved into it from their home of 23 years at 1260 North Wetherly Drive. After sleeping in their new home for the first time on September 8, they were almost immediately off to Europe.

The Stravinskys had known Catherine d'Erlanger as a patroness of Diaghilev in the 1920s. As Hollywood neighbors during the 1940s and 1950s they had dined together quite regularly at her home or the Stravinskys', but more frequently, during my period, in one of the three restaurants that she owned successively in the area of Sunset Boulevard and La Cienega Drive. The food in the first of these, The Deauville, was excellent—Marie Le Put, the wife of the chef, became the Huxleys' cook a little later—but the raison d'etre for all three was to provide the Baroness's paramour, Johnny Walsh, a café-style singer, with a place to perform. From March 1952 until the Baroness's death in 1959, I lived in a tiny upstairs apartment over the garage at the back of her property but with an entrance on another street, parallel to Wetherly Drive. I paid the rent by reading to her for two-hour stints three or four times a week; she was in her eighties by this time, and her eyesight was failing.

When the Stravinskys took possession, they had the ground floor of the garage turned into a maid's room and installed a swimming pool between this structure and the wall of the next property on the Sunset Boulevard side. The Stravinskys also converted one of the Baroness's living rooms into a library and music room, built a guest room and bathroom in the basement, another bathroom adjoining the kitchen, and still another, for a total of five, between Stravinsky's upstairs bedroom and studio. The studio was a replication, as faithful as possible, of the one at 1260 North Wetherly Drive.

The move had become inevitable. The many steps from the street to the Stravinsky house had become increasingly difficult to negotiate— whereas the new home was built on flat ground with a driveway leading to the porte cochere and front entrance (no steps). Moreover, the old house was too small. The only bedroom was so tiny that if Stravinsky had needed a night nurse, Mrs. Stravinsky would have had to sleep in a hotel. But the new house was not without drawbacks. The stairs that connected the upper and ground floors were steep—a plan to install an elevator was never realized—and the dining room was smaller than the one in the old house.

The move upset Stravinsky emotionally and psychologically. He was deeply attached to the "nest" that he had lived in for so long and in which he had composed so much music. It was the first home that he had owned, rather than rented, since leaving Russia before World War I. He did not love the new house and never entirely adjusted to it. Mrs. Stravinsky was happy to have a large bedroom of her own, and she enjoyed the pool-side balcony adjoining it, but at 76 she was too old to look after the house, and in the first place would have preferred to live in New York or Paris. When the Stravinskys closed the doors of 1260 North Wetherly Drive for the last time, Yvgenia Petrovna, their housekeeper and cook of some 22 years, also a woman in her seventies, knowing that she could not manage the future, three-times-larger residence, retired (on a pension that the Stravinskys provided for the remaining 16 or so years of her life). For a time, before the reign of Hideki Takami in 1967, the Stravinskys were dependent on cooks and housekeepers from Czechoslovakia, young women, married and therefore unlikely to defect, but allowed to accept employment from abroad for no more than two or three months.

The Baroness's property had to be relandscaped. This entailed the removal of one of her most original architectual fancies, a wall about 20 feet long and 8 feet high made of stacked-up empty beer bottles. The eccentric old lady, dressed in a dirty flannel nightgown and wearing a tiara on her bright orange hair, delighted in showing this eyesore to visitors who, naturally, could find nothing to say.

🍃 *1965*

March 30. Letter from Spender in Ames, Iowa: "This is a very dreary place. . . . The corridors of the campus buildings, instead of being lined with photographs of alumni and ex-presidents, have row on row of photographs of bulls, pigs and hens. The members of the Faculty I've met are far duller than any of these animals."

March 31. Our arrival at the Austin, Texas, airport is filmed for CBS by Haskell Wexler. A motorcycle escort is provided from the airport by the chief of police, Michael Barrie's brother.

April 1. I.S. is filmed on the University of Texas campus looking at student paintings and attending an art class busily drawing a nude girl. Party at Robert Tobin's.

April 2. I.S., V. seated on stage behind him, is filmed answering students' questions. At one point, he turns to her and asks for an English translation of *"znatok."* "Connoisseur," she says, but pronounces it *à la française*, which provokes laughter. (This reminds me of the story of Mark Twain arriving in a German town, sneezing, hearing someone say *"Gesundheit,"* rejoindering "Thank heavens someone here speaks English.")

April 13. I conduct the inaugural concert of the Los Angeles County Museum's music program: Schoenberg's *Begleitsmusik* and Cello Concerto (his arrangement of G. M. Monn's clavicembalo concerto), with Laurence Lesser as soloist; I.S.'s two Little Suites, *Abraham and Isaac*, with Richard Robinson as soloist, and Movements, with Karl Kohn as soloist.

April 20. On the flight from Chicago to New York, I.S. gives me a page from his pocket music pad, on which he has written the series of the Variations and inscribed it: "For you, dear Bob who performed Saturday April 17/65 my Variations for the first time. ISTR."

May 12. Paris. CBS films our visit to Giacometti in his rue Hippolyte-Maindron studio. He is thinner than last year but otherwise looks the same, *i.e.*, like an unmade bed. Apart from the rumpled clothes and dishevelment, his skin is coriaceous, like a piece of old luggage, his hair has apparently never been trained by a comb, his fingernail dirt is paleo-

400

zoic, and his tartared teeth alternate yellow, black, and absentees, like the keyboard of a broken harpsichord. In the street, where he comes to greet us and to see us off, he blends into the *quartier;* or, at any rate, the *blousiers* who pass by, *baguettes* under arm and talking about food, do not notice him.

The clutter in his studio gives an impression of spareness, like the art it contains. Giacometti has fitted the walls of the alleyway entrance with a Della Robbia (?) and other reliefs. In the room, small, with a high skylight, one notices the graffiti first: all the walls are scratched, scribbled on, painted, like those of a catacomb or cave. Next we are aware of the sculptured figures, a hundred or more of them, it seems, some as small as lead soldiers, two or three larger then life. Several of them appear to walk about the room, but most are gathered in a corner where their thin gray trunks look like trees after a forest fire. Two others are wrapped in canvas tied with rope; from time to time Giacometti sprinkles these newest creations from a watering can, as if he were tending flowers.

We sit on a cot, after clearing it of paints, bottles, papers, books, sketches, canvases, palettes; these last are remarkable in that the daubs are bright colors, the paintings all dark gray. The other furniture consists of a battered table, a potbellied stove, and a small tree which comes up green through the dirty floor like a medieval miracle. The paintings, all in great need of dusting, are turned to the wall. The artist shows them to us only very reluctantly, supplying a running commentary on the degree of failure in each: *"Je n'ai pas réussi . . . je dois travailler . . . c'est mauvais ça . . . toujours la même chose, chaque fois la même"*—and in truth, the uniformity in the portraits of seated people and in the sculptures of walking men *is* somewhat stultifying. The shrug of failure is withheld only for a sheaf of pencil portraits of Matisse done in 1954, and it is even conceded that one or two of them might actually be acceptable. "Matisse was a difficult subject," he says. "He hated to pose and would give me only two minutes at a go. To make it even more difficult, he kept assuring me as I worked that nobody knows how to draw any more: 'I can't draw, Giacometti, and *certainly* you can't,' he would say, and of course he was right. He knew he was dying, and said he regretted it because he needed 20 more years to complete his work." A dozen times during the visit Giacometti interrupts himself or ourselves to remark, 'C'est curieux, ça," about something which does not seem at all curious to me. Shortly before we leave he pours Scotch for us from a bottle with a whiskey label, but the contents taste like turpentine.

May 13. I.S. is filmed in the Théâtre des Champs-Elysées, both on stage and in the audience, by seat No. 111, where he heard the beginning, at least, of the first *Sacre.* But who was with him in seat 109, for which he also preserved a pass? In the afternoon I drive to Chambord, stopping, near Orléans, at the Stravinsky family cemetery of S. Catherine des Bois.

May 14. Henri Michaux for lunch in I.S.'s rooms. His eyes are so striking—a little exophthalmic, a little too high up and close together, a little

1965 oriental ("like two jewels in a Chinese idol," I.S. says, and *"Il n'y a que des yeux dans ce visage"*)—that the other features are difficult to remember, the light red, dandelion-fluffy brows on an otherwise entirely molted cranium, the something rodent-like, but agreeably so, about the forehead and mouth. *Voilà*, that's it: Michaux is a polymath mouse; a mouse that sits on its hind legs and clasps the table with long, white, very clean paws; a mouse out of *Alice*, intellectually superior both naturally and by experience. It follows that this extraordinary creature emits an extraordinary laugh, a serious and thoughtful laugh, which at the same time offers a dental survey that proves him to be a chrysostomos in the literal as well as the poetic sense.

Do his gray flannels and blue sports jacket express a desire for a way of life that his shyness will not allow him to lead? When he is unfolding an idea, in any case, a different character emerges, as if the machinery were being removed from automatic controls, and when mescaline is mentioned, his phrasemaking is both more rapid and more original. One of the joys of this drug is that "while the thing outside you, the thing you have made, becomes greater, you yourself become more and more detached from it. As the lines in your drawing begin to seem more important to you, so you forget about your own importance, with the result that you feel *royalement bien.*" I.S. takes issue with this, saying that he has no wish to leave himself outside or behind and that detachment does not attract him. Michaux graciously provides him with the counter-argument: "It is true that life has difficulties enough without adding new ones. That, after all, was Balzac's stand against drugs, and it may be preferred to Baudelaire's drug-taking-for-literary-exploitation." Michaux's use of the word "understanding" during mescaline intoxication raises another demurral from I.S. "I prefer thinking to understanding; thinking is active and continuous, like composing, while to understand is to bring to an end."

Proposing a new category of "superbly boring literature," Michaux says he would award the palm to Proust's letters: "The ennui is really masterfully composed." From Proust he turns to Lou Andreas-Salomé, who "could wiggle her shoulder in a way to imply that Nietzsche"—he pronounces it to rhyme with pizza—"was somewhere within. She used geniuses like maquillage, wearing Freud like a face powder, showing off Rilke as if he were a new kind of lipstick. When I first met this flaming redhead—stoking a blaze in her fireplace that exactly matched the color of her hair—she was talking about Rilke. After a while it occurred to her to inquire about my own profession. I will never forget that look of disbelief when I said that *I* was a poet. But what a temperament she had! *Une femme ravagée, mais ardente, ardente!*" And as he goes on to imitate her Russian accent, I wonder if his sensitivity to accents is attributable to his own Belgian one, for he does not gargle his "r's" in the way that Parisians do.

Talk about Tibet and a recent trip to Katmandu—"in airplanes I look at

my watch all the time and wonder when my head is going to explode"—
lifts him to his highest pitch of excitement. "How primitive and empty we
Americans, Russians, Europeans are next to these people, though compared
to Montagnards, even the Hindus are hysterics. What a *maîtrise* of philosophy and psychology they have attained, and not only in their tantras but
also in their lives. You feel, with them, that they are simply waiting for us
to grow up to their height." Which is pretty much what I feel with
Michaux.

Giacometti arrives, to draw I.S., as Michaux is leaving, and as they pass
each other, the sculptor compliments the writer on his new paintings.
They are amateur work, Michaux says, and Giacometti does not dispute
the word, but says that he cannot see any difference between the paintings
done under the influence of mescaline and the others, an observation that
earns him the silent study of those two piercing oriental jewels.

After the mental positiveness and physical neatness of Michaux, the
contrast that Giacometti brings is almost too extreme. The artist is
obsessed with failure, or the idea of failure, and the conviction that he will
fail yet again is apparently a necessary goad for each new attempt. His
talk in the main is a nervous patter of questions, "*Eh?*" "*N'est-ce pas?*" "*Non?*"
"*Vous croyez?*" "*Ce n'est pas vrai?*" which he accompanies by tapping his nico-
tine-stained fingers on the table cloth and turning his light brown, very
kind eyes in a restless search from face to face. "*J'ai beaucoup travaillé mais la
sculpture est là, et je reste toujours là,*" he says, tracing two areas on a napkin to
show how he cannot bring them together.

Preparing to draw, he sheds his jacket, thereby exposing several inches
of underpants overlapping the soiled blue shirt above the belt line, the belt
itself having missed three of the loops. He then rolls up his sleeves and
with the blade of a small pocket knife whittles several hard-lead pencils to
fine points. Proposing to practice on me before trying I.S., he explains
that, just as a pianist must wind or unwind a piano stool to exactly the
right height, so for him the main problem is in finding the exact distance.
In fact, he works very close to me, but shifts positions twice. When I ask
whether he would like more light, the answer is that the light is immaterial
to him. "If we change, it would only be different, but not easier or better."
Taking a sheet of slightly rough paper, adjusting his spectacles, folding his
right leg over the left, he peers into my face. "*Je ne vois rien,*" he says, not
very flatteringly. Then: "*Je suis complètement incapable . . . Je suis à zéro . . . Je dois
recommencer . . . Je me trouve toujours devant la même difficulté et je ne peux rien faire.*"

Finally deciding to take the plunge, he begins to draw, looking rapidly
back and forth from my face to his paper about three dozen times. He
talks incessantly, and I am reminded of the loquacious dentist and the
gagged patient, for if I talk or budge, so I have been warned, he will
destroy the drawing. He works at great speed and makes almost no era-
sures, but in the moment of finishing, exclamations of failure pour out in a

1965　torrent: *"Mais, c'est mauvais ça . . . c'est mal fait. . . ."* When not drawing, he chain-smokes (Camels)—ashes falling where they may—and his cigarette cough could be studied for extra realistic effect by even the most accomplished Mimi or Violetta. After completing two drawings of me, he starts on I.S., who steers him to the subject of Picasso. *"Il m'étonne,"* Giacometti says, *"il m'étonne comme un monstre, et je crois qu'il connait aussi bien que nous qu'il est monstre."* A minotaur no doubt. Two very fine portraits are achieved during this one-way conversation.

May 15. A CBS car to Vevey. We stop in a five-star restaurant in Saulieu, where the S.s eat mounds of crayfish. The Theodore Stravinskys are waiting in the Vevey Palace Hotel, which infuriates I.S., exhausted from the long trip. He goes to bed leaving V. to deal with his family.

May 16. Filming in Clarens and on the balcony of the hotel, overlooking Lake Geneva. I.S.'s granddaughter for lunch, the Theodores at 4, since the two generations are not on speaking terms.

May 17. I.S. conducts an on-camera search for the *pension* in Clarens in which he composed most of *Le Sacre du printemps*, though Les Tilleuls, as this residence is called, was already tracked down during a rehearsal excursion yesterday morning and in any case is well known locally. Whereas yesterday's experience obviously affected him, to judge by his blindman's bluff directions to the driver and the general fuddle in his usually powerful memory for this sort of thing (he has no recollection of having shown the house to me in October 1951), today, returning to his old home, he seems calm and unafraid of whatever peeps into the past the visit might hold in store.

In spite of the plural name, a single linden shares the entrance, 51 rue Gambetta, at the intersection with the avenue des Chatelards. Entering the *pension*, I.S. is allowed to climb one floor too high before CBS men direct him back to the *premiere étage* where, thanks to their fieldwork, one buzz of the doorbell admits him to his old lodgings. He goes at once from room to room impatiently looking for his quondam studio, but soon announces it is not here and that this is the wrong apartment. At this point CBS springs its coup, Madame Louise Rambert, a red-nosed and frumpish old lady, who actually lived in the building at the same time as I.S. and has never changed her address. She fusses her way in, alarmed and confounded by the TV cameras, the powerful lights, the sound equipment, and the crew who, in full gear, standing by for a Stanley and Livingstone scene, *do* look as if they might be part of a Martian invasion. When the old lady sees I.S., her voice chokes and she appears to be on the verge of bursting into tears, except that the explosion takes the form of volubility instead, a cascade of memories from which there seems to be no prospect of shelter. Though ordinarily contemptuous of anyone who allows the past to obtrude in the present, I.S. is deeply interested in and moved by the old lady's recollections.

The two of them sit in an alcove with a view, down the hill, of La Pervenche, another of I.S.'s homes, and beyond that, below some railroad tracks, of the site of yet another residence, the former Hotel du Chatelard. Still farther below is Lac Léman. I.S. recalls that work on *Sacre* was interrupted each morning by a train and that he used to anticipate it with hatred and baited nerves.

The old lady remembers that Madame Stravinsky did her hair in a bun, and that she and her children were always wan and sickly. I.S., himself, she continues, spent all day in his studio, which was on the *rez-de-chaussée*— a fact he denies, maintaining that it was on the same floor as the apartment. When she reminds him of some fellow tenants of the time, among them a German ex-admiral and an Austrian countess, he himself supplies details about these people.

Madame Rambert would like us and the CBS crew to know that at one time the address had aristocratic as well as artistic tenants, partly by way of apology for the present occupants of I.S.'s old apartment, a migratory worker and family from Spain. She recalls, too, that the other residents used to complain that "Monsieur Stravinsky plays only wrong notes." This does not amuse I.S., who returns to the charge of 1911: "The wrong notes for them, the right ones for me."

Eventually Madame Rambert leads a disbelieving and protesting I.S. downstairs to the room she assures him was his studio. Recognition is immediate. As he enters this amazingly tiny and constricting cubby hole, his face floods with pleasure; reminders of long-dead loved ones and friends are pushed aside by reminders of the creation of a masterpiece. He walks to a sofa, exactly as he says he used to do 54 years ago and, sitting there, tells us and the television audience that he was fully aware at the time that he was "writing something important." In fact, he inscribed some words on the inside door of the closet—nicked them out with a knife, like a schoolboy's declaration of love on the bark of a tree—to the effect that *Sacre* was composed here. (On other occasions he has said that the verb was active: "I am composing.") He looks for this carved autograph, but the incumbent of the apartment, Madame Carrell, says that the door was re-lined a decade ago and that she does not know of anyone who would be able to say whether the signature had been found on the former surface. In 1930 Nicolas Roerich told a New York lecture audience that he and I.S. had inscribed beams to commemorate the room in the house at Talashkino in which they first conceived the *Sacre*.

That the music was created here, that such power—one pictures I.S. at the piano holding handfuls of volts—was unleashed in this dingy anteroom, is wondrous. (Does the room resemble his childhood bedchamber in St. Petersburg? It is exactly the sort of room, in any case, claustrophobic to me, that he loves, and not only loves but compulsively needs, to crowd still further with the objects and artifacts that to him signify order.)

1965 The wonder is in the neighborhood, too, in the townsmen with whom I.S. was rubbing elbows and in those fellow boarders, the admiral, the countess, Madame Rambert herself, and, at one time, just down the street, Maurice Ravel and his Basque-speaking mother. How in this torpid village, which was also the scene of the creation of *La Nouvelle Héloïse*, did I.S., or the powers that mediate, manage to keep the fuse to his taproots so directly and fully open? But then, the same question might be asked in connection with *Tristan und Isolde*, that most un-Swiss flood of passion, much of which was brought forth not so many kilometers from here.

When I.S. departs, the old lady, now in a high state of emotion, gives him an ink-press *cliché* of Les Tilleuls and begins to weep; her moment has come and gone, the witness has been called, the content of waiting emptied. But the encounters of the morning must have run an even more difficult course for I.S. The "universal eye" of television has tried to rub his nose in former emotion in the hope that he might be able to say what it is "like," though of course he cannot say, but can only repeat conditioned answers a little differently, changing a bead here and there in the mosaic of semi-fictions out of which true history is composed. Ultimately, too, ghosts, souvenirs, and even the opening of tombs may be less hard than the realization that the 54 intervening years have produced nothing to equal the music composed here, this, at any rate, being the weight of opinion behind the promiscuous lens that has been prying down on him all morning, focusing on *Sacre* of all his work.

Drive to Basel, the Hotel Drei Königen.

May 19. To Paris. Lunch in Strasbourg, after which, on Giacometti's commendation, we go to the Cathedral to see Pigalle's monument to the Maréchal de Saxe.

May 23. At 7 A.M., David Oppenheim and I board a Caravelle through the rear, like stuffing going into a turkey, and fly to Warsaw to prepare for I.S.'s arrival there in two days. Our first glimpse of Poland is of lettuce-colored fields, thin strips of newly-plowed land, and a highway with as little traffic as it must have had 40 years ago. The closer the view, the more skeptical we are of the stewardess's promise that Warsaw is "a fun city," though it could be with her along. Did she notice an effect on us of the other passengers, all of them returning Poles and every face an advertisement of how grim life in Poland must be?

The airport porters find us worthy of sustained curiosity, which, regrettably, is not the case with the girl from the PAGART agency sent to nursemaid us through customs and currency control. This wall of indifference and *sang-froid* selects certain of our questions to answer, but shoves the others aside as if we had simply not asked them. Except for a few tile-roof prewar buildings, and some barrack-style postwar ones, the road to the city is lined mainly with empty or rubble-filled lots. The Warsaw skyline is dominated by the tower of the Palace of Science and Culture, which so resembles one of the towers of Moscow University that I expect a city with **1965** Russian-style architectural features.

The Europejsky Hotel—the name seems to suggest that Europe is somewhere else—is modern with respect to date and the intention of its conveniences, but is so bleak and institutional that we expect to hear the clank of a lock and chain after crossing the threshold. While Miss Permafrost enrolls us at reception (and probably with SMERSH as well), we wait in a restaurant as large as a city block in Peoria and as square. Nor do the potted palmettos standing at lonely intervals around the room conjure any atmospheric benefits of southern seas or serve any other decorative purpose that I can discover. Are they bugged?

The menu, on the other hand, *is* exotic, but linguistically rather than in the actual promise of culinary delights, one of which is "gravy soup." The foreigner orders by reading translations in any of four languages and pointing to the Polish equivalents, none of the waiters being able to speak more than a word or two of any other tongue. This is surprising, at first, in view of the wartime diaspora, but as the room staff proves to be no less crampingly monolingual, the reason must be attributed to "security." One built-in defect of this pointing system is the lack of allowance for variable detail ("Can you bring mine without the sauce?"). A more serious difficulty is that most of the listed dishes do not exist. No fruit of any kind is available, not only no Vietnam pineapple and Cuban cantaloupe (lots of Cuban crystal sugar, though, or is it ground glass?), but even no Polish cherries or grapes. Each dish is priced by weight, like caviar in Western restaurants. Thus a certain amount of *zlotis* will buy 38.08 *ogs* (grams) of beans or 15.29 *ogs* of jello. Miss P. has recommended ham, and advisedly; in fact, after only a few experiments I resolve to stick to a Gadarene diet for the duration. The wine, though nicely served with a towel tied around the neck of the bottle like a flapper's scarf in the twenties, is a Bulgarian off-white with the consistency of mineral oil. The dessert is a plate of almonds in a dune of hot salt.

I accompany Miss P. on a tour of inspection of the S.s' suite, now being readied for their arrival. Its vast and cavernous living room could well be, at other times, the main meeting place of the Central Committee of the Party Presidium; the only furnishings are a round table with six straight-backed chairs and a huge painting of a naval disaster. When I reckon aloud that the ceiling must be 40 feet high, Miss P. provides the exact information. "The entire apartment is above a hundred square meters," she says, in a special tone of achievement, and as if we intended to spend our spare time flying toy airplanes. But rentals *are* determined by spatial volume, just as foods are priced by weight. "This is because of the inspectors," Miss P. adds, without explaining who these mysterious people are, or otherwise developing this promisingly Gogolian, or Scotland Yard, theme.

I must stop saying "Miss P." She has a beautiful name, Jolanta (the "J" pronounced like the "i" in Spenser's "His sports were faire, his ioyance innocent"), and is herself, by very evident attractions, deserving of more personal, in fact full-scale attention. She is tall, strawberry blonde—when at last she removes her Andean-Indian-woman's bowler—and very fair of complexion. Overconscious of the slight strabismus that affects her light brown eyes, she tries to find an angle to conceal it when she talks.

Her fingers are nibbled at the tips like a pianist's, which they may be since they seem to be performing piano exercises wherever they alight. Finally, her manners are pre-proletarian and ladylike. I suspect a deep romantic temperament beneath the capping of *froideur* being shown to me, but a de-brainwashing would be necessary to prove it; which, come to think of it, could be an agreeable assignment. One thing that puzzles me is her quick and open expression of dislike for everything Russian. Is this to draw me out, a part of the East-West game? I think not, but if she is a stooge, congratulations to the Party on having found such an attractive one. If only she would lose that New Year's party hat!

My room is a different matter. Mascot-sized—its measurements could be expressed in *ogs*—it might have been chosen for me by a status-conscious capitalist. After squeezing through the door, I see that to "stay flat in bed" would be an impossibility, though a heavy comforter has been folded over the middle of the mattress to disguise the fact. Of the lights, the one on the ceiling hums E above middle C almost loud enough to cushion the noise of the passing tram-cars; and the reading lamp, which has the strength of one aged lightning bug, is remote from the bed, even when its strangling length of wire—if it should come to that—is stretched to the full.

Strolling on the Nowy Swiat, David and I enter the Church of the Order of the Visitation, attracted by its Venetian façade; Warsaw is still an Italianate city in its church architecture. The church is surprisingly crowded, and we find full congregations in three other churches, all with fairly large sprinklings of young men in cassocks and calottes. Does the West underestimate the church, I wonder? We tend to forget that even the radical agrarian reform program of the National Liberation Committee of 1944 did not apply to Church-owned estates. Clerical habit is more common in the streets here, in any case, than in any other European city except Rome and Dublin.

Sidewalk traffic, in other ways as well, is much less drab than it is in Russia, the political parent. A type of trench-coated, bereted, and brief-case-carrying pedestrian is endemic here, as he is in Moscow, but the quality of these accouterments is marginally better here; and Warsaw, though I should have begun with this observation, is bountiful in good-looking women.

A bookstore window on the Nowy Swiat displays photographs of death and devastation resulting from U.S. air raids in North Vietnam; but com-

pared with some of the protestations to the same purpose currently deco-
rating the walls of Paris, this one is mild, inconspicuous, and less damaging
to the U.S. "image" hereabouts, I would think, than some of the U.S.'s own
propaganda pictures of the apple-pie-eating spouses and baseball-playing
progeny of the latest astronauts.

Two American exchange students, here to study cinematography, take
us to dinner in the Club for Film Artists and Writers, a prewar building, I
assume, though to distinguish the restored from the genuinely old is practically impossible. The women here, waitresses as well as actresses, are
strikingly handsome, with auburn hair, milky skins, high bosoms, the dark
eyes of Maria Waleska. And the American students confirm the French air
hostess: Warsaw *is* a fun city, they say, and the "loosest" in Europe.

May 24. Jolanta, this morning, is unable to conceal her annoyance
because of our unchaperoned sortie to the Film Club, and she goes so far
as to request particulars of other places visited and of people met. Is she
required to fill out a report? I ask, but with that her tone changes, and
back we go to the superior nursemaid of yesterday. It is now becoming
clear that if we are to act out a charade, she as Ninotchka, myself as "the
American," the rule of the game will be that the more serious she, the more
I intend to laugh. Is the plot also beginning to resemble the film *Ninotchka?*
Flirting with her, in any case, could easily become involuntary.

Arriving for rehearsal in the concert hall on Henryka Sienkiewicza
Street, I am shown to a dressing room whose furnishings include a portrait
of Emil Mlynarski, founder of the Warsaw Philharmonic, as well as Artur
Rubinstein's father-in-law, and a clock with a heavily premonitory tick and
a minute hand that jerks like a taxi meter. The conductor, Witold Rowicki,
introduces me to the orchestra, before delivering me to one of those mysterious "inspectors," a panjandrum who announces the order of the pieces
to be rehearsed and calls the intermissions, during which everyone drinks
tea, Russian style, from a glass. I address the musicians in English, which
the concertmaster translates, prefacing each remark, before relaying it,
with the Polish for "colleagues." At one point a player voices a question in
German, which I answer in that language. A commotion follows. Will I
please continue in German, since more than half of the orchestra understands it, whereas no one knows more than a word or two of English and
French? And from then on we communicate in the language of the
wartime invader, a fact no one seems to feel as an irony.

The players are willing, patient, good-humored, slow; but I, too, am
slow to adjust to their radically different time scale, which is that they are
not going anywhere and have lots of it, and that I have a date in Paris next
week and am in a hurry. They play with energy and passion, but their
instruments are of poor quality, their mode of attack is not well or uniformly defined, and their ears are innocent of any sensitivity to intonation. (I.S.
often remarks that in the first decades of the century little attention was

1965 paid to intonation even in the best Western European orchestras.) In view of what happened here in 1939–45, the wonder is that an orchestra exists at all, a miracle that it is such a good one.

Lazienki Park, where I walk with Jolanta in light rain, is surrounded by the kind of wrought-iron fences that were melted into the war effort elsewhere; were the Germans never short of scrap metal? The semi-wild beauty and the romantic trappings of the park, the ghostly palace swaddled in mist, the swan lake, the nut-begging red squirrels, the forest of tall larches, poplars, beeches, firs exert no evident effect on Ninotchka. Her only emotion, so far as I can see, is patriotism, the colors of which, in the little lecture she delivers in front of a monument to Chopin, are as bright as the Polish flag. This is an official stroll, she seems to say, and I must not expect her to exceed her office by a whit or a word.

Taxis are not plentiful in Warsaw, and most of the few that exist would have been declared unfit for General Gallieni's 1914 expedition to the Marne. All automobile drivers being warranted to sell taxi service, we hire a ride back to the hotel with one of the beret-and-briefcase types.

Jolanta takes us to an evening rehearsal of *Sacre* by the National Ballet in the not-yet-finished—no seats!—Teatr Wielki. This is said to be the largest opera house in the world, but the less said about its other qualities the better, especially of architectural imagination, which gave out near the level of the basement. The choreography is of the so-called kinesthetic variety, but with alien touches: the "adolescents" imitate ponies, and their dance alternately suggests a school of equitation and a movie Western, except that the Indians do not actually whoop. In "Spring Rounds," hands tremble over heads to suggest sprouts on the way up. This sort of thing, tying the music to something not essentially musical instead of leaving it to its own description, can soon reduce even the *Sacre* to gag music. But if the triviality of these exterior associations is obvious, so *any* visual complement, accompaniment, commentary to a piece as powerful as the *Danse de la terre* is bound to be absurd. The ballet ends with the *Elue*, one of those slender shoots, falling on her back, in which position she writhes, curls, and grinds.

May 25. I have been trying to picture the ruins of the city at the end of the war, but Cibrowski's *Warsaw, Its Destruction and Reconstruction* does the job for me horribly well. Photographs of the rubble heaps of 1945, on facing pages with photographs of the same sites from the same angles today, make apparent that the feat of reconstruction here far surpasses that of any other city, German, Dutch, and Russian included. But to look at this book is to lose the power of criticism and to come away feeling guilty for ridiculing not only the new architecture, as I have been doing, but anything whatever.

Cibrowski does not include a photograph of the prewar Ghetto (or is this tautological, in that a postwar Ghetto does not exist?). The enormity of the crime here is of course unimaginable, yet one has some sense of it simply because nothing has been built in its place, the site now being an empty square framed by slab-style apartment houses: of the largest home of the Jews in Europe, no trace is to be found. A monument has been erected, a prismoid pile of black granite flanked by black marble Menorahs which, to remind the world that the Jews of Warsaw chose to die fighting, are sustained by pairs of rampant Maccabean lions. The monument includes an unfortunate attempt to depict the murder of the Ghetto—as if anything so monstrous could be represented in a vignette tableau, even a good one—a sculptured relief of resisting people, all impossibly heroic. What should stand here is a candelabrum of seven eternal flames. Someone has chalked the figure 6,000,000 on the base of the stone, and as I look at it, an old woman in black, leaning on a small boy, slowly makes her way to it, kneels, and spreads a handful of posies under the six zeros.

The kiosks in the Nowy Swiat contain announcements in Hebrew, among them the production of a play by Isaac Babel, and a few dishes on the hotel menu are described as Jewish. (Are there Jews to eat them?) I question Jolanta about the Jewish population of Poland today, but all she will say is, "We make no distinctions," and her pretty face turns poker. Then suddenly, unasked, she tells me, "Polish youth have no sense of belief that such things as Oswiecim really happened." And no doubt this is true, for what else is the failure of history? (V. says that in her childhood Poles never used the word "Hebrew," but only the contemptuous "Zhid"; she also recalls a visit to the Warsaw Ghetto with her father, who told her it was famous for its beautiful women.)

Ninotchka is changing, nevertheless, and I suspect that in a little time and with no undue pressure, the carapace could be penetrated and even crumbled entirely. The first crack, still hardly visible on the outer edifice, is that she has begun to show strong feelings, if only of national pride. She is no mercenary, then, and if a bureaucrat, at least one with a soul for the job. What she wishes to bring about, the cause she is working for even through me, is the cultural autonomy of Poland and a new *Regnum Poloniae* of the arts. I offend her most, I have been slow to realize, when I fail to distinguish the Polish from the Russian in that, to me, gray area where the two seem to shade into each other. In remark after remark I have implicitly blanketed the Slav under the Russian and consistently failed to identify what for her is so vividly individual; and I am aware of this even now only because she is so quick to correct me. That I ever could have questioned the ingenuousness of her Polish sentiments and suspected that her animadversion to the USSR was simulated now embarrasses me. Big Brother *is* listening, of course—we may already have swallowed detector capsules, and the chauffeur and the waiter could very well be governmental gumshoes—but not through Jolanta's attractive antennae, not at any rate in the way I at first assumed.

Patriotism and the suppression of feelings to duties exact their price in a woman, a price of femininity, usually, though that, too, may be a planned part of the job, to keep such quarries as myself at bay. Jolanta, in any case, needs an eye-do and a hair-do for a start. What rules has she been given concerning me, I wonder? Surely it is unintentional that her lips open farther outward and more flower-like pronouncing English (she now addresses me as "yourthelf") than Polish, and as surely she cannot be completely unaware that the result is a tempting, if somewhat graceless, pucker.

For I.S.'s arrival this afternoon, CBS has asked the Ministry of Culture to "lay on a cheerful crowd, if possible in regional costume." The request is turned down with the explanation that "Poles are not a very cheerful people." "What about the Polonaise and the Mazurka?" CBS comes back, but the Ministry will not be drawn into a more specific definition of the national temperament, which, after all, has become a question of ideology. Whether "cheerful" is the word, and the larger question of "Poles" apart, the people of Warsaw seem to me remarkably light-humored.

When I.S. leaves the plane, cameras crackle like a pine-woods fire. As he steps to the ground, I see signs of a bibulous lunch. Soggy with Polish vodka as he in fact proves to be—does he mistake the TV men poking their light meters in his face for breathalyzing traffic cops?—his happy-to-be-here speech manages to say the right things.

The S.s are no sooner out of the airport than they begin to react to the Poles as Russians of 50 years ago might have done, and a few minutes of conversation are enough to revive the national prejudices of their youth. These amount to something like Dostoyevsky's anti-Polish sentiments; doesn't Dmitri Karamazov denounce someone as a "typical cheating Pole"? I.S., in any case, recalls Russian expressions mocking "Polish" pomposity, "Polish" servility and obsequiousness—which V. describes as especially dripping: "I am already on my knees" or "Already prostrate before you" (*"Padom do nog ooshe lezhoo"*)—while Polish hypocrisy, so both I.S. and V. aver, even exceeds the Viennese kind, whose alleged failings, or successes, in this field are so famous. And to some degree, no doubt, these attributions are true, for how could the character of a people with a thousand years of *that* geopolitical background, or non-ground, *not* develop in these directions?

V. asks Jolanta about changes in the language, which before the war still employed the polite form of the second person and was therefore well suited to the fawning and the niceties the S.s have been ridiculing. Her answer, that the spoken language has been greatly vulgarized since 1945, puts her firmly on the side of the ancien régime. I.S. says that to Russian ears, Polish sounds like a comical *argot*, full of malapropisms; or, if not quite that, of closely-related but strangely off-target words, like saying of a good perfume that it stinks. The transliterations on the dinner menu amuse the S.s, but when they speak Russian to the room waiter—who looks like Nijinsky with Boris Karloff bangs—*he* laughs: the exchange evidently works both ways. For whatever reason, laughter at this point is welcome, V., after a stroll through the lobby, having announced her intention of "staying in bed until the plane to Paris."

May 26. The orchestra does not know how to greet I.S. when he appears at my rehearsal today. Some of the players applaud, some stand, some remain seated, but all hesitate until Maestro Rowicki gives them a signal, at which they leap to their feet and give forth with a genuine, if too-late-to-be-spontaneous, ovation. This uncertainty followed by late but fervid action is interpreted by V. as an example of the effect on the Polish character of historical habits of palliation. She claims, moreover, that I.S. shares this character, that it is a mark of his—as she says with no great fondness for it—Polish side: "When I ask whether he would prefer this or that and he says, 'I don't know, what would *you* prefer?,' I recognize the voice of his Polish ancestors." Not only do I see what she means, but I also think I am now able to see wherein some of his manners are more Polish than Russian, and whereby the almost over-politeness distinguishing him in Moscow three years ago was more than a question of tsarist versus commissarist styles.

We soon *do* hear some of those voices, in the persons of relatives, cousins-german every one, so they pretend, for people with the Strawinsky name are swarming to him like a gathering of the clans. The name is said to be common here, and the letters and calling cards piling up with the concierge—telephone directories do not exist—are proof of it. A distant female cousin, armed with family photograph albums, calls on him during lunch today, but though he recognizes some of the faces in her pictures, we correctly deduce, when she pulls him out of earshot, that genealogical research is a lesser object of her visit than *zlotis*. One *bona fide* relative is Dr. Konstanty Strawinski, the director of the Zoological Institute of the University Marie-Curie Sklodowska in Lublin; but he has contented himself with sending a letter.

Another correspondent, no kin, is the poet Anatol Stern, who encloses a reprint of an interview that he conducted with I.S. in the Warsaw Bristol Hotel in November 1924. In it the ill-humor of both I.S. and V.—indiscreetly identified as a "Russian lady-friend"—with Warsaw, the hotel, and the interviewer himself comes through saliently and characteristically, though apparently not to Stern. Still another letter, from the daughter of I.S.'s family doctor in Ustilug, reminisces about I.S. at Ustilug in her youth. This Dr. Backnitsky was a friend and correspondent of the Marxist philosopher Plekhanov, whose letters I.S. also read, "as they were written in an unusually intelligible German." Regularly, since 1950, I.S. has sent money to the doctor's daughter.

With Jolanta to Chopin's birthplace at Zelazowa Wola. The road is

1965 brick-paved for about half the way, and better suited to the wagon traffic of the time of its construction than to trucks and automobiles, though these are rare compared to trough-shaped carts, horse-drawn but with large rubber tires, as if the mechanization process had broken down after this first step. Farm machinery is nowhere in evidence, but only hand implements, yet most of the low-lying thatched-roof houses along the road have TV aerials. Jolanta says that some of the land in the region is privately owned. And, she adds, a few privately owned restaurants survive, "the only good ones in Poland," though these mavericks are expected to be taxed out of existence.

The Zelazowa Wola relics are unremarkable—a plaster cast of the composer's left hand, some nursery chairs and other petite furniture, manuscripts of juvenilia—but the STEINWAY stenciled in large white letters on the grand piano *is* surprising in a country so wholly free of advertising.* The attractions of the place, the sylvan walks and willow-washed stream, fail to work any spell on Jolanta, but she is doubly careful today to treat me as an assignment. Poland's climate is pluvial, and we are soon fleeing from torrential, after four days of merely heavy, rains. I note that Poles do not like to hear the name of their national musical idol pronounced as if he had been a Frenchman.

Back in Warsaw we attend a reception by the Union of Composers at their home in Rynek Starego Miasta. This is in the heart of the old city— or, more precisely, of the rebuilt old city, for it was pulverized during the insurrection of 1944. Since then, every edifice has been replicated, the Rynek (market) again being recognizable from Canaletto. Much as the spirit of the rebuilding must be applauded, these five-year-old medieval houses, in which even the creak of the ancient floorboards has been restored, are as eery as a movie set. I prefer the new city, no matter how ugly.

The composers are shy, hospitable, well informed—as people who stay home and read *are* well informed. Their pride and patriotism are on a par with Jolanta's; one of them tells me that though Moszkowski may not have been any great shakes as a composer (no argument), "he *was* Polish." Again and again I.S. is asked for details about Szymanowski, whose *Stabat Mater* is hereabouts compared not unfavorably with *Symphony of Psalms;* but Szymanowski was more V.'s friend than I.S.'s, and she has avoided the party. Before deciding on the Polish trip, I.S. feared he would be "kidnapped by the official musicians and the academics of the older generation." To some extent this might have happened; none of the younger progressives, not Penderecki, Serocki, Baird, Gorecki, or even Lutoslawski (whose *Three Poems by Henri Michaux* is Polish music's pop-modern display

---

* The instrument was installed for the use of visiting pianists from the West.

piece) is present.* But officialdom is always conservative, and a guest of I.S.'s stature could hardly expect to escape it. I nonetheless regret the absence in this group of any of those representatives of the musical renaissance—composers, conductors, instrumentalists—who have enriched Poland and brought it world prestige. If I emphasize the latter, it is for the reason that while the Polish arts movement may have come into being in protest against the Stalinist East, it is the Western export business that they—Grotowski, Penderecki, Jerzinsky, and the film directors—have most eagerly sought.

Speaking for myself, I would like to hear something from anyone about the music of the Jagiellonian Dynasty and the influence of Marenzio in Cracow; and I would like to hear from unabashed living lips (except that they could only be abashed ones) the Marxist interpretation of Renaissance culture as propounded in the State Publisher's luxuriously embellished editions of early Polish music. In *Music of the Polish Renaissance* "ideological progress" is equated with "the democratic current of homophonic structure," and "the abandonment of forms for the select few in favor of simpler but more expressive types." In *A Thousand Years of Polish History*, published in 1964, "the flourishing of Romanesque art" is attributed to, of all things, "social and ideological fermentation." Now it seems to me that if the phenomenon of art can be accounted for by circumstances other than the appearance of talent, then Poland today is an argument for the theory that great suffering provokes strong feelings, and that these feelings *might* at least be artistically fertile. But no one, abashed or otherwise, will come to grips with that most unprogressive idea.

Toasts are proposed—in French, the language of nearly all of the conversation—each one ending *"Vi-ve Stra-win-ski!"* I.S., toasting the Union in turn, strays into politics, and even begins to castigate Russia, blaming her for the largest share of Poland's miseries. He has taken for granted that his audience is anti-Russian, as Poles generally were in his youth. Twice, too, he refers to the Iron Curtain, and both times one can fairly hear the creak of those new-old floorboards.

May 27. The Cleveland Orchestra, on its way home from the USSR, rehearses this morning just before we do. What a contrast to the Warsaw Phil.! The American ensemble seems nearly perfect. The playing is polished, refined, and beautifully in tune, the notes sitting squarely in the center of the pitch, whereas they tend to circle around it, trapeze-like, with the Warsaw Phil. We have become accustomed to the Polish players, however, even to the extent that the efficiency and finesse of the Clevelanders work inverse returns, actually making us feel somewhat fond of the crudities in the Warsaw Orchestra that the Cleveland machine has

---

* They were attending a modern music festival in Germany.

1965 been at such pains to steamroller out.

Appeals to the Soviet embassies in Washington and Warsaw, and directly to Madame Furtseva in Moscow, have failed, and we learn today that permission for I.S. to visit his old home in Ustilug will not be forthcoming. Ustilug is in a pink zone, automatically off limits to foreigners. We had hoped for permission, nevertheless, since the reasons for the zoning, according to the Poles, are not military but economic. The neighborhood is reputed to be poor, the people ill-clothed and shod; understandably the Russians prefer to keep such places swept under the carpet, or at any rate not advertised on American television.

From 1919 to 1939 Ustilug was a hundred miles or so within Polish territory. In the late 1930s, I.S. managed to sell a part of his land there. When the Soviet Union annexed eastern Poland up to, approximately, the Curzon line, in effect moving the whole country a hundred miles to the west, Ustilug came out on the Soviet side of the frontier by the margin of the Bug River. Since the war, I.S. has received letters from actual and would-be* visitors to the village, and photographs of his home there have appeared in both Russian and German publications. But Warsaw is as close as he will come to it again himself.

In the course of a conversation with a young Polish writer about the comedies of Alexander Fredro, I learn that Joseph Conrad is widely read here, and that Polish translations of him are "well redacted." Interest in the work of Conrad's father, Apollo Korzeniowski, has revived, too, and only last year his *For the Love of Money* was staged in Warsaw with considerable success. Like his son, Korzeniowski was enamored of the English and French languages, becoming an expert translator from both; two of Shakespeare's plays are performed here exclusively in the versions by Conrad *père*. Then, quite by accident, the talk turns to politics, and my young acquaintance reveals himself as a neo-orthodox Marxist. To him, history is a kind of Gulf Stream, a steady current flowing in a fixed direction. Moreover, the travel time to any point in this current, meaning to any point in the past to the present, is equal, and involves no awkward apparatus of cultural contexts and comparisons.

---

* "Lublin, December 8, 1968. Dear Mr. Stravinsky, Among your mail will be this modest letter. I decided to write you because of my holiday event. . . . It were so: holiday 68 I went to a Polish village on the edge of River Boog. I lived there and I talked with the old peoples living there. Among others, I have heard about the village on the Russian edge today. The old people told me that in this village lived in former times good lords named Stravinskys. They were very kind lords and their fame is living the peoples on both edges of the river. The peoples say that in Stravinskys' palace visible on the Russian edge there were great dances and musics of several tens years ago. I heard and I asked many questions so I suppose this is your familiar possession. I am very curious if I am right. I would be happy to hear your answer. Excuse me for my mistakes in English language. I hope I traced your home place and I would like to know it for myself. Respectfully, Tadeusz Wojnicki."

The only factor, applied everywhere and unmodified, is the evolution of the Marxist concept. Westerners, he contends, are over-concerned with pattern in history, including, as it may be, the pattern of change. This leads them to discover parallels that are not really parallel, rhymes that do not rhyme. "The capitalists still fear a cyclical repetition of the stock market crash," he says, "and they still look for the overthrow of the socialist revolution, after which they expect to return to their old innings." On the subject of corrupt individualism in the West, the young man is entirely convincing, though it must be admitted that the picture he draws of us, each in his "existential void," is not unattractive. Jolanta's conception of history, as I discover in our most intimate late-night conversation so far, is expressed entirely in cultural terms. To begin with, she draws a firm distinction between Slavic and Germanic cultural watersheds. Then, too, she subscribes to the idea that the Soviet Union is simply the contemporary manifestation of Russian history, as Nazism was of German history. Furthermore, she believes that "While nationalism may have declined at the end of the war, owing to the Late Roman Empire-type East-West division, it is again more important than ever in the socialist countries." *Is* the East-West fracture so very sharp in Poland? I ask, and she persuades me to "look at the country from the point of view of a middle ground, an Eastern language with a Western alphabet, an Eastern people with a Western church." What does "the West" mean to her? "Ideas of liberty and democracy, never much cultivated here," she answers, very readily. "Nevertheless, we believe that our socialism is more profoundly democratic in its aims than your democracy."

If Jolanta is changing, so am I. And if we are correctives to each other, the corrective action is also bringing us together. The worm has turned so far, in any case, that I have become almost overly respectful of her Ninotchka seriousness and correspondingly ashamed of my native inclination to laughter, with its detestable implication of superiority. How embarrassing now to recall my bumptious bonhomie on arrival, the tactless references to the West, the specious analyses and superficial comments on everything I have seen! But Ninotchka, at the same time, has become infected with my former laughter—which would be less regrettable if she knew how to laugh, did not respond too excessively in terms of volume, and were not seduced by only the lowest and most depraved examples of my own "wit." When I inquire about what one does for nighttime amusement in this fun city, the Ninotchka guise instructs me to go to that Stalinoid monster-building, the Palace of Science and Culture, "and look at the Book Fair." But when the problem is underlined—"I mean, what does one do between 1 and 4 A.M."—the point is at length seen, the funny-bone tickled, and the night air shattered with the reaction. How far will this dangerous transformation go, I wonder, for she is also becoming a little impish and coy, as when, at parting, I bestow pecks of *amitié* on each cheek,

Russian style, she lets me see that she is well aware of how much more I would prefer the sunflower in the middle. If she continues to concede at this rate, it will be difficult before long to distinguish the truly adamant from the false.

May 28. A telephone call from Giulio Razzi, Puccini's nephew, in Rome, an invitation to the three of us to attend a concert in I.S.'s honor in the Vatican, all expenses paid Warsaw-Paris-Rome-New York-Los Angeles.

A shopping expedition, to buy a rug for V. and wine for I.S. Clerking, it seems, is for women only. Another apparent qualification is the ability to maintain a total indifference to customers: wares are displayed only on request, and then reluctantly, with no effort to engage any interest. This absence of the commercial spirit has a surprisingly depressing effect, except that, considering the merchandise, neither party in a buying-selling transaction could be greatly exhilarated. In one food store, about 50 people have queued before a clump of what will surely prove too few *kilbassa* to go around. In another, an even longer line has formed to buy tins of peanuts "From Hanoi," as the label pointedly advertises in English. This second store, in which we find one bottle of Beaujolais, is open to tourists, as well as to natives, and licensed to accept their *zlotis;* most stores not altogether off-limits to foreigners are designated "for foreign currency only." Hard money, of course, is avidly coveted by a government desperately trying to keep prices pegged to the international index at the official rate, which is six times less than the unofficial. The government is said to be so dollar-hungry that the black-market speculators parading like prostitutes between the two "American" hotels are widely suspected of being Treasury Department employees.

The audience at our concert has come to see a famous live animal more than to listen to music, in this case I.S. conducting *Firebird* and *Psalms*, myself the Variations and *Sacre*. The event is very gala and along with several standing ovations, I.S. receives countless bouquets of carnations in the national colors of red and white. David Oppenheim, CBS's director, and I go to a post-concert concert, a jazz *jeunesse musicale*, according to the American film students who neglected to say that the jazz is not the grooviest. The young people are good looking, well behaved, and well groomed—spitcurls and Beatle-type forelocks but no beards. During an intermission an older woman tells me that she "grew up under Stalin and therefore never dreamed of seeing Igor Stravinsky." At this point, a younger girl contributes the only political utterance of the sort I have heard in Poland: "Things were going so well under Krushchev, but now we are very frightened again." Oh, you poor stomped-upon Janus-headed Poles, though not even Januses, for as real estate you belong to the East (that watchtower of the Palace of Science and Culture standing over your town), no matter how ardently you pursue the *ignis fatuus* of a middle ground.

May 29. Telegram from Razzi:

Following my phone call stop June twelve Radio Televisione Italiana offers homage concert in Vatican where your Symphony of Psalms is performed by our orchestra and choir stop his Holiness Pope Paul VI has expressed his desire of having your presence and invites you to attend concert sitting next to him stop concert is taken by Eurovision and Mondialvision stop beg to consider enormous signification of this ceremony and accept invitation stop travel and stay expenses for you and accompanying persons are completely at our charge stop enough being Rome June 11 but arrival and departing dates are at your choice according your convenience please advise dates and hotel for reservations stop thanks and regards—Giulio Razzi, Director Programma, Radio Televisione Italiana, Via Babuino 9, Roma.

A new attitude is noticeable in Jolanta this morning, and from her first words I am aware that she is not being frank. We have hired a car to Malbork on Monday, and from the very variety of her arguments against the trip, it is obvious that her superiors have countermanded it. The simple truth, it later appears, is that they themselves wish to entertain I.S. on that date at a formal luncheon and have charged Jolanta to maneuver us out of the other arrangements. Yet I foolishly act as if she herself were guilty of a misprision; and this exaggeration makes me aware of how much I have put my trust in her, which in turn leads me to reflect on her responsibilities as an employee. From the beginning, after all, her orders must have contained lists of things we were not to know and things we were to be prevented from doing or made to do. Hasn't she, in effect, been steering me from the moment of arrival? Since I am not by any means the first of her charges, hasn't each stage of my adjustment been coolly observed by a professional eye? And isn't she also aware, as the psychoanalyst is aware when a similar crisis overtakes a patient, of the true nature of my feelings for her? And to how many of her charges has that happened before? This sobering and jealous thought leaves me feeling not only naive but also nakedly transparent. It also hurts.

Telephone from Los Angeles: the S.s accept an offer of $45,000 for the 1260 North Wetherly Drive house.

May 30. Today being the first without threat of rain, we drive through the Praga to Wilanow. It is National Election Day, too, and though no signs of election fever or hustings (*could* there be any with a choice between Gomulka and Gomulka?) are visible, every factory on the way is flying the Red Flag of the Revolution side by side with the red-and-white Polish flag.

The view of *Urbs Warsowia* from the Praga is a popular angle in old prints, the viewer looking over plumed riders on prancing horses in the

Praga foreground and noble ladies in fur-lined pelisses (Watteau's *"La Femme polonaise"*). This was the view of the Red Army in 1944, when it failed to cross the river and raise the German siege against an insurgent army, standing by for political reasons as is now generally believed, while a quarter of a million people died in Warsaw. But the Vistula, from here anyway, is not vital to the life of Warsaw as the Danube is to Vienna and Budapest.

May 31. We pack, pay bills, spend leftover *zlotis*, and go to the composers' luncheon in the rebuilt Poniatowski Chateau at Jablonna. The trans-Vistula landscape—brown wooden houses, pigeons perching in mud pools, fields of broken corn stooks, farm lands covered with mulch— reminds the S.s of Russia, as does Jablonna itself, with its circular saloon and veneered-birch furniture.

Amazingly, the cuisine is of a quality to match the surroundings. The chef, now 86 and former chief cook to the Tsar, is sent for at one point (he looks like Bruckner) and presented to I.S., whose hand he kisses as a peasant would have done a century ago; everyone applauds and says that his *service royal* is the only good cooking in Poland, but no implications are drawn from the fact, at least not out loud. At table I try to make Ger-French conversation with, on one side, Stefan Sledzinski, president of the society, who chairs the proceedings, and, on the other, the writer Tomaszewski (a face like that of the Polish hero Lelewel, but with blunter features, like a Wit Stwosz peasant). Toasting comes to the rescue, at long last, except that because of tail ornaments, I fail to recognize myself in the one to "Robertowi Craftowi" and have to be nudged. At the heady high point of the *fête*, the composers stand, face I.S., and sing an old Polish song in "unison": "May he live to be a hundred." Whereupon a remarkable event occurs. I.S., suddenly, and, I am convinced, unconsciously, switches from French to Russian, and in a trice the entire company follows him, as though they had only been waiting out of politeness for him to give the signal. And whereas most of them, only moments before, had been dropping mildly denigrating digs about the Russians—"they have not played as much modern music as we have," which is true, "and therefore their orchestras are not as quick as ours," which is false—all seem perfectly at home now speaking the Russian language.

While post-prandial drinks are passed around, I escape with Jolanta to the Chateau park, where we follow a meandering path to the roiling river. Here are the tall, soughing trees, the lush meadows with buttercup and dandelion of my adolescent daydreams of Tolstoy and Russian novels. And here, finally, on the riverbank, against a bilious soundtrack of frogs and a dovelike wind, it is the turn of the middle, which is yielded silently, seriously, persistently, and with no outwardly escaping sign of pleasure.

Back in Warsaw I try to collect the impressions of a week, wondering if even two or three have survived the mass reversals. But none has; and the subject of my Polish peroration must be my reasons for the impossibility of composing it. Some of them—the brevity of the experience, the language barrier, and the lack of both general and specialized knowledge—are obvious. At least one other difficulty is the same for every foreigner: Warsaw is not Poland, and hardly even a continuation of the city it once was, having been clinically murdered and, as medics say, left alive only biologically. Nevertheless, the greatest obstacle to the visitor is the ambivalence of the Poles themselves—as shown in that nonplussing switch to Russian today at Jablonna. In Russia, the attitude to the Westerner, substantiated by power, is always clear. But what are the psychological strategies of a people whose map has changed with every major European power shift and who, during the whole of the 19th century, were deprived of political and territorial existence? (It seems to me that the ethnological problems of the territory are soluble only by transplanting minority populations to new demographic gravity centers, by moving the people of Lwow westward, for instance, as Muslims migrated to Pakistan from other parts of India.) And what of a people who, when reconstituted at Versailles, found themselves a century behind the West—whereas before the partitions, in the age of Stanislaus Leczinski, they had been in the vanguard of the Enlightenment? Were they not an easy prey, first to corruption and later to fascism? And, finally, what are the feelings of a people who, at the end of a terrible war of liberation, find themselves more hopelessly the instrument of another power than ever before?

To read even as little as I have done in Polish affairs is to be astonished by the survival of Polish culture at all. The explanation can only lie in the integrity of the people. They were a heroic people during the Occupation, when, in spite of the suffering, no Quisling appeared and collaboration was almost unknown.

At 11:30 P.M., I.S. is filmed conducting a few measures from *Sacre*, himself and the orchestra in full dress, the house empty. This videotape will be dubbed so that I.S. will appear to be conducting a performance by the Warsaw ballet.

June 5. Paris. To the *"Spectacle Igor Strawinsky"* at the Opéra, *Sacre*, *Noces*, and *Renard*, staged by Béjart and conducted by Boulez. The *Noces* musicians and chorus are in the pit, the chorus wearing brown robes with cowls. The half-lowered backdrop, a reconstruction of Goncharova's curtain for the 1929 *Firebird* revival, seems to represent an *Arabian Nights* city, hence is too southern by several thousand versts. No less remote are the village weddings, not only of the subtitle but of the whole character of the work, the bridesmaids in their taffeta dresses and ermine muffs resembling ladies-in-waiting to a tsarina. V., who was to have mimed and danced the bride in the original performance and who rehearsed the role in Monaco, recalls that she stood stage center during the combing and plaiting of the tresses, which were several yards long.

The second scene is no closer to the geographical target, the costumes of the "best man" being a cross between gaucho and Music Hall Cossack, the dance half Siberian, half Argentine folk ballet. Beginning with this scene, a choreographic device divides the spectator's attention. Bride and groom, got up like fairy-tale royalty, are doubled, except that the alter egos are naked, embodiments, presumably, of sexual fantasies. Diverting as this could be in a satire on a Victorian costume piece, the notion is wholly out of place in *Noces*, for the visions, dancing like shadows by the sides of their projectors, imply a psychological interior contradicted by the hard musical surface. Worst of all, the gratuitous psychological dimension, like the sentiment of the staging, which is that of an exotic "musical," dilutes, or undercuts, the severity of the musical emotion, which, at the end, is tragic emotion of a rare kind. The visions, moreover, are optically confusing, the eye naturally preferring to travel with the naked *Doppelgänger* rather than with the overclothed original. And the naked thoughts obtrude too much, getting in the way of their thinkers, then taking over from them completely. *Noces* is musically mechanized ritual. Failing to match the demands of the score as such, the choreographer's next best course is to stage the piece straightforwardly as an album of village wedding scenes.

To judge by the costumes, the geography of the third tableau is even farther afield. The headgear might have been confected by a Cambodian pastry cook, the bride's mother's minks by a Parisian furrier interested in the program credits. But the great scene of the two weeping mothers is ruined less by couturiers than by an excessively slow tempo—when no change is warranted at all.

The backdrop of the final scene is an iconostasis befitting a church of the Hagia Sophia class. Here the bride is veiled like a Muslim, the groom hatted like a Tibetan, perhaps to keep company with the five no less oddly clad clowns—marriage brokers?—who pop on stage to "play" Pelegai. The surpassing vulgarity, however, is saved for the very end. As the wedded couple enters the nuptial chamber, the relatives and guests should seat themselves on a bench against the wall outside the door. The immobility of the scene, frozen in the music, frozen on stage, and everlasting in its minute and a half of time, is unique in theater history. But instead of a realization of one of the simplest and most beautiful pages in modern music (and more than "modern"), the "visions" are joined upstage, where they copulate in synchronicity with the piano chords. Commenting on this afterward, I.S., who did not attend, remarks to Rolf Liebermann, who sat with V.: "The most dangerous compromisers of art are the second-rate geniuses, the interpreters, the people who tell us what art means, what it symbolizes, the stage directors, orchestra directors, directors of every kind."

The *Renard* staging is less offensive, both because the scope for harm is much smaller and because the work justifies a degree of experiment. In this version, Stravinsky's four animal actors are given spectators' vantages to the rear and sides of the stage, thus forming a stage arena, while the action, a total enigma to me, is entrusted to their human representatives—more visions, perhaps—in Flapper Period bathing garb. During the introductory and the final marches, this aquatic troupe is taxied on stage in a Hispano-Suiza. Renard, marvelously slinky and possessing great guile, is danced by Claire Motte.*

The backdrop, half-lowered from the boom, exposes a collage of photographs, most prominently of Diaghilev, Astruc, Groucho Marx, Picasso's I.S., while the orchestra and singers are perched on a pile of automobile tires, about 20 *pneus* high, at the back of the stage. The screaming singers—all senses—are almost miraculously bad (though the feat of finding a worse vocal quartet than that in *Noces* seemed impossible), and the voice of the tenor crying the cock's part is in more terrible tatters than the fowl itself after his mauling by the fox.

When the *"Spectacle"* is over, Boulez, who has conducted the triple bill without visible exuviations—a literal example of "It wasn't any sweat"—tells us that part of his success formula is: "Be a Robespierre in rehearsals, a Danton in concerts." But *he* is a Napoleon the year around.

June 6. After lunch with Boulez, in a restaurant near Versailles, we take the night train to Italy.

June 12. Rome. I.S. is extremely nervous during the Vatican concert, which I watch from the side balcony next to one of the camera positions. Fortunately, V. sits beside and steadies him, helping him to stand and sit. The *Symphony of Psalms* annihilates the pieces by the other composers, Milhaud, Malipiero, and Sibelius (represented by his son-in-law), and one feels embarrassed for them. A tense moment occurs after the *Psalms* when I.S. attempts to kneel and kiss the Fisherman's Ring, but slips and momentarily loses balance. He recovers with V.'s support, but not in time to avoid some commotion. Seeing him totter, an elderly gentleman, seated on the aisle comes forward to help; as we learn later he is Giovacchino Forzano,** the librettist of *Gianni Schicchi*. Back in the hotel, I.S. receives Manzù in the bar, and drinks too much.

At Razzi's post-concert dinner at the Hilton, I.S., flanked by two exclusively and effusively Italian-speaking ladies, both unknown to him, soon gets very drunk. By testimonial time, his arm is on the table, his head on his arm. Seeing this state of affairs, V. walks around the round table, comes up behind him, and whispers in his ear that he absolutely *has* to acknowledge the host's congratulations. This piece of intelligence takes some time to sink in, but when it does, I.S. bravely raises his head, slowly but clearly forms the syllables "*Gra-zi-e*," sinks back into his lees.

---

* The late wife of Mario Bois, who was Boosey & Hawkes's representative in Paris. She died prematurely in the mid-1980s.

** Died October 28, 1970, Rome.

1965   **July 1**. After my Muncie performances of *Histoire* and *Oedipus*, we drive to a Holiday Inn near Indianapolis, where one of the baggage porters, a fan of I.S.'s and in particular of the *Symphony of Psalms*, has opened the Gideon Bible in I.S.'s room to Psalm 150 (the text of the last part of the *Symphony of Psalms*).

August 11. Hollywood. Letter from Gerald Heard: "Hoping you can be seen before . . . you will be shining on the other hemisphere."

September 24. New York. Party in the S.s' rooms at the Pierre with Isaiah Berlin, Robert Lowell, Spender.*

October 5. Lowell and Lizzie Hardwick to dinner. I.S. is very funny about a Soviet edition of Chekhov, in which "a footnote identifies 'pince-nez' as 'a French expression,' which anyone can see, but does not say what it means." I.S., in a high mood, serves the caviar. Everyone quite drunk.

🐚 **Postscript 1994**. The diary for 1965 devotes too much space to an absurd flirtation in Warsaw and too little to other events; I can only hope that David Oppenheim kept a diary as well; as director of the CBS film portrait of Stravinsky, he was with us in Austin (Texas), Chicago, Los Angeles, New York, and throughout the European tour. David was a keen observer and, in spite of suffering torments about his ex-wife, the actress Judy Holliday, who was dying of cancer in New York, a good traveling companion. After Poland he flew from Paris to visit her, then rejoined us in Rome.

David and his cameraman Haskell Wexler sailed to Europe with us in May on the North Atlantic route. The sea was rough all the way, however, and Stravinsky kept to his cabin; the crossing did not yield any usable footage. Furthermore, our flight to Paris from the port of Göteborg, Sweden, entailed a longer in-transit stop in Copenhagen than the whole of the flight time from New York to Paris.

David accompanied us on our automobile trip to Vevey, Basel, Strasbourg, and back to Paris. We left the Champs-Elysées quite early in the morning of May 15 with the intention of "lunching" in a five-star restaurant in Saulieu. But by 11 o'clock Stravinsky wanted to stop somewhere for bread, wine, and cheese, the result of which was that we ate too much and drank two bottles of Pommard. At the stellar establishment an hour later, the Stravinskys, to David's and my envious amazement, were able, and with no ill effects, to ingest a mountain of crayfish and, in addition to pre- and post-prandial compotations, impressive quantities of wine.

But back in Hollywood, in the summer, Stravinsky was not in good form. He had agreed to a week of recording sessions but was cranky during them and physically unable to conduct his Variations, though he had

---

* Spender's *Journal* dates this occasion September 25, conflating his two evenings with the Stravinskys, September 23 (dinner) and 24.

thoroughly studied and marked the score in preparation; or, rather, he did **1965** record the work once through, with several breakdowns, in order to "cover" the piece in case of criticism that the final product had been pieced together from my "rehearsal takes"—which, as of course the orchestra knew, was the case.

🎵 1966

January 15. New York. We see the edited CBS *Stravinsky*, then dine at David Oppenheim's with Saul Steinberg, the Meyer Schapiros, Lionel Abel, Noah Greenberg's widow, Jean Stein (later). Lionel A. to me: "Until I met Bertrand Russell, I grew up thinking that all non-Jews were stupid."

January 16. Auden for dinner in the S.s' suite (1716) at the Pierre. He has expanded ventrally in recent months. Apart from the glittering jewels of his intellect, he wears a dark brown flannel shirt, black necktie, wicker beach shoes, and—on departure—dark glasses, with which he might pass for a jazz musician. After confounding the room-service waiters by ordering mushrooms as a savory (*amuse-bouche*), and using "quite" for "yes"— "More wine, sir?" "Quite"—he expatiates on anti-opera. *Fidelio, Boris, Pelléas*, and Janáček's *House of the Dead*, which has "no characters and no tunes," are the high-cult examples, but he chooses to dwell on an out-of-the-way specimen, Godard's *Dante*, "pronounced 'Dant.' Whereas the whole of Act One simply sets the Florentine scene, the subject of Act Two is the entire *Divine Comedy*. Act Three unites 'Dant' and Beatrice in, of all places, 'a nunnery, near Ravenna.' "

More in his element with German operas, Auden says that "*Elektra* is so definitely non-U that a singer who suits the part could not attempt Isolde." This leads to the observation that "Dramatic movement in the first act of *Tristan* is limited entirely to exits and entrances." Complaining about the numerous excisions in the new Vienna production of the *Rake*, he asks I.S. to proscribe cuts in future by the publisher's contract with the opera house. "After all, the *Rake* isn't exactly *Götterdämmerung*, where the stage director can claim he has to give people a chance to pee."

Talking about more recent operas, he pretends to be concerned "lest the Britten pendulum swing so far the other way that people begin to say they are *all* bad. . . . By the way, I hear that Barber's *Cleopatra* is to be tried out in New York; Verdi saw that the subject wouldn't do, though it might have done in Boito's Italian. Now obviously the only Shakespeare that could be made into English-language opera is *Love's Labour's Lost*, and that would take a great deal of making."

Gently teasing I.S. about money ("Has he scads now?" he asks me), Auden suggests that *millionen* would be a good word for him to set to music. "Think how you could aspirate the final syllable, Igor, and keep it going, page after page, like the compounding of interest."

Confessing to homesickness for his house in Austria, he says that he buys a Vienna newspaper from time to time, "to see what the weather is doing there—I don't need to be told what it is doing here—though having bought it, I sometimes peek at the obits, too." Recalling his Ford Foundation year in Berlin, he describes a brush with the law one night on suspicion of inebriety: "The police there pay people to inform on pedestrians who appear to be tight. *I* was informed on once, and the police refused to believe I was a Herr Professor. I had no trouble passing their mental and coordination tests" (who *would* have, under any condition, with *that* intellect?), "but evidently the alcohol level in my blood was high" (as well it might be after a demijohn of Chianti). He claims that in Kirchstetten, he is always immaculately abstinent driving his Volkswagen and was ever so "in motor cars," since first piloting one in 1925. The date reminds I.S. that *he* began to drive in the same year* but gave it up because the gendarmes stopped him so often, and because he habitually burned up the brakes; which, Wystan observes to me, "is another figure in the pattern of the pills and the salting away of securities in Helvetia."

His literary targets today are the "scholars who refuse to consider the possibility that Shakespeare could have made a mistake." He also cites several mistranslations in the new Bible but avoids clerical and theological talk, apart from one reference to the Pope as "publicity mad" and the remark that "when God said 'Let there be light,' which Longinus quotes as exemplifying sublimity, He must have realized that He was saying something extraordinarily pretentious." He mentions Eliot's "very good ribald verse that will probably *not* be collected. I once submitted a poem to him for the *Criterion* that included a then unprintable word, and he suggested the more decorous, 'like a June bride . . . sore but satisfied.'"

Books referred to include Auerbach's *Literary Language*; Tolkien's *Silmarillion* ("J.R.R. is 'in' with the teenage set, you know, and is no longer the exclusive property of dotty school teachers and elderly cranks"); *In Cold Blood* (can he really have read *that*, or did he merely sink a trial shaft?); *The Ambidextrous Universe* ("I knew *that* all along, of course—even nucleic acid is left-handed—but my generation was brought up to think of God as someone like Zäzilie, Christian Morgenstern's symmetry-loving housemaid"); the new David Jones: "I'm sorry about my name preceding yours on the subscribers' list, Igor, but it was only because of 'A,' which I can't help; still, the way it was printed did make it seem as if I were somehow next in rank

---

* Stravinsky's driver's license is stamped "Paris, December 2, 1925."

1966 to the Queen Mum."

Apropos the Capote, he says, "I understand that the author is remarkably changed now, and looks like a banker—which I suppose he is." The question of capital punishment arising in connection with *In Cold Blood*, he says, "At least in England they don't keep them waiting about for five or ten years." I point out that in the Christie case they should have and ask whether he thinks the death sentence is ever justifiable. "Well, there *have* been people on whom I can picture it being carried out. Brecht, for one. In fact I can imagine doing it to him myself. It might even have been rather enjoyable, when the time came, to have been able to say to him, 'Now let's step outside.' I'd have given him a good last meal,* of course. Still, you must admire the logic of a man who lives in a Communist country, takes out Austrian citizenship, does his banking in Switzerland, and, like a gambler hedging his bets, sends for the pastor at the end in case there could be something in that, too."

Listening to I.S. and V. converse in Russian, he remarks on the beauty of the language. Because he has never hinted at a remotely favorable opinion of Russia before, this raises the alarming thought that his German period may be running out, or *would* have raised it except that he is unusually mellow tonight in other ways as well. Though Randall Jarrell's death has shocked him, he observes, "It's not very nice for the driver of the truck you decide to jump in front of." Then, as if reflecting on his own mortality, he says, "A schoolgirl, quoting one of my poems in a class recently, astonished her teacher by insisting that I was among the living. It seems that a newspaper did refer to me as deceased. I saw the correction myself in a later edition: 'Auden not, repeat, *not* dead.' Naturally I tried to inquire what it was thought I had died of."

January 24. At the same time that I.S. finishes the *Dies Irae*, he learns that the Second Vatican Council has banned the reference to the Delphic Sybil. I ask if Thomas of Celano's hymn, *"Dies irae, dies illa solvet saeclum in favilla teste David cum Sibylla,"* is the origin of his dreamed tune in the *Soldat*, or is the explanation simple coincidence. He says that he was thinking of Liszt's *Totentanz*.

January 27–28. Our Los Angeles Philharmonic concerts: I conduct the *St. Anne Fugue* (Bach-Schoenberg), *Zvezdoliki*, Symphony in C, and I.S. conducts *Vom Himmel hoch* and *Psalms*.

February 1. In the Los Angeles Airport, the S.s see the announcement of Anna Akhmatova's death in the *New York Times* and accompanying recent photo of her, which greatly upsets them, her changed appearance in the photo as much as her death. I.S. and I fly alone to St. Louis for our con-

---

* According to Glob's *Bog People* (Cornell University Press, 1969), the condemned man or *élu* in Iron Age Denmark was fed a gruel containing some 60 different varieties of grain, evidently to propitiate the gods and induce the return of spring.

certs. Our plane is the last to land before a snowstorm closes the airport.

April 9. Letter from Virginia Rice: The *New York Times* wishes to commission me to write two articles for the June 26 paper, the week of the opening of the New York Philharmonic's Stravinsky Festival, one about I.S., *ONE BY HIM!!!!*

May 4. Letter from Virginia Rice: "On May 1 I received an ecstatic phone call from the *New York Times*. Seymour Peck is delighted with your pieces."

May 8. We fly to New York (Newark), and, on the 12th, to Paris. Most airplane conversations between strangers follow a pattern. Stage one begins with a search for mutual acquaintances, shared opinions and impressions of places. The common knowledge of even a restaurant or hotel will help people to feel weighted together, proving to them that "the world is very small," when in fact it proves only that people with pro-rata incomes tend to be found in the same places, hence on the same highways leading to those places. Stage two, marked by the settling-in-of-cocktails, moves on to the exchanging of scraps of personal confidences. And more than scraps. My remarkably unreticent neighbor, a New Man type—foundation representative, or Rand mathematician, the sort of person who would like to chat about Quine's set theory or Bohr's complementarity principle— manages to deliver himself of several very substantial installments of autobiography between some 20 or so foot-trampling trips to the lavatory. It turns out that he is on his way to an important lunch the day after tomorrow in Africa.

Stage two depends on the quantity and effectiveness of the libations. Owing partly to the tensions of flying, partly to the limbo psychology that abrogates not only responsibilities but also the sense of time, the establishment narcotic is an especially potent confessing drug in airplanes (to say nothing of its biochemical effects—on blood sugar, on the salt content in the hypothalamus, etc.). Alcohol at high altitudes pushes forward suddenly-remembered connections, stories, comments, which, for a moment, are of supreme importance and insist on being voiced, but which a moment later turn away as peremptorily as a cat and defy recalling. If we are but loosely in control of our thoughts ordinarily, how much less so are we under alcohol and over 40,000 feet?

Stage three, flirtation, depends on individuals, but a great deal of it transpires in airplanes. The reasons re-include those for stages one and two, with the added factor that flying itself is sexually stimulating, both mentally—all flying dreams are sexual, after all—and physically, in the tingling sensation aroused by the wheels touching the ground, in the pressure of braking, and in the desire to re-embrace life, each landing being a birth. Yet the central sexual ingredient in air travel is none of these but the stewardess, toward whom the male passenger harbors, and often attempts to navigate, the most ardent wishes.

1966   The stewardess is not merely a new amalgam of receptionist, party host-ess, geisha, waitress, mother, mistress, nurse (bringing clean napkins every few minutes as if symbolically changing our diapers), but an entirely new aspect, or hitherto unexploited aspect, of Woman. Just as landscape paint-ing did not exist before Giotto, though landscapes evidently did, or the cult of literary tears before *Manon Lescaut*, though the flow of actual ones must have been fairly constant, so the combination of female beauty and bravery was unknown as a commercial asset before the age of air travel. A handsome girl, ever the most desirable traveling companion, is now the most exemplary as well, her valor or indifference shaming the male passen-ger and helping him to collar his cowardice.

Our stewardess's lecture on flotation seats and life-raft inflating, on the donning of life jackets and the manipulation of lanyards, sounds like so much fun-filled fashion modeling. But her perpetual cheeriness gives way for a moment when, nearing the French coast, the plane begins to bump coltishly and to yaw and shake, at which point the sternness of her com-mand to buckle seat belts and put out cigarettes is in such contrast to her earlier manner that I suddenly become aware of the Holy Bible on the magazine rack, along with *Playboy* and *Time*.

I.S. objects to the stewardess's tone of voice, nonstop smile, relentless salesmanship ("Your personal airline," she says, parroting the slogan of this giant, totally impersonal enterprise), and interminable translations of such useless information as "the outside temperature is minus 42^0 Centigrade"—as if we were planning to eject—and "Captain Smith hopes you have enjoyed your flight. 'Bye now." "*Le capitaine* Smeet. . . ." I might add that our stewardess's very busy path to the cockpit with trays of vodka, wine, cognac, champagne, and Pernod has not increased *my* store of confidence in *Hauptmann* Schmidt.

I.S., though he has been slaking his thirst with Scottish antifreeze, is far from sozzled. He talks to me about Chekhov, whom he is systematically rereading and with whom he identifies to the extent of defending *Ivanov* against the performance of last night's Broadway cast: the wife who might have been reading from a teleprompter; the uncle who, judging by the way he picked each overly decrepit step, might have been on an obstacle course of rubber tires; and the Ivanov himself (Gielgud), whose method of expressing bitterness and suffering was to curl his mustached lip, thereby merely conveying the impression that someone in his vicinity had made a rude smell. I.S. admits that the plight of provincial Russians wanting to go to Moscow is not exactly spellbinding any more, "Yet Chekhov manages to make us care whether they go or not, and he manages it, as he manages everything else, with great tact."

Apart from Chekhov, I.S.'s in-flight reading is confined to Michel Phillipot's *Stravinsky*, which the book's subject is obelizing—correcting, annotating, rephrasing, deleting words and substituting better ones of his own, rewriting whole chunks, and, in short, polemicizing with the author **1966** and posterity.

As we approach Paris, I.S. is relieved when we drop below the iridescence of an afterstorm and toward a cloud bank on which the shadow of the airplane flashes like a wheeling bird. At a lower layer of weather, we dive through the storm itself—which is like traveling backward in time. The encasing element establishes relativity and creates a sobering impression of the velocity of the plane, not least in the specific sense of the dispersion of alcoholic vapors. In consequence, already pouchy faces seem to become pouchier and roomier for returning anxieties.

At Orly, watching an old woman standing as if hypnotized by the beam-controlled, electric-eye glass doors, I notice that older people, *i.e.,* with acquired rather than innate confidence in mechanics, approach the miracle with arms protectively extended.

May 19. Malraux's newly cleaned Paris is the color of white skin from which black greasepaint has just been removed. To the Balthus exhibition at the Louvre. Berman arrives from Rome. I receive a check from the *New York Times,* attached to a voucher describing the sum as payment for my article, "A Master at Work," which describes, in advance—the *Times* wants the dateline of the piece to be I.S.'s birthday—how I.S. *will* behave in Strasbourg next month.

May 22. I.S. is complaining of a *crise de foie,* as might be expected after so many bibulous meals; nor are we allowed to remain in ignorance of his fecal fears, and of an absorbing scatological disquisition with digressions on purgatives and piles. How much more at home he is in Paris than in California! He prefers the gender language, for one thing, and, for another, he is entertained by French society, no matter how much he scoffs at it, especially by that climate of intrigue compared with which the smog-darkened atmosphere of Los Angeles seems pure and clean. In Paris, above all, conversation has not yet been entirely superseded by television, though in truth the cutting off of all that oral libido, the national satisfaction of the mouth, is unimaginable. All the same, I wonder whether his Russianness is not at least as apparent here as his Europeanness is in America, French social structures being so much more closed than American.

At Chartres, every approach to the cathedral is impeded by the booths of an agricultural fair. Returning through Maintenon, we eat Camembert sandwiches Chez Loulou, then go to Paris 2, which is the French idea of American *luxe intégral:* termitary architecture, swimming pools, shopping *géants,* and other tokens of *le bonheur*—as distinguished from *la culture,* which of course Americans cannot hope to understand, let alone acquire. In Paris 2, unlike Paris *tout simple,* the bidets do not outnumber the bathrooms, the elevators do not hobble, and the telephone earpieces—"*Ne quittez pas, monsieur*"—do not reverberate like seashells. This horrendous Utopia adjoins the toy village of Marie Antoinette.

1966   **May 23.** Athens and dinner in a seaside restaurant with Lina Lalandi.

May 24. In the stuffy hotel dining room, I.S.'s two small lamb cutlets are wheeled in under an egg-shaped silver container the size of an iron lung. During the meal an elderly woman approaches our table flourishing a photograph of herself with I.S.'s brother Gury and reminding I.S. that they knew each other in St. Petersburg in 1900. Whatever his curiosity, I.S. is not in a mood to grapple with unforeseen reminders of the more tender years of his past; he scolds her for disturbing him and sends her away. The upshot of this is that V., though not interested in the woman's story, feels sorry for her, follows her to the lobby and hears her through to the bittersweet end. I.S.'s reactions in such cases are capricious. Tomorrow he would be capable of inviting the intruder to a banquet.

To Corinth in the afternoon, a five-hour jolt on a narrow and bumpy road in 1956, now a 90-minute spin on a divided superhighway. Automobiles are a hundred times more evident than a decade ago, too, and the jogging donkey carts of that remote date rarer in the same ratio. In fact, all of Greece is so transformed, touristically speaking, that the view *of* the Hilton *from* the Acropolis is as frequently spoken of now as the other way around. It is even said that in the most popular vacationing waters, signs have had to be floated warning of the danger of dropping anchor on the scuba divers.

Shrines survive along the road and, near Athens, a few touchingly ugly churches with cypress-shaded cemeteries, but the roadside exposures of all other buildings are covered with hoardings. Only the sweeping hillsides seem the same as 10 years ago, which is to say stony and lacking in tilth. At Megara, the scent of pines, anticipated from memories of 1956, is swamped, if it exists, in the fetors of refining petroleum and, more agreeably, in clouds of spume blowing over small islands that seem to have fallen like crumbs from the cake of the mainland. The tourists at Nero's canal lean over the sides of the bridge like seasick steamship passengers at the taffrails, and at Corinth the proportion of tourists to natives must be roughly equivalent to that of Persians to Greeks at Thermopylae. Where, a decade ago, I posed against the deserted ruins—for an excitable photographer, wearing an artist's smock, Lavallière, Taras Bulba mustaches, and ducking his head under a black tent to take the picture—hundreds of Americans are posing and snap-shooting each other. Returning to Athens, we are detained at a railroad crossing by a toy-sized but clangorous and fuliginous—like black wool—Sparta Express.

May 26. Our concert, in the Amphitheater of Herodes Atticus, goes very smoothly, blessed by an ambrosial night and the circumstance that I am not distracted by an awareness of myself, as if from another dimension or body, or from the helicopter of my superego, which ordinarily makes a deafening noise. A singer's mistake puts I.S. into a lather, and when Lalandi asks him to acknowledge the continuing applause, he refuses with brandishes of his cane. Afterwards I go to Piraeus with Lalandi and her husband to listen to bouzouki music.

June 1. Lisbon. In the interval of our concert, I.S. receives the Order of Santiago from an Admiral who is said to govern Portugal in Salazar's name.

June 6. Paris. To Le Grand Véfour with Cartier-Bresson and Mme Lazar of the *New York Times*. I.S. is greeted, from another table, by Don Antonio de Gandarillas; the two of them, coevals and friends of 50 years, study each other to see who is in worse shape. Mme Gandarillas was I.S.'s mistress after Chanel.

June 9. Walking in the rue St.-Honoré this morning, I am accosted by a display of recordings in a shop window and in the next instant recognize them as mine, whereupon I feel ill. Why does the sight of my name in print, of a photograph of myself, of any kind of publicity concerning myself, even the sound of my voice on a playback or in an echo chamber during a long-distance telephone call, upset me so much? I put the question to I.S. later, but instead of explaining the neurosis, he adds to its documentation, saying that I neglected to sign the first letter he received from me, because of which he had to trace me through Nicolas Nabokov. We attend the beginning of a concert in the Hotel de Sully, but leave after a performance of Schoenberg's Chamber Symphony.

June 11. With I.S., Xenakis, Béjart, Marcello Panni to a screening for French critics of CBS's I.S. documentary, which is unanimously condemned as an American-style cover story with interpolated gratifications for minority groups, critics excepted. Above all, the French object to the mass-appeal diversionary gimmicks: the reception by the Texas cowboys, the hansom ride on 72nd Street in Central Park, the ballet of little girls—to whom, nevertheless, I.S.'s parting words, "Grow up well, little *demoiselles*," provide the film's most endearing moments. Nor do the French warm to the relentless hyperbole of the narration, the oh-so-famous Mister Balanchine, the great, great Mr. Benny Goodman, and now just look who this is, and in fact it is the Pope himself. (And very pleased his Holiness was to be on American television, though the Vatican concert honored not only I.S. but also Malipiero and Milhaud, both unceremoniously shunted to a back row, at the request of the CBS cameramen, by the obliging Papal Public Relations Department.) What the French critics see as most American of all is the McLuhanite message of the TV screen itself, which says, in effect, that great artists are rewarded with riches, the company of the famous, TV biographies.

The Giacometti episode alone wins praise, as much for the reason that it is conducted in French as for the relief it brings from the tone of an overly excited TV commercial surrounding it. Giacometti never notices the camera, never emerges from his absorption in his work, and talks only of his failure: *"Je n'arrive pas; c'est abominable."* None of the viewers notices, or mentions, that in I.S.'s two drawings of Giacometti, the artist's eyes are closed as

1966 if he were a dead man, which was I.S.'s presentiment that May day six months before the event.

"Is the film a true portrait of I.S.?" one of the disgruntled critics asks me afterward, meaning, I take it, that although I.S. has said and done everything he is seen to say and do, have the editing, cutting, transposing of contexts unduly distorted the resulting picture? I answer that the contexts of the critic-fustigating are immaterial and that the drawing of a few more beads, or potshots, in the direction of Richard Strauss requires no contextual preparation. (I.S. had answered a student's question at Austin as to "what specifically" he dislikes in the music of Strauss with "I do not like the major works, and I do not like the minor works," adding, off camera, that for him Strauss's music is too homogenized.)

The film inevitably offers valuable reflections of I.S.'s mind: for instance, his misquotation of Tertullian's "*Credo quia absurdum*" ("I will give it to you in the original Latin [!] of St. Paul: '*Credo in absurdum*'"), which can be interpreted as an indication of his dogmatic side and of his supposed respect for rubber-stamp forms (formulae, formats), time-hallowed ideas, apparent traditions. The received idea of I.S. as a composer for whom rules precede emotions, and frames come before pictures, is still widespread in Paris, but it is also, or was also, a self-promoted view, whether or not an actual hedge against rampant feelings.

If the film seriously misleads, it is not in any out-of-context or too locally circumstantial remark, but in the inference that Poland was important in I.S.'s life and that his concert there was something of a pilgrimage, whereas the reasons for filming in Warsaw were entirely budgetary. The implications of the Vatican episode are also false. In a sudden, ill-advised gesture of recognition toward the arts, the Throne of St. Peter decided to honor four composers of four faiths, choosing Sibelius to represent the Protestant world (did anyone know that he was dead?), Milhaud the Jewish, I.S. the Orthodox, and Malipiero the Catholic. But I.S. has not been *pratiquant* in *any* faith for more than a dozen years, and if religious affiliations could be classified by feelings rather than by declarations and acts of worship, he might be described as a lapsed Jansenist. He continues to be anti-Pelagian, and, as strongly as ever, he sees a teleological pattern, though what it is remains secret and defies labeling.

June 22. New York. The steam rising from open manholes and grates of subway catacombs reminds me of Doré's "*Inferno*," and doormen's whistles for taxicabs, like shrieks of Beelzebub, make the picture lifelike, or afterlife-like. Unlike Dante's Florence and Ravenna, parts of which have remained much the same for some time, New York is a never-completed city. "What will it be like in five years?" I think aloud to my driver, on the way to the Port Authority Terminal. "Mister, I'm wondering what it's going to be like in five minutes," he says, adding sourly, when we reach the destination, "Have a nice trip. Please write." His New Yorkese is characterized by the disappearance of *L*'s (awready) and the transference of *R*'s from where they should be to where they shouldn't (I sawr that in the papuh).

June 30. I spend the afternoon with Marianne Moore eliminating archaisms from the Narrator's part in *The Flood*. Though Twiggy-thin, wispy, and as bent as a woman carrying a shoulder load in a Hiroshige print, she still bustles about her apartment at high speed and works with enviable energy and concentration. The book-lined walls are embellished with pictures of birds and animals, and with photographs, one of them of a young, unfamiliarly fleshy and smiling T. S. Eliot.

Miss Moore has marked scansions and circled words which, she contends, "can be read but not narrated, if the audience is to understand." Her own reading is difficult to follow: the alveolars failing to come through, the volume small, the delivery, though refreshingly nonemphatic, uninflected. Moreover, she fails, orally, to cross her "t's" ("crea-a[t]ure") so that the unfocused vowels surging around the unpronounced consonants are as broad and undefined as the river, at springtime, whose name classifies her accent.

The blur in enunciation is in striking contrast to the matter enunciated, for her thought is distinct, her intellectual vigilance unflagging. Of the libretto generally, she commends the idea of assigning the lines from the Bible to a narrator and the guild-play lines to actors, saying that "The stylistic fusion of Genesis, Anonymous, and *Paradise Lost* is natural." She is also the first critic to remark that the sea itself is the symbol of chaos and to catch the connection with *Timon* in the "salt flood." As for the replacements of the words she rejects as too obscure for a textless audience, I concur in every instance, if only, in one or two of them, in gratitude for the privilege of watching her work.

She fetches several "bulwarks" (dictionaries)—one at a time, to my relief: those precarious, stilt-thin arms and legs—including German, for she has revised the German translation as well. But a sere and yellowed rhyming dictionary is the only tome made use of, not to say systematically ransacked. As we discuss the candidacy of each word, she points a long fescule-like forefinger to keep her place. Her method is to preserve the rhyme words wherever possible and to exchange the bodies of the lines, which is like *bouts-rimés;* failing in that, she re-orders the rhymes themselves. Since quantities are of little importance in these transpositions, templates and purely musical ornaments are expunged. To achieve her goal, and eliminate ambiguity and obscurity, she will retain anachronisms and let stylistic questions fall by the board. Her rules, in short, are rules of thumb and ear, *her* thumb, *her* ear.

"I cannot use a word I feel contempt for," she stipulates, changing "Hares hopping gaily can go" to "Hopping briskly hares can go," justifying "'briskly' because of its greater dignity." She amends "Here cats can make it full carouse" to "Here cats make full carouse," and repairs

1966   And here are bears, wolves set
             Apes, owls, marmoset

to

             And here are bears, wolves, leveret,
             Ape, owl, and marmoset

which is superior but may raise the question whether the singular might have been too sophisticated for the fifteenth-century guild plays, coupling being the raison d'être of the Ark. She also changes "Here are lions, leopards in" to "Here come lions . . ." and finally alters the "briskly" versus "gaily" stanza to:

             Both cats and dogs also
             Otter, fox, fulmart, too,
             And, hopping briskly, hares can go.

Her most dramatic revisions are in Noah's last speech, where she re-renders "And multiply your seed shall ye" as "And so shall your lives be saved" (which lacks a syllable for the music); and "Sons, with your wives shall ye be stead" as "Sons with your wives gain new estate." Objecting to "bairns" (which Basil Bunting is trying to keep in circulation), she adjusts "Your bairns shall then each other wed" to "The youths and maids shall then be wed." Finally, she changes "And worship God in good degree" to "And thus your god be served," and "Shall forth be bred" to "Shall thus be bred."

Accompanying me to the street, Miss Moore provides a rare spectacle for devotees of extraordinary millinery among her neighbors: *La dame au tricorne* is bareheaded! As William Empson guessed, she talks "without stress, and only could be scanned by counting syllables."

In tonight's opening concert of the Stravinsky Festival at Philharmonic Hall, Bernstein conducts Rivuelta's *Sensamaya*, Ruggles's *Men and Mountains*, and *Sacre*, this last a good performance on the whole, with the exception of a rubato in the next-to-last section of the *Danse sacrale*. Afterward, Bernstein bows in the direction of the deafening applause, then to I.S. in his loge, at which the audience stands, shouts, and applauds until the theater seems likely to collapse. I.S. stands for a moment and V. helps him to walk backstage, where he asks for Scotch, drinks half a glass, reaches for the *Sacre* score. When Bernstein comes offstage from his sixth bow, I.S. points to the place where the liberty in tempo occurred. Bernstein: "But I learned it that way from Stokowski and I can't do it differently. God how I love the music." We wait in Bernstein's dressing room for nearly an hour before returning to the hotel.

July 19. Santa Fe. When I enter the empty orchestra pit tonight to begin the piano-dress rehearsal, Linda A. follows me. I turn suddenly and kiss her, an action that is the more novelettish for being our first encounter of any kind apart from eye contacts. She is about 25, but has baby-dimples and is babyish in other ways as well (the closed-eyes pucker, the dental braces, blue jeans, gray sweatshirt). She wears contact lenses (to judge from the squinting and peering), a thick gold wedding band, but no make-up (her lips are a purplish litmus color).

July 21. After the *Rake* rehearsal, I fly to El Paso in a chartered Cessna, and from there at midnight, joining an American Airlines flight from Mexico City, to New York. The worst of the Cessna is the noise—the raspings and explosions as we roll down the sizzling concrete-and-melting-tar runway and slowly lift into the sky—and the roar thereafter. The flimsiness of the plane—the pilot flings my bags aboard like a balloonman loading ballast—and the thinness of its insulation are more evident the greater the altitude. The pangs of acrophobia are replaced by an unnamed worse sensation that afflicts me when the plane is seized by paroxysms of shuddering. What is the significance of those drops of oil shivering on the window? I ask, by pointing to them. The pilot assures me that "it was like this three days ago" (a tertian ague, then?), or at least this is what his mouthing and gesturing (three fingers) seem to say. A great deal of gesticulation on his part in the direction of the instrument panel is answered by a corresponding amount of ambiguous shrugging and head-shaking on mine, my mechanical aptitude being such that I can hardly tell the difference between a flooded carburetor and a flat tire.

Numbed by the noise, I begin to fly backward in time (as positrons, or electrons, are said to travel temporally backward) until transported to another evening hour when, standing in a field loud with katydids and tightly holding my father's hand, I am watching the take-off of the first airplane I ever saw on the ground. The aviator spins the two-bladed propeller himself, running back and forth from it several times before the motor, which makes stuttering, dynamite-like detonations, finally "turns over."

I see myself as well, a short time later, greatly disturbed by the vision of an ace stunt flyer and daredevil parachutist whose chute has failed to open and who has volleyed to his death at the Kingston Airport 100 yards from a horror-stricken crowd. This plummeting-man image, and image of the body penetrating the ground to the depth of a grave, has remained in my mind's eye until now. In spite of this incident, I flew with my father in a Ford trimotor in, I think, the same year, rising over the city higher, it seems, than I have ever flown since, though it must have been very much lower, since I could see both the Ashokan Reservoir and our house, which looked like a toy model. I remember that we were unable to talk over the blast of the motors at that time, too, and that the noise bothered me more than the bumping. But then, I used to hide in the cellar or attic on the Fourth of July; and at the circus, waiting for the human cannonball to be catapulted from the cannon to a net, suffered agonies of suspense, as much

1966 because of the explosion as for the safety of the man. Then 35 years hurtle by, and I am I, here and now, attributing the unlocking of memory to similarities of sensation between the two airplanes and thinking that the most evident difference is that I am probably greener in the gills now.

Like a scenic-route bus driver, the pilot, who grips his steering wheel much less tightly than I grip mine, points out the site of the first atomic explosion and calls out the names (unheard) of mountains, rivers, towns, sometimes shouting anecdotes connected with them, of which I fail to get the drift. Again, as it was 35 years ago, we fly low enough to follow an automobile map and to construe details of the landscape down to haystacks and spinning dust devils. Patches of water, gleaming from the earth like metal reflectors, are evidence of recent storms, as the choppiness, scudding clouds, and aerial bombardment-like flashes of sheet lightning are promises of imminent ones.

Suddenly the pilot begins to twiddle the dials and hammer the instrument panel with his fists as if it were a rigged pinball machine. Removing and shaking his earphones—his only "gear"—he tells me, in sign language, that the radio is out of order and that to land without it in El Paso is unthinkable. Accordingly, we head west toward a small strip along the river, where, if the weather is clear, we should be able to touch down without difficulty. (He rapidly scribbles this information on a piece of paper.) And it *is* clear, clear*er* at any rate, a sliver of sunset still showing on one side of the plane while a net of stars ignites on the other, and the lights on the converging highways below turn on as if by a switch.

The Rio Grande coils blackly between the electrically gaudy American and the electrically faint Mexican cities. We come in, swaying like a swing, at hardly more than rooftop height, then bump down uncushioned on a short, narrow, and ancient concrete strip, rebounding like a roller-coaster. "Fillerup?" a cowpoke with paprika freckles asks, as I emerge, weak-kneed, onto the wing and into a light warm rain. I count out $220 for the pilot and call for a taxi to the main airport.

July 22. In New York at 8 A.M., a limousine takes me directly to Philharmonic Hall. Two visits from M.O. in my dressing room there, before and after the morning rehearsal. *During* it, she goes to one of her tri-weekly talking sessions, now in their 12th year (her illness is that she is seriously rich), so that by my arithmetic her analyst has heard more stories from her than the Sultan from Sheherazade. I tease her about this, reminding her of Karl Kraus's "Psychoanalysis is the disease of which it pretends to be the cure," likening analysts as outlets for talk to manicurists and coiffeurs, and warning her that today's aggressiveness, like tomorrow's meekness, is all a matter of how her shrink pulls the strings.

She is caparisoned, the first time, in sheath pants, gold waist chain, ear ornaments resembling an insertable appliance that used to be worn before the advent of The Pill. The second time, this outfit has been exchanged for a paneled bakelite micro-mini with fluorescent buttons, fishnet stockings, and hoop earrings the size of canaries' trapezes. Sometimes she herself seems as easily changeable as her wardrobe, but that is untrue; she is charming, genuinely unaffected, and ravishingly beautiful. Still, the talking cure is not yet a complete success, and more sofa work is undoubtedly in store—to judge by her habit of packing her bags at 4 in the morning and tiptoeing out, like Santa Claus, or a thief, for the declared reason, if caught and pressed to reveal it, that "I feel rejected."

July 23. Our concert: I conduct the Symphony in Three and a slightly cut *Flood*, and I.S. conducts *Psalms*.

September 15. Louisville, the Brown Hotel. After the evening rehearsal, we attend a screening of the Liebermann-Leacock film. It preserves the most natural view of I.S.'s genial side that, at this date, can ever be made, and is also the least scripted, least manipulated by technicians, advertisers, ax-grinders. The one misrepresentation is the jumbling of the time sequence. And the one drawback is that, like all such documentaries, it is essentially an obituary. Yet it is worth seeing for five remarks alone. The first is I.S.'s disarming explanation, in reply to a question about his anti-Wagnerism, that "everybody who makes something new does harm to something old." The second is prompted by a question, raised during a tea party with Isherwood and Heard, about the creative process: "There is no creative process for me, only the pleasure," he says, adding, off-sound, "Imaginative processes have their laws, but if I could formulate them, they might stop being useful to me." A marvelous remark comes in response to a question as to whether he cares if his music is performed: "Of course I am interested to hear if I was right or not." But the two most valuable statements in the film occur, transposed, at the end. "I am always happy when I am awakened," he says, "and it is the same with composing." Finally, the 84-year-old says: "In the morning we think differently than in the evening. When I come to a difficulty, I wait until tomorrow. I can wait as an insect can wait."

September 17. I.S. has planned his post-concert getaway with the thoroughness of a bank robber, but we are captured by a reception in the hotel and made Kentucky Colonels.

October 8. From New York to Princeton by limousine, for an afternoon rehearsal. Shortly before the beginning of the concert, a note is delivered to I.S. in his dressing room: "We shall try to see you briefly at the intermission or the end. If you are in Princeton Sunday, let us bring you home for a few quiet minutes. In respect and devotion, Robert Oppenheimer." Defying the injunction in the program not to applaud the *Requiem Canticles*, Oppenheimer leads a standing ovation for I.S. at the beginning of the concert. At intermission, Oppenheimer, spectral and towering over I.S., chats with him about his new pieces. After the concert, in a room adjoining the hall, President Goheen pays his respects: "We

1966 hope to have you with us again." I.S.: "I am a very old man and that is unlikely."

I.S. talks to every member of the audience who comes to greet him, from the top dressing of professional musicians to countless students. And he listens sharply to every comment on the new work, 60 years in the arena not having insulated him from opinion. The younger people, especially those just learning to become the old man's contemporaries, seem to be astonished that an octogenarian can create music of such newness. In the limousine returning to New York, he talks about the student reaction, saying that he thinks about the problems of both the bloom-is-off ex-youths and the overthrowing of the biblical tradition of "the wisdom of the elders" by "youth culture." The repudiation of the past in favor of the newest and latest (*"cupidus rerum novarum"*) is by no means a new disease. His own rapport with young people, he says, is a better one than he had with their parents and grandparents at the same age, and he attributes this to a natural desire to cling to an old man with a good enough safety record.

I.S. says that when he first saw Oppenheimer, in his Princeton home in August 1959, "I was struck by his feet. Some people, Oppenheimer among them, have intelligent hands. But he also has—it was a hot day and he had removed his sandals—intelligent feet."

October 12. On the flight to Los Angeles, the S.s watch a film, but I.S.'s closest attentions to such entertainments does not guarantee that he is successfully following them. Near the end he asks for help identifying a character who has already appeared numerous times. *"Kto eto?"* ("Who is that?"). V.: *"Ubiytsa, konechno"* ("The murderer, of course"). I.S.: *"Kak ty eto znaesh?"* ("How can you tell?"). What I.S. likes most about flying is the cocktail hour, that sudden tide of alcohol washing away the good fences between neighbors and unloosening torrents of talk. This ritual begins, for him, with a course of medical hors d'oeuvres, Glutovite (for memory), and "leapies" (pep pills). "There is no way of knowing whether they help," he says, "but if you are willing, maybe they do." And down they go, sloshed by a variety of libations—whiskey (three under-the-counter refills from his own stores), claret, armagnac—each new glass aromatically savored before being upturned, for I.S. is no run-of-the-mill intravenous boozer but a discriminating taster.

October 14. I.S. on the origins of the *Requiem Canticles* says simply that he expanded certain "intervallic designs" into contrapuntal forms from which, in turn, he conceived the larger form of the work. The twofold series was also discovered early on, while he was completing "the first musical sentence." So, too, the instrumental bias of the piece, the triangular instrumental frame—string prelude, wind-instrument interlude, percussion postlude—was an early idea. He began with the interlude, the formal lament, but acknowledges that the prelude puzzled the audience more (having overheard comments comparing it to Bartok and to the beginning

of Mozart's "Dissonant" Quartet). "The preluding manner is precisely suit- **1966**
ed to the musical matter to be expounded," he says, and he refers to the
whole piece as a mini-Requiem, claiming that it is "the easiest to take
home" of his last-period, or last-ditch-period, music.

October 30. Hollywood. Rehearse *The Owl and the Pussy-Cat* with
Ingolf Dahl. I.S. calls the piece a musical sigh of relief, adding that a
Requiem at his age rubs close to home. He says that the origins of the song
are in the trimeter rhythms of the title, and that the rhythmic cell suggested a group of pitches, which he expanded into a 12-note series in correspondence to the stanzaic form of the poem. The piano octaves are at the
same time a syncopated canonic voice and a double mirror reflecting the
movement of the vocal part between both the upper and the lower notes:
"Octaves are peculiarly pianistic," he says. "No other instrument produces
them so distinctly." But what of the other origins, the "To Vera" dedication? The "elegant fowl" kept the composition a secret until he could
"sing" and play it for her, not in a "pea-green boat," naturally, but in his
soundproof roost.

November 5. Pasadena. Some Cal Tech students have invited I.S. to a
"wine" party (Glenlivet for the composer, Gallo for the young boffins) after
tonight's rehearsal. He accepts and even enjoys answering their questions,
"because of the chance that one or two of these young people might keep
going."

November 7. Lately I.S. has been suffering from bouts of sneezing during noontime meals. ("There are conditions under which the most majestic
person is obliged to," George Eliot wrote.) "Here comes my allergy," he
announces (allergy to what?), and then, either nine or eleven times,
sneezes.

November 14. Honolulu. A letter from L. rawly exposes what I have
known, but out of vanity not been willing to admit. I mind especially
because others must have seen it so transparently.

> When amorists grow bald and amours shrink
> Into the compass and curriculum
> Of introspective exiles, lecturing. . . .

Stevens's lines come to mind as, swimming across the warm lagoon and
the warmer reef to the surf, I notice that I am the only over-20s, to say
nothing of 30s and 40s, in a group of still bald-chested surfboarding boys.
This makes me aware that age differences have been suspended and that
the mask I have been wearing against myself has now been lifted. Now I
must oust the feeling or cauterize it.

Will writing about it help? One of the oldest forms of surgery, after all,
is the exploratory operation called The Anatomy of Love. Perhaps I can
discover whether the ego-tumor is malignant. Here goes:

1966   1. All love is self-love, all talk of sacrifice for the other is rhetoric. (The formulation is too *dix-huitième*.)

2. Love is like talent in that he who knows it truly, has not mistaken an identity or used it as a form of conquest, can never lose it entirely.

3. We are more agreeable when in love than at less enchanted times because the best of reality is intensified, the worst hidden.

4. The opposite of love is the fear of possessing or, which is the same thing, of being possessed. (Cliché.)

5. Love is uncharitable; we cannot beg it. (Cliché.)

6. The paradox of love is that we are more aware of its limitations during it than at any other time. (A Stendhal novel in this.)

7. Infidelity is natural for all "true" lovers, "true" love being dependent, and the deprivation of the other "unbearable," which explains the recourse to substitutes, as in the supposed high incidence of posthumous cuckolding, and the need of all about-to-be-unfaithful wives and husbands to assure themselves and their adulterers that they *really* love the wives or husbands they are about to betray; these assurances are, of course, perfectly "sincere."

8. Even a single experience of the depths of love's labour's lost should have taught us that our "inconsolable" feelings will change. Yet we continue to pretend that it is within our power to mortgage future ones, as if we could pledge our love "forever" and promise that "death cannot abate"—by which, even in love's exaggeration, we do not mean some extension beyond time, but an experience endlessly in it, and therefore, above all, now.

9. After the first fall, experience in love does not count, in the sense that we do not learn more from more of it. How otherwise explain Lothario's successiveness and the length of Leporello's catalog? And how explain the experience of encountering a former till-death-do-us-part lover a cold interval later and wondering how we "ever could have."

10. While our "rational" parts are aware of the circumstantiality of life, our far more powerful "irrational" ones prefer to cling to false absolutes, including the idea of an absolute love. (A parochial observation.)

11. Memory is no less circumstantial, and, in the radically different circumstances of Hawaii, it is already dimmer and less poignant; even that last encapsulated moment together, our last full exchange, is beginning to dissolve, as capsules will; and involuntary, purely glandular proclivities, the recognition of which made me feel disloyal only a week ago—acknowledgment even of the existence of anyone else representing a move away from L. and confirming the possibility of a post-L. world, which in my "heart" I did not want—are now invested with a decidedly voluntary element, if not yet a full return to normal nympholepsis.

12. We talk about swallowing our vanity and our pride, but love, more frequently and convincingly described as sickness than as health, is the bit-

terest and least digestible of these in any case unnourishing metaphorical meals.

13. The unresponsive mistress may prove to have been a more fertile theme for poetry (Campion, Donne) than the fully cooperating and aggressively abetting one (in the area of Marvell's *To His Coy Mistress*).

14. All lovers are ridiculous. (See 1–13 above.)

I empty out today's bag of platitudes—the circumstantial brain—on the beach, to escape not only the throb of Hawaiian music in the bar, but also the people, for if the air is "like silk" and the sea "like satin," then the texture of the tourists is gunnysack. But will I, after this exercise of penmanship, be able to work at last? "Weeping Eros is the builder of cities," Auden says.

November 25. To Columbus, Ohio. The flight is not smooth, the plane bouncing in an atmosphere like "snow" on a TV screen. At one point I.S. remarks that without seat belts we would be clinging to the ceiling like bats, and when we are again on terra firma, he confesses that he had been afraid we were going to be front-page news. I.S. likes to fly, nevertheless, and positively basks in the attentions of the stewardesses, except when they call him "folks" and deliver smiling pre-take-off lectures on the emergency exits. The landing in Columbus terminates in an abrupt, "eyeballs out" pull-up. As we leave the plane, the stewardesses and an old lady passenger who, except for her blue eyelids, looks like George Washington, ask for and receive I.S.'s autograph.

November 28. Our concert is in an auditorium on the transpontine side of the Scioto River (*sigh-otto*) and next door to a casket factory that advertises itself in a deathly mauve neon.

November 30. I.S. attends a terrible student performance of *Histoire du Soldat*, after which we fly to Chicago, Seattle, Portland, arriving in the middle of the night at the Hilton, where, not having a room, I sleep on the S.s' couch. The baggage is delivered hours later.

December 5. Portland has a good orchestra: what a wealth there is in America of excellent underpaid musicians! I conduct Beethoven's First and Schoenberg's Five Pieces, after which Governor Mark Hatfield comes backstage, says that he "cannot accept the Schoenberg as music." At dinner—in the hotel, because of perpetual rain—the Japanese waitresses quickly learn to ask I.S.: "You wish care more Scots whiskey, pease?"

December 7. Los Angeles. When I go with I.S. to his studio this morning, he looks around at the photos on his walls, piano, and desk, says, "All these people are now dead," a wrenching remark because he seems so little attached to the past and so rarely expresses feelings about it. The contents of a man's room speak back and forth to him, nevertheless, and his own are heaped with mementos.

December 13. A visit from Yevgeny Yevtushenko, which the S.s enjoy. He arrives an hour late with translator and publicity team in tow, but as

1966 soon as he has been immortalized peeling off his jacket under the tropical glare of his photographer's lamps, his entourage retires to another room. Conversation begins with a discussion of Anna Akhmatova, during which Yevgeny Alexandrovitch offers to recite a poem of his about her funeral. His rendition is stirring, and the most accomplished of maudlin actors might have envied the voice and delivery, even if these attributes do not show to best advantage in stageless, pulpitless, and merely medium-sized parlors. When the declamation finally ebbs, he candidly confesses to an inability to warm up (*that* was cold?) "before audiences of fewer than two thousand people." But the S.s liked the poem and say so, thereupon being rewarded with two encores, about which my only area of judgment is one of admiration for the poet's memory.

V. chats with him about Gorodetzky, Kuzmin, Vladimir Nabokov, and other writers she had known during the Revolution and of whom, she says later, Yev. Alex. reminded her. He listens carefully to her description of Osip Mandelstam in Alushta in August 1917.

Of the many cultural ambassadors from the USSR who have visited the S.s, Yevtushenko is the first to notice the contents of the house. He looks at everything, as one might do in a flea market, and admires the paintings, especially one by V., thereby being presented with it on the spot, which is called Russian hospitality. Near the end of the visit he suffers one minor setback. Trying to turn the talk to Shostakovitch, Yev. Alex. provokes I.S.'s point-blank dismissal, but recovers in time to mention several favorite compositions by I.S. himself.

The family affection that Russians are able to turn on at first acquaintance, even Russians of such different origins and ages and such different views as the S.s and Y.Y., amazes me once again. "Are you coming back to America?" the S.s ask, as Yevgeny Alexandrovitch bids them *"Do svidaniya!"* and the anachronistic answer, "God knows," reminds me that the poet is a compatriot of Daniel and Sinyavsky. His visit left the S.s homesick.

Why am I recording this not very momentous encounter? I had not intended to, nor was I attentive during it, remaining out of sight in the dining room during most of it. Then I saw how animated the S.s became speaking the *lingua materna* not, for a change, with other emigrés, but with a representative of the younger generation of the actual Russian-speaking state. It seems to me, too, that they were more natural with Yev. Alex. than they are with their closest American friends.

December 15. I.S. learns of Arthur Lourié's death, but makes no comment. In the new CBS Studio, Sunset and Vine, I record the soundtrack for the United Air Lines film, *Discover America*. I.S. is interested in the reasons for mating certain sections of his music with certain scenery. The winning combination, he thinks, is that of the "Apotheosis" from *Apollo* to underscore (undermine?) a tour of the District of Columbia's most hallowed monuments. The other most successful associations are the use of the last section of the *Agon* "Interlude" as a requiem for Arlington's Unknown Soldier, and of the beginning of the "Nurses' Dance" in *Petrushka* to accompany a narrow-gauge Rocky Mountain train ("huffa-chuffa"). Predictably, *Firebird*, as the richest in mood clichés, is the film-makers' chief resource; each of the passages chosen had long since borne the moviemakers' own stamp of a character, the "Berceuse," for example, responding to the "eeriness" of Monument Valley to their complete satisfaction. When one of them says this to I.S., he says, "Eerie it may be, but in 1910 I scarcely thought I was composing music for Utah landscapes." Walt Disney's death is announced during the recording session, and a minute of silence is observed.

December 21. I.S. pretends to believe that coincidence is the only force at work, or play, when a line he composes turns out to have twelve different pitches in succession, though if this phenomenon were reported of someone else, he would be the first to see that hearing and thinking in that measurement is to some extent a matter of habit. When I ask about the role of habit he says, in essence: All composers eventually become obsessed with numbers, the rapport expressed between them being so much greater than most expressions of rapport in reality. I cannot explain this to non-musicians, and the point is not transferable or demonstrable in another medium, though some parallel sense of it might possibly appear in an example from photography. Certain kinds of rapport—of distance and balance, let us say—are more clearly seen in a black-and-white than in a color photograph, though the color photograph is more real. So, too, certain musical relationships are more clearly expressed as numbers. It may well be that the love of combining twos, threes, fours, and sixes is compulsive and that a composer who works this way is behaving in music like the man who has to lock his door three times, or step on all of the cracks in the sidewalk. But if this is true, and musical composition involves nervous disorders, I would not want to be cured.

December 22. Among the adverts on the Sunset Strip: "Christmas Trees Painted Any Color You Want"; "Have A Kool Yule With Aerosol Snow"; "The Naked Lunch" ("Serving Double-Breasted Milkshakes"); "The Body Shop: Kama Sutra Is Here"; "Lee Harvey Oswald, We Need You Now"; "Down With Blue Fascism" (the police).

December 23. Chicago, the Drake Hotel. A gooseflesh sky, in harsh contrast to the pavonian colors and rich sea changes of Hawaii. The waves of Lake Michigan seem to have turned to ice at their crests, and the surf to have frozen in mid-spray, but the S.s, answering the call of their septentrional childhoods, go for a walk after dinner and probably would like to "play" in the snow.

December 29. I.S. is received with a standing ovation after our concert, and the "tusch" from the orchestra.

At Maxim's with Bill Bernal, talking about music in films. The gist of

1966 I.S.'s remarks is that music should be used only where logically required by contexts—scenes of concerts and in the imagination of a musically-minded character. There can be no real relationship between what one sees and what one hears, but only habit relationships. Film-makers continue to treat music as sound effects and wall-to-wall emotional carpeting, in other words, on more or less the same level as commercials for cat food. Not only do they try to tie music to concrete sentiments and things, but they also attempt to synchronize its own events to movements of the camera, making the horn "sting" coincide with the "zoom-in," the "expansive theme" with the "pan-across," and the orchestral crescendo with the visual tilt-up.

December 30. I.S. dispatches a telegram to the *Chicago Sun Times* in response to an idiotic review denigrating the quality of the pick-up orchestra: "Most of my recordings, of which your critic's approval makes me uneasy, were made with pick-up orchestras such as the one I conducted Wednesday and which was a credit to Chicago. Your reviewer is a local disgrace. Happy New Year. Stravinsky." What has angered him in the newspaper article is that his departing gesture, hoisting his hat on his cane from the door, after bowing from center stage, has been interpreted as an insult to the audience. What the gesture is meant to convey is that he cannot walk out front again and must signal the end.

Postscript 1994. With the completion of the *Requiem Canticles* and *The Owl and the Pussy-Cat*, 1966 marked the end of Stravinsky's life as a composer, though he continued to make sketches for new works and in 1968 scored the piano accompaniment of two Hugo Wolf songs for a double quintet of strings and winds.

The year's principal events were the Stravinsky Festival at Lincoln Center, New York, in June and July, and the premiere of *Requiem Canticles* at Princeton, October 8. The *Canticles* performance had been planned for the celebration of the composer's 85th birthday, but when it became known that he had completed the opus (on August 13), the University decided to present it in conjunction with his trip east in September. So, too, the Lincoln Center festifications had been advanced a year as a result of reports about the uncertain state of Stravinsky's health. Both decisions proved to be fortunate, as it happened, since he did not conduct again after May 1967 and was seriously ill during the latter part of that year.

The *Canticles* premiere was a moving occasion. The music was wonderfully new; Stravinsky, in his 85th year, had created new instrumental colors and new harmonies. Moving, too, was the realization of old friends that they might be seeing the composer for the last time. The University's presentation of the concert was elegant: rehearsal time was generously provided, intrusive publicity tactfully avoided.

In contrast, when Stravinsky said that he would not be able to conduct the recording, scheduled for the following week, and that I would have to *1966* substitute for him, Columbia Masterworks dismissed the professional singers in the chorus and retained only the unpaid amateurs. He attended this recording session very briefly, leaving after an altercation between Mrs. Stravinsky and the recording director, during which she accused Columbia of treating both me and her husband shabbily in pretending that he was supervising recording sessions at which he had not been present and of failing to acknowledge my work for what it was.

❧ *1967*

January 7. New York. Arnold Newman photographs I.S. with Balanchine. Afterward, I.S. copies one of Edward Lear's drawings of *The Owl and the Pussy-Cat*, in an amazingly steady hand, with great speed and no false starts, adding waves around the boat to "place" the picture. When Newman goes we listen to a test pressing of the *Canticles*, I.S. deploring the many errors (the fault of a corrupt text) that deform the performance. Balanchine, on the other hand, imagining a choreographic presentation, is deeply moved: "Every measure that Igor Fyodorovitch ever wrote is good for dancing," he tells me, and he proceeds to illustrate the claim—arm and hand movements only, and with no embellishments of costume apart from his rumpled shirt and bolo tie, souvenirs of his frontier days (*Western Symphony* and Maria Tallchief).

January 9. A breath-fogging night. Party at Newman's with Marcel Duchamp, who is tight-lipped and *sec* in aspect only. And what an aspect! The profile might have served for a Renaissance numismatic or medallion portrait, the posture and backward tilt of the head for an equestrian hero, such as Pisanello's "Leonello d'Este," a far-fetched comparison attributable partly to something equine about Duchamp himself, partly to his talk about the armor of scorpions. Neat, well barbered, tightly tailored, he sports a daunting pink shirt and blue necktie. When complimented on this natty combination, he dismisses it as "Christmas-present clothes." Conversation revolves around Giacometti, but when someone remarks that this mutually lamented friend must have been "a *triste* person," Duchamp objects: "Not *triste*, tormented." Certainly neither word could have occurred to anyone seeking to describe Duchamp and his raptorial acuity.

What *are* the feelings of a man who, when the subject gravitates to airplane crashes—I am flying tomorrow—contributes the thought that "death in the air is a good way because you explode"? (vs death in bed from a heart attack because you implode?) They are not morbid, anyway, the thought being purely logical to him, with no more emotional coloring than one of his chess moves. What may seem untrue to type in a crystallizing

448

mind such as his is the keen susceptibility to outside amusements. He tells a story about the Queen of England at an exhibition of his work at the Tate Gallery questioning an embarrassed curator about an object Her Majesty did not seem to see was ithyphallic, then quickly follows with the observation, "A freedom we are all much in need of at present is freedom from bad wit."

Tunneling a chimney through an after-dinner cigar with an ice pick, he handles the awkward awl so adeptly that we watch as if he were sculpting a new anti-masterpiece, which of course he is. I.S. and Duchamp have not seen each other in a long time, and when we leave, Duchamp says, "Well, Maestro, see you in another 50 years." A meeting of two veterans, then, two who challenged and changed the values to which they were born, two survivors of artistic revolutions, who occupied lonely outposts once, and whose currency, now part of the whole world, was at one time theirs alone.

February 15. Hollywood. Gertrude Schoenberg is dead.

March 1. Seattle. I conduct *Histoire* for an audience of school children: Narrator: Basil Rathbone; Princess: Marina Svetlova; Soldier: John Gavin. I.S. gives interviews and poses for photographs by local and British newspapers. The *Seattle Post-Intelligencer* quotes him: "You can't tell where music is going any more than you can tell where people are going. Each time creates its own needs."

April 3. Boston. Drive to my sister's at New Paltz. "Samantha has recovered," she says, surprised herself to be pleased at the news, Samantha being a white rat rescued from a laboratory at Cornell by my niece, and since then living, uncaged, in New Paltz. Until three mornings ago, when discovered on her back, breathing heavily, legs outstretched and deathly stiff, the rodent had inspired the strongest revulsion in my sister, but the sight of the stricken creature emboldened her to cuddle the invalid in a blanket and rush it to a veterinarian, worrying the while about bubonic plague. The diagnosis was acute constipation; the prescribed treatment is an injection of antibiotics and hourly spoon-feedings of prune juice. This morning Samantha's legs began to flex, and tonight she is her old self again, playing with the cat and dog, her best friends except when she receives more than her share of attention—which tends to bear out Lorenz's theory that real aggression takes place only within the species. My sister believes that because Samantha has not seen another rat for two years, she may be assuming herself to be one of us. Speaking for myself, I hope that she recognizes me as a sinking ship.

April 4. Kingston. I come across a paragraph in Wallace Stevens's letters this morning, dated August 1942, that bumps head-on into my own life. Describing "a visit to the Dutch Church at Kingston . . . one of the most beautiful churches that I know of," the poet says, "The janitor told me that at one time there were nine judges in the congregation . . . and he gave me a pamphlet by one of them . . . Judge Hasbrouck, containing an

1967 article on this particular church. The Judge starts out with this: 'When Spinoza's logic went searching for God, it found him in a predicate of substance. The material thing.' Now, 'the predicate of substance' in this case, was this church: the very building," Stevens says, adding that "if a lawyer as eminent as Judge Hasbrouck went to church because it made it possible for him to touch, to see the very predicate of substance, do you think he was anything except a poet? Another thing that this episode makes clear is that Spinoza's great logic was appreciated only the other day in Kingston."

It was also being read at the same time and place, though I doubt with much appreciation, by me. A consuming interest in Spinoza came over me in my 18th year, though I have no idea why, except perhaps a quest of reasoning power for its own sake. Determined to master his "great logic," I mounted assault after assault on the *Ethics*, only to recoil again and again from some step in the narrowly consecutive argument on which I had stumbled and could not get past. In due course I developed a strongly secular bias that relegated Spinoza's monism to my Index, along with all related claims that the mind of God is reflected in His works and that human notions of evil are only further proofs of God's perfection.

With Stevens's letter in mind, I walk to the Dutch Church, the center of the city even now, as it was of the stockade of 1658. The outlines of the latter are still marked by ridges and glacis, and the 18th-century houses within are rich both in numbers and quality; nor are the few modern buildings with Dutch gables a serious eyesore.

The fastigate steeple is the radial point of the entire valley. Halfway up is a small window in which, after dark, a ghost used to appear to children, for which reason I avoided short-cutting through the churchyard cemetery at night. George Clinton, the first and longest serving Governor of New York, Jefferson's and Madison's Vice-President, is buried under a granite obelisk in this picturesque boneyard, along with many veterans of the War of the Revolution whose graves are marked by iron wreaths stuck like tiepins in the ground in front of their headstones. Civil War graves, grouped around a statue commemorating the 120th Union Regiment, are more numerous. But the most interesting stones are the ones scratched with crossbones-and-skulls and morals in terse verse. According to legend, a system of underground tunnels once connected the church with burial vaults. The thought of this, together with an early reading of *Edwin Drood*, fired my Gothic-novel imagination with ghoulish thoughts of incarceration, and, even now, my claustrophobia may be more literary than real.

The interior of the church could have been a syndics' meeting room in a late-17th-century Dutch town. No cross or other Christian image is exposed in it, and it is Dutch-clean: the walls and ceiling are immaculately white, the floors newly red-carpeted, the pews and their knee-high gates spotlessly upholstered. When no pamphlet-distributing janitor appears, I sit for a moment and involuntarily see myself, aged six, deposited by my mother at my first choir rehearsal,* where the older boys sniff me over as if I were a new dog. In the very effort to banish this memory, I begin to explore it, wondering what I owe to my years as a pre-cracked (vocally speaking) chorister. An ear well-trained in four-part harmony and voice-leading, for one thing, and hence a love of J. S. Bach. Also a morbid concern with death, for the choir was employed at funerals, and imbursed with grand sums (50 cents to a dollar) for singing them, scaled down from the oldest alto bullies to such lowly sopranos as myself. My fellow *decani* regarded the passing of any well-heeled churchman as the greatest good fortune, but I dreaded these occasions and would cry at night long after them, foreseeing my own mother's death. Although supervised while reciting my bedtime prayers, I am certain no one ever suspected the reason for my half-suppressed sobs. The cure for them, in any case, was to have an extra chapter of *Uncle Wiggly* read to me, a fact recently restored to my memory by seeing the word "pipsissewa" in a newspaper and realizing that it is a real flower, which I had not supposed—such being the parlous state of my nursery culture—when hearing the name in *Uncle Wiggly*.

The Holy Communion disturbed me, too, but much later, in my twelfth year, and as a result of conflicts prompted by arguments divulged to me by my older and more enlightened sister, then immersed in "atheist" literature. These tracts, which included H. G. Wells's *Crux Ansata* and Bertrand Russell's *Why I Am Not a Christian*, seemed to dwell on the barbarity of the theophagous impanation ritual ("This is my body. . . . Take ye and eat"), so that when finally receiving the Eucharist itself, I felt profoundly deceived. The perfumed sweet wine ("my blood. . . . Drink ye") and the pasty wafer, shaped like money and served on a ciborium that looked like a collection plate, cheapened and degraded the symbolism, while the prayer, "Jesus Christ our only mediator and advocate," made Him sound like a union boss.

But I have not come to the Dutch Church looking for memories. What *would* interest me is an encounter with my younger self as an object, a meeting that could be brought about only by the discovery of my childhood poems, letters, and musical compositions. With this material in hand I would avoid the error of most autobiographers, which is in forgiving themselves.

Dutch names—Neukirk, Swarthout, Van Deusen, Tenbrouck—are inscribed on rosters in the entranceway. Encased there, too, are the colors of the 120th Union Regiment, and a letter from General Washington thanking the city for its hospitality to him in November 1772.

May 17. Toronto. Our Massey Hall concert, *Oedipus* with Marilyn Horne, I.S. conducting *Pulcinella*. Leaving the hotel, we pass a crowd come to stare at Princess Alexandra. No one in the gathering can be aware that

---

* Not at this church, but at St. John's Episcopal.

the unscheduled parade of the little old man is a far rarer sight than the one they are waiting for, creative geniuses being so much harder to come by than merely well-born ladies.

Backstage, answering a question about the "wooden Indian" staging concept of *Oedipus*, I.S. says that it is not very different from his earlier works with voice. "The singers are in the pit, the dancers on the stage, in *Renard*, *Noces*, *Pulcinella*, and the title part in *Nightingale* should be performed in the same way. The music is more important than the action, just as the words were more important than the action in Shakespeare."

For the first time in his life, I.S. conducts sitting down, though this probably gives him more trouble than he avoids by not standing. He *is* unsteady on his feet, however, and, in spite of the chair, grips the podium railing with his left hand during much of the performance. Remembering how vigorously he conducted in Chicago five months ago, V. is alarmed. Worse still, as she can plainly see, the orchestra is not really following him but the tempi of my rehearsals of the piece. At the start of the "Tarantella," about half of the players interpret his first gesture as a 1-beat, the other half as a 2-beat, which results in about 10 measures of excruciating "augmentation," after which the playing thins out almost to the point of stopping completely.

The performance over, I.S. moves to a chair at the front of the stage, averts his eyes from triple-pronged TV exposure, and listens to accolades in both French and English by dignitaries who then bemedal him. This ceremony affects him, too, as it would not have done a year ago, when he probably would have been contemptuous of it, and of the special warmth of the audience, whose applause has distinctly said: "This is obviously the last time." As I know him, I.S. is more conscious of this than anyone.

In the greenroom afterward he tells one of the medal-conferers that he suffered an "occlusion" two months ago, adding that "my blood is like puree." The remark startles us because until this instant he has betrayed no sign of suspicion that a stroke is what might have occurred. I am unable to sleep after the concert, seeing the I.S. of the past, as if on one side of a divided movie screen, skipping across the stage to the podium, his movements twice as fast as anyone else's, and in this, as in everything he did, leaving everyone around him far behind; and on the other side, I.S. tonight, old, frail, halting, and, I fear, conducting in public for the last time. What makes it all the more disturbing is his super self-awareness. A long decline and withering away would be a great cruelty to him.

May 24. To New York. I.S.'s physician, Dr. Lewithin, says that he is amazed by the findings of the electroencephalogram. I.S.'s responses are as rapid as if in a man of 30. Nor is there any sign of senility, of the brain softening that is 3normal in a man his age, or any onset of brain sclerosis; but then, I.S. lives entirely in his brain. He is greatly interested in the encephalogram himself, comparing it to "an electronic score with unreadable avant-garde notation," and adding that the 18 electrodes attached to his head made him look like a bald woman trying to scare up a mane of hair.

At the same time, Lewithin warns, the composer's body is a ruin. The blood-lettings and three Roentgen-ray treatments scheduled for the week are a matter of life and death, which I.S. not only knows but is already processing and overcoming in his powerful psychological machinery. Armed with an understanding of the apprehensible biochemical data, he will begin to "think positively," harnessing his formidable "esemplastic will" to the favorable factors and ignoring the unfavorable. A more difficult enemy to subdue is another part of the same mind, the intelligence which has not aged with the body and remains so ruthlessly aware of it.

May 25. Attending to a medical problem of my own, I go for kidney X-raying, the first stage of which is a two-hour wait in a room permanently piped with very loud "pop." Served up to the photographing eye semi-naked on a freezing platter, I am interrogated about my susceptibilities to sodium injections, and advised, now that it is too late to retreat, that "some people become violently ill." In the event, the injection, in the median cephalin vein, is followed by cramps, tumescence, hot flashes, vesical burning, and a tidal wave of nausea. (Psychologists would classify me as an "augmenter" rather than a "reducer," but I do not see how that helps.) At this point the radiologist warns me that the slightest movement, let alone retching, during the next 30 minutes will spoil the test and oblige me to start over, with three ounces of castor oil. I "endure," of course, and an hour later learn that I have prostatic calculi and must take up a regime of Eau de Vittel.

Still feeling radioactive, I take in the Royal Ballet's *Romeo and Juliet* at the Met, though the more arresting spectacle is the Met itself. The whole ensemble—lowest-bidder architecture, sculptured plaza, Chagalled foyer, retractable chandeliers—might have been intended for an Eastern European People's Republic, then sold to the capitalists by some sharp Ministry of Culture *apparatchik* who saw what had gone wrong. Yet Eastern Europe is where the two principal ingredients of the ballet, Prokofiev's music and Nureyev's charm, come from. In fact, Nureyev's broad Bashkir Tartar face contrasts no less radically to the pinched Anglo-Saxon features of his fellow dancers than to his other attractions (*Chacun à son goût*), the muscle-bound buttocks and steel-thewed thighs. In contrast, the bosoms and bottoms of Juliet and her attendant goslings are concealed by floor-length skirts.

Act One offers two opportunities for musical depth, Juliet's return to the deserted ballroom and the balcony scene. Prokofiev makes nothing of either, merely substituting loudness for intensity of feeling, as if "passion" and "full orchestra" were synonymous. The music accompanying Romeo's approach to the balcony is so over-agitated, moreover, that it momentarily

1967 casts the hero as the villain. And, finally, Prokofiev cannot perorate, but only repeat. But I should have said in the first place that the play is poor material for ballet, pantomime a poor exchange for poetry. And the choreographer seems to agree, at least in those far-from-rare instances where the dancers stand about gesturing like singers whose sound systems have gone dead.

June 2. Hollywood. As Stendhal says, *"Une partie de la biographie des grands hommes devrait être fournie par leurs médecins."* Item: I.S. opens and confiscates his doctors' reports of their examinations, though they are addressed to V. and not intended for his eyes. But no harm is done. On May 24, Dr. Donald Simons found him "very alert, bright. . . . An electroencephalogram was made in my office. It reveals a normal, well-formed 9/sec alpha pattern. There was no trace of any abnormality in the left central-parietal. There was no evidence of the slowing of the frequencies which is commonly found in elderly people. . . . The patient stated that he has some difficulty in comprehending women's voices, but he was able to hear fingers rubbing at twelve inches, which is much better than most people at his age can do. . . . When asked to multiply 7 by 11, he gave the answer as 77 and said there was 23 left over." (Looking for a point to the question?) "He admits to getting angry at least once a day"—I like that "at least"—and "he has an alert intellect." This leaves the patient feeling conceited. A letter in the same mail from Dr. La Due addressed *to* I.S. remarks on his "voracious consumption of books" and reassures him that "no impairment whatsoever to your mental faculties has occurred."

June 16. At the Hotel del Coronado, Coronado Beach, the receptionist asks, "Are you Mr. Stokowski, the conductor?" I.S. nods affirmatively but is less amused later seeing his real name in a letter from Public Relations asking whether he would mind being photographed. The hotel, venerated locally as ancient, is 10 years younger than I.S. It might have come from another country, as well, but which one would be hard to determine. It sets out to be tropical and overdoes it. And colonial-oriental, though I may be over-ascribing this side of it because of prior knowledge that Chinese coolies comprised the original construction force. Still, the window ventilators, transoms, verandahs, balconies, wicker furniture, valentine-lace panels, and tinderbox whole remind me of the Repulse Bay Hotel in Hong Kong, except that the airplane-propeller ceiling fans are missing. The pavilion tower reminds the S.s of a Russian cupola, and, in its general shape and dark red shingles, of a stave church as well. The religion urged on the congregation inside, however, is from Utah; each dressing table is furnished with a copy of *The Book of Mormon.*

And what a congregation! "Ex-passengers from the *Queen Mary,*" I.S. says. And the Coronado *is* spinsterish, prudish, dead-as-Lugano, and as sad as all old-fashioned resorts. A creaky mahogany and dark-oak corridor leads to an elevator cage, then to a kind of Crystal Palace dining room in which a dozen or so occupied tables are huddled to one end against the gloom of two hundred or so unoccupied ones. Mammoth coronado-shaped chandeliers are suspended from the high, woven-basket ceiling, but they shed precious little light. Whether because of the inhibiting empti-ness of the room or the annoying sobriety of the other diners, we drink too much and become too loudly effervescent.

June 18. Writing from the Coronado in April 1905, Henry James com-plained of having been kept awake by the "languid list of the Pacific." The rumble of waves curveting on the rocks opposite my window keeps me awake.

The beach is wide, the sand very fine and soft, though only apparently white: our footsoles are tarred after a few steps. During low or eddying tides, the shore is a congeries of vegetation from "the ooze and bottom of the sea": clumps of kelp and amber algae; chains of seaweed with spiculed, fin-shaped leaves; a plant, from some fantastic underwater garden, with a snout-of-an-oil-can proboscis. Jellyfish, purple-veined blobs of glycerine shaped like the human pancreas and looking like *tête-de-veau*, quiver in the sand, along with amputated jellyfish tentacles, like soft icicles. We uncov-er a dead gull, claws up as if to fight off an enemy; and a dead skate, cuneal wings partly buried in the sand. V. extends her camera over these birds as if it were a Geiger counter and as if she feared their spirits. Live, all too live, are the beetle-size beach crabs that Japanese fishermen gather for bait, meanwhile leaving tall fishing poles and piles of gasping perch untended in the dunes. (Auden used to compare himself to a beach crab—Talitrus—saying that they both knew when it was mealtime not by hunger but by the time of day.) In mid-afternoon, scores of tentlike sails appear, tipping and careening in the wind. An airplane begins to skywrite, scraping a white path on the blue background like a figure skater; but the wind strengthens, the aerial chalk blurs, and the drifting bits of alphabet are soon indistinguishable from natural clouds.

I.S.'s birthday party is launched with a bottle of Stolychnaya and docked with a cake baked by his daughter, who brings it into the room parading with V., who carries a tray with 85 lighted candles. When we sing "Happy Birthday," I.S. makes a remark about *"son et lumière."* But he says little else, and to read his feelings is not easy.

After he cuts the cake, we open some of the four hundred cables and telegrams that have been piling up from all over the world. Whereas the President of Germany has wired a two-page homage, no word has come from any public official in America, where "the poor procession without music goes." Nor has any message come from the Mayor of that despoil-ing of the desert in which I.S. has lived for 27 years. The only acknowl-edgment of the anniversary in his home community was the concert by the Beverly Hills Symphony, conducted by both of us four months ago at greatly reduced fees not yet received. So, let the record stand. While the

1967 composer's 85th birthday is being celebrated all over the world by entire festivals and countless individual concerts, performances, and publications, no organization in the vale of smog-induced tears that *he* has long honored by his residence has dedicated a single program to the event. Not the local Philharmonic, it goes without saying, but also not the Ojai Festivals, which were pleased to have him at a fraction of his normal fee at a time when they needed his name but which had been distracted this year by the glare of momentarily more expensive, if in the long run much cheaper, attractions. In fact, the *art* critic of the *Los Angeles Times*, Henry Seldes, alone recognized the necessity, for Los Angeles' sake, of a concert and attempted to organize one months before the date, but the Musicians' Union refused on grounds that it would "set a precedent." A precedent for whom? Is a proliferation of Stravinskys imminent? In Los Angeles?

As V. unwraps gifts that have accumulated during the past weeks, identifying the senders for I.S., I cannot help thinking of how utterly lost he would be without her and hope for his sake that it is destined to be the other way around. She translates bits of talk for him that he fails to catch and supplies quick Russian synopses of American jokes. To be with her for even a few minutes, he will walk to, and even brave the terebinthine fumes inside, her studio. She is kinder and more patient with him each ever-more-difficult day, and she has lately begun to take him with her to the supermarket because he can hold on to the cart, instead of his cane, and even push it, thus feeling useful to her.

The emotional strain of the birthday must be very great, and some of the messages, especially from old friends who broke down and said the things old friends want to but seldom do say, must have moved him; a letter from Nadia Boulanger, for example, was transparently about death. I.S. was never one to brood over the certitudes of insurance companies, nor has he betrayed any sign of dotardly sentiment concerning his age today. Still, I will be happy to see him more combative again, for which reason his answer to a well-wisher's question whether he would like to live to the same age (111) as his great-grandfather—"No, taxes are too high now"—is reassuring; and we are greatly relieved when, after the party, he says he is in a hurry to be rid of the birthday and resume composing.

July 15. Hollywood. Nureyev and Fonteyn come for aperitifs, directly from a rehearsal, which partly explains Nureyev's get-up: white tennis shorts, white sweater, white sandals. From the front he may be "faun-like," as claimed, but seeing the back of his head first, with the long shaggy hair, one could easily mistake him for a tousled woman. So far from resembling the thrasonical exhibitionist of the copywriters, he is more gracious and gentle with I.S. than almost anyone I can remember. His first words are: "This is a very great honor for me and I only hope I am not taking your time."

"I learned a great deal from Bronislava Nijinska's revival of *Noces*," he

456

says. When the S.s, in turn, talk about their experiences in the USSR, he is clearly uneasy, and when V. quotes Nancy Mitford on the "clean feeling in the Soviet Union that money doesn't matter," he breaks in with: "Of course it doesn't. There is nothing to buy: no houses, no automobiles, no edible food." He speaks gratefully of Madame Furtseva, and of her "discovery" of him during a Kirov Ballet season in Paris. "She pointed to me at a reception for the dancers one afternoon and told one of her minions, 'Next time this one will dance the solo.' But we were quartered in a very poor hotel near the Place de la Bastille and never saw anything of Paris. One day I learned how to use the Metro and took it to the Champs-Elysées. Suddenly Paris seemed the most wonderful place on earth, and while walking from there to the Seine, I resolved not to leave. Tell me, why are Russian emigrés, in Paris, California, and everywhere else so nostalgic for a Russia most of them have never seen?" V. suggests that part of the answer is in Russian literature, and it is true that many of the refugees she knows are walled up in a world of Russian books and have never even learned the local language. Nureyev's rejoinder is, "A refugee should live according to the way of life in the country of his adoption." Just as *he* lives?

Next to I.S., as thin and shrunken as Mahatma Gandhi, Nureyev is almost impertinently healthy-looking. Entering the room, he identifies a postcard-size Klimt, and he continues to study the art objects on tables and walls, glancing back and forth from them to I.S., as if trying to crack the "object language" of the house (people being implied by their possessions, after all), which, as he must see, is simply I.S.'s obsession with the minuscule.

Dame Margot, lissome and lovely, describing her arrest in San Francisco a few days ago on suspicion of possessing marijuana, says that she was searched skin-deep by a jailoress who had been to all her performances and claimed to "idolize" her.

After trying to avoid the visit, I.S. was especially lively during it, partly because of a hint from V. that his state of health is a subject of rumor nowadays, a consideration that apparently had not occurred to him before.

In the evening we listen to Fischer-Dieskau recordings of parts of *Dichterliebe* and the Opus 39 *Liederkreis*, as well as a batch of Brahms *Lieder* and Wolf's *Spanisches Liederbuch*. I.S.'s fingers play along with the piano in the Schumann songs, one of which, "*Am leuchtenden Sommermorgen*," he asks to hear three times. He also cues vocal entrances, flips pages back in search of details and points of comparison, and two or three times turns ahead impatiently to the next song. His highest expression of approval is a staccato grunt, but the same kind of noise turns into a groan when something displeases him or is *too* beautiful, "Beautiful, but not for me." Brahms, on the whole, wearies him: "There are too many *Regenlieder*, and compared with Schumann it is formalism; what I admire in Brahms is his knowledge, which isn't quite the right thing." But he likes "*Herbstgefühl*," "*Du sprichst*," the

1967 third of the *Ernste Gesänge*, and of the Wolf songs falls heavily for *"Herr, was trägt der Boden hier."**

July 24. Santa Fe. Dress rehearsal of *Cardillac*. The general weaknesses of the work are set forth at unnecessary length in the rhythmically square, block-like overture, which all too perfectly matches the pedestrian pace of the ideas, a relentless flow of notes, rather than of invention, expended, hit or miss, like flak. The orchestration emphasizes the overweight in the stern, the tuba playing as continuously as the flute, with nearly every other line doubled, octavized and double-octavized.

The opera could be presented to greater advantage by treating the first act as a masque: the plot and characters are self-contained, and, figuratively speaking, the action takes place before the curtain, as in the *Ariadne* Prologue. The other acts could then stand as two equally balanced scenes, which would help to concentrate the evening, as well as to justify Cardillac's own peculiar musico-dramatic position in not singing until—as it is now—the second act. The restriction of singing to Cardillac alone during the royal visit to his workshop, while the others move in dumb-show, is the opera's one theatrically effective device.

Hindemith seems not to have trusted voices, that or his ability to write for them. Thus the aria of Cardillac's daughter is an instrumental piece primarily, a trio-concerto, and the instrumental frame is awkwardly large. The duet between Cardillac and the Gold Merchant contains the best instrumental idea in the score, the trio for violin, viola, and piano.

July 26. Tonight, in prickly heat and heat lightning, I conduct the American premiere of the original version of *Cardillac*. And tonight, anyway, my feelings are that Hindemith's goldsmith opera, at its rare best, is not an unalloyed disaster, and this in spite of the composer's lack of aptitude for the theater, and in spite of many patches of really wretched music (villainous muted brass, etc.) and umpteen patches of indifferent, banausic music (fugal exercises not only conveying no message bearing on the dramatic action but also seeming to belong to another opus entirely, as if some packer at the factory had mixed up the parts). Surprisingly, some sections of the work are stage-worthy, even though, except for Cardillac, the cast is made up of mannequins unbreathed on by any form of life, and though Cardillac himself, after his metallurgical recitative with the Gold Merchant, declines into crazy Cellini, the mad-genius inventor of the comic strips. The saving grace, if any, is that the subject has inspired

---

* In a single afternoon, May 15, 1968, in San Francisco, Stravinsky arranged the piano part of this song, along with that of *"Wunden trägst du mein Geliebter,"* for three clarinets, two horns, and solo string quintet. One of his reasons for the transcription, so he said at the time, was that "Wolf used octaves only for more sound. He had an ear and a sense of invention but very little technique." Another reason, not said, was that Stravinsky wanted to say something about death and felt that he could not compose anything of his own.

Hindemith—no mean feat—into surpassing himself at times, his routine self running after, if rarely catching up to, his inspired self, and in one scene even trying to scale a peak (blowing into his hands to stave off frostbite). The performance goes smoothly, except that the offstage conductor has an attack of offstage fright.

July 27. During breakfast, a telephone call brings the shocking news of an unscheduled Wagnerian finale: a fire, starting at about 3 A.M., has burned the stage and auditorium to the ground, incinerating not only the *Cardillac* sets, costumes, and orchestra parts, but also the cellos, basses, harp, and everything combustible that had been left in the theater area, which is now a sickening prospect of ashes and charred remains. Fly to Los Angeles.

Seeing the S.s again after even a short separation moves me nowadays almost more than I can bear. They are the most marvelous people in the world, the last survivors of a bigger and better humanity, a whole continent in themselves. But they are so old and creaky and fragile now, and so terribly alone. They know the hour of my flight and when to expect me; if I am late they will go to the window again and again and play their rounds of solitaire more anxiously. When I do arrive, the sight of them in the doorway, to which they come at the sound of my taxi, is heartbreaking. They seem desperately out of place, the more so after the ride through the junkyard and *dreck* of Los Angeles, as well as out of time. When away, I tend to think of them as they were in the past, and coming up Wetherly Drive, I picture my arrival in 1948, I.S., as always thereafter, bestowing a wet, messy lips-to-lips kiss, V. loosely embracing me and smooching the air behind my head, left, right, left. To see them after an interval is a sudden acute reminder of age, a reminder full of the pain of impending loss. I simply cannot accept their passing as natural, as I have had no insurmountable trouble doing in other cases; to me, I.S. is part of the order of nature. Dinner with them tonight is sad, all the sadder because they are so happy to see me.

August 15. To New York to complete my Gesualdo recording, overdub the singer in *Abraham and Isaac,* and record *The Owl and the Pussy-Cat.*

August 21. An alarming call from V. during my recording session tonight: I.S. has a bleeding ulcer, has in fact lost more than half of his blood, and is in Cedars of Lebanon Hospital. I arrange to fly back immediately.

September 13. Hollywood. The 14 days in the hospital and 9 subsequent days in bed at home have weakened I.S. critically. He has lost 18 pounds, one wonders from where, since he was already so thin. Nor can he regain much weight on his frugal diet. His rib cage reminds us of photographs of Buchenwald, and he complains that every nerve ending in his skin-and-bones body is raw and painful. His hematocrit stands at only 35, whereas the platelets have risen to 1,200,000, meaning that the one com-

1967 ponent is anemic, the other too rich; and, to complicate matters further, the indicated medicine for each is counter-indicated for the other. The uremic acid level is high as well, and each finger of his left hand throbs like a toothache, supposedly from gout. Worst of all, and unspeakably depressing to observe, is the defeat, I pray only temporary, of his powerful will. He does not even read today, and when I switch on the television for him to watch his favorite African animal program, he refuses to turn toward the screen, saying, "I only like to look at it in Vera's room." He tells V. that he saw his birth certificate in a dream last night and "it was very yellow."

V. has draped a towel, with a print of a cat on it, over the couch in his room, as if to represent her in absentia, though she is seldom absent any more. How fitting, if it is so destined, that his last creations should be a statement of his religious beliefs, and that a Requiem, and then a personal postlude for the human being who has meant most in his life.

September 25. A marked upturn today, the symptom of which is an old-time tantrum over some of the contents of the mail: a fulsome fan letter; an application form for a self-paying *Who's Who*; a request to fill in a sexual questionnaire (he is regularly circularized for this); a tape of a "ballad composed on a harmonica by an airline pilot during flight," herewith submitted for I.S.'s opinion, which is: "I would be afraid to fly again." Reaching for a Kleenex and finding it to be the last in the container, he angrily flings the empty box to the floor. V. gently admonishes him, as one would a small child, telling him that the box will probably have to remain where it is until a pile accumulates, "Then perhaps the thrower will realize that we have no one to pick up such things."

The bedside night table holds an array of pens, music pads, pliers, secateurs, the Fabergé gold clock that Alexander II gave to and inscribed for I.S.'s father; and the small gold cross and silver roundel of the Virgin that I.S. has worn around his neck since his baptism.* Books, dictionaries, boxes of man-size Kleenex are stacked on the floor around the bed. To remind him to drink water, V. has written "H_2O" on a dozen sheets of paper and taped them to the walls, furniture, and even to the wastebasket with the Tchaikovsky photograph on one side. V.'s Russian translations of medicine schedules are attached both to the head of the bedstead and to a dressing table otherwise crowded with trays, thermos bottles, glasses, and cartons of milk with Mickey Mouse straws in them, packages of crackers, paper cups for quarter-hourly doses of Gelusil, plastic and glass medicine vials. I.S. keeps his own pharmaceutical inventory and his own records of medicines consumed, entering this information in a red diary, an extraordinary chronicle that sometimes takes note even of a cough or sneeze. On better days, prescriptions are spelled out in full and reactions elaborated in detail. On worse ones, the identification is brief: "Took one *foncée* capsule

---

* These were buried with him.

460

at 2:30, two white ones at 3:45."

He sits up during most of the afternoon today, telling me with some of his old zest that the Japanese ideogram for noise is the ideogram for woman repeated three times. (He has learned this during a drive with Hideki, who is so small that, at first glance, other drivers do not see anyone behind the wheel at all.) He also talks about Gorky's *Mother*: "I read it when it was first published and am trying it again now, probably because I want to go back into myself. But it is not good. Gorky is not the 'big' writer I had hoped he might be, the writer that Tolstoy is, even at his worst. Gorky's indifference to 'style' would be acceptable only if he had invented something to replace it. And surely it is more important to show what one likes than what one dislikes." The comparison with Tolstoy brings to mind Gorky's remark about his great predecessor, and which exactly describes my own feelings about I.S.: "I am not an orphan on the earth as long as this man lives on it."

George Balanchine for dinner, snorting and sniffing as if from hay fever, twitching as if he might have caught the *tic douloureux*. He is dressed in check pants, silver-buckle shoes, double-breasted blazer with gold buttons, sideburns to the ear lobes. On arrival, he goes to the basement music room and puts in a half-hour of piano practice. At table, describing the *Salomé* ballet now planned for Suzanne Farrell, he uses mudra-like movements, and asks me to choose music for it by Berg; but *Reigen*, the only possibility I can think of, is too large orchestrally, and, like the Variations and Adagio from *Lulu*, which he has also been considering, too brooding in character and too explicit dramatically. I wonder if Balanchine's inspiration has been kindled in any degree by the circumstance that nowadays the seven-veil striptease, like that of Astarte-Istar, would inevitably conclude in a complete disrobing, and the dance would be able to show Salomé, like the Queen in *Alice*—"Off with his head!"—wanting a different part of the victim's anatomy than the one she gets. Herod, too, would be revealed today as the archetypal Humbert Humbert, marrying the mother for the daughter (the Baron de Charlus buttering up Mme de Surgis because of her sons).

Mr. B. wants I.S.'s new piece, whatever it is, and in reply to the composer's damper that very little is finished, says he would settle for even two minutes of music because "they are bound to be an atomic pill." Showing *The Owl and the Pussy-Cat* score to Mr. B., I.S. says that the song "should be impersonated: a little hooted, a little meowed, a little grunted for the pig." Just before leaving, Mr. B. asks a number of questions about *Russlan*, which he will direct in Hamburg. He still looks to I.S. for ideas—as well he might, considering that some of the most successful ballets (*e.g.*, the Bizet Symphony) began from suggestions by him.

When Mr. B. first entered the room, I.S., very self-conscious about his weight, said: "Like all Americans, I am reducing."

1967   October 8. At about 4 P.M. I.S. complains of a chill, and his teeth, as he says, begin to *"klappen."* By 5 his temperature is 101, which in his weakened state is alarming. He can hardly navigate across the room now, and his shoulders and torso are as fleshless as a coat hanger; pneumonia, though his lungs are clear, or influenza, could kill him. The fulminant pains he complains of are abdominal. When I ask him to describe them, he sits bolt upright and says "FEAR." Soon after this he begins to urinate every few minutes, which could indicate an infection from the bladder crystals formed by the high uric acid.

Reentering the room at 7 I find him praying, *"Gospodi, Gospodi,"* over and over, with his head turned to the wall. At long length (it is Sunday) a doctor arrives and prescribes Gantrisin. At the beginning of the examination, I.S.'s pulse is very fast, but as soon as he is convinced that a bladder infection is the true complaint, the rate drops to normal, and the temperature to a bit below; he has had a death scare and was as frightened of pneumonia or flu as we were. All night, says V., who spends it on a couch at the foot of his bed, he twists, turns, fumbles with the sheets trying to make a nest but is unable to forget the specter.

That a man's life has been rich, long, and perfectly fulfilled does not make him any readier to leave it; the contrary, rather, and the more so in I.S.'s case because of his and our knowledge that there is more of it in him. Nor does "naturalness" enter into consideration, except from afar, where the termination of a life of 65 years of continual creation must seem more just than the savage extinction of wholly unfulfilled young lives in a senseless war. But what may seem the most natural of events at a distance can be the most unnatural at close range. Death, at any age and in any circumstances, is immeasurable loss; but if I even *try* to measure the loss of I.S., it comes to something very like life itself. And though it may be special pleading, future joy can be the consequence of his continuing existence, whereas so many other existences only compound the general misery, a thought that affords neither compensation nor consolation.

> . . . blown husk that is finished
> But the light sings eternal. . . .

But the light eternal hardly matters now, only the life which I pray will go on in that—well, I.S. is still far from a husk.

I realize that I have hidden my true feelings for him in recent years precisely because of this dread. Yesterday evening those feelings came irrepressibly flooding out in an extraordinarily clear hour during which he talked with me and discussed his ideas in the way it used to be between us years ago. I understood that he has no thoughts of *not* going on. But of course he *can* go on only in that undamaged and undaunted mind of his; and this is the tragedy. Ever since I have known them, I.S. and V. have

July 1948. At the Stravinsky home, 1260 North Wetherly Drive, Hollywood.

March 22, 1949. Drawing by Stravinsky of a desert landscape and its reflection, from a letter to the author.

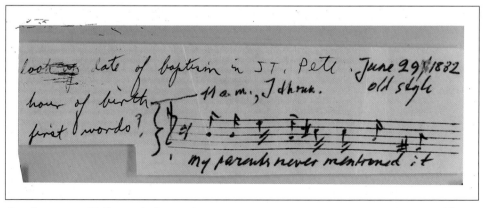

1260 N. WETHERLY DRIVE
HOLLYWOOD 46, CALIFORNIA

October 7/49

Dearest Bobsky,

        Today just this:
By now you must have received the PRIBAOUTKI materiel I sent you one week ago via B. & H. Please, acknowledge!

        Paul Sacher (of Basel) was here the other day – on his way (from Mexico) to New York. He will be there on October 10th at the Ambassador Hotel. I promised him to write you – he wanted so much to get in touch with you and to come at your concert. He leaves New York on October 26th.

        Let us heare from you very soon

October 7, 1949. A letter from Stravinsky.

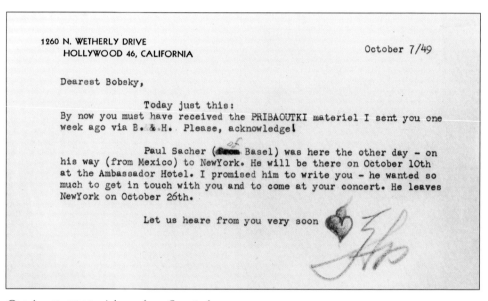

October 1960. Hollywood. Stravinsky's answer, "My parents never mentioned it" (from *The Rake's Progress*), to the author's questions about the hour of his birth and date of baptism.

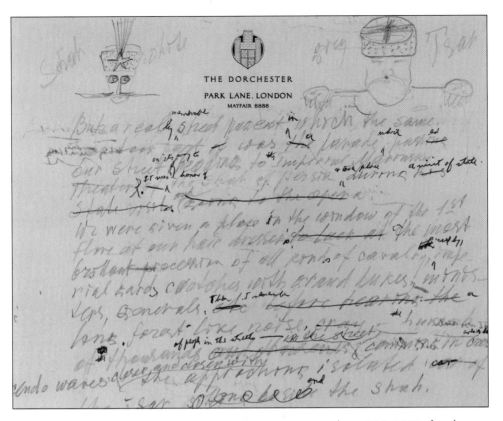

THE DORCHESTER

PARK LANE, LONDON
MAYFAIR 8888

August 11, 1957. London. Stravinsky's illustrations for his recollections of Tsar Alexander III and the Shah of Persia during a visit by the latter to St. Petersburg. The text, with the author's changes, appears in *Conversations with Igor Stravinsky* (Doubleday, 1959, p. 92).

October 20, 1960. Venice. Cartoon collage by Vera Stravinsky.

Photo by Robert Cato (CBS)

August 26, 1964. New York.

December 18, 1969. New York. Stravinsky, hand to head, is at the opposite end of the table from W. H. Auden (ditto). Vera Stravinsky is seated at the poet's left. George Balanchine, the author, and Lincoln Kirstein are seated at the composer's left.

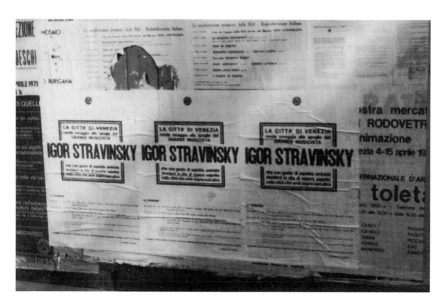

April 13, 1971. Wall in Venice.

April 15, 1971. Venice. Stravinsky's funeral at the Church of Saints John and Paul.

Stravinsky's funeral. The recessional.

The water hearse.

August 1981.
Mohonk, New York.
Vera Stravinsky and
the author.

May 1982. Pompano Beach, Florida. Vera Stravinsky.

kissed each other at first sight of the new moon, a promise of renewal. The moon is new tonight, but they do not see it.

October 28. I.S. is keen and alert with Suvchinsky, as he has been since his arrival yesterday. We listen to *Noces* together, and, after I.S. goes to bed, to the *Canticles*. "The Postlude, Suvchinsky says, is one of those endings, like that of *Noces*, which do not end, or end in infinity. And here Stravinsky has added a dimension to Western music beyond the classical composers. For comparison, think of the ending of a Beethoven or Brahms symphony, which simply thumps more loudly with each repeat."

Suvchinsky contends that a neurosis is at the root of I.S.'s passion for order, and, just having read a study on "Religious Order and Mental Disorder in a South Wales Rural Community" (in *Social Anthropology of Complex Societies*), I agree. Suvchinsky argues, too, that I.S.'s Russian background constituted a greater handicap to his development as a composer than the misunderstanding and opposition that were Schoenberg's fate. "If you had seen what he came from in Russia, in both the family and musical senses, you would believe in genius." (I already do.) "Stravinsky's creative psychology, that of a 'walled-in' artist, was fully formed by the time of *Firebird*, and it never veered in any essential thereafter. Obviously he neither invented nor followed any doctrine of 'neo-classicism,' but simply made music out of whatever came to hand. Which was all he *could* do, given the limitations of the tradition from which he sprang. But it is high time that the Diaghilev myth was exploded. So far from discovering Stravinsky, Diaghilev never really understood how big Stravinsky's genius was." And Suvchinsky repeats I.S.'s story about Diaghilev's reaction to the ending of *Petrushka*: "'But you finish with a question?'" "Well," I.S. used to say, "at least he understood that much." But this is unfair to Diaghilev.

November 2. I.S.'s "gouty" left hand has suddenly turned black. A new team of doctors, in consultation early this morning, attributes the discoloration to circulatory blockage from a sludge of platelets, a rate of some 2,000,000 at last count, which is 10 times normal. The finger pains of the past eight weeks were caused not by gout, in other words, but by circulatory failure, and all the anti-gout medicines he had been taking were not merely powerless to relieve the hand but were dangerous for the ulcer. The discovery is infuriating. Why were a competent vascular cardiologist and a gout specialist not called in two months ago, as soon as the colchicin and the wonder-drug anti-gout medications failed to alleviate the pain? And is sudden gout even a remotely reasonable prognosis for a man of I.S.'s build, temperament, and lifelong habits? How, furthermore, could four doctors, whom I would not now trust with a hangnail, accept the gout theory of the fifth while overlooking the possibility of circulatory blockage, and this in a man who has had polycythemia for 12 years and whose platelet count stands at 2,000,000? A miracle of modern medicine, indeed.

To try to dilate the coagulated capillaries, a decision is made to block

1967 the nerve with Novocain injections. Since this entails risks in a man of I.S.'s age, he must go to the hospital. Choking with tears and fears, I pack his bag and take him to Mount Sinai in the early afternoon, practically carrying him from his room to the car, for he is heavily drugged and scarcely able to walk.

The injection is postponed until 7 o'clock, pending a second consilium with a second vascular cardiologist. When we return to the hospital at 11, the fingers are even more horribly black: gangrene is mentioned, and the gruesome possibility of amputation, and we are further warned of the danger of pneumonia, the patient having been so long in bed. I drive V. home, then go home myself, but I cannot pass I.S.'s studio and bedroom or look at his dark window from my room or, of course, sleep. Going to bed, I use my childhood prayers.

November 3. The color of the finger has improved slightly since the third Novocain injection, but the hand is still gangrenous. Sick as he is, and despite the haze of pain-killing sedations, I.S. shines like a beacon, replying precisely, ironically, originally, I.S.-ishly to his doctors' forensic inquisition, replying to them, moreover, in English and German, to me in French, and to V. in Russian, without once mixing or confusing the languages or fumbling for words. One of the new neurosurgeons asks if he dreams under the drugs, and his answer, to our great relief, is that he does and that the dreams are "good"; he was always a hyperactive, total-recall dreamer. When the doctors leave the room for a consultation, he drops his voice to a whisper to ask V. if she has been painting, apparently having no sense of his own volume, except that at the same time he overhears *our* whispers through the pall of the drugs.

His extreme fastidiousness is giving him no end of trouble. He insists on staying in the *gabinetto* unaided and on brushing his teeth unseen, charging me to explain to a voluble nurse that he does not mean to be rude but is unable to converse with her. To me he says, "I can offer you nothing here but ennuis." As I leave, the nurse, no doubt annoyed by my anxieties and imperfectly stifled feelings, follows me into the corridor with the advice that "it is a mistake to get too involved." Is "involving" oneself a matter of choice, then, and would a noninvolved life be worth anything?

November 4. The nerve will not be blocked today, the index finger being slightly less black this morning, and the palm of the hand a little rosier. Because the amelioration is in some degree ascribed to a trickle of alcohol in the intravenous fluid, a decision is reached that I.S. should be allowed to *taste* the stuff, if it *can* be tasted through all the lactation he would have to swallow before and after. He is to receive three half-jiggers of Scotch, at wide intervals, blended to obliteration with milk. The prescription provokes a flap among the floor nurses, who say that this is the first time "drink" has been administered in the hospital in the social sense.

I.S. is untrusting. Nor will he take my word for the contents of the bottle, until I uncork and hold it to his nose, after which we can almost see his olfactory bulb turning on. What follows is a Finnegans Wake. He sits up—as if from smelling salts after a dead faint—and his eyes widen with each inward waft. To prove that we are not misleading him with a stratagem of flavoring or perfume, I play Petronius and sample the liquid in front of his eyes. The head nurse then fills a paper cup to the halfway mark, inserts a straw, holds it to his mouth. Drugged to the bones as he is with codeine, Darvon, Demerol, I.S. nevertheless protests the miserable dram— "Half?"—then, resigning himself, throws out the straw, and with inimitable panache touches the paper cup to mine. Whereas he has slowly and torturously sipped his milk and medicines these three months, the whiskey is downed in one gulp. A smile spreads over his face, and we quote Goethe to him on the beginning of the French Revolution: "From today forward, a new chapter in the history of mankind." In fact the whiskey, strongly opposed by the gastroenterologist, is a desperate expedient, the last trick up one of those white surgical sleeves.

November 5. The left index finger is still blue-black today, but the others are normal, and the nacreous, color-of-death streaks in the palm of the hand have disappeared. I.S. insists that all the fingers hurt, adding, characteristically, "Each pain has its own manner." No less characteristic is his response to a doctor who asks if he can endure the pains from three to five minutes longer without more codeine. Out of a profound stupor—his eyes roll like ball bearings when he first tries to open them—but also out of a fathomless vitality comes the accepted challenge: "Five minutes."

Returning to the hospital in the afternoon, I spoon-feed him and hold his bad hand: he says the warmth diminishes the pain. Because he is naturally affectionate but also a deeply lonely man, feeling now pours out of him. And not a little of it pours into me, for we are very close now, as we were in our first years together. He asks me to sit by him all the time, and will allow me to leave only if I promise to return immediately. This directness of feeling, which each of us in other circumstances would be the first to flee, makes it difficult to control my not abnormally suffusion-prone eyes. It is the power of creation in him that always fascinated me, yet the threatened extinguishing of this power is not my uppermost concern today, but the impending loss of the human being to whom I have been closer than to anyone else since childhood, around whom my life has revolved for 20 years, and my feelings of admiration for the fight, the will, and the courage of an old man.

To what extent death is in *his* thoughts I have no idea; that will appear later, if he lives. But it is clear that much of his mental suffering in late years has been caused by the lack of a proper sense of himself as old. In his own mind he is not 85.

A resurrection has occurred between my second and third visits tonight and, of all providential ironies, the whiskey may have turned the tide. His

1967 face has more color, the grasp of his hand is firmer, his voice is stronger, his conversation is quicker, and his criticisms of the nurses are as caustic as they would be if he were not ill. He wants to know today's date, and, on hearing it, seems as surprised as Rip Van Winkle on being told how long *he* had slept. Only yesterday he was uncertain whether he was even in the hospital, at one point asking the name of the hotel and the city. The finger is clearer tonight, too, and as the doctors concur in ascribing at least some of the improvement to the whiskey, we tipple once more.

November 6. An electric vibrating mattress has been brought in to stimulate circulation, and his left arm has been thickly swaddled in cotton to increase the flow of blood. A fluid of glucose, vitamins, alcohol, and vasodilators is fed to him intravenously through his right arm, which is already as needle-marked as the "golden" arm of a "mainliner," as well as bandaged in several places.

His watch is now on his right wrist, having been transferred from the left after a struggle that did not succeed in removing his two wedding rings and signet ring from the painful fingers, except during an X-ray, and then virtually by force.

I spend the entire day in the hot, stale, ill-lighted, and medicine-flavored room and return again in the evening, after attending a Monday Evening Concert to hear Michael Tilson Thomas and friend play the four-hand version of *Sacre*. The concert includes a group of Schubert songs as well, sung with no *Schwarmerei* and little enough voice; Webern's piano minuet, which is just long enough for the question to cross one's mind whether any composer has ever been so quickly picked so clean; Stockhausen's *Adieu*, which contains some novel wind-instrument sounds suggesting weeping; and I.S.'s *Pastorale*, which, with quarters rather than eighths as the unit of beat, is nearly twice too fast for the character of the piece. The *Sacre* performance is rousing, though the timbre is monotonous, the main lines are frequently swamped, and the tempi, pianos being unable to sustain, are generally too fast. The effect on me is extremely depressing, having made I.S. himself seem remote and expendable and making me realize that his music can never have an existence for me apart from him. The evening is a foretaste of a time in which his absence will be felt and regretted by no one but me; which means simply that I have never been able to separate the man and his music.

At the hospital afterward we find him drugged but lucid; Suvchinsky, who comes for a last look-in, and to collect a signature on a contract, describes him as a "flambeau." We do not stay long—the room is as stifling as a greenhouse—even though I.S. asks us to, with imploring looks as well as words, and the departure is painful.

November 11. The patients' list today includes Jennifer Jones, a would-be suicide, brought in during the night still dripping from the sea, like Botticelli's "Venus." The nurses are goggle-eyed, not with scientific amazement at her apparent amphibiousness and the phenomenon of *1967* Anadyomene, but for the banal reason that Miss Jones is a "movie star."

I.S. has a new nurse today, a tough old trout with a scabrous tongue and the personality of a warden. She treats him as if he were an ancient, puling baby, and offends his decorum with questions such as, "Do you use Poly-Grip on your dentures?" and remarks like "I've wiped more bottoms in my time. . . ." The patient serves as a lever of compensation in her own life, as I have come to think most patients do for most nurses; which is the reason she so clearly resents V.'s place next to the bed and I.S.'s rapt gaze toward her, as if she were a peri from another world. "Can you see this?" V. asks, holding up a book of photographs for him to peruse. "I think so," he says, "but I would rather look at you." What I am beginning to fear now is that unless I can find a way of spreading her burden, V. will collapse.

November 13. A Dies Irae, the worst crisis since August. A new abscission must have occurred in the index finger, which is blacker than ever. Equally upsetting is I.S.'s semi-delirium. His senses of time and distance are virtually inoperant, and his memory is a jumble. He repeatedly asks where he is and confounds names and places (though verbal resemblances are evident in this, the name "Dr. Marcus," for example, starting him off on Markevitch). He talks to the nurses in Russian, too, mistaking them for V. Worst of all, he says he cannot see and is clearly unable at times to identify objects in the room, or even ourselves. At one point he says: "I have left my passport behind and cannot return."

Fearing that he has had a major stroke, I ask for a consultation, summon the two neurosurgeons, and return to the hospital in the evening to witness their examination. The result is an amazing display of I.S.'s always amazing and still very much intact mind. He is fond of medical interrogations, one must concede, but he rises to the occasion now with some impish *mots d'esprit* as well. Dr. Rothenberg: "Will you answer a few silly questions, Mr. Stravinsky?" I.S.: "No." But the questions come. "Do you ever see double, Mr. Stravinsky?" "Yes." "How long has this been going on?" "All my life, when I am drunk." "What month and year is it?" The best I.S. can say for the former is "autumn," but he gets the year right. "Did you see people or animals in the room at any time today and later realize that they weren't there?" "Yes. Two boys were sitting in that chair this afternoon." "Did you see a black cat?" "No." But he claims to see vivid color mixtures in the curtain even now, while at the same time maintaining that he knows it is a drab brown because it was that color yesterday. A reading test reveals that he sees the letters a half-inch to the left of the print as well as the print itself. What distresses him more than this, he confesses, is his inability to relate events. "Something is wrong both in my sense of time and in the reasoning faculty," he says, and he goes on to describe an awareness that a philosopher in perfect health and a fraction of his age might envy. One of the doctors, in the interests of an analogy I fail to follow, puts a question to

1967 him about time in music but bungles his concepts, whereupon I.S. sets him straight by "time is a matter of speed, and rhythm is a matter of design."

The doctors seek to assure him that his new complaints are the result of his new drugs. "I am *consolé*," he concedes at last, adding, "I looked hard in myself for the cause of the failure and was distressed because I was unable to reason about it exactly enough.* I want to be more exact in my thoughts." But *is* he "*consolé*"? He pleads for "a more powerful pill, so that I will not have to think anymore tonight." A stronger sedative is forbidden because of the danger of pneumonia if he does not move enough.

The examination has allayed V.'s worst fears, at least temporarily. His imagination is unimpaired, certainly, and his repartee says the same for his spirit. But it is obvious that he has had a new thrombosis. And what of that black finger? And of the effects of more pain and more drugs when he has already endured so much of both for so long? As Exeter says of King Henry V:

Now he weighs time/Even to the utmost grain.

November 14. Finally, eight weeks late, I.S. is given an arterial injection of radioactive phosphorus, by a doctor in a rubber suit and what might be a welder's helmet. Three nurses, like the three queens accompanying Arthur to Avalon, wheel the patient to a lead-lined room in the basement, and immediately afterward a thrice-daily series of abdominal and subcutaneous heparin injections is begun.

The mental wanderings are more alarming than they were yesterday. Before the trip to the X-ray room, he asks me to look after his wallet, which he has not had on his person for three months. (He was always concerned about pocket valuables when disrobing for X-rays.) On the return to the room, he asks if we have "enough *Frantzuski Geld* to tip the porters." When dinner comes, he insists on eating from his own tray, thinking himself in his room at home, and when V. says that it isn't there, he points to where she can find it. As we leave for dinner ourselves, he asks to come to the restaurant with us. He will be able to do that very soon, I tell him. But after considering this for a moment he replies, heartbreakingly, "Oh, I realize I am not able to eat with you, but I could watch." He also begs to be taken for a "promenade" in the car. And no doubt troubled by his mistake in thinking he was home, he asks how are things there now. Very bad, I say, for we miss him all the time. I add, "You remember

---

* Stravinsky's habit of intellectual self-accusation, a lifelong trait, was a great trial to him during his convalescence, simple failures of memory being enough to precipitate fits of anger. In Zurich, almost a year later, his inability to recall some incident during a discussion at table seemed to be responsible for a nightmare. At about midnight, at any rate, hearing him get up, I went to his room and found him sitting on the edge of his bed with his truss in his hand to use as a weapon against "the guards" who, in his dream, were coming to take him "to the madhouse."

how you used to describe us as a *'trio con brio'*? Well, please hurry and get well so we can be one again."

He has a period of hallucinations—a side effect of heparin, the doctors say—and apprehends people who are not present but fails to see us and his nurses only inches away. Once he asks why there are two watches on his right wrist, from which even the one has been removed. His comments in Russian, V. says, are "nonsensical" and "delirious," which greatly upsets her; nor is she impressed by my argument that this unreality is better for him now than the truth.

His mind seems to be divided into two parts, of which only the part dealing with the outer world and the present is confused. Yet surely this is natural, given the disruption of his time sense by medicine schedules and drugs, and the dislocation as a consequence of staring at hospital walls, not, after all, so very different from his bedroom walls at home.

The other, the creative part of the mind, appears to be unaffected. In the evening, during one of his lucid spells, I tell him that the BBC has asked him to compose from six to ten seconds of music which, together with a multicolored eye by Picasso, would form the signature of a new color-television channel. Instantly the creative mind seizes the idea and moves ahead like a prow. "The limitation to six seconds rules out chords, as well as rhythms in any conventional sense, though many notes can be used at once. And an eye means transparency: the sound should be produced by very high instruments, possibly flutes, compared with which oboes are greasy and clarinets oily."

November 18. The depredations are showing. I.S. is so thin now that his nose seems to have grown, and his long-untrimmed mustache overhangs his lip, suggesting a walrus or fox terrier. The finger remains blueblack and painful, though less so in the mornings, when he is still comatose from sedatives. As for the intensity of the pain, the doctors assure us that he performs for our sympathy, following normal patient behavior, and that he has dispatched his nurse for codeine or Darvon but fallen asleep before she has had time to give it to him. Nevertheless, he has pain, and he moans from it throughout the afternoon. Once the nurse gives him a pill, warns him it is a big one, goes to fetch water to help him swallow it. When she returns, he says: "Already done."

As a result of yesterday's midnight consultation, which introduced a new vascular surgeon into the medical-opinion pool, new ingredients are compounded in the I.V., arm and hand exercises are begun, and mild heating therapy is applied to the forearm and hand. Thanks to computerized filing systems, too, a former victim of the same ailment has been traced, and his case history, treatment, progress studied and compared. The man was I.S.'s junior by 20 years, and his hand became gangrenous after a coronary. We learn from his case that recovery was extremely slow and that in the matter of pain he would "prefer 10 coronaries to that ache in the fingers."

1967   The main effect of the change in the I.V. fluid since the midnight medical powwow is soporific. The new strategy, apparently, is to keep the
patient "under" until the radioactive phosphorus begins to work, which is
like waiting in a heavily besieged fort for the relief column of cavalry.
Why am *I* suffering so much, asks a new, analysis-jargonized ("intropuni-
tive") nurse? Father figure? Identification? I do not give my answer, which
is that I love him, not wanting to hear the word translated into a neurotic
symptom.

What are the answers to her questions? To borrow Rank's terminology,
wasn't there a narcissistic basis for the object-choice of I.S. 20 years ago?
And to borrow Freud's terminology, haven't I identified my ego with the
disappearing object? Perhaps, in both instances, and I can be fooled by my
ego as well as the next person by his or hers. But the main hinge of Freud's
explanation, the transformation of the object-loss into the mourner's ego-
loss, does not apply.

November 19. The new I.V. formula, with the new anticoagulant,
Priscoline, has not changed the finger color, but it makes I.S. so drowsy
that I get only a few words out of him the whole day. "They are giving me
phenobarbital now, probably to keep me polite," he says, and a great while
later, as if he were reading our minds: "My impression is that the doctors
haven't the faintest notion what to do." Once he describes the finger pain
as "crackling," and at another time as "needling." Yet I suspect that a
resourceful nurse could keep him off painkillers entirely. He displays the
finger ceremoniously to the new, analysis-wise but otherwise resourceless
one, saying, "*We* can't touch it." His failing sight is more alarming than the
finger, and while he identifies us by our voices, hardly turning his head to
left or right, what he *does* see, the anti-corona of someone walking past the
bed, is not there.

November 20. Letter from Berman: "With the best medical science
and care that's supposed to exist in the U.S., it is hard to believe that the
ineptitude and incompetence of L.A. doctors has aggravated or even
caused I.S.'s new condition! Incredible, atrocious, heartbreaking. I
embrace poor Igor in thought and Vera and you who are living these hours
in a personal agony of watching helplessly the tremendous struggle for survival by this wonderful, indispensable man."

"Where are you?" I.S. asks, hearing me enter the room this morning, and
as I approach the bed, he puts his good hand to my face as if he were totally blind. He is so heavily drugged that he speaks only at great intervals.
"How long will it last?" he says at one point, and again, "How much
longer?" Then for the first time in all these months: "I don't want to live
this way." I try to make him believe that he will soon be home and composing, but he nods his head weakly toward his left hand, saying: "I need
my hand; I am maimed in my hand." I am more worried about his eyes,
and most worried of all about the amount of fight left in him. Already, as

the Duke of Albany says in *Lear*, "The oldest hath borne most."

November 22. Letter from my great mother: "As soon as I put *Firebird* on the player, the tears come. I can't help thinking of his misery, in contrast to the beauty of his work. When it was over I wrote a short note to thank him for his creations but later tore it up."

November 23. It is Thanksgiving Day in the most wonderful way possible: the miracle has happened. The finger color has returned to normal, and I.S. has not complained of pain or taken painkiller in 72 hours. His sight is not restored, and he is unable to distinguish faces in what, as he describes it, seems to be a dioramic blur; but his eyes turn rapidly toward and focus quickly on us. He sits on a chair for a while, too, looking much thinner there than in the bed. While he is up, his daughter reads to him and is quickly pounced on for mistakes in Russian pronunciation. Incredible man! Only three days ago he was in a semi-coma, his left hand a half-silted estuary of gangrene, his body worn out by months of sickness and pain. Now he has come out of it, recrossed the Styx. "How much is it costing?" he asks me suddenly, and in all these weeks no words have sounded so good. I.S. is back in decimal-system reality. Hallelujah!

Pepped up from glucose, jumpy, brittle, anxious, he is ready to fly off the handle at anything and everything. "I have had enough medical philosophy," he informs his most discursive physician. He is suffering drug withdrawal, of course, and a mountain of after-effects. But I like the friction.

V. is ill and in bed today. The diagnosis is flu, but "battle fatigue" would be more accurate. The crisis last weekend was too much for her, and her fear has been kept inside too long.

November 25. Letter from my marvelous mother: "There is much to be thankful for with Mr. S. He has been spared to brighten this earth to the age of 85. Think how many old masters died in abject poverty. Your devotion to him leaves no room for regret on your part."

November 28. I bring I.S. home at noon, his departure having been delayed by requests for autographs from every nurse on the floor, which he gives, embellishing some of them with musical notations. Outdoors, out at last from that stultifying hospital, he looks as pale as junket and, dressed in a suit, terribly thin, shrunken, frail.

As I help him from the car into the house, he says that it must seem to me as if I am "towing a wreck." Weak though he is, he props himself on the couch and will not go to bed. Contemptuous of medicines now, he balks at his quarter-hourly doses of milk. "Milk is the Jesus Christ of the affair," he says, to which profanity V. responds with: "Now we see how much better you are." "Not better, bitter," he corrects. To divert him, V. plays Patience and asks him to keep the tally for her in his head. His scores, she says—not meaning any pun—are perfect.

He asks for today's newspaper (which says that Zadkine, a coeval, has

1967 died) and the mail. The latter contains Malraux's *Antimémoires*, with the author's dedication: *"Pour Igor Stravinsky, avec mon admiration fidèle."* I.S. jumps on this. "When was he ever '*fidèle*'? He once said that music is a minor art." So I.S. is still I.S.

Later in the day, when the doctors come to congratulate themselves, he flummoxes them, too, as he has done at every stage: "The finger and the eyes are from the same cause." The chief neurosurgeon corroborates this to me privately, saying that not one but three thromboses occurred just before that tardy radioactive phosphorus, and that some peripheral vision in the left eye is permanently lost. At the moment, I.S. is distressed less by the damage to his eye than by a gas pain; and when the doctors seek to remind him that he has not suffered alone, he snaps at them with "Maybe, but you don't have this pain." (Apostrophizing them later, he remarks: "It was very well-paid suffering for them.") But he is beginning to talk like a doctor himself. "Is the pain merely spasmodic," he asks, "or could it be organic?" One of the medics, in parting, tells him that healing takes longer at 85. I.S. turns on this: "Damn eighty-five."

He watches *Daktari* in V.'s room tonight, but tosses and turns in his bed afterward, tormented, he says, about the state of his mind. At 11 o'clock I go to V. to see if she is all right and find her in her dark room, quietly crying, tears streaming down her face. Not once during the whole ordeal did she ever lose control, and only now is it clear that she had begun to lose belief and was only continuing to pray that he would ever be home again. After an hour of trying to talk her into some "peace of mind," I am summoned by the night nurse to help with I.S., who is not asleep in spite of his pills. I try to fake some more good cheer with him, but he says he is "in a bad way psychologically." When I leave him, he answers my last inane "Please stop worrying" with "I am not worrying any more, only waiting," a wrenching remark. "Old people are attached to life," Sophocles says, condemning it as a fault.

I write a letter to Thomas Messer, Guggenheim Museum, for V. to copy in her name:

> Your telegram arrived at the very darkest hour of the most difficult period we have ever been through. Igor had a bleeding ulcer in August, but recovered quickly, X-rays showing it to be almost healed after only three weeks. Then he began to complain of acute pains in his left fingers. His uric acid was high, and gout was diagnosed. During the next two months he was fed anti-gout poisons harmful to the ulcer. Then at the beginning of November, his hand turned blue, with no let-up in the pain. At this point a gout specialist said the trouble was vascular. The next four weeks in the hospital were a nightmare. Igor was pumped full of "vasodilators" and to increase circulation the nerve was repeatedly blocked, a

dangerous operation at his age. The pain, the drugs, the hell of **1967** the hospital, the exhaustion, and the discouragement have been terrible for him.

December 1. The platelets have fallen to 900,000, and the white count—"my blood policemen," as I.S. tells it, though he is also using such nonmetaphorical terms as oenosyllophyl—is down to 17,000, from 37,000 a few days ago. His diet is less strict now, and henceforth the taste of milk can be cut with larger swigs of Scotch. This news raises I.S. out of the apathy and black melancholy into which he had fallen the day after his homecoming, when he had apparently expected to be able to skip rope. After dinner we listen to the C sharp minor quartet and *Dichterliebe*, the first music to sound in the house since he entered the hospital. He comes to life with the music, grunting agreement with Beethoven at numerous moments in the quartet and beating time with his left hand, which is protected by an outsized mitten, like the claw of a fiddler crab. Whereas he has been unable to read words, his eyes travel easily with the score (being guided by a quite exceptional "ear").

December 6. A marvelous day, sunny and warm, though the San Bernardino Mountains glitter like Kilimanjaro with new snow. My leave-taking is the hardest I have ever had to go through. It will only be for a few days, I tell I.S., and I blame his music as the reason for the trip in the first place. To which he says, *"Je crache sur ma musique."*

December 9 and 10. Ithaca. I conduct I.S.'s Piano Concerto, *Canticles*, and *Psalms*.

December 16. New York to Los Angeles. Meeting me at the door, V. says that I.S. had been waiting for me since early morning but became tired and fell asleep. He is awake when I enter his room, nevertheless, and he actually sheds tears when he sees me. He is utterly changed, better than I had ever hoped to see him again. V. says a delayed shock has occurred. A veil has dropped over the worst of the illness, mercifully eradicating all memory of the hospital. He even refuses to believe he had been ill at all, on grounds that he had no temperature, and though he remembers that we were all much concerned about his hand, he does not recollect that it had ever pained him. Yet he flexes the hand as we converse, tightening and loosening its grip on a toy-size exercising football.

The greatest difference is in communication. Whereas two weeks ago he would follow conversations abjectly, contributing little himself, talk flows from him now. Telling me about a Christmas letter from the conductor James Sample, he recalls several incidents touching the lessons in composition that he gave Sample's father-in-law more than 25 years ago, and describes how he wrote much of his pupil's symphony for him. After dinner we listen to the great quartet movement that I.S. calls "the *Sehr grosse Fuge*," and to the Debussy *Etudes*, which, not for the first time, he names as

1967 his favorite piano opus in the music of this century. Having dreamed about Debussy a few nights ago, he says, "I clearly recalled the strong scent of his eau de Cologne when we last embraced each other."

Both I.S. and V. seem happier and are looking better than at any time since August, for which I thank I.S.'s invincible spirit.

December 25. It now seems likely that the infection to which I.S. is supposed to have succumbed on the 19th, and against which he was murderously over-dosed with antibiotics, was a new thrombosis, though we cannot be certain, precisely because of the debilitating effect of the drugs. He is extremely low, in any case, seems to have aphasia at worst, and at best, forms words with great difficulty. He cannot walk at all without the aid of his nurse, but resolves to come to the dinner table because it is V.'s birthday and Christmas—in *that* order: "Christianity is a system," he says, "but Christ is not a system." His only other words during this extremely depressing meal are a *cri de coeur*: "Something new has happened to me. What is it? I was walking so well last week."

At the end of the dinner he says *"Ne bougez pas!"* to me, then climbs slowly up the stairs with the help of the nurse, and again all the way down, bringing me a Christmas present, a gold clasp. "It belonged to my father and to his father," he says, and apologizes because it isn't wrapped.

It seems so brutal that, having endured so much, and at last reaching the threshold of recovery—walking unaided and even mentally digesting his ordeal—this brave and miraculous man should again be struck down. What can we do now except pray that the thread by which his life seems again to be suspended will prove, as it did before, as strong as someone else's rope? When I greet V. with a "Merry Christmas and Happy Birthday" this morning, all she says is: "I went to his room a few minutes ago and thanked God he was still breathing."

&❧ **Postscript 1994.** As the diary reveals, the autumn of 1967 was the most anxious period since Munich in 1956. It was also a turning point for me in that henceforth and until Stravinsky's death I devoted almost all of my time and energies to him, which is to confess that in the two prior years I sometimes avoided the medical discussions that preoccupied the Stravinskys. I hardly need to say that my account of Stravinsky's medical history in the last months of the year is unprofessional and may be inaccurate, but the diary is a reliable record of my feelings for him, feelings that I tended to suppress in the years when he seemed indestructible.

It must also be said that the publicized picture of the composer functioning as usual was far from the truth. He was not conducting and not composing, and because of this, his lawyers, for purposes of tax-deduction, urged me to publish interviews with him as proof that he was still active.

Jean Stein Vanden Heuvel reentered my life in 1967, partly because I was an unresolved problem from her remote past (1954). Though she probably explained my behavior in relation to her as well as to the Stravinskys as neurotic, she did not attempt to explain me to myself in that light. She gave me much-needed support during my concert tours to Boston, New York, Lexington, Toronto, Santa Fe, Los Angeles, and Ithaca and was wonderfully considerate of my feelings and responsibilities throughout the ordeal of Stravinsky's illness. Moreover, she was immensely helpful in providing high-level medical advice from Dr. Corday, her father's physician; in fact, her efforts led us to the brilliant young hematologist, Dr. Weinstein, who found the formula that regulated and stabilized Stravinsky's blood chemistry for the next three years.

Stravinsky's career as a conductor came to an end in May 1967. His recording of the *Firebird* Suite in January was the only one of several scheduled sessions that actually took place and that was to have included *Song of the Nightingale, Danses concertantes, Abraham and Isaac, Japanese Lyrics,* all of which I recorded for him. The two orchestra concerts that we shared in February, the one in Toronto in May—televised, though Stravinsky never saw the film—and the staged performances of the *Soldat* in Seattle in March, were his last public appearances.

During the terrible month of November, it became clear to me, but not yet to Vera Stravinsky, that her husband could count on no help from his son-in-law, who lived only a few blocks from the hospital but never visited him there, and on precious little from his daughter, who did visit him there, but briefly and only three times. Unfortunately, too, Edwin Allen, on whom the Stravinskys had come to rely during his Los Angeles stopovers in the year before—he worked as a salesman for Oxford University Press—spent all of 1967 in London.

Never, after 1967, did I take Stravinsky for granted.

❧ 1968

January 1. I.S. is none the worse today for some 12:01 A.M. sips of champagne, but he discharges a thunderclap by remarking that certain legal actions, of which he has just learned, were necessary, "in case I had died in the hospital"; no acknowledgment of the possibility of death has crossed his lips heretofore. When we prod him to exercise the bad finger, he says, "I will be able to use the finger only when I can get it out of my mind."

One of his Christmas presents is a canary. Remarking somewhat acidly on the volume of its "song," I am challenged in the use of the word: "Musical elements—pitch, color, intensities, rhythmic patterns—yes—and the bird even gives notice before signing off. But the result isn't 'song.'"

Although I.S. tends to resist Handelian grandeur, he likes Colin Davis's zippy and well-articulated *Messiah*, which we listen to in the evening; also bits of *Hercules*—Dejanira's mad scene, Iole's recitative "Forgive me, gen'rous victor"—but he gives up because in this case the performance is excruciating.

January 16. Spender calls from London asking I.S. to respond to the appeal to help condemned Soviet writer Pavel Litvinov. I.S. agrees, tells me what he wishes to say, and we draft the following statement together, which he translates into Russian for recording next week for the BBC:

> I remember the sufferings of my teacher Rimsky-Korsakov from both the threat and the exercise of tsarist censorship. Sixty years later, while the world stands in admiration of so many achievements of the Revolution, Russian writers and readers still live under the censor's Reign of Terror. The spirit of the Revolution is with the condemned writers, who must be counted among their country's most valued patriots if only for the reason that they love her language. But writers cannot live, and poetry and people cannot grow, under censorship. The Soviet Union can prove its greatness more profoundly by pardoning the condemned writers than by conquering all of outer space.

Privately, I.S. denies that tsarist and Soviet censorship are comparable:

476

"There was hope under the old regime, now there is none. But what a fatuous notion is this 'patriotism.' The world being what it is, how can a writer or anyone else be patriotic?"

January 17. I.S. discovers that his Swiss Bank account records were removed from his office while he was in the hospital, presumably by Andre Marion, since he alone knew where they were kept.

January 18. With Isherwood and Don Bachardy at Chasen's. I.S. cables to Ampenova in London: "Bergman appealing my intervention. Must advise you whatever cause of impasse I am more interested in having his superb performance seen than in realizing money myself. Please try to reach accord and telephone me." *

January 24. I.S. says that he does not want to go on with his piano opus because he has "a bigger piece in mind," but no further information about this newer composition is forthcoming. Of the abandoned piano piece, he says, "I had no sooner forbidden myself to use octaves in one place than I saw what richness I could extract from them in another place where I used them all the time."

January 25. We play Schubert's E-minor Fugue and F-minor Fantasy four-hands, then dine at Chasen's with the Stalveys. Groucho Marx, at another table, approaches I.S., points to Mr. Stalvey, asks, "Is that your grandson?" I.S.: "He's young enough to be my *great* grandson." Groucho (very fast): "But he'll never be as great as you are."

January 27. V. is disturbed today because I.S. cannot remember where they were married, though why he should remember New Bedford, Massachusetts, from an hour's visit 28 years ago is a mystery. Furthermore, after 19 years of what already amounted to matrimony, the ceremony itself could scarcely be expected to become an indelible event. The lapse *is* curious, however, in that the day before the thrombosis, in November, he began to talk with exceptional distinctness about his life in Massachusetts in 1939–1940, a period rarely mentioned. Is this merely the long arm of coincidence, or were the cells encoded with those particular memories in that particular file of the information bank undergoing exposure as a result of strain just before the eclipse?

February 10. To San Francisco with the S.s for my concerts on the 13th, 14th, and 15th with the Oakland Symphony: *Scherzo à la Russe*, Symphony in Three, *Requiem Canticles*, *Psalms*. The view from our rooms in the St. Francis Hotel encompasses an electric letterboard flashing time and temperatures in the name of Equitable Life Insurance; an electric sign interspersing news of local and world disasters with appeals to drink, smoke,

---

* Bergman had cabled me asking for help in persuading Boosey & Hawkes to drop a $25,000 preliminary requirement for filming his staging of *The Rake's Progress*. Stravinsky agreed to pay the $25,000 himself in order to preserve Bergman's realisation of his opera, but Rufina Ampenova, of Boosey & Hawkes, refused.

1968 deodorize, and wipe with products that are bigger, better, newer, cheaper, sexier; girders, slanted jibs of cranes, showers of sparks from welders of tomorrow's skyscrapers, dwarfing today's skyscrapers and promising more and still larger executive suites; a column, possibly a reject, for a Central American version of the Place Vendome, topped by a globe and a disproportionately diminutive but coyly draped dancing nymph carrying a thyrsus and trident.

A hurdy-gurdy, performing for the empty benches of Union Square below, reminds I.S. that this low-fi but very loud music machine, audible even above the demolition squads, was so popular in St. Petersburg that to find two competitors grinding at the same time, as in *Petrushka*, was not uncommon. "Sometimes they accompanied dancers, and as a child I watched more than one hurdy-gurdy ballerina from my window, throwing coins tied in a rag to the *artiste* afterward." Another, much louder, concert is pealed up in late afternoon by off-key carillons somewhere in the all-too-near environs. This angelus consists of the principal theme of Tchaikovsky in B flat minor. Even the pigeons forsake their eyases on the ledge below us.

"Loud" is again the word for tonight's Chinese New Year parade, the firecrackers suggesting not merely an old-fashioned Fourth of July but the blunderbusses and cannonades of the Revolution itself. The din and wail of Chinese music combine ominously with the subterranean rumble of the cable-car chains, and the procession itself is sinister, with its real (caged) gorilla—this is "the year of the monkey"—and a scaly, block-long cardboard dragon intended to propitiate Confucius-knows-what malevolent powers. Some of the marchers carry paper hares and paper tigers, and some of the onlookers hold balloons in clumps resembling models of molecular structures. San Francisco itself has a Chinese aspect tonight, in the shapes of hills under the nesting fog, in the stylized Chinese clouds, and in the Chinese moon over the Bay.

The Haight-Ashbury district might be a movie set for an earlier America. The sidewalk people are nomadic, semi-pastoral, carrying duffel bags and guitars and wearing long hair and Smith Brothers beards, Civil War capes and frontiersmen's leggings, Indian ruanas and headbands; berdache—Indian transvestitism—is in evidence, too. A sign in a store window reads: MIRRORS FOR SALE, NEW AND USED. The Barbary Coast North Shore, in contrast, caters to the American businessman's tax-deductible night out in a flesh market, sold on the hoof. "Bottomless Shoe Shines" are advertised, and "Topless Weddings," "Thoroughly Naked Millie," "Miss Freudian Slip," "Naked Orphan Fanny," "The Nude Bat Girl" (what is the added attraction of the aliped?). One establishment lures its customers with a busty, sparsely clad girl standing in a glass telephone booth elevated about 25 feet above the sidewalk. We are lured here ourselves for a moment, though more to observe the audience than the entertainment, which is very dull. In view of the mental level and the potential lactation, the place would be more useful as a nursery.

February 11. A navy training jet has grazed the Bay Bridge in thick early-morning fog and drowned. Little trace of debris has been found, and though frogmen discover an oil slick, a clue to them, as spilled blood is to the police in a murder case, the plane is not recovered.

To Muir Woods, over the red bridge from which known *salto mortale* number 340-odd has been tabulated this week. The number of unknown opters of this way out—down—is estimated at between three and ten times as many. San Francisco, from the bridge, is a white city and Muir Woods a small pocket of Natural resistance.

At the rehearsal of his "requicles" in Oakland, I.S. asks the *Libera me* chorus to speak in triplets, and to speak, not mumble; but then the words come out as if from the cheering section at a football game.

Germain Prévost, the violist and friend of I.S.'s for 50 years, tells me he finds the composer less pale than might have been expected after such an illness, but weak-voiced. It is true that I.S. has never regained his full voice (there were spells of total aphonia in the hospital), but we are accustomed to the new timbre and do not notice the difference. Undoubtedly he strikes other people as very thin, too, though to us, comparing the present with a few weeks ago, his face seems almost bloated, as in Auberjonois's portrait, which, by slanting the eyes and distorting the head, makes him look fishlike, reminding us of the sculptures of Lepenski Vir. "Eat more," the portly Prévost advises, and I.S. says that he swallows two raw eggs "like oysters" each morning. Prévost's autograph album, submitted for a fresh inscription, contains a manuscript poem by Schoenberg and the chronicle of a concert tour in the twenties featuring I.S.'s Concertino. What most impressed Prévost about the tour was I.S.'s price of 500 francs per performance, the highest that the Pro Arte Quartet had ever been paid.

After the rehearsal, chatting about love in the pill paradise with the orchestra's pretty blonde cellist, who is a member of the Bay Area Sexual Freedom League, I put forward the a priori, or a priapic, notion that such groups are expressions of reaction to Salic laws, and more important to women than to men because they give women the freedom to choose. As an informed student of mating behavior and an advocate of sexual freedom *à la Fourier*, she says that the point for men is that the prospect of new females increases the possible number of copulations, as is the case with other male mammals; bulls, for example, are able to mount new cows (and Pasiphaës) shortly after dismounting old ones. She says that her husband and their two children are most "understanding" of her new life. Whatever the truth of her contentions, and a priorisms are proved or disproved not by philosophy but by experiment, she believes that most participants in group sex suffer from third-sex repressions. She also says that apart from sounds of zippers and of clothes dropping to the floor, group sex takes place in total silence, and that names are never used. Pot is seldom taken at Bay Area League meetings (orgies?), she further enlightens me, but she justifies her own occasional use of it by citing the laudanum-taking of De Quincey, Coleridge, Elizabeth Barrett. This conversation has made me feel very ancient.

February 12. The attractive cellist comes to my hotel room at midnight, disrobes, lies on my bed. I am well up to the occasion, but may not be after one experience, since her natural attributes do not conform to the desiderated ideal ones of my imagination. And with me, *brevis voluptas* is the rule. "What would you like to do?" she says, which suggests a large and perhaps kinky repertory, whereas my experience as well as the parameters of my interest are limited to the most ordinary methods. I am able to sustain her for no more than an hour, after which, disappointed in me, she leaves early and I read.

February 13. At tonight's concert I do not look at the cellos when cueing them. After it, I.S. stands in front of his seat in the hall to acknowledge the ovation and, Russian style, applaud his applauders; but the audience rises, too, and blocks the composer, who is the smallest man in the room, from the view of all except his immediate neighbors. Emotional dangers beset him from several sides tonight, the concert marking at the same time his first appearance in public since May, first exposure to live music-making, first live audition of the "requicles" since Princeton. No wonder that he trembles slightly in the car afterward. But back in the hotel, it is clear that he has had a boost and a much-needed restoration of confidence.

His comments on the concert show that, as always, one cannot know what is going on in the engine room from the perspective of the top deck. He is well aware that the *Canticles* can have generated only a small part of the ovation. "People come first to see if *you* are still there, and second to see if you are still there in the music, hoping, of course, that you aren't." With this he begins to autograph a pile of scores—pirated editions, in the main, of his early ballets. As if the buccaneering were not injury enough, one of the stolen *Sacre* publications adds the insult of subtitling it a "Ballet Suite." I await an outburst, but, untrue to form, he calmly and neatly blacks out the offending description, saying, "Why not call it a Gavotte?" Signing a score of *Petrushka*, he tells me that an aunt of his, "married to a man with whiskers like a Schnauzer," refused to see the ballet because she was "not going to the theater to look at a lot of peasants."

February 21. New York. To *Die Walküre* at the Met, or some of it, for the second act affects me like chloroform. Visual interest in the first act focuses on the arboreal confusion in Hunding's tree house. The two limbs that sprout like *phalloi* from either side of this mammoth log—the only one in the whole forest primeval—appear to have been grafted from a cactus (*Girl of the Golden West?*), and although a Plantagenet profusion of

480

branches was probably not to be expected, the poverty of connection implied by only two is really too poor and too bastard; besides which there *must* be another part of the forest. The tree is hewn through at the base, not merely like the redwood that straddles a highway somewhere in northern California, but as broadly and openly as the Eiffel Tower. In proportion, Siegmund's sword, uneasily sheathed in the shin bark, is hardly as big as a thorn, albeit a most sensitive thorn, blushing at every mention of it, flickering and gleaming at every hint of the "sword motif." No one is surprised, therefore, that when finally extracted, after much strenuous but unconvincing tugging, it comes out as highly charged electrically as a bolt from Thor. The "action" in the Fricka scene, what I see of it in my sleepless moments, takes place on what might be the rim of a recumbent flying saucer or other UFO; but whatever it is dwarfs the gods who, following my prejudices, should look like Giulio Romano giants in a clouded skyscape. The duel takes place in a kind of mobile Monument Valley, in which two great monoliths come together symbolically and most effectively.

March 3. Los Angeles. "I have been thinking about the Picasso eye," I.S. says, out of the azure, and as the subject has not been mentioned since the hospital, the remark falls across the conversation like a newsflash on a television screen during a "detergent opera." "A thousand notes could be spent in those few seconds, but what matters is that the form—the music must begin and end, after all—must remind the listener of an eye. I have considered many ways of composing it and many kinds of measurement. But my brain is not clear enough yet, and my body has to be re-educated. I was thinking as I left my bed this morning that I walk like a turtle."

At *The Graduate* tonight, as always at the cinema, I.S. cannot be restrained from commenting aloud and from loudly and frequently applying to V. for Russian translations. At one point he provokes a chorus of shushes and a scramble for seats remote from him. In fairness to our fleeing neighbors, it must be admitted that his observations are annoyingly detached (if also marvelously acute, especially on errors of length), or would be to anyone engrossed in the film. After bailing out the car from the parking lot to meet the S.s at the curb, I find them drawing blank stares from the long line of young people filtering inside for the next showing, people as faceless and undifferentiated, even by the effects of Crest on their grins, as eggs on a conveyor belt; which makes the two old people seem more radically differentiated than ever and turns the flow of my own, well, philoprogenitiveness away from the egg faces and toward I.S. and V.; and which further makes the old man's desire even to *go* to the movies, and this is his second time for *The Graduate*, seem like a manifestation of the same tremendous life force that impelled him, at the age of most of these eggs, to stay home and compose *Le Sacre du printemps*.

March 20. Phoenix, the Casa Blanca Inn. I am feeling euphoric, owing,

481

1968 I think, to differences of climate (if the word can be borrowed back from political jargon) between Los Angeles and Phoenix, to chemical-free and even orange-blossom-scented air. Another explanation for the sensation of looseness is inadvertently proposed by the snub-nosed photographer who meets the S.s at the airport. She says that certain supersensitive small parts of her cameras come unfastened during flights. What then of the effects of flight on such a comparatively sensitive appurtenance as the human nervous system?

The Casa Blanca Inn is in the desert, with a view in zoom-lens distinctiveness of two humps of rock inevitably called Camelback Mountain. The mosque-shaped central building, as well as each outlying motel unit, is protected by spiny saguaro, prickly pear, bristling ocotillo, tall cucumber-shaped and small porcupine-shaped cactus—a statement that may reflect my hostility toward the golfers who are our only Inn mates. Beyond the swimming pools, the fairway, and the putting greens, the desert is tinged with lupines and golden poppies. In Arizona, the color of spring is gold.

Just how mortal the desert can be is made clear by a traffic warning: DON'T END UP A LITTLE WHITE CROSS—unless, of course, the sign was erected by B'nai B'rith or a society of agnostics. We refrain from questioning our driver on this point, since to do so would be to interrupt an exceedingly slow-moving disquisition on the, as it turns out, not inconsiderable differences between a butte and a mesa; and we are already late for the dress rehearsal of the *Rake*.

This takes place in Gammage Auditorium in Tempe, designed by Frank Lloyd Wright for, it is said, an emergent African republic that in the event failed to emerge. Completed by one of Wright's pupils three years ago, the building is something of a freak, possibly because the change of destination did not result in any impious modifications of the master's plans. In any case, the building would certainly look better in Cairo, or adjoining the Casa Blanca Inn. On second glance, whatever it is seems to be sea-faring, a stranded ark, perhaps. The side entrances are in the form of gangplanks and the lights on the walls are shaped like portholes. For a building so recently finished, it is astonishingly tacky and out of date (Wright the irrepressible stuccodore), and the atmosphere it provides is more appropriate to a Ziegfield folly than to a "mod" opera. Perhaps Gerald Heard, who was Wright's guru, will he be able to enlighten us.

Before beginning the rehearsal, I introduce I.S. to the assembled cast, chorus, orchestra, bystanders; except that the only person actually to stand, out of respect for the composer and older man, is our friend Robert Tobin; which means that some of those present undoubtedly take Mr. Tobin (who is distinguished-looking himself in his resemblance to Buffalo Bill) to *be* the composer.

Returning to the Casa Blanca, we stop at a diner, but the food—plastic shrimps, chopped-rubber-tire hamburgers, a dessert made of old pancakes—is a front for jukeboxes with video screens showing "conservative striptease."

Finding no restaurant open after the performance, and going to bed hungry, we are awakened at 3 A.M. by a noise that V. fears is being generated by a rat, but proves to come from a half-starved I.S., nibbling a gaufrette.

The musical reading of the opera would have been better with some 50 more rehearsals and several other changes of circumstance. The Rake's English, for one of them, is unintelligible, owing in part to tracheal congestion—to judge by the struggles with mucosities and the emanations of Vicks reaching to about the 30th row. From the same cause, perhaps, his pitch is only intermittently *not* a quarter-tone flat, but the fitfully in-tune notes, obtained at the cost of an excruciating fortissimo, are worse. The harpsichord is distinguished by a no less painful pitch discrepancy in the upper direction, and the instrument is amplified to something near the level of the Mormon Tabernacle organ at triple forte. In the first scene a singer anticipates an entrance by several beats, and the others follow him, sheeplike, instead of taking their cues from the orchestra, with the result that the denouement occurs somewhat sooner on stage than in the pit.

I.S. likes the male Baba both dramatically and vocally ("voyce of unpaved Eunuch," Cloten says, in *Cymbeline*), and the sound *is* good, except for an alarmingly clamant bark on the A in *alt*. "After all," I.S. remarks, "the opera is supposed to take place in the age of Farinelli," when operatic sex-swapping was conventional. True, except that in the period of tonight's staging, universal transvestism constitutes a stronger justification for the switch. Perhaps unnerved by considerations involving his, or her, muliebrity—or bilateralism—tonight's Baba is forgetful. "Speak to me," she croons, and the Rake, dependably flat, asks, "Why?" This is followed by a freezingly long pause, then a backing up, by Baba, for yet another try at "Speak to me," as if she had suddenly become extremely fond of that particular line. At this point, and because her next lines are a cappella, I clear my throat and prepare to give way to a swell of lyricism myself.

The breakfast scene, in which the running commentary of photographic slides includes a view of Baba doing a sit-in at the *Last Supper* (Leonardo's), is too campy with a male Baba, and anyway, a more fundamental objection, the opera needs a second woman, even a bearded one. Then, too, hermaphroditism seems to be less happily represented by a division down the middle, as the case is here, than by the over-endowing of the female, as in the Hellenistic reclining nude in the Villa Borghese. In last year's Boston performances, the resurrected Baba, after the hibernation under the wig, was projected on the curtain through closed-circuit television. This suggested psychic manifestations and ectoplasmic transubstantiation and was superior as an idea to the new one, in which the garrulous androgyne reappears on a standard-size television set exactly like the evening news.

1968   **March 31.** Hollywood. Twenty years ago today I first met the "Stravs," that same day on which Auden delivered the book of the *Rake;* and to mark this vicennial anniversary, I.S. gives me the sketches of *The Owl and the Pussicat* [sic]. But the greatest gift is that we are celebrating together as, so short a time ago, with I.S. straddling two worlds on Mt. Sinai's Death Row, I hardly dared hope we would. At dinner, Christopher Isherwood—boyish, but with eyebrows like tussocks—wonders how to designate the anniversary, whereupon we decide to call it a marriage of Craft and Art. Then, since the S.s have a corner and more in Isherwood's autobiography, he asks them for *their* impression of *me* at that first meeting. They recall only that I was "very nervous, hardly said a word, and had apparently never before touched alcohol!" Well, I am still nervous, but do talk a bit now and then, and do not invariably refuse a glass of French anodynes. Finally, Isherwood wants to know "whether it was love at first sight," and I am happy to say that the three of us answer YES at the same time.

May 7. Letter from my great mother: "It will do something for Mr. Stravinsky to appear at Berkeley and be acclaimed. To stay at home after so much traveling and to disappear from the world of concerts after so many years of them must be difficult."

June 3. Drs. Knauer and Corday. I.S. is put in traction because of a broken vertebra.

June 30. A second visit from Maya Plisetskaya, this time with some Russian herbs for V.

August 15. V. writes to Caryl Steinberg, the McCarthy-For-President Committee: "My husband is sending this silver spoon, which has served him all his life and which bears his initials, *Igor Fyodorovitch Stravinsky.* He wishes the future owner *bon appétit.*"

August 25. A birthday party at Chasen's for Isherwood, who laughingly tells us that one of his presents was a copy of the book *Victoria: Sixty Years A Queen.*

September 6. Because of the demand for tickets, our concert at The Los Angeles County Museum, filmed by NET, is performed twice, at 7:30 and 9 P.M. Michael Tilson Thomas plays the first piano part in *Noces.* Tremendous ovation for I.S.

September 23. New York. I.S. receives a poem and a letter from Robert Lowell: "I think you must be the best critic now in any of the arts."

September 25. Zurich. Entering his suite at the Dolder Hotel, I.S. says: "I don't want to go back to California."

October 7. To Basel and the Swiss Bank Corporation with the S.s and Rufina Ampenoff, in a car from the hotel. I.S. enters the inner sanctum of the bank alone. Then, several minutes later, the bank's agent, Jean-Pierre Puenzieux, comes to fetch V. It seems that she could not accompany her husband because of an agreement making Messrs. Marion and Montapert I.S.'s sole beneficiaries, and giving them, but not her, access to the account.

The discovery of this treachery has put I.S. in a rage; he tears up the agreement, demanding that a new one be made for him and V. alone, but leaving Montapert's name, at Puenzieux's prompting, as lawyer-liaison. **1968**

As the S.s leave, I enter by a special door, where a guard impounds my passport and obliges me to write the number of my account on a paper, with which he disappears into the interior, to verify my handwriting and identify my face against a photograph. Another guard escorts me to a conference room—incarcerates me there, to the extent that he continues to stand watch outside the door; the bank wishes to protect the privacy of its depositors and spare them embarrassing encounters with each other, such as Truman Capote colliding with Gore Vidal. One imagines the room, when not occupied by the usury squads of the Swiss Monetary Police, being rented out in the evenings to abortionists or psychoanalysts. When I realize that it is soundproof and that a murder next door or clank of chains would not be heard, I am convinced that, off hours, it must serve some sinister purpose, perhaps a confessional cell for important criminals.

The furniture is sparse: a leather couch, leather-backed chair, table stacked with picture magazines of Swiss scenery and skiing resorts, mimeographed sheets of stock-market quotations, and a telephone—severed, no doubt, or tuned to a record saying, "Normal service will never be resumed." At some point I become aware of a peculiar odor—money, obviously, except that, apart from those market averages, nothing in the bank hints at anything so crass. The very last feature that I notice is the barred window, for the bars, the most discreet imaginable, are partly hidden; but they remind me of the bullion somewhere below, and of all those nests, glittering with golden eggs, of the rich and super-rich.

Puenzieux arrives—eyes sterling cold, clothes as crisp as newly minted dollars—and requires me to recite my account number, as if it were the password in a speakeasy or the combination to a safe. He is male-voiced but sexless, and the mini-skirted courier who joins him after the inspection of credentials is icy enough to be able to copulate adiabatically. She brings a folder containing the numbered but nameless records of my own paltry investment.* I receive no accounting and have no documentary proof of any connection with the bank. Within five minutes I am bundled out of a back door and into the S.s' car—after an all-clear from the guard lest in that instant some international celebrity is entering or leaving as well.

October 10. On the way to Lucerne, I.S. expresses the need of a "Watyer Closyet" (Russia having had so few of these facilities that it did not bother to make up a word for them). The caretaker of Wagner's villa at Tribschen is unbelieving after reading I.S.'s signature in the visitor's book,

---

* This account had been opened in my name in 1966 by William Montapert, Stravinsky's lawyer, in order, as I later learned, to blackmail me, numbered accounts being illegal. I closed it after this visit.

1968 but she recovers her composure, and composer, in time, and guides us through. The collection of musical instruments on the second floor contains many beautiful examples by Renaissance and Baroque craftsmen, along with such Wagnerian instruments as the tenor tubas, not only of the *Ring*, but also of *Le Sacre du printemps*.

October 11. Theodore and Denise Stravinsky bring the manuscript full score of *Sacre* from Geneva, and the sight of penciled changes made during the final rehearsals reminds I.S. of the premiere, a memory so disturbing to him even now that he adds a P.S. on the last page, berating the first audience for "the derision with which it greeted this music in the Théâtre des Champs-Elysées, Paris, Spring 1913." When Ampenoff tries to stop him from writing in the score, he brings it across the hall to my room and does it there. All in all, a strange tension prevails in the room, on Theodore's part as if the manuscript were his, and on Ampenoff's as if it were, well, if not hers, then also not I.S.'s. After Ampenoff leaves for London and Theodore for Geneva, I.S. gives the manuscript to V., who puts it in one of his suitcases.

October 19. To Einsiedeln, crossing the lake on the causeway at Rapperswil, where V. photographs the cloister and Schloss. The valleys are still green, but the vineyards are yellowing, the ivy is already mulberry red, and the road south of the lake is clogged with wains. The exterior of the great Benedictine monastery, *"Coenobiu Eremitaru"* on old maps, reminds us of the Escorial except for the church in the center, which, with volutes like treble clefs, is pure South German Baroque. The interior disappoints, partly because we have anticipated the gleaming white and gold of Die Wies and other Bavarian churches, but a choir of shavelings, kneeling in a circle before the Madonna and Child in the nave chapel, sings a Vesper service with great refinement of intonation. The monastery library has two Latin eclogues from Nero's period in a 10th-century manuscript. Outside again, in the arcades that form a semicircular approach to the church, we buy photographs from a man who manages to inject so much kindness into the transaction that he sticks in my mind, together with the idolatrous choristers, for the remainder of the day.

October 24. Paris. On the recommendation of Dr. Thirolroix, the S.s employ a nurse, Rita Christiansen, through the Centre des Infirmières Danoise Diplome, 31 rue de Poissy, certainly the most attractive member of the profession that the S.s have had.

October 25. I.S. complains that the Ritz's furniture is *"décoratif mais pas très utile,"* whereupon Count Zembrzuski, the managing director, calls for a more effulgent lamp and promises to install an electric buzzer between I.S.'s and V.'s rooms. A piano, probably unheard in these sedate precincts since the death of Chopin across the street, will be brought in next week. IN CASE OF FIRE BE SURE TO INFORM THE VALET OR MAID, a notice reads, and another, USE ONLY FIREWOOD IN THE CHIMNEY GRATES

AND CALL IN THE VALET TO LIGHT THE FIRE WHEN REQUIRED, turns *1968* my thoughts to the Louis Quinze chairs, if it should come to that. While a valet helps I.S. to unpack, V. worries aloud about a missing garment. *"Un rien vous habille, Madame,"* the valet remarks, making one reflect that whatever the truth of the dictum "Paris is too good for the French," such gallant wit is found nowhere else. My own room is acoustically ideal for listening to the chauffeurs in the Place Vendome discussing their employers.

October 26. Tonight's concert in the Théâtre de la Musique is the culminating event of a *"journée Xenakis."* The other principal event, billed as a discussion-debate, turns out not to entail any lobbing back and forth but only some very heavy "questions" that are really self-answering statements much longer than the "replies." Pop-cult hero Lévi-Strauss attends, and young people, both dandy and hippie, overflow both affairs. Several times the audience lathers into a Beatles-type hysteria, though the causal connection between the character of these responses and the contents of the program is beyond my comprehension. I sit next to Messiaen in a loge designed for people with no knees.

Xenakis is not one of the two or three contemporary composers who can survive the exposure of a one-man concert, let alone a one-man day. But this difficulty is nowhere dealt with or acknowledged in the purple program folders, whose sheafs of Xeroxed press clippings, biographia, film-strip photos of the master at work, and a booklet of Pataphysical bull called *La pensée de Xenakis*, spill across the stage most colorfully later in the evening when jettisoned there by the protesting minority.

One of the publicity releases assures the reader that Xenakis's "time" is "in some cybernetic future." But tonight's reception shows all too patently that his time is right now and that the future, cybernetic or otherwise, is precisely what he will soon have to worry about. Despite all the advance warnings about the abstruseness of the composer's cogitations and the inaccessibility of his mathematical methods, the music itself is both absurdly predictable (in fashionable cant: "The mind makes probabilistic assessments") and astonishingly naive, the latter being the case with some timpani rolling of the type that had gone out, one thought, with the *Symphonie fantastique*.

The program's centerpiece is an avalanche of electronic noise called *Bohor*, which, pronounced as one syllable, partially describes its effect. An experiment in sonic sadism, *Bohor* is inflicted by "quadruple stereophony," bruited, in other words, by eight loudspeakers shaped like dryers in a beauty salon and aimed at the audience like death-ray machines. A jet motor seems to switch on *in* one's penetralia. When the theater itself begins to tremble like a tuning fork, the "reactionaries" head for the exits—as I would do, except that I go on thinking from second to second that *Bohor* cannot last a second longer. After a while, and inasmuch as the noise is so little varied, one suspects that the machine must be stuck or the tape

1968 derailed. If at all, *Bobor* should be detonated in a football stadium for an audience in air-raid shelters many miles away.

The one point of interest would be in comparing impressions of duration (10 minutes? an hour?), but even that is frustrated, for when the noise finally subsides, the outburst of booing, jeering, catcalling, accompanied by a hail of program folders, like the refuse thrown into a bull ring after a bad corrida, nearly equals *Bobor* in volume. The counter-assault ("*Bis!*") is hardly under way when the string orchestra returns to the stage, and the demonstration turns to whistles imitating the slow glissades which are what, in the main, the strings play. When the conductor, Lukas Foss, signals the start of the next piece, a shout "*Du Mozart!*"—a "plant," surely— goes up and is answered by a rich assortment of uncomplimentary epithets, of which the most popular is "*Con!*" But surprisingly, the opus passes without further outward incident. And without much inward incident either. The layout of contrasting blocks of sound effects is the same in every piece, except that "contrasting" misleadingly implies movement. If this is "sound architecture," as advertised, then it should go back to the drawing board.

The real trouble with the evening after *Bobor* is that live players, a conductor, "trad" instruments, and the concert routine itself are exposed as glaringly obsolete. Nor are the instruments functionally adapted to their work. The design of a violin, after all, and its tuning in fifths, corresponds to an evolution in music itself. In sum, Xenakis's *"pensée"* seems more fittingly served by filters, sonotrons, oscillators, potentiometers, sine-wave generators, ring modulators, and other such hardware. Most disturbing of all, the conductor's straight beat patterns do not have any evident bearing on, or relation to, the noise.

Xenakis receives his ovations in the blue-denim uniform of a factory worker and in footwear showing him to be ready for tennis. Well apprised that the turnover in the reputation market is more rapid on the Paris Bourse than anywhere in the world, he emerges afterward, inveighing against the Parisian process of becoming à la mode. BECOMING?

I emerge thinking about Verdi's "Progress could be in the reverse direction." I think about it, with rapidly diminishing interest, until 2 A.M., at which hour girls for hire—"shop workers who want to buy more clothes," Miss Christiansen says—are trying to give a basic idea of their wares in nearly every doorway of the rue de la Paix all the way back to the Ritz.

November 1. At the Trianon Palace Hotel, Versailles, I.S. walks an even greater distance than he did yesterday. We stop at Debussy's birthplace in St. Germain-en-Laye on the return. Visit from Nadia Boulanger.

November 17. New York. Letter from Berman: "It seems tragic not to have a home at I.S.'s age."

November 19. Pompano Beach. Senior Citizens and Golden Agers greatly outnumber gilded youths, and nearly all the customers in the barber shop have lost their wool. "Hair transplants" of a kind are performed on the beach, where palm trees are being placed in front of new condominiums, then bent for that natural blown look. And on the beach, the last two of the Seven Ages of Man are far more conspicuous than the first five, thus raising the thought that perhaps beach-wear should be restricted to the under-thirties, a remark that risks the wrath of age-lib. Ages Four and Five definitely would benefit from the revival of whalebone corsets, which I should not say, having signed a petition to "Save the Whale." The latest fashion among Age Three females is to expose the lineaments of the natal cleft and exaggerate the dichotomy of the derrière.

And the Second Age? Jesus loves them, this I know. Still. One of them, with a toy mine detector, auscultates the sand near me for buried treasure, while another refuels a gull in flight, flinging crumbs into the air and attracting a flapping, squawking, excreting flock. Prejudiced by Hitchcock's *The Birds*, I am relieved when they take off on a mission somewhere else. A buzzard hovers *hors concours*, even higher than the airplane advertisements.

The sight of a jogger, Fifth Age, obese and puffing, turns one's thoughts to the oxygen respirator in the Beach Patrol Tower, but the Tarzan in Kelly-green sweatsuit who normally roosts there is out sprinting—past lollygagging lovers, past recumbent bodies glistening with embrocations guaranteed to patinate with the perfect tan ("Under the influence of sunlight, Vitamin D synthesizes in the skin"), past the gasping jogger, and as if racing the aerial advertisers.

December 6. Los Angeles. I receive the Académie de Disque Française Prix Florent Schmitt for my Schoenberg recordings, Paris, November 28, 1968.

December 9. Dr. Anderson comes: I.S. has herpes zoster. My farewell appearance at the Monday Concerts, conducting *Pierrot Lunaire* and Messiaen's *Couleurs de la Cité Céleste*.

&♠ **Postscript 1994.** 1968 was an upswing year, a time of recovery and comparative stability. By January, Stravinsky's ulcer had healed and he rapidly regained strength, even to the extent that he practiced conducting. He was more frail than before the illness, of course, and the resonance in his basso profundo voice had disappeared. But he was able to travel to San Francisco in February and to Phoenix in March, which boosted his morale. Moreover, the three of us had complete confidence in his new medical team: Dr. Weinstein, the hematologist, Dr. Rothenberg, the neurologist, and Drs. Marcus and Pincus, the cardiologists. A Russian-speaking night nurse was retained, not because Stravinsky needed her but to ease Mrs. Stravinsky's burdens.

The second stay in San Francisco, in May, was a high point for Stravinsky in that he was able while there to complete his instrumentations

1968 of Hugo Wolf songs. But the concerts in Berkeley, for the inauguration of Zellerbach Hall, put me in an embarrassing position. They had been falsely advertised. Both the concert agent and the University were aware that Stravinsky would not be able to conduct, yet the publicity up to and including the day of the concert pretended the contrary. The audience read the truth on a placard in the lobby, which, no doubt, was preferable to an announcement from the stage greeted with a groan from the sold-out hall, but when I learned about the duplicity I felt like running away. The program began with a greeting to Stravinsky read by Gregory Peck, an alumnus, that included a substantial passage from one of the composer's books. (My friend Bill Brown, the painter, standing offstage with me, remarked: "That must have been written on your day off." It was from *The Poetics of Music*.)

Back in Hollywood Stravinsky seemed to be suffering from lumbago, but X-rays showed a displaced vertebra. In the beginning of July he was strapped into a tight corset, but tore it off in a fit of anger, never wore it again, and was apparently none the worse without it. The Swiss vacation in September and October lifted our spirits—until a doctor advised Stravinsky that hematology was more advanced in the United States than anywhere in Europe and that after a few weeks he should return to California. Stravinsky did not have a nurse during his stay in Zurich, and he received only two visits from a doctor, both of them for injections against osteoporosis.

In Paris, the Stravinskys visited with old friends—most frequently Nadia Boulanger and Nicolas Nabokov—saw *Le Sacre du printemps* at the Opéra, and went on excursions to Chantilly, Saint-Germain-en-Laye, and Versailles. Their Paris doctor suggested that they employ a day nurse in order to give Mrs. Stravinsky more freedom to enjoy the city, see her friends, and go to museums. The young Danish nurse they engaged was fluent in both English and French. She accompanied the Stravinskys to California and, except for brief holidays in Mexico, Paris, and Copenhagen in the summers of 1969 and 1970, remained with Stravinsky until his death. I married her some months after that and, on February 22, 1972, we became the parents of Robert Alexander.

ஆ *1969*

February 1. In the two weeks since the discovery of the clot in the lower left leg, the anti-coagulants have proven to be too strong, and I.S.'s and our nights are now almost wholly sleepless; that any of us still functions according to a circadian rhythm is surprising. Yet the response to the last injection was good, and he is decidedly better now. How much suffering he has had to endure since December! We desperately need a doctor for the whole man, someone who can talk to him and gain his confidence, instead of which we have specialists who come at all only for huge fees and only after we plague them with telephone calls.

February 5. I.S.'s fighting spirit is showing through quite literally: this morning he threw a pillow in the direction of one of his nurses. The log of his medications for the day and night include:

10:00 A.M.	1 Pronestyl
11:00	100 mg. Heparin
12:30	teaspoon Butisol
3:00	1/2 comp. Tylenol
4:00	1 comp. Pronestyl
6:30	1 teaspoonful Butisol
9:00	Myloran tablet. Darvon tablet
9:50	Pronestyl capsule. Placidyl tablet (500 mg)
12:25 A.M.	Placidyl 200 mg p.o.
2:00	Placidyl 200 mg p.o.
3:45	Placidyl 200 mg p.o.
3:50	Pronestyl 250 mg. p.o.
6:15	Tylenol tablet

February 15. Write to Columbia Records apropos I.S.'s "talk" record: "The circumstantial nature of the remarks will be overlooked and thesis writers will seize on the contradictions, yet this rehearsal record *is* characteristic of Stravinsky, and probably at any period in his life."

February 17. Write to Ampenoff: "We have four nurses, in 6-hour

491

1969 shifts. Mr. S. sleeps more during the day than at night, walks only when forced to, but likes automobile rides. He plays the piano every morning, reads constantly, but comes to intense life only in the evening when, for one-and-a-half hours, we listen to music."

March 31. Montapert invites me to the Telephone Booth, a restaurant on Santa Monica Boulevard near La Cienega. Lunch here turns out to be no ordinary feed, except that food is not the point, but the topless and bottomless waitresses—"only the salad comes with dressing"—who serve it and take turns "dancing" on a dais. The ringside seats for these ballets are at the bar, but the performers' charms, fore and aft, are in mirror if not direct view of every table. The room is dark, the more fulgently to set off spotlighted and powdered epidermises and at the same time to shield the viewers, some of whom, perhaps fearing a televised police raid, hide behind smoked glasses as well.

Who are the diners? Leering lechers? Inveterate voyeurs? Well, not all of them. The grim faces of two men at a back table suggest that they represent an anti-topless, pro-stuffed-shirt movement, while the bashful gastronome in the booth next to ours hardly bothers to glance in the direction of the performers, or, for that matter, away from his plate. I note that the more overt and steady watchers share a predilection for the lactiferous organs, seldom lowering their sights from that level. But if more bizarre penchants existed, would they be discernible?

Despite the salad-only advertisement, the girls wear black pajama-top jackets during their stints of waiting on table (*i.e.*, pushing drinks), shedding the garment only on the dais, to which each dancer is cued by a recorded theme song (the only tune she recognizes?). So little is concealed in the first place that this last strip is teaseless. All the same, the first disrobing provokes a "Get a load of that!" from an ogler newly installed at the bar. "That" is a case of bouncy overendowment which the girl seems to defy the customers to notice, looking them straight in the eyes, if that is where *they* are looking. But her act is an indescribable (pussyfooting?) dilly.

A platinum *Playboy* blonde appears next, with fluorescent pasties, very sheer panty-hose—against the chill? not enough time for body make-up?—and a bad case of the moues. She is half bombed, but her dance, so far from a bacchanal, might have been copied from a circus pooch. Obviously repelled by sex and contemptuous of men, she raises the questions: at what more halcyon time of life—she is probably in her late twenties, which is middle-aged in this profession—did she discover that her virtue was irretrievable, and how many more years as an itinerant go-go stripper graduating to call girl will she be able to take?

The next "waitress" is, at the other extreme, tough and able to take care not only of herself but of every man in the room—some of whom, to judge by her claque, may have been taken care of already. She inspires no lewd ambition in me, apart from a Theseus-like curiosity concerning the hidden portion of her gold-chain G-string, but this could be no more than a sign of Craft ebbing. Nor would she have fetched the top price in a seraglio, being too angular for Ingres (*Le Bain Turc*) and, at the same time, showing a localized tendency, perhaps from usage, to pleat and sag. But whereas her colleagues do no more than go through their paces barely, she puts soul into hers, simulating the throes of denouements with excruciating thrusts and gyrations, and clenchings and unclenchings of the pyge. "Hey, that hurts," one castration-threatened spectator cries out, and a dirty old man at the bar chimes in with "How d'ya like to take *her* home?" The answer this time evidently comes from a married man: "Yeah, only anywhere but *there*." Strutting off after her number, the nymph remarks out loud, "These mornings are really getting to me." This provokes the comment from the floor that perhaps she is working too hard at night.

The next girl, tall, Junoesque, a brunette postiche down her back, is the beauty of the bevy, at least as an example of theater in the round. Her movements are muzzy, perhaps from "grass" or oncoming menses, yet she alone—that cadent, if rented, hair—could raise my libidinal temperature a therm. (Only a necrophiliac could be "bothered" by the other exposures.) As she passes our table after her exhibition, I tell her that of all the girls she would look best in clothes (see-through clothes, anyway), but she is uncertain whether the remark is a compliment, and what started as a smile turns to a "level-with-me-Mister" expression. She is the least at home here, at any rate, and that in itself goes some way toward making her the most attractive.

The male spectator's "kicks" from contemplating the sexual object under a glass bell depend in part on aesthetic gratifications governed by his psychological make-up as a whole. (The "kicks" of the female object, apart from money, are apparently similar to those of the child discarding its clothes in order to gain attention; but I know nothing about "the female," and Tiresias, the only male who did know, said that her pleasure is the greater of the two.) Experiments to isolate and measure male susceptibility to female form, qua form, are carried out by projecting adjustable outlines of female shapes on a screen and enlarging, shrinking, and otherwise modifying them to the subject's desiderations. The latter are not simply avowed—the subject's imputing of the tendency of the attraction to his own impulses is unreliable—but also determined by electrical sensing devices. The findings of the tests thus far, after comparison with personality data, indicate that the breast-fixated American male is better adjusted than the bottom-fixated one. Furthermore, those who opt for comparatively large amplitudes—a rise in the graph—earn correspondingly higher marks in psychosocial stability.

In the absence of coordination between the natural and the social sciences, this result cannot be accepted as pragmatically conclusive, or even

1969 as a fact at all, in view of the present low repute of this kind of psychological measurement. Until recently, the retardation of the heartbeats of submerging crocodiles was thought to be one of all-wise Nature's protective devices for the conservation of oxygen, but the slow-downs are now known to be caused entirely by fear of the scientific experimenters. (In *crocodiles?*) Further research along these adjustable lines will no doubt continue as sex is further removed, and eventually separated entirely, from procreation.

Meanwhile, to "make love, not war" is obviously preferable, and no matter that the biological overlove in lovemaking is as wasteful as overkill: a mere 17 nuclear missiles are said to be enough to destroy human life on the planet, yet hundreds of thousands exist; so, too, though a single sperm cell is enough to create human life, every ejaculation of male seed contains at least 250 million.

Whatever, if anything, love may have to do with the sex explosion—as distinguished from Marcuse's long-awaited and more profoundly subversive Revolution of Eros—one already looks forward to a time beyond, when to make love, forget about it, and even go on to other things, will again become possible. "We liberate sexuality not in order that man may be dominated by [it]," Freud wrote (in 1908!), "but in order to make a suppression possible." Voilà! Temptation exists to be resisted.

April 4. The S.s sign a deed transferring their Arizona citrus groves to the Marions, a gift intended for division among all of I.S.'s children in equal shares.

May 2. New York. Following a consultation with I.S.'s doctors, we take him to New York Hospital at noon; he has been complaining since yesterday of sharp pains above the left knee, which may indicate that the clot, discovered in January, has grown. At the hospital, the femoral artery is found to be entirely blocked and circulation in the by-pass veins so dangerously reduced that surgery is necessary as soon as the patient can be prepared. Autographing a release for the operation, I.S. remarks, "This is like signing your own death warrant." It begins at 7 P.M., under halothane and sodium pentothal,* with simultaneous oxygen feeding to ventilate the heart, lungs, and blood. At 10, he is taken to an intensive care unit, where Dr. Jack Bloch, the operating surgeon, explains that an 11-inch embolus has been removed through a catheter inserted into the crural artery by means of air pressure from below.

May 3. We learn this morning that a second clot was found in the other

---

* I.S. described this later: "It seems as if you had just extended your arm for the injection when you are told the operation is over." Sylvia Plath:
  Fuzzy with sedatives and unusually humorous.
  . . . At the count of two
  Darkness wipes me out like chalk on a blackboard. . . .

arterial branch and that another embolectomy and a left lumbar sympa-thectomy, to open all pipelines as widely as possible, will have to be per-formed today. Can a man of 87, weakened by long illness, survive major surgery for the second time in 24 hours?

At 11:20 P.M., after waiting outside the operating theater all evening, we are admitted to an intensive care unit, where one of the occupants is invisi-ble beneath bandages like the padding of an ice-hockey goalie, and the heartbeats of another, muzzled with breathing machinery, bounce across the screen of a cardiac monitor in the form of green blips. I.S. is clear-headed, sprightly (from digitalis?), and wholly in character. When I tell him that V. is anxious, he says, "Why? What's the matter with *her*?"

May 12. I.S. has been moved from his small, bleak cubbyhole with its view of Spanish Harlem to the spacious room 1719, which is reserved for sick bigwigs; it looks over the barred sun terrace of the psychiatric clinic, a few floors below, to Welfare Island, where rookie firemen are extinguishing practice blazes in dummy buildings. Because he is able and eager to listen to music now, I play a recording of Handel's *Theodora*, assuming it to be emotionally unharmful for him. "Beautiful and boring," he says, not far along: "Too many pieces finish too long after the end." After a nap, he becomes intransigent, refusing to talk and excluding us all from the privacy of his mind. Though literally skin and bones now, he will eat no more than a smidgen of caviar, and that only for the ration of whiskey allowed with it, knocking back the liquid in an amount disproportionate to the small substance of the solid. The skin of his buttocks hangs like laundry when we lift him, and his fingers are so thin that his sapphire signet ring, an apotropaic power to him, has to be removed; his slippers are cross-garter bandaged to the calves as if they were ballet shoes. On the other side of the ledger, the danger of infarction has passed, the carbuncular swelling has diminished, the toe is no longer pustular, and sensation is restored to the foot. The surgical scars, too, from which long threads pro-truded a few days ago like hairs of the metamorphosed Gregor Samsa, are healing, and the skin around them, covered with black-and-blue maculae, is squamous and starting to peel.*

May 20. When I enter the room, I.S. proudly tells me that he has scored four more measures of the B-minor Fugue from Book I of the *Well-Tempered Clavichord*. But in mid-afternoon his temperature flares up to 39 (the New York Hospital uses the apothecary system) from the 38.2 that has been "normal" since the operation and aroused our suspicion that he may have the so-called hospital infection ("staph disease"?). His cough is more congested, like croup, and the respiration rate has accelerated to 44. X-rays are taken and bacterial cultures dispatched for analysis. But

---

* This was before ultrasonic suturing.

1969 whatever the diagnosis, it is not the pneumonia* all of us fear, the "all" including doctors and nurses whose anxiety is unprofessionally apparent but humanly welcome. After leaving the hospital at midnight, I receive hourly calls from a nurse reporting small fluctuations of temperature.

May 24. An offended letter from one of I.S.'s old friends, who, like others of I.S.'s old guard of former eras, freely assures me what is best for him, tells me exactly what he needs, where he should go, what he should do, what my own attitude should be. This last should not include any unrealistic optimism. Return to Hollywood, she says, leaving I.S.'s feelings wholly out of consideration—whether he himself might wish to escape depressing reminders of illness there. I should do this even while unable to imagine the sheer physical impossibility of life there now for both S.s, neither of whom can manage the stairs any more, let alone look after the house.

I myself am unable now, or unwilling, to sympathize with the point of view of my critics, especially the kind who are often wrong but never in doubt. That I have been guilty of mistakes and misjudgments in trying to take care of I.S. is perfectly clear to me. But at least I have given *all* of myself to him and to the job, and if I hadn't, a great deal more might have gone wrong, while his musical life, passive as it is, would have come to an end. As I see it, I.S.'s true friends as well as his children are indebted to me for that. The responsibility for every decision has been mine, furthermore, with no help from anyone but V., and the responsibility is becoming intolerable, equilibrium ever more difficult to maintain. I am increasingly aware of a new tendency to avoid the burden, thanks to my habit of assessing every liability of a course of action, then backing down from the indicated choice and opting for another course simply to shirk the blame for any unfavorable consequences. But it could be that I am becoming ill myself. Abulia, perhaps. (Or is it bulimia?) Self-justification, certainly.

May 25. Letter from my mother: "With your affection for the Stravinskys it is impossible for you to be the least bit objective about them; keep up your courage. I don't know what they would do without you. It is probably one of the things you are supposed to accomplish on earth."

May 26. I.S. has taken an upturn and emerged from the limbo in which he has been suspended for three weeks. Best of all, his demon is still there. "I want to work," he says, "and if I can't work, I want to die." Accordingly, we hoist him out of bed to a gantry-type table with a windlass-like device to adjust the level, and there, cocooned in blankets and with his feet resting on a pillow labeled "Feet," he copies out keyboard Bach for strings. Glancing back and forth from the printed page, propped on a reading stand, to his penciled score, he might be a monk copying a manuscript, or Carpaccio's Augustine at his desk.

---

* It was pneumonia.

After 20 minutes or so we lift him back to bed, with the difference that a small gleam of confidence is showing in his eyes; and he is soon up again, and up and down a total of four times during the afternoon. He wants to listen to music, too, "my own only if you have nothing else." I begin with his tiny two-trumpet *Fanfare*, which draws the comment, "Well, I have nothing against *that*," then Mendelssohn's Octet, Schumann's first string quartet, Beethoven's C-minor Variations. He follows the printed music of each piece, betraying no sign of pleasure or pain except during the Mendelssohn (pleasure).

His bed oscillates like a bunk on a slowly rolling ship. The "sheet" is a sheepskin paillasse, but he is so thin now that his back soon becomes sore at every point of pressure, and his position must be shifted every few minutes. About once an hour he is obliged to lie totally flat while his left leg, crooked like a pelican's most of the time, is forcefully, painfully, straightened by a nurse. "I hurt everywhere," he grumbles. But the *longueurs* of medication schedules, of permutated tests for prothrombin time, of bombardments from a humidifier (like the steam from a manhole cover in a New York street), to say nothing of the indignities of bedpans and the occupational disingenuousness of nurses, with their alternating *Grosspapa* talk and baby-talk ("upsy-daisy"), must gall him most of all.

Still, he *is* better, and a thousand hosannas for that. His recuperative powers have again proved themselves and astonished those who see only the outward and belying decrepitude. His temperature is normal, too, for the first time since May 20, though whether as a result of the river of intravenous effluents that has been poured into him I cannot say. Once, in a pique, he moves his arms as rapidly as he ever did conducting an orchestra, thereby provoking a sybilline nurse to remark: "Obviously God doesn't want you yet, Maestro." But he will not eat. Nor heed our arguments that only by eating can he return to his piano, which, he says, is his one wish. And the hunger strike is more difficult to break than the silence strike, since he can seldom forbear to provide the word one of us may be groping for in some backchat he is not supposed to be tuned in to; or resist the temptation to correct my French (no end of opportunities; I am unable to pronounce the French *"muscle"* to his satisfaction, for example, and the word regularly recurs in reference to the dystrophy in his abdomen and left leg). Once he seems to be on the verge of talking of his own volition, but he stops short dramatically (aposiopesis) and expresses the futility of it all with a wave of the hand. Yet when the head floor nurse—a "yenta" whose own vocal equipment could drown out the brass section of the Berlin Philharmonic—asks him if he will please say something, anything at all, just to oblige us, he fairly yells at her: "MERDE!"

From the hospital, where the parking attendants have begun to call me "Doc," I go to the ballet, where the main attraction, more stared at during intermission than the stage during the performance, is Mrs. Onassis. The

1969   seats are knee-jamming and ill-raked, and the applause, except for a brief volley mocking the abstract antlers above the proscenium arch and the ascent of the retractable chandeliers, is misplaced. The conductor stretches the tempi to the groaning point for Fonteyn, while Nureyev, Tarzan-maned and with the hocks of a Percheron, seems to spend less time dancing than bowing, which he does with his right arm straight up like a chief of MGM Sioux. But then, I am hardly present, being unable to take my thoughts from room 1719 and the man lying there, who has enlarged the imagination and changed the sensibility of the world as much as anyone alive in it, but who had to be helped this afternoon in transposing a clarinet part.

June 18. After being on the rota for discharge since Sunday, I.S. returns to the hotel, and not only from the hospital but also from a place so close to The Other Side that few who have ever been as far ever return. Before he leaves, the floor nurses bring a birthday cake with musical notes on the icing. He smiles, seeing it—a genuine, not a Ritalin-induced smile—and when the women in white break into "Happy Birthday," he conducts them. The party continues in the hotel, where 30 baskets of flowers await him, and where, as V. opens 50 telegrams, he sips champagne. One of his birthday gifts is a recording of *Le Coq d'Or*, to which he listens for about three minutes before it puts him out of sorts.

Going to his room at night, I find him wide awake, his nurse unarousable. "I'm accustomed to the undulating bed," he explains. "Besides, I am afraid of dreaming music, and I realize now that I will never again be able to compose." I protest, of course, trying every tack I can think of to persuade him that he is wrong. But he does not believe any more and is impervious to bonhomie and cheer. It is becoming difficult even to record the depression.

June 20. Having failed to trace Montapert anywhere via telephone, telegram, and letter, and to get a straight answer from Marion, V. sees a new lawyer, Mr. Brinn.

June 29. Television commercials are well into the exploitation of the third-sex market. "For women only," the husky contralto proclaims on behalf of Virginia Slims, which seems to have been promoted as a Sapphic cigarette. And an advertiser for an electric lawnmower, demonstrating the superiority of the machine over a grazing sheep, considers whether the animal might be roasted for dinner, but concludes: "That would be like eating the gardener." The advertiser, moreover, identifies himself as "Dick Palmer."

June 30. V., Miss Christiansen, and I go to a preview of *Oh! Calcutta!* for which Goddard Lieberson has sent tickets. Though the show is for regular guys, or seems to be, unless the men are the real attraction and the women merely decoys, and though all the episodes deal with country matters and none can be construed, except wholly transposed, as a form of gaiety, the largest part of the audience is made up of men in pairs, fissiparous sex. Whatever the viewers' sectarian proclivities—and its other conspicuous feature is the absence of the very young and freaked-out—the performances inhibit. Communality on so large a scale at a peep show violates long-ingrained notions of privacy, at least in our culture. (Cf. Roheim on group onanism in the Intichiuma ceremony in Australia.) Nor does the awareness of the collective ever let up, thanks to the univocal laughter, embarrassed at first, and first, last, and at all other times, embarrassing. Spasms of it afflict my neighbor at the drop of a trouser.

Until now, the limitation of pornography to male fantasies has been explained as a consequence of the involvement of "more extensive higher cortical control" (Lionel Tiger) in male sexual activity than in female. Whatever the truth of that, the desacralization of sex has challenged both the taken-for-granted supremacy of the female nude and the bartered-bride system, which encourages women to think of their bodies, and men to think of women's bodies, as their most valuable possession. Which cannot be a welcome development to the woman of the streets.

On stage, the male nude is still handicapped, if that is the word, by the ban on virile members, at least in amorous action pieces such as *Calcutta*. A young man in the buff, approaching a young and reasonably comely woman in the same, is expected to register a visible physical reaction. But the unattired young men in *Calcutta* do not meet the minimum realistic requirement of the circumstances. The spectator wonders about the reasons for this sexlessness, whether androgen deficiency, sexual shell-shock, saltpeter, or milking the male cast, like vipers, before each performance. In sum, while no holds are barred on stage, tumescence is not permitted, and the actor is therefore denied the opportunity to perform at the top of his bent. The damaging consequence of this is that it exposes him to prejudicial reflections on his manhood and character, the audience being left to assume that if he rises to the occasion at all, he must do so like Blake's worm, a thief in the night, a moral invertebrate. The double standards of stage and screen, of public and cable television, are tripled and quadrupled when compounded with bookselling laws and actual sex laws, different in every state. Critics subject to the current Blue Laws of the Independent Government of Television are forbidden even to describe *Calcutta* with apt and ultimate brevity, that particular Anglo-Saxon tetragram being outlawed on the public-channel medium.

Nudity wears off quickly—and clothes are off in *Calcutta* only long enough for the observation of details reassuring on the whole to the male ego—before the audience is ready for an entirely new cast of bodies. (You could hardly call it a dramatis personae.) The interchangeability of anatomies and the greater uniformity in nude than in clothed ones are premises of the depersonalized presentation of sex, the only possible presentation if the third-party role of the audience is not to be intolerable.

1969   A further premise is that to start over again fully clothed can invigorate. It does, to some extent, in the sadomasochist fantasy scene. A young, fully-dressed English housemaid enters carrying a rod, which she hands to the master of the house whose duty is to punish her. She kneels head to floor, bottom high and audienceward, and, one by one, artfully forestalling the final one, upraises her numerous petticoats. The ultimate revelation, abetted by good countdown technique, is a comparatively *foudroyant* effect, and the sheer effrontery (or backery) of it holds the audience in a brief trance. But an unrelated-to-other-features derrière loses its identity, and *we* lose our bearings, forgetting what it is—an enlarged peach? an idée fixe?—and why we are basking in it.

On balance, and for purely negative reasons, *Calcutta* is worth the while of anyone concerned with improving the prevailing standards of "erotic culture." For one thing, it obviates further demonstration of the dullness of sex as a subject for a full evening in the theater. For another, it neglects variety—no same-sex playlet, no satire on the 500 positions (cuissades, croupades, flanquettes, etc.). The bedwork scenes should have been interspersed with illustrations of the polymorphous perverse, peeks at selected fetishisms, and especially bestiality, which would at least allow for a bit of horseplay.

Calcutta also shows the undesirableness of puerility in pornography (as in everything else), particularly in the two episodes that had starting possibilities as social satire, the takeoff on "swinging" via the sexual want-ad columns, and the send-up of Masters and Johnson. The latter is the most nearly successful caper of the evening, both because its clinicalism fits the genre and because it turns the tables to show that the "sexual response" of the volunteer lovers, who are attached with electrodes and wired to a computer-like console that lights up when copulation begins, is less worthy of study than that of the kinky institute staff.

What, I wonder, not breathlessly, will be the use of the artistic-merit and redeeming-social-value clauses when our moribund "living theaters" move on from group therapy to the theater of intercourse? At the present rate of escalation, onstage erections may soon be de rigueur.

Does *Calcutta* celebrate sexual freedom as much as it does sexual frustration? Catharsis, in any sense at all—well, what *was* that function old Reich once made so much of?—has never seemed more remote. "I want it now," a singer moans at the end, but *does* anyone, do even sexual have-nots, as a result of incitement by these exhibitions? Or are the latter something of an anti-arouser, in the sense that while substitute performances may nourish the imagination, they can also reduce it. Will the decriminalization of sex contribute to desexualization?

Perhaps the unclothed state may have been intended only for the gods, and the gods at home: sea-changed Venus had to be draped before entering the mortal sphere. Or intended for those who, like the Doukhobors and the Digambora, practice it in the name of a god. But that is to over-look those rites of passage well suited for the condition: Naked I came into the world, naked I shall go.

July 12. Los Angeles. At 12:20 A.M. I.S.'s nurse calls me to say that his temperature is 104, and the respiratory rate alarmingly fast. I telephone Dr. Bernstein, who instructs me to bring him to the emergency entrance at UCLA Medical Center—which I do in an ambulance and with a nurse, not being certain that I can carry him inside. The doctor in attendance is busy antidoting hippies poisoned by mushrooms (botulism toxin?). When at length he examines I.S.—under my proctoring, since the nurse is only sketchily aware of his medical misadventures—the verdict is pneumonia. A little later, X-rays reveal no more than his 30-year-old tuberculosis scars. Two other doctors, arriving for consultation, are as baffled as were their New York colleagues by the incident on May 20. An oxygen cylinder is wheeled into the room, nevertheless, and I.S. spends the night with a plas-tic mask clapped over his nose and mouth. It is 4 A.M. when I take V. home; she drove to UCLA alone, a further worry in view of her very poor automobile night-vision.

Temperature and respiration normal, I.S. returns at 6 P.M., undiagnosed. V. fears that his tuberculosis may have become active again; an enclosed and dormant TB bacillus is virulent if released, and could be after thou-sands of years. She believes, moreover, that people are born to their dis-eases—Bartok to his leukemia—and that I.S.'s born-to disease is tuberculo-sis. Poor V. All she can do is wonder from which direction the next blow impends.

July 13. Letter from my mother: "I hesitate to think about what today brings you. I am sure you are reluctant to open your eyes in the morning. My heart aches for you, and it does for Mr. and Mrs. Stravinsky, too. After having lived such glamorous and exciting lives, how prepared are they to take these old age blows that come to them? Wish I could say something to cheer you but can't think of anything except that I am very proud of your behavior. You are displaying the greatest loyalty."

July 16. I take I.S. to Cedars of Lebanon for tests, on Dr. Bernstein's hunch that the coughing spells, the halituous constriction, and the rale may be due to clotting in the lungs, a not-uncommon development in polycythemiacs; but the diagnosis on the admission card is tracheal bron-chitis. I.S. coughs only when swallowing liquids, however, *not* when he eats, which raises the possibility that the spasms are caused simply by pres-sure on the esophagus.

July 18. "The tests will prove nothing," the patient protests. *"Le mal est dans mon âme."* Overhearing our discussion as to whether a Practical Nurse will be needed for the night, he cuts in with, "All my nurses are *im*practical, anyway, and since I already have pains everywhere else, why must you give me a pain in the neck, too?" When V. gently asks if he wants anything, the

1969 answer is soft and poignant: "I want to compose." As we leave the hospital, she reasons, "He would suffer less if he had a smaller endowment of intuition, but then he wouldn't be *him*."

July 19. Yesterday's lung-scanning has unfounded our fears of clotting but not dispelled the specter of tuberculosis or ended the suspicion that the alveolae may be dilating, the small lung sacs fibrillating, as they do with emphysema. Unable to account for the coughing fits and dramatic rises in temperature, the doctors are obviously grasping at straws.

Back from the hospital, I.S. says the worst of the experience was that yesterday he received someone else's lab report, which was less good than his own. But he needs analeptic medicine now, or, like an athlete, anabolic steroids. He weighs only 87 pounds!

Haydn's Opus 76 Quartets, in the evening, elicit three of his long-unheard grunts of pleasure (at measures 45–50 of the Largo, at measures 169–72 of the Presto of No. 5, and in the last measures of the Adagio of No. 6). Nor does his attention ever stray, except when objecting to the thicker layers of unctuousness in the performance. "To say that the music is '*like* Beethoven' is hindsight," he says. "It should not be played as if it were *by* Beethoven." But he does not cough at all during the two hours of music, and he has not swallowed any linctus. We carry him upstairs afterward on a seat of crossed hands.

August 1. The first half hour of *Skin*, said to be representative of the new sex flicks, takes place at the San Francisco Botanical Gardens. One supposes that this is to compare phalli to flora, except that no human appears, and the audience soon begins to suspect that the title refers to lemons and oranges. The dermatological mystery deepens in the second scene, a drama about the Bay Area needle set, but in the scene after that, a blotched and mottled rump (rondures only, no connecting anatomy!) canters about the screen in time with Bach's D-minor Fugue from *Fantasia*. What was it Socrates said about "the desire and pursuit of the whole"?

August 9. Unable to extract a financial statement from Montapert, the S.s decide to dismiss him and to retain Arnold Weissberger, whom they telephone in New York.

August 17. The Marions and Soulima Stravinskys come to see I.S., to determine how long he might last. In order to cut the visit short, he stays in bed and pretends to be ill, then dresses and goes downstairs to receive Michel Yelachich.* The Soulimas and Marions pass V.'s door without speaking to her or even inquiring about her. A novel waits to be written about all this, ideally by Mauriac (*Nest of Vipers*), the Marions being devout French Catholics.

August 22. Milene pays her father a quick visit, after which V. asks why her brothers have not thanked their father or herself for the gift of the

* He later married Stravinsky's granddaughter Catherine.

502

citrus groves four months ago. "Ask Andre," Milene blurts out, rushing **1969**
from the room.

August 26. The turnover in nurses has been so rapid of late that I.S.
pretends he cannot remember their names. He has taken to summoning
them with "Hello," spoken weakly at first, then repeated three or four times
con crescendo. If a response is still not forthcoming, he will shout in a *Boris
Godunov* voice that we are surprised and reassured to find he still possesses.
But he is always aware of his nurse's language and always chooses the right
one (Russian, German, English, or French) in which to be understood by
her when criticizing her to V. This afternoon, he greatly offends his dot-
ing Russian *nanya* by asking us, deliberately within her earshot: "Why
must I spend the whole afternoon in the company of an idiot?"

At table now, he prefers, if he can get away with it, to officiate and to
direct traffic, rather than to exert himself. Thus he will nod his head or
crook his index finger toward some food on his plate that he wishes to be
fed to him, but if the nurse is not around, he spoons or forks it quite easily
by himself.

A birthday party for Christopher Isherwood, after which we listen to
Dargomizhky's *The Stone Guest,* following a score that I.S. acquired in his
youth. "If you were to ask me about the music today," he says, when it is
over, "I would be less generous than I was at one time. Now I prefer the
libretto to the music, and so far as the performance is concerned, I prefer
the diction of the singers to their singing. Still, it is an original work,
whose best and worst qualities are the same: the evenness." Isherwood,
meanwhile, has fallen asleep in front of the television.

September 15. To the airport in two automobiles, one of them driven
by Milene. Fly to Newark, nurse Miriam Pollack with I.S. He has a good
room, Suite 1270, on the Park side of the Plaza Hotel.

October 3. Berlin. A fierce rain. With Rita Christiansen and Nabokov
to the airport at 5 A.M. for the early flight to Munich, Zurich, and Basel
(the Drei Königen Hotel). A brass band, parading on the Rhine bridge,
rocks me but not to sleep, and at 3 P.M. Montapert calls, asking me to meet
him on the street outside the bank. Inside the bank, I sign papers that I am
not given a chance to read. Afterward, Montapert drives me to a taxi
stand, and, as I step out, says that we will never see each other again, that
he owes I.S. $10,000, given by Marion from I.S.'s account. Back in the
hotel, a telephone from V.: they have leased an apartment in the Essex
House for two years (!).

October 4. Drive to Zurich with Rita, whom I persuade to return as
I.S.'s nurse. She flies to Paris and I fly to New York, which is a multi-layered traffic tangle: in the air (a two-hour "holding pattern"), at the airport
(waiting for baggage and in Customs), queuing for taxis, on the express-
ways, crossing 61st Street to the hotel. Excepting his calves, as thin as
those of Donatello's St. John in the Frari, I.S. looks almost hale, and his

1969 weight is up to 106, the same as it was before the operations.

October 6. I urge the S.s to repatriate the money in their Swiss bank to the U.S., whatever the tax penalties, and we inform Weissberger.

October 14. We move to the Essex House.

October 21. Svetlana Stalin Alleluyeva, an attractive woman with a ruddy complexion, calls on an unusually talkative I.S.

October 25. I.S. signs a new agreement with Boosey & Hawkes (Ampenoff) for the publication of his "archives." He writes to George Seferis about the translation of *Poetics of Music*: "I, too, prefer the second version. In the opening sentence, 'to do as I pleased' (first version) sounds brash in tone and too wide in scope compared to 'if I could freely choose' (second version). But, then, translations are one of life's necessary frustrations. . . . Thanks for the instance of the form 'Oedipoda' in Seneca's play. . . . I am much obliged to you, also, for an epigraph (*The Woman of Zakynthos*)."

November 18. Theodore arrives from Geneva. He did not know that six and a half months ago, through Marion, V. and I.S. had given him one-third of their citrus groves! And he does not react or answer when she asks why he thinks Marion did not inform him of the gift.

November 21. Inscribing a copy of *Retrospectives and Conclusions* for Lucia Davidova, I.S. writes his name in Russian on the flyleaf, then turns to the biographical blurb on the inside of the dust-wrapper, and, below the phrase "lives in California," adds the heart-breaking words "No more."

November 22. I.S. files suit to recover his manuscripts from his son-in-law, Andre Marion, and former lawyer, William Montapert, to whose joint stewardship they were entrusted in February 1967. The story is carried by newspapers and television nationally. But not, of course, the *full* story. Two months ago, after becoming a New York resident, I.S. requested the return of his manuscripts. Marion answered with the demand that I.S. first sign a "release" not to prosecute him. Marion also referred to a "dispute over the ownership of certain manuscripts," though I.S.'s manuscripts were incontestably I.S.'s property, nor had he ever indicated his intentions with regard to them, except to give them to libraries for tax deductions. The "release" also described some seven or eight categories of employment ("business and investment manager, holder of various powers of attorney, bookkeeper, recipient and disburser of funds, corporate officer and director of Verigor International, manager of Stravinsky's citrus farm," etc.) for which the S.s had been paying Marion, but of whose functions Marion denied any knowledge when V. sought his help during the hospital crisis last May. The "release" further demanded I.S.'s protection from prosecution by the government (as if he could contravene a legal investigation): "Stravinskys agree to hold Marion harmless from claims of any governmental agencies, whether state, federal, or foreign . . . and hereby expressly waive the benefits of the Civil Code of the State of California which reads:

'1542. A general release does not extend to claims which the creditor does **1969**
not know or expect to exist in his favor at the time of executing the
release, and not a mere covenant not to sue.'"

But why should Marion have reason to fear that his father-in-law might
sue him? And what could an honest man have to hide from government
agencies, local, federal, and even foreign?

Nicolas Nabokov for dinner, after which the 10 o'clock television news
includes an announcement of I.S.'s suit against Marion.

November 26. I.S. signs an authorization for the Swiss Bank
Corporation to purchase U.S. municipal bonds with all the funds in his
account and to send the bonds to New York.

December 11. I Draft a letter to Lawrence Morton in answer to one
from him concerning my strictures of Los Angeles for its disregard of I.S.
on his 85th birthday.

> I am glad to have your views on my "general condemnation" of Los
> Angeles in its treatment of Stravinsky. But my remarks were pro-
> voked only by comparing what Los Angeles did in observance of
> Stravinsky's 85th birthday (*i.e.*, nothing) with what was done in
> other cities of the world, many of them with far fewer resources.
> Obviously I should have been more explicit. I should have men-
> tioned the failure of the Los Angeles universities to mount a
> Stravinsky festival. No less obviously I should have excepted you,
> Ingolf Dahl, Sol Babitz, and a few other individuals.
>
> But why do you mention John Vincent and the Cantata "com-
> mission"? Although Stravinsky did eventually receive a minute
> sum for the piece, above his conducting fee, this was used to cover
> costs of part-copying and of importing a tenor; and weren't you
> present at the rehearsal when Stravinsky offered to pay for an extra
> oboist (or English horn player) out of his own pocket and *was
> accepted?*
>
> And Werner Janssen, yet, among the wronged! Stravinsky used
> to tell it the other way around, and the evidence in his files sup-
> ports him. But, then, the files tell much the same story all the way
> down, a story of skimping on rehearsal time, of the composer
> being asked to waive music rentals and performance fees, of pro-
> gramming based on first-performance publicity.
>
> But what has happened to *you?* Not long ago you would have
> been the first to agree with my "condemnation." When Stravinsky
> was only eighty and not yet safe to praise, you helped him to write
> a letter protesting the *Los Angeles Times's* defamation of *The Rake's
> Progress.*
>
> You say that the Museum concerts were "costly" as well as "sin-
> cere appreciations of Stravinsky's presence in the community." *I*

say that they were not costly enough. Nor do I consider three Stravinsky concerts an extravagant number, even if personal homage had not been a consideration.

Besides, "the Museum," in the sense of initiator, does not exist. The concerts took place only because *you* were there. And the third and final one, the belated so-called birthday concert, was a face-saving afterthought. If Basel, Berlin, Edinburgh, Amsterdam earn an "A" for good intentions simply by announcing their programs a decent interval in advance, then Los Angeles deserves a "Z." And even at that final event Stravinsky *was* exploited. Television had him for nothing.

So, not pretending to any detachment and claiming a perspective no larger than what I have learned by reading Stravinsky's mail, I feel that Los Angeles's treatment of him on the occasion of his 85th anniversary was shoddy. What matters far more is that the Stravinskys felt it, too. Yet I concede, and Stravinsky concedes, that this treatment was probably no worse than it would have been if he *didn't* live there.

December 17. We bundle I.S. into the car for an evening ride through Central Park and down 5th Avenue to see the Christmas lights, then, back in the hotel, listen to the Adagio and Fugue from the *Hammerklavier* Sonata. ("What do you think of that?" I ask at one point, but he shuts me up with "*Je ne pense pas, j'écoute.*") V. advises him to go to bed early: "Auden is coming for dinner tomorrow and you will have to be sharp. Please try to be a little less gloomy, too," she adds, to which his answer is: "Then give me a larger Scotch." She also reminds him that "Nabokov is coming in the morning to say *au revoir.*" I.S.: "Without saying *bonjour* first?" And she suggests that he be a little more *méchant* with his nurses, "just to get back in form." I.S.: "I already started today."

December 18. After Nabokov talks at length about his recent trip to the USSR, V. asks I.S. if he remembers who attended the banquet in his honor in Moscow in 1962. When he says, "Well, *I* was there, which means that *you* were probably there, too," it is clear that the presence of no one else in the world would matter to him in the slightest. Nabokov asks him to autograph *Retrospectives and Conclusions,* and V. encourages him to "add a few notes of music as well." "Which notes?" he asks, whereupon she hums something that he writes down in a novel way.*

Auden, who comes with Kirstein and Balanchine, is ornery before din-

---

* Stravinsky *never* autographed the same way twice, and he *always* had ideas. Meeting his San Francisco friend Hans Popper in Tokyo in 1959, after having seen him in Vienna and New York shortly before, I.S., in no time at all and with no apparent forethought, decorated Popper's keepsake album with a map ingeniously relating the three cities.

ner and not on his best mettle during it. His uppermost concern nowadays is to adhere to the split-second timing of his daily routine. He replies to I.S.'s "How are you" with, "Well, I'm on time, anyway," and for the poet's sake, dinner has to be served at exactly 7 o'clock. He even gets sozzled on schedule, and to the extent that, as far as he is concerned, the Chateau Margaux could be acetified Mogen David. At one point he exclaims, on no evident provocation, and as if unaware that the remark is *outré*: "Everybody knows that Russians are mad"—which might be described as emotion recollected in alcohol, except that the recollecting is ahead of time, this being tomorrow's. Toward the end of the evening, while V. looks on in horror, he opens three closets before finding the urgently needed one. But the refractory mood finally gives way to one of deep affection for I.S., who becomes the object of a tender speech *in German*.

After his departure, the S.s speculate on the reasons why Auden's standard of living has failed to keep pace with his income, why he inhabits the same kind of hovel that he did 20 years ago, and why he is still wearing some of the same garments. Are the dark glasses, the tattered coat, the frayed bedroom slippers that he reserves for winter social outings a protective disguise for "greatest living poet"? Not, anyway, according to his own interpretation of the psychology of clothes ("They enable one to see oneself as an object").

Whatever the answer, if he had had a tin cup in his hand, it would have been filled with coins shortly after he reached the street, especially since he sang so merrily on the way out.

December 30. New York. Write to Berman:

> I was in Florida for one week (the longest time I have been away from the Stravinskys for three years!), because my mother has had another operation. Happy to report that Mr. S.'s health is better, and that he has improved steadily since our arrival in New York, mentally as well as physically. He has gained 20 pounds since leaving the hospital, thin and chlorotic, last June and is much more *vivant*, more aware, more active than at any time in the past year. Still, no one, certainly none of us and not his doctors, expected that he would be celebrating (or deploring) the beginning of the 70s.
>
> Mrs. S., however, is showing the strain not only of worry about him—she reflects every fluctuation in his health—but also of the legal and financial responsibilities thrust on her. (She is four years older than the date on her passport. Sudeikin made the adjustment in Tiflis when they were applying for new documents, the old ones having been destroyed in the flight from Sebastopol; she was born in 1888.) Not being able to paint or to go out in the evenings, she is frustrated, and we are all weary of hotel life. The

1969   rooms at the Essex are more ample than those in the Pierre, but the neighborhood is worse, the food is inedible, and the difficulties of transportation are greater, even though the S.s have their car in the garage. When you leave a hotel room in New York, where do you go? Lincoln Center? Broadway? In Paris, at least, Mr. S. was able to stroll in the Place Vendome, which was worth the bundling up and the long trek through the hotel corridors.

December 31. The main event in I.S.'s life at Christmas 1969 has been his re-reading of Lermontov in a new edition of his works, a gift from Lucia Davidova.

❧ **Postscript 1994.** This was the worst year of Stravinsky's life, as concerns both health and personal relations. The diary describes in considerable detail the emergency operation in New York and the protracted recovery but says little about the rift in family affairs, which had now become an active San Andreas Fault. The Stravinskys' N.Y. doctor, Leon Lewithin, had urged them to move to New York in 1967, promising superior medical care. They had wanted to go but at their advanced ages could not face another uprooting. The decision to resettle in New York in 1969 was only partly medical, the larger part being the complete estrangement between the Stravinskys and his daughter and son-in-law. The facts of this became known only in 1977, in the course of long litigation. Suffice to say here that in August 1969 the Stravinsky children entered into an agreement with a lawyer, Montapert, working against, rather than for, the Stravinskys, and using the lawyer's power-of-attorney to remove all of the Stravinskys' money from their Swiss bank and deposit it, 50% in the lawyer's name and 50% in the names of the children; this embezzlement was actually carried out until the lawyer discovered that although the numbered account was illegal, so was the embezzlement.

After October 1969, when Stravinsky's son-in-law refused to return his manuscripts, Stravinsky never again mentioned the name of his daughter or her spouse. In a life of so many uprootings, the old couple undertook still another, flew to New York, and lived in a rented suite in the Essex House, while all of their belongings were placed in storage.

❧ 1970

January 4. I fetch Auden in a limousine, taxis being scarce both because it is Sunday and because the unremoved snow in streets like his keeps them away. The chauffeur's raised brow when we enter the neighborhood and pull up at 77 St. Mark's is not a reaction to driving conditions, however, and he inquires twice whether I am certain of the address.

Auden is gentleness personified with the S.s, and the evening is smooth, quiet, affectionate. How different he is from his public persona. Not long ago, he wrote, "A writer's private life is, or should be, of no concern to anybody except himself, his family and friends." Why, then, does he invite so many journalists to his Austrian hideaway? And why is he apparently gratified with their descriptions of his very private life?—as in the recent *Esquire* piece and the one in the current *Life*, which he actually commends to us. At the same time he has become almost impossibly touchy (from loneliness and frustration, no doubt, Chester hardly being a family), as well as tyrannical and quixotic in his opinions, tending to speak almost exclusively in absolutes: "This is right, that is wrong; one must, one mustn't." His approbations and condemnations are total and final. Consider his rave review in the *New Yorker* of Eiseley's *Unexpected Universe*, a likable book, certainly, but by no means free from "romance of Nature" gush. (Describing Captain Fitzroy of the *Beagle* in the act of slitting his throat, Eiseley writes: "In the dim light the razor glinted." How does *he* know? Did Fitzroy leave a last-minute note? And does it matter?)

But the poems continue and excuse a great deal; and not only the poems but the man who wrote, not long ago: "Every time we make a nuclear bomb we are corrupting the morals of a host of innocent neutrons below the age of consent."

January 6. After Rita tells me that I.S.'s left foot is cooler than the right, V. calls Dr. La Due, who comes promptly and says that the patient has suffered a spasm. But because the symptoms are the same as a year ago when a clot was found, and to hesitate could be fatal, I call Nabokov and ask him to send *his* doctor, Henry Lax, who duly arrives, says it *is* a clot, and prescribes anti-coagulants. The foot is warmer now and my *apologia pro vita sua*

509

1970 is defined: I am an Early Warning Station.

But *not* a Boswell. Which I say because no reference to me neglects to call me that. This may be attributed, in part, to the Great Cham's own observation that "nobody can write the life of a man, but those who have eat and drunk and lived in social intercourse with him." Except that the second half of the statement, "but few who have lived with a man know what to remark about him," takes away what the first gives. The difference is that Samuel Johnson needed a Boswell and I.S. doesn't, even though he clearly thought of me as one, even going out of his way to tell me secrets—about his brother Gury's homosexuality, about his own early sexual corruption by his nurse Bertha—that he seemed to want recorded. If I reject the Boswell role, it is to claim one more like that of a Goncourt (in category, of course, not quality). In fact, the beginnings of a Goncourt partnership go back to our first week together, I.S. having inducted me into his letter-writing service from the start. The method was exactly that of the Goncourts' "dual dictation." I would lean over his shoulder as he wrote, each of us acting as the other's intercessory, contributing words or phrases, suggesting changes, beginning sentences which the other would finish, as we still do in conversations. For this reason I can go through my journals and point to words and expressions that were his; and go through his writings, stumbling on phrases (flippancies and pomposities, all too frequently) that were mine. In short, and presumptuous as it is for me to say so—as well as difficult to substantiate because our only taped conversations, at a public forum in Cincinnati a few years ago, reveal me only in my feed-in function and him only in his "public personality" one—a merger (exchange, symbiosis) *has* taken place between the senior and the junior, the creative and, in late years, the executive branches of our firm. And, ill-assorted a pair as we are in many ways, our musical responses (which is what brought us together, after all) are kindred.

· **March 3**. In reply to an inquiry about his children, I.S. says: "They are more concerned about my wealth than my health." Yet in fairness to them, I.S.'s double life has left them in an anomalous position throughout the longer part of their own lives. Very likely their strongest feelings toward him have always been those of fear. Nor can it ever have been easy to have such a man for a father. Even biologically, being born of first cousins, their first legacy was the threat of the recessive gene.

Simply to get their work done, all great artists must be selfish, must sacrifice the people around them, as I.S. sacrificed his children to his art. From my own early years with him, I can imagine exactly what life must have been for them. When in the throes of composition, he would come to the table for days in succession without saying a word and forbidding everybody else to speak as well. He was capable of throwing things, of locking himself in his room, and of shouting orders at anyone in his vicinity, which meant, first of all, his family. Even at 86, ill, and in bed, he could and did so terrorize his daughter on at least one occasion that she came from his room in tears, saying: "It was always like that with Papa! He always got his own way. He killed my mother."

The truth of his relationship with his children is that they have been remote from him not merely during his illness but for the past 30 years, not seeing him at all in his first decade in America and in the subsequent 20 years, his two sons, anyway, only very rarely. Of the reasons for the remoteness—understandable envy of the superior qualities of their step-mother, jealous hatred of me—not the least is that the children are older and mentally less elastic in their 60s than I.S. is in his 80s. But to do them justice, they know this and admit it.

The real puzzle is in connection with the S.s' gift of their Arizona citrus groves to the three children and granddaughter in equal shares. The gift never got beyond I.S.'s daughter and her husband, who did not inform the brothers of the parental intentions. V. discovered this by a fluke, in con-versation with her older stepson. But, as she says, describing the imbroglio to a friend today, the strain of premature interest in matters of inheritance began to show in the daughter and son-in-law some years ago. Their remark that "the paintings are disappearing from the walls of father's house" (actually, Picasso's portrait of I.S., lent for an exhibit in The Hague), repeated to the S.s, first alerted us to the hidden attitude. V. then learned that I.S.'s will—which, incredibly, she had not read!!—denied her the right to a will of her own and that I.S.'s son-in-law had blanket powers of attor-ney and actually would have become her parcener.

What is baffling about this sordid turn of events is that, far from follow-ing traditional novercal behavior, V. has always shown the greatest munifi-cence. It was she who convinced I.S. to buy new houses for his children, something he never would have done on his own. Of all ironies, too, it was *her* idea to bring them from Europe after the war, to take care of him in his old age if anything should happen to her. Even now, her strongest feel-ing in the matter is one of concern for the damage to I.S., both physically and morally, the doctors having told her that his recuperation has been set back.

And the feelings of the paterfamilias himself? Does he feel like King Lear? He had ranting, Lear-like moments at the time of the suit over the manuscripts, but this soon turned to irony. Then one day not long ago he said, "*Il arrive un moment où on ne veut plus savoir.*" This very afternoon he inquired as to the whereabouts of the manuscript of *Jeu de cartes*. "It is in the other room," I say. "Do you want to see it?" "No, but I would like to know what the price tag on it says."

March 4. Write to Berman: "I.S. has suffered new setbacks, including an attack of cystitis three weeks ago, and a small thrombosis, which is manifested in a severe headache followed by a day or two of drowsiness, then recovery. Even so, the doctors say that nothing is seriously wrong,

1970 no disequilibrium in the components of the blood, no weakness of the heart. . . . Much of our time is wasted with lawyers, going from Jarndyce to Jarndyce. The fees are prodigious and the work accomplished minuscule. I.S. is enjoying Henri Troyat's *Pushkin*."

March 5. During the night, after months of painful deliberation about the matter, V. composes a letter of instructions for I.S.'s funeral and burial in the Russian corner of the cemetery island of San Michele, Venice. She does not represent this as his wish, which none of us has ever been able to determine because of the unmentionableness of the subject: all we know for certain is that he does not want to be cremated and scattered to the winds. V. says simply that she believes he would have concurred with the decision. (Well, you could hardly say that it would have *pleased* him.) When his nurse fetches me this morning with the words "The maestro wants to talk to you about Venice," I am momentarily electrified, but then not especially surprised: I have always believed that I.S. is deeply psychic.*

Later in the day we play the *Requiem Canticles*, which V.'s letter has specified as the work *she* wishes to be performed in his memory, when the time comes, "since *he* and *we* knew he was writing it for himself." But at the *Libera me*, where, it seems to me, the music leaves the concert hall and becomes part of an actual requiem service, she rushes from the room in tears.

March 6. I.S. awakes with a fever. Examining him two hours later, Dr. Lax diagnoses pneumonia in the lower left lobe. Tetracycline, dijoxin, and other medications are sent for, and happily the temperature does not rise.

March 7. His fever having disappeared, I.S. greets us in the "good-morning-everybody" mood of the Emperor of China in *The Nightingale*, after *his* nightlong struggle with "Death." To the doctor, however, I.S. describes his condition as "*Comme çi, comme ça.*" Which, Lax says, "is not only proof that his spirit is intact, but a precise scientific answer. . . . I have never seen such inner vitality and life force," he goes on, "to say nothing of the alertness, the powers of observation, the acuteness of the critical faculties—for he can formulate the subtlest distinctions. And the inner physical elasticity is no less amazing, considering the restricted outer mobility. Few people of his age are able to respond to medication, not only the way he does but at all."

Speaking of China, the eclipse of the sun today, which I.S. watches, is accompanied by an eerie quiet, the opposite of the great din that the Chinese keep up during eclipses to frighten off evil spirits. Is it because the whole city has stopped to sky-gaze? And does the greenish, deathly penumbra remind I.S. of the shadow that has passed over him during the night?

---

* Shortly after Stravinsky's death, V. lifted his Russian Bible from his bed table, and a picture of St. Michael fell out, a copy of an icon that I.S. had owned since childhood.

March 16. Letter from my mother: "It is not right that Stravinsky can-
not enjoy his last days peacefully. Patience, courage, strength and faith to
do all the chores that are thrust upon you."

March 27. 1218 North Wetherly Drive is sold for a pittance.
Hardened refugees though they are, the S.s are sad about this: But I am
not, having been happier when they lived at 1260. Moreover, it seems fit-
ting that I.S. should be on the move again, like Tolstoy at the end.

April 5. On the Seaboard Express, nearing Palm Beach, I am inundated
by memories of an automobile trip through Florida with the S.s 20 years
ago. We entered the state from the west then, partly because I was gather-
ing local color for an article on such improbable one-time residents as
Macpherson, the author of the "Ossian" forgeries (Pensacola), Prince
Achille Murat (Tallahassee), Harriet Beecher Stowe (near Jacksonville),
George Inness (Silver Springs), Maeterlinck (St. Augustine), and Delius
(Solano Grove, the would-have-been pantisocracy, or Rananim, of D. H.
Lawrence). In February 1950, we drove from the Prince Murat Motel,
Tallahassee, to Tampa and St. Petersburg; and from there crossed the Bay
by ferry, in spite of I.S.'s fears that the boat would capsize and he would
"drone"—in which prospect V. attempted to console him with the thought
that at least the water would be "lukey warm."

In Sarasota, finding ourselves short of money and unable to pay our
hotel bill, I.S. asked Mr. and Mrs. John Alden Carpenter, who were in their
winter home there, for a loan, and their generosity saw us through to New
York.* We visited the Museum, then drove to Key West, and, finding no
rooms there, to Miami. The next day we went to an alligator farm, the
only incident of the trip that I.S. still remembers because the keeper told
him that a giant gavial, between whose jaws the keeper had inserted a strut
in order to show the teeth, was born during the lifetime of Dante. (I.S.
still pronounces the last syllable of "crocodile" as if it were a pickle.) We
spent that night in Daytona and the one after in Charleston, where V. had
lived for the month of February 1940, shortly after coming to America.

These daydreams are interrupted by the arrival of the train at West Palm
Beach. Or, rather, at its black-belt backyard. Social stratigraphers must
have an easy time of it in Florida, status being almost entirely a matter of
distance from the beach. The farther inland, the lower the social order,
and for black people the railroad tracks and bascule bridges provide addi-
tional demarcations to stay on the wrong side of.

April 6. Pompano Beach. I have hardly begun to bask in the sand and
eye the Nereids when V. calls from New York to tell me that I.S. has pneu-
monia and is to be taken to the hospital. She is naturally distraught but
has tears in her voice, too, because of anxiety about his heart, this for the

---

* Stravinsky had known the Carpenters since his first American tour in 1925 and had
stayed with them in Chicago in November 1940. She was Adlai Stevenson's mother-in-law.

1970 first time, weakness having been detected in the left ventricle. And, according to her description of the symptoms, he may be suffering from Stokes-Adams Syndrome. Not yet having unpacked, I go directly to the airport and add my name to several waiting lists for cancellations, flight reservations being unobtainable because of the air traffic controllers' strike. Luckily finding a seat on a 7:30 flight, I arrive at the Essex House in time to hear the 11 o'clock newscaster announce that "the condition of composer Igor Stravinsky, now in the Lenox Hill Hospital Cardiac[!] Unit, is described as critical." This stuns us, not the statement itself but the publicity, since I.S. was admitted to the hospital under an assumed name in order to avoid the inevitable flowers, telegrams, and letters that will add to V.'s burden. She now realizes that Lillian Libman is talking to the press behind our backs.

One prays, of course, in spite of Galton's *Statistical Inquiries into the Efficacy of Prayer* (*i.e.*, the *in*efficacy), which I have just been reading. And the thought of Galton makes me wonder about a statistical inquiry into the efficacy of "symbiotic relationships," if the phenomenon can be extrapolated and distinguished from "coincidence," whose numerical expression is comparatively simple: This is the third time in as many years that I.S. has been taken to the hospital when I have gone away.

Not *that* thought keeps me awake, but the emptiness of his room, which is across the hall from mine; and the silence, for I have listened to his cough, his calls for the nurse, his movements in and out of bed every night for the last six months. And not only listened, but gone to his room several times each night, quite regularly at his worst hour, 4 A.M., talking to him, giving him water, primping his pillow, helping him to turn or sit up, or simply holding his hands—which look more and more shriveled, as if they had been too long in water—when he seemed confused or surprised, perhaps waking from a dream, his eyes questioning for a moment, and the next moment knowing the answers all too well.

V. asks me to leave the light on in his room tonight. But I hate to enter it, hate to see the icons and the photographs of the Turin shroud in the empty corner; and the Bach fugue he had been playing, still open on the piano; and, worst of all, that terribly sad wheelchair *by* the piano. Only three nights ago we listened to the *Canticles* together, after which I tried to encourage him to compose "even two notes." "But they must be the right two," he came back, and the meaning of the man was in that answer. Last week, a nurse who urged him to "try" to compose was rebuffed with: "I never *try*, I compose or I don't compose."

April 7. The first volunteer pall bearer is the BBC. Early this morning its New York office calls to ask Rita "whether Mr. Craft will be available for an interview if Mr. Stravinsky dies."

While waiting to see I.S., we watch his heartbeat on a master console of monitors, one for each patient in the unit, which reminds us of Space

Flight Control, Houston. The range of his graph seems small (indicating weakness?) and the beat itself syncopates about once in every two trips across the screen. But the graphs of others are far more erratic. One of them seesaws bumpily, one is as jagged as lighting, one is like last week's stock market, one is alarmingly flat, and one hovers very high above the equatorial line, like a profile map of the Himalayas.

I.S., in a pressure breathing unit, has clumps of wires like the viscera of an old radio set attached to his chest; a nasal cannula, like a diver's nose-guard; and a catheter, which drains into a plastic canteen and which is the worst of these trammels, he says, provoking an unassuageable urge to urinate. He begs to get out of bed, turns from side to side, and finally kicks his blankets away, revealing strap-on sheepskin heel-pads (as they are called, though the heels are uncovered) with which he looks incongruously Mercurial. But he betrays not the slightest opacity of mind, and knows exactly what he wants, whether word, object, or action.

He is a minefield of medical problems, to be sure, what with polycythemia, chronic bronchitis, and numerous other complications to be contended with. Yet the visit is not disheartening. His strength, inner and outer, is far from depleted, and his lifeline is more steel cable than silk thread. He may once again play havoc with medical laws of averages.

April 8. An avalanche of well-wishing cables, telegrams, letters from all over the world—and, unlike last year, almost no quack-religious get-ready-to-meet-your-Maker mail. Xenia cables from Leningrad, Ahron Propes from Jerusalem. Proud parents in Holland say they have named their newborn baby after I.S. ("Igor," presumably). A lawyer in Portugal, using no other address than "Neuva Iorque," seeks to convey his gratitude for the music. A school in Delaware petitions I.S. to get well with pages of its pupils' signatures. Scores of cables from every European country express appreciation for the music and hopes for its creator's quick recovery. A cardiologist in Ventura, California, telegraphs, unprofessionally, that of all hearts in the world, I.S.'s is "the most worth keeping going." Whereas the Composers' Union in Moscow has been quick to send its sympathies, comparatively few composers in America—in view of the dozens he has lettered to Guggenheim juries, seconded for nomination to the American Academy, recommended to publishers—have thought about him, or acted on the thought. Among the exceptions is Leonard Bernstein, who has shown the greatest feeling for I.S. since the beginning of his illness.

As for the messages from anonymous lovers of his music everywhere, the people I.S. *doesn't* know, these attempt simply, forthrightly (no panegyrics, no dithyrambs), and very movingly to tell him how much his music has meant to them. I should add that "everywhere" includes New York. Scores of people here have stopped at the hospital to inquire and leave messages, some signed with peace decals and the word "Woodstockers." Two young Juilliard students have even made their way to, and stood vigil

1970 at, his door.

April 10. Entering the room toward evening, we find I.S. alone, sitting in a chair, and trembling—from cold, he says: his Buddhist-monk-like saffron robe is far too big for him. He has a bell to ring for the nurse but because of its strange shape did not understand what it was; and the nurses, unrung, twittering in the corridor just outside his room, have not looked in at him for some time. We cover him with blankets and hold his hands until the chill is over and the pulse meter, which had been running riot, subsides. In consequence of his fright, he presses V.'s hand to his cheek and never turns his eyes from her. Is he in pain? we ask, and he ventures a cautious nayshake. Does he feel exhausted, then? No, again. In that case, is it boredom? A large "Yes." The only alleviation we can promise is that tomorrow he will have his own nurses and be able to amuse himself outwitting them, as he does at home. Is tomorrow's moonshot of any interest to him? It is, on the contrary, the essence of acedia (though I should add that the astronauts' dream-world weightlessness and slow-motion dancing used to fascinate him). Is he pleased by our report of the many performances of his music in New York this week? He could hardly care less. What does matter, and uniquely, is our insistence that he can, and will again, compose. At this, anyway, he smiles. Can it be possible that he is still undiscouraged, that he still wants to go on? I had feared this time, not that he would capitulate but that he might at least allow the dangerous debate to get on the floor.

April 13. The retention of urine since the decatheterizing—which on other occasions was followed by enuresis—has not been noticed until too late. (One wonders what happens to quite ordinary, as distinguished from VIP, patients, who are *not* in intensive care and cannot afford the supplementary ministrations of private teams of nurses.) By evening the blood urea nitrogen (BUN) count has shot so high it flies off the chart. The symptoms, which V. and I recognized long before the lab tests were completed, are the same as in October 1967: trembling hands and chattering teeth. A danger of tubular necrosis?

One of our own standby nurses—herself with an intensive-care cough, aggravated, perhaps, by her odd perfume (glue?)—tells us that the nurse who performed the suctioning operation on I.S.'s bronchial tubes during the night asked for and received an autograph immediately after.

April 14. Now in another intensive care unit, I.S. is especially miserable today ("So far, so bad") because his left elbow, to keep the I.V. in place, has been bound to a splint. He changes position quite suddenly once, causing the complex in his cardiac monitor to invert and bringing a nurse on the double. She adjusts the focus of the machine, spreading out the rills (like an affine-geometry transformation) in order to read the graph from a different and enlarging perspective, but nothing is wrong.

A woman burned nearly to death is installed in the next cubicle.

Obviously it would have been better if she had died: she will never regain consciousness, and, except through total dependency on machines, be able to maintain even the most tenuous connection with life. It seems, too, that her family is fully aware of this. Yet while the whole horrifying spectacle directs my thoughts to the problem of death control—hardly less important in the future, perhaps, than birth control—I overhear the family talking in the corridor, and they, at least, no matter what, do not want her to die.

In another cubicle a man lies near death from knife wounds inflicted in the unsafety of a local jail. He is in a bad way, in any case, being in an oxygen tent most of the time, and all the while chained to plasma pumps and I.V. Yet three formidably armed cops, bandoliered as if for a siege, stand in shifts at the foot of his bed, presumably to stop his escape even by dying. Meanwhile, the patient, who might have a case against the City for its *lack* of protection in durance, is visited by several pretty girls. The last of them, a freckled redhead wearing a wedding ring, is accompanied by a "spiv" lawyer who cross-questions the nurse-in-charge as to whether "experimental" drugs have been used.

April 15. The apical averages and BUN are normal today. And, just as I.S. is aware of most things about himself in advance, so he knows now, by some sixth sense, that another crisis has been surmounted. (How can he still respond to antibiotics, after the saturation bombing of the last 10 days?) His eyes—which changed in color in November 1967, the left turning darker and the right, both iris and pupil, becoming more blue—are alive with the knowledge. A tough old nurse tells us we should be relieved: "Most of them go from intensive care to perpetual care." Leaving the room for a moment, she warns I.S. not to "run away." Which, I suppose, is an example of nurse-ry wit.

April 17. Theodore and Denise arrive from Geneva, but too late to go to the hospital. He spends the evening telling stories about his father, of which the best are about trying on Wagner's beret, in the Werner Reinhart Collection in Winterthur, and finding that it almost covered his shoulders as well as his head; and about I.S. interviewing wet-nurses at a breast-feeding agency and insisting on sampling the milk of each candidate himself. I learn, too, that I.S. had a collection of antique wood-sculpture puppets that he painted himself, in many colors, and that both Jawlensky and Malevich, his neighbors in Switzerland during the first war, greatly admired the composer's talents as a painter.

April 29. Returning to the hotel this afternoon, I.S. sits at the dinner table with us and listens to music afterward: Schubert's B-flat Sonata, first, but not much of it, because it ill suits his mordant mood and because, as he says, "The theme itself is everything—it doesn't need development"; then Beethoven's Fourth Symphony ("*Ça nourrit l'âme*"); my own new recording of Gesualdo's Book Six, which avenges his uxorcide by plunging the knife

1970 into the composer himself: the performances are murderously bad; and, finally, I.S.'s String Concerto, which he obliges me to switch off before the end because of the messy, out-of-tune playing.

I write Berman: "Three weeks ago I.S. was hospitalized with pulmonary edema. He recovered rapidly but then developed a kidney infection. Granted that his medical scheduling is a computer-sized project, can you believe that even with private and staff nurses he was not watched closely enough and had to be returned to intensive care with uremic poisoning, or nephritis? But he is home at last."

April 30. In answer to a question from Scriabin's biographer, Faubion Bowers, I.S. says that he *was* present at the first performance of *Poème de l'Extase*.

May 3. Write to Berman:

> Dr. Lax has just given I.S. permission to fly to Europe, but not to go by boat because of the fragility of old bones. We plan to be in Paris by the first week of June. Think, only, that a year has passed since the embolectomies! . . . The Stravinskys' financial affairs are in a parlous state, and the California house has been sold for less than two-thirds of the sum once considered an acceptable minimum. They have thought of auctioning manuscripts but are deterred by the "protective reserves" required from the seller. I cannot pretend to be confident about the trip. I.S.'s main worry is not himself, however, but the French political situation and the frequent wildcat strikes in Paris.

May 7. Balanchine comes to say *au revoir*. Wearing pajamas and beret, the crooks of his arms black and blue from injections, I.S. listens with close attention and mounting appetite as Mr. B. discusses a recipe for *bitochki*. When he finishes, I.S. demands in a loud voice, *"Kogda?"* ("When can I eat some?")

May 15. Letter from Berman about "the see-saw struggle of the great man, almost hopeless one day, much better the following. I.S. was in good form when I last saw you in Paris at that bistro beyond the Bastille. He moved with difficulty, as he did for years before, but he was alert."

May 20. Dr. Lax, on a routine visit, tells I.S. he is in good health. I.S.: "I wish you would come when I am sick." But I.S. is crusty and capricious with everyone today, and so spiteful to his nurse that even after defeating her at "three-dimensional checkers," he knocks the "tryptic" over and sends the lucite marbles rolling about the room. The asperity is undiminished at table. He demands a proper whiskey-glass for his Scotch, a proper spoon for his demi-tasse (he flings the teaspoon to the floor), and he describes the omelette as *"une sottise réchauffée."* It is really wonderful to see him like this again.

June 11. Jean Stein comes to see us off, V. and I going to the airport in a taxi, I.S. with Rita in an ambulance, this being the only way we can get permission for him to board the plane directly from the tarmac. He reads most of the night.

June 12. Geneva at 7 A.M. *"Prudence,"* a large sign advises on the south-shore exit from the city, but immediately on the French side of the border the emphasis switches to food, from *"casse-croûtes"* (snacks) all the way up to *"alimentation générale."* In one small village alone we count three shops selling *"charcuterie."*

The Hotel Royale in Evian is a glorified sanitorium for the very *vieux* and the very *riches*, the latter including both *nouveaux* and second-generation types (themselves "elders of scions," one might say). On one side are Alpine vistas and Grand Roc. Directly in front and below is the lake, arc-tic-white when we arrive, then, after the mountains on the Swiss side emerge, resembling a heat-vapored valley in the California desert. In late afternoon the surface becomes glassy, and the boats—spinnakers, racing sculls, a speedboat buzzing like a Brobdingnagian wasp—seem to be sail-ing in the sky. Immediately below our rooms are shrub terraces and beds of roses, coleuses, begonias, hortensias; and below that, poplars, pines, tall red oaks. At night the Swiss shore is defined by the lights of the towns in which I.S. wrote so much music, and its distance is measured by the beetle-like Evian-Lausanne ferry plying between.

June 14. In the church at Neuvecelle, just beyond the hotel grounds and a field of clover and buttercup—we have literally "gone to grass" here—I.S. dips his fingers in the stoup, touches his forehead, then uses the holy water to smooth down his hair. Though today's analysis shows mild anemia, he is in marvelous form, more active both physically and mentally than at any time since he was in Europe two years ago and as if the ordeals visited on him in his New York dog days had never occurred. An after-noon visit from his granddaughter and great-granddaughter, who are leav-ing for a holiday in Corsica, upsets him briefly, as no doubt it did them. "What is the little girl's last name?" he asks, and the granddaughter answers, "Stravinsky." "Has she no father, then?" "No."

At St. Gingolph, a village half in Switzerland, the streets are so narrow that we are obliged to enter the Swiss half in order to turn our large car around, which means that we are obliged to clear the border controls re-entering France. Storms are breaking in a dozen directions at this end of the lake, but many sails are out, and, in view of the lake's reputation for ici-ness, a surprising number of swimmers. At several points along the shore, plaques remind compatriots—SOUVENEZ-VOUS, FRANÇAIS—of victims of the Nazis shot while attempting to escape to Switzerland. We pass a hayrick loaded with greens and as fragrant as a salad.

Dinner with Arnold Weissberger and Milton Goldman on the hotel ter-race, which has five waiters per table, versus the five tables per waiter aver-

1970 age in New York. Another advantage here is that a few francs and a bottle of white wine are enough to bribe the "Tea for Two" orchestra into taking an intermission.

June 15. Bingeing is less conspicuous than rechabitism, dieting more in evidence than gluttony in this health resort, yet the Royale does not lack for gourmets, the most deeply devoted of whom is in residence at the table on our right. This gentleman—who also and not infrequently appears to be deeply ingrained in alcohol—directs all operations concerning his own fare, at one point summoning the whole staff for a conference, at another obliging the maitre d'hotel to swallow a scoop of Cavaillon melon for confirmation as to some insufficiency of flavor or freshness. The second, but by no means the main, course in his lunch today is a trout drowned in Armagnac and grilled before our eyes on a crackling pine-branch fire. The gourmet bones the fish himself, starting from the tail and folding the skin back like a coiffeur center-parting a head of hair. Yet this elegant performance, followed by no less elegant ones at subsequent stages, concludes with an indecently loud and vigorous quarter-of-an-hour's probing with a toothpick.

Later, by the swimming pool, the same ever-famished one kisses the hands of the female bathers of his acquaintance, absurd as this seems in view of the brevity of their garments—so loose and low in the bottom in the case of some of the younger naiads loping about that my own impulse is to go around pulling them up. Some are transparent, too, there and elsewhere, and in at least one instance the upper containers seem to exist only to allow the contents to slip outside. False nipples are "in," too—though also outside—but French bosoms, on the sampling of the Royale, are seldom outstanding, and in the over-thirties more often than not resemble fried eggs. Bottoms, too, seem to have a national character here, Boucher-cum-Bouguereau in the case of the French female, jodhpur hips in the case of the British.

June 16. Although the sky is always dramatic and expectant, storms are nonetheless sudden, usually coming from the south, over the mountains, which are snow-topped (when you can see them). And it raineth every day.

June 17. Marcel Falco, our *niçois* room-waiter, not only leaves no "e" mute and inglorious, but also singsongs the language like a stage Italian immigrant speaking English. *"Une tête comme ça,"* for example, comes out *"Oon-a-te-ta-com-ma-ça."* Even so, the words are less important than the operatic gestures that accompany them and outline the actual proportions of this big—*i.e.*, smart—head. Marcel is a philosopher, storyteller, almanack, quack physician, and, it follows, a man of enormous if winsome conceit. Like Figaro, he can turn the tables on those he serves, as I discover when he deliberately confuses my name, calling me Mr. Starke (Kraft=strong, Beethoven's joke in the letter to E. T. A. Hoffmann). He has recipes, remedies, prescriptions, explanations for everything from the weather, which is "bound to be good if you can't see Switzerland," to a long catalog of cures for maladies both physical and mental. "Carrots clear the complexion," he says, and "asparagus are healthy for the kidneys if not eaten too often." He advises me to singe my hair to delay the retreat—or, as it has seemed to me lately, rout.

As a waiter, Marcel supplies mind-reading service, appearing at the propitious moment with the martinis we didn't ask for but are pleased to have, sending an *omble chevalier* when in his opinion we have chosen something less delectable. *"Il est dynamique, comme un Américain,"* he says about someone, with more richness of vowels than this spelling indicates, but the description would apply to himself only if American "dynamism" were more likable.

Not surprisingly, Marcel's storytelling is theatrical, but it contains insights and illustrates moral virtues besides, counting sympathetic observation itself as a high moral virtue. (He has shrewdly observed our preferences from the first, of course, and thus made himself the master of our tastes.) To illustrate his point that children lead their parents about nowadays, he says he wanted to spend last Christmas in Rome, but his son, now 25 and a Mercedes salesman in Berlin, wished to go to Brussels. And Brussels prevailed, except that at Cambrai father and son were detained by the police for crossing a double line on the left. As the policeman approached their car, which had a "D" (Deutschland) license plate, Marcel Junior instructed Marcel-the-one-and-only to "Pretend you don't speak French." Hence the policeman's *"Qui parle français?"* was answered only by Marcel's uncomprehending smile. *"Trop 'links,'"* the *flic* said, showing off his German before letting the frightened foreigners go. Marcel's point, however, is that his son had thoughtlessly exposed him to risk, and he dubs the story the *"Bêtise de Cambrai."* His younger son would not have done that, he goes on, proudly informing us that this later offspring is "the first in our family to wear spectacles, our first intellectual." V. questions him about the older brother. "How could you have a son of 25?" she asks, and his long-drawled answer is: *"Par-ce que j'ai fait un-e bêtis-e."*

Marcel is assisted by a dark, handsome, 15-year-old and still gauche Sardinian, Raffaello, who stands to attention while Marcel bids him take copious mental notes on a wide variety of matters. During the more protracted of his partner's yarns and vaudeville acts, Raffaello's faraway eyes betray no flicker of concern for the outcome. But when Marcel says something particularly outrageous—*"Je suis un vedette du cinéma,"* for instance (he once *was* a stand-in for John Gavin on long shots, and he claims to have received 2,000 francs for saying *"Scusi"* in a Sophia Loren film), or, *"Ce soir j'avais un peu plus de fantaisie"* (this refers to a new arrangement of his thickly brilliantined hair)—Raffaello flashes his stagey superior a withering look of disbelief.

1970 Describing a scene in a cowboy film, Marcel not only blazes away from the hip but also blows the smoke from the barrel before holstering the imaginary weapon. It is a convincing bit of buffoonery, but as Raffaello does not watch, cannot be brand new. Later Marcel confides in us about his minion, saying, "*Il est très sensible, Raffaello, mais un peu sauvage. Il faut faire attention avec lui.*"

June 18. Waking from deep dreams this morning, I.S. says: "*Je veux que Bertha vienne me féliciter.*" Is he thinking himself back 80 years, or simply telling us that he would indeed like to see his old nurse again? In either case the remark tends to confirm, as he has always claimed, that in his infancy and impressionable years Bertha was closer to him than his mother. The burden of the birthday anniversary *has* been weighing on him, and he has been talking about the remote past as, unprompted, he seldom does. Shortly before lunch he complains of nausea, and of "another pain, just behind the nausea": the identification of a pain behind a pain is typical of him. At our celebration lunch he has no trouble swallowing two prodigious helpings of caviar, nor do we see any ill effects from the vodka and champagne on top of a stiff medical aperitif. He replies to our toasts to 88, moreover, with allusions to 90.

A cable informs us of the death, in New York, of I.S.'s physician and friend of eight years, Leon Lewithin. Seven months ago, on his last visit, finding I.S. reading Herzen, the doctor advised: "At your age you should be reading pornography." A year ago today, Dr. Lewithin supervised I.S.'s discharge from New York Hospital. Who would have believed then that a year hence the patient would be flying to Europe and the much younger doctor would be dead?

June 20. The only sounds reaching our rooms at night are the chugging and the two-note hoot of a rickety train, the plaints of crows, and the bells of Neuvecelle celebrating the hours.

Letter from Berman: "Just received your good news of the safe landing and am enormously relieved to know that Maestro was able to make it. More power to his amazing will power and resistance."

June 21. Marcel loses his bet in the races at Deauville today; he had gambled on the numbers of his sons' birth dates. But his spirits are undampened. Having worked in Deauville at one time, he treats us to a description of the arrival there of the Friday afternoon "*train des cocus*"—husbands down from Paris for the weekend.

He acts out the Evian cure for us, too, playing the concierge who delivers the bottle of spring-fresh water outside the door at 6 A.M., like a milkman; and the sleepy guest fetching it, cutting his thumb while removing the sharp tin cap (half of the people in Evian go about with Band-Aids on their fingers), drinking two glasses, then returning to bed and snoring for another hour or so before eating too much breakfast.

June 26. Several times during a walk in the dewy fields this morning, V.

stops to pick mushrooms that I do not see and almost trample. I prefer to blame this blindness on differences of culture rather than personality.

July 4. Suvchinsky having arrived from Paris last night, we drive around the lake to Clarens and "Les Tilleuls," the birthplace of *Le Sacre du printemps*. The sight leaves I.S., to all appearances, unmoved; he seems more interested, back on the French side, in La Tourronde, a one-time home of St. François de Sales. Since Suvchinsky is my only *tutoyer* friend, I am obliged to think about verb endings before every remark addressed to him. It seems odd to say *"tu"* to him and, after 22 years, *"vous,"* as well as "Monsieur" and "Madame," to I.S. and V., though it would be still odder for me to use the intimate.

July 12. Unwisely, Marcel has again gone to the *guichet*, this time staking his all on a horse called "Igor." But others must have wagered, too, for the *"comptes rendus de la course"* blare from transistors on the terrace all afternoon. At dinner, the now two-time loser talks scoffingly about *niçois* superstitions: never open an umbrella indoors; never pass a saltcellar directly from hand to hand, and never thank for salt, because one thanks for what it may bring; never stop to converse in the doorway or on the threshold of a house; never put the picture of a loved one on a sideboard shelf or other eminence whence it might fall; never measure a child's height, since it might be for a coffin; never put flowers on a bed, which could become a grave.

July 13. A letter from Lincoln Kirstein:

> Dear Bob: Balanchine's "unfortunate" recension of *Firebird* is quite simply a tasteful equivalent of the Chagall, and it is much more about the Chagallerie than Stravinsky's music; it is very rich, very neat and *very* successful. . . . While Wystan's poems get better and better, his temper gets worse and worse; irascible, impatient, unyieldingly touchy; I have discovered with rapture the Stravinsky Concerto for Piano and Wind Instruments, which I should have known, but which Balanchine even said he had forgotten existed. It would make a marvelous dance piece. . . . Have you read Lifar's *Ma Vie?* It makes strange reading, somehow touching and not ill-tempered. A rather devoted and very silly man, but the portrait of Diaghilev sounds alarmingly like.

July 14. A listless morning, the mood of the *cor anglais* in *Tristan*—or so I reflect until the hotel comes to life, breakfast trays appearing on balconies, waiters going through their paces on the terrace, bathers by the poolside smearing themselves with suntan oil. At noontime, the surface of the lake is so unrippled, despite the internal hemorrhage of the Rhone, that the rhumb line of the ferry vacillating between the two countries survives for a quarter hour after each passage.

1970   Wagner's pipeherd does not express the mood at dinner, which is simply the *flanerie* of the overfed, nor does the actual dinner music, a potpourri of *La Traviata* played by our "Tea for Two" band; snatches of martial airs mix with this, as they float up from the festivities in the town below. V. recalls that she first heard *Traviata* with Lina Cavalieri, the mistress of a Grand Duke who rewarded her, a little too specifically, perhaps, with a diamond-studded gold bidet.

The fireworks display from our balcony begins with magnesium flares and detonations, introduced by long, swooping whistles, like an old-fashioned bombardment. But the girandoles and the spangles that hang in the sky like parachutes, then fizzle and dissolve in an instant, compensate for the noise. One great burst of white chips falls all the way to the ground, like manna. V. is nostalgic. Her liaison with I.S. began in Paris on *le quatorze*, 1921.

July 18. I.S.'s niece, Xenia Yurievna, comes from Leningrad, via Paris, on the 5:22. The reason for her three-day visit is immediately clear. The USSR wants I.S. to "come home" and, to borrow an expression from the Wild West, dead or alive. If the latter, he can be assured of "the world's best medical care, as well as a house, car, chauffeur, and every comfort and even luxury." If the former, he will be accorded the highest state burial honors, as well as a niche next to Pushkin.

Like all Soviet citizens abroad, Xenia seems to wear blinders, seeing neither to right nor left, a result, no doubt, of the inculcation of the idea that all this will pass away—as, no doubt, it will. Here, in Evian, the contrast between the old-fashioned gentility of this comrade of a Communist state and the boorishness of the hotel's *haute bourgeoisie* is especially striking. Xenia is a little slow in grasping the point of some of our conversations, but understandably, never having been outside the Soviet Union. Yet she is really interested only in what we have to say about the USSR. When the S.s describe their meeting last year with Svetlana, née Stalin, Xenia actually takes notes. A tea drinker in the Russian tradition, she remarks on the comparatively rare addiction to this brew in France. When V. mentions her own preference for Peking tea, Xenia's hands go up in protest (a tempest in a teacup): "Oh, no, please. *Nothing* from China."

Or from Israel. Xenia says that both wars passed near I.S.'s old home in Ustilug, devastating the neighborhood, but not his house, which sustained only a scratch, a chimney shot off but now restored. The house is still known locally as his, she adds, and a few elderly people there claim to remember him. For my part, I tell her that during our first tour of Israel eight years ago, a kibbutz of emigrés from Ustilug presented I.S. with a history of their former Russian community. At this, hardly less agitated than by the thought of Chinese *chi*, Xenia says, "Probably they lie," though one wonders what could be lied about in that, and what would be the purpose.

The oddest incident in Xenia's visit is that, seeing a copy of *Bravo*

Stravinsky on I.S.'s table, she leafs through it, mentioning pages snipped out by the censor in her copy at home (the picture of Yevtushenko among them), but evinces no curiosity about the reasons for the excisions.

As for her Leningrad news, we learn that not long ago she shared the exercise yard of a Leningrad hospital with Shostakovitch, who suffers from the same heart trouble as she does.

July 22. Drive with my sister and her family to Menthon (where I.S. composed *Dumbarton Oaks*), Annecy and Talloires (*Le Baiser de la fée*), and, via Thonon, back to Evian. Campers' bivouacs are everywhere, and *pique-nique*-ers who literally squat on the roadside as if car and truck exhausts provided an indispensable condiment. The towns are architectual farragoes of chalets, modern maisonnettes, barrack-style apartment buildings, and, as I.S. used to say of Geneva suburbs, "the villas of retired dentists, each with a copy of Rodin's 'Thinker' in the garden."

Back in the hotel we learn that I.S. will require a third transfusion of *globules rouges lavés* next week, the worst of which is that an amount of painful harpooning is entailed nowadays to find an infrangible vein.

August 5. I.S. sends for me in the afternoon, saying, "I have two things to tell you. First, I, personally, do not feel very well. Second, I am *très inquiet* about Vera"—V. having gone to Geneva for the day. But the order of the anxieties is typical; he would have said the same 20 years ago. A touching reply from him tonight, when I promise to play music with him tomorrow afternoon: "Good. I am free."

August 17. A visit from faithful Hugues Cuénod, the first Sellem in the first *Rake*.

August 18. I.S. listens to recordings with Nikita Magaloff.

August 23. Rita returns after a week's vacation in Copenhagen. Letter from Shirley Hazzard Steegmuller: "Life has become like one of those old movies where one is tied to the railway track with the train approaching."

August 24. Lord Snowdon arrives to photograph I.S. Joining him in the bar, I find him taller than photographs have led me to expect, more freckled, more wrinkled, more blond—as well as less, in fact not at all, o'erweening. His young companion—Beatles hairdo, black velvet suit, pink shirt unbuttoned to a gold cross, high and super-shiny shoes—opens with: "I'd like to drive a very fast car through this hotel." His Lordship—himself rather trendily gotten up as to hair-length, shirt, cravat, gold-chain bracelet, gadgety Omega wrist-clock—orders a vodka and tomato juice (*not* a "Bloody Mary") and opens with a reference to something of mine he has read. I retaliate with a compliment on his film about old age, which inspires him to put on a droll imitation of the jactations, German accent and all, of the great rejuvenator, Dr. Niehans.

August 26. Lunch with François-Michel. The send-off party at the Geneva airport includes all of I.S.'s nurses and doctors but not Soulima and family, though this should not be surprising, since he has spent the summer

1970 only 150 miles away without telephoning to inquire about his father's health, or even sending a postcard. The reason for the neglect, as Theodore quotes his brother, is that "I can't bear to see Father so old and frail." Which raises the question of what condition a man in his 89th year should be in not to upset his son.

September 10. New York. Letter from Berman: "Natasha Nabokov has just arrived and told me that you are all back in New York. She feels it was the right move. I am happy that Natasha confirmed the amazing change and improvement in I.S.'s condition you reported, which is really a wonderful thing. Still, I am afraid that New York is a bad place for I.S. or for anybody."

September 13. Write to Berman:

> You characterize our return as folly, yet the move was inevitable. In Evian the Stravs never visited the town, the buvette or the Casino; and when the hotel prepared to close for the season, they had to leave—were, in fact, the last guests to do so. We looked at houses in Switzerland, but they were ugly, expensive, and inconvenient. . . . I.S.'s blood is normal—no traces of his polycythemia, which, after 15 years, appears to have given up on him—and his heart is strong. Thanks to a new therapist, he is walking better than before. The chief obstruction to walking is the thirteen-year-old inguinal hernia. His teeth give him more trouble than anything, probably because of his constantly changing weight. He will soon have two extractions. We have had a dreadful heat wave accompanied by a pall of carcinogenic air. The search for an apartment has not been successful, the prices being out of sight.

September 25. Visit from Balanchine.

October 23. A medical check-up of my own, the first in three years. Whatever the verdict, so much of the medical machinery resembles instruments of torture that I feel fortunate in surviving the ordeal. I am wired for a cardiogram like a man condemned to the electric chair; my head is fitted to the chin rest of an X-ray machine as if for guillotining; I am obliged to run up and down stairs like a hazed recruit in the Marines; and, the ultimate indignity, made to go on all fours for a painful probing of the prostate.

I.S. has acute ochlophobia: he is no sooner out for his afternoon sorties on 59th Street than he insists on returning. He is not declining into "anility," not "crossing over" but softening and slowing down. And the vital signs are good: his blood pressure is perfect, his heart, Lax says, is "of a man of 30," and the neurological evidence has not shown any cardio-vascular spasm for at least eight months. Although we were assured a year and a half ago that the sympathectomy would deprive him of the use of his left leg, he is able to walk, and his muscle tone improves with each visit of the therapist. Because of poor circulation, he has necrosis in the left toe, but the condition is responding to dermatological treatment. He uses four languages, both in reading and in conversation. He plays the piano daily, and though he sometimes wears a hearing aid, when listening to music he removes it and nearly always complains that the volume of the record player is too high.

His state of mind is more difficult to describe, but always was; one *never* knew exactly what was transpiring there. I *do* know that at times he behaves like a character in Beckett, turning off simply because he feels nothing *can* be said or is worth saying. Yet he takes in everything. On a recent visit, reading aloud and translating the paragraph that I.S. appended in 1968 to the last page of the *Sacre* manuscript, Nicolas Nabokov found himself stuck for a word that I.S., who did not seem to be following, instantly supplied, "guarantee." Thus, too, at dinner tonight, when V. cannot remember the Russian and German words for certain precious and semi-precious stones ("jasper," "chrysoberyl," "garnet," "amethyst"), I.S. provides them with the speed of an infant prodigy on a rigged quiz show. Nor has his lifelong quest for precision lost its force. The well-worn dictionaries and encyclopedias are still stacked on his reading tables and still resorted to. "Which is more correct, 'every day' or 'each day'?" he asks me this afternoon, and a friend who asks whether he is "drinking," is rather curtly told that "I *drank* a while ago, but am not drinking now, obviously."

If his critical faculties are unimpaired, he remains loyal to most of his old prejudices. He has been execrating Berlioz as harshly as ever, dismissing most of *Les Troyens* as "*N'importe quoi*," and to my question about what he would like to hear after tonight's dose of it, replying, "Something better." When at length I am able to prise a more specific critique out of him, it is that the music does not evidence any real harmonic and melodic gifts; and he cites the "flatness" of Chorèbe's *Cavatina*, speculating as to what Verdi might have done. Nor is the comparison unfair, for the big choral scene, "*Châtiment effroyable*," is handled in a Verdian manner, and, so I think, almost as ably as Verdi.

What he likes in *La Prise de Troie* are some of the orchestral novelties: the high strings and woods at the very end of Act Two; the two-note orchestral figure at "*J'ai vu l'ombre d'Hector*," and the following six measures in 18th-century-suite style. What he dislikes are the long March and Hymn, with its dull "*Dieu des mers*" choral echoes. And the waltz finale, which he describes as "bad French ballet music," thereby committing, I think, a double pleonasm.

November 2. David Frost offers I.S. a huge sum to appear on his television talk show. When V. explains the kind of question he would be expected to answer, he interrupts her, protesting, "Is this already a rehearsal?"

1970   Buñuel's *Tristana*, tonight, is disappointing, except for the restfully vita-min-deficient color. Perhaps the predominance of eerily filtered yellows and the viridescence are symbolic of the heroine's (Catherine Deneuve's) gangrenous, later-to-be-amputated leg. What we actually see of her com-plexion is so pale that one suspects Buñuel of whatever is the next stage beyond necrophilia (laying a ghost?), for at times he seems to suggest that she is not merely cold but also not really there. Her icy beauty is compro-mised less by the low temperature than by the over-dubbing, the lips being contorted by the discrepancies between the sounds they form and the ones we hear. (The same may be said for the facial expressions with which she accompanies her rendition of Chopin's "Revolutionary" Etude; and as I seem to be dwelling on the subject of synchronization, I should add that the titles, apart from many wrong nuances, are left too long on the screen, the eye having assimilated the sense in most cases long before the words appear; which is one-up for McLuhan.) The grimness and social cruelty of Spain are not overdone, but some of the other messages—the anti-clerical-ism, the sexual hypocrisy—are embarrassingly tendentious and simplistic. Nor is the erotic element very effective; a glimpse of Deneuve's left leg, early on, is too pointedly aimed toward the dramatic irony of the later views of its gruesome wooden replacement lying about on chairs and sofas.

November 3. Write to Berman: "I.S. likes automobile outings, but these are difficult to arrange in New York. Mrs. Stravinsky shudders at the mention of a winter in the South, and the logistic problems of such a move are formidable; but he always smiles when these projects are discussed and immediately wants to know exactly when we plan to be under way. Nabokov and Dominique come regularly, and Lucia."

November 12. I.S. is in high spirits today, even though his hemoglobin is down to 6, his hematocrit to 20, and a transfusion is scheduled for tomorrow. He pens a message for a Festschrift to be presented to Aaron Copland the day after tomorrow in our hotel: "Dear Aron, 70 is pretty good. Congratulations, Stravinsky." Happening to read this testimonial, V. remarks that Mr. C. spells it "Aaron," whereupon Rita suggests that I.S. write a small "o" over the "A," this being the Scandinavian sign for repeat-ing a vowel. I.S. vetoes that idea on grounds that "Copland isn't Scandinavian," and rewrites the whole, grumbling that "If he doesn't like this, *je m'en fous*."

Rita reads to him, but he is impatient and keeps asking, "How long does this description go on?" "Well, you can't get into the book without an introduction," Rita explains, not mollifying him in the slightest. "*Well*," he says, imitating her, "it's very boring. Let me read it myself, if I must." When Rita gives it to him, he slams it shut. "We're not being very nice today," she says, going out. This time he withholds his retort. Five minutes later, not at all contrite but having found the compromise that suits him, he calls to her, saying, "After all, I've decided I'd like to read a bit *this afternoon*."

November 16. Francis Steegmuller comes to tea, and V. gives him carte blanche to write I.S.'s biography, also permission to take the archives to another room in the hotel, a box at a time, to be returned at night. I am of two minds about this but more in favor than not, both because Francis will take the heat off me and because he is a good writer. The other side is that the archives do not provide a biography, and a biographer, I think, would have to be a musician.

November 17. David Storey's play *Home* tonight compensates for last night's *Sleuth*, a short story with *grand guignol* ending, never as good as the Agatha Christie it seeks to parody, and made into a long evening of forced jokes redeemed only by the three minutes during which the future murderer plays a recording of the end of the first movement and the beginning of the second movement of Beethoven's Seventh. *Home* is a good-enough play, superbly performed, but an inaccessibly large part of its appeal is in the contrast with the various kinds of theater that it is *not*, ranging from several species of New Theme Drama to the equating of the physical closeness of the actor with closeness in communication. Among other welcome absences are those of shouting, both in what is said and in how; of all Bedlamite, mad-as-a-hatter, *Marat-Sade* funny business; and of the philosophy of "the kids," Storey's people being naturally ravaged elders. As for positive virtues, the language of clichés is well observed. One shrewd structural invention is the introduction of a fifth character, the lobotomized boy wrestler, at the beginning of the second half of the play. Until then the straying thoughts and the forgetfulness of the two leading men could be attributed to daydreaming, their excessive reactions to trivia to "nervous disorders" well within the bounds of normalcy. Until this point, too, even the women, who are more obviously "off" than the men, and whose imaginations are more lurid, might pass as eccentric boarders in a seedy "rest home" instead of inmates in a lunatic asylum. It is by drawing his women from a lower social order than his men that Storey finds the dimension of comic relief, for the shabby-genteel Jack and Harry are quite incapable of the coarse jokes of their female counterparts. But the boy wrestler puts the play where it is.

The beginning may be, and the end definitely is, too long, with moments that threaten to become over-poignant, not to say sugary, as in the case of the slow, final blackout, which has been prepared for by an amount of mood-filled cloud studying of the *Dances at a Gathering* type. Moreover, the two-couples idea threatens to become as symmetrical as a tennis match—mixed doubles inevitably following the men's and women's singles—though better that than the formlessness which would have been inevitable otherwise. As for the cast, the women are natural comediennes. Whereas Ralph Richardson *is* the character Jack, Gielgud, who can cry real tears on cue, is untransformed Gielgud. But David Storey is the star. He can show not merely the despair and emptiness behind the mental door but also the bravery that can keep these emotions there, enabling people incompletely in charge of the knob to go on living.

November 22. Before we go in to dinner, I tell I.S. that V. has trudged about in bad weather to buy the ingredients of his favorite soup, *Shchi*, and that he must remember to say he likes it. At table, when I ask his opinion of the wine, he says, "I can't tell you; I'm still thinking about the soup."

We listen to two Haydn piano trios, of which I.S. is particularly fond of the first movement of No. XXX in D; and to Liszt's *Transcendental Etudes*, one of which, *Feux follets*, might make a good solo number in a ballet, I.S. suggests, though another, *Mazeppa*, makes him laugh out loud. After Opus 127, hoping he will have had enough music for the night, I say: "What could we possibly listen to after the Beethoven?" "That's easy," he answers: "*lui-même*."

December 1. V. purchases an apartment at 73rd Street and 5th Avenue, binding it with a check for $27,000; the date of occupancy is fixed for February 1.

Today's *Times* carries an article to the effect that I.S.'s manuscripts and archives are for sale at $3,500,000, and it names the USSR as a bidder. A *Times* reporter seems to have interviewed I.S.'s agent, Lew Feldman, who divulged both the top asking price and the information about the non-existent inquiry from the Soviet Union, which was a lure to induce a buyer to come forward in the U.S.; the USSR does not part with hard currency in such amounts, and, anyway, a lump-sum sale, as one to the USSR would have to be—after taxes, commissions, lawyers' fees—would leave little for I.S. In spite of this, the telephone is busy all afternoon conveying congratulations to the new "millionaires."

December 2. A summer's day—so warm, in fact, that some of the trees in the Park seem confused in the absence of a proper cue whether or not to shed their leaves.

Auden for dinner, in top, even euphoric form, dispensing much needed shots of mental B12. "I've just done Igor's obit for the *Observer*," he tells me in an elated, or at any rate not conspicuously bereaved, voice. "I talk about him as the great exemplary artist of the 20th century, and not just in music."

He eulogizes I.S. more than I have ever heard him do before. When I ask him to distinguish between the love that he feels for him and the mere admiration that he feels for Wagner ("indisputably a genius, but apart from that an absolute shit"), he links his own discovery of the sense of the Modern to I.S.'s music. I.S. dislikes being told such things to his face and a few weeks ago was rude to Nicky Nabokov for telling him much the same. But I.S. is on his best behavior tonight—he *can* be *très enfant de la nature!*—listening very intently and telling V., in Russian, "Auden has marvelous ideas." Otherwise he obdurately refuses to talk, except once when V. asks why he did not respond to a joke: "I smiled inside."

Auden is preparing a lecture on Freud for a public reading in Philadelphia next month, and his homework is taking him back through the *New Introductory Lectures* and *The Interpretation of Dreams*: "Now the trouble with dreams, of course, is that other people's are so boring." All that we hear about the content of the lecture is that "it makes a case against analysing works of art as if they were people. I was delighted, by the way, to find that Freud has so much common sense. He *does* see that a cigar could be simply a cigar. Incidentally, I have been doing a bit of amateur psychiatry myself. Young people. You know the type: every experience of life by age 20 except work. Most are on drugs, and all have sex problems. I'm no advocate of the purely Uranian society myself. I mean, *I* certainly don't want to live *only* with queers."

He reels off a list of books we should have read—Blythe's *Akenfield*, Leontiev on Tolstoy (well, I *have* read that), the new biography of Scott. "By the way, how much Scott have you actually *read*?" he asks, but luckily doesn't wait for an answer. "Rereading him now, I see that he was more of an 18th-century rationalist than I'd thought."

"I have given up sleeping pills," he confesses. "Too difficult to procure in Austria. Instead, I keep a glass of vodka by my bed, which tastes better." Is his greater sociability attributable in any measure to this chemical change, I wonder? *Some* of it, in any case, is owing to expanding royalty statements. "I can't complain any more," he says, "and my credit in the neighborhood has increased remarkably ever since a TV cameraman began following me about." Answering my question about the fortunes (Tyche sense) of his operas, he tells me, "Henze wears a Mao tunic now, but with lots of money in the pockets."

The poet has not given up gaspers, though, and at regular intervals he forges a chain of them from a pack of Lucky Strike. "We all know that smoking is bad, but I can't see why anybody should ever stop drinking." In that case, would he care for another martini? I ask, and the answer is "Jolly." He has a remarkably spruce, almost-washed appearance tonight, and his slippers are in better repair than the floppy tartans he was wearing last time. His mind, of course, is *always* tidy, and even after the martinis, the claret, the champagne, he can remark, "Every artist must see for himself the relationship and balance between tradition and change. But does anyone see it any more? Now surely you, Igor, composed what you *had* to compose without asking yourself: 'Well, let's see, what sort of thing should I be doing now?'"

Switching to his social life in Kirchstetten, he says, "The Burgermeister cannot be invited to dinner because he hasn't got a degree, and for this reason it would embarrass him to be asked; but the chemist can be asked because he has one—at least I *hope* he has. Incidentally, the village priest's name is Schicklgruber, and he is actually a relative."* Wystan's own reli-

---

* A relative of Hitler, that is, whose father was the illegitimate son of Maria Anna Schicklgruber, a domestic, who kept her name until changing it to Hitler in 1876, age 39; but Schickelgruber is not a rare name, and the connection here seems unlikely.

1970 gious affiliations are now turning toward the Greek Orthodox Church, because "I can't put up with all the Reformist nonsense in my own."

When I congratulate him on *The Aliens*, he owns to being "pretty well pleased with it," and he admits that *A Certain World* is "at least fun." Promptly at 9 o'clock he looks at his watch, mutters something about bedtime, and bolts from the table and the apartment.

December 9. A note from Nadia Boulanger to I.S., scarcely readable because of her failing sight, remembering the death of his daughter (32 years ago!): *"Mon ami, je suis si proche, Dieu nous garde. Je vous embrasse."* What a great lady!

December 12. Elliott Carter for dinner, after which we follow scores, Carter on one side of I.S., myself on the other, while listening to my test pressing of *Chant du Rossignol* and to Klemperer's *Magic Flute*.

December 28. I.S. writes to Georg Solti: "I am very sorry but we had a substitute secretary the day you called. Your name, found on a pad, was never given to me. I would very much have enjoyed seeing you again and meeting your wife, and I am very happy about the great success you had here with what I have long considered to be the world's finest orchestra."

&. **Postscript 1994**. The year began with signs of improvement in Stravinsky's health, but the New York winter, too severe to permit more than a few outings, was defeating. Stravinsky was hospitalized with pneumonia for most of the month of April, but once again he recovered. By mid-May he was able to take short walks in Central Park and, on June 11, to fly to Geneva and travel from there by car to the Hotel Royale in Evian, where he spent the summer. A note in Mrs. Stravinsky's diary dated May 18 says that Stravinsky "resents his old age, especially in that it prevents him from hearing everything and taking part in discussions. . . ." Most people are resentful of failing powers, of course, but Stravinsky's resentment must be attributed less to his enforced withdrawal from social participation than his losing struggle to find sufficient energy to concentrate on composition. This was a greater torment to him in the last four years of his life than the physical pains and indignities that he was forced to endure, and the neglect by his children.

The summer at Evian was a period of recovery. Friends from London, Rome, Paris, Leningrad, Los Angeles, and from across the lake in Switzerland came to visit him. His son Theodore and wife came several times from Geneva. A Swiss doctor, Della Santa, appeared every few days and began a treatment in the nearby hospital at Thonon, after which, and until the end of his life eight months later, Stravinsky no longer suffered from polycythemia.

Theodore had been friendly to Mrs. Stravinsky and myself during the summer, but on our return to New York he stopped corresponding, then sent an accusing letter to Mrs. Stravinsky that had to be answered by a lawyer. The lines were now clearly drawn, and Theodore was no longer in the middle. Mrs. Stravinsky could not look for help to any member of her husband's family and was henceforth to divide her time between lawyers and taking care of him.

1970

Speaking for myself, my life as a musician came to a halt, except that I spent every evening in the depressing precincts of the Essex House—the Stravinsky apartment overlooked not the Park but the ugly gulch of 58th Street—listening to music with Stravinsky. A bright note was that Hideki Takami came from Hollywood to cook for the Stravinskys, even though the kitchen was the size of a galley in a very small boat.

ᚨ *1971*

January 1. Pompano Beach. Playing tennis this morning for the first time in years, I paunch about, panting and perspiring, sometimes missing the ball entirely, three times sending it on a straight-up aerial course, twice lobbing it over the fence, and once adding it to the game in the neighbor court, where it must have made the players feel like jugglers.

Orthography along federal highways tends to purely alphabetic forms: "ex" is "x," as in "xpert," "y" is "why," as in "Y not buy a . . . ?" a motel calls itself the "C-Breeze," a new household appliance is advertised as "E-Z-ER," and the established way of writing a certain synonym for rapid is "Kwik." But some of this roadside epigraphy is genuinely puzzling. While poor proofreading may be responsible for "Mery Xmas," and "plumr" (send for one if your faucets don't work), who could be certain in the case of "Enter, Rest, Pay" on the door of a church? Other manifestations of innovatory roadside English add verb forms ("Orange Juice Freshly Squozen") while destroying syntax, as the parts of speech become interchangeable ("plus" as a verb: "to plus or not to plus"). The Floridian language is compulsively alliterative and euphemistic: a garage is a "Collision Clinic."

At the beach, the dunes are littered with palm fronds, coconut husks, shells—one of them, found after an hour's hunting, exquisitely gadrooned. Swift-legged sandpipers, like tightly wound-up toys, flee and follow the surf at less than an inch. When a dead fish is washed ashore, a gull instantly swoops on it, plucking out its eyes. The majority of bathers are elderly women who anoint themselves with protective lotions and regale each other as "gals." Another of their ghastly euphemisms is "shedding a tear" (micturition). Some of their male coevals are as much in need of bras as they are themselves, if not more so (two sets of boobs).

The expression "rubber goods" does not mean here what it does on 8th Avenue, nor are there any uterine double entendres in "inner tubes," and "skin-diving sheaths." The reference is simply to bathing caps, snorkels and fins, inflatable beach furniture, surfing mats, rubber surfboards with sharklike rubber fins, and tublike rafts large enough to hold three paddlers, as in the nursery rhyme. I ride the waves myself, trying to catch them between the curl and the break, my only thought being how quickly "Thought" disappears under the pressures of the apolaustic life.

The sky, lightly flaked at first, suddenly turns stormy, like a Winslow Homer, at which point a blimp appears above the beach trailing an advertisement from the nacelle: *TRY THE LIBRARY AT THE HILTON.*

January 12. New York. I.S., very cast down when I first returned, has brightened as a result of the music we have listened to together since then. Seeing that I am able to raise his morale this way, I should do so for however long I will have the opportunity. Dr. Lax says that to judge from the neurological evidence no thrombosis has occurred in nine months, and that heart, circulation, blood pressure, and lungs are in good order. Still, we are only at the beginning of winter. Dr. Lax is also saying that I.S. did not have polycythemia *vera* but only polycythemia *spuriosa*. Apparently the symptomology was not sufficiently developed a decade ago to enable doctors to make the distinction. If true polycythemia had been the disease, Lax says, I.S. would already have been dead.

January 16. A cold spell, everyone breathing steam—buildings, too: smoke plumes hover over Harlem like anti-aircraft balloons. Earflaps and woolen headgear, unexpectedly rural touches, appear in the Park and on 59th Street. A pity on all those unskirted knees.

After two hours at Bonnier's, V. buys a Calder-type toy, a bouquet of hollow, billiard-size balls attached to flexible wire stems and anchored in a wooden plaquette; when knocked together, these globes emit a variety of soft, rather agreeable clucking noises. How are such objects packaged and transported? This one, at any rate, was fitted into a cylindrical plastic tube, large enough, perhaps, for a missile or nerve-gas shell, and with a violin-case handle at the center. Boarding the 57th Street bus with this cargo, V. cuts a wide swathe—the other passengers suspecting the contents of being an arsenal of some kind, until she is overheard asking the driver to stop at Carnegie Hall, at which point speculation switches to the nature of the instrument in the parcel, her Russian accent obviously marking her as a musician.

At tea time we receive a visit from the violinist Leonid Kogan, whose accent is thickly Russian, but who does not mention fiddling. His *Mavra*-like conversation with I.S. focuses on the servant problem in the USSR. As bad as here, Kogan says.

January 20. Playing Patience with I.S., Rita tells him not to forget to make a wish if he wins. He does win, naturally, whereupon Rita asks him to reveal his wish, which is "To win."

To Peter Brook's circus-like *Midsummer Night's Dream*, the bad taste of which, as I.S. would say, is often quite profound. (One line would have delighted I.S.: "I never heard so musical a discord.") The play itself may be boring, but that can justify only the intention, not the quality, of Brook's distractions, which include the fat man's pants falling down, and not once but twice. Nor does Brook's busy-ness dispel the tediousness of the lovers' symmetries, so that one wonders if the thing will in all senses ever come out of the woods.

January 23. With the Goddard Liebersons, Leonard Bernsteins, and Richard Avedons to a screening of Ken Russell's *Delius*, which moves us so deeply that when the lights go on, I find V. in tears. The film contains striking resemblances to I.S. in his present condition, the locked-in musical imagination, the portative papal chair, and—perhaps in a similar way, as V. no doubt thinks—the death.

January 31. Carlos Chavez, in the course of a visit, goes to his knees while talking to I.S. and hardly manages to hold back the tears, all of which greatly disturbs I.S. and leaves him upset all evening.

February 3. Dr. John Stansfield extracts I.S.'s last two teeth.

February 12. Nabokov comes in the afternoon to say good-bye, but makes the mistake of asking I.S. how he is. "You can see how I am, miserable," he shouts, and so angrily that N., who loves him more than anyone, leaves with wet eyes.

February 19. Asked by a friend what he would have chosen to be if he weren't a composer, I.S. frowns suspiciously and says, "Why, who wants to know?" (He might have chosen to be a linguist, among many possible alternative careers, as I realize at table when he conjugates a Russian verb for my edification, a hopeless goal.) Pursuing the matter from another angle, the friend asks him to "suppose that when you were a young man a beautiful goddess had offered you any career *other* than that of composer, what would you have chosen then?" "Well, if she were *really* beautiful, probably I would have chosen *her*."

February 23. Pompano Beach. Calling New York this noon, I talk to I.S., my first long-distance telephone conversation with him since August 1966. The experience is startlingly like old times, his voice sounding much deeper than it does in person nowadays. His breathing is clear, too, which I say because it sometimes sounds like a soda fountain. After a moment of indecision as to which ear to apply to the receiver, he comes on gruff and laconic, as he always was on the telephone. "It arrived to me" (*i.e.* happened), he says, explaining an indisposition, but "I gathered all my forces" (which sounds like a general remembering a campaign, but means physical and moral strength). I suggest some music to listen to on the day of my return. "I have nothing against it," he says, and though the negative could imply a residue of skepticism, this much-used expression of his is actually a sign of something akin to enthusiasm.

A dependable guide to the true situation of motels and hotels vis-à-vis the beach is the degree with which they overdo their claims to be directly on it. While the "Briny Breeze" and "Vista del Mar,' modest enough appellations, are only a few blocks from the shore, the "Sea Spray," "Surf-Side," "Sea Wash," and "Sandy Toes" are miles inland. On the whole, too, the true proportions of these establishments can be determined by inverting the measure of exaggeration in their self-descriptions. The "Ocean Manor" and "Castle-by-the-Sea" turn out to be glorified bungalows. Whatever the Miami hotels intend with *their* names, the partiality to the Scottish and the French is hardly borne out by architectural resemblances, at any rate in "The Kenilworth," "The Ivanhoe," "The Balmoral" (there is also a "Prince of Whales"), "The Versailles," the "Eden Roc," "The Fontainebleau," and "The Fleur de Lit" (sic: this may be a way of indicating room service beyond the routine).

Whereas hotels frequently advertise their accommodations in vowel-less acronyms—"SGL," "DBL"—most flying ads are spelled out to a tee. One small airplane buzzes our beach at crop-dusting level, trailing what looks like a tennis net lettered: "KEEP FLORIDA GREEN: BRING MONEY." Another low-flying machine drapes the warning: "LIFE BEGINS AT 40 BUT EVERYTHING ELSE BEGINS TO GIVE OUT, WEAR OUT, SPREAD OUT: WATCH YOUR WATE." This is a pitch for macrobiotics, unbleached bread, and health food markets, and for more of the unhealthy-looking types who seem to be their principal patrons and in whom last year's saccharine panic evidently failed to arouse any suspicion. Related appliances such as "wiglets" are widely available hereabouts, and related stimulants such as "Stagarama" cinemas. But to most outward appearances, the "life" that "begins at 40" centers on lawn-trimming, bridge, and the phosphor dots.

I am alone on the beach this afternoon except for a man feeding dog biscuits to gulls unable to fend for themselves. "After all," he tells me, not quite analogously, "the mother wolf nourishes her youngest and weakest cubs first." One-legged birds, losers of contests with predators of the deeps and shallows, are common. These unipeds reduce their landing speed with a flurry of flapping, but alight off-kilter, nevertheless, and attain balance only by hopping about. The older birds are yellow and scruffy, the younger ones sleek, white-and-gray, like West Point cadets, which I say for the further reason that they look so much like sentinels. Nor is there any amorous billing and cooing among them, but only the squawk of the pecking-order top sergeant.

March 1. New York. Talking about the Mayakovsky vogue, I.S., who knew the poet in Paris, remembers him as "*très arrogant*," while V. recalls that when she first saw him, in Petrograd in 1917, the point was that he should not see her. "I was in a cabaret in the Champs-de-Mars one night when Mayakovsky came in: Sudeikin quickly put a napkin over my head and pushed me under the table. Mayakovsky was supposedly irresistible to women."

The color of the midnight sky, where the glow of the city strikes the fog bank, is topaz. Whether in spite or because of the cold and damp, the male professionals on Central Park West are hustling, as are their brawnier

1971 female rivals on Central Park South, some of whom bask under the infrared, meat-grill marquees of the 59th Street hotels. A young man, long hair in urgent need of a shampoo, is picketing the Plaza, but for a remote cause, it seems to me, in view of the cruelty to the ancient nags on this very block who haul the tourist hansoms. STOP THE BRUTAL CANADIAN SPORT OF CLUBBING BABY SEALS TO DEATH, his placard reads on one side, and, on the other, instead of letting it go at that, KILL SEALS HUMANELY. Why not leave them alone?

March 3. I.S., at a two-year peak, composes this morning for the first time in months, as the greater intensity of his playing makes us aware, as well as the complexity of the harmony—though, talking about it later, he says that he "had an idea beginning with a combination of *tièrces*." His memory is wide open, too, and his verbal powers are quick and fluent. I ask about his working method in translating *Noces* with Ramuz, and he describes how he prepared several crude French versions for his collaborator, one of which they would refine, always opting for the best musical solution. Would you like to hear *Noces*? I ask, but he refuses: "I like to compose music, not to listen to it. All my life I have been pursued by 'my works,' but I don't care about my works. I care only about composing. And that is finished."

March 4. Still in marvelous form, I.S. composes again today, this time for about an hour. And he is clairvoyant, above all about himself, though he also describes everybody's mood in the morning before seeing anybody (which, around here, may be simple prediction). "Sometimes I am frightened because I can't remember," he says. "Tell me, when did Bertha die?"

March 11. A cable from Richard Buckle in London asks I.S. to orchestrate one of the pieces by Bach on the list drawn up in July 1913 by Diaghilev, Nijinsky, and Benois in Baden-Baden and recently discovered in the archives of the Paris Opéra.

I.S. makes the *Congressional Record*, his tax predicament with regard to his manuscripts and personal papers being cited by Senator Frank Church in connection with a proposed revision of the law. "One extremely important collection denied to the Music Division [Library of Congress] has received public attention," the senator remarks. "Because of a change in the law, Igor Stravinsky has been forced to place his manuscript collection, valued at $3.5 million, on the open market when, prior to the change, he could have donated it to the Library and not been penalized financially." The last phrase indicates that the senator reads the *New York Review*. He goes on to quote the *Washington Star*:

> A few months ago Igor Stravinsky's original manuscripts and personal papers were put up for sale in the open market. The price tag was $3.5 million, and considering their importance, anyone buying them would be getting a bargain.

These days it costs $25 million per mile or more to build a super-highway. Are the thousands of items offered by Stravinsky, including the manuscripts of compositions which altered the entire history of twentieth-century music, worth less than one-fifth of a mile of concrete?

March 14. I.S. is hypersensitive to the weight and textures of clothes and bedding. When I first knew him, he was always shielded by layers of coats and sweaters, and it was the same when he was young: that awning-stripe blazer which he wears in so many old photographs, and which dates from Ustilug, concealed several thicknesses of clothing. Now he prefers to go about in shirtsleeves and to sleep under one not-tucked-in blanket (though a beret is also part of his night garb). As with the princess and the pea, a fold or wrinkle in the back of his pajamas is enough to keep him awake.

March 15. The Philharmonic's announced plans for a Liszt survey provoke us to listen to half a dozen of the tone poems tonight, but we make no headway with any of them. Several times I.S. actually giggles; at other, rarer times, he follows the score for a few moments with real interest and expectations always unfulfilled.

March 16. A letter to I.S. from a certain John Bell in Perth, Scotland, describes a performance of *Firebird* in Queens Hall "in 1913 or 1914" at which I.S. and Bernard Shaw were present: "I rather fancy you may have forgotten a little incident outside the door of the little café at the entrance to the stage door of the Lyric Theater. You had driven round in a taxi from the Café Royal with your companions Lillian Shelley and Joseph Simpson. Lillian Shelley opened the cab door and you fell out bang on the pavement, striking it with the back of your head." I.S. has no recollection of this, though it could have happened in February 1913 or June 1914.

March 18. Tikhon Khrennikov calls from Moscow, but V. will not talk to him until I have looked up his patronymic. "Tikhon Nikolaiitch," as she then greets him, invites the S.s to spend the summer in the USSR, assuring V. that they will be treated like Tsar and Tsarina, which is exactly what she fears.

I.S. is unwell. His pulse is labile, his coughing spells are deep and prolonged. Pulmonary edema, Dr. Lax says, and within an hour I.S. is litter-borne and on the way not only to the scene of last year's crimes, but also to the very same room (891). "What should I do? What should I do?" he asks V. again and again in the ambulance, but V., choking back her tears and trying to calm him, can only say, "You do nothing. Other people will do."

Do they ever! He is processed like a product on an assembly line, chest clamped with cathodes, trachea scoured by a vacuum cleaner, nostrils invaded with plastic oxygen tubes, right inner elbow embrocated to expose a vein that a Draculess then punctures to draw a remarkably copious "specimen." The left arm, meanwhile, is strangled by a sphygmomanometric

1971 pump, implanted with a tube for intravenous feeding (a rivulet of diuretics to flush the fluid from the lungs), and bandaged to a small ironing-board splint. Last and worst, he is catheterized, the deed done by the head of the Urology Department who, apologizing for the discomfort, says afterward, "Maestro, I hope we are still friends." But the maestro angrily demolishes the assumption that they ever were.

The graph on the cardiac monitor slopes like a *télépherique*, sags in a deep catenary, drops out of sight, then stabilizes briefly in what looks like Persian script, the upper loops of which, recorded by a yellow light blinking on another part of the machine, plot the contractions of the heart. At least some of the disjunct movement is caused by nervous agitation, for the patient is too clear, not sick enough to have been subjected so suddenly to such a shocking experience. Trapped in this maze of machinery and plastic lariats, he refuses to eat, but when Rita reasons with him, ignores the indignity, takes up his fork, and valiantly goes on.

Throughout the ordeal, the quality of the man most to the fore is his precision of language and the absence of confusion in switching from one to another according to the addressee. *"Ustal, ustal"* (tired), he says to V., and "Send them to the devil!" Turning to the doctor, he describes the characteristics of his pangs in German, and, to Rita, complains about them in French. As for my language, when I joke with him to the effect that he did not have to go to this length to avoid Liszt, he smiles.

The view from I.S.'s window is almost as depressing as the scene in the intensive care unit: standing-room-only buildings, different in size but nearly uniform in ugliness, all with the same TV antennae, same window-sill air-conditioning boxes, same chimneys, skylights, water tanks, and, in the penthouses, bits of shrubbery; even the narrow spire of a church, shoe-horned into the middle of this squeeze, is inhabited, a vase of forsythia and some books being visible beneath the half-drawn Venetian blind of a window near the base. The ICU is brisk and businesslike—infectiously so, to judge by a clergyman who pops in to administer last rites and who leaves soon after, as insouciant, if possible, as the doctors and nurses. The gravest faces in the ward, so far as I can tell without peeking under oxygen masks, are those of three solicitors, come, I think, to witness a noncupative (oral) will.

At one point, in reply to V.'s "Why do you call me every minute and rap on the bed railing with your rings when you *know* I am here?," I.S. says, marvelously: "I want to be sure that *I* still exist."

March 22. The edema is worse today, and he suffers a moment of mental confusion, asking for "Katya." V. answers that "Katya is in Paris," telling me afterward: "If he had asked *where* in Paris, I would have *had* to say, 'in the cemetery.'" This revenant has been aroused, I think, by a nurse's question as to how many children he has. He has heard "had" for "has" and held up four fingers. Otherwise he refuses to talk, and we resort to pantomime.

540

March 25. V. buys a canary for I.S. (A bird was in the next room to Mozart's when he died.)

March 28. With I.S. still in the hospital, we go about our last day in the Essex House. Trying to induce I.S. to drink water, Rita explains, as a last resort, that he is dehydrated. "Well," he says accusingly, "no one told me," and he promptly swallows a quarter of a litre. He receives a transfusion in the afternoon and another in the evening.

I spend the afternoon with Aaron Copland and Virgil Thomson trying to judge pieces for the Pulitzer Prize, an impossibility because of incomparables of media and styles—how does one choose between an electronic Mass and a string quartet?—and very largely because of the unknowns, meaning the operas one has not seen, the multi-media pieces one cannot visualize, the scores whose notation is purely verbal, the scores not meant to sound the same way twice, and the complex works one cannot digest in a single read-through and without the aid of performance tapes. Furthermore, how can three jurymen with radically different inclinations hold their natural prejudices in abeyance long enough to agree even on the stylistic area of the choice? Today's midway answer—lacking a really obvious winner, we do not bring down the gavel—is that we begin to introduce such criteria as sensitivity to color and whether or not we can outguess the composer. We are beginning to veer toward established reputations, in the sense of giving them the benefits of our doubts. After each rejection, Virgil says: "Another redskin bites the dust."

March 29. At the ages of 82 and 89, V. and I.S. move to their new home, 920 5th Avenue, he directly from the hospital, she from the hotel (bringing bread and salt, in accordance with superstition). Weak though he is, I.S. insists on two full tours of the apartment, which seems to please him: he kisses V. and thanks her again and again. Of all the new furnishings and accouterments, his greatest interest is in the new occupant of the birdcage, Iago, the canary, which is not surprising from a man who once composed music for a "real" as well as a mechanical nightingale. When Iago, who trills like Galli-Curci, repeats a note several times at near A-440, I.S. says, "He must be tuning up." Flowers, messages of welcome including one from Berman: "*Vita nuova, vita buona, vita felice, vita lunga.*"

Auden comes at 7, sniffs the fresh paint, observes (without overtaxing his acumen) that the apartment "needs to be lived in," embraces I.S. (saying to me, "You never know when it's the last time"), accompanies V. and myself to the Pavillon, where he orders a British dinner. Waiting for it, he shows me the typescript of his book of clerihews, reciting a few yet to be included. Some are about composers, and when we reach the "B.s," he asks V., "What made Igor stop being catty about Beethoven?"

Turning to his most recent lecture tour, he holds forth on what is "in" on the campuses. "Lévi-Strauss still is, though he writes such bad prose. And Buckminster Fuller—it was very unkind of the *Times* to publish that full-page 'poem' of his the other day." The audience for his own Philadelphia Freud lecture "consisted entirely of analysts and hippies," he says, adding, "I read it from my own longhand, which made it seem even longer than it is." In Toronto, he found himself in a symposium with Marshall McLuhan, "a confrontation that, according to the press, I won. Vosnezensky was there, too, and I read *for* him. Speaking of Canada, I now own tax-deductible Dominion oil stocks, an arrangement that looks a little *louche* to me, but my lawyer seems to know what the traffic will bear."

Recalling a symposium in Stockholm last year, he says, "The scientists were bigger prima donnas than artists ever are, and though they may know everything about microbiology, they don't know their ass from a hole in the ground about human beings. Furthermore, when a speaker is asked to limit himself to 20 minutes, it is infuriating to have him take 45." All of this is said in a voice whose normally very substantial carrying power has been appreciably increased by the effects of two double vodka martinis and several glasses of champagne; which seems to be the reason that so many people at other tables find us more and more deserving of their undivided attention.

Switching to the subject of old age, he confesses to sleeping longer, "From 9 to 9, in fact," and is astonished to hear that I.S. rarely retires before 11. He is incredulous that I.S. had two teeth extracted last month—that he *had* two teeth—and he mentions some recent work on his own "lowers" by Dr. Kallman, Chester's father, "who, incidentally, charged only $250, though in the case of a genius like Igor, it would certainly be more"—surely the non-sequitur of the decade. "I could never live in a siesta culture," he goes on. "If Mama found me resting in the afternoon, she would say, 'Are you ill?'" And the thought of his mother reminds him that he received a letter from her shortly after her death, in 1941, written just before. "I tore it up, of course. I simply could not bear to open and read it."

His enthusiasm of the moment is Oliver Sacks's book on migraines, a review of which he expects to finish next week in Pisa. He confesses that he "turned down the Norton Lectures because I didn't have anything to say. Now I think that at least one requirement for a lecturer is that he should have something to say," which may become one of Auden's immortal apothegms. He tells us that his adaptation of "*L.'s L.'s L.*" does not contain any anagrams. "They would have been too patent. Plays are for people who like that sort of thing, not operas. But this opera is more fun than the play, I think, in the sense that *Kiss Me Kate* is more fun than *The Taming of the Shrew*." But why Pisa? Are migraines in some way related to an architectural slant there?

March 31. Twenty-three years ago today I met the Stravinskys. We observe the date with a short musical banquet, the First "Rasumovsky" Quartet and the beginning of the *Pathétique* Symphony. I.S. is in good spirits and much amused by a remark today, in a *TLS* review, on Herder's concept of *Kraft*: "a . . . hovering in status between an inanimate causal agency and a personified and intelligent agency."

April 1. Happy as he is in his new home, I.S. is greatly concerned whether he can afford it. *"Vraiment, tout ça appartient à moi?"* he asks, and it is hard to convince him that it does indeed belong to him.

April 2. I.S. writes a short note in Russian, but forgets and signs his name in Latin letters. V. asks him to do the signature over in Russian, whereupon he takes the pen, and, aware that she is watching him, writes not his name, but "Oh, how I love you!"

April 3. Drive to New Paltz with Rita for a walk in the still snow-patched woods. Back in New York, I leave her at the Essex House and go to 920 5th Avenue, where I notice that I.S., who should move frequently, is sleeping too soundly on one side. Has the substitute nurse, unaccustomed to his restlessness, given too strong a sedative? I want to wake V., but she is soundly asleep and exhausted.

April 4. We can hardly wake I.S., and his breathing is very labored, in spite of which the nurse, another substitute, dresses him and takes him to the dining room for breakfast. It is soon obvious that he has pulmonary edema again. The nurse calls Lax, apparently not describing the condition as an emergency. Worse still, she does not call Rita, who would know enough to give Lassix or another diuretic immediately, along with dijoxin. Happening by at about 2:30, Rita says that the pulse is dangerously rapid. The breathing is like that of a fish out of water.

When at last the doctor arrives, we reject his recommendation of the hospital, an unthinkable trauma for I.S. now, convenient as the removal would be for the medical functionaries. V. insists that the intravenous apparatus be installed here and that an intern or doctor remain in attendance during the night. The I.V. equipment is delivered surprisingly quickly, but a weak vein is chosen, the needle slips, and a full hour is lost before it is reinjected and the clysis begins to flow. Lax, meanwhile, trying to explain I.S.'s chances to V. and myself, is oddly drawn to anecdotes about the last days of his one-time patient Bela Bartok. He quotes Bartok: "One of the most important things I learned from Stravinsky was daring." Is Lax deliberately hinting to V., or, is he unable to eject the memory of the other composer's death?

Two large green torpedoes of oxygen are trundled in, but the twin-pronged nostril-clamp feeder can be kept in place only by stretching a rubber band around the head. We cushion I.S. from the pull of the elastic by putting large tufts of cotton under it, on each cheek, where they remind me of dundrearies and Ibsen's sideburns (and bring to mind the Norwegian's "To write is to judge one's self"; but surely a simpler use of writing, calling down no judgment if not exempting the writer from it, is the double-edged, partly cathartic, desire to remember?). I.S. is fearfully

1971 anxious, squeezing and kissing our hands, crossing himself and ourselves, but still and always panting like a stranded fish. And his body is *not* responding, the Lassix is *not* mobilizing the fluid, he does *not* pass any urine during the entire afternoon, and the lungs are no less audibly congested.

Worst of all, his pulse is wildly irregular, and the signs of heart failure are alarming. At about 8 P.M., Lax and the night-watch intern he has assigned decide that morphine must be given to slow the heartbeat, even though it may perilously retard other functions. Just before the injection, I talk to I.S., his big eyes studying my face as I promise that he shall have music tomorrow. He responds with a smile. "Do you want Beethoven?" I ask. But he does not answer. "Well, then, Stravinsky?" But at this he makes a sour face and firmly shakes his head to left and right.

About an hour later, when he is still not reacting to the medications, Rita disregards her nurse's uniform for the first time in two and a half years, and says, "Robert, you must hope that he dies now—for him. And I will tell you that already this afternoon *we* thought he would." I do not want him to die—or, of course, want him to suffer; but if the choice were mine, it would be for more suffering, and I would take the responsibility for it on pain of perdition because I know there is more life in him still, life of the most precious kind. At this point V. enters the room, and at first seems not to comprehend the gravity. Then, after gazing at him for a long time, she says: "He is tired and would like to sleep 'forever,' but his mind is still making distinctions and he knows that 'forever' and 'death' are the same." We take turns moistening his open mouth and lips with lemon water—"Like Christ and the vinegar," she remarks.

Then a little later, strangely, ominously, and for no reason except that the record is on the turntable, I start to play the finale of the *Pathétique*. Four days ago it delighted him; "Tchaikovsky's best music," he called it. But I have no idea why we played it then; in all our 23 years we have never listened to it together. Now, at the first sound of the last movement, V. runs from the room, begs me to turn it off, says that to Russians it predicts death.

April 5. No change occurs during the night; the diuretics are having no effect, and no urine is passed. The breathing is still like that of a runner after a race, and the sound of it is more and more like a death rattle. The intern, Dr. Raymond E. Moldow, on his way out at 7 A.M. (after an excellent night's sleep on a pile of pillows near the bed), tells me that in his opinion nothing can be done and that life cannot go on for more than an hour or two. But Dr. Lax, on his rounds, finding an accumulation of water in the bladder, summons Dr. George Slaughter (*sic*), chief urologist at Mt. Sinai, noted for his work in the development of renal bisection, to catheterize him, and Dr. (Miss) Shelley Brown to take blood for a BUN. Lax tells V.: "It is not 100 percent hopeless. His strength is incredible and he is a man of surprises."

544

1971

The catheterizing is accomplished without complications, but by 1 P.M. the life signs are failing: the pulse is weaker and even less regular, the lungs are still congested, and the catheter has drawn only 44 ccs of urine. At one point the blood pressure drops below 80, the pulse climbs to 140, and the respiration remains at 40. Nor can morphine and dijoxin be given again for two more hours. Three times when we are briefly out of the room, Rita calls us back to his bedside for what she says may be the end.

Then suddenly a change comes over him. His *in*spirations sound less labored, his lungs begin to clear, his blood pressure rises and his pulse falls (to 120). He responds to Rita's directions, too, turning from side to side when she explains how important it is for him to move, but he fights her like a wildcat when she attempts to insert a nasal suction tube. Whereas he was holding my hand loosely an hour ago, he clasps it now with a powerful grip and will not let go. Finally, in the late afternoon, when the BUN report is not favorable, it is clear that the outcome rests entirely with that mighty heart, which is so much more than a muscle in I.S.'s case but which has already endured more than 40 hours of superhuman strain.

He seems much improved in the evening. Yet when I sit by his bed, he kisses my hand and holds it to his cheek as if he were saying good-bye; and when V. sits on the other side and he slowly strokes her cheek with the back of his left hand, which is bandaged to keep the I.V. needle in place, that is obviously what he means. His eyes are aware of some new change, moreover, and he always was and still is ahead of everybody. V., nevertheless, after dabbing his face and neck with eau de Cologne, goes to bed slightly more hopeful than last night, and soon falls into an exhausted sleep. Rita, too, with whom I have been lifting him every few minutes to change his position (with *his* help, too; he has strength in his arms), actually returns to her room at the Essex House, "for some sleep if I am to work well tomorrow," a disastrous decision, but evidence that she, who knows him best—the other nurses, Grace Buck, Dorothy Hawkes, Catherine Sealon are not familiar with his characteristics as a patient—believes in the rally.

April 6. While the new intern, Dr. Sam Berger, and one of the new nurses adjourn to the living room to play a few hands of cards, I pace the floor, looking in at him every two minutes, praying for a change in that terrible breathing. But it does not come. And the elderly relief nurse who arrives at midnight confirms my fears that it is, if anything, more labored. Dr. Berger tries to reassure me that the breathing will ease soon as a result of the last morphine injection. Unmollified, I go to my room, then back to him; he looks weaker but more peaceful: "My life is light, like a feather on the back of my hand/Waiting for the death wind." Returning to my room I doze off until awakened by Lillian Libman, who frightens me since she has been avoiding us, keeping to the back office room and preparing her press lists. "He is sinking," she says, and I go to him, find the oxygen mask

1971 still in place, touch his feverish, perspiring forehead and face. His eyes are open and life is in them, but a moment later Dr. Berger stethoscopes the chest, says he hears nothing, and, with all the feeling of a filling-station attendant disengaging a hose from an automobile tank, removes the intravenous tube. "Gee," he says. "He went just like that." While Berger calls Lax and certifies the time of death as 5:20, I wake V., who is uncomprehending. Together we hold his still-warm hands and kiss his still-feverish cheeks and forehead. V. asks the nurse to put blankets over the mirrors (the Russian superstition that the Devil can enter through them), kisses him once more, and, crying, leaves the room not to return; for her, the spirit remains in the dead body for 40 days. Rita arrives from the Essex House in time to close the eyelids and to prepare the body, pull the sheet over the head, disinfect the room, brush his hair, insert his dentures.

Then comes the brutal "loved one" business. We are obliged to decide questions relating to the two funerals and burial; whether the casket is to be sealed for the New York service—it should be, we agree, for V.'s sake, though this is contrary to the barbaric Russian Orthodox rule.* Rita takes over the macabre jobs of selecting burial clothes (it is especially painful to think of his three Venetian-made shirts with "I.S. 1," "I.S. 2," and "I.S. 3" on them to distinguish them from mine in the laundry), and of choosing the casket and flowers. His gold cross and silver medal go with him, but V. keeps his sapphire ring** and gives me his wristwatch,† which I can hardly bear to look at, remembering how he had to lift his sleeve halfway to the elbow to find it and tell us the time, his arm having become so thin.

In 40 minutes Dr. Lax arrives—if only he had been as quick on Sunday!—and gives V. a sedative and an antibiotic for her pulmonary infection. After him, Arnold Weissberger comes, partly to take photographs of the body, which V. forbids, and to advise V. of her financial and property rights and direct her to begin the inventory of the effects. Soon, attendants from the funeral home arrive for the "transferral of the decedent." Meanwhile, in the back office, Libman is euphorically telephoning every news service in the world—the story is on all the 6 A.M. news programs—and, as we discover in the evening, identifying herself as having been at the bedside with Rita Christiansen, a fib that will be repeated until the day that Rita and the records of the Essex House confirm that she was in the hotel. By noon, hundreds of telegrams and hand-delivered

---

* This requires that a priest place an icon on the chest, cross the deceased's arms over it, and fasten a ribbon containing a printed prayer to the deceased's forehead.

** She had given it to him in the 1920s, having purchased it with money received as compensation in an automobile accident, and wore it until her death, after which I gave it to Lawrence Morton.

† A gift from Eugenia Errazuriz in the 1920s, inscribed on the gold underside with an imprint of her handwritten first name. The winder is a sapphire.

messages have arrived, and many flower baskets, while the telephones are so busy that one of our two lines breaks down and requires emergency repair (by a young man who says: "Stravinsky is my favorite composer"). But this worldwide response, instead of helping to establish the reality, makes it less believable.

The regular morning mail brings two supremely ill-timed letters, one from Theodore's lawyer proposing that a committee of custodians be formed to supervise I.S.'s affairs; the other from lawyers representing the estate of Vaslav Nijinsky and claiming a share of the royalties from *Le Sacre du printemps* on the basis of a Société des Auteurs *"déclaration,"* signed by I.S., Nijinsky, and Roerich, June 9, 1913.

At 6 P.M. we go in a daze to Campbell's Madison Avenue funeral home, where the flower-decked coffin seems unreal, a grotesquerie in no way related to I.S. A prayer service is held for V. and a few friends—Lincoln Kirstein, weeping like a child, Balanchine, very calm, who embraces and thanks me for "everything you did for him," Paul Horgan, Richard Hammond, George Martin, the Elliott Carters, Ed Allen, Natasha Nabokov. The service is long and V. is able to stand for only a few minutes of it. Bishop Dmitri's generous dispensing of incense, moreover, nearly asphyxiates us. But a wondrous thing happens. As we leave the apartment an unseasonable snow begins to fall and the winds to howl. Now, as the Bishop pronounces the name "Igor," three great bursts of thunder reply, as if Nature were acknowledging the departure from the world of a natural force.

To read the late newspapers, and to see and hear the event related on television with the completed dates 1882–1971 in the foreground, is a shock. Worst of all are old film clips of I.S. conducting. All of this seems like an attempt to make him remote, to say that he is no longer ours. Telephone from Berman, in Rome, asking about our travel plans and other information, with RAI hooked in, recording everything we say.

April 7. I talk with V. half the night, afraid of sleep, of forgetting in sleep and remembering again, then sleep, but wake from it like a bolt at exactly 5:20. V. and I do not want him to be with Bach and Mozart, as commentators and messages of condolence are saying. We want him in the next room, old, frail, and weak as he was, but wonderfully alive. And I want to hear his voice calling "Hello"; or, to give egoism its due (though I feel no "ego identification," no "guilt," and no other application of transference theory), "Where's Bob? Can we have some music?" ("What music, Maestro?" one of his nurses used to ask, and not wanting to say "Josquin des Prez" to her he would say "Bob's music.") I want to hold his hand, in which the pulse between the right thumb and forefinger throbbed almost nakedly. And laugh with him; and provoke one of his inimitable ripostes; and raise a glass to him, for he never failed to smile and raise his in return. And I want to look into his eyes, always so full of questions, though we always felt that he knew all the answers, and knew the moment of death. I

1971 cannot believe and cannot accept that he is not and will never again be there.

V., whose deeper reactions are always delayed, is worse. Yesterday she was simply numb, having gone to bed Monday partly believing he would be well in the morning, as had happened so often before. Today, too, she is suddenly aware of the monstrously cruel joke of the "new apartment," for which she has spent months in planning and preparation, reconstructing his room after his old California studio, filling it with his music, icons, pictures, photographs, books. His piano is exactly as it was there, with the manuscript drawingboard over the keys, and, on top, the portraits of Monteverdi, Mozart, Beethoven, and Bach, and the *Well-Tempered Clavier*, Book I, is still open to the Prelude in E-flat minor, which he had been playing on Saturday. No wonder V. can hardly bring herself to pass the closed door of the room. And no wonder she says she cannot live in the "new home" now, even though the few happy days that he lived here bless the house as much as the death darkens it. Or so I argue. But she says, "It is as if he only came to pay a visit, for my sake."

And Rita. What must she feel, having washed his body almost every morning for two and a half years, dressed him and brushed his hair, read to him, played cards with him, pampered him, and joked and fought with him?

I drive V. to the Cloisters, as she wishes, but she does not go inside.

Once again we talk half the night, dreading to be alone and fearing to fall asleep, to wake again, and to remember.

April 8. I wake at 5:20, but do nothing all day except read some of the cables and letters from scores of friends known and unknown. One of them says, "No other contemporary composer passes the test of a one-man concert, but Stravinsky survives about 20 of them." Another says: "He was keeping so much alive besides himself." And another, from George Perle: "This is the first time since Guillaume de Machaut that the world is without a great composer." Claudio Arrau cables from London: "Now he joins the immortals where in any case he has already been for fifty years." Shostakovitch says: *"Potriasen ujasnym izvestiem o Konchine velikogo Russkago Kompozitora Igoria Fedorovicha Stravinskovo Stop Vmeste s Vami Razdeliaiu Vashe Tiajoloe Gore."* In the afternoon we take the *Sacre* manuscript to a bank vault for safekeeping while we are abroad for the funeral.

April 9. It is Good Friday, the one day in the Church year that I.S. observed, keeping a strict fast, except for music (the Couperin and Tallis *Tenebrae*, the Schütz and Bach Passions—Bach's *St. John* was the last music he heard before being taken to the hospital on March 18); but he would not work (compose) on that day, now the day of his funeral.

V. can hardly walk, and has been ordered by Lax to stay in bed and see and talk to no one. But I.S.'s children have arrived, and his elder son has asked to see her; he will take her refusal in bad grace. "Why didn't they come to see him when he was alive?" she asks. And, in truth, while she has not been away from him for more than two hours in two years, the children, the same son excepted, have not been two hours *with* him. No doubt his death has momentarily grieved them, but they were remote from him at the time, and for a long time; and their loss at a distance is simply not comparable to V.'s, who, moreover, in spite of all the anguish, still has to face decisions relating to the Venetian funeral and interment. The children spend two hours before the funeral discussing questions of inheritance and the Swiss bank with Weissberger and two attorneys of their own. In short,

> Some natural tears they drop'd/But wip'd them soon. . . .

A few minutes before 3 o'clock, we go to the funeral home at 81st and Madison, where a crowd is gathered in front of the door and a line stretches around the block; we are ushered into a waiting room, then to the front row, right side of the chapel—the children are on the left—and given candles to hold throughout the service. Just before it begins, Ampenoff, representing Boosey & Hawkes, enters the room, sits on V.'s side, but, treacherous and two-faced as always, makes a sign to the children that she is with them. The hardest moments are the sound of I.S.'s own *Otche Nash* at the beginning, and, near the end, the sound of the name "Igor" as if he were a little boy, in the mouth of the priest. The *"Gospodi pomiluy"* ("Kyrie eleison") is also painful, reminding me, as it does, of the Russian services I used to attend with him in Hollywood two decades ago; and the three "Alleluias" which, as he once acknowledged, were part of the inspiration for the *Symphony of Psalms:**

After the service, V. says that she cannot "stand on a receiving line, as if it were a cocktail party" and cannot return to the apartment. Accordingly,

* The Slavonic "Alleluia," which adds, and stresses, a penultimate syllable

is possibly a source of a two-note motive endemic to Stravinsky's music. The word is written thus in the Slavonic prayer book which was at Stravinsky's bedside when he died, and which had belonged to his father:

549

1971 Rita, Ed Allen, and I fly with her to Miami, where a car takes us to the giddying glassed-in top of the Boca Raton Tower, a lonely skyscraper that, for even a mild acrophobe, is like trying to sleep at the top of the Tour Eiffel.

April 10. Again we wake at 5:20 and are still unable to comprehend, but at least manage for a time to talk about something else. I rent a car, and, with Rita, drive a short distance to an empty beach, where I skid while trying to turn around and bury the car axle deep in a dune. Walking far enough from the bogged vehicle—which looks as if it might be sinking in quicksand—to rule out the suggestion of any link between it and ourselves, we attempt to hitchhike back to the hotel, but inspire no confidence, probably because of my Fellini-like apparel: red bedroom slippers, wet-through checkered pants, two large suitcases (from the trunk of the sand-swamped car). V., even more restless than yesterday, is eager to return to New York, which we arrange to do from Miami tomorrow.

April 12–13. New York. Letter of condolence from Isaiah Berlin saying that nothing will ever be the same for me again.

We fly in the evening to Rome and Venice. V. has 'flu and a temperature, but insists on being on the same airplane (a 747 flying auditorium, large enough for a memorial concert) as I.S.'s body. Also aboard is a man carrying I.S.'s passport, a Gogolian requirement of the Italian government.

We arrive so late in Rome that our connecting plane to Venice has to be recalled from the runway to take us aboard.

In Venice, fog-wrapped, phantomal, only the nearest and tallest towers—San Francesco della Vigna, the *pigna* of the Madona dal'Orto—stand out in silhouette. We enter the great stone labyrinth beneath the Ponte Sepolcro. An *affiche* on many walls reads, in effect:

THE CITY OF VENICE HONORS THE GREAT MUSICIAN IGOR STRAVINSKY
WHO WITH A GESTURE OF EXQUISITE FRIENDSHIP WANTED IN LIFE TO BE
BURIED IN THE CITY HE LOVED MORE THAN ANY OTHER

This is not true: he never expressed any desire to be buried here; the responsibility for that decision is V.'s and mine. Moreover, St. Petersburg was the city he loved more than any other. But Venice reminded him of St. Petersburg, and he did love Venice. If he had died in California, the interment would have been there, but New York was only a way-station in his life, while burial in the USSR would have betrayed his good years in the U.S. France had become remote.

I am obliged to rehearse in the foyer of La Fenice; a rehearsal of *Carmen* is on stage: Bizet's passions mingle profanely with our *Requiem*.

April 14. At 9 this morning, a water-hearse moves the *salma* (coffin) from the Campo San Tomà to Santi Giovanni e Paolo, pantheon of the doges, where it is placed in the Cappella del Rosario, and where people file around it for the rest of the day, some of them condoling with V. when she arrives for the evening rehearsal of the *Canticles* in the cold and too reverberant church; the sight of the flower-decked bier in the chapel is even more disturbing than in New York, if such feelings can be measured. Walking back to the Gritti Hotel, we pass the Stravinsky children in conference in front of the Bauer Grunwald, where, of all ironies, they are staying. They look in the other direction.

April 15. And so the day of burial has come. At 11:30 A.M. a *motoscafo* takes us to S. Zuan e Polo, as it is written on old maps. The Campo is thronged (500, the *Gazzettino* says), as are windows, roofs of houses, and the great Gothic church itself (3,000, the *Gazzettino* says), whose front doors are left open so that the people outside may be included in the ceremony. The Campo is also crowded with memories and, as we cross it, I see I.S. as he used to come to the Ospedale (Scuola di San Marco) in a blue water-ambulance, for his weekly blood tests, and see him at the Caffè al Cavallo, to which he sometimes walked, or was boated, in the evening for a grappa; only two months ago, by some coincidence, he referred to the Cavallo itself (the Verocchio).

Entering the Basilica through the *Porta laterale*, we proceed to the left transept, where a row has been reserved for the *"famiglia"* (V., myself, Rita, Ed, and, like an ambassadorial wall between us and I.S.'s children, Nicolas Nabokov). The rose-covered bier rests on a black cloth ornamented with white Maltese crosses; huge tapers, in large gold *candelabri del presbiterio*, burn at each corner. A young acolyte, in a black vestment with a pattern of white flowers and crosses, stands at the foot of the *salma*, facing the altar and holding a tall *croce astile* (processional cross), base to the floor; in a ceremony of more than three hours (here and on the island) he never fidgets, and his bearing is always far more commanding than that of the attendant *carabinieri*. The service is a standing (*kathistos*), not a sitting (*kathisma*) one, and when V. sits for a moment, from fatigue, the archimandrite glances in her direction with noticeable lack of compassion.

The young cross-bearer cannot conceal his incredulity at the antics of the paparazzi, those nonstop camera-snappers who are on the verge of infiltrating the archimandrite's beard. (But without flapping him; not so me: a posse of them follows me to the podium, no doubt sensing that a photo of me keeling over is imminent; it is 9 A.M. for me, biologically speaking, besides which I have slept no more than minutes at a time in days, have conducted only once since I.S.'s illness two years ago, and am wholly unable to detach myself from the event; only by constantly thinking of what I.S. would say about every detail of the performance am I able to get through it.) The obsequies begin with Alessandro Scarlatti's *Requiem Missa Defunctorum*, added for bad measure to show off the chorus, but the music is featureless and in no way relates to I.S. (or, being Neapolitan, even to Venice). The three organ pieces that follow (Andrea Gabrieli's

1971

Praeambulum quarti toni, Toccata del decimo tono, Pass'e mezzo antico), played by Sandro Dalla Libero, would have pleased him; I remember walking with him from the Madona dal'Orto to San Marco, tracing the route of the Lepanto victory procession, for which Andrea Gabrieli composed music. After the Scarlatti, Mayor Giorgio Longo delivers an address, quoting encomia of Venice by I.S. and Ezra Pound; *il miglior fabbro* himself is present and has been in the church since early morning, before the casket was moved from the chapel to the *navata centrale*.

The *Requiem Canticles* follows, faltering at first, the staccato accompaniment in the Prelude suffocating in the acoustical wool, the *Rex Tremendae* wobbling like pasta, and the *Libera me* sounding more like a mob scene than the *"bisbigliare"* (background patter) I.S. wanted. Worst of all, the celesta player fills in one of the pauses in the Postlude, nearly ruining that explicit structure: the chord of Death, followed by silence, the tolling of bells, followed by silence, all three thrice repeated, then the final three chords of Death alone. (No wonder everything I.S. composed after this was meant both to preserve it as his last work and to prevent it from becoming so too soon.)

At 12:30, Archimandrite Cheruvim Malissianos, gold cope and black hood (*klobuk*), with veil trailing over his shoulders, parades down the center aisle to a vermilion throne at the entrance to the apse. Two acolytes follow him and stand, one on each side, a step below him, where together they hold the euchologion from which the archimandrite reads part of the service, while they, together or individually, sing the responses. Malissianos, a young man with the dark eyes, olive skin, black hair and beard, and the allure of a Byzantine Pantocrator, is a dazzling performer, both to listen to and to watch, although his gestures are simple: whether raising his hand; or lowering the fourth finger, in the Orthodox way, touching his temples and heart (which is how I.S., too weak to trace the transverse, crossed himself the night before he died); or slowly swinging the thurible around the coffin, with prolonged fumigations in the direction of the head. He is ostentatious only in the way he closes his eyes, but this has the effect of hushing the entire congregation and of asking it to pray.

What wonderful music these chants, remnants of Byzantium bedizened by corruptions from the Syrian, Hebrew, and Arabic Orient, albeit bastardized for want of a Rosetta Stone relating the different systems of notation. And no wonder hymnographers were so important in Byzantium! How beautiful, too, are the Greek words: *"makarios"* and *"philanthropos"* and *"eleos"* and *"hosios."* The singing is an art of agogics, of the *kratema*, the *parakletike*, the *apodema*; and an art of ornaments, such as the *kylisma*, and whatever the names for that "break" of emotion in the voice and the effect of trailing off to the last note, so that the listener is uncertain whether or not it has actually been sung. This high art would have delighted and been best understood by the man who lies dead.

Alleluiatic antiphons begin the service, which celebrates the joyous pas- sage from death to eternal life (and the Orthodox Church seems to emphasize the Resurrection as much as the Roman Church emphasizes the Crucifixion). Whereas in the Russian service the music is harmonic, syllabic, and tonal, here, in the Greek, it is monodic, melismatic, and plagal— falling whole-tone cadences, exquisitely sung by the mellifluous Malissianos. Psalm 118 follows (Josquin's setting of Psalm 118 was one of I.S.'s favorite pieces), the Four Beatitudes of John the Damascene, the Fourth Chapter of the First Epistle to the Thessalonians, and the Song of Exodus. Again the most painful moment comes with the name "Igor." Until then, art and ritual have helped to make this celebration of the mystery of life—ending in death and beginning in death—less personal.

At the end, the archimandrite summons V. to kneel before the coffin and say good-bye. Then four gondoliers—black sashes, black armbands, black shirts showing at the neck beneath white blouses—wheel it slowly down the center aisle, V. walking behind, and out into the sunlight and azure and the Campo banked with flowers. Here it is transferred to the water-hearse, a gondola with gold lions of St. Mark on the sides, and a border of pink-and-white roses, like those on the bier; the gondoliers' oars are black-tipped, and a long tongue of black drape trails in the water. The archimandrite, seated, and his cross-bearer, standing, ride in the first gondola, V., with me, in the one behind the bier. As the bier passes, the people on the Fondamenta, in front of San Lazzaro dei Mendicanti, in windows and doorways, and in boats and on bridges—all packed to the parapets—bow their heads and cross themselves.

When the cortege sails under the Ponte dei Mendicanti and into the lagoon, the archimandrite stands behind the cross-bearer, cope and *klobuk* now blowing in the breeze. The faster boats of the TV crews and the paparazzi cut in on the procession and confound the protocol, and as a result the heavy hearse-boat is the last to reach the island and be unloaded. (When it has been, the thought occurs to me that I.S., who could not swim and was always nervous in gondolas, would be relieved.) We wait for it before the gateway with Gothic pinnacle over the frieze of the Archangel Michael (who as Metatron stayed the hand of Abraham), receiver of souls (scales in one hand, spear in the other) and sounder of the last trump, "When the dead shall be raised incorruptible, and we shall be changed."

As the procession resumes and we enter the old Camaldolensian cloister, I reflect that *Apocatastasis* is not a consoling thought. The flower displays are borne ahead now, President Saragat's first, and a large red one from the Soviet Union behind, along with those of many other countries, *not* including the U.S.A. The archimandrite follows, then the bier on a caisson, and ourselves with our own bouquets. The gondolier pallbearers, not yet having found their terra-firma legs, are held up for an awkward minute or two by a small flight of stairs. Moving on, we follow a crunchy gravel path past

1971 a wall of kennel-like mausoleums and through a field of small white crosses, each with photograph of the deceased. The "*Rep. Greco*," so designated over the portal, is a garden of laurels, cypresses, and expired Orthodoxists, bordering the outermost wall of the island. The chapel at the end of the path is barely large enough, lengthwise, for the coffin and for ourselves; the paparazzi and TV cameramen have installed themselves atop the vined wall over the grave-site. In the chapel, the archimandrite and acolytes disappear into a shallow, curtained-off prothesis, ostensibly to prepare for the final rites—he strips for a moment to his black cassock—but primarily to stall until a call can be put through to the *sindaco* for clearance to begin the service without him. It starts behind the curtain, Malissianos chanting now in a dolorous, weirdly "white" voice, answered by one of his acolytes with three sepulchral "Kyries," after which the other one begins to wail and to lead the coffin outside to the grave, where he stands under a tree, keening his unearthly music throughout the burial.

Before the interment begins, and while the scaffolding is being removed, Malissianos banters with two of the gravediggers, Hamlet-like, but sotto voce, telling them in Venetian vulgo to get it right because burial is a more or less permanent condition. But he does so without compromising his sacerdotal dignity (which may be inviolate, in any case, as I suspect at the end of the service when we are required to kiss his hand and find that this is impossible: *Noli me tangere*). Then the terrible moment: ropes lower the coffin, the archimandrite accompanies V. to throw the first handful of dirt, and the IGOR STRAVINSKY on the steel nameplate gleams for a last instant in the sun.

April 16. During the flight to Paris, the clouds break suddenly as we are over Evian, and we can make out the Hotel Royale.

Suvchinsky, at dinner in the Ritz, encourages V. to write her memoirs, "the one really valuable book and the least postponable." He counsels her to "write it, or tell it to a tape recorder, in Russian, English, French, German, or a mixture of them all." But this is a different Suvchinsky. Why, of all people, did he not come to the funeral? I.S. has supported him in the material sense for five years, after all, and for longer than that by the gift of friendship. He talks too much about "*les archives*" for someone who knows nothing about them.

My role, he says, airing a theory, differs from the examples of I.S.'s earlier associates only in degree; and in that, being a conductor, I was more broadly serviceable. At the beginning of the 1950s, so the thesis goes, I.S. lacked a sense of direction, and supposedly found one in, or by reaction to, me. I was not so much an "influence" as a catalyst, therefore, in the sense that I.S. responded not only "in his own ways," which would be obvious, but in ways that often ingeniously contradicted what I may have seemed to be espousing. Thus, if my advocacy of Schoenberg appeared to be uppermost, he would devote himself exclusively to Webern; and if I seemed to think that chromatic equality was a built-in tenet of serialism, he would opt for a diatonic species. Which may or may not be true, *I* say, but all that anyone *else* can say, for certain, is that in my role as housedog I was more Cerberus than spaniel.

"The feelings of the children are plain enough," he goes on. "You took their place.* But never mind. It is more important to remember that a hero must be blameless. Which is the reason the USSR will blame you because he was not buried there, even though everyone knew that his visit there in 1962 was possible only because of your—in this instance the word is correct—influence."

April 17. Impatient as she was to leave Venice, V.'s, decision to come to this even more deeply memory-laden city was wrong. Her face streams with tears during our drive through the Bois de Boulogne, and, on the return, stopping at the rue Daru church, she cries harder than at any time since his death. Nor does "the beauty of Paris" provide much balm. After the "coziness" of Venice—I.S.'s word and one of his reasons for wanting to be there—the Louvre looks pompous, and the "restored" Place des Vosges seems as new as a Disneyland replica.

April 19. To Marrakech, to visit Ira Belline, I.S.'s niece and one of V.'s closest pre-1940 friends. The two have not seen each other since then, Mademoiselle Belline having lived in Morocco since the war. Nor, for a nerve-wracking half-hour, is it at all certain that they will see each other now, our Royal Moroccan Caravelle having developed convulsions on the descent at Fez. With no respect for our imaginations, the captain refers to "motor trouble" and says that our course has to be shifted toward the larger runway at Casablanca. We drift down like a glider thereafter, and at a drastically reduced speed. The runway, when we touch down, is flanked by ambulances and firetrucks with hoses at the ready. Hours after an announcement about a short delay for repairs, when no noticeable step has been taken in that direction, we hire a taxi and complete the trip by car.

The cactus, prickly-pear, and adobe landscape is New Mexican, if not the traffic: donkeys, whose passengers sit far back as if to keep the animals from tipping forward; camels, dark brown and shaggy except for a young, milk-white one tethered to a telephone pole; and women, in the same category as the donkeys except limited to freight, which they carry like canephoroi. Nor has Women's Lib made conspicuous inroads in other directions. Almost all females are veiled, and not only to the eyes but also over them, which in the case of white with a white garment (*haik*) is distinctly djinnish. Women turn away at our approach, but the turbaned and djellabahed men turn into salesmen, holding up clutches of eggs, bouquets

---

* No. None of them had performed the same role in their father's life that I did. Moreover, when I appeared on the scene, the children were married people in their 40s, leading lives independent of their father in every way except financially.

1971 of wild flowers, and, near the muddy Oum er Rebia, catches of fish skewered on sticks. These are the unchosen few who lack the gift of doing absolutely nothing, the majority being asleep or seated, legs akimbo, by the roadside. It is this inertness that makes our driver's feat in capturing a wasp with his hands and actually tweaking its wings seem the more remarkable.

No sooner do we reach the palm and eucalyptus oasis, Marrakech, with its kilometers of medieval walls, and enter the brass-cuspidored lobby of the hotel, than we feel the emptiness at the center more acutely than ever. "I want to be near him," V. says, asking the concierge for airplane schedules to Rome and Venice.

Ira comes at six, a tall, handsome woman strikingly dressed in red turban, sweater, Spahi pants, Moorish gold bracelets. Both women are nervous, chain-smoking and fidgeting, and at first the meeting is stiff. I go for a walk in the gardens, but the gravel paths and the trees are reminders of San Michele.

Averroes lived here, perhaps walked near these same ramparts. All that I can remember of him, and that vaguely, is his argument for the validity of alternative modes of access to truth, and, which follows, his defense of the right to the coexistence of conflicting truths. This seems reasonable enough, at least to one who believes in "permanent" musical and poetic truths, fallible and, at best, highly adjustable scientific truths, and modal philosophical working hypotheses, that the answer to Jesting Pilate is circumstantial, the formulation of the culture and the age. In other words, *not* "revealed" truth. Why not? Because that is also the expression of a cultural mode. Why am I intolerant of "revealed" religion as fact? Simply because I cannot believe, am incapable of belief? But why, too, these outpourings, this soliloquy, these particular questions? Because I have been more deeply shaken than ever before in my life and because I am surprised—naively surprised, perhaps—to find that the arts, science, and philosophy are no succor at all, that the only help is to be found in other human beings. The change in me is that I am at least prepared to believe that other modes exist.

We eat in the hotel, where the headwaiter is from the Royale in Evian. (I quickly recognize and greet him, having an excellent memory for waiters, drivers, and all "menials," unlike V., who was taught to take no notice of her "surroundings.") At sundown the sky turns indigo, the olive trees turn silver, the palms dark green, the mountains (below the snow line) purple, and the hum of nesting swallows fills the jasmine-sweet air. After a signal of distant cock crows, the night itself begins to snore in and out, like a concertina.

April 20. Dinner at the home of Ira and her brother Ganya, a man so startlingly "Russian" in appearance—Tolstoy nose, "Russian" goatee, old-fashioned silver rimmed "Russian" spectacles—that he might have been made up for a part in Chekhov. The trip takes 20 minutes from the Mamounia Hotel in our one-camel-power taxi, not including a skirmish, on arrival, with the dogs, for the house is guarded by 10 vociferous canines: they bark in concert throughout the evening, then suddenly fall silent when we leave—not for that reason, I think, but because they must be hoarse.

If the atmosphere of the house, once actually owned by a granddaughter of Tolstoy, is "Russian," the impression is attributable less to the occupants, or even to the many mementos of the Diaghilev Ballet, than to a similarity between a way of life of the Arab fellaheen and Russian peasants, the peasants of I.S.'s creations; the principal *domestiques* in the Stravinsky household during I.S.'s own youth were Tartar Muslims.

As if reading my thoughts, Ira tells a story remarkably akin to the world of *Noces*. It seems that when her Arab houseboy announced his forthcoming marriage, she unthinkingly asked a question about his betrothed, which obliged him to confess that he had never seen her and that the wedding had been arranged by his mother. Ira's wedding present to him was a brass bedstead which, at the ceremony, she found in the center of the one-room shack, with about 20 veiled women seated on the floor around it. The bride, swaddled in white from head to toe, sat in a corner. When the marriage had been consummated, the sheet, proof of *hymen intactus*, was held up for the inspection of the 20 women. Ira says that the bride is 15 now, has two children, and that she prepared tonight's couscous—which has cauterized my tongue.

Ira lived in Ustilug during I.S.'s last summers there but was too young to remember much about him. Her recollections of him in Morges in 1919, when her family reached Switzerland after a six-month trek fleeing the Bolsheviks, are more vivid. But most clearly of all she remembers her uncle as a worried investor in the Chateau Basque, her father's restaurant in Biarritz. She tells V. that her Russian friends called her "Verinka," then, "but uncle called you 'Verusha.'" I hardly listen, being distracted by a lizard on the wall devouring a moth, whose rescue I fail to attempt only partly out of respect for the ecological balance. (I resolve to conduct a careful search of my room and bathroom for lacertilians, scorpions, millipedes.)

Returning to the Mamounia—same one-camel-power taxi—V. is bursting to describe the evening to I.S. and missing him more than ever.

April 21. A sandstorm blows over the oasis, followed by violent rains.

We dine Moroccan-style, beginning with *harira* (a soup), a fish, succulent but viscous to touch—and *everything* here is eaten with the fingers—a sugar-and-cinnamon pancake dunked in a bowl of orange juice and milk. The waiters wear tarbooshes, babouches, white jackets, pleated white *serwaks*, and ankle-length bloomers. To keep the food warm in transit, their trays are covered with conical wicker lids, and to keep us from smelling fishy, in *ditto*, at the end of the meal, perfume is squirted in our cupped

1971 hands from silver syringes.

April 22. The *souks* and the Jemaa el Fna are muddy from yesterday's rain; which reminds Ira of Ustilug, and me of I.S. talking about the mud there. Mere mud does not interfere with the storytellers, the scriveners, the mullahs and holy men reading from the Koran, the barbecuers, teeth-pullers, water vendors, and snake charmers, all of whom live in the open air. Whether charmed or not, one of the snakes squirms very actively when suspended by the tail, but seems to suffer stage fright the moment it is set down.

The *souks* are mazes of narrow alleys roofed with rushes and dense with animals and people, the latter on bicycles and motorcycles as well as on foot. We visit carpet stalls and caftan stalls (silk, satin, nylon); wool dyers and leather tanners; a saddlery; metal embossers; spice and herb merchants (baskets of freshly picked mint); and fruit and vegetable *charrettes*. But colorful and exotic as it all is, one sight haunts me the rest of the day: a line of 13 blind, ragged, barefoot, and no doubt diseased and consumptive beggars chanting, "Allah is good," over and over, as they tap the ground with their white canes and hold out cups for alms. "Then let Allah give," a blasphemous boy jibes at them, himself a beggar, asking Ira for a groat, or a dirham, but being effectively shooed away by whatever she says to him in the demotic. Nor can I forget the sight of an old man displaying a few pieces of candy on a dirty handkerchief. *"On vend ce qu'on peut,"* Ira says, truly enough, though this is hardly the point.

April 23. The Evian waiter tells me that whereas the poor are still imprisoned for infractions of Ramadan, the King has a harem of 150. But my first and most truthful feeling about the latter part of the statement is more one of envy than of injustice.

To Ourika, at the beginning of the Atlas mountains, stopping at Berber ksour on the way. The women, colorfully dressed and not veiled—they display the family-identifying tattoos on foreheads and chins—apparently do all the work, swinging scythes and even turning waterwheels.

April 24. After farewells to Ira,* we drive to Casablanca, a filthy, noisy city, with radio music blaring in the streets from loudspeakers. The red fez is less popular here than the gray or black, and the turbans look like bandages after skull surgery. Face-curtains are fewer, though girls on motorcycles wear them. Are these veils exploited in the Venetian-masquerade sense, I wonder, as well as in the sense that probably many a disguise does not contain a blessing?

April 25. Casablanca to Rome, leaving for one of the two airports at 5 A.M. because of uncertainty as to which one is the dispatcher of our flight,

---

* Ira Belline died September 11, 1971, after an operation—of complications attributed to abuse of cortisone, according to her friend Sanche de Gramont, writing from Tangier. See the obituary by Cecil Beaton, the *Times* (London), September 30, 1971.

and the fear that to switch to the other will take a long time. As it happens, the extra time is needed because of herds of sheep and camels on the road and because of the rigmarole of document-stamping, taxpaying, customs-declaring, and multiple inspecting of passports. Airborne at last, we land only a few minutes later at Rabat, over a muddy, meandering river where everyone including ourselves is obliged to leave the plane with all baggage for another wait, before being hurried aboard again. André Chénier's father, who was French Consul here in the 18th century, described life in Rabat even then as a succession of inconveniences. The flight to Rome, just above white clouds, is like a sleigh ride.

April 26. Rome. Dinner at Passetto's with Berman, who reminisces about I.S. on our trips to Paestum and Gesualdo in 1959.

April 27. The drive to Florence and Venice reminds us of our 1959 excursion with I.S. to Canossa, the site, in the 11th century, of Ghibelline Henry's three barefoot nights in the snow (surely with chilblains) outside Pope Gregory's castle.

In Venice, V., with a jolt, hears herself referred to for the first time as *"la vedova Stravinsky."* The Royal Suite at the Gritti—beamed and coffered ceilings, baldachined and sparvered bed, canopied bath—reminds her of I.S.'s return to Paris from his first American tour: "He cabled from the boat asking me to reserve the most luxurious suite in the Grand Hotel for a few days; which I did, but without seeing it and discovering that it was decorated in a nouveau-riche style; Diaghilev was so shocked when he saw it that for days he wondered what could have happened to Stravinsky in America."

April 28. And so we go again to San Michele, past the Zanipolo, where the poster—*"La Città di Venezia . . . del Grande Musicista IGOR STRAVINSKY"*— is still on the door; and past the Mendicanti, once renowned for its orchestra of young females (praised by Goethe), but as neglected and impoverished now as the people—"Blessed are the poor"—it was meant to comfort. And into the lagoon, silent and empty today. And again to the walled isle of cypresses, the isle of the dead. Again, too, we pass beneath Saint Michael's pointed arch, a wind now blowing his rusty iron balances this way and that (so much for weights and measures). And again pass through the Convento, a solarium at this hour for a lazing tribe of cats. I.S. would have spoken to them and picked one of them up by the scruff; when the *Gazzettino* published a photograph of him after the funeral, it was *not* one of him conducting in San Marco, but one showing him feeding the cats behind San Fantin.

And again we follow the path to the Orthodox section, where lilacs and oleander are in bloom, and it is full springtime, except for the man who created a spring of his own that of all mortally begotten versions will give Nature its longest run for everlasting joy. And again we walk to the chapel, the vined wall, and the iron gate, ajar today, framing a *veduta* of the lagoon.

1971   The moment has come, too, when we must raise our eyes toward the mound of newly turned earth, which is exactly where we know it will be, the most cruelly certain of all places in our memories, now covered with flowers, like Rakewell's springtime grave. But the new earth is terrible to see, and terrible the bedlike form of the mound. V. weeps, laying her flowers on his head, and turns away. (Does she think of an afternoon long ago when, calling her and finding *her* fast asleep, he composed that most beautiful of all *berceuses* for her, Perséphone's *"Sur ce lit elle repose"*? And of that afternoon only a month ago when, instead of his name, he wrote, "Oh, how I love you?") Three times, as we walk slowly toward the gate, she is stopped and asked the direction—it is already venerated ground—"to Stravinsky's grave."

My turn to look away comes when I notice the word "Strasvischi" scrawled beneath the "36" on the marker; this is exactly what I.S., in one of his ironies, might have invented himself so short a time ago. And it is impossible not to see and hear him saying it now, just as it is impossible to believe that the man whose immortal celebration of the resurrection of Nature, and all his other continuations of the highest humanizing art of man, lies beneath that mound of earth. Yet it is not *that* man we mourn, but the old one, ill, frail, skin-and-bones, who was still so wonderfully alive. And it is that ill and frail *old* man I miss so much, miss more than I ever thought it was possible to miss anybody.

And again we leave. But will be back soon. And soon permanently, when my promise to him is fulfilled, if it should be V. first. And another promise, my own and unasked for, and I am somewhere nearby.

à Postlude

June 26, 1971. Rome. Following Berman's suggestion that we ask Manzù to design I.S.'s tombstone, we call on the sculptor in his hillside home at Campo Fico, near the ancient Roman town of Ardea, which may seem prettier than it is simply because the drive through the suburbs of the new Rome is so ugly. *"Attenti al cane,"* a notice warns at the gate, but "attention" to the high wire fence should be given priority, a chewing by canines being a less terrible prospect than electrocution. We ring up, drive up, park behind the maestro's new Cadillac—not the only sign of the increasing marketability of his art—are warmly received by him and only once growled at by the *cane*.

The maestro is so portly now that one wonders how, from certain angles, he can work at all. Otherwise he seems the same, which is to say that his hair is still migrating from his head neckwards and that his quick brown eyes are as soft and, at the same time, as strong as ever. The route to the sitting room contains a shelf of his hats, two pieces of his sculpture, and a gallery of Japanese prints. Some of his drawings are displayed on the walls of the room itself, but the furniture, a low glass table and capacious bucket chairs, is ultra modern.

I explain that V. wants a simple stone with the name (no dates) and a cross. The stone should be white, Manzù suggests, probably in two layers, the upper slightly indented, and the frame in porphyry. "I can procure the marble from the Vatican, but the cross must be gold as befits a great king." The name could be in lapis lazuli tesserae, he adds, but he would want time to consider this (and so would V.). I promise to send the measurements of the plot from Venice next week, and he promises to join us there at the end of August with a model of the tomb. He tells V. that I.S. was the greatest inspiration to him, whereupon she embraces him, and says, revealing more of her own loneliness than she allows me to see, "I can't get over the feeling of expecting him to come back."

561

July 4.   Venice.   Clearly it was a mistake to return here where we have so many intense memories of I.S.   Even the colors and odors of the city remind us of him.   He used to say that the primary Venetian "color" is black—gondola black, the black bombazines of gondolier pall-bearers, the black of the Virgin in the Scalzi, of the Christ with gold breechclout in Santa Sofia, of the wooden Moors (those Venetian cigar-store Indians). But then, he preferred the black and white Venice to the polychromatic one of the iridescent Favile glass, the Santa Maria della Salute when "composed" with foreground ecclesiastics in black cassocks to the façade of the Palazzo Dario.

July 16.   Biarritz, the Palace Hotel.   As we enter the restaurant, an elderly maître d'hôtel tells V. that he had met her here with Stravinsky and Diaghilev in the 1920s.   When she is out of earshot, he whispers to me *"Je pense que Monsieur et Madame n'étaient pas encore mariés en ce moment."*   Which says something about the French memory.

Biarritz has changed virtually beyond V.'s recognition, the "bastard Tudor" Basque style of black-and-white timbering almost having disappeared in the mess of new buildings, though *not* the Basque language, which, on road signs, looks something like IBM's "magnetic writing."   The Russian Church, facing the hotel on the rue de Russe, is surprisingly large and, whatever the Russian population may have dwindled to now, it must have been considerable in the time of the grand dukes, and of Stravinsky.

August 11.   Paris.   The air in the Jaquemart-André's Proust exhibition is as hot and stuffy as the living Proust would have wanted, but nothing else in the show evokes him, least of all the morbid mannekins of his major characters dressed in period costumes.   The black coverlet of his deathbed, in the last room, has apparently not been dusted since 1922.   The original of I.S.'s drawing of Bakst is here, much smaller than expected from reproductions.

April 10, 1972.   Our hostess at the Manzù Museum in Campo Fico is the sculptor's model, Inge.   So many of the maestro's figures are of the nude Inge herself that to refrain from mentally undressing the original is impossible, if impolite.   Manzù's world centers so closely on her—straying to any large extent only to *natures mortes*, helmets (he is obsessed with headgear), priests and their raiment—that one looks for her features in all his women, including the female partners in two tempestuous copulations in bronze.

The theatrical designs section is more revealing of the artist as a whole. Whereas the sets are generally successful, friezes exploiting pleated drapery in the same way as the sculptures, the costumes are often naive, as that of the Devil in *Histoire du Soldat*:   the fallen angel has a tattered black wing and a fig leaf of solid gold.

The gate to the artist's hilltop home still threatens the intruder with canine dismemberment, but the maestro's mastiffs are nowhere in evidence (bite each other and die of rabies?), and the barbed wire is less obviously dangerous now than the cactus.   The maestro greets us outside, against a landscape as undulant as the flanks and *fesses* he loves to mould, for Manzù is an "old man mad about hills."

His studio is the size of a B-52 hangar but not tall enough to shelter a mammoth opus-in-progress that stands outside the entrance as mysteriously as the Trojan horse. Whatever it is, the scaffolding and canvas covering suggest that the sculptor has struck oil and that he prefers to keep his discovery secret. The studio is cluttered with plaster nudes; mitred heads, both in relief and in the round, the latter including two of Papa Giovanni; three dollhouse models of a set for Strauss's *Elektra*; and, oddly, a clump of Winterhalter-period hunting horns tied to the wall like dead game, though not oddly at all as one looks a second time at the instruments' rounded tubing, flared and infundibular bells, female curves.

The *bozzetto* of I.S.'s tomb is a flat oblong block, actual size, set in a troughlike frame that is to be capped with porphyry. Manzù shows us a piece of the milky marble of his choice but asks V. to decide between lapis lazuli and light green stone for the lettering. "Blue was our color," she says, but the green, in any case, is unsuitably veined. Taking a square sheet of gold, Manzù draws the cross to be encrusted between the name and the foot of the stone, and draws it at high speed, in contrast to the way he writes, which is like a backward child. In fact, he succeeds in writing the difficult word "Stravinsky" at all only thanks to Luisella, his American-speaking ("He's not kidding") secretary, who somehow pulls him through, though for a time the outcome is in doubt. V. wants to be certain he does not make a "w" of the fifth letter, which is the German spelling, or an "i" of the final one, which is the Polish.

He promises that the *pietra* will be in Venice by June for the *sistemazione* and tells V. that he wishes to make a gift of it, and not only of his art but of the materials. Then, as we leave: "I would like to have made something that could last as long as Stravinsky's music, but stone, which won't, is all I have."

April 11. During the drive to Venice I am obsessed by the thought that I.S. is happy V. is on the way, just as he used to be when she returned from a drive in Hollywood. Our arrival is an unbearably empty homecoming, made all the more depressing by an unseasonable inundation: half of the Piazza is submerged and the Molo is not navigable. Venice is dying on its feet (fins?).

April 13. The archimandrite—in mufti: black suit, black shirt, gold cross on a gold neck chain—comes to discuss Saturday's Panikhida service. He says that souvenir hunters have stolen three crosses from the grave, but that the mayor has now had a name plaque cemented to the wall. The archimandrite's only language, apart from Greek, is the Venetian dialect, which limits conversation.

April 14. The high waters having receded, we go to the cemetery, where a transformation has taken place. In the midst of death we are in life. The secluded corner is a five-star tourist attraction now, and the traffic to I.S.'s grave is directed by arrows. Business at the florist's has doubled, the postcard and curio stall is sold out, and the *ortodosso* wing has actually been weeded. Above all, the surly gardeners and gravediggers of last summer have become obliging receptionists. Proud of the sudden importance of the island, the staff has taken a new lease on death.

Passing the tightly packed, pectinate tombs of the poor, my thoughts turn to *ex*carnations, to "A bracelet of bright hair about the bone," to "dogsbody" and "nobodaddy," and to the likelihood of "God" versus the likelihood of accidents and chains of events leading over millions of years from amino acids in volcanic lava to Stravinsky; and, more concretely, to the underlying attraction of cemeteries, which may be in the answer they offer to the pretense to equality in the institutions on *this* side: namely that rich and poor, great and humble, are alike, for in San Michele, apart from the price of the name plate and memento mori, they *are* alike. Thus "God" becomes an invention before which, at last rather that at first, we can be equal.

It is Easter week in the Eastern Church, and lighted candles have been placed on many graves, including I.S.'s. Spreading her flowers on the still tombless ground, V. says: "I am unable to believe it even now, except that the marker says so" ("Stravinsky, Igor" in black paint on the mayor's plaque). Just then a loudspeaker startles us, *"Attenzione, Attenzione,"* as the word booms out in airports. *"Quattro spiriti sono. . ."* But the disembodied voice is interrupted by static—supernal, it may be—until the final words, *"al porto principale."* Workmen are apparently being summoned to receive four coffins—unless four escapees have been discovered and the authorities are trying to close all exits including resurrection.

April 15. The Panikhida this morning begins in San Giorgio dei Greci and ends, an hour and a half later, at the graveside. In the church we stand with Nicolas Nabokov and Adriana Panni before a laurel wreath on a table covered with red cloth (like the "red table" of *Noces*), which is in the same position in the bema as the bier in the Zanipolo a year ago. Small golden balls, like the silver rattles of the censer, are attached to the wreath. (Are they related to the golden balls, clustered like stars in the firmament, on the domes of San Marco and the Zanipolo?) Tall candelabra and silver lamps on silver chains have been placed on each side and beyond the table.

Much of the service, which includes a Mass, takes place behind the iconostasis, some of it visible through the open door, some merely audible. A procession (*vkhod*) enters the church through the iconostasis, the archimandrite, bareheaded, vestments of brocaded gold, in the center, censing to right and left, a server on one side carrying a tall candle, and on the other a deacon who proceeds to an agalogion to sing the responses. When the archimandrite turns to the altar and begins a chant, that day a year ago is instantly brought back. The music is unornamented, apart from cadential *échappées*, and at times the deacon, in a hollow voice, chimes in at an octave below. At the high point of the ceremony, the archimandrite raises the ancient red book of the Gospel of St. John to his forehead for our veneration, then turns to the altar and in a radiant voice sings a verse from it. At the end, he dons his *klobuk*, another reminder of a year ago, and places a piece of the antidoron (bread) in V.'s cupped hands.

On San Michele, the deacon shakes smoke over the grave while the archimandrite lays the laurel wreath at its head and sings a prayer ("*sophia*," "*makarios*"). As it was a year ago, the most painful moment occurs when he invokes the name "Igor."

October 2. Manzù's tomb, expected at Mestre since last week, is still not here, evidently for the reason that last-minute authorizations by bureaucrats Roman and Venetian had been overlooked. V. telephones the sculptor, who assures her that the stone is on its way and will reach Venice "*domani*." All wrapped up in red tape, no doubt.

Gravitating to the familiar places first (looking for a former self and the reasons why the new one is different?), I go to "Mozart's house," next to the Barcarolli bridge, and to the Legatoria Piazzesi to talk to the bookbinder who used to make sketchbooks for I.S. and who still wears a black smock, as he did then. But I feel lonely afterward, intensely so in the Basilica at sunset and walking in the white and gold Piazza after dark.

Dinner at Harry's with Nabokov (scarlet socks and braces, psychedelic tie). The restaurant is like a subway car at rush hour, and only fragments of his talk—about Mediterranean bull culture versus Persian lion culture—are audible. He brings I.S. to life by quoting one of his expressions: "*On compose la musique avec la gomme.*"

October 5. The stone has finally arrived and, thanks to the mayor's intervention, has already been ferried to the island and entrusted to a *marmorista*.

Bill Congdon comes from Subiaco, where he lives in monastic retreat (10 miles to the nearest telephone) not only from the U.S.A. and his New England Brahmin background but from the last 15 centuries as well. Of all those who knew I.S. more than superficially in his later years, and whose lives were profoundly affected by him, Bill is one of the most perceptive. Moreover, he remembers I.S.'s every word, gesture, inflection, from their first meeting in the airport canteen in the Azores in March 1955, to their final ones, in Assisi, October 21, 1962, the day I.S. learned of Goncharova's death, and in Palermo and Rome in November 1963. But it was during the summers in Venice from 1956 that the camaraderie developed.

Painting is Bill's art, but he is more spectacularly gifted as a linguist. Like Baron Corvo, he speaks the Venetian dialect, having been a gondolier, and is fluent in a half-dozen Mediterranean tongues. His leaves of absence from the cenobitic life in Subiaco have led to long periods in India and

Africa—especially Mali—from which he has just returned.

I do not know whether Bill ever took the Franciscan vow of poverty, but he is a voluntary have-not, uncharitable only about the "American system." He remarks that "protest art cannot be of any value unless the frustration is at the creative level. Besides, the artist's first problem is always the same, to understand his motive; the second is to be patient." I admire this man, though I cannot enter into his intellectual religiosity; for Bill *is* an "intellectual" despite himself, forever discussing concepts and making distinctions, always acutely self-aware. At one point he observes, astutely: "If the maestro had been younger, he would never have accepted me. He was too crisp and precise as a young man for the likes of me. Age expanded him."

When V. and I go to San Michele in the afternoon, Bill returns to Subiaco and the world of the sixth century, except for his collection of I.S.'s recordings from the world of the twentieth. But he will come every April, as he did last year and this. Nor will I forget his words when he raised his glass at lunch today: *"A noi quattro."*

The tide is low, exposing scabs of plaster on brick walls that make the city look more diseased than ever. Rickety docks, loose moorings, creaky pintles: the whole of Venice seems to rattle, scrape, and grind. The cloacal function of the canals is especially conspicuous, too, the wash in the wake of our boat, and the drains from pipes and spiles suggesting that the city is either flushing itself or foaming at the mouth. Today the Archangel Michele seems to promise not that the graveyard will yawn but only that Death Will Out.

"Vietato Fumare," a sign reads above the inner entrance. (A question of "no smoke without fire," hence the fear of connection with the eternal flames?) The thin autumn foliage within the walls exposes the grotesquerie of the decor, both iron (a monument with a raven, wings spread as if violently struggling to fly) and marmoreal: wreaths, roses, *putti*, coats-of-arms, busts—of Garibaldian males and weeping-willis (*le villi*) females with bindweed in their hair. In the lane segregating the ranks of deceased *"Religiosi"* and *"Suore,"* we fall behind a procession in which a priest, preceded by a cross-bearer, is followed by a coffin cart pushed by four men in black suits and black tam-o'shanter caps, moving in step as if in some macabre pavane.

The names in the *Reparto Greco* read like the cast in *War and Peace:* Wolkoff, Potemkin, Galitzine, Bagration (Princess Catherine, her tomb under a fig tree with large, blush-sparing leaves), Princess Troubetzkoy (née Moussine Pouchkine; was her husband the Troubetzkoy who gave the Ca' d'Oro to a ballet dancer?). And why the "de" in Serge de Diaghileff? I.S.'s stone is not yet here, and a litter of kittens is romping on his grave. Why, in all the length and breadth of the island, at this one place? Because I.S. possessed what Novalis described as the awareness of the inter-relations of all things, of conjunctions and coincidences?

Looking up, I discover that *my* grave, Number 38, is occupied! And *newly* occupied at that. I touch the ground, flex my limbs—as Lazarus must have done—say "*Cogito ergo sum*," ask V. to verify me. But neither of us recalls any mention of my death in the recent obits, no epipsychidion in the *Daily American*. So if I am still *here*, who is *there*? And, in the language of "The Three Bears," what is he or she doing in my grave?

October 6. The stone has finally reached the path in front of the actual site of the grave. Since its two sections have not been joined, we are unable to form an impression of it, even after workmen unwrap the upper layer from its bed of excelsior—then stand by, brown paper hats in hand, awaiting the widow's tokens of appreciation.

I go to the cemetery's administration building, to pick a bone with the Direzione about the usurpation of my final resting place. It is a lugubrious room piled with ledgers, each with a year stamped on the spine. The sallow bookkeeper, Signora Mondovecchi, coldly listens to my story, grimly removes "1971" from the shelf, and opens it to a map showing coffins stacked like jereboams in a wine cellar. Pointing to an area marked "*Spazi Perpetuità*," she explains that in practice "perpetual" means 99 years, to which I reply that this will not be long enough in I.S.'s case, whatever may become of Venice. His name has been entered in red ink, V.'s, next to his, in black. But in the place where *I* had expected to be stretched out, the mortal remains of Aspasia of Greece, widow of Alexander I, King of the Hellenes, languish, her name freshly blotted on the page. A flustered Mondovecchi assures me that the regina's remains are to be transplanted to her native country "as soon as money has been raised to pay her debts in Venice." A case of squatter's rights, then? But another thought seizes La Mondovecchi: if this money is not forthcoming, if a moratorium is denied, and if the exhumation does not take place, the sale to me will have been lost. Whereupon La Mondovecchi, who is very "old world" indeed, urges me to put a deposit on the adjacent plot for the reason that Aspasia's companion and closest friend is rumored to be "*molto malata.*"

As La Mondovecchi turns to shut the Domesday tome, I inquire about the mosaic-encrusted mausoleum facing I.S.'s grave on the other side of the path and occupying 20 times the territory, a sarcophagus of such dimensions that one pictures the resident cadavers not resupine but striding about. In La Mondovecchi's ultimate roll call this House of the Dead is registered under the name Messimis, which, I suppose, out loud, to be that of a Greek shipbuilder. But La Mondovecchi corrects me: "No, Signor. Maestro Messimis was a very important music critic."

June 8, 1973. Venice. We wait to dock at San Michele until after the departure of a *convoi funèbre* led by a gilded water hearse with gold-winged orb. The Orthodox section is a blaze of poppies, found nowhere else on the island, which raises the thought that they might be an ancient mark of heresy. I.S.'s stone is hardly larger than his own body and so narrow that the letters of his name, on a single line, look crowded. While we are here, visitors bring flowers, one of them, to judge by her legs and interest in the Diaghilev monument, an ex-ballet dancer. Searching among the newer graves for Ezra Pound's, we find only those of one "Oreste Licudis" and one "Pericles Triantifillis," the company of whose *names*, at any rate, the poet would have appreciated. The long walk in the cemetery exhausts V.

June 12. In San Giorgio dei Greci we stand before a laurel wreath in thick incense, the smoke obscuring the images of Simeon Stylites that flank the altar's center portal. The Panikhida differs from last year's in that the genuflections are fewer, the tempi of the chanting faster. Most of the latter is performed by a boy who at one point loses his place, whereupon the archimandrite sings the page number to him disguised in melismas. We are able to follow most of the service, from the first *"thanatos"* to the final *"makarios,"* and can join in the repeated Kyries and Alleluias. At the end of the service the archimandrite places crusts of consecrated bread in our hands. The name "Igor" occurs six times in the prayers.

During the ride to the island, the archimandrite chats about the fame that has come to him from I.S.'s funeral. He cannot pronounce the Italian *ci,* or even *gio,* and he says *unditsi* for *undici, vetsio* for *vecchio,* and greets a workman on the dock with *"Buon zorno."* The crown of laurel is on the stone when we arrive, and lighted candles have been planted in the ground at its head. Once again the grave is like a bier.

&. **Postscript 1994.** Mrs. Stravinsky's diary for 1975 records dreams, one of them, while we were in Venice, about being "happy together with Igor," but his absence was still an emotional bomb crater in her life. In the summer, in Switzerland, she was very moved during the excursions we made to his former residences, which I say because she had never betrayed great interest in the earlier part of his life before she entered it.

Visits to doctors were noticeably more frequent in 1974–1975 than in previous years, and her blood pressure was becoming a matter of concern. She complained of fatigue more than before, but attended the opera, the ballet, the theater, dinner parties, galleries, and gave interviews, painted several hours a day, read until late every night. Most entries in her chronicle keep count of the many, often 30 to 40, blocks walked during the day: at 87!

* * *

April 6, 1976. New York. 6 PM. The fifth Panikhida, in the Russian Church at Park Avenue and 90th Street, is private, attended only by ourselves, Lucia Davidova, and Balanchine, who remains on his knees throughout the half-hour service.

March 5, 1978. London. Today's *Sunday Telegraph* color magazine feature is a three-page story, "The Moon Goddess Who Lived History," about the forthcoming show of paintings by V. The article quotes the director of her gallery: "On the very day Madame first called to discuss her exhibition it so happened that Prokofiev also came by with his portfolio." But since Prokofiev died a quarter of a century ago, the reader must conclude either that the arrangements for the exhibition were fixed an unusually long time in advance or that the Prokofiev in question was not the composer. (It was his painter son, Oleg, who is not mentioned.) The article also fumbles her anecdote about an encounter with swashbucklers on the Black Sea, saying that the ship on which she fled from Baku to Marseilles in 1920 "was over-run by Turkish brigands. 'They spoke Russian like Stalin,' Madame recalls." But these cutthroats, like their infamous successor, were Georgians, not Russian-speaking Turks.

A more serious misquotation, from another interview, has landed on the front page of the *Guardian* and resulted in an international *retentissement*, as we learn from calls to New York and the Continent. What V. actually said was that at I.S.'s request she had burned his love letters before coming to America in 1940. What she is reported to have said is that she intends to burn these letters on returning to America. Messages arrive from every-where, some of then drawing an analogy between V. and Clara Schumann, who actually destroyed some of *her* husband's last compositions, as well as correspondence.

September 1, 1982. V. is failing rapidly. I go to her at all hours, whis-pering in her ear, to which she responds by opening her eyes and squeez-ing my hand. Day and night I wait for the nurses' knock on the wall, a sig-nal that she is asking for me.

September 12. Before dawn, at nurse McCaffrey's request and without my knowledge, a Roman Catholic priest administers extreme unction to V., for whom this passport-stamping viaticum could have meant only the con-firmation that she is dying. (Who could imagine a god for whom "last rites" would make any difference?) V. herself decided to spare I.S. the shock of seeing a cleric.

September 13. The Russian last rites are administered, nurse McCaffrey having arranged for them with an Orthodox priest. He warns me that the ceremony can take place only if the dying woman is fully con-scious, which, though clearly not the case, does not stop him. V. stares intently at him for a few minutes, then seems to sleep while he anoints her forehead, feet, the palms of her hands, and presses a silver cross to her lips (*Svadebka*: "And we kiss now the silver cross"). Since he is not wearing clerical garments, she may have thought he was another doctor. Still, to hear *Otche Nash* intoned in her mother tongue at a time when she knows herself to be gravely ill must have terrified her, if indeed she heard it. The heat of the afternoon is intense and the priest continually mops his brow.

September 15. When I enter the room in the morning, V. almost shouts my name. Dr. Tyson's argument against life-sustaining devices is that she has recently shown no sign of recognizing *him*. But she rarely recognized him, seeing him too infrequently. And how could he disregard the varying experiences of those who have been with her all the time, and fail to perceive that her condition might differ according to the hour? After 34 years with her, I believe that she is still too much alive to justify his proposal for an abject surrender, and I insist that she be fed intravenously, at least for a trial period. He sabotages this by ordering only a single bottle for the early evening and nothing for the night.

September 16. V. is much weaker; and I consent to cut the life line. At 6:30 the therapist arrives and proceeds to exercise the semiconscious patient's leg, until I tell him to collect his check and depart. Yet V. had been fond of him earlier in the summer, especially when he helped her from bed to chair and, on that glorious day, the high point of the last three months, wheeled her into the dining room, where we applauded her. She smiled then, but did not believe me that she would soon be outside again taking her daily rides. A week later, when I said the same thing, tears rolled down her cheek.

I sit by the bedside all evening, crying in the dark, except for the flickering light of the nurses' television screen. I.S. died in this same room, in the same kind of hospital bed, even facing the same way. At 11:00 I take pills to try to sleep but cannot and at midnight return and hold her hands.

September 17. At 3:15, nurse McCaffrey calls me from my room: "You had better come!" "Is it over?" "Yes." V.'s forehead and cheeks are still warm, and her silver hair has been smoothed behind her on the pillow. When the nurses begin their business of preparing the body and remove her pink woolen socks, I take them. Nurse McCaffrey says that V. turned to her left side and died looking at the icon on the wall above and behind her head, the icon she had made herself as a young girl.

Dr. Tyson arrives minutes after being notified, looking even more dour in his black suit and carrying his black bag than he had in the afternoon. He enters the room without a word, not even an "I am sorry," though tears are streaming down our faces, and curtly refuses my request to close her eyes. After the perfunctory ritual with the stethoscope, he retreats to the living room to write the death certificate ("consequence of a stroke"), then creeps out. I kiss her forehead, her hair, her hands, and leave the room.

The undertakers appear as quickly as if they had been waiting in the lobby. After the first sight of the lifeless body, the worst shock is the view of the empty bed. At 7 A.M. the funeral home representative arrives, the same, it happens, who accompanied I.S.'s casket to Venice with us in the night of April 12–13, 1971. At 6 P.M. we go to a small chapel at Campbell's on Madison Avenue. The casket is covered with my blanket of roses. As the priest shakes his censer, a young man and woman in jeans stumble through a Russian prayer, one line of which is unbearably poignant: ". . . thy servant Vera, who has fallen asleep." A dormition, not a death.

September 20. The two sacred choruses by I.S. that begin the early-morning service revive the memory of his funeral. Father Gregory addresses the congregation briefly, explaining the meaning of the service and its use of Old Slavonic, ending with the words "Vera Stravinsky's passing is that of an era, the civilization of pre-1917 Russia." He and five superb choristers sing antiphons, after which we kneel by the casket.

September 21. After a long wait in Paris, changing terminals and airlines, I am grateful to find Venice invisible in a thick haze, and, another piece of luck, that the only available hotel rooms are in the Lido, for me a no-man's-land without memories.

September 22. Stepping from a *motoscafo* directly to the canal entrance of the Greci, I am greeted and consoled by Adriana Panni, Francesco and Chiara Carrara, Bill Congdon, Bobby Fizdale and Arthur Gold, Baron Ernesto Rubin de Cervin. But the casket is still en route: V. will be late for her funeral. When it finally arrives, in a water hearse, gondolier pallbearers carry it to a black and gold carpet at the center of the church, with tall candles at the four corners. The archimandrite, black headdress with drape flowing down the back of his red and gold cassock, intones prayers from behind the iconostasis, then approaches the casket singing florid alleluias and an archaic oriental chant. His Kyrie Eleison is sung in echo by the same sepulchral-voiced old man who participated in the Panikhida services that we held in I.S.'s memory in 1972.

Between S. Giorgio and the island we pass the church of SS John and Paul, scene of I.S.'s funeral: V.'s death brings his death back to life. At San Michele, the casket is lifted to a wagon and wheeled to the *Reparto Ortodosso*, past the pointer marked "Igor Stravinsky." Here all is familiar, the dark cypresses, the old tombstones, and the gravel paths, all except the sight of the newly dug earth. The graveside ceremony is brief, the casket quickly and creakily lowered. I sprinkle a handful of dirt over the length of the coffin. Now they are together, only a few yards from Diaghilev, who introduced them to each other 61 years ago.

September 23. New York. Five minutes after I enter the apartment, a call from Sotheby's invites me to inspect the manuscript of the draft score of *Sacre*, which will go to London tomorrow for auction in November. Though feeling half dead, I make the effort and am infused with a little more life by examining the writing, which is so bursting with energy that the notes seem ready to leap off the page. At the end of the manuscript, before what should be the *Danse sacrale*, I.S. has scrawled in large letters: "That idiot Nijinsky has not given the *Danse sacrale* back to me." (Presumably Nijinsky's heirs still have it.)

September 24. The silence and emptiness in the next room is cruel. I dread sleeping, and the pain of waking with the thought that a terrible thing has happened, and the realization. I am beginning to understand those who, in the hope of a vision, or the sound of a voice ("Oh my goodness, oh my goodness," I can hear her say), turn to spiritualism and table-tapping. The imagination insists on conjuring her face at the time of death, instead of past images, and the only photographs I wish to see are the most recent; the very old woman is the one I so sorely miss.

Curiously, the first music I happen to hear since her death is I.S.'s *Orpheus*, which was the first music I heard *with* her, at the New York City Ballet rehearsals in the wonderful month of April 1948. Orpheus is the most human of the myths, and the score, which observes the moment of death by silence, moves me again as it did then. But the music I most miss is V.'s quiet singing. In all my 23 years with I.S., I remember her singing only one melody in his presence, a mushroom-gatherers' song from her childhood that he notated in one of his 1920s sketchbooks. After his death, she regularly sang songs, especially "Cheezhik" and "Fontanka." If the chatter of dinner guests ignored or bored her, she would sing these and other melodies very softly and to herself. Nurse McCaffrey tape-recorded some of them, but I could not bear to listen now. During the final months, V. did not sing at all.

September 30. V.'s name day. A letter from Bobby Fizdale: "Arthur and I have always felt it was one of the great privileges of our lives to be able to feel we were friends of the Stravinskys. You enjoyed that privilege more profoundly than anyone else they ever knew. Each of them gave us the feeling that they felt it was a privilege for *them* to have *you* in their lives. Vera Arturovna was one of the most beautiful women who ever lived. She was not only born beautiful, but she inspired beauty, created beauty, and lived to make the lives of those around her more beautiful."

December 25. Pompano. Walking on the beach this morning, V.'s birthday, does not help to erase memories of the night of her death. The end was said to be "expected," but is it possible to expect the instant transformation of a living person into a motionless image, and can anyone anticipate the beginning of an eternal separation, "the slamming of the door in your face, and the sound of bolting on the inside"? I must believe Joseph Conrad: "Life . . . will close upon a sorrow like the sea upon a dead body, no matter how much love has gone to the bottom."

At times since the death I have been tempted to believe in Coleridge's existentialism, "We lived ere yet this fleshly robe we wore." But Betjeman's poem, "I haven't hope, I haven't faith," speaks for me, and Whitman's "that may-be identity beyond the grave is a beautiful fable only." So does the Sudanese (Dinka) chant:

> The sun is born, and dies, and comes again.
> And the moon is born, and dies, and comes again.
> And the stars are born, and die, and come again.
> And man is born, and dies, and does not come again.

"Soul," "spirit," the Buddhist idea of a continuity, a rebirth of minds not connected with a self: even if I understood and believed in these notions, I doubt they would console me. Thinking about death, the mind is unable to imagine something other than life, and I want the resurrection of the person: her face, her smile, her eyes, her voice, her gestures—the way she lighted a cigarette—and she smoked until the last days, puffing rapidly, as if each one might be the last. The empty bed was terrible.

During the last months, nurse McCaffrey, who kept her elegantly dressed and groomed, would walk with her from her bedroom to the front part of the house and call to me: "Look who's here," or "Someone is coming," with which I would jump up from my desk, run to the corridor, and kiss the elderly lady. Until the last months, she went out every day, sometimes no farther than the bench across the street, from which she would wave to me in my fourth-floor window. Twice a week we drove to midtown stores and into the country, and in the last year of her life she flew to Florida four times and once to London.

But May 29 was the last time she left the city, for a visit to my sister's in New Paltz. In June, she attended my orchestra rehearsals with the New York City Ballet and waited for me in the car after the evening performances. At her last public appearance, for my June 15 New York Philharmonic concert, she was warmly applauded and stood in her front loge in acknowledgement. She had resolved to honor her husband's memory by attending the ballet rehearsals, but she did not go to the performances. As soon as the festival was over, she seemed to have made another resolve: not to live any longer. She stopped painting, did not go out, was silent much of the time, and began to refuse food. By mid-August she had taken to her bed.

December 30. One evening last spring, seeing her lost in meditation, I asked for her thoughts: "They are good for me, bad for you. It will be hard for you." I should have been grateful for her death and considered it a blessing when the labored breathing stopped, the relentless pumping of her left knee ended. But in truth I would have let her pain continue in exchange for a little more life.

December 31. New Year's Eve. A year ago, at the party for V. in this room overlooking the ocean, she wore the pink dress in which she is now buried.

Index

OF STRAVINSKY'S WORKS MENTIONED IN THE TEXT

575

General Index